online resource centre

www.oxfordtextbooks.co.uk/orc/chenwishart5e/

This book is accompanied by an innovative Online Resource Centre offering a range of resources to support learning. The fifth edition Online Resource Centre includes **downloadable versions of the diagrams** and a **selection of PowerPoint presentations** demonstrating how key diagrams in the book, and their different elements, come together. These presentations are accompanied by audio recordings, scripted by the author, which talk you through the difficult concepts illustrated in the diagrams, breaking these down into smaller and more manageable steps.

PRESENTATIONS ARE AVAILABLE FOR THE FOLLOWING DIAGRAMS:

These resources are password protected. The login details to enter this part of the Online Resource Centre are:

Username: **chenwishart5e**
Password: **Diagram5**

CONTRACT LAW

FIFTH EDITION

MINDY CHEN-WISHART

OXFORD

UNIVERSITY PRESS

OXFORD
UNIVERSITY PRESS

Great Clarendon Street, Oxford, OX2 6DP,
United Kingdom

Oxford University Press is a department of the University of Oxford.
It furthers the University's objective of excellence in research, scholarship,
and education by publishing worldwide. Oxford is a registered trade mark of
Oxford University Press in the UK and in certain other countries

Second Edition 2007
Third Edition 2010
Fourth Edition 2012

Impression: 1

Published in the United States of America by Oxford University Press
198 Madison Avenue, New York, NY 10016, United States of America

British Library Cataloguing in Publication Data

Data available

Library of Congress Control Number: 2014954268

ISBN 978–0–19–968916–3

Printed in Great Britain by
Ashford Colour Press Ltd, Gosport, Hampshire

To my parents, Peter and Jean Chen
Lotung—Taipei—Dunedin—Oxford

To my sons, James, Zachary, and Max—
You take my breath away.

PREFACE TO THE FIFTH EDITION

Students sometimes come to contract law with the preconception that it will be dry, rule-based, technical, and confusing, not to be understood but to be learnt by rote for the examination. I aim to counter any such impression by conveying the accessibility and practical importance of contract law, by provoking students to honest and critical engagement with the subject, and by imparting an appreciation of the interests, values, and concerns that must be balanced by the law and by the courts. Thus, this book seeks to:

- give a clear and accessible description of English contract law;
- give an overview of the interests, values, and concerns that arise in each area of contract law;
- encourage readers to critically assess the law; and
- assist readers to engage in the constructive process of law reform.

Over many years of teaching, I have evolved diagrams and tables to help explain concepts and give overviews to my students. I include some in this book. People learn in different ways; if these don't suit you, ignore them; the text can stand on its own. The law is updated to August 2014.

New material in this edition includes the following:

- In Chapter 1 Introduction, new cases on human rights as it intersects with contract law: *Bull v Hall & Anor* (2013), *Jitesh Salat v Mindaugas Barutis* (2013), and *Ashworth v Royal National Theatre* (2014).

- In Chapter 2 on Agreement, there is a new section on electronic contract formation and new cases on certainty: *MRI Trading AG v Erdenet Mining Corp LLC* (2013) and *Jet2.com Ltd v Blackpool Airport Ltd* (2012).

- Chapter 3 adds three new cases on consideration: *Teat v Willcocks* (2013), *Spreadex Ltd v Cochrane* (2012), and *Attrill v Dresdner Kleinwort Ltd* (2011) and (2013).

- Chapter 4 on Privity discusses *Great Eastern Shipping Co Ltd v Far East Chartering Ltd (The Jag Ravi)* (2012).

- Chapter 5 on Misrepresentation discusses the Consumer Protection (Amendment) Regulations 2014 (SI 2014/870) and the Consumer Insurance (Disclosure and Representations) Act 2012; and offers revised sections on contractual estoppel and no reliance clauses, and on the assessment of reasonableness under UCTA (*Lloyd v Browning* (2013)).

- Chapter 6 on Mistake includes a revised section on rectification in the light of new cases *Daventry District Council v Daventry & District Housing Ltd* (2011) and *Cherry Tree Investments Ltd v Landmain Ltd* (2012).

- Chapter 7 on Frustration adds *Cosco Bulk Carrier Co Ltd v Team-Up Owning Co Ltd (The Saldanha)* (2011).

- Chapter 8 on Duress adds *Progress Bulk Carriers Ltd v Tube City IMS LLC* (2012).

- Chapter 10 on Terms and Interpretation:

  - introduces a new section on implied term of good faith (discussing *Yam Seng Pte Ltd v International Trade Corp Ltd* (2013), *Compass Group UK and Ireland Ltd v Mid Essex Hospital Services NHS Trust* (2013), *Hamsard 3147 Ltd v Boots UK Ltd* (2013), *Bristol Groundschool Ltd v IDC Ltd and others* (2014), *Emirates Trading Agency v Prime Mineral Exports Private Ltd* (2014));

  - and a new section on implied limits on the exercise of discretionary powers (including *Barclays Bank plc v Unicredit Bank AG* (2014));

  - discusses new cases on interpretation: *Aston Hill Financial Inc v African Minerals Finance Ltd* (2013), *BMA Special Opportunity Hub Fund Ltd v African Minerals Finance Ltd* (2013), *Aberdeen City Council v Stewart Milne Group Ltd* (2011), *Lloyds TSB Foundation for Scotland v Lloyd's Banking Group plc* (2013), *Napier Park European Credit Opportunities Fund Ltd v Harbourmaster Pro-Rata and others* (2014), and *Cherry Tree Investment Ltd v Landmain Ltd* (2012);

  - new cases on admissibility of evidence in interpretation including *Scottish Widows Fund and Life Assurance Society v BGC International* (2012);

  - new cases on the interpretation of exemption clauses: *Greenwich Millennium Village Ltd v Essex Services Group plc and others* (2014), *Astrazeneca UK Ltd v Albemarle International Corp* (2011), and *Kudos Catering (UK) Ltd v Manchester Central Convention Complex Ltd* (2013); and

  - new cases on implied terms: *Lomas & Others v JFB Firth Rixson Inc & Ors* (2012), *Jackson v Dear* (2013), *Stena Line Ltd v Merchant Navy Ratings Pension Fund Trustees Ltd* (2011), and *Fitzhugh v Fitzhugh* (2012).

- In Chapter 11 on Direct Control of Terms, there is discussion of the proposed Consumer Rights Bill, and of new cases on the scope of UCTA (*Avrora Fine Arts Investment Ltd v Christie, Manson & Woods Ltd* (2012)) and UTCCR (*West v Finlay & Associates* (2014)).

- Chapter 12 discusses new cases on termination: *Telford Homes (Creekside) Ltd v Ampurius Nu Homes Holdings Ltd* (2013), *Urban I (Blonk Street) Ltd v Ayres* (2013), *Geys v Société Générale, London Branch* (2012), and *Ioannis Valilas v Valdet Januzaj* (2014); and on affirmation *The Isabella Shipowner Ltd v Shagang Shipping Co Ltd (The Aquafaith)* (2012).

- Chapter 13 on Damages discusses new cases: *John Grimes Partnership Ltd v Gubbins* (2013), *Trebor Bassett Holdings Ltd and the Cadbury UK Partnership v ADT Fire and Security plc* (2012), *Edwards v Chesterfield Royal Hospital NHS Foundations Trust* (2011), and *Ageas (UK) Ltd v Kwik-Fit (GB) Ltd* (2014).

- Chapter 14 on Specific Enforcement discusses *AB v CD* (2014) on inadequacy of damages, and cases on the penalty rule: *Makdessi v Cavendish Square Holdings BV* (2013) and *Andrews v Australia and New Zealand Banking Group Ltd* (2012). There is also a new flow diagram offering an approach to determining the remedies for breach of contract.

In Additional Chapter 2 on Illegality which is available on the Online Resource Centre, there is discussion of *Sibthorpe v Southwark LBC* (2011), *Simpson v Norfolk &*

Norwich Hospital (2011), *Parkingeye Ltd v Somerfield Stores* (2012), *Jamaican Redevelopment Foundation v Real Estate Board* (2014), *Patel v Mirza* (2014), *Les Laboratoires Servier & Anor v Apotex Inc & Ors* (2014), and *Hounga v Allen* (2014).

Many people are owed thanks. My students past and present have taught me far more than I them. By asking the questions that prompt consideration and inquiry, and giving me repeated opportunities to explain the complexities and fascinations of contract law, they have deepened my understanding and provoked new lines of inquiry. I am extremely grateful to my colleagues at Oxford and elsewhere for stimulating discussions, to the OUP team for its expert handling of the production side, and for the capable and efficient research assistance of Robert Mullins and Kelry Loi. I also thank my sons for the insights that parenting them continues to give me into law-making, law-enforcement, and the doctrine of precedent ('because I am the Supreme Court and I said so!'). They have shown me the rough comparability of the roles of parent, teacher, and, by extension, perhaps also the state via contract law; that is, to enable those in its charge to live self-directed and worthwhile lives—be it as an artist, a physicist, or a manga artist cum quantum physics researcher. Thanks to James Chen-Wishart for the cover artwork.

Mindy Chen-Wishart
15 September 2014

ABOUT THIS BOOK

Contract Law by Mindy Chen-Wishart is a resource rich in learning features. These pages will show you how to make the most of this textbook by illustrating each of the features used by the author to explain the key concepts of contract law.

In each chapter

Pause for reflection boxes

These boxes are ideally placed to help you stop, reflect on, and assess the law described. How the law works in practice, its consistency with other principles, its policy ramifications, possible alternatives, and other key issues are considered. References are given to related articles of interest to further your reading.

> **Pause for reflection**
>
> 1. *When* will a court imply an offer to consider? The Court factors in *Blackpool*:
>   - the invitation was made to a small number of parties;
>   - the duty to consider was consistent with the parties' ir
>   - the tender process was 'clear, orderly and familiar', en eral offer with reasonable precision.

Counterpoint boxes

These boxes highlight criticisms of the law described and identify options for reform. Use these boxes to identify areas of controversy, problems with the current law, and possible alternatives.

> **Counterpoint**
>
> Arguably, section 1(1)(b) goes too far in permitting third pa merely 'purports to confer a benefit' on him:
>
> 1. *Uncertain*: When does a contract which 'purports to con a rebuttable presumption that the contract parties int benefit?
>   √ *Beswick v Beswick* (1968, see 4.1.5.1) is clearly with widow would now be able to sue in her own right.

Diagrams

Overviews are given and key concepts are explained visually using clear and informative diagrams and tables. Read the relevant text in conjunction with each diagram for a clear explanation of even the most complex concepts.

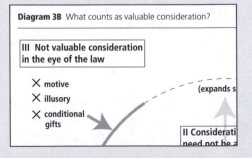

Diagram 3B What counts as valuable consideration?

III Not valuable consideration in the eye of the law

× motive
× illusory
× conditional gifts

(expands s

II Considerati need not be a

End of the chapter

Questions to consider

Use the exam-type questions to test your understanding of the topics covered. Hints on how to answer these questions appear on the Online Resource Centre.

> **QUESTIONS**
>
> **1** To what extent, if any, is there room to award reliance or account of profits for breach of contract?
>
> **2** 'Monetary awards for breach of contract should do no innocent party for his loss.' To what extent is this true?
>
> **3** What counts as 'loss' in the context of damages for bre
>
> **4** 'Contract law recognises non-pecuniary loss reluctan Discuss

Further reading

Select titles from the further reading lists at the end of each chapter in order to broaden your knowledge of the individual topics covered.

> **KEY FURTHER READING**
>
> See generally, Burrows, A (2004), *Remedies for Torts and*
>
> Friedmann, F (1995), 'Good Faith and Remedies for Breac Friedmann (eds), *Good Faith and Fault in Contract Law*
>
> Goetz, C, and Scott, R (1977), 'Liquidated Damages, Pena *Rev* 554.
>
> Jones, G (1997), 'Specific Performance: A Lessee's Covena 488.

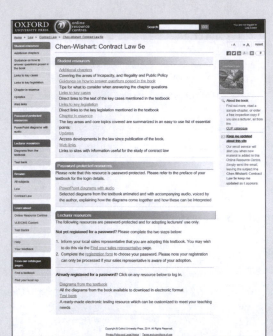

www.oxfordtextbooks.co.uk/orc/
chenwishart5e/

An Online Res ource Centre accompanies this book providing students and lecturers with ready-to-use teaching and learning materials. These resources are free of charge and are designed to maximise the learning experience.

Student resources

PowerPoint® presentations with accompanying audio recordings

A number of diagrams from the book have been drawn in PowerPoint®. The presentations show the order in which the various elements of each diagram come together. The presentations are accompanied by audio recordings, written by the author, which talk you through the difficult concepts illustrated in the diagrams and help you to break these down into manageable steps.

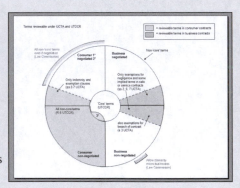

This resource is password protected. The login details to enter this part of the Online Resource Centre are:

Username: chenwishart5e
Password: Diagram5

Diagrams from the text

The diagrams from the text have been provided in high resolution format so that you can download them for use in your own study and revision notes.

Regular updates

Access changes and developments in the law which have occurred since publication of the book on the Online Resource Centre. These are added to the website as necessary and include page numbers enabling you easily to identify which materials have been superseded or supplemented.

Annotated web links

A selection of annotated web links helps to guide you in the right direction for important legal resources including legislative developments, key cases, and related EU documents.

> **Web links**
>
> **Legislation**
>
> Links to key legislation referred to in the book are available by visiting the 'Links to key legislation' resource.
>
> OPSI website for **statutes and statutory instruments** from 1988 onwards.
> www.opsi.gov.uk/legislation/about_legislation
>
> **Bills currently before Parliament:**
> www.publications.parliament.uk/pa/pabills.htm
>
> **Law Commission:** Annual Reports, Consultation Papers, Reports, Law under Review
> www.lawcom.gov.uk
>
> **Cases**
>
> Links to key cases referred to in the book are available by visiting the 'Links to key cases' resource.
>
> **Court of Appeal** Website: includes Court of Appeal (since 1964), Chancery Court (since 1994), Queen's Bench Division, and other judgments since 1996.
> www.hmcourts-service.gov.uk/cms/judgments.htm

Guidance on how to answer questions posed in the book

Advice from the author on how to approach each question posed in the book and how to structure your answers, to ensure you are successful in demonstrating your knowledge and critical understanding of contract law.

> **Chapter 5**
>
> **1. How can you tell whether a pre-contractual statement is: (a) a term, (b) an actionable misrepresentation, or (c) a puff? Why does it matter?**
>
> See 5.1.1 Representations and terms.
>
> This question invites you to discuss the remedial consequences of classifying statements made in the context of contract negotiations. The sub-questions you should address are:
>
> - What are the theoretical differences between (a)-(c)?
> - How is the distinction between (a)-(c) made in practice?
> - To what extent is the distinction based on the parties' intention and to what extent on other considerations (what?)?
> - What differences does it make at the remedial end (what can a claimant receive for breach of term, misrepresentation or an untrue puff? See 5.1.1.1 The remedial importance of the distinction)?
> - What difference might it make whether the claimant made a 'good' or 'bad' bargain?
>
> **2. Are statements of opinion, intention, or law actionable as misrepresentations? Give examples.**
>
> See 5.1.2 Statements of fact.
>
> In so far as these are *not* statements of fact as such, they may, nevertheless, be actionable if they *contain* an untrue statement of implied fact. What implied statements of fact might be contained in apparent:

Chapter in essence

The key areas and core topics covered are summarized in an easy-to-use list of essential points.

Additional Chapters

Available to download are two Additional Chapters: 'Incapacity' and 'Illegality and Public Policy'. These chapters, combined with those in the book itself, provide complete coverage of the key topics on undergraduate contract law courses and both are fully indexed, and referenced, in the book itself.

Lecturer resources

Test bank

A fully customizable resource containing ready-made assessments to test your students' grasp of key concepts as they progress through the course. The test bank contains 150 multiple-choice/response questions with full answers and feedback linked back to the textbook. It offers versatile testing tailored to the contents of each chapter and can be downloaded into Questionmark Perception, Blackboard, WebCT, and most other virtual learning environments (VLEs) capable of importing QTI XML. The test bank questions are also available in Word format suitable for printing directly.

Chapter 03 - Question 09
On 4 April, Alison offers Betty an antique clock for £2000. Betty spends a week mulling over the offer. On 13 April she sends Alison a letter stating she'd be willing to buy it for £1500. The next day while looking through an antiques catalogue she sees that a similar clock has recently been auctioned off at £5000. Betty realizes that if Allison refuses her counter offer she may lose the clock altogether. She immediately sends another letter on 14 April accepting the original offer. Betty's first letter containing the counter offer arrives on 16 April, her second letter accepting the original offer arrives on 18 April. Have the parties concluded a contract and, if so, when?
○ No, Betty's counter-offer killed off Alison's original offer on 13 April.
○ Yes, Betty has accepted Alison's original offer of £2000 on 14 April.
○ No, Betty's counter-offer killed off Alison's original offer on 16 April.
○ Yes, Betty accepted Alison's original offer of £2000 on 18 April.

Diagrams from the text

The diagrams from the text have been provided in high resolution format for downloading into presentation software for use in lectures or seminars.

OUTLINE CONTENTS

TABLE OF CASES

Page numbers in this table which are preceded by a 'W' (e.g. W1, W2) indicate where cases are covered in the chapters that appear on the Online Resource Centre. These chapters cover Incapacity and Illegality.

Page references given in bold indicate that the facts and decisions of the case are included in the text.

European Cases

TABLE OF STATUTES

Page numbers in this table which are preceded by a 'W' (e.g. W1, W2) indicate where statutes are covered in the chapters that appear on the Online Resource Centre. These chapters cover Incapacity and Illegality.

TABLE OF SECONDARY LEGISLATION

Page numbers in this table which are preceded by a 'W' (e.g. W1, W2) indicate where secondary legislation is covered in the chapters that appear on the Online Resource Centre. These chapters cover Incapacity and Illegality.

TABLE OF EUROPEAN LEGISLATION AND INTERNATIONAL CONVENTIONS

Page numbers in this table which are preceded by a 'W' (e.g. W1, W2) indicate where European legislation and international conventions are covered in the chapters that appear on the Online Resource Centre. These chapters cover Incapacity and Illegality.

ABBREVIATIONS

Where the following authors' works are referred to, the relevant textbooks are:

J Beatson, A Burrows, and J Cartwright, *Anson's Law of Contract* (29th edn, OUP, 2010)
P S Atiyah, *Introduction to the Law of Contract* (5th edn, Clarendon Press, 1995)
H Beale (ed), *Chitty on Contracts* (31st edn, Sweet & Maxwell, 2012)
H Collins, *The Law of Contract* (4th edn, LexisNexis, UK, 2003)
E Peel, *Treitel on the Law of Contract* (13th edn, Sweet & Maxwell, 2011)
S M Waddams, *The Law of Contracts* (6th edn, Canada Law Books, 2010)
C von Bar, H Beale, and others (eds), *Principles, Definitions and Model Rules of European Private Law—Draft Common Frame of Reference* (Sellier, 2009) ('European Draft Common Frame of Reference')

PART I

Introduction

Making contracts is part of our everyday experience. We do it to get, and sometimes to sell, goods and services (food, travel, accommodation, banking, employment). Doing so expresses our freedom and, at least potentially, enhances our welfare. Through contracting, we can determine the shape and direction of our lives. Contract law supports this activity by conferring power on parties to create binding agreements enforceable in law. By giving greater security to private arrangements, contract law helps people to do things they could not otherwise do or do as easily; it is a form of state subsidisation of a valuable activity. However, that subsidisation is not given in an unqualified way. Since contract is an activity that we engage in with others, the state must also regulate the basis on which we deal with others in order to preserve justice between parties, to differentiate trading from taking, bargains from exploitation.

This section explores:

- the sources of contract;

- the values reflected in contract law;

- the different theories about why agreements are enforced;

- the types of human interaction governed by contract law;

- the relationship of contract law to other branches of private law governing the relationship between individuals; and

- how contract law fits in with European law, with international commercial law, and human rights law.

1

Introduction

'What is contract law?'

1.1 **What is a contract?**

What is a 'contract' that contract law applies to? The common law offers no formal definition of a contract, but textbooks generally define a contract as *an enforceable promise (or agreement).*[1] We can derive three elements from this.

(i) **Promise**: the focus here is *one-sided*. The focus is on the *voluntariness* and *seriousness* of the undertaking given by the promisor.

(ii) **Agreement**: the focus here is *bilateral* or multi-lateral. We cannot make contracts by ourselves. It is something we do with others by reaching consensus as to our respective rights and liabilities.[2]

(iii) **Recognition by the law**: it is the *state* which provides the legal apparatus to enforce contracts; this enhances the reliability of voluntary exchanges, and bridges any gap in trust and sanctions between parties by guaranteeing redress for breach, backed up by the coercive power of the state. While agreements would still be made without legal enforcement, parties would tend to regard each other with suspicion like participants of hostage swap, and adopt a 'you first!' stance. They would have to devise alternative enforcement schemes (think of the Mafia) or bias exchanges towards those that take place instantly, with family or friends, or towards persons with a reputation for keeping their promises. Thus, 'the supportive role of the law helps make contracts outside the framework of ongoing relations much more common',[3] and allows individuals to project their intentions into the future and plan actions that require concrete pre-commitments. Moreover, whatever the parties intend, if a dispute arises, it is ultimately contract *law* that determines:

- whether, when, and what the parties have agreed;
- whether one party can escape from the contract;
- how breach should be remedied; and
- what happens when the contract is silent or uncertain on a disputed matter.

1.2 **What is contract law?**

'Promises' or 'agreements' are not ' "things" that exist outside the law . . . [or] physical objects which can be perceived by the senses. They are themselves abstract concepts, just as much as the concept of contract itself' (Atiyah at 38). For example,

---

[1] *Anson's* at 1, describes contract law 'as that branch of the law which determines the circumstances in which a promise shall be legally binding on the person making it'. Treitel at 1, states: 'a contract is an agreement giving rise to obligations which are enforced or recognised by law'. The US Second Restatement of Contracts states: 'a contract is a promise or a set of promises for the breach of which the law gives a remedy, or the performance of which the law in some way recognises as a duty'.

[2] However, deeds (see 3.2) are enforceable by beneficiaries even if they are ignorant of them when made; thus, agreement is unnecessary.

[3] Joseph Raz, 'Promises in Morality and Law' (1981) *Harvard L Rev* 916, 934.

Diagram 1A What does contract law *do*?

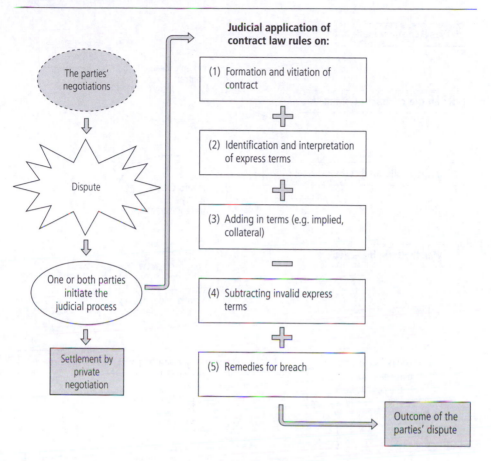

the law *deems* certain conduct, such as signing a document, as showing agreement to be bound by its contents, irrespective of the signer's knowledge, understanding, or intention in respect of it. It is contract law as developed and applied by the courts that defines how the practice of making agreements should be conducted; how the contracting game should be played.

Diagram 1A shows that, although contract law rests on the foundation of the parties' voluntary assumption of obligations, that is only the starting point. The outcome of cases depends on the process of judicial application of contract law rules or on the parties' own bargaining in the shadow of the law.

1.2.1 **The questions contract law addresses**

Diagram 1B gives an introductory overview of the questions addressed by contract law in the chronological sequence they arise in the life of the contract, and reflects the structure of this text. What follows is the briefest of overviews.

Diagram 1B Overview: legal questions arising in the life of a contract

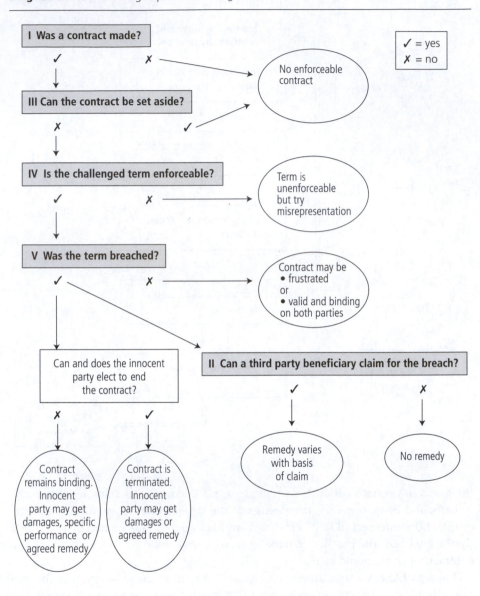

Part **II** of this text deals with contract **formation**: contract law determines the types of arrangements that will be recognised and supported *as contracts*. The court first looks for an 'agreement' between the parties; contract law:

(i) adopts an **objective test** of the parties' intentions;

(ii) adopts the **mirror image approach** to finding agreement: one party's *offer* must be matched by the other's *acceptance*;

(iii) requires sufficient **certainty of agreement**; and

(iv) presumes that commercial agreements have, but agreements made with family and friends do not have, the necessary '**intention to create legal relations**'.

As well as agreement, a claimant must satisfy one of the following to *enforce* the defendant's promise:

(i) **'consideration'**, meaning that the claimant has given or promised something *in exchange* for the defendant's promise; or

(ii) that the defendant's promise is contained in a **deed** (ie certain formalities such as writing are satisfied); or

(iii) **'promissory estoppel'**, meaning that the claimant has relied on the defendant's promise and it is inequitable for the defendant to renege on it.

Part III deals with **privity**: *who* can *acquire rights* or *be subjected to liabilities* by a properly made contract (ie who can sue and be sued in respect of the contract)? The general (privity) rule confines the legal impact of contracts to the contract parties. It seems right that contract parties should not be able to impose burdens on third parties. However, the traditional position that they cannot give third parties the right to enforce a contract made for their benefit is now subject to a wide statutory exception.

Part IV deals with **vitiation**: *when can one party be excused from (get out of) the contract?* Contract law contains *defeasibility rules* determining when arrangements which satisfy the requirements of contract formation will, nevertheless, not receive legal support. Namely, when there is: misrepresentation, mistake, frustration (ie radical change of circumstances), duress, undue influence, unconscionability, an unfair guarantee, incapacity, or illegality or contravention of public policy.

Part V deals with the **contents** of the contract: *what are each party's respective rights and liabilities under it?* Contract law:

(i) determines *what* the agreed terms are;

(ii) interprets what the terms *mean*; and

(iii) tempers the parties' express agreement by:

- *adding* to them (eg implied and collateral terms), or
- *subtracting* from them (eg making certain terms unenforceable), or
- refusing to enforce contracts which are *illegal* or contrary to public policy.

Part VI deals with **the remedies for breach**: *when one party does not perform the contract, what can the law do for the other party?*

(i) If the parties have explicitly agreed on what should happen on breach, contract law decides whether this is enforceable.

(ii) If it is not or if the parties have not expressly agreed on the remedies, contract law provides a menu of default remedies to the aggrieved claimant who satisfies their requirements, so long as there is no double recovery:

- *termination*—the claimant may be allowed to discontinue his or her own performance of the contract,
- *damages*—the claimant may be awarded a sum of money designed to put him or her in the position he or she would have been in had the contract been performed,
- *specific performance*—the claimant may be able to compel the contract-breaker to perform the contract.

1.2.2 **Sources of contract law**

The sources of contract law are the common law and legislation. Legislation is readily understandable as statutes and regulations made by Parliament, but the expression '**common law**' needs more explanation. Broadly, it means *judge-made law*, which has evolved from a pragmatic case-by-case analysis over time. Its line of reasoning is *inductive* (ie from the particular case to general principles, although courts are reluctant to give formal recognition to any overarching principles). In this sense, it contrasts with the legal *codes* of European continental civilian systems of law. These codes adopt a *deductive* style of reasoning (applying general principles to specific cases). In 1965, the Law Commission of England, Wales, and Scotland announced an ambitious plan to codify contract law. Eight years later, it was abandoned when many disagreements over substance proved irresolvable. The danger is that codes can be either too general (eg a rule that 'all agreements will be kept' is useless when applied to specific problems) or too specific (eg requiring all contracts to be evidenced by signed writing is apt to be inflexible and to give rise to many exceptions). As Waddams observes (at [5]):

> Human conduct is infinitely variable, and no codifier can foresee every problem that will arise, especially in an area covering so many different kinds of human interaction as contract law. The attempt to impose on a highly developed and developing common law system a code sufficiently specific to implement useful changes and yet not so specific as to set up inflexibilities and anomalies in unforeseen cases proves to be almost impossible.

The expression 'common law' *includes* but can also be used to *contrast* with **equity**. Before the late 19th century there were two separate systems of courts:[4] the courts of law ('common law courts'), and the courts of equity ('Chancery'). Every legal system must contain elements of certainty, predictability, and stability on the one hand, and elements of flexibility, fairness, and justice in the individual case, on the other. In English law, these competing sets of values were once institutionalised in these two separate systems of law. This separation remains important in understanding modern contract law. In its original role of controlling the activation of proceedings in the (common law) courts, Chancery took increasing account of factors beyond those considered by the common law and so alleviated the rigidities of the common law. Moreover, someone dissatisfied with a result obtained from a court of law could appeal to the Chancellor, the king's deputy, for discretionary relief on the grounds of natural justice and fairness. Where the rules of common law and equity clash, equity prevails. It was said, disparagingly of the early Chancery court, that 'justice varied according to the length of the Chancellor's foot'. But, just as elements of discretion crept into the common law, so, over time, rules grew up to govern the Chancellor's discretion, and equity itself became extremely rigid and inflexible.

Principles of fairness and good conscience have cut through the severity of some legal rules. Indeed, these rules may be utterly reversed by their equitable gloss. For example:

- common law regards written documents as conclusive of the parties' legal rights, but courts of equity can *rectify* the document so that it conforms with the parties' common intention;

---

[4] See *Anson's* at 9–19, on 'The History of Contractual Obligations in English Law'.

- it is irrelevant at common law that an agreement is harsh or unfair, but courts of equity can set aside *unconscionable bargains*;
- an innocent misrepresentation inducing a contract attracts no relief at common law, but equity can set the contract aside.

The Judicature Act 1875 fused the two courts so that a *single court* now administers both common law and equity. However, this fusion of the courts did not result in a fusion of the laws; common law remedies were still tied to common law actions and equitable remedies to equitable actions. For example, even after fusion, no damages were available for innocent misrepresentation and statutory reform was needed to allow this (see 5.2 and 5.3.3). It seems anomalous for modern courts to restrict their own powers by reference to those of courts abolished over 100 years ago. Rather, modern courts should use the power inherited from *both* courts to develop appropriate and flexible responses to contractual problems.[5]

Legislation (or Parliament-made law) is the other source of contract law. Some statutes are *codifying*; they collect together and restate the common law (including equitable) developments in a particular subject (eg the Sale of Goods Act 1893). Other statutes are *reforming*; they remedy deficiencies in the common law.[6] Reforming statutes free judges from adherence to previously decided cases ('precedents'), a self-imposed restriction which occasionally inhibits necessary judicial development in response to changing circumstances. Indeed, it is arguable that much legislation would be unnecessary if courts were more prepared to develop the law (as on equitable mistake see 6.3.3) rather than abdicate the task to the legislature. As Lord Wilberforce said:[7] 'The law on this topic is judge-made: it has been built up over the years from case to case. It is entirely within this House's duty, in the course of administering justice, to give the law a new direction in a particular case where, on principle and in reason, it appears right to do so. I cannot accept the suggestion that because a rule is long established only legislation can change it.' The danger of legislative reform is that it can stifle judicial development by hardening developing rules at an interim stage[8] or by curtailing judicial development in related areas.[9]

Judicial conservatism has necessitated legislation aimed at protecting certain vulnerable groups, such as consumers, employees, and tenants. Such legislation has broadly followed judicial leads and would have been unnecessary if judicial initiatives had been pushed home. Judicial conservatism is also evident in the tendency towards overly narrow interpretations of legislative innovations. Beatson argues persuasively that courts should treat legislative innovations as policy guidance on how to develop related areas of the law on rational and consistent lines.[10]

---

[5] See A S Burrows, 'We Do This at Common Law and That in Equity' (2002) 22 *OJLS* 1.

[6] Eg the Law Reform (Frustrated Contracts) Act 1943 (ch 7), Misrepresentation Act 1967 (ch 5), and Contracts (Rights of Third Parties) Act 1999 (ch 4).

[7] *Miliangos v George Frank (Textiles) Ltd* (1976) 469.

[8] Eg Law Reform (Frustrated Contracts) Act 1943 on the calculation of restitution, see 7.6.

[9] Eg Contracts (Rights of Third Parties) Act 1999 on promisee actions, see 4.1.3.

[10] J Beatson, 'The Role of Statute in the Development of Common Law Doctrine' (2001) 117 *LQR* 247.

1.2.3 **Understanding legal reasoning**

Contract law is *applied by the courts* and courts have considerable *latitude* in determining the outcome of cases. At its most basic, legal rules take the following form:

Rule 1: $a + b + c = X$ (the legal result), unless d is present, in which case Y results

Assuming:

Rule 2: $a + b + e = Z$

Rule 3: $a + b + f = Q$

Judicial latitude resides in:

(i)   determining whether facts a–f are present; and

(ii) selecting which rule to apply (1, 2, or 3) by highlighting certain facts of the case and minimising or ignoring others, thereby determining the outcome (whether X, Y, Z, or Q).

For example, whether the parties have reached agreement is assessed *objectively*. Thus, it is for the *court* to say how a *reasonable* person would interpret the relevant conduct as consenting. A contract can be set aside when both parties enter it under a fundamentally mistaken assumption, but it is up to the *court* to decide whether:

(i)   both parties were mistaken about a matter;

(ii) the matter was of fundamental importance; and

(iii) the mistake doctrine applies or a related doctrine such as misrepresentation (mistake induced by the other party's statement), or undue influence (mistake resulting from the claimant's unquestioning trust in or dependence on, the other party).

The degree of *flexibility or indeterminacy* in the system is such that a range of fact-findings is possible and a range of rules can be applied without the courts being demonstrably 'wrong'.

Judicial discretion in the true sense is exercised when courts are required to apply broad standards such as *reasonableness*. For example, courts once said that when circumstances change radically after the contract is made, they look for the parties' intention to decide whether the contract comes to an end. Absent express agreement, the courts ask what *reasonable* parties (not what the actual, perhaps unreasonable, parties) would have intended had they considered the matter. As Lord Radcliffe said (at 728) in *Davis Contractors v Fareham UDC* (1956):

> [I]t might seem that the parties have become so far disembodied spirits that their actual persons should be allowed to rest in peace. In their place there rises the figure of the fair and reasonable man. And the spokesman of the fair and reasonable man, who represents after all no more than the anthropomorphic conception of justice, is, and must be, the court itself.

Value judgments may, consciously or unconsciously and unavoidably, affect the particular facts found, the selection of applicable rules, and the way in which discretionary standards are applied by the courts. Atiyah observes (at 58) that, although courts present themselves as reasoning *forwards* in resolving disputes (*from* the fact-findings and the relevant legal principles *to* the solution), they in fact often engage in **backward reasoning** (*from* the desirable solution *to* the selection of the most suitable legal principle and the finding of the necessary facts). Where courts reason backwards, the ostensible legal analysis merely *justifies*, rather than *explains*, the outcome.

This has led the *Critical Legal Studies* theorists (CLS)[11] to deny that the law is largely scientific and determinate: they point to the coexistence of contradictory norms (each principle can be countered by an opposing principle) and the imprecision of doctrines that fail to dictate a result, aside from the rare 'easy' case.[12] Mainstream theorists concede the latitude that courts have in 'hard' cases, but they regard the CLS view as exaggerated. Judges are not free to decide *whatever they like*; the answer does not vary according to the length of the Chancellor's foot, or the contents of his breakfast. As Hart observes:[13] 'nothing can eliminate [the] duality of the core of certainty and a penumbra of doubt when we are engaged in bringing particular situations under general rules'. 'Hard' cases may often be decided either way and considerations of policy will often be determinative. However, to see legal questions as matters of pure policy, as if there were no authoritative legal context of judgments or statute, goes too far: it would destroy the essence of law and the point of legal education.

CLS theorists concede that legal outcomes *are* often predictable but only, they say, because the indeterminacy is bent towards results that reinforce the existing power structures (the 'legitimising thesis'). Whatever precise stance one takes on this, it is clear that law is not a value-free enterprise. Rules cannot be mechanically applied. Merely studying contract law *rules* does not tell us how they will be *applied* to particular disputes. To understand what is really going on, we must also appreciate the underlying and competing values which nudge the courts' decision-making.

1.3 **Values reflected in contract law**

Warning: the discussion that follows includes details of substantive contract law rules that may go over the heads of first-time readers. *Do not worry about the details at this stage*; the purpose here is just to give a **sense of the direction of contract law, the issues in play, and the broader context within which contract law operates.** You should *revisit these sections* after studying the substantive law to help you to:

- pull together the strands;
- consider the big questions (see the 'questions to consider' at the end of the chapter); and
- obtain a deeper understanding in revision.

---

[11] See M Kelman, *A Guide to Critical Legal Studies* (Harvard University Press, 1987).

[12] J Feinman, 'Critical Approaches to Contract Law' [1983] *UCLA L Rev* 829; C Dalton, 'An Essay on the Deconstruction of Contract Doctrine' (1985) 94 *Yale LJ* 997, 1010–11.

[13] H L A Hart, *The Concept of Law* (3rd edn, OUP, 2012) 123.

Contract law reflects an uneasy mix of competing values ('ideals', 'influences', 'policies'). People contract for a variety of reasons and contract law supports the activity of contracting by making transactions legally enforceable. At the same time, contract law places restraints on contracting behaviour, shapes the type of obligations that are created, and limits the means by and extent to which parties may enforce their agreement. Thus, contract law both *facilitates* and *regulates* the practice of contracting. These functions of contract law can be understood by reference to the *classical* model of contract law (influential in the late 19th century and early 20th century), which highlights the *facilitative* role of contract law, and the shift in emphasis as *modern* developments incorporate increasing elements of *regulation* in *neo-classical* contract law.

During the latter half of the 19th century, a concept of contract developed together with a body of legal doctrine which is now generally referred to as the '**classical law of contract**'. This was 'invented' in the sense that it was a synthesis and interpretation of case law into a coherent body of law by treatise writers such as Anson, whose *Law of Contract* (written for students) was first published in 1879. The major features of this classical model loomed large in the justificatory language (reasoning) of the courts and was, paradoxically, reinforced by detractors who criticised them as unrealistic, unreflective of modern practices, and stifling of desirable developments.[14] Classical contract law reflects the dominance of laissez-faire economic attitudes in the 19th century. Its somewhat absolute assumption is that personal freedom and wealth creation go hand in hand. The corollaries of this emphasis on ***freedom of contract*** are that:

- the contract parties are sovereign: it is up to them to decide whether, when, and on what terms they wish to contract;
- the law should impose *minimal restrictions*: its primary function is simply to *give effect* to the parties' agreement;
- contract law rules should therefore be *few, clear, and consistent with commercial expectations* and apply to *all* contracts;
- a contract should be *interpreted within its four corners*, without reference to the external context.

These ideals were reinforced by a particular *paradigm of contracting* in which:

- there is presumed *equality* between the parties (aside from infants, lunatics, and, for a time, married women);
- the contract is *negotiated, freely agreed*, and therefore *fair*;
- the contract is *discrete* in the sense that its boundaries are clear and performance more or less instantaneous (eg buying a coffee or DVD), and contract parties act only out of *self-interest* and adopt an *adversarial* stance.

While this 'story' did not hold absolute sway, in that it was minimally tempered by fairness and public policy (eg doctrines such as duress, and the rules against penalties

[14] Eg M Horwitz, 'The Historical Foundations of Modern Contract Law' (1974) 87 *Harvard L Rev* 917; P S Atiyah, *The Rise and Fall of Freedom of Contract* (Clarendon Press, 1979); G Gilmore, *The Death of Contract* (Ohio State University Press, 1974).

and forfeitures could invalidate the whole contract or particular terms), it was the predominant model upon which cases were resolved.

In very simplified terms, the story of modern or **neo-classical contract law** is characterised by a move away from these classical values and towards doctrines and statutory provisions that *regulate* the practice of contracting in the interests of fairness and flexibility. The movement is masked because:

(i) the classical law still casts a long shadow in the justificatory language of the courts. Rather than abandon outmoded legal concepts or adopt new ones, the doctrine of precedent bends the courts towards reinterpreting or according different weight to established legal concepts;

(ii) particular types of contracts that attract greater legal regulation (eg employment, tenancy, or consumer transactions) are usually ignored in the discussions of the 'general' law of contract;

(iii) the bulk of cases that actually reach the courts still mirrors those disputes which forged the classical model of contract law (ie commercial disputes involving large sums of money) and they, in turn, reinforce the rules derived from the classical model. This can paint a misleading picture of contract as a whole.

The following discussion gives a flavour of the values that must be integrated by contract law. It reveals the, albeit inconsistent and subtle, shift in the balance of values discernible in modern contract law. To assist understanding and exposition, the discussion is presented as pairs of competing ideas and methods of legal reasoning, broadly categorised as *classical* as opposed to *modern* (see **Diagram 1C**). However, contract law does not reside only at one pole. Its complexity and interest result in large part from

Diagram 1C Policy tensions shaping contract law

Values and emphasis identified with 'classical' contract law: Freedom of contract.	Values and emphasis identified with 'modern' contract law: Limits on freedom of contract.
1. Freedom and autonomy	1. **Limits on freedom and autonomy**
2. Minimal legal intervention	2. **Regulation and channelling of contracting**
3. Equality	3. **Responding to inequality**
4. Negotiated contracts	4. **Standard form contracts**
5. Assumed fairness of exchanges	5. **Unfairness of some exchanges**
6. Discrete contracts; self-interested individualism	6. **Relational contracts; cooperation, trust**
7. Literal interpretation	7. **Contextual interpretation**
8. Rules	8. **Discretionary standards**
9. General law	9. **Specialisation and differentiation**

the simultaneous presence and interaction of *both* sets of values; the tension between the individualist and the interventionist strands is the constant theme of contract law. How and why the current law strikes the balance in different circumstances is the subject of contract law. For example, in **'The Ideologies of Contract Law'** (1987) 7 *LS* 205, **Adams and Brownsword** argue that the rules and principles of contract law should be interpreted in the light of two 'ideologies'; 'Market-Individualism', which is aimed at facilitating competitive exchange, and 'Consumer-Welfarism', which leans towards consumer protection and principles of fairness and reasonableness.

1.3.1 Freedom and limits on freedom

'Freedom of contract' demands that parties be free to choose whether, when, and to what they bind themselves via contracts. This enhances freedom by allowing individuals to achieve a wider range of desired outcomes through cooperation. It also enhances welfare because parties will only give up something to obtain something they value more highly. The idea that this freedom should not be restricted is characterised as 'negative' liberty. Paradoxically, some restrictions on freedom have long been recognised as necessary to *preserve* freedom. Thus, contract parties are protected from fraud, duress, and other conduct, which inappropriately interferes with their exercise of choice. Courts also refuse to enforce agreements that permanently destroy freedom (eg contracts of slavery) and that involve perceived gross immorality and criminality.[15] Thus, contract law will not support all free choices. Indeed, there is an increasing recognition that inequalities in resources, knowledge, and competence can result in oppressive or undesirable outcomes that should not be supported by the law. For example, Collins (at 29) notes that choices to injure oneself, to sell one's property at gross undervalue, to enter into economic relations which give others oppressive power over major aspects of one's well-being, and even to harm the environment, do not seem to be valuable choices which the law should support. Collins[16] explains the notion of *'positive' liberty*, according to which: 'the law can tolerate a considerable range of economic transactions and give the benefit of the doubt to activities which seem of little worth to most people, but the law sets limits to freedom of contract when the choices made do not appear worthwhile on any reckoning'. On this view, the ability to make contracts is not unlimited but is a power to be exercised for *worthwhile* purposes. While the commitment to freedom means that the concept of 'worthwhile contracts' must have a large margin of tolerance, it nevertheless gives greater scope for legal regulation.

1.3.2 Minimal regulation of contracting

The classical model assigns contract law a non-interventionist role, ideally confined to identifying and enforcing the parties' agreement. The argument runs that, once the rules of the contract 'game' (which should themselves be minimalist) have been

---

[15] See Additional Chapter 2 on illegality available on the Online Resource Centre.
[16] Citing the work of J Raz, *The Morality of Freedom* (OUP, 1986); and see R Brownsword, 'Liberalism in the Law of Contract' (1988) 36 *Archives for Philosophy of Law and Social Philosophy* 86; S Smith, 'Future Freedom and Freedom of Contract' (1996) 59 *MLR* 167.

observed, the courts should respect the outcome as the expression of the parties' exercise of freedom; if the procedure is fair, the outcome must logically be fair. Thus, contract law's legitimate sphere of control is traditionally confined to ensuring *procedural* fairness (in the negotiation process).

On the other hand, concern with *substantive* fairness (the outcomes of negotiation) may be justified in terms of ensuring a broadly acceptable 'pattern of welfare' in a liberal society, ready examples are the minimum wage legislation and control of exorbitant interest rates in consumer credit contracts. While contract law adopts no systematic response to substantive unfairness, it has taken a piecemeal approach to trouble hotspots where the problem is serious and recurrent (eg in consumer or standard form contracts, and clauses which exclude liability or impose harsh remedies for breach). Moreover, procedural and substantive unfairness overlap: in setting the standard of fair *procedure*, the law is unavoidably influenced by the fairness of the *outcome* that is likely to result.

1.3.3 **Equality/inequality**

Classical contract law is strongly identified with the ideology of equality in the sense that it assumes that everyone is free to choose to enter any kind of transaction to improve his or her position in life. The corollary is that the distribution of wealth and power in society is said to depend upon one's merit (ie success in playing the contract game). This contrasts with traditional social orders which determine a person's welfare by reference to such factors as social status or rank, political power, religion, race, or physical force. This is the meaning of Sir Henry Maine's famous statement that 'the movement of the progressive societies has hitherto been a movement *from Status to Contract*'.[17]

The reality is that *initial* inequalities in the distribution of wealth, power, and knowledge will be reflected in the inequality of the *outcomes* of contracts. In this sense, the *same* treatment is not necessarily *equal* treatment, for there is no greater inequality than the equal treatment of unequals. Contract law has given increasing recognition to the need to protect weaker parties. But, since inequality of bargaining power is ubiquitous and a matter of degree, only the most vulnerable parties can be protected from the worst excesses of contractual exploitation.

1.3.4 **Negotiated/standard form contracts**

The classical paradigm of contract is the arm's-length individually *negotiated* exchange. But, the modern reality is the *standard form* contract, pre-drafted by the stronger party to:

- maximise protection of its own interests;
- minimise its own liability to the other party; and
- avoid legal control.

---

[17] *Ancient Law, its Connection with the Early History of Society and its Relation to Modern Ideas* (John Murray, 1861; reprinted edn Tucson: University of Arizona Press, 1986) 141.

The stronger party imposes its terms on a 'take-it-or-leave-it' basis, attracting the label of 'adhesion contracts'. In combination with monopolies and cartels, there may be no meaningful freedom as to whom one contracts with and on what terms. A feature of the modern law is to restrict the advantages that can be obtained via standard form contracts.

1.3.5 Fairness of exchange

Classical contract law emphasises the *subjectivity of values*; the idea is that since individuals value things differently, it is impossible for courts to assess the fairness of exchanges. A contract freely entered into is fair by definition; courts should not second-guess the parties' preferences. Moreover, consistent with social Darwinism, the law should not protect parties from grossly unbalanced exchanges that result from foolishness and carelessness, lest it reduces their incentive to be more careful in future.

On the other hand, increasing recognition of the contract parties' unequal bargaining power is coupled with the law's increasing, albeit piecemeal, legal control over the fairness of the exchange. While modern law tolerates considerable disparity of prices, it is increasingly sceptical of 'choices' that amount to extreme under- or over-value.

1.3.6 Discrete or relational contracts; self-interested individualism/ cooperation, trust, and altruism

Where an exchange is practically simultaneous (eg buying groceries, petrol, or a cup of coffee), parties rarely need the support of contract law. But legal support is necessary to protect parties who enter non-simultaneous or deferred exchanges. Suppose that I commission you to paint a portrait of my father for his birthday:

- if I pay *in advance*, you may take the money and run, or demand a higher price once it is too late for me to obtain another in time;

- if I only pay *on delivery*, you are vulnerable to my change of mind or my insistence on paying less since you cannot sell it elsewhere.

Contract law facilitates voluntary exchanges by ensuring the enforceability and security of the original deal.

The classical model of contracting pictures antagonistic individuals entering discrete transactions to further their self-interest. The emphasis is on *detachment* and the assertion of *rights* contained in the contract. In contrast, Macneil and others criticise this as unreflective of actual business practice, where more emphasis is given to the *relational* aspect of contracting,[18] in the sense that:

(i) *all* contracts must be interpreted in the context or 'social matrix' in which they are made;

(ii) many contracts involve *long-term* or *continuing relationships* (eg employment and construction contracts, leases, franchises, and commercial agreements for the

---

[18] I Macneil, 'Contracts: Adjustments of Long-Term Economic Relations under Classical, Neoclassical and Relational Contract Law' (1978) 72 *NWU L Rev* 854; 'Relational Contract: What We Do and Do Not Know' (1985) 3 *Wisc L Rev* 483.

supply of goods or services over time) which affect the way they should be interpreted. The more long term an exchange, the less likely it is that the parties can plan for future contingencies. Rather, they rely on *relational norms* to fill any gaps in their contract. These are characterised by cooperation, trust, flexibility, altruism, and a willingness to make adjustments in response to changing circumstances. This contrasts with the classical ideal that *all* the answers to contractual problems can and should be resolved by reference to the parties' intention *at formation*, as expressed in their contract. Relationalists argue that contract law should recognise or impose certain duties of cooperation which are implicit in the particular contractual relationship.

1.3.7 Literal or contextual interpretation

Classical contract law focuses on the parties' intentions *as embodied in the contract*. Barring exceptional circumstances, factors external to the four corners of the contract are irrelevant (this is the 'parole evidence rule'). The apparent advantages of this approach are: increasing certainty and predictability; preventing courts from injecting moral or political values into contractual interpretation; and encouraging contract parties to spell out what should happen in future contingencies.

However, absolute certainty is unachievable. Anyway, predictability and fidelity to the parties' intentions are also undermined when courts ignore the social context which gives contractual behaviour its meaning and purpose. Modern contract law has done this by, for example, gap-filling contracts in ways which are consistent with the parties' *reasonable expectations*, and minimising or negating the impact of express terms that contradict such expectations.

1.3.8 Rules/discretionary standards

Classical contract law is identified with a preference for clear and certain rules rather than broad and uncertain discretionary standards. *Rules* ostensibly narrow the judicial inquiry by predetermining what is permissible and what is impermissible, leaving courts to determine factual issues on a finite set of questions. In contrast, *standards* leave both the specification of what is permissible and the determination of the facts to the court.

In practice, there is *no bright line* between rules and standards: the supposed gap between them is reduced by the judicial tendency to make standards more certain (more rule-like, by developing subsidiary principles), and as courts exercise more discretion in their interpretation and selection of rules. Rules which require judges to decide in a particular way on the basis of 'triggering facts', regardless of the context or equity of the case, are likely to lead to *backward reasoning*. Standards such as reasonableness, fairness, good faith, and unconscionability, and structured discretions play an increasing role in modern contract law.

1.3.9 One law or many laws of contract

Classical contract law was developed in an era when most litigation involved commercial transactions. This common fact situation nurtured the idea of a *unified* (and so more certain) law of contract applicable to *all* contracts, irrespective of their context, subject matter, or the nature of the parties. However, such a law was ill-suited to the fair and flexible resolution of non-commercial contractual disputes. The injection of broad standards into contract law opens the way for the different treatment of different types of contracts. Legislation embodies the most significant innovations of modern contract law by hiving off certain types of contracts for specialist treatment (eg consumers and traders, employees and employers, landlords and tenants). These specialist regimes shatter the unity of the law of contract. Their emphasis on avoiding domination and unfairness and encouraging cooperation 'demand a reconsideration of the fundamental assumptions of the classical model' (Collins at 38).

1.3.10 Conclusion on the values reflected in contract law

The story of the evolution of contract law is by no means straightforward. Although the tensions are presented as *rival clusters* of values, current contract law does not coalesce clearly around one or other cluster. There is much academic debate about whether contract law facilitates individual *freedom* or defers to broad principles of *fairness*. However, it is misleading to highlight one at the expense of the other. Indeed, debating which side 'wins' is a somewhat futile exercise. Individualist and interventionist principles share the stage. Contract law is an evolving *integration* of ideals which is informed by, and which in turn informs, social views about contract's role in society.

1.4 **Why are contracts enforced?**

Why does the law recognise some promises and agreements as legally binding but not others? Theories of contract law provide answers by explaining the basis of contractual obligations and, by implication, the main features of contract law. Thus, all contract theories are both *descriptive* and *normative*; they tell us what the law is and what it should be. There is an obvious overlap with the contract *values* or policies just discussed, but contract *theories* exist at a higher level of generality. A contract theory purports to give the 'big picture': it generates relatively open-ended propositions that do not necessarily dictate specific detailed *rules* or how such rules are *applied* in particular situations. Moreover, the detailed rules are often compatible with many different theories because ideally each theory offers a different explanation for them. A theory can 'run out' of predictive power at the level of practice where specific policies may prove more illuminating.

The limited aim of this section is to give a taste of the *range* of explanations for contractual obligations and to begin the task of evaluating them. Interested readers are directed to writings on each main theory and synthesis of different contract theories.[19] (See also **Diagram 1D**.)

---

[19] See S Smith, *Contract Theory* (Clarendon Press, 2004) for further sources.

Diagram 1D Contract theories: why enforce contracts?

1.4.1 Promissory and will theories	*'You should keep your promise.'* *'We agreed.'*
1.4.2 Reliance theory	*'You induced another to rely on your undertaking to his detriment.'*
1.4.3 Efficiency theory (wealth maximisation)	*'Everyone is better off if you keep your bargain.'*
1.4.4 Promoting distributive justice	*'Contract law does or should further wealth distribution.'*
1.4.5 Transfer theory	*'Your contractual performance is already mine.'*
1.4.6 Positive autonomy	*'Contract law does or should support worthwhile choices.'*
1.4.7 Mixed theories	*'Contracts are enforced for a variety of reasons including all of the above.'*

1.4.1 Promise-keeping and will theories

Broadly speaking, promissory and will theories explain contractual liability in terms of respect for *voluntarily assumed obligations* and the corresponding *voluntarily created rights*. Such *self-imposed* obligations are often contrasted with obligations (eg in tort or unjust enrichment) which are externally *imposed by the law*. Fried[20] famously relies on the morality *of promise-keeping to* explain contractual liability. The promisor creates a moral obligation by purposefully invoking 'the convention of promising' (ie conducting himself or herself in a way that is generally understood as making a promise). Enforcement of such promises enables promisors to 'determine their own values' (at 20). 'If we declined to take seriously the assumption of an obligation . . . to that extent we do not take [the promisor] seriously as a person' (at 20–1).

The promissory and will theories can explain much of contract law, for example:

(i) they are consistent with *the justificatory language of the law* (the concepts and reasoning used by courts);

(ii) they explain *who* is affected by the contract. In general, a contract only generates *personal* rights and liabilities in the contracting parties and not third parties;

(iii) they explain *when* the parties become bound. Liability attaches from contract formation, even if the claimant has not relied on it and would suffer no harm if the contract were not enforced;

(iv) they explain why statements of fact ('this car runs well') or of intention ('I will fix your car') generate no contractual liability, while *promises* ('I promise this car runs well', 'I promise to fix your car') do;

---

[20] C Fried, *Contract as Promise: The Theory of Contractual Obligation* (Harvard University Press, 1981).

(v) They explain why the *contents* of the contract depend, in the first instance, on what the parties have expressly agreed;

(vi) they explain doctrines such as mistake, frustration, duress, and undue influence in terms of a defect in one or both parties' consent to the contract;

(vii) they explain why courts can compel the performance of the contract or measure damages by reference to the position that the aggrieved party would have been in had the contract been performed.

On the other hand, promissory and will theories attract some criticisms, for example:

(i) they are *inconsistent with the objective test of intention*. The law enforces promises that parties *appear* to have assumed rather than those that they have *actually* assumed;

(ii) they cannot explain *why the promisee should benefit*. Even if the promisor should keep his or her promise as a matter of self-consistency, they do not explain why the promisee is owed the right to sue for it as a matter of justice. The law could respond in other ways (eg by making promise-breaking an offence). To enforce a promise is essentially to compel the promisor *to benefit* the promisee. Fuller and Perdue famously observed that the expectation damages standardly given for breach of contract represent a 'queer kind of compensation' since they give the promisee something he or she never had.[21] As such, they seem to contradict the foundational principle of modern liberalism, the 'harm principle', according to which the state should only interfere with individual liberty to *prevent harm* to another; mere disappointment is not enough;

(iii) they cannot explain *the requirement of consideration*. The promissory principle cannot explain why, in general, something must be given in exchange for the promise to make it enforceable;

(iv) they have difficulty explaining *legal control of the contents of contracts*. Contract law may render certain unfair terms or even entire contracts unenforceable, or may *imply* terms into contracts. These may owe more to conformity with an ideal of minimum justice in particular types of contracts (eg sale of goods or employment), than to the search for the parties' unexpressed intentions;

(v) they cannot explain why many rules on *remedies* do not reflect the morality of promise-keeping, for example breach is not punished, there is a distinct reluctance to compel performance, and various doctrines reduce the amount of damages payable on breach from that which would truly put the claimant in the position he or she would have been in had the contract been performed.

1.4.2 **Reliance theory**

The essence of the reliance theory[22] is that contractual liability arises (and should arise) where *A* makes a promise to *B* and *B* suffers loss by relying on it. Accordingly,

---

[21] L Fuller and W Perdue, 'The Reliance Interest in Contract Damages' (1936) 46 *Yale LJ* 52, 53.

[22] See P S Atiyah, *The Rise and Fall of the Freedom of Contract* (Clarendon Press, 1979); G Gilmore, *The Death of Contract* (Ohio State University Press, 1974); L Fuller and W Perdue 'The Reliance Interest in Contract Damages' (1936) 46 *Yale LJ* 52, 53.

contractual obligations are primarily aimed at ensuring that people are not made worse off by relying on others' reliance-inducing conduct. These are obligations *imposed by law* because of what people *do* and not because of what they *intend*. Accordingly, Atiyah argues that consent is only an *admission* of pre-existing obligations arising from reliance suffered or benefit conferred. Since contract law's primary aim is to negate the harm caused by induced reliance, much of it belongs in the law of tort and unjust enrichment, supplemented by principles of justice and public policy; contract is only treated as a distinct category for historical and pragmatic reasons.

Reliance theories have a number of attractions.

(i) *Moral justification*: reliance theories are consistent with the 'harm principle'; the state only interferes with individual liberty (by imposing obligations) to prevent harm to others. In their famous article, '**The Reliance Interest in Contract Damages**' (1936) 46 *Yale LJ* 52, **Fuller and Perdue** compare the relative merits of a contract party's restitution, reliance, and expectation interests:

- the **restitution** interest has the strongest claim to protection because where *A* causes *B* to lose one unit (−1), which is transferred to *A* (+1), there are two units of injustice to be remedied. On the Aristotelian ideal of *corrective justice*, aimed at maintaining the equilibrium among members of society, *B*'s restitution interest is twice as strong as his or her

- **reliance** interest (ie −1 without any corresponding enrichment to *A*, although reliance can also incorporate unjust enrichment where *B*'s −1 results in *A*'s +1),

- in turn, *B*'s reliance interest is stronger than his or her expectation interest; where *B*'s material position is unchanged (0), non-fulfilment of *B*'s expectation simply leaves him or her no 'worse off'.

Fuller and Perdue argue that fulfilling expectations passes from the realm of corrective justice to the realm of distributive justice; the law is not just responding to a disturbed status quo but bringing about a new situation.

(ii) *Explains the objective test of intentions*: the protection of reliance readily explains why courts are not concerned with what a contracting party *really* (actually or subjectively) intends, but with what a reasonable person would understand his or her conduct as intending. A party who acts as if he or she intends to contract when he or she actually does not is liable because they thereby induce the other party to rely on this apparent intention.

(iii) *Explains restraints on unfair conduct*: a reliance-based duty is broadly a *duty to take reasonable care of the interests of others*. This can explain the concept of good faith inherent in a number of contractual doctrines such as unconscionability, undue influence, misrepresentation, and promissory estoppel.

On the other hand, reliance theories are open to criticism.

(i) *Reliance is not of the essence of liability*: since people can also rely on statements of fact, the reliance theory does not explain why a *promise* is necessary for the imposition of contractual liability. The rationalisation that only reliance on a promise is worthy of protection free rides on the voluntariness rationale; your reliance is not my problem, *unless I have given a voluntary undertaking*, which seems to be the true source of my obligation.

(ii) *When obligations arise*: contractual liability is not dependent on reliance; it arises when an exchange is agreed, even *before* any acts of reliance on the contract. The exchange element ('consideration') is met by simply *promising* to do something; the promisor need not *actually* have done it.

(iii) *Failure in explaining remedies*: the logical remedy for reliance-based obligations is to negate the reliance loss suffered. However, the remedies for breach of contract can compel performance or, more commonly, the payment of expectation damages.

(iv) *Judicial language*: protecting reliance is not what judges say they are doing.

1.4.3 **Welfare maximisation**

Welfare maximisation theorists see contract law merely as the *means* to the proper *end* of maximising total welfare (alternatively 'happiness', 'utility', or 'efficiency'). Welfare is broadly and subjectively defined as encompassing 'everything that an individual might value—goods and services that the individual can consume, social and environmental amenities, personally held notions of fulfilment, sympathetic feelings for others, and so forth'.[23] Contract law promotes wealth maximisation by giving parties the incentive to act efficiently, and the disincentive to act inefficiently. Something is efficient if its *benefits* outweigh its *costs*. Since efficiency theories deploy economic analyses to defend their claims, they are also called 'economic' theories of contract law.

The core assumption is that voluntary exchanges in free markets should be supported because, by pursuing self-interest, people make themselves and, by extension, society in general, better off. As 'rational maximisers' of their own welfare, parties will only give up resources in return for something they regard as more valuable. I will only offer you £10 for your book if I value the book more than the £10; your acceptance shows that you value the £10 more than your book. Such exchanges tend to move resources to those who value them the most.

The efficiency theory has a number of attractions.

(i) *Value neutrality*: it offers a rationale that claims to be largely objective, determinant, and divorced from politics. Efficiency theories are preferred by those who are fearful that law may be used to destroy autonomy and individuality.

(ii) *Explains the value of voluntariness*: only if exchanges are voluntary will resources be moved to higher value users.

(iii) *Explains the consideration doctrine*: the requirement of an exchange is explicable by the greater efficiency of exchanges in general over gratuitous promises.

(iv) *Explains vitiating factors*: doctrines such as duress, misrepresentation, undue influence, and mistake are explicable not only in terms of ensuring the voluntariness of consent, but also in terms of countering *market imperfections* such as imbalances of power, information, or knowledge which lead to inefficient outcomes.

---

[23] L Kaplow and S Shavell, 'Fairness v Welfare' (2001) 114 *Harvard L Rev* 961, 980.

(v) *Explains the legal control of the contents of contracts*: contract law implies terms and cures uncertainty to fill the gaps in the parties' agreements. This enhances efficiency by releasing parties from the time, cost, and practical impossibility of making a 'complete' contract to govern every conceivable eventuality. Furthermore, the *contents* of the gap-fillers are claimed to be efficient because they: (a) express the parties' genuine but unexpressed intentions, (b) mimic what parties would have agreed had they bargained over the matter with perfect information and without transaction costs, or (c) put the risk of what has happened on the 'superior risk avoider' or the 'superior risk bearer'.

(vi) *Explains remedies*: restrictions on the remedy of specific performance are explained by the theory of *efficient breach*. The argument is that it may be more efficient for parties not to perform the contract, but to breach it; for example, where performance for a third party would generate more profits than the loss suffered by one's contract partner, breach is the efficient option. Thus, remedies should not inhibit efficient breach, but should also not leave the contract partner worse off by the breach. Thus: deliberate breach is not punished; courts rarely compel performance, but instead award money as the primary response to breach (allowing contract parties to choose between performing and paying money not to perform); the measure of compensation is the value of the promised performance (this gives the promisor the incentive to perform unless breach is more profitable); and specific performance *is* granted when the value of performance is too difficult and costly to assess.

Conversely, efficiency theories are open to trenchant criticism.

(i) *Difficulties in calculation*: one commentator observes:[24]

> any serious pursuit of efficiency . . . will often require complex rules. After all, the goals and constraints relevant to a given policy are likely to be numerous, and the legal rules, in order to be efficient, must take account of, and be tailored to, each of them. Accomplishing this may necessitate a system of multi-factored rules, complex defences, complex party structures, sequential burden shifting, and so on.

Eric Posner famously observes that: [25]

> Economics fails to explain contract law . . . And economics provides little normative guidance for reforming contract law. Models that have been proposed in the literature either focus on fine aspects of contractual behaviour or make optimal doctrine a function of variables that cannot realistically be observed, measured, or estimated. The models do give a sense of the factors that are at stake when the decisionmaker formulates doctrine, and might give that decisionmaker a sense of the trade-offs involved, but in the absence of information about the magnitude of these trade-offs- and the literature gives no sense of these magnitudes- the decisionmaker is left with little guidance.

---

[24] P Schuck, 'Legal Complexity: Some Causes, Consequences, and Cures' (1992) 42 *Duke LJ* 1, 37.
[25] Eric Posner, 'Economic Analysis of Contract Law after Three Decades: Success or Failure?' (2003) 112 *Yale LJ* 829, 880.

(ii) *The 'efficient breach' claim is open to question:*

- the cost of negotiating around the breach and of reselling the contractual subject matter to third parties is often ignored. As Macneil observes:[26]

> the whole thrust of the [efficient breach] analysis is breach first, talk after-wards . . . despite the fact that 'talking after a breach' may be one of the most expensive forms of conversation to be found, involving, as it so often does, engaging high-priced lawyers, and gambits like starting litigation, engaging in discovery, and even trying and appealing cases . . . [these are] uncooperative and—ironically enough—highly inefficient human behaviour.

- Specific performance is arguably the more efficient remedy since it avoids the often difficult and uncertain calculations of damages;

- even if specific performance were widely available, wasteful performance would not happen. *Rational parties would negotiate around the remedy* so that they share the profits (or savings) from breach rather than allow the contract-breaker total retention;

- even if we can identify all the relevant factors in the efficiency equation (including eg whether specific performance or damages give parties the bet-ter incentive to contract in the first place), it is impossible to attach accurate figures to them.

(iii) *Unrealistic assumptions*: efficiency theories are too simplistic in assuming, for example, that parties act rationally with the single motivation of maximising their welfare, *measured by willingness to pay*. This ignores the complexities of human psy-chology, the irrational aspects of human behaviour and conduct which expresses preferences unrelated to wealth (broadly conceived) such as altruism, relational com-mitment, and integrity.

(iv) *Moral objections:*

- critics object that by accepting the starting point of pre-existing wealth dis-tribution and measuring efficiency by reference to willingness to pay, *the theory favours the rich*. For example, it assumes that welfare is maximised by allocating a pair of shoes to someone willing to pay £100 for those shoes although he or she has hundreds of other pairs, rather than to the poor per-son without shoes who can only pay £20;

- efficiency theories do not take individual rights seriously.[27] For example, the idea that damages are preferable to specific performance because this gives the right incentives for efficient breach rests on the morally repugnant idea that one is free to take another's right or breach a legal duty so long as one is willing to pay the 'price' for it. The latter is not even necessary so long as the efficiency gains *overall* (however distributed) exceed the loss to any particular individual;

- by refusing to engage with questions of whether preferences are good or bad in terms of the welfare of individuals and of society in general, and whether

---

[26] I Macneil, 'Efficient Breach of Contract: Circles in the Sky' (1982) 68 *Virginia L Rev* 947, 968–9.
[27] R Dworkin, *Taking Rights Seriously* (Harvard University Press, 1978) 184–205.

some ordering or hierarchy of an individual's preferences is possible or desirable, efficiency theories simply suppress the inescapable balancing between individual freedom, individual welfare, and the interests of society.

(v) *Lack of transparency*: judges rarely explain what they are doing in terms of promoting overall efficiency.

1.4.4 **Promoting distributive justice**

Kronman argues[28] that 'distributive justice not only *ought* to be taken into account in designing rules for exchange, but *must* be taken into account if the law of contracts is to have even minimum moral acceptability'. In his view, contracting cannot be understood except as a distributional concept. The notion of individual autonomy, taken by itself, provides no guidance on which of the many forms of advantage-taking possible in exchange relations should be permitted. While it is generally thought that taxation and welfare are the primary tools for wealth distribution in a liberal society, contract law should also be used when alternatives may be more costly or intrusive.

This explanation of contract law may claim:

(i) *moral attractiveness*: it expresses a more robust emphasis on equality in liberal democratic societies in its concern with the distribution of resources and opportunities; if not equally, then at the level of some irreducible minimum;[29]

(ii) consistency with vitiating factors such as misrepresentation and duress as legal restraints on the exercise of power, rather than the absence of 'real' consent;

(iii) consistent with legal controls *of substantive unfairness*: such as implied terms, the invalidity of certain unfair terms, and restrictions on remedies such as specific performance.

However, a distributive theory of contract encounters enormous obstacles, for example:

(i) contract law is a poor tool for altering existing distributions of wealth. Indeed, contracting is a major cause of distributional inequalities;

(ii) distributive contract law rules (eg increasing quality or reducing price of goods or services) can be neutralised by the parties changing other terms of subsequent contracts. Strongly distributive contract rules will make parties more reluctant to contract with the protected group.

1.4.5 **Transfer theory**

On this theory, contracts are like property.[30] The ability to *create* property rights (to obtain the exclusive use and possession of a *thing*) and to *transfer* property rights is a

---

[28] A Kronman, 'Contract Law and Distributive Justice' (1980) 89 *Yale LJ* 472.

[29] J Rawls, *A Theory of Justice* (Belknap Press of Harvard University Press, 1971); R Dworkin, *Law's Empire* (Belknap Press of Harvard University Press, 1986).

[30] For a summary of this debate, see P Lee, 'Inducing Breach of Contract, Conversion and Contract as Property' (2009) 29 *OJLS* 511, 513–20. See also *OBG v Allan* [2007] UKHL 21, [2008] 1 AC 1, [309] (Baroness Hale). For criticism of this view, see eg A Goymour, 'Conversion of Contractual Rights' (2011) *LMCLQ* 67, 68–9.

necessary precondition of individual autonomy. Contract law facilitates the creation of present **ownership** of the right to the promisor's future performance and this right is held by the promisee as part of his or her *present wealth*. Benson argues that a contractual right entails a right to *exclusive* possession of the goods or services promised; it is proprietary in character. The wrong of breach of contract consists of depriving the promisee of the thing promised, including its value and use.

This theory is consistent with:

(i)   the importance of voluntariness in contracting;

(ii) the 'harm principle' because breach is not just failure to benefit, but is interference with what *already* belongs to, the promisee;

(iii) the remedies of specific performance and the expectation measure of damages.

The main objections are:

(i) *timing*: contractual *rights* are transferred at formation prior to any later performance, while there is normally no such time lapse between the transfer of property ownership and performance. **Benson** replies that:[31] 'It is not the physical delivery of property that confers ownership of property; most legal systems allow for ownership without physical possession, there can be no objection to contracts transferring ownership without transferring possession. The important issue in both contract and property is consent';

(ii) *contract rights are personal*: they do not, as property law does, give the promisee rights of a proprietary character. The major implication is that contractual rights, unlike property rights, give no priority to the right-holder on the other's bankruptcy; he or she can only share in what is left along with the other creditors. Douglas argues that the label of property is not useful in determining the extent of legal protection that contractual rights should receive.[32] Instead, it is better to examine the specific characteristics of contractual rights, to see whether they can fit within the framework of protection established for the core examples of property, such as physical objects. He concludes that they cannot.

1.4.6 **Positive autonomy**

Raz[33] sees the role of the state as not to hold people to their promises (which is mere legal moralism), but to create the conditions of 'positive autonomy': 'it is the goal of all political action to enable individuals to pursue valid conceptions of the good and to discourage evil or empty ones' (Raz at 133). Hence, 'the autonomy principle . . . permits and even requires government [ie law] to create and support morally valuable opportunities, and to eliminate or discourage repugnant ones' (Raz at 417). To support

---

[31] P Benson, 'Abstract Right and the Possibility of a Nondistributive Conception of Contract: Hegel and Contemporary Contract Theory' (1989) 10 *Cardozo L Rev* 1077.

[32] S Douglas, 'The Scope of Conversion: Property and Contract' (2011) 74 *MLR* 329, 335–7.

[33] J Raz, *The Morality of Freedom* (OUP, 1986) 369; R Brownsword, 'Liberalism in the Law of Contract' (1988) 36 *Archives for Philosophy of Law and Social Philosophy* 86; S Smith 'Future Freedom and Freedom of Contract' (1996) 59 *MLR* 167.

contract-making is to support people in making **worthwhile (positive) choices**. It facilitates special relationships with others; special, because contract provides a reason for one party to treat the other's interests as superior to all others' interests in relation to the contract's subject matter. This is distinct from freedom of contract in the *negative* sense of freedom *from* coercion or intervention which does not guarantee the exercise of *positive* autonomy.

Raz[34] regards the purpose of contract law as that of protecting 'both the practice of undertaking voluntary obligations and the individuals who rely on the practice'. Its role is *supportive* rather than initiating: it reinforces existing norms and practices, thereby increasing confidence in them and extending their use ('But for the support of the law, contracts between complete strangers would not be as numerous and common as they are' (at 934)). It 'acts as a conservative force, hindering influences that tend to undermine the practices it reinforces'.

Collins' **transformation thesis** takes this further, arguing that contract law does and should regulate the practice of contracting to ensure conformity with three ideals of social justice (at 28–35):

(i)   the avoidance of unjustifiable domination;

(ii)   ensuring the substantive fairness of the exchange; and

(iii)   fostering cooperation.

This theory has the following main attractions.

(i) Consistency with *the harm principle*: unlike reliance theorists who focus solely on harm to the *individual,* the relevant harm in question here includes *institutional* harm. Preventing the erosion in or debasement of the practice of contract is therefore a 'fit object for the law to pursue' (Raz at 937).

(ii) It explains *the objective test of intentions*: people must be prevented from abusing the *practice* of contracting by making it appear that they have agreed to obligations when they have not.

(iii) Consistency with *contextual interpretation*: it explains why courts do and should refer to the *social norms* which inform the practice of contracting when interpreting contracts, gap-filling incomplete contracts, and formulating default rules.

(iv) It *explains the vitiating factors*: contracts resulting from duress, misrepresentation, undue influence, unconscionability, or fundamental mistake are not the sort of exercises of positive (worthwhile) autonomy that should be supported by the law. To enforce them would debase the practice of contracting.

On this view, the practice of contracting is a collective good which requires steering, channelling, and supplementation. Whilst the positive autonomy theory accords considerable respect to the parties' self-regulation, it also makes room for the law's role in regulating contractual practices *with a view to controlling the types of relationships established through contract and the distributive consequences.*

---

[34] J Raz, 'Promises in Morality and Law' (1982) 95 *Harvard L Rev* 916.

1.4.7 **Mixed theories**

Contract theorists do not generally claim total explanatory power for their favoured theory. Given the complexities and competing norms in contract law, they are pre-pared to concede some limited role to values highlighted by other theories, although not at the level of justifying first principles. The alternative is to say that no single theory can explain all of contract law but that *each contributes vital insights into the nature and basis of contract law.*[35] On this view, contract law does not need to fit neatly or even largely into any slot. It recognises that contract law includes apparent con-tradictions, is subject to competing norms and various exceptions, and is fragmented by special rules applying to distinct kinds of contracts. This being so, contract law reflects the legal system's practical compromises over a multiplicity of methods, val-ues, and goals. This is unsurprising since it would be unrealistic to expect one unified theory to explain every aspect of a body of law which has evolved over hundreds of years in the hands of many individuals. We should be wary of theory's potential for excessive abstraction, reductionism, and oversimplification.

However, this is also the main criticism of a mixed theory view; namely, that it is a largely ad hoc and unstable mix which is anti-theoretical.[36] One response is the 'vertical integration strategy' put forward by Kraus,[37] according to which different theories have a different role to play within one overall theory. Thus, he argues that while autonomy theories are normatively *foundational*, they are fundamentally vague, essentially contestable, and not sufficiently fine-grained to determine the many issues that fall within the grey area. They lack the resources to translate the value of auton-omy into concrete analysis. Other theories, especially the efficiency theory, might then provide an *operational*, but subordinate, principle; useful for providing practical answers for questions raised in actual situations.

1.5 **How far does contract law *reach*?**

Three factors limit the impact of contract law:

(i)   contract law's reluctance to intervene in family or social arrangements;

(ii) specialist regimes which have replaced general contract law in many important areas; and

(iii) empirical studies which indicate the limited relevance of contract law in 'real' life.

1.5.1 **Family and social arrangements**

Contract law is largely concerned with *economic* exchange taking place in the *market* (eg buying and selling, leasing and hiring, employment and services,

---

[35] See R Hillman, *The Richness of Contract Law: An Analysis and Critique of Contemporary Theories of Contract Law* (Kluwer, 1998); S M Waddams, *Dimensions of Private Law: Categories and Concepts in Anglo-American Legal Reasoning* (Cambridge University Press, 2003).

[36] J Feinman, 'The Significance of Contract Theory' (1990) 58 *U Cin L Rev* 1283.

[37] Jody S Kraus, 'Reconciling Autonomy and Efficiency in Contract Law: The Vertical Integration Strategy' (2001) 11 *Philosophical Issues* 420.

money-lending and borrowing). It is reluctant to get involved in *non-market* trans-actions which take place in a *family* or *social* context (eg 'You cook and I'll wash up', 'I will help with the cost of your rent, car, or education'). This reluctance is expressed in the strong presumption that, even if all the other requirements of an enforceable contract are satisfied, there is no 'intention to create legal relations' in such agreements (see 2.7).

Pause for reflection

The doctrine of 'intention to create legal relations' is conceptually important because it marks one boundary of contract law. The question is how far the *state* should intervene in the private activities of individuals by state coercion. Collins (at 56–7) offers two persuasive reasons against the 'contractualisation of social life'.

1. It may amount to an *excessive intrusion into the private lives of the citizens*. Informal arrangements may be binding in morality or etiquette (to be settled by compromise or informal social sanctions), but they should not be the subject of state intervention (in the form of awards of damages for breach).

2. It may *subvert the values of the relationship*. For example, to see relationships such as those of husband–wife, parent–child, or friend–friend in contractual terms seems to suggest that they can be reduced to measurable obligations. This can inhibit the open-ended and diffuse obligations characteristic of such relationships (eg trust, affection, commitment, and altruism). The same can be said of the teacher–student relationship.

1.5.2 Specialist areas: law of contract or law of contracts

In reality, the *general* law of contract is only applicable to a small portion of contracts actually made: it is not directly applicable to enormous swathes of contracts which are subject to *specialist statutory regimes* (eg contracts involving employment, land, hire purchase, consumer credit, financial services, companies, and sale of goods). Thus, it can be said that we do not have a *unified* law of contract but a *differentiated* law of contracts. Contract is not a monolithic phenomenon.

Atiyah questions the significance of general contract law rules which are 'general only by default, only because they are being superseded by detailed ad hoc rules lacking any principle or by new principles of narrow scope and application'.[38] There is truth in this. However, general contract principles remain important as the foundation on which specialist regimes are built. Moreover, specialist regimes emphasise discernible values and policies which qualify the fundamental assumptions of classical contract law. For example, statutory regimes identify categories of persons warranting special protection (eg consumers, employees, borrower, and tenants) and aim

---

[38] P S Atiyah, 'Contracts, Promises and the Law of Obligations' in P S Atiyah (ed), *Essays on Contract* (Clarendon Press, 1986) 19.

to promote fairness (eg by specifying mandatory procedures or terms or by employing standards such as reasonableness, fairness, and good faith).

1.5.3 Empirical evidence: contract law in the real world

Studies[39] show that, in practice, even business people often do not:

- plan or draft agreements carefully;
- consult lawyers;
- think in terms of their legal rights;
- understand the legal ramifications of their contracts; or
- resort to the law when something goes wrong.

Rather, the importance of establishing and preserving long-term business relationships and good reputations favours flexibility, compromise, and resort to customs or non-legal sanctions, over standing on one's legal rights.

Relational contract theorists argue that classical contract law is *unsuitable* for regulating most modern business arrangements as it ignores their *relational dimension*. However, numerous contract rules and standards *do* invite courts to analyse the implicit understandings and expectations of its participants.[40] Moreover, despite the rarity of business parties resorting to the law, they nevertheless settle their disputes 'in the shadow of the law'. Furthermore:

(i) contract law allows people to choose whether to enter a *binding* agreement rather than rely on purely informal arrangements; and provides a framework at the planning stage, especially where parties do not know each other or the contractual subject matter is unusual, important, or risky;

(ii) contract law helps to resolve *disputes* when flexibility and compromise run out or relationships break down irretrievably.

1.6 Contract law's relationship to other branches of private law

Seeing contract *law* in the context of neighbouring branches of private law:

(i) gives another perspective to the *nature and role of contract law*; and

(ii) shows when other branches of private law may apply to resolve problems arising in the life of a contract. They may operate to fill perceived gaps in contract law, or take over where contract law naturally leaves off.

---

[39] Notably S Macaulay, 'Contract Law and Contract Research (Part II)' (1968) 20 *J Legal Educ* 460; H Beale and A Dugdale, 'Contracts between Businessmen: Planning and the Use of Contractual Remedies' (1975) *2 Br JL & Soc* 45.

[40] See generally D Campbell, H Collins, and J Wightman, *Implicit Dimensions of Contract: Discrete, Relational, and Network Contracts* (Hart Publishing, 2003).

The subject is complex and controversial. *Again, don't worry about the details.* At this stage, it is enough to get a flavour of the issues that will be more fully explained in the text.

1.6.1 Contract law's place in private law

Public law is concerned with the relationship between the citizen and the *state* (eg constitutional, administrative, or criminal law). *Private* law is concerned with the rights and obligations *between citizens* generated by their interactions. Contract law is part of *private* law.

In **Diagram 1E**:

Row I shows that private law comprises the laws of contract, tort, unjust enrichment, and property.

Row II denotes the *causative events* which generate the different types of liability. Whilst the matter is not free of controversy, the orthodox view is that:

- *contractual* obligations are generated by voluntarily undertaking obligations to another who gives a reciprocal voluntary undertaking or performance;

Diagram 1E Comparing contract, tort, unjust enrichment, and property law

I. PRIVATE LAW	CONTRACT	TORT	UNJUST ENRICHMENT	PROPERTY
II. Causative event	(a) Reciprocal undertakings (b) Deed	(c) Engaging in conduct that may cause harm to others	(d) Receipt of unjust or undue enrichment	Property obtained by (a), (b), (c), or (d)
III. Source of the duty	'Self-imposed'	Imposed by the law		
IV. Nature of the duty	To perform one's undertaking	To avoid causing harm by the prescribed conduct with the specified state of mind	To return unjust enrichment	To respect property rights
V. Rights generated	'Law of obligations' generating *personal* rights			'Property law' generating *proprietary* rights
VI. Potentially enforceable against	Only the party owing the duty (*in personam*)			Everyone (*in rem*)
VII. Nature of the remedy	Actual performance or compensation for non-performance	Compensation for harm caused	Restitution of benefit gained	Return of property; and account for the fruits of the property (actionable as *torts* or equitable wrongs)

- obligations in *tort* are generated by engaging in conduct which can cause harm to others;

- obligations in *unjust enrichment* are generated by the receipt of an unjust enrichment at the expense of another;

- obligations in *property* law arise on another's acquisition of property rights (the latter may arise from the same events that generate personal obligations).[41]

Rows III to VI compare the source and nature of the duty, the rights generated, and the nature of the remedy in each branch of private law:

In **contract**, duties are traditionally seen as *self-imposed*. The duty is, broadly, to do what one has undertaken (ie perform the contract). It follows that the other party is entitled to the performance and their remedy for breach is actual performance or its money equivalent (expectation damages).

In contrast, duties in tort, unjust enrichment, and property are generally said to be *imposed by the general law*. In **tort law**, the duty is not to cause harm, by engaging in the proscribed conduct with the specified state of mind (whether deliberately, carelessly, or even innocently (ie strict liability torts)), to another's physical well-being, property, economic position, or reputation. This points to remedies measured by the claimant's reliance and aimed at restoring him or her to the position he or she would have been in without the wrongful infliction of harm.

Unjust enrichment law rests on the corrective justice of reversing one party's unjust enrichment at the expense of another. The duty is to return the unjust enrichment and the corresponding remedy is the restitution of benefits received. The classic restitutionary claim arises where you pay me money by mistake. You can seek the return of the sum even if there is no contract between us and I have committed no tort against you.

Property rights include rights in the 'thing' itself and in the *fruits* (profits) of the thing. Correlatively, there is a duty to respect others' rights in property (eg in land, tangible chattels, or intangibles such as a debt, shares in a company, or a patent).[42] However, it is *tort* law (including equitable wrongs) which generates the wrongs arising from the infringement of property rights. A myriad of common law and equitable remedies aim to negate the infringement:

- by ordering return of the 'thing' itself;

- where this is impossible (eg the 'thing' has been used up, altered, or sold on) or inappropriate (eg the 'thing' has merely been used to generate profits or savings), or where the right was never 'to' the thing anyway (eg a right merely for its use), then by declaring trusts, or by awarding monetary relief in the form of damages measured by some combination of the value of the property, the value of the *use* of the property, or by an account of profits (such monetary awards may equally be said to belong in tort); or

- by ordering people to take action (or not to take action) calculated to protect the property right.[43]

---

[41] P Birks, *Unjust Enrichment* (2nd edn, Clarendon Press, 2005) 28–30.

[42] See F Lawson and B Rudden, *The Law of Property* (2nd edn, Clarendon Press, 1982).

[43] Eg a *quia timet* injunction restraining a trespass or a breach of a restrictive covenant; an eviction order or a mandatory injunction correcting such wrongs *ex post*; an order replacing a corrupt trustee.

Row VII shows that property rights (rights *in rem*) are potentially enforceable against the whole world.[44] In contrast, voluntary undertakings, wrongs, or unjust enrichment (collectively known as the 'law of obligations') give rise to personal rights (rights *in personam*): the right-holder can only enforce them against the specific party with whom their interaction generated the right. Voluntary undertakings, wrongs, and unjust enrichment can give rise to personal or sometimes property rights. Property rights belong in the law of property and personal rights belong in the law of obligations.

Pause for reflection

This brief overview is a useful starting point but it is, inevitably, an oversimplification. For example:

1. The contrast between 'self-imposed' duties (in contract) and duties 'imposed by the law' (in tort, unjust enrichment, and property) is false in the sense that all (legal) duties are imposed by the law. People can only impose duties on themselves (eg by making contracts) where that is what the *law* allows. In this sense, the real contrast is between the different kinds of reasons why the law imposes a duty.[45]

2. Tort and property law duties may also arise from voluntary undertakings (ie can be described as self-imposed); for example, a tortious duty of care can arise from an 'assumption of responsibility' and property rights can arise from voluntary transfers.[46]

3. Conversely, contractual liability may arise from other than a voluntary undertaking (eg for breach of implied terms, especially where that liability cannot be excluded). Many features of modern contracting are not fixed by the parties but by the courts and the legislature. Some of these default rules may be modified by the parties to some extent (eg the remedies for breach), others may not be changed at all (eg when contracts are vitiated).

4. Damages for breach of contract are primarily aimed at fulfilling the expectation created by the contract, but they may, sometimes, be measured by the claimant's reliance or restitution interest.

5. The contrast between contract and tort damages is blurred where reliance damages include loss of opportunity to make an alternative similar contract so that, in practice, they mimic expectation damages.

It is impossible to maintain the bright lines which ostensibly distinguish contract law from the other branches of private law. This is seized upon by those (eg Gilmore and Atiyah)[47] who call for the categories to be merged into a unitary law of obligations, reclassified according to the nature of the claimant's interest sought to be protected. This view is not generally accepted

➡

---

[44] But they do not generally bind everyone absolutely and always.

[45] I am grateful to Simon Gardner for this point.

[46] It is true that when property rights operate against third parties they do so without a voluntary undertaking by the latter, but that is a facet of their legal quality as *in rem*, rather than their mode of creation.

[47] G Gilmore, *The Death of Contract* (Ohio State University Press, 1974); P S Atiyah, *The Rise and Fall of the Freedom of Contract* (Clarendon Press, 1979).

> ➡
>
> and it is questionable whether it would necessarily represent an improvement. Legal thinking demands some classifications, and a united law of obligations would need to include a category (whether called contract or not) which is concerned with the protection of expectations based on another's voluntary undertaking of obligations.

1.6.2 Applying tort, unjust enrichment, and property law to contractual problems

Disputes arising in the life of a contract are not the exclusive preserve of contract law. It is not a matter of 'contract law or nothing'. The law of torts and unjust enrichment and property law may also apply. For example, conduct during contract negotiations which do not result in a contract may still result in the transfer of property rights and yield liability in tort or in unjust enrichment. Again, although the general rule of privity is that contracts only create rights and duties between parties to the contract, third parties may have claims under, and be bound by, other branches of private law. Further, while the contractual measure of damages is expectation, a claimant may, in certain circumstances, opt for the *reliance* measure, the restitutionary measure, or even claim the profits made by the contract-breaker from his or her breach.

1.7 External influences on English contract law

English contract law operates in a world where markets are increasingly international in scope and interdependent in nature. International trade, the rise of instantaneous electronic communications, multinational enterprises, and the creation of free trade blocs such as the European Union, mean that sources of contract law external to domestic law can affect the legal significance of contracts. In fact, English contract law has been hugely influential around the world for three reasons. First, English law has been spread through its colonial history (hence it is the basis of the law in the United States, Canada, Australia, New Zealand, Hong Kong, and Singapore). Second, England and specifically the City of London, has historically been a great commercial centre. Third, parties in a position to dictate the choice of law may opt for English contract law, which is relatively more respectful of the agreement and so more certain, and untrammelled by principles of disclosure, good faith, and fair dealing. It is unsurprising that English lawyers are unenthusiastic about the creation of European or international contract law to supplement or replace English contract law.

The UK government opposes any form of comprehensive codification. The problems of codification, mentioned earlier (see 1.2.2), are multiplied when it comes to harmonisation at the European level. Significant differences exist not only at the level of *substance* but also at the level of *legal reasoning*. The deductive style of reasoning of civil law systems (applying general principles to particular cases) can be contrasted with common law's preference for inductive reasoning (case-by-case analysis from which general principles may emerge). Adaptability is facilitated by the common law's ability to ignore or revive earlier lines of authority. An important consideration is whether the pragmatic and inductive qualities of common law legal reasoning would be stifled by the influence of the formal deductive style of reasoning characteristic of legal systems governed by codes.

1.7.1 **European law**

The UK's membership of the European Union means that European law may govern domestic contractual disputes. The Council of the European Union can adopt measures that have as their object 'the establishment and functioning of the internal market' (Art 100A Treaty of Rome). The aim is to facilitate the European internal market by reducing the deterrent effect on contracting resulting from variations between the contract laws of Member States. This aim of **harmonisation** has, to date, borne fruit primarily in the field of consumer protection, for example:[48]

- the Consumer Rights Directive (2011/83/EU; implemented by the Consumer Contracts (Information, Cancellation and Additional Charges) Regulations 2013 (SI 2013/3134));

- the Unfair Terms in Consumer Contracts Directive (1993/13/EEC; implemented by the Unfair Terms in Consumer Contracts Regulations 1999 (SI 1999/2083));

- the Electronic Signatures Directive (1999/93/EC; implemented by the Electronic Communications Act 2000 and the Electronic Signatures Regulations 2002 (SI 2002/318));

- the E-Commerce Directive (2000/31/EC; implemented by the Electronic Commerce (EC Directive) Regulations 2002 (SI 2002/2013));

- the Unfair Commercial Practices Directive (2005/29/EC).

Since 2001, the European Commission has taken steps towards a European Contract Law. The most recent are the Draft Common Frame of Reference (DCFR),[49] published in 2009; the European Commission's Green Paper (COM (2010) 348 final), and the *Expert Group Feasibility Study* published in 2011. A range of options are currently being debated. Among them are, from the least to the most assertive models:

- a '**non-binding instrument**, aimed at improving the consistency and quality of EU legislation'; this is a set of model rules that does not have the force of the law;

- a non-binding '**toolbox**', which the Commission and Member States can draw from when drafting or reforming national or EU contract law;

- an '**optional instrument**' that would exist alongside the national laws of Member States and which contract parties can choose between to govern their contract. This would add a layer of complexity to the contract law of any Member State;

---

[48] See H Beale, 'The "Europeanization" of Contract Law' in R Halson (ed), *Exploring the Boundaries of Contract* (Ashgate, 1996).

[49] C von Bar, H Beale, and others (eds), *Principles, Definitions and Model Rules of European Private Law—Draft Common Frame of Reference* (Sellier, 2009). This is largely based on Lando and Beale's *Principles of European Contract Law*, published in 2000 under the auspices of the Commission.

- a Directive setting out the **'minimum common standards'** for Member States;
- a Directive setting out a **uniform set of rules** 'including mandatory rules affording a high level of protection for weaker parties' that could replace national laws;
- a **'binding instrument'** setting out an alternative to the existing national law. This is highly unlikely to be accepted by the UK.

On 26 February 2014 the European Parliament voted in favour of introducing an optional **Common European Sales Law** (CESL). CESL must now be adopted by the Council of Ministers before it can become law. Even then, it would only apply to cross-border contracts (eg online or phone transactions) and only if both parties agreed. It covers both business-to-consumer (B2C) and business-to-business (B2B) contracts for the sale of goods and supply of digital content (eg video, audio, and digital games), and related service contracts, such as installation, maintenance, and repair. The proposal passed with a vote of 416 for, 159 against, and 65 abstentions. In November 2012, the UK government criticised the 'fundamental flaws in both the principle and practical operation' of CESL. In particular, it said:

- 'The instrument is: too complex, incomplete in parts (some significant aspects of a contractual relationship are not covered), unworkable for certain types of contract, uncertain, both as to whether a contract is valid and as to the certainty of its terms; and unclear on its applicability, in particular how its provisions interact with other EU law.'
- The general duty to 'act in accordance with good faith and fair dealing' is 'likely to be abused or lead to protracted disputes'.
- CESL 'does not serve in resolving the specific problems that B2B, B2C and digital sectors may have'. In some situations, such as telephone sales, the regime would be 'unworkable'.
- Doubts surrounding various provisions and definitions in CESL undermine the certainty that businesses need.

1.7.2 International commercial law

The drive towards harmonisation of contract law goes beyond Europe. The primary mechanism is the production of **non-binding statements of principles or model contracts**. The UNIDROIT Principles of International Commercial Contracts were drawn up by a team of, mainly, legal academics from all over the world, published in 1994, expanded in 2004 to 185 Articles, and expanded again in 2010 to 211 Articles with accompanying commentary. Contract parties can incorporate these Principles as terms of their contract or as the law applicable to the contract. While the latter is not recognised in national courts, the UNIDROIT Principles play an important role in international commercial arbitration.

There is also a growing number of **international standard form contracts** on particular subjects that have been widely accepted by contract parties, for example the INCOTERMS (sponsored by the International Chamber of Commerce) on international sales and the FIDIC (Fédération Internationale des Ingénieurs-Conseils) Conditions of Contract for Works of Civil Engineers for international construction contracts.

Mandatory schemes are more controversial. For example, if a country ratifies the United Nations Convention on Contracts for the International Sale of Goods 1988 (also known as the 'Vienna Sales Convention' or 'CISG'), it is applicable to all international sale of goods contracts, unless the parties specifically opt out of it. The Convention has been ratified by over 60 countries including the United States, France, Germany, and China, but not the UK. Supporters of ratification argue that it will reduce the cost of negotiating international sales since parties can simply look to the Convention to govern their agreement. However, uniformity does not necessarily bring certainty: the Convention is the product of many compromises and is likely to receive varying interpretations in different national courts. Moreover, such a 'code' will be difficult to amend in response to the changing needs of international trade. The same could be said of any European contract code.

1.7.3 Human rights law

The Human Rights Act 1998 incorporates the European Convention for the Protection of Human Rights and Fundamental Freedoms 1950 by making Convention rights enforceable in domestic law. Section 6(1) makes it 'unlawful for a public authority [which includes 'a court or tribunal'] to act in a way which is incompatible with a Convention right'. It is therefore clear that the Convention applies to a contract between a *public authority and a private party*. By virtue of section 3, it also applies to contracts between private parties *when legislation must be interpreted*; it must be 'read and given effect in a way which is compatible with Convention rights'. Beyond that, it is arguable that the court, as a public authority, must act consistently with Convention rights, in the sense that it must observe Convention rights *in adjudication* between private parties. Thus, for example, enforcement of a contract of slavery would contravene **Article 4** of the Convention if it was not already invalid in English law. However, the precise impact of the Human Rights Act on domestic contract law is still unclear. Potentially relevant Articles include the following.

- **Article 1** of Protocol 1 the *protection of the peaceful enjoyment of possessions*—this could invalidate legislation which overrides traders' contractual rights or retention of property rights in pursuit of consumer protection.

online
resource
centre

- **Article 6** the *right to a fair trial*—this may override the current refusal of courts to enforce contracts that are illegal or against public policy or to grant restitution of benefits conferred under them (see Additional Chapter 2 which is available on the Online Resource Centre). The Law Commission recognises[50] that by denying enforcement and restitution, the courts are at risk of contravening a claimant's rights to a fair trial, to the protection of his or her property (Art 1 of Protocol 1), and to not being punished without due process (Art 7). If so, such contraventions must be justified by the public interest exceptions of the Convention (*Shanshal v Al-Kishtaini* (2001)).

- **Article 8(1)** the right to respect for a person's home and private and family life.

---

[50] *Illegal Transactions: The Effect of Illegality on Contracts and Trusts* (Law Com Consultation Paper 154, 1999).

- **Article 9(2)** *the right to manifest one's religion or belief,* 'subject only to such limitations as are prescribed by law and are necessary in a democratic society in the interests of public safety, for the protection of public order, health or morals, or for the protection of the rights and freedoms of others'. In *Bull v Hall & Anor* (2013) Christian hoteliers refused to let a double-bedded room to two homosexual men in a civil partnership because of their policy to only let such rooms to heterosexual married couples. The Supreme Court held (at [44], [51]) that they contravened regulation 3(1) of the Equality Act (Sexual Orientation) Regulations 2007. The limitation on the hoteliers' right to manifest their religion was a proportionate means of achieving a legitimate aim—the protection of others' rights and freedoms.

- **Article 10** the *right to freedom of expression and information*. In *Ashworth v Royal National Theatre* (2014) the court refused to grant specific performance or a mandatory injunction to musicians requiring the Royal National Theatre to re-engage them in a production of a play (*War Horse*) because to do so would interfere with the theatre's right of artistic freedom under Article 10 of the European Convention on Human Rights 1950 and prevent it from continuing to stage a play in the form which it judged to be artistically preferable.

- **Article 11** the *right to freedom of association*. This may be used in support of the ideal of freedom of contract and against rules which restrict that freedom.

- **Article 14** against *discrimination* on any ground such as sex, race, colour, language, religion, political or other opinion, national or social origin, association with a national minority, property, birth, or other status. This and Article 8(1) were used to interpret provisions of the Rent Act 1977 (granting a statutory tenancy to the 'surviving spouse' of the original tenant) to include homosexual cohabitees (*Ghaidan v Godin-Mendoza* (2004)).

Wilson v First County Trust Ltd (No 2) (2003) shows that courts will be slow to use their powers under the Human Rights Act 1998 to undermine modern regulation of contracts in the name of protecting property rights and freedom of contract (and see *Jitesh Salat v Mindaugas Barutis* (2013)). The case relates to section 127(3) of the Consumer Credit Act 1974, which seeks to protect consumers by making a consumer credit agreement unenforceable by the creditor if the contract is not made in the prescribed form. The Court of Appeal declared this a contravention of Article 1 of Protocol 1 (since the creditor is barred from taking possession of any security in the event of the debtor's default), and of Article 6 (since the more appropriate response is to give courts the *discretion* to do justice between the parties in view of the seriousness of the breach and the degree of prejudice to the consumer). However, the House of Lords overturned this because the court had no jurisdiction (the events predated the operation of the Human Rights Act 1998)[51] and anyway, the relevant provision was not incompatible with Convention rights.

---

[51] However, in *PW & Co v Milton Gate Investments Ltd* (2003) Neuberger J held that the requirements of the Human Rights Act 1998 could be applied to a lease made before the Act came into force so long as it did not impair 'vested rights' or 'otherwise create unfairness', [107]–[115].

(i) There was no breach of **Article 1** of Protocol 1 because, in view of the social problems caused by money-lending transactions and the inequality of bargaining power between borrowers and lenders, Parliament was entitled to decide that the appropriate way of protecting the borrower was to deprive the lender of all rights under the agreement, including the rights to any security, unless the statutory requirements have been strictly complied with. It was a *proportionate* means of achieving the legitimate aim of consumer protection.

(ii) There was no breach of **Article 6** since it is really aimed at *procedural* bars preventing *access* to the courts.

Pause for reflection

Chitty (at paras 1-079, 1-083) supports the 'indirect horizontal effect' of the Human Rights Act in relation to the tests of validity of terms under UTCCR and UCTA. That is, courts should legitimately take into account consistency with Convention rights (including that of the right to redress) when applying the reasonableness or unfairness tests as between private parties. The EU right to effective judicial protection against unfair terms goes much further than the English interpretation of Article 6(1) ECHR (see eg *Oceano Grupo Editorial SA v Roció Murciano Quintero* (Case C-240/98), *Pannon GSM Zrt v Erzsébet Sustikné Győrfi* (Case C-243/08), *Cofidis SA v Jean-Louis Fredout* (Case C-473/00)). This should encourage English courts to adopt a very robust and substantive (rather than purely formal) approach to evaluating terms that have the object or effect of depriving the adhering party of redress.

THIS CHAPTER IN ESSENCE

online resource centre

The key areas and core topics in this chapter are summarised in an easy-to-use list, ideal for revision purposes, on the Online Resource Centre at http://www.oxfordtextbooks.co.uk/orc/chenwishart5e/. Links to websites relevant to the topics covered and any updates to the chapter can also be found on the Online Resource Centre.

QUESTIONS

1 'Contract law probably works well enough in practice but its theory is in a mess.' Discuss.

2 To what extent does contract law enforce promises?

3 Does contract law interfere too much with contractual freedom?

4 What problems are caused by the prevalence of standard form contracts?

5 What values are, and what values should be, promoted by contract law? Illustrate with examples.

 For hints on how to answer these questions, please see the Online Resource Centre at http://www.oxfordtextbooks.co.uk/orc/chenwishart5e/

KEY FURTHER READING

Adams, J, and Brownsword, R (1987), 'The Ideologies of Contract Law', 7 *LS* 205.

Atiyah, P S (1986), 'The Modern Role of Contract Law' in P S Atiyah (ed), *Essays on Contract* (OUP).

Beatson, J, and Friedmann, D (1995), 'Introduction: From "Classical" to Modern Contract Law' in J Beatson and D Friedmann (eds), *Good Faith and Fault in Contract Law* (Clarendon Press) 3.

Collins, H (2003), *The Law of Contract* (4th edn, Butterworths) chs 1–2.

McKendrick, E (1997), 'English Contract Law: A Rich Past, an Uncertain Future?', 50 *CLP* 25.

Simpson, A W B (1987), *A History of the Common Law of Contract* (OUP).

Smith, S (2004), *Contract Theory* (Clarendon Press).

Steyn, J (1997), 'Contract Law: Fulfilling the Reasonable Expectations of Honest Men', 113 *LQR* 433.

PART II

Contract formation

'I say there is a contract and you say there isn't'

INTRODUCTION

Contract law applies to contracts. But what arrangements are *recognised as* contracts and so attract the application of contract law rules? What are the 'entry requirements'? We saw in Chapter 1 that a contract is commonly defined as a *promise or agreement recognised by the law*. This yields three distinct areas of inquiry that will be examined in Chapters 2 and 3.

(i) Each party must *intend* to enter the contract: the voluntariness of the parties' consent to be bound by the contract they have made is *foundational* to most explanations of why contracts should be enforced (see 1.4). Chapter 2 addresses:

- the question of how contractual intention is assessed; and
- the problem of contracts entered under mistake as to terms.

(ii) The parties must be *in* agreement *about* the contents of their contract: the remainder of Chapter 2 examines the requirements of an agreement:

- offer,
- corresponding acceptance;
- certainty; and
- intention to create legal relations.

(iii) The agreement must pass an *additional* hurdle to be enforceable in law: Chapter 3 examines these hurdles, namely:

- consideration ('the claimant paid for the promise');
- formalities ('the parties went through a ceremony'); and
- promissory estoppel ('the claimant reasonably relied on the other's promise').

2

Agreement

'Have the parties reached agreement?'

Disputes over contract formation usually arise when party *A* asserts that party *B* has failed to perform particular obligations owed to *A* under a binding contract. *B* may counter either that he or she owes *A* no contractual obligations *at all*, or not the *particular* obligation that *A* asserts. Three questions arise.

(i) **The commitment question**: *was* a contract concluded at all between the parties?

(ii) **The content question**: *what* did the parties contract for?

(iii) **The timing question**: *when* were the parties locked into the contract?

These distinct questions are merged in the traditional 'mirror image' approach (also called the 'offer and acceptance' approach). Its deceptively simple proposition is that a contract results from an offer made by one party to another who accepts it. That is, at a definite point in time one party intentionally makes an *offer* by words or conduct, and the other party *accepts* this offer (hence the expression 'mirror image'). At the precise moment of acceptance, the formation questions (whether?, when?, and what?) are answered simultaneously. Before we examine the details of contract formation, we must address how contract law determines the intentions of the parties.

2.1 **The objective test of intentions**

The voluntary nature of contract parties' assumption of obligations is the foundation of contract law. It distinguishes contractual liability from liabilities arising in tort, property, and unjust enrichment law, which rest primarily on reasons other than the defendant's consent to them (see 1.6.1). Faced with various problems arising in the life of a contract, the traditional approach is to say that the answer lies in the parties' intentions. But, how do we know what a party intended? How is the meaning of another person constructed, communicated, interpreted, or accessed?[1] The court may adopt:

- the *subjective* approach, which refers to a party's *actual* intention, regardless of appearances; or
- the *objective* approach, which refers to how a reasonable person would interpret a party's intention from his or her conduct in all the circumstances.

The dominance of the objective approach is affirmed in *Smith v Hughes* (1871). Lord Blackburn (at 607) said:

> If, whatever a man's real intention may be, he so conducts himself that a reasonable man would believe that he was assenting to the terms proposed by the other party, and that other party upon that belief enters into the contract with him, the man thus conducting himself would be equally bound as if he had intended to agree to the other party's terms.

As May LJ explains: 'Subjective intention or understanding, unaccompanied by some overt objectively ascertainable expression of that intention or understanding, is not relevant' (*Ove Arup v Mirant Asia Pacific Construction* (2004) at [62]). The often stated requirement of *consensus ad idem* ('meeting of minds') must be understood in this light, lest it should be thought that courts concern themselves with the parties' actual or subjective state of mind. In short, there is no need for genuine agreement; the *appearance* of agreement alone is enough. A person's conduct may indicate his or her consent to a contract even though he or she had no such intention or he or she believed they were consenting to different terms.

2.1.1 The justification for objectivity

The subjective/objective distinction is real. Although a party's objective intention will usually correspond with his or her subjective intention, this is not always the case. Parties *can*, without any dishonesty, misrepresent their own meaning and misinterpret the meaning of others. The objective approach would seem to seriously undermine the view of voluntariness as the distinctive touchstone of contractual liability insofar as it ignores the parties' actual/subjective intentions. Why then, should the objective approach be preferred?

(i) **Accessibility**: it is impossible to determine what was *really* in a party's mind at the relevant time. As Brian CJ said: 'the intent of a man cannot be tried, for the Devil himself knows not the intent of a man'.[2] An objective approach overcomes the evidential difficulties in determining the parties' intentions.

---

[1] See further, C Dalton, 'An Essay in the Deconstruction of Contract Doctrine' (1985) 94 *Yale LJ* 997, 1039–65; J Finnis, 'The Priority of Persons' in J Horder (ed), *Oxford Essays in Jurisprudence* (OUP, 2000) 1, 11–13.

[2] *Anon* (1478) YB 17 Edw 4, Pasch. fo. 1, pl. 2.

(ii) **Avoidance of fraud**: to determine a person's intention simply by reference to his or her assertion as to his or her subjective state of mind at the time is to invite dishonesty and chaos. Once a conflict between the parties has arisen, a person's incentive to distort the truth in favour of his or her self-interest (whether consciously or subconsciously) should disqualify such evidence.

(iii) **Certainty and the protection of reasonable expectations**: great disruption would ensue if one party could escape the liability he or she appeared to have assumed to the other party by simply asserting that they really meant something else. A vital function of contract law is to facilitate the security of transactions: it should enable people to plan on the basis of an apparently enforceable contract. This function would be hopelessly undermined if a party could be heard to say (ie if legal significance attaches to the claim): 'When I said "white" I meant "black"'. The objective approach allows parties to know in advance how their conduct will be interpreted and how they are entitled to interpret the conduct of others.

 Pause for reflection

1. *Objectivity is intrinsic to contracting* and subjectivity simply irrelevant to it. Objectivity is indispensable when one seeks to relate to others in any way. Making a contract is essentially an exercise in the *communication* of choice, and communication is impossible without objectivity (ie the context of *conventions* which gives meaning to conduct). Intention is wholly dependent on manifestations interpreted in a context of shared meaning, that is, on the signs made, the moves in the language game being played. Any legal concern with undisclosed intention is senseless: it contradicts the very idea of contract as an agreement between parties who convey and receive meaning. In **'Objectivity, Subjectivity, and Incomplete Agreements'** in J Horder, *Oxford Essays in Jurisprudence* (OUP, 2000) 151, **Endicott** argues that contract law takes the objective approach not for evidentiary or policy reasons, but because communication is objective by definition. The meaning of words is not determined by the speaker's intention, but by the *reasons* the speaker gives for another person to believe that he or she has one intention or another.

2. Paradoxically, although valid contracts are not necessarily voluntary in the subjective sense, *voluntariness* can still represent the *distinctive feature of contractual liability*. Raz argues that contract law should protect the *practice* of undertaking voluntary obligations. Parties are held to the objective standard to protect the integrity of the *contracting process* and to prevent the abuse of a *cooperative practice*.[3] The objective approach:

   ✓ prevents parties from reneging on their undertakings;

   ✓ gives parties a strong incentive to take care neither to misrepresent their own intentions (even innocently) nor to misinterpret the intentions of others; and

   ✓ extends the practice beyond pre-existing relationships where it would otherwise not exist.

---

[3] J Raz, 'Promises in Morality and Law' (1982) 95 *Harvard L Rev* 916, 928–38.

2.1.2 **The meaning of objectivity**

While the case for objectivity is clear, compelling, and generally accepted, its precise meaning and scope is less so. The questions are as follows.

(i)   Objectivity from *whose* point of view?

(ii) Objectivity on *what evidence*?

2.1.2.1 Detached, actor, or addressee objectivity?

In **'The Meaning of Objectivity in Contract'** (1984) 100 *LQR* 265, **Howarth** sets out three perspectives from which courts have assessed objective meaning: 'detached', 'promisor', and 'promisee'.

Detached objectivity takes a viewpoint that is independent of that of either contract party. The main authority for this approach is *Upton on Severn UDC v Powell* (1942). P called for U's fire-fighting services, both parties mistakenly believing that P was within U's area and entitled to U's services free of charge. The court found a contract by P to pay for U's services although neither party intended the services to be paid for. This decision is inconsistent with the majority of English cases, has been discredited, and is now generally regarded as an instance of restitution for failure of basis.[4] As Spencer observes (at 113), while '[i]t may be acceptable for the law occasionally to force upon *one* of the parties an agreement he did not want . . . surely there is something wrong with a theory which forces upon *both* of the parties an agreement which *neither* of them wants'.

'Promisor' objectivity adopts the interpretation of the honest and reasonable promisor. 'Promisee' objectivity adopts the interpretation of the honest and reasonable promisee. These labels are unnecessarily confusing since in a bilateral contract, each party is both a promisor and a promisee.[5] It is preferable to distinguish between *'actor* objectivity' and *'addressee* objectivity'. On this terminology, each party's actions should be interpreted as they would be reasonably understood by an honest and reasonable person in the *addressee's* position.[6] It is **'*addressee objectivity*'** that counts in determining what obligations each party has undertaken.

2.1.2.2 Conventional rules in attributing meaning: 'formal objectivity'

When determining a party's intention from the addressee's viewpoint, what evidence should be taken into account? Two versions can be contrasted: one can be labelled 'formal objectivity', and the other, 'contextual objectivity'.

The traditional and narrower formal objectivity limits the kinds of conduct that count and prioritise them according to a fairly strict *hierarchy* of probative value as follows:

(i)   *signed final writing* contained in a contractual document is the best evidence of intention[7] and is superior to

---

[4] P S Atiyah, *The Rise and Fall of the Freedom of Contract* (Clarendon Press, 1979), 663; J R Spencer, 'Signature, Consent, and the Rule in *L'Estrange v Graucob*' (1973) 32 *CLJ* 104, 110, 112 n 46; *TTMI v Statoil ASA* [2011] EWHC 1150 (Comm), [44].

[5] J Vorster, 'A Comment on the Meaning of Objectivity in Contract' (1987) 103 *LQR* 274, 276–8.

[6] Blackburn J in *Smith v Hughes* (1871); *Freeman v Cooke* (1848) at 653; J Vorster, 'A Comment on the Meaning of Objectivity in Contract' (1987) 103 *LQR* 274, 283, 278; *Destiny 1 Ltd v Lloyds TSB Bank* (2011), [15].

[7] See the parole evidence rule and signature rule (see 10.3.1, 10.3.3.1).

(ii) *unsigned final writing* contained in a contractual document, which is superior to

(iii) *other writing or to speech*. This, in turn, is superior to

(iv) *non-verbal conduct* (a nod, a wink, contractual performance) and that, in turn, is superior to

(v) silence or omissions.[8]

Examples of formal objectivity are the specific rules on what words or conduct are conventionally *deemed* to be 'offers' and what are 'invitations to treat' (see 2.2.1), and the signature rule as instanced by *L'Estrange v Graucob Ltd* (1934). There, the court upheld a signed document excluding all the seller's liability for a defective slot machine, although the seller knew that the buyer did not read the 'regrettably small print'.

2.1.2.3 Attributing meaning in the whole context: 'contextual objectivity'

Whilst formal objectivity continues to influence some decisions, there has been a general move away from literalist interpretations of contractual documents, towards a more contextual interpretation, culminating in Lord Hoffmann's restatement in *Investor Compensation Scheme Ltd v West Bromwich Building Society* (1998) (at 912–13, and see 10.5). The modern approach exhorts the court to place itself in the same factual matrix as that in which the parties were at the time when the contract was made and to take into account *absolutely everything* reasonably available to the parties which would have affected the way in which the contractual documents (and logically, any other manifestations of intent) would have been reasonably understood. It adopts 'the common sense principles by which any serious utterances would be interpreted in ordinary life'. What this yields is the meaning *of the person*, and not merely *of the conduct*. It offers a more realistic and accurate approach to ascertaining intentions. The drawback in admitting a larger body of evidence is the potential problem of multiple and contradictory meaning,[9] but this is a question of weight for courts to assess.

This contextual objective approach to the ascertainment of intentions is applied in the mirror image approach in determining the existence of agreement between the parties. At its simplest, this approach looks for an offer matched by a corresponding acceptance. A party may *deny* the existence of a valid contract by arguing that the alleged offer was invalid because it was:

(i) mistakenly made (see 2.1.3);

(ii) not an offer at all (see 2.2.1); or

(iii) no longer valid at the time of the purported acceptance (see 2.2.3).

2.1.3 Objectivity and 'mistaken offers'

Since the reference point for fixing *whether* the parties intend to be bound, and *what* they intend to be bound by, is *objective*, this must trump a party's assertion of a different

---

[8] Silence does not generally constitute acceptance even if clearly intended, see 2.3.3.2.
[9] C Staughton, 'How Do the Courts Interpret Commercial Contracts?' (1999) 58 *CLJ* 303.

subjective intention. Yet, a number of distinguished commentators[10] state that contract law recognises exceptional cases where the subjective approach trumps the objective approach to void the parties' agreement for so-called 'mistake as to terms'.

However, the authorities put forward are entirely consistent with the objective approach on the more expansive contextual version of objectivity. This:

(i)   assumes the addressee's honesty in interpreting the actor's conduct;

(ii)   is infused with the standard of reasonableness; and

(iii)   can 'run out' in the case of latent ambiguity.

Each is discussed below.

2.1.3.1 Knowledge of the other's 'mistake as to terms' and the objective interpretation of intention

In *Hartog v Colin & Shields* (1939), a seller offered to sell 3,000 Argentine hare skins at a fixed price '**per pound**' when he really meant '**per piece**'. Since there were three pieces to the pound, he mistakenly offered the hare skins at one-third of his intended asking price. The buyer purported to accept and sued for damages when the seller refused to deliver at that low price. The court found no contract since, in the context of the custom of the trade and the negotiations (verbal and written) between the parties, which always discussed the price '**per piece**' and never 'per pound', the buyer 'must have realised, and did in fact know, that a mistake had occurred' in the seller's offer. The conventional interpretation of this case is that the seller's subjective intention trumps the buyer's objective interpretation when the buyer knows that the seller has made a mistake as to terms (ie knows of the seller's subjective intention): he or she is prevented from '*snatching a bargain*' known not to have been intended for them.

Smith v Hughes (1871) has been interpreted in the same way. There, a racehorse trainer agreed to buy oats from a farmer after inspecting a sample, which the trainer believed to be old oats. When the oats turned out to be *new* and useless to him, the trainer refused to pay. The jury found for the trainer but did not say which of the two possible reasons suggested by the trial judge applied, namely:

✗   that the parties had *agreed on old oats*, so the buyer was not obliged to pay for the new oats—the appeal court rejected this basis because the seller had given no such undertaking, and the oats delivered corresponded with the sample inspected and agreed to by the buyer.

✓   that the *seller knew that the buyer 'believed . . . that he was contracting for old oats'* (at 602)—the appeal court found this direction by the trial judge failed to distinguish clearly between the seller's knowledge that the buyer believed:

(i)   the oats to be old (which does not void a contract); and

(ii)   that *the seller* was *promising* them to be old (which *does* void the contract).

---

[10] Treitel, at 8–048, refers to 'three exceptional situations, in which the objective principle does not apply, so that the mistake is *operative*'. Atiyah at 84 writes, 'In this case the law abandons the objective interpretation of the first party's intentions.' E McKendrick, *Contract Law: Text, Cases, and Materials* (6th edn, OUP, 2014) 21 discusses '[c]ases in which it has been argued that the courts have resorted to a subjective approach'.

The lack of evidence for (ii) suggested to the appeal court that the jury had erroneously voided the contract on (i). The verdict being unsafe, a new trial was ordered.

▶◀ Counterpoint

We should reject the interpretation of both *Hartog v Shields* and *Smith v Hughes* as instances of a category of operative mistake (as to terms known to the other party) where subjectivity exceptionally trumps objectivity.

1. It *contradicts* the compelling case for objectivity.

2. It is *unnecessary*. *Hartog* is entirely explicable in terms of the **contextual objective approach to intentions**; there were sufficient reasons for an honest and reasonable buyer to treat the seller's meaning as 'per piece'. In the context of the practice in the trade and the pre-contractual negotiations, the buyer 'could not reasonably have supposed' the seller intended to quote the price 'per pound' (at 568). There is no need to resort to talk of 'mistake' or 'knowledge of the mistake' or a subjective test of intention. Indeed, one could go further and conclude that an honest and reasonable buyer knew that the seller meant to offer 'per piece', which he accepted.

3. It is *logically impossible*. In **'Objectivity and Mistake: the Oxymoron of** *Smith v Hughes*' in J Neyers, R Bronough, and S G A Pitel (eds), *Exploring Contract Law* (Hart Publishing, 2009) 341, I argue that a *mistake* as to terms must refer to a deviation from the objective interpretation of the contract (in *Smith v Hughes*, the objective agreement was for 'new oats' because this is what the buyer inspected and gave the seller reason to believe he was agreeing to). In that case, it is logically impossible to find that the buyer also gave the seller reason to believe that he thought he was contracting for something else, that is, 'old oats'. That is to say, the court cannot find that the seller simultaneously believed that (i) the buyer was contracting for 'new oats' and also that (ii) the buyer was contracting for 'old oats'. The first belief makes the second logically inconsistent.

In *Hartog*, the seller's mistaken use of the words 'per pound' when he meant 'per piece' should simply be seen as a case where an honest and reasonable buyer *had reason to know* that the seller's words 'per pound' reasonably meant 'per piece'. This makes 'per piece' *the objective reference point*. The seller makes no relevant mistake because his or her meaning does not deviate from the objective point of reference.

Smith v Hughes is weak authority for the doctrine of mistakes as to terms known to the other party. The case itself is not an example of it. The actual decision was only to order a new trial in the light of the distinction drawn between:

  ✓ (i) mistake of *terms* known to the other party (which void the contract irrespective of importance of the mistake);[11] and

---

[11] The Singapore Court of Appeal has imposed a requirement of fundamentality in such cases, although it left open how fundamentality should be determined (*Chwee Kin Keong v Digilandmall.com Pte Ltd* (2005), [34]).

✗ (ii) mistaken *assumption* about the subject matter of the contract (ie not as to term, which does not void the contract unless it is shared and fundamental, see Chapter 6).

Since the judges expressly stated that there was no evidence of (i),[12] they must have regarded it as a case of (ii) and believed that the jury was wrong to set aside the contract. Moreover, no other decision clearly and necessarily falls within (i). *Smith v Hughes* should be regarded as a straightforward case of contextual objectivity. It establishes that what a party *actually* knows (insofar as that is distinguishable from what he or she has reason to know) must be taken into account as part of the context in which meaning is honestly and reasonably attributed to another's conduct. On this approach, the court found that the parties' objective agreement was for the oats that were inspected (new oats). On retrial, the buyer could only win if new evidence shows that: (a) there was actually a contract for 'old oats'; (b) the seller made an actionable misrepresentation that the oats were old (see Chapter 5); or (c) there is no objective agreement at all because of latent ambiguity (see 2.1.3.3).

The same analysis can be applied to *Centrovincial Estates plc v Merchant Investors Assurance Co Ltd* (1983). During a rent review negotiation, the landlord mistakenly stated the figure of £65,000 (he meant to say *£126,000*), which the tenant immediately accepted. The previous rent was £68,320. The Court of Appeal held that the rent of £65,000 would stand *unless* the landlord could prove that the tenant knew or ought to have known that the landlord's offer was mistaken when the tenant purported to accept it.[13] An internet example is *Chwee v Digilandmall.com Pte Ltd* (2005). D's employee mistakenly advertised online a commercial laser printer for $66 (actual retail price $3,854). By the time the error was detected, 4,086 orders had been received and confirmation notes automatically dispatched within a few minutes. D resisted C's action to enforce its order for 1,606 printers. The Singapore Court of Appeal rejected C's contention that it was unaware of D's mistake. The Court required *actual* knowledge of the mistake to void the contract (at [53]) but held that it could be established by inference from circumstantial evidence (at [35]): 'Phrases such as "must have known" or "could not reasonably have supposed" are really evidential factors or reasoning processes used by the court in finding that the non-mistaken party did, in fact, know of the error made by the mistaken party.' It also includes '"Nelsonian knowledge", namely, wilful blindness or shutting one's eyes to the obvious' (at [42]).

Where it is clear to the unmistaken party merely that the other party did not intend to contract on the literal terms, there is no contract. However, where it is *also* clear to the unmistaken party what terms the other party *does* intend, and he or she purports to accept that, then there is a contract on that basis (*Bashir v Ali* (2011) at [42]). On this basis, if, in *Hartog v Shields*, instead of the seller simply refusing to proceed with the sale, the seller had insisted on selling the hareskins at the price the seller must have known was intended, there should be an enforceable contract on those terms.

---

[12] Blackburn J (at 608) could 'not see much evidence to justify a finding for the defendant ... if the word "old" was not used ... it does not seem a very satisfactory verdict if it proceeded on [the mistake] ground'. Hannen J (at 611) also found 'very little, if any, evidence to support a finding upon [the mistake ground] in favour of the [buyer]'.

[13] The tenant was given leave to defend the landlord's action for a declaration that the tenant must have known of the landlord's mistake.

2.1.3.2 Misleading offers: fault

In *Scriven Brothers & Co v Hindley & Co* (1913), the buyer successfully bid for a lot he believed to contain hemp when it actually contained tow, a different and much cheaper commodity. He refused to pay. In finding for the buyer, Lawrence J (at 568) appeared to apply a subjective test. He said there was no contract because 'the parties were never *ad idem* as to the subject-matter of the proposed sale', one intending to sell tow and the other intending to buy hemp. The crux is that this non-coincidence of subjective meanings, which was unknown to either party, would have been irrelevant without the seller's *misleading auction catalogue*. This described the goods as so many bales in different lots all bearing the *same shipping marks*, which witnesses explained never happened for different commodities from the same ship. Thus, it was reasonable for the buyer not to have foreseen the potential for confusion: being only interested in buying hemp, he had only inspected the hemp on show and not the tow bearing the same shipping marks. Lawrence J (at 569) found that, since the confusion was deliberately perpetrated by the seller in order to swindle the bank financing the shipment, 'it was peculiarly the duty of the auctioneer to make it clear to the bidder . . . which lots were hemp and which lots were tow'. Thus, while auctioneers are generally entitled to assume that bidders know what they are bidding for (making their mistakes legally irrelevant), they cannot do so if they have carelessly induced the bidder's mistake.

Pause for reflection

The objective approach is not only contextual; it is also reasonable. It is infused with a *bias in favour of the just interpretation*, and against the unjust. It treats a contract party as an honest and reasonable person who will not take an unjust view of the other party's intentions, nor give a dishonest or misleading view of his or her own intentions. This aspect of justice is built into the identification of an agreement and its content on the objective approach.[14] The same idea underlies Collins' reference to the need for 'clean hands' and his identification of a 'duty to negotiate with care' and 'refrain from unconscionable conduct' (236–7).

2.1.3.3 Latent ambiguity

It can be particularly difficult to determine what the parties agreed where there is nothing in writing. In *South East Windscreens Ltd v Hamid Jamshidi* (2005), the court noted that 'the confused and informal way in which the deal was struck', attributable to the trust between the parties, gave 'enormous scope for confusion in what was discussed and agreed' (at [79]). The court concluded that the parties were 'at cross purposes . . . [there was] no true agreement about the terms upon which the sale of the business was to take place' (at [80]). '[N]either party has discharged the burden of proving, on the balance of probabilities, that their version of the agreement is correct' (at [84]).

---

[14] T Endicott, 'Objectivity, Subjectivity, and Incomplete Agreements' in J Horder (ed), *Oxford Essays in Jurisprudence* (OUP, 2000) 151, 164–5.

The same problem can arise even with written contracts if they lack sufficient specificity. In **Raffles v Wichelhaus** (1864), the parties contracted to buy and sell goods 'to arrive ex Peerless from Bombay', the buyer intending its delivery via the ship *Peerless* arriving in *October* while the seller delivered on a different ship, but also called *Peerless*, arriving in *December*. The court upheld the buyer's refusal to pay but without giving its reasons. The decision is commonly explained on the basis of the non-coincidence of the parties' *subjective* intentions (eg *Anson's* at 254).

◀▶ Counterpoint

This explanation is unnecessarily wide. Exact coincidence of intentions must be rare in contracting: non-coincidence is not generally a ground for voiding the contract (eg contracts can be enforced although the parties disagree on whether they have reached sufficient agreement (see 2.6 on uncertainty), what terms bind them, and what these terms mean (see Chapter 10)). The case does not depart from the contextual objective approach if it is recognised that even this approach is not omniscient. It may not always be possible to choose between different, and each reasonable, versions of the contract by reference to the parties' conduct, even taking into account the full factual matrix of the case. In such exceptional cases where, moreover, the non-concurrence is over an *important* matter,[15] it is impossible to give sufficient content to the objective agreement to enforce it. The parties *were* objectively agreed, but the agreement suffered from *latent ambiguity* which was both important and impossible to resolve by reference to the context: objectivity simply 'ran out'.

2.2 **Offer**

An offer is a manifestation of intention (whether orally, in writing, or by conduct) by the **offeror** of a willingness to be bound by the terms proposed to the **offeree** (the addressee), as soon as the offeree signifies acceptance of the terms. Thus, it contains:

(i) a proposal of the terms of the exchange; and

(ii) an expression of willingness to be bound as soon as the offeree manifests acceptance.

An offer puts the offeror *on risk*: it confers a power on the offeree to bind the offeror at the precise moment of acceptance; thereafter, the offeror loses his or her ability to withdraw from or further negotiate the arrangement.

2.2.1 **Offers and invitations to treat**

A party seeking to deny the existence of a contract may argue that what the other party purported to accept was not an offer, but something less. Whether a party's

---

[15] Existence of the seriousness threshold can be inferred from cases where ambiguity or vagueness does *not* invalidate the contract, see 2.6 and the suggestion that concurrence on the 'material terms' can overcome the problem of a battle of forms, see 2.3.1.3.

words or conduct amount to an offer can be difficult to determine because parties themselves are often ambivalent in the negotiation process. Each seeks the greatest commitment from the other whilst conceding the least possible commitment themselves. Parties should be able to spell out the terms on which they are willing to contract and to look for the best deal, without being locked into a contract before they are ready to commit to it. The law must uphold not only the parties' freedom to contract, but also their freedom *from* contract. But the point will be reached when it would be unfair for one party to induce another party's reliance while still remaining free to pull out. The law must strike a balance between giving the parties adequate *room to manoeuvre* and protecting their *reasonable reliance*.

2.2.1.1 General principles

Generally, no offer is made when a party communicates his or her proposed terms unless he or she also communicates their *commitment to be bound* on the other's acceptance of the terms. This is the substantive sense of 'intention to create legal relations'; not to be confused with the sense that there is a presumption that agreements made in a social or domestic context are not intended to be enforceable (see 2.7).

A communication may not be an offer, but merely a **request for or supply of information** which is not open to acceptance. For example, in *Harvey v Facey* (1893), H sent a telegram to F asking: 'Will you sell us Bumper Hall Pen? Telegraph lowest cash price.' F replied: 'Lowest price for Bumper Hall Pen, £900' and H purported to accept this 'offer'. The Privy Council found no binding contract because F merely supplied information in response to H's request. F evinced no intention to be bound by H's acceptance.

Alternatively, a party's communication may not amount to an offer because it is only an **invitation to treat**, that is, an expression of willingness to embark on negotiations with the other party to see whether agreement can be reached, further down the path. Even if serious terms are proposed, an offer is only made if the speaker confers on the addressee the *power to bind* the speaker on the addressee's acceptance. Two cases involving negotiation over the sale of council houses by the Conservative-controlled Manchester City Council illustrate this distinction. In both, the sale was in the process of being made when the local election returned a Labour majority and the policy of selling off council houses was reversed. The issue was whether the particular negotiation had reached the point of a binding contract, making reversal impossible.

✓ The answer was 'yes' in *Storer v Manchester CC* (1974). The council sent a brochure advertising the details of a scheme for tenants to buy their council houses. S ascertained the price and sent a formal application to buy. The council responded by letter: 'I understand you wish to purchase your council house and enclose the agreement for sale. *If* you will sign the agreement and return it to me *I will* send you the agreement signed on behalf of the corporation in exchange' (emphasis added). S signed and returned the agreement, but control of the council changed at that point. The Court of Appeal held that a contract *was* concluded because the council's letter evinced an intention to be bound by the terms of the agreement as soon as S accepted it (by signing and returning the agreement to the council). The new council could not halt the sale.

✗ In contrast, no concluded contract was found by the House of Lords in *Gibson v Manchester CC* (1979). In response to G's inquiry, the council wrote to G informing him of the price at which the 'council may be prepared to sell the house' and giving details of a mortgage proposal. The council expressly stated that its letter should *not* be 'regarded as a firm offer of a mortgage' and that G should complete a further form if he wished to make a 'formal application'. G applied and, after unsuccessful negotiation over the price and certain repairs, asked the council to proceed with his application. G then made the repairs himself and the council took the house off the list of tenant-occupied houses and put it on the house purchase list before the council changed hands. The House of Lords held that the council's letter did not confer power on G to bind the council to sell the house as soon as G manifested assent. On the contrary, the council warned against regarding their letter as a firm offer and invited G to make a 'formal application', the latter becoming the offer. The council's conduct indicated its *intention* to accept G's offer, but it had not yet completed the acceptance by *communicating* it to G. G had jumped the gun in his reliance and could not insist on the sale.

The *general* approach to making the distinction between offers and invitations to treat is superseded by some relatively **specific rules or conventions** applicable to particular common situations. These conventions have largely *replaced the search for the parties' intentions* in many common contracting situations. It is possible to displace these rules by evidence of contrary intention, but where the parties are silent, they will apply without reference to the intention of the maker of the statement.

2.2.1.2 Displays and advertisements

When goods are displayed in stores or advertised in newspapers or catalogues with clearly marked prices, the reasonable consumer or reader is likely to believe that the storekeeper or advertiser intends to offer the items for sale. However, the general rule is that displays or advertisement of goods for sale are *not offers* to sell those goods, but *only invitations to treat*. This is so even when the word 'offer' is used because the court may determine that it was not used in its legal sense (*Spencer v Harding* (1870)). Thus, the customer is generally regarded as making the offer when he or she presents the goods at the cash desk or otherwise evinces an intention to buy. This leaves traders with the all-important power to accept or reject the customer's offer.

This rule was established and reinforced in a line of cases on statutory offences relating to the sale of specific goods. The leading case is **Pharmaceutical Society of GB v Boots Cash Chemists** (1953). The Pharmacy and Poisons Act 1933 required that certain drugs be sold under the supervision of a registered pharmacist. When Boots introduced self-service shopping, the pharmacist was positioned so as to supervise the sale at the cash desk. Whether or not Boots contravened the Act was translated into the legal question of *when* offer and acceptance combined to complete the sale. If the display was an offer, and the customer's putting the item in his or her basket or presenting it for purchase was the acceptance, then Boots *would* have contravened the Act since the pharmacist's supervision of the transaction only comes later, at the cash desk.

The court held that Boots did not contravene the Act since **displays and advertisements are not offers** (merely invitations to treat). It is the customer who makes the offer when he or she presents his or her selection for payment at the cash desk, where the pharmacist could stop the sale. None of the reasons given for this conclusion are very convincing.

(i) If displays were offers, then the customer's act of putting it into the basket amounts to acceptance, **preventing the customer from changing his or her mind** thereafter without breaching the contract: this problem is easily met by finding no acceptance until the customer presents the item for payment;[16] only then does the customer *communicate* his or her acceptance to the offeror. But on this view, the pharmacist's intervention thereafter would still come too late.

(ii) If displays or advertisements were offers, then vendors would be deprived of their **freedom not to deal** with particular customers and this would contradict the idea that a shop is a place for bargaining, not for compulsory sales. Bargaining is not the reality in shops today where goods are presented on a 'take-it-or-leave-it' basis. Even if it is, the customer could be regarded as making a counter-offer, which the trader could reject. The crux is that traders should not be allowed to refuse to contract with any customers (consistent with legislation prohibiting discrimination),[17] or refuse to contract on the marked prices (in order to discourage deceptive trade practices).[18] The pharmacist's supervision could be the subject of an implication that the offer is 'subject to the pharmacist's approval in relation to restricted drugs'.

(iii) If displays or advertisements were offers, vendors would be obliged to supply goods to everyone who accepts, even if the vendor **runs out of stock**:[19] this problem is easily met by implying a commonsense limit that the offer is 'subject to availability' or only applies 'while stocks last'.

The actual issue in *Boots* was not whether a vendor could refuse to sell an item to a particular customer: rather, it was whether a more efficient self-service pharmacy (where a pharmacist supervises sales generally, rather than serving each individual customer) complied with legislation requiring supervised sales of restricted drugs. It is understandable that the court would not want to deter self-service pharmacies by convicting Boots of the offence. *To achieve this result*, the display had to be treated as an invitation to treat.

However, an inflexible application of the rule established in *Boots* could lead to error in different contexts. In **Partridge v Crittenden** (1968), Bramble finch cocks and hens were advertised for sale at a stated price. The advertiser was charged with the offence of 'offering for sale' wild live birds contrary to the Protection of Birds Act 1954. The advertiser was acquitted because the court rigidly applied the convention that an advertisement was only an invitation to treat and not an offer, citing some of the

---

[16] This was held in the US decision of *Laskey v Economic Stores* (1946).

[17] See *Timothy v Simpson* (1834), where a person was asked to pay 7/6d on an item marked 5/11d and a shop assistant said: 'don't let him have it, he's only a Jew; turn him out'. Note now, the Equality Act 2010.

[18] Criminal liability is imposed for misleading advertisements or indications as to price of goods under the Consumer Protection Act 1987 and the Consumer Credit Act 1974.

[19] See *Partridge v Crittenden* (1968) at 1209–10.

unconvincing reasons mentioned above, which were irrelevant to the case. Similarly, in *Fisher v Bell* (1961) it was held that a display of a flick-knife in a shop window was not an offer to sell the item in contravention of legislation restricting the sale of offensive weapons.

⏪ Counterpoint

1. Such decisions bring the law into disrepute. Statutes prohibiting the offer of certain items for sale in *all* circumstances raise quite different issues (eg conservation or prevention of crime) from a statute prohibiting the offer of certain drugs for sale without pharmacist supervision (as in *Boots*), or contract formation in general (eg protecting reliance and preserving freedom of action). The mischief behind statutes in *Partridge* and *Bell* can only be met by preventing the display or advertisement of the prohibited items, if necessary by construing them as 'offers' in law, or by construing the statutes as impliedly prohibiting both offers and invitations to treat.

2. A rigid application of the decision in *Boots* can expose *consumers* to unfair trade practices (eg refusal to sell an item unless the customer pays more than the price displayed or advertised). The trader may be subject to criminal sanctions under the Consumer Protection from Unfair Trading Regulations 2008 for misleading customers, but the customer cannot insist on buying at the advertised price.[20] 'Bait advertising' (ie attracting customers by the prospect of heavily discounted items, when in fact there are few or no such items; the hope is that disappointed customers will buy other more profitable items) would also go unchecked. In the American case *Lefkowitz v Great Minneapolis Surplus Stores Inc* (1957), G placed a newspaper advertisement for the sale of three valuable fur coats and one lapin stole for $1 each, 'First Come, First Served'. L was first in the store on the dates advertised, but G refused to sell the goods to him, stating that the sale was intended only for women. The court held that the advertisement was an *offer* and not an invitation to treat: it was clearly defined and explicit in its terms, leaving nothing to negotiate between the parties.

Courts have exceptionally treated **displays and advertisements as offers** in order to reach just solutions.

- In ***Chapelton v Barry UDC*** (1940), it was held that the *display* of deckchairs for hire on a beach with a notice of the charges was an *offer*, which was accepted by a customer taking a chair. This meant that the ticket issued to the customer thereafter, which contained an exclusion of liability for injury, was not part of the contract.[21] This cleared the way for the customer to claim compensation when the deckchair collapsed, injuring him. Treating the display as an offer allowed

---

[20] The Draft Consumer Protection from Unfair Trading (Amendment) Regulations 2013 from the Department for Business, Innovation and Skills, would give consumers the right to redress for eg misleading actions, in the form of unwinding the contract, discount on the price, or damages.

[21] In this case the customer received the ticket containing the exclusion clause at the same time as taking the deckchair but the court recognised that it could just as well have been later.

Diagram 2A Inconsistent approaches to whether displays and advertisements are offers

	① Display or advertisement	② Customer selects	③ Trader agrees	Results:
General legal rule	Invitation to treat	Offer	Acceptance	Contract at ③
Boots	Invitation to treat	Offer	Acceptance	No contract at ②. Boots has not contravened legislation
Chapelton	Offer	Acceptance		Contract at ②. Supplier cannot thereafter introduce term (here harsh)
Carlill	Offer	Acceptance		Contract at ②. Seller must pay up according to the contract

the court to *bring forward the time of contract formation* in order to keep out a harsh exclusion clause, which was introduced later.

- An *advertisement* may also, exceptionally, be treated as an offer rather than an invitation to treat. In **Carlill v Carbolic Smoke Ball Co** (1893), the manufacturer advertised the 'carbolic smoke ball' and offered to pay £100 to anyone catching influenza after using it in the specified manner, adding that £1,000 had been deposited in the bank to show their 'sincerity in the matter'. C successfully sued for £100 when she caught influenza after proper use of the smoke ball. The court rejected the manufacturer's claim that the advertisement was too vague and not seriously made. The Court held that: (i) the advertisement was an offer to the whole world; and (ii) a unilateral contract (see 2.3.5) was made with those who met the condition 'on the faith of the advertisement'.

Pause for reflection

These cases smack of 'backward reasoning' (see 1.2.3). Where a court concludes that it would be unfair to leave the claimant without a remedy (*Chapelton v Barry*) or to allow traders to make wild claims in support of quack remedies (*Carlill v Carbolic Smoke Ball*), it is prepared to treat the display or advertisement as offers to reach the desired outcome. A different analysis was applied where the court concluded that it would be unfair to impose liability (here criminal) on Boots. This is illustrated in **Diagram 2A**.

2.2.1.3 Timetables and automatic vending machines

It has been held that railway and bus **timetables** are offers which can be accepted by passengers who buy railway tickets[22] or board buses.[23] However, most timetables

---

[22] *Denton v Great Northern Railway Co* (1856).
[23] *Wilkie v London Passenger Transport Board* (1947).

now contain express *disclaimers of any obligation* to provide the services contained in the timetable.[24] In *Thornton v Shoe Lane Parking Ltd* (1971), Lord Denning held that an **automatic machine** outside a car park stating charge rates makes an *offer*, which the motorist *accepts* by driving in and prompting the machine to issue a ticket. Thus, the exclusion of liability contained on a notice *inside* the car park is not part of the contract; it only comes to the motorist's notice after the contract is made and (like *Chapelton v Barry* in the previous section) cannot bar the motorist's claim for his or her injury. Lord Denning explained that there is no expectation or opportunity for negotiation; once the consumer drives in, there is no scope for withdrawal since the product or service cannot be easily returned and the likely queue of cars behind will prevent the driver from backing out. These reasons would extend to analogous situations such as self-service petrol stations and vending machines, which dispense an ever-increasing range of goods.

2.2.1.4 Auctions

The law analyses a sale by auction in the following steps:

(i) the *advertisement* that an auction will take place on a certain day is merely an invitation to treat (*Harris v Nickerson* (1873));

(ii) putting up goods for sale is also an invitation to treat (*British Car Auctions Ltd v Wright* (1972));

(iii) a bid by the purchaser is the **offer**; and

(iv) *the fall of the hammer* indicates the **acceptance**.

This is codified in section 57(2) of the Sale of Goods Act 1979. On this analysis the auctioneer can refuse to hold the auction at all (eg if it is poorly attended) or to refuse to knock down to the highest bidder if the bid fails to reach the reserve (a minimum) price. Otherwise, an auctioneer could be exposed to a multiplicity of claims if the advertisement were to be construed as an offer, accepted by all those who turn up. It would be difficult, if not impossible, to quantify the loss of those disappointed (their wasted expenditure or loss of the chance to bid successfully?).

However, where the words '**without reserve**' are added to the advertisement, this increases bidders' expectations that: (i) the auction will take place; (ii) no minimum price will be set; and (iii) the item will be sold to the highest bidder. Martin B stated obiter in *Warlow v Harrison* (1858) that the transaction should be analysed as **two separate contracts**.

(i) A *unilateral collateral contract* between the highest *bidder* and the *auctioneer* by which the auctioneer is obliged to accept the highest bid from the bidder making it. This can be understood as a *procedural contract* (to regulate the procedure for making the main contract).

(ii) The *main contract* for sale of the main subject matter between the highest *bidder* and the *owner*.

---

[24] Moreover, regulations made under the Transport Act 1962 and the Railways Act 1993 effectively prevent contractual liability from arising.

This is confirmed by the Court of Appeal in *Barry v Davies (t/a Heathcote Ball & Co)* (2001), where two machines worth £28,000 were auctioned without reserve, but the auctioneer refused to accept B's bids of £200 each. B was awarded £27,600 in damages.

> ### ▶◀ Counterpoint
>
> The words 'without reserve' would be meaningless if the auction could be called off altogether or halted once bidding starts. This would allow the auctioneer to ignore his or her own statements about the auction and refuse to sell to the highest bidder (either by not giving a chance to make the highest bid or not accepting the highest bid). However, that conclusion fits rather awkwardly within the offer and acceptance framework.[25]
>
> 1. It departs from the convention that an advertisement is merely an invitation to treat.
> 2. If the sale is not held or the item is withdrawn, it would still be impossible to identify the highest bidder to whom the obligation is owed since, until the hammer is brought down, a bid can always be withdrawn, or outbid.

2.2.1.5 Tenders

The same issues arise in contracts resulting from a tendering process. The traditional analysis is set out in ***Harvela Investments Ltd v Royal Trust Co of Canada (CI) Ltd*** (1986):

(i) *an invitation to tender* for a particular project is merely **an invitation to treat**;

(ii) the **offer** is made by those *submitting the tenders*; and

(iii) the **acceptance** is made when the person inviting the tenders *accepts* one of them.

However, where justice has demanded, courts have invoked the **two-contract analysis** to impose liability for failure to consider, or to accept, the lowest or highest tender. In *Harvela Investments*, R decided to sell their shares by sealed competitive tender between two parties stating that they would accept the highest complying 'offer'. H tendered a *fixed bid* of $2,175,000. X tendered a *referential bid* of '$2,100,000 or $101,000 in excess of any other offer . . . whichever is the higher'. R accepted X's bid as one for $2,276,000. But the House of Lords held that R was bound to accept H's bid. R's invitation to tender was held to be an offer of a unilateral contract to sell the shares to the highest bidder, even though the invitation asked the bidders to submit an 'offer'.

---

[25] See the debate between C Slade, 'Auction Sales of Goods without Reserve' (1952) 68 *LQR* 238; criticised by L Gower (1952) 68 *LQR* 456; in reply C Slade (1953) 69 *LQR* 21; C Cox, 'Auctions without Reserve—A Schematic Approach' (1982) 132 *New LJ* 719.

> ### Pause for reflection
>
> In *Harvela*, X's bid was invalid because the object of the vendors' invitation was to ascertain the highest amount that each party was prepared to pay and this purpose would be frustrated by a referential bid. If *both* parties had bid referentially, it would have been impossible to determine which was the highest bid. The relevant policies are: (i) the encouragement of fair play; (ii) the protection of a tenderer's reasonable expectation that the process would be determined by fixed bids; and (iii) the tenderer's reliance on this by investing the resources in putting together the bid. These concerns are mirrored in other cases.

In **Blackpool and Fylde Aero Club Ltd v Blackpool BC** (1990), the council invited tenders for a concession to operate pleasure flights, but stipulated that 'the council do not bind themselves to accept all or any part of the tender. No tender which is received after the last date and time specified [noon, 17 March 1983] shall be admitted for consideration'. At about 11 am that day, the Aero Club posted their bid in the town hall letterbox on which there was a notice stating that it was emptied at noon each day. The letterbox was not duly processed and the council did not consider the Aero Club's 'late' bid, awarding the concession to another party with a lower tender. The court used the **two-contract analysis**: one between the council and the party whose tender is actually accepted; the other the procedural contract, comprising of the council's invitation to tender which constitutes a *unilateral offer to 'consider'* any conforming tender which was accepted by any party submitting such a tender. The council breached the contract to consider the Aero Club's tender.

Bingham LJ articulates the concern to protect the more vulnerable party in the tendering process (at 1201–2):

> A tendering procedure of this kind is, in many respects, heavily weighted in favour of the invitor. He can invite tenders from as many or as few parties as he chooses. He need not tell any of them who else, or how many others, he has invited. The invitee may often . . . be put to considerable labour and expense in preparing a tender, ordinarily without recompense if he is unsuccessful. The invitation to tender may itself, in a complex case . . . involve time and expense to prepare, but the invitor does not commit himself to proceed with the project, . . . he need not accept the highest tender; he need not accept any tender; he need not give reasons to justify his acceptance or rejection of any tender received . . . The invitee is in my judgement protected at least to this extent: if he submits a conforming tender before the deadline he is entitled, not as a matter of mere expectation but of contractual right, to be sure that his tender will after the deadline be opened and considered in conjunction with all other conforming tenders or at least that his tender will be considered if others are.

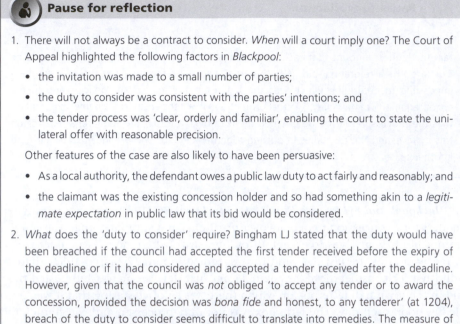

Pause for reflection

1. There will not always be a contract to consider. *When* will a court imply one? The Court of Appeal highlighted the following factors in *Blackpool*:
   - the invitation was made to a small number of parties;
   - the duty to consider was consistent with the parties' intentions; and
   - the tender process was 'clear, orderly and familiar', enabling the court to state the unilateral offer with reasonable precision.

   Other features of the case are also likely to have been persuasive:
   - As a local authority, the defendant owes a public law duty to act fairly and reasonably; and
   - the claimant was the existing concession holder and so had something akin to a *legitimate expectation* in public law that its bid would be considered.

2. *What* does the 'duty to consider' require? Bingham LJ stated that the duty would have been breached if the council had accepted the first tender received before the expiry of the deadline or if it had considered and accepted a tender received after the deadline. However, given that the council was *not* obliged 'to accept any tender or to award the concession, provided the decision was *bona fide* and honest, to any tenderer' (at 1204), breach of the duty to consider seems difficult to translate into remedies. The measure of damages was not in issue in the Court of Appeal, but assessment of the Aero Club's 'loss of a chance' (see 13.2.5.5) of winning the tender must be speculative.

2.2.2 Overview of considerations in determining the existence of an offer

Contractual consequences depend on finding an offer, which has been accepted. Thus, finding an *offer* is *pro-liability*, while finding a mere invitation to treat is *anti-liability*. The factors mentioned in the discussion in the previous section which influence this determination are summarised in **Diagram 2B**.

Diagram 2B Overview of policies in determining existence of an offer

	Pro-liability: 'offer'	Anti-liability: 'invitation to treat'
Factors relating to the alleged offeror	Prevent exploitative trade practices, such as bait or misleading advertising, or failure to observe the offeror's own rules	Need for room to manoeuvre
Factor relating to the alleged offeree	Protection of reasonable expectation or reliance	
Other factors	Promote consumer protection; control of unfair exclusion clauses	

2.2.3 Termination of offer

A party denying the existence of a contract may argue that, although a 'live' offer once existed, it was 'dead' (had ceased to exist) by the time the offeree attempted to accept it. Conceptually, the issue of termination of offer belongs with the topic of offer, but in practice the issue will not arise unless and until there is an alleged *acceptance* which has been communicated to the offeror. Thus, it makes sense to fix the point of acceptance first before asking whether its effect is negated by the termination of the offer (see 2.4).

2.3 Acceptance

An acceptance is an unequivocal expression of consent to the proposal contained in the offer and has the effect of immediately binding both parties to the contract. It locks the door on the contract 'room': neither party can get out of the contract or vary its contents. We noted that an apparent acceptance is not binding if the offeror knows that the offeree was mistaken as to the offer (see 2.1.2). In addition, a valid acceptance must:

(i) *correspond* with the offer (2.3.1);

(ii) be made *in response* to the offer (there must be a *nexus* between the acceptance and the offer) (2.3.2);

(iii) be made by an appropriate *method* (2.3.3); and

(iv) be *communicated* to the offeror (this fixes the time of contract formation, crystallising the terms and making withdrawal impossible) (2.3.4).

A party can deny the existence of a contract by establishing the absence of *any* of these requirements. Again, the scope and operation of each requirement reveal the competing influence of considerations of certainty, fairness, and respect for the parties' intentions.

2.3.1 Correspondence of acceptance with the offer

The mirror image approach to contract formation requires the acceptance to mirror the offer. This requirement of exact correspondence means that a purported acceptance that deviates in any way from the offered terms is unlikely to conclude a contract. Three situations warrant special mention.

2.3.1.1 Conditional acceptance

'Acceptances' which contemplate further conditions being satisfied or steps being taken, such as a more formal contract, generally render the agreement incomplete and not binding (see further 2.6.1).

2.3.1.2 Counter-offer kills the original offer

An offeree whose response *deviates* from the terms of the offer will usually be regarded as having made a *counter-offer*. A counter-offer terminates the original offer. If the offer is rejected, it is no longer 'live' for acceptance. On receiving the offeree's counter-offer (rejection of the original offer), the offeror should be immediately free to deal elsewhere and not be required to wait further. The practical effect is that the offeree loses the power to accept the original offer. In *Hyde v Wrench* (1840), W offered to sell his farm to H for £1,000. H said he would only pay £950; this was rejected by W. H then agreed to pay £1,000, which W also rejected. It was held that H's proposal of £950 was a counter-offer which terminated the original offer, making it incapable of subsequent acceptance.

The offeree can retain his or her power to accept the original offer if the court finds:

(i) that the original offeror's rejection of the counter-offer includes a *renewed offer* on the original terms; or

(ii) that the offeree's response was not a counter-offer but merely a *request for information* or clarification about the availability of better terms. In **Stevenson, Jaques & Co v McLean** (1880), M offered to sell S iron at '40s per ton net cash'. S asked whether M 'would accept forty for delivery over two months, or if not, longest limit you would give'. M then sold the iron to a third party. Hearing nothing, S accepted the original offer by telegram before M's revocation reached S. The court held that S merely made an inquiry, not a counter-offer extinguishing the offer, and so could bind M with his subsequent acceptance. The line between a counter-offer and a request for information can be a fine one. The lesson is that the offeree should be careful not to appear as if he or she is rejecting the original offer, so as to preserve (rather than destroy) their power to accept the original offer, as a fall-back position.

2.3.1.3 Battle of forms

The offeree's counter-offer must itself be accepted before the parties are bound. If there is a signature or other clear manifestation of acceptance, all is fine. But, two common contracting practices lead to acute difficulties when parties dispute the *content* of the contract, although they have commenced performance. The issue is less '*whether* there is a contract', and more '*what* is the contract for?' The first problematic situation is the so-called '**ticket cases**'. They concern the enforceability of terms in unsigned standard form documents which one party hands over to the other when making the contract. Essentially, the terms only bind if the recipient of the unsigned document has *reasonable notice* of the challenged term (see 10.3.3.2).

The second situation, the so-called '**battle of forms**' cases, arises where the parties purport to conclude a contract by an *exchange of forms* containing incompatible terms (variously labelled 'offers', 'quotations', 'tenders', 'invoices', 'orders', 'delivery notes', and so on). For example, X offers to sell goods on its standard form terms X^{**} and Y 'accepts' by placing an order on its, different, set of terms Y^{**}. X then delivers the goods accompanied by its invoice X^{**} and Y receives the goods without objection. There is an agreement of some sort, but on whose terms? The conventional answer is that it depends on which party '*fired the last shot*': the party that presents its terms *last* without provoking objection from the recipient who acts on the 'contract', succeeds in binding the recipient on its terms (X, in the above example). For example, in **Brogden v Metropolitan Railway Co** (1877), M sent B a draft agreement for the supply of coal. B amended the agreement and returned it. Nothing further was done to formalise the agreement. M ordered coal from B, which B supplied and M paid for. When a dispute broke out, M denied any binding contract. It was held that B's amendment amounted to a counter-offer, which M *accepted by conduct* when M placed the order.

A more difficult case is that of **Butler v Ex-Cell-O Corp (England) Ltd** (1979). B quoted the price for manufacturing a machine for E on B's standard terms *B*** with a price variation clause. E then placed an order on their standard form *E***, which mentioned no price variation. *E*** contained a tear-off slip which invited the supplier's signature acknowledging the order to be on *E*** terms. B signed and returned this slip, *but also* attached a letter stating that they were supplying the machine on their original terms *B***. B relied on *B*** to claim an additional sum on delivery of the machine. E successfully denied any obligation to pay the extra sum. The Court of Appeal held that B's *original* offer was met by E's counter-offer, which B accepted when B signed and returned the acknowledgement slip in *E***. B's accompanying letter was not a counter-offer, but simply a means of identifying the order.

In *Tekdata Interconnectors Ltd v Amphenol Ltd* (2009), the Court of Appeal reaffirmed the 'last shot' rule, but held that the rule can be displaced where the parties' common intention is that some other terms were intended to prevail.

It is even possible for the court to conclude that there is a contract but on neither party's terms. In *GHSP Inc v AB Electronic Ltd* (2010), the issue was whether the contract was on the claimant's terms (which imposed unlimited liability on the seller), or on the defendant's terms (which effectively excluded liability for all consequential loss and damage). After reviewing the correspondence between the parties, Burton J concluded that they were in deadlock: 'both sides buttoned their lips, or fastened their seatbelts, and hoped that there would never be a problem'. Nevertheless, it was clear that a contract existed and had been performed. The court filled the gap by implying in the term contained in section 14(2) of the Sale of Goods Act 1979, namely, that the 'goods supplied under the contract are of satisfactory quality'.

Pause for reflection

1. Whether a situation falls within the normal rule or the exception will be a matter of judgment on which reasonable courts can differ.

2. The 'last shot' approach set out in *Butler* is open to criticism.

   (i) *It can hide the real basis for decisions*: the court found a contract although, objectively interpreted, no agreement was ever reached. The letter accompanying B's signature on the tear-off slip plainly evinced B's intention to assert their terms and so was really a counter-offer. This was rejected by E when they refused to pay the extra sum. However, the parties had acted in *reliance* on their arrangement (B manufactured the machine to E's specification, and E made no alternative arrangements). To protect this reliance, the court *had* to find a contract: to do this, the court construed B's signed return of E's

   ➡

➜   tear-off slip as an acceptance and discounted B's contradictory letter. Where contractual performance has begun or is completed (the contract is executed or partly executed), courts strive to impose liability even if this means constructing an agreement out of disagreement. In **'Contract Law: Fulfilling the Reasonable Expectations of Honest Men'** (1997) 113 *LQR* 433, **Lord Steyn,** writing extrajudicially, explains (at 435):

> Each party insists on contracting only on his or her own standard conditions. In the meantime the work starts. Payments are made. Often it is a fiction to identify an offer and acceptance. Yet reason tells us that neither party should be able to withdraw unilaterally from the transaction. The reasonable expectations of the parties, albeit that they are still in disagreement about minor details of the transaction, often demand that the court must recognise that a contract has come into existence. The greater the evidence of reliance, and the further along the road towards implementation the transaction is, the greater the prospect that the court will find a contract made and do its best, in accordance with the reasonable expectations of the parties, to spell out the terms of the contract.

(ii) *It may not fit what actually happens*: contract parties tend to put forward their own standard terms for reasons of ease, efficiency, and self-interest, but may not insist on the other's overt acceptance of them for fear of aggravating the other party and losing the deal (see 1.5.3).[26] Each party proceeds on the optimistic expectation that no problems will arise and that, if they do, he or she will be able to sort out the problem. Indeed, it is conceded that '[c]ommerce could not be carried on, and no contract could ever be concluded if merchants were required to use the precision of solicitors in contracts with each other.'[27] So, it is not surprising that, when disputes arise, courts may have the greatest difficulty in untangling the strands and fitting them into an offer and acceptance analysis.

(iii) *It may produce unjust solutions*: it may be a matter of chance which party gets the 'last shot' in and, although courts have some latitude in how they interpret the particular facts to decide which set of terms should prevail, the solution is still 'all or nothing'; the contract will be *entirely* on one party's terms. The solution in *Butler* was arguably just. Since there was nothing that could be unequivocally construed as *E*'s acceptance of B**, *B*'s signature and return of the E** tear-off slip had to be construed as the acceptance, and *B*'s inconsistent letter discounted. Lord Denning MR also noted that *B*'s performance was five months late and *E* could only take delivery two months after that.

In *Butler v Ex-Cell-O Corp*, **Lord Denning** puts forward **an alternative approach to finding agreement** (see also 2.5.3). He says (at 404–5): 'In many of these cases our traditional analysis of offer, counter-offer, rejection, acceptance and so forth is out of date.' The 'better way' is for the courts to determine reasonable compromises on

---

[26] H Beale and T Dugdale, 'Contracts between Businessmen: Planning and the Use of Contractual Remedies' (1975) 2 *BJLS* 45, 49–50.

[27] *Anglo-Newfoundland Fish Co v Smith & Co* (1902) at 276.

the disputed terms if the parties are agreed on all material terms. This separates two hitherto merged questions:

(i) **the commitment question**: assessed by looking at the correspondence as a whole and the parties' conduct to see whether or not they 'have reached agreement on all material points, even though there may be differences between the forms and conditions'; and

(ii) **the content question**: '[i]f [the parties' terms] can be reconciled so as to give a harmonious result, all well and good. If differences are irreconcilable, so that they are mutually contradictory, then the conflicting terms may have to be scrapped and replaced by a reasonable implication.'

Pause for reflection

Lord Denning's approach is criticised for uncertainty and for making the contract for the parties. In **'The Battle of the Forms'** (1979) 42 *MLR* 715, **Rawlings** emphasises the difficulty and essential arbitrariness of distinguishing between 'material points', 'material differences', and residual terms. He concludes that while not all the arguments are on one side, the traditional analysis should be retained for its simplicity. On the other hand, Denning's approach provides a more flexible framework for reconciling inconsistent terms and apparent lack of consensus. Indeed, it is broadly mirrored in:

• the US Uniform Commercial Code (§ 2-207);

• the Vienna Convention on Contracts for the International Sale of Goods (Art 19);

• the UNIDROIT Principles of International Commercial Contracts (Art 2.11); and

• the European Draft Common Frame of Reference (Arts II.-4:208–II.-4:209).

The basic idea is that only 'material' inconsistencies will prevent contract formation, while relatively minor ones will not. The Vienna Convention provides a non-exhaustive list of '*material*' terms, namely, those relating to 'price, payment, quality and quantity of the goods, place and time of delivery, extent of one party's liability to the other or the settlement of disputes'. The common law's attempt to resolve the battle of forms problem within the mirror image model is hardly free from uncertainty. Ultimately, the courts must decide whether the parties should be bound by:

(i) the last shot fired; or

(ii) more radically, a reasonable compromise between the parties.

2.3.2 **Nexus between offer and acceptance**

A valid acceptance must be made *in response* to a *known offer*. This *mens rea* (state of mind) requirement means that conduct purporting to be an acceptance is ineffective if it is done in ignorance of the offer, even if it matches the offer. The issue arises in cases of cross-offers and offers of rewards.

2.3.2.1 Cross-offers

Two identical cross-offers made in ignorance of each other do not amount to a contract, unless or until one is further accepted. In *Tinn v Hoffman* (1873), H wrote to T offering to sell him 800 tons of iron at 69s per ton. On the same day, T wrote to H offering to buy on the same terms. It was held obiter that these simultaneous offers, made in ignorance of each other, would not bind the parties.

Pause for reflection

A shared intention or a meeting of minds does *not* create a contract. There must be a *causal nexus* between them. It is only when there is an offer on one side, and an acceptance *of that offer* on the other, that each party *knows when* he is contractually bound, when it is safe to act in *reliance* on there being a contract, and when liability will be incurred for departure. In practice, no problems arise from cross-offers unless one party changes his or her mind.

2.3.2.2 Rewards

The offer must not only be *known* to the offeree, it must also *induce* the offeree's performance. However, the cases show that they are easily satisfied for meritorious claimants, perhaps because the offeror who receives the benefit sought is thought to suffer no prejudice in paying what he or she promised for it. Moreover, public policy calls for claimants who perform beneficial acts (eg returning lost pets or providing useful information) to be encouraged and rewarded for doing so.

- ✗ In *R v Clarke* (1927), a reward was offered for information leading to the arrest of certain murderers. C was charged with the murders and gave the relevant information in order to absolve himself. C's claim for the reward was rejected because he admitted that when giving the information he had forgotten about the reward. The claimant did not perform the act to get the reward.

- ✓ In *Gibbons v Proctor* (1891), a police officer was allowed to claim a reward because the court found that although he was ignorant of the offer when he gave information to a fellow officer, he knew of it by the time the information reached the superintendent after passing through other hands.

- ✓ In *Williams v Carwardine* (1833), the informant acted because she believed she would not live long and wished to ease her conscience. The court held that she was entitled to the reward because she 'must have known' of the reward and interpreted the reward as payable even if the informant did not act from the desire to receive the reward.

2.3.3 **Method of acceptance**

An acceptance must be made in an appropriate way. The method of acceptance may be stipulated in the offer. Otherwise, any words or conduct that objectively evince the offeree's intention to accept are enough. A *signature* on a contractual document is a clear example of acceptance, but acceptance can also be made by *conduct* in reliance on and consistent with the terms of the contract (eg *Brogden v Metropolitan Railway Co*) or by *failing to object* (acquiescence) to the last shot fired by the other party in battle of forms cases.

2.3.3.1 Method of acceptance prescribed

If the offer *requires* the offeree to comply with a particular method of acceptance, a purported acceptance that deviates from this may not bind the offeror unless the offeror *waives* his or her right to insist on compliance. However, courts lean towards treating the stipulated mode as *permissive* rather than *mandatory*: they are slow to conclude that the offeror *only* intends to be bound by the stated method of acceptance unless very clear words to the contrary are used. The offeror will be bound if the actual method of acceptance did not disadvantage him or her (eg by occasioning delay) compared with the method prescribed. In ***Manchester Diocesan Council for Education v Commercial and General Investments Ltd*** (1970), M invited tenders (ie offers) on a particular form stating that the person whose bid was accepted would be informed by a letter sent to the address contained in the tender. However, M sent an acceptance of C's tender to C's surveyor rather than the address in C's tender. C sought a declaration that no contract was concluded. The court held that the mode of acceptance specified in the invitation to tender was not the sole permitted means of acceptance. Since C was not disadvantaged by notification to its surveyor, M's acceptance was effective. Moreover, since it was really M who made the stipulation, M could waive strict compliance.

2.3.3.2 Acceptance by silence

The general rule is that acceptance cannot be inferred from the offeree's silence. In ***Felthouse v Bindley*** (1862),[28] F offered to buy his nephew's horse, adding that: 'If I hear no more about him, I consider the horse mine at £30 15s.' The nephew did not answer the letter, but told B, the auctioneer, that the horse had already been sold. B mistakenly sold the horse, and F sued B for conversion (ie for infringing F's ownership of the horse). The court held against F because his offer to buy the horse could not be accepted by his nephew's silence.

Three reasons support the rule that **silence cannot constitute acceptance**.

(i) In general, silence is *ambiguous*: it will often be difficult to infer an intention to accept from it.

(ii) Acceptance must generally be *communicated* to the offeror so that he or she knows *when* a contract binds both parties.

(iii) The rule prevents an offeror from *exploiting an offeree's inertia* (by imposing liability unless he or she actively rejects the offer). The Unsolicited Goods and Services Act 1971 allows recipients of unsolicited goods to treat them as unconditional gifts in certain circumstances and prohibits suppliers from demanding or threatening legal proceedings for payment.

---

[28] See C Miller, '*Felthouse v Bindley* Revisited' (1972) 35 *MLR* 489.

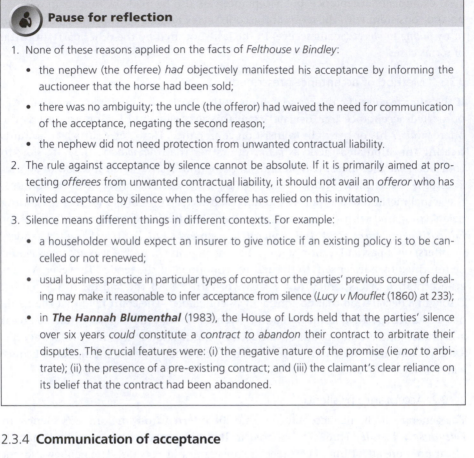

Pause for reflection

1. None of these reasons applied on the facts of *Felthouse v Bindley*:

   • the nephew (the offeree) *had* objectively manifested his acceptance by informing the auctioneer that the horse had been sold;

   • there was no ambiguity; the uncle (the offeror) had waived the need for communication of the acceptance, negating the second reason;

   • the nephew did not need protection from unwanted contractual liability.

2. The rule against acceptance by silence cannot be absolute. If it is primarily aimed at protecting *offerees* from unwanted contractual liability, it should not avail an *offeror* who has invited acceptance by silence when the offeree has relied on this invitation.

3. Silence means different things in different contexts. For example:

   • a householder would expect an insurer to give notice if an existing policy is to be cancelled or not renewed;

   • usual business practice in particular types of contract or the parties' previous course of dealing may make it reasonable to infer acceptance from silence (*Lucy v Mouflet* (1860) at 233);

   • in **The Hannah Blumenthal** (1983), the House of Lords held that the parties' silence over six years *could* constitute a *contract to abandon* their contract to arbitrate their disputes. The crucial features were: (i) the negative nature of the promise (ie *not* to arbitrate); (ii) the presence of a pre-existing contract; and (iii) the claimant's clear reliance on its belief that the contract had been abandoned.

2.3.4 **Communication of acceptance**

The general rule is that the offeree must communicate his or her acceptance to the offeror. Only at that moment does the offeror know that the contract is binding, and each party know that they can safely rely on the existence of the contract. Two practical problems are posed by the communication requirement.

(i) **Timing**: when there is a delay between the sending and the receiving of the acceptance, should the offeror's revocation or the offeree's rejection of the offer in the intervening period be effective?

(ii) **Failure of communication**: which party should bear the risk if the acceptance does not reach the offeror without either party's fault?

The answers to these questions have traditionally depended on whether the method used to communicate the acceptance is classified as postal or instantaneous:

• Where it is **postal**, acceptance takes effect when the letter is *sent*: the offer *cannot* be rejected or revoked afterwards.

• Where it is **instantaneous** (eg by telephone), acceptance takes effect when and where it comes to the offeror's attention: the offer *can* be rejected or revoked before that time.

2.3.4.1 Acceptance by post

A letter of acceptance is posted, arrives some time later, and later again is read by the recipient. When does acceptance take effect? An offeror can only revoke the offer and prevent contract formation if his or her revocation takes effect before acceptance.

(i) The postal acceptance rule

If it is reasonable for the offeree to accept by post, acceptance takes place *when the offeree posts his or her acceptance* (*Adams v Lindsell* (1818)). Two consequences follow:

(i) The offeror is bound before he or she knows of the acceptance, even if its arrival is delayed, and even if he or she never actually receives it (***Household Fire & Carriage Accident Insurance Co Ltd v Grant*** (1879)). These risks lie firmly with the offeror.

(ii) The offeror cannot revoke his or her offer after the offeree's acceptance is posted. In ***Byrne v Van Tienhoven*** (1880), V sent an offer to sell tin plates on 1 October. When it arrived on 11 October, B immediately sent an acceptance, concluding a contract on 11 October. However, on 8 October, V sent a letter revoking its offer; this reached B on 20 October. It was held that a contract was concluded on 11 October. Since the *postal acceptance rule does not apply to revocations*, the revocation only took effect on 20 October, by which time a contract was already in existence.

(ii) Justifications for the postal acceptance rule

Many justifications have been ventured for the postal rule, none very convincingly. For example, the following have been put.

(i) The Royal Mail is the *agent of the offeror*, so that communication to the agent is as good as communication to the offeror. *However*, the Royal Mail is an agent to transmit the message, not to receive its contents. If anything, it is the agent of the offeree who pays for its services.

(ii) *The offeror who initiates negotiations through the post* should assume the risk that the postal acceptance may be delayed or lost. *However*, the offeree may just as likely have initiated postal negotiations (by inviting the offeror to treat or to tender by post). Use of the postal system is not unusual and does not indicate that either party should particularly assume the risk of any delay or loss.

(iii) *The offeree is less likely to detect* that his or her acceptance letter has gone astray, because he or she expects their letter to arrive in the normal course and expects no further communication to conclude the contract. In contrast, the offeror, waiting for a response, is more likely to inquire if he or she does not hear from the offeree (ie the offeror is the best risk-avoider). *However*, the offeror may equally interpret the absence of a response as a rejection of his or her offer.

(iv) *The offeror can always specify that the postal acceptance rule* does not apply (ie stipulate that acceptance only takes effect when it is *actually* communicated to the offeror), *but* the fact that the parties can contract out of a rule does not explain the rule itself.

(v) *Once the offeree posts his or her acceptance, he or she cannot know whether and when the offeror acquires notice of it*, unless the offeror writes to tell them of its arrival. This would only multiply the problems of communication sought to be resolved. The *offeree* would be disadvantaged since the offeror can safely rely on the existence of a contract while the offeree remains vulnerable to revocation until he or she knows that their acceptance has arrived. This leaves the timing to the offeror; he or she may not admit to receiving the acceptance and may try to revoke his or her offer if the contract turns out to be a bad one. *On the other hand*, the postal acceptance rule disadvantages the *offeror* by allowing the offeree to rely on the existence of a contract before the offeror can, and barring the offeror from revoking their offer before he or she can know of its acceptance.

 Pause for reflection

1. In truth, no really convincing reasons support the weight of the postal acceptance rule. The law cannot avoid preferring the offeror or the offeree and it must choose one in the interest of *certainty*, rather like the decision about which side of the road cars should be driven on. There is no particular reason to choose the left or the right, but making a decision is important for certainty.

2. Even so, a rigid application of the postal acceptance rule can yield perverse outcomes. An offeree *A* (accepting the offer) who changes their mind after posting their acceptance and communicating their rejection to the offeror *O* by a quicker method, is bound even if his or her acceptance arrives after their rejection (see 2.4.2). This is absurd since *A* does not want to contract, and *O* knows that any acceptance later received does not reflect *A's* intention. Neither party can reasonably rely on there being a contract, nor is either prejudiced if no contract is found. The only reason for binding *A* to his or her postal acceptance is to prevent him or her from withdrawing from the contract if the market fluctuates against them. However, it may not even do that. A rigid application of the postal acceptance rule has the bizarre result that *O*, who relies on *A's* apparent rejection and sells to a third party, may find themselves in breach of contract if *A* subsequently chooses to rely on his or her postal acceptance.

3. In **'Trashing with Trollope: A Deconstruction of the Postal Rules in Contract'** (1992) 12 *OJLS* 170, **Gardner** finds none of the traditional justifications for the postal acceptance rule convincing. He ultimately explains the rule by reference to the historical context in which the original cases were decided. The introduction of the uniform penny post in the 1840s brought great general enthusiasm for the post along with the idea that posting was as good as delivery. The second wave of cases in the 1870s and 1880s involved attempts to escape regretted applications to buy shares after posting and evince a preference in favour of companies. Gardner concludes that the postal acceptance rule is now 'something of a museum piece', and that we should be careful not to go down the same route with newer forms of communication, where delivery rather than mere transmission should be the rule with qualifications based on business practicality.

Rather than abandoning an outdated rule, the courts are more likely to marginalise it through lack of use. Emphasis is placed on dicta in *Holwell Securities Ltd v Hughes* (1974) that the postal acceptance rule does *not* apply where:

(i) it is expressly or impliedly excluded in the offer. In *Holwell*, a contract stipulated that HS could accept an option to purchase certain property 'by notice in writing' to H within six months. HS's solicitor sent an acceptance by mail to H but it never arrived. The court held that the stipulation of 'notice in writing' required *actual* notice. Absent this, no contract was concluded between the parties.

(ii) 'it would produce manifest inconvenience and absurdity' (at 161). With the abundance of new communication technologies, the postal acceptance rule will seem increasingly inappropriate and exceptional.

2.3.4.2 Two-way instantaneous

The assumption with instantaneous methods of communication is that *both parties are present*, there is no delay between the sending and receiving of the acceptance, and any failure of communication is usually detectable immediately. *Brinkibon Ltd v Stahag Stahl und Stahlwarenhandelsgesellschaft mbH* (1983) held that, in cases of instantaneous communication (specifically face-to-face dealing and telephone), acceptance takes effect **when and where it is actually brought to the attention of the offeror**, unless one of the parties should reasonably have detected and rectified the communication failure. Lord Denning gave the following examples in *Entores v Miles Far East Corp* (1955):

- if a face-to-face oral acceptance is drowned out by a noisy aircraft flying overhead, the offeree must repeat his or her acceptance once the aircraft has passed;
- if the telephone goes 'dead' before the acceptance is completed, the offeree must telephone back to complete the acceptance;
- if the offeror does not catch the clear and audible words of an acceptance or the printer receiving a telex runs out of ink, but the offeror does not bother to ask for the message to be repeated, the offeror will be bound.

Where *neither* party is blameworthy, the general rule requiring actual communication of acceptance favours the offeror. Lord Denning (at 333) said that if 'the offeror without any fault on his part does not receive the message of acceptance—yet the sender of it reasonably believes it has got home when it has not—then I think there is no contract'.

2.3.4.3 One-way instantaneous

Lord Wilberforce justified the rule on instantaneous communication 'where the condition of simultaneity is met' (in *Brinkibon v Stahag Stahl* at 42). This allows us to draw a distinction between *two-way* instantaneous communications 'where the condition of simultaneity is met' (the telephone, face-to-face conversation), and *one-way* instantaneous communications where the condition of simultaneity is *not* met. For example, with emails, text messaging, answerphone messages, faxes, or telexes,[29] the message arrives almost instantaneously, but the recipient does not necessarily access the message instantaneously. *When does the acceptance take effect?* A flexible approach is required. As Lord Wilberforce said, 'No universal rule can cover all such cases: they must be resolved by reference to the intentions of the parties, by sound business practice and in some cases by a judgement where the risks should lie' (at 42).

Three possibilities can be mooted; acceptance can take place.

✗ When it is *sent*: this prejudices the offeror who may not know of it at that time.

✗ When it *actually comes to the offeror's notice*: this prejudices the offeree because it allows the offeror too much control over whether and when the contract is concluded. The offeror could revoke his or her offer without reading the acceptance or only read it after an unreasonable delay.

✓ **When a reasonable offeror would access the message, taking account of all the circumstances.** This allows a court to balance the parties' respective interests. *Tenax SS Co Ltd v The Brimnes* (1975) is instructive. In determining when a *revocation of offer* by telex (like a fax) was communicated, the Court of Appeal held that, *if the telex* was sent to *a place of business during ordinary business hours*, the revocation was effective when it was received on the telex machine, even if it remained unread. This implies a different result if the message was sent *out of office hours* or to *non-business premises*. If the mode of acceptance is permitted or invited by the offeror, he or she can be expected to act reasonably by checking the technology he or she puts into use in a timely manner (unless he or she indicates when they are otherwise likely to access any messages). This standard of reasonableness must also apply to acceptances made by post where the postal acceptance rule does not apply (see 2.3.4.1).

2.3.5 **Contract formation by electronic means**

Contract formation involving email, websites, or instantaneous messaging have largely superseded previous methods of electronic contract formation, including facsimile and telex communications.

2.3.5.1 **Offer**

Existing common law principles point towards the conclusion that websites advertising goods and services and inviting customers to make an online purchase are not making contractual offers, but rather invitations to treat (*Pharmaceutical Society of Great Britain v Boots Cash Chemists (Southern)* (1953)). However, **traders** are required by the Electronic Commerce (EC Directive) Regulations 2002 to set out clearly for their customers the procedure for completion of a contract (reg 9). Failure to comply with these requirements renders the merchant liable for breach of statutory duty (reg 13).

---

[29] A telex machine is similar to a fax machine, in that a message is generated on one machine and sent to another machine on the telex network. Although the *Brinkibon* case classifies the telex as an instantaneous method of communication, it is distinguishable from telephones and face-to-face conversations since both parties are not necessarily present when the telex is used.

The regulation also requires the trader to offer the purchaser 'appropriate, effective and accessible means allowing him to identify and correct input errors prior to the placing of an order' (reg 11(1)(b)). Otherwise, the purchaser can rescind the contract (reg 15(b)). Communication of an offer by email or electronic message will normally be presumed to have occurred when the message arrived in the server inbox of the recipient.

2.3.5.2 Acceptance

A valid acceptance must be successfully communicated to the offeror. The issue has not been settled decisively in the English courts, but the problems arising from the postal acceptance rule point overwhelmingly against any extension of the rule to cover electronic contract formation. This is reinforced by existing decisions. *Entores v Miles Far East Corp* (1955) held that contracts, like those made by telex, that are 'virtually instantaneous' are not covered by the postal rule (at 332, 337). Similar reasoning was endorsed by the House of Lords in *Brinkibon v Stahag Stahl mbH* (at 41–2 and 48). In *Chwee Kin Keong v Digiland Mail plc Ltd* (2004), Rajah JC noted at [101] that being generally instantaneous, contracts made through websites fall outside the scope of the postal rule exception.

In online purchases, an offer will be deemed to have been accepted either by the conduct of the trader (eg the delivery of goods) or upon communication of acceptance. Traders are required to acknowledge receipt of payment under regulation 11 of the Electronic Commerce (EC Directive) Regulations 2002. Whether or not this acknowledgement amounts to acceptance will depend on its precise wording.

The previous discussion on one-way instantaneous acceptance expressed a preference for the view that the acceptance is operative when it ought reasonably to have come to the attention of the recipient (see 2.3.4.3). The alternative is that acceptance takes effect when the email or electronic message arrives in the server folder. This is supported by Art 24 of the UN Convention on Contracts for the International Sale of Goods; § 68 of the US Second Restatement of Contracts (1981); the UN Model Law on Electronic Commerce (Art 15(2)), the US Uniform Computer Information Transactions Act (§ 102(a)(52)(B)(II)), and the Law Commission's 'initial view' that emails should be deemed to be received when the message reaches the recipient's internet service provider (Law Commission, *Electronic Commerce: Formal Requirements in Commercial Transactions* (2001) para 3.56). In *The Pendrecht* (1980) a telex notice was 'served' for limitation purposes when it was received at the registered office of the other party, whether or not this was during normal business hours.[30]

Is it the offeror or the offeree who should bear the risk if there is a **failure of communication** (ie the offeree's acceptance fails to reach the offeror)? Fault or responsibility should be determinative. If the offeree has knowledge actual or constructive that the message has not got through, then no contract exists. Otherwise, the risk should lie with the party best placed to avoid the risk. Thus, if the mode of communication is within the offeror's control, such as an answerphone, it is arguable whether he or she should bear the risk since they have invited reliance on it for acceptance. Otherwise,

---

[30] See also *Bernuth Lines Ltd v High Seas Shipping Ltd* [2005] EWHC 3020 (Comm) (concerning service of notice by email received by the server but wrongly discarded).

as with emails, which are processed via servers outside the control of the parties, failure which is neither party's fault or responsibility should leave the default position requiring actual communication. The risk lies with the offeree.

2.3.6 **Unilateral contracts**

Contracts are often *bilateral*, involving an exchange of a promise for a promise. However, a contract may be *unilateral*, involving an exchange of a promise for a completed act (or refraining from an act). The distinction matters in determining (i) what constitutes valid acceptance and (ii) whether offers are revocable.

2.3.6.1 Acceptance

Bilateral contracts are concluded by *communication of the acceptance* (eg *A* promises to pay *B* £1,000 *to* complete the London marathon and B accepts). B undertakes to run and can be sued if he or she does not. In contrast, unilateral contracts are only concluded by the *performance of the stipulated act* (eg *A* agrees to pay *B* £1,000 *if* he or she completes the London Marathon (and see reward cases, 2.3.2.2)). The unilateral offer is only accepted when *B* performs the stipulated act. *B* need not run and need not communicate to *A* his or her intention to do so; any such communication is legally irrelevant. In **Carlill v Carbolic Smoke Ball**, C accepts the offer when she buys and uses the smoke ball as instructed, although she is only entitled to the £100 when she satisfies the further condition of catching one of the illnesses named in the advertisement. She need not communicate this to CSB to conclude the contract, although in practice she must do so to claim the payout.

> **Pause for reflection**
>
> The justification for fixing the point of acceptance at the offeree's *completed* performance is symmetry of treatment.[31] The offeree is not bound to perform and it is thought that the offeror should not be bound either until the stipulated act is completed. This means that the offeror may be bound before he or she becomes aware of the completed performance.

2.3.6.2 Revocation

In the marathon example in the previous section, it would be unjust to allow *A* to revoke his or her offer to pay when *B* has almost completed the marathon.[32] The injustice lies in *B*'s induced reliance and, in some circumstances (eg say *B* was to wear running gear advertising *A*'s products), *A*'s receipt of unpaid-for benefits. *Chitty* states that the unilateral offer can be accepted 'as soon as the offeree has unequivocally begun

---

[31] I Wormser, 'The True Conception of Unilateral Contracts' (1916) 26 *Yale LJ* 136.

[32] This is distinct from the 'entire obligations rule' (see 12.2.2.1 III) where, eg, the painter only earns the sum promised on complete or substantial performance since the customer could not prevent him from doing so and the painter cannot fail to complete without breaching the *bilateral* contract.

performance of the stipulated act or abstention . . . , so that the offer can no longer be withdrawn' (at para 2-079). Alternatively, the courts can imply an obligation on the offeror not to revoke the offer once the offeree has started performance. But the law is not as clear-cut as this suggests.

The clearest case in favour of no revocation on commencement of performance is *Errington v Errington* (1952). There a father promised his son and daughter-in-law that if they paid off the mortgage, amounting to two-thirds of the value of the house that all three were living in, it would be theirs. The father died nine years later after a substantial part of the mortgage had been paid. As the couple had commenced payment, the Court of Appeal prevented the father's representatives from revoking the arrangement, provided that their performance was not left 'incomplete and unperformed' (at 295). Aside from this family case, the position is only supported by Court of Appeal dicta in *Daulia Ltd v Four Millbank Nominees Ltd* (1978), at 239 (involving an unenforceable oral agreement for property) and *Soulsbury v Soulsbury* (2007), at [50] (where no question of revocation arose because the stipulated performance of a family arrangement was completed).

On the other side, ***Luxor (Eastbourne) Ltd v Cooper*** (1941) denied an implied obligation barring revocation. The House of Lords refused a real estate agent's claim for £10,000 in commission payable on completion of a sale; the agent found buyers but the owners refused to complete. The commission was the equivalent of a Lord Chancellor's annual payment, for work which had been done within eight or nine days. The court held that the common understanding was that estate agents take 'the risk in the hope of a substantial remuneration for comparatively small exertion' (at 126). Likewise, the Federal Court of Australia in *Mobil Oil Australia Ltd v Wellcome International Pty Ltd and Others* (1998) allowed Mobil to revoke its offer to give nine additional years of franchise free if the franchisee obtained at least 90% in the annual 'Circle of Excellence' judging for six years. The court rejected the suggestion 'that the attainment of 90% in the first year or even perfect operation of the service station for a day, a week or a month, albeit by reference to the offer, represents a commencement of attainment of 90% in all six years so it is immediately to bind Mobil not to revoke' (at 224).

 Pause for reflection

1. It is tempting to opt for a clear rule prohibiting or permitting revocation of the modifying offer once performance has commenced. However, the answers 'never' or 'always' will sometimes yield unintended and unjust results. In *Morrison Shipping Co v The Crown* (1924), the Lord Chancellor doubted (at 287): 'whether a conditional offer in general terms, whether made to the public (as in the *Carbolic Smoke Ball* case) or to a class of persons, is converted into a contract so soon as one of the persons to whom the offer is made takes some step towards performing the condition.' The Federal Court of Australia in *Mobil Oil Australia* declined to recognise a 'universal proposition that an offeror is not at liberty to revoke the offer once the offeree "commences" or "embarks upon" performance of the sought act of acceptance' (at 228). The issue is one of construction, but also of protecting

➡

➜ a performing offeree from exploitation by the offeror. These features will vary greatly from case to case.

2. The offeror's implied obligation not to revoke his or her offer requires a two-contract analysis. Aside from the main offer to pay on completed performance, the court implies a separate unilateral offer of a procedural nature, not to revoke the main offer once the offeree commences performance.

2.4 Termination of the offer

A party denying the existence of a contract may argue that, although a valid offer once existed, it had ceased to exist by the time of the offeree's attempted acceptance. An offer can be terminated by: (i) revocation by the offeror; (ii) rejection by the offeree; (iii) lapse of the offer; or (iv) death of either the offeror or the offeree.

2.4.1 Revocation by the offeror

An offeror can revoke his or her offer any time before the offeree communicates his or her acceptance. The exception is a **unilateral offer**, which may be irrevocable once the offeree has commenced performance (see 2.3.6.2). The same need to protect the offeree's reliance may be present in offers to keep an offer open for a specific period of time (**options** or **firm offers**), but the rule is that they are revocable before the expiry of the specified time, even if the offeree has relied on the promise. To enforce this firm offer, it must be contained in a deed (see 3.2) or the offeree must have given consideration (see 3.1). The Law Revision Committee[33] recommended, and Article 16(2) of the Vienna Sales Convention stipulates, that firm offers should be enforceable without consideration.

A revocation only becomes effective if it is *communicated* to the offeree before their acceptance takes effect. A *postal revocation* is not effective on posting, but only when it is 'brought to the mind' of the offeree (*Henthorn v Fraser* (1892) at 32, 37), or when it would be reasonable to expect the offeror to acquire notice of it (eg when it arrives at business premises during office hours; if it arrives near or after closing hours, it takes effect the next business opening, see *Tenax SS Co Ltd v The Brimnes* (1975) at 966, 969 and see 2.3.4.3). An offer in a newspaper advertisement is revoked by a similar advertisement even if unseen by the original offerees (*Shuey v US* (1875)).

Dickinson v Dodds (1876) establishes that an offer can even be revoked by a *reliable third party* acting without the offeror's authority. Mellish LJ said (at 475): 'once the person to whom the offer was made knows that the property has been sold to someone else, it is too late for him to accept the offer'. However, courts will be slow to conclude that the offeree should lose his or her power of acceptance on the say-so of a third party. The onus will be on the offeror to show that, in all the circumstances, it would be *unreasonable* for the offeree to doubt the accuracy of the information.

---

[33] Lord Chancellor's Office, *Statute of Frauds and the Doctrine of Consideration* (Sixth Interim Report) (Cmd 5449, 1937), para 38.

2.4.2 **Rejection by the offeree**

An offer is terminated as soon as the offeree communicates his or her rejection of it to the offeror. Recall (at 2.3.1.2) the fine distinction between a counter-offer (which is regarded as a rejection and so 'kills' the offer) and a request for further information or clarification of the offer (which preserves the offeree's power to accept the original offer).

A rejection only takes effect when it is actually communicated to the offeror. This can logically lead to unpalatable conclusions when combined with the postal acceptance rule.

- Where an offeree posts his or her acceptance, then changes their mind and notifies the offeror of their rejection by a speedier means (eg telephone), the parties are still bound by the postal acceptance (2.3.4.1).

- An offeree who posts his or her rejection, then changes their mind and posts their acceptance before their rejection letter arrives, can bind the offeror, although their acceptance arrives after their rejection letter.

2.4.3 **Lapse of the offer**

An offer may lapse on:

(i) the *expiry of the stipulated period* for which the offer is open;

(ii) the *expiry of an express or implied condition*, other than time, for the validity of the offer (eg 'while stocks last'); and

(iii) the passage of a *reasonable period of time* where no time limit or other condition is imposed. What is 'reasonable' depends on all the circumstances, including the urgency of the matter, the nature of the subject matter, the practice of the trade, and the previous mode of communication used. In *Ramsgate Victoria Hotel Co Ltd v Montefiore* (1866), M offered to buy shares in a company. Although shares were allotted to him five months later, he was not bound since his offer had lapsed.

2.4.4 **Death of the offeror or offeree**

An offer is generally terminated by the death of the offeree[34] or of the offeror.[35] However, *Errington v Errington* shows that an offer remains open if the offeror could not have terminated the offer during his or her lifetime, and the performance of the contract does not depend on the offeror's personality but can be satisfied out of their estate (see 2.3.6.2).

---

[34] *Reynolds v Atherton* (1921) at 695. In *Re Irvine* (1928) an acceptance handed by an offeree to his son for posting, but not actually posted until after the offeree's death, was invalid.

[35] *Coulthart v Clementson* (1879). The offeree cannot validly accept, whether or not he is aware that the offeror has died, *Re Whelan* (1897).

> ### ◆◆ Counterpoint
>
> The present rule that the offeror or offeree's death automatically terminates an offer is too rigid. It may leave the offeree's reasonable expectations and reliance unprotected. Contracts other than those for personal services are usually enforceable against a party's executors and an option can be exercised by the option holder's estate. Analogously, an offer should be capable of acceptance by the offeree's estate. Unless the terms of the offer indicate that the offer is only valid during the offeror's lifetime, or is only addressed to the offeree personally, it should be possible for the offeree to accept (after the offeror's death) or the offeree's estate to accept (on the offeree's death), if performance can be satisfied out of the parties' estates and is independent of the parties' personality.

2.4.5 Change of circumstances

Three approaches have been taken to deal with the situation when the subject matter of the offer deteriorates between offer and purported acceptance.

(i) The court can **imply a condition into the offer** that the offer will lapse if the subject matter of the contract is not, at the time of acceptance, in substantially the same condition as it was when the offer was made. In *Financings Ltd v Stimson* (1962), the court held that no valid contract was concluded when, after the buyer offered to buy a car from a finance company, the car was stolen, damaged, and subsequently recovered and sold for £224.

(ii) In *Dysart Timbers Ltd v Roderick William Nielsen* (2009), the New Zealand Supreme Court held that, as a **rule of law** (rather than based on the offeror's implied intention), an offer can lapse if there has been a **fundamental change in the basis of the offer** (by analogy to the doctrine of frustration, see Chapter 7).

(iii) The court can find a concluded contract but **interpret** it as being for the undeteriorated subject matter. For example, in the Singaporean case of *Norwest Holdings Pte Ltd v Newport Mining* (2010) phosphate mines and production facilities in China sold for $10 million were damaged by an earthquake between the offer and the acceptance. The court found a contract, but for both the company's shares and a *fully operational phosphate mining, processing, and production business*, which the seller could not deliver. This entitled the buyer to terminate the contract and get its deposit back.

2.5 Assessment of the mirror image approach

2.5.1 Criticisms of the mirror image approach

2.5.1.1 Unsuitability: cases that don't fit

Many common contracting situations 'do not fit easily into the normal analysis of contract being constituted by offer and acceptance' (*Gibson v Manchester CC* at 297).

In *New Zealand Shipping Co Ltd v AM Satterthwaite & Co Ltd (The Eurymedon)* (1975), Lord Wilberforce noted some awkward cases (at 167): sale at auction, supermarket purchases, boarding a bus, buying a train ticket, tenders for the supply of goods, offers of rewards, acceptance by post, warranties of authority by agents, manufacturers' guarantees, gratuitous bailments, and bankers' commercial credits. In his view: 'These are all examples which show that English law, having committed itself to a rather technical and schematic doctrine of contract, in application takes a practical approach, often at the cost of forcing the facts to fit uneasily into the marked slots of offer, acceptance and consideration.'

2.5.1.2 Insufficiency: other requirements of enforceability

Offer and acceptance are necessary but insufficient to establish the formation of a contract. In addition:

- the agreement must be sufficiently *complete and certain* (see 2.6);
- there must be intent to create legal relations (see 2.7);
- the agreement must satisfy one of the requirements of enforceability: *consideration, formalities, or promissory estoppel* (see Chapter 3).

Even then, the contract may be set aside for *vitiating factors* such as duress or misrepresentation (see Part IV). Moreover, the *contents of a valid contract* are subject to legal interpretation and regulation (see Part V); the resulting contract may comprise a ragbag of things that the parties agreed, things which they could not resolve, and things to which one or both gave no thought.

2.5.1.3 Misleading: concerns beyond consensus

While the mirror image approach points to a search for the parties' matching intentions, departures from this in the rules on contract formation reveal the influence of competing concerns (see 2.5.2).

(i) The **objective test** of intention 'bites' precisely when a party's actual intention differs from his or her apparent intention, so that an enforceable contract may not reflect any genuine consensus.

(ii) Courts can cure agreements which are **vague or incomplete**, by interpretation and gap-filling, but they do so by reference to factors *external* to the parties' objective intentions (see 2.6).

(iii) The **situation-specific rules** may contradict the objective test as to whether there is an 'offer' or an 'acceptance' (eg displays do not generally constitute offers, and acceptance cannot be made by silence). Or the courts may find an agreement despite the evident lack of consensus (eg the 'last shot approach' to the 'battle of forms', or the two-contract analysis).

(iv) The courts may find that an agreement has come into existence before one of the parties can know of the other's agreement (eg the postal acceptance rule or the unilateral contract analysis).

2.5.1.4 Backward reasoning

Judges often give the impression that they reason deductively (ie *'forwards'*), assess-ing the facts of the case for compliance with the legal requirements and *thereby* arriving at the solution (ie offer + acceptance = agreement). This is reinforced by the long-standing fiction that judges merely *apply* settled rules without reference to the justice of the rules or the outcomes they yield. Indeed, Scrutton LJ describes concerns with justice as 'well-meaning sloppiness of thought' (*Holt v Markham* (1923) at 513). However, any attempt to understand the formation cases as the product of a mechani-cal application of the rules is doomed to failure.

Judicial reasoning may sometimes be described as *'backwards'* in the sense that the judges *reason back* from their sense of the 'right' solution *to* 'find' the presence or absence of offer and acceptance necessary to *justify* it (see 1.2.3). On this view, findings on questions of 'offer' and 'acceptance' are less the outcome of an empirical examination of the parties' conduct than an expression of the court's *conclusion* of the labels that justice requires. The reasons must be sought elsewhere.

2.5.2 **The policy considerations**

Many factors enter the equation when courts have to decide whether contractual con-sequences should attach to the parties' dealings.

(i) Respecting the parties' intentions

- Courts are genuinely concerned to ascertain whether the parties have committed to a binding contract (see 2.2.1.1).

- Courts are also concerned to give parties some room to manoeuvre (to negotiate, compare alternatives, clarify details, and resolve differences) without the risk of making binding commitments. This can be done by finding a particular commu-nication to be *less than* an offer (merely an invitation to treat) or an acceptance (merely a counter-offer or request for further information), or by concluding that the agreement was too uncertain or lacking in intention to create legal relations (see 2.6 and 2.7).

(ii) Certainty

- Sufficient certainty in the agreement is necessary in order to enforce it (see 2.6).

- The objective test of intentions and the rules on how specific and common con-duct will normally be interpreted (eg display, advertisement, postal acceptance) allow parties to know where they stand.

(iii) Preventing unfairness

- Some rules discourage opportunism and encourage fair negotiating practices (eg the rule that silence is no acceptance, see 2.3.3.2).

- The use of the unilateral contract analysis (recall *Carlill v Carbolic Smoke Ball* at 2.2.1.2, 2.3.5) and the two-contract device (in auctions and tenders) prevents one party from acting inconsistently with the reasonable expectations or reliance induced in the other party.

- Courts are more ready to impose contractual liability to protect *reliance* where a party has commenced performance of an apparent or anticipated contract, 'even if it is impossible to identify the coincidence of offer and acceptance' (*Fitzpatrick Contracts Ltd v Tyco Fire and Integrated Solutions Ltd* (2008) at [9]) or a contract 'cannot be spelt out by a classic analysis of the sequence of offer and acceptance' (*RTS Flexible Systems Ltd v Molkerei Alois Müller* (2008) at [65]).

- Unfair terms (eg unfair exclusions of liability for breach) can be excluded by moving forward the time of contract formation to *before* the offending clause is introduced (recall *Chapelton v Barry* at 2.2.1.2).

- Deterioration of the subject matter of the contract between offer and acceptance can be remedied in various ways (see 2.4.5).

2.5.3 **Alternative approaches to formation**

Despite its instability, lack of transparency, insufficiency, and, at times, unsuitability, the **offer and acceptance** model is still the dominant approach. In its favour are the following.

(i)   Many contracts are naturally susceptible to this analysis.

(ii) It is *analytically convenient* and provides a degree of *certainty* (especially important in commercial transactions) about the general framework that courts will adopt in resolving questions about the existence or content of contracts.

(iii) Considerable *flexibility* is built in to take account of other policy concerns. This is merely the corollary of the criticism of uncertainty often levelled at the mirror image approach.

(iv) The offer and acceptance model is well established and has the weight of *authority*.

The flexible and discretionary elements of the mirror image approach are hidden behind the current formalistic facade. **Lord Denning** advocated a **more transparent approach** to resolving minor differences in the parties' intentions (see 2.3.1.3). In *Gibson v Manchester CC*, he added (at 523): 'It is a mistake to think that all contracts can be analysed into the form of offer and acceptance . . . You should look at the correspondence as a whole and at the conduct of the parties . . . [to decide] *whether the parties have come to an agreement on everything that was material*' (emphasis added). Where the parties' terms are mutually contradictory, it should be possible for a court to 'scrap' the terms and replace them by a 'reasonable implication'.

Lord Denning's suggestion contradicts the mirror image approach by separating the *commitment* and *timing* questions from the *contents* question. In essence, a contract will be found if the parties are sufficiently committed to the *material* terms, leaving the court to iron out the differences on *immaterial* terms. The approach has been criticised for uncertainty and for judicial rewriting of the contract. The approach has not found favour with the House of Lords. In *Gibson v Manchester CC*, Lord Diplock viewed contracts that could not be analysed in the traditional way as 'exceptional' (at 297). English law remains firmly committed to the mirror image approach.

> **Pause for reflection**
>
> A number of arguments support Lord Denning's suggestion.
>
> 1. It is a less radical departure from actual practice than might first appear: eg where the primary *commitment* question is answered affirmatively (especially where performance has begun), we have seen that 'minor' inconsistencies in the *content* can be resolved by the 'last shot' approach (see 2.3.1.3). The cases on uncertainty also reflect this general attitude (see 2.6).
>
> 2. It is a more accurate reflection of business practice (see 1.5.3).
>
> 3. It is supported by European and international commercial law.
>
>   • Article 2.1 of the UNIDROIT Principles of International Commercial Contracts states that: 'A contract may be concluded either by the acceptance of an offer *or by conduct of the parties that is sufficient to show agreement*' (emphasis added).
>
>   • Article II.-4:211 of the European Draft Common Frame of Reference states that the rules relating to offer and acceptance 'apply with appropriate adaptations even though the process of conclusion of a contract cannot be analysed into offer and acceptance'.

2.6 **Certainty**

Even if there is sufficient correspondence between offer and acceptance, there is no enforceable contract if the agreement:

- expressly anticipates the need for further agreement (the 'one more step' problem); or
- impliedly does so because it is too vague (the 'fuzziness' problem); or is silent (the 'gap' problem) on material points.

Certainty as to the material contract terms is necessary in order to decide whether a contract has been properly performed and, if not, the position that the remedies for breach are aiming for. Moreover, the nature and extent of the agreement's uncertainty may indicate that the parties have not yet committed to be bound. Maugham LJ said (at 13) in *Foley v Classique Coaches Ltd* (1934) that 'unless all the material terms of the contract are agreed there is no binding obligation. An agreement to agree in the future is not a contract; nor is there a contract if a material term is neither settled nor implied by law and the document contains no machinery for ascertaining it.' Note that only 'material' terms, not all terms, need to be agreed. The judicial task is to draw the line between uncertainties that are:

- ✓ *curable*, by a process of judicial construction of the parties' implied intentions (resulting in an enforceable contract); and those that are
- ✗ *incurable*, being a mere 'agreement to agree' (where the agreement is unenforceable, but a claimant who has done work in anticipation of a concluded contract may be able to sue on unjust enrichment (see 2.8)).

2.6.1 **Conditional agreements**

An agreement may stipulate that a further step should be taken (eg it may be made 'subject to contract'). The question is whether the stipulated step is:

- *a pre-condition* of the contract's *existence* so that if one of the parties refuses to perform the stipulated step there is no contract; or
- merely indicates the *manner of performance* of an *already enforceable* contract so that one party's refusal to take the next step does not prevent contract formation.[36]

In general, agreements that are expressed to be 'subject to contract' or 'subject to solicitor's advice' indicate that there is no binding contract.[37] That is one reason why agreements to buy land expressed in these terms may be worthless to buyers in a time of rising prices. They postpone formation until a formal document is drafted and signed. Even if a prospective buyer has invested in surveys and lawyers, and paid deposits, he or she can be jilted (or 'gazumped') for a more attractive offer.

However, the presumption of unenforceability attached to such expressions is **rebuttable by clear evidence to the contrary**. The court may enforce an agreement although it is expressed to be 'subject to the signing of a mutually agreeable contract' if:

- the expression is meaningless and can be **severed** because there is nothing left to be negotiated and no need for any further formal contract, and both parties had proceeded on this basis (*Michael Richards Properties Ltd v Corp of Wardens of St Saviour's Parish (Southwark)* (1975)). Recall *Storer v Manchester CC* (at 2.2.1.1) where the council stated: 'If you will sign the [agreement] and return it to me I will send you the agreement signed on behalf of the corporation in exchange.' A contract was formed on S's return of the signed agreement although the council never signed and returned the agreement;[38]

- there is a clear intention to be bound and the non-signing party's subsequent words and conduct amount to a **waiver** of the stipulated step. In *RTS Flexible Systems Ltd v Molkerei Alois Muller GmbH* (2010) the parties entered into a contract formed by a 'letter of intent' to enable work to begin while the parties were negotiating the full formal contract. On 5 July, a draft final contract was produced, which stipulated that it was ineffective until each party had executed and exchanged a counterpart. This was never done. However, substantial work was carried out and, on 25 August, the draft agreement was varied in important respects. R claimed payments for work done at M's factory after the expiry of the letter of intent. The Supreme Court found clear evidence of the existence of a contract because: it made no commercial sense to say that the parties agreed

---

[36] *Von Hatzfeldt-Wildenburg v Alexander* (1912) at 288–9.

[37] *Winn v Bull* (1877); *Chillingworth v Esche* (1924); *Eccles v Bryant and Pollock* (1948).

[38] The Law of Property (Miscellaneous Provisions) Act 1989 now requires contracts for the sale of land to be in writing.

to the work without any relevant contract terms; R had carried out substantial works, which M had paid for; and none of the issues outstanding after 25 August were regarded as essential matters requiring agreement before the contract could be binding. The parties had impliedly waived the requirement of execution.

In *Benourad v Compass Group plc* (2010) at [106] Beatson J helpfully identifies the following guidance from the authorities.

(i)   The more *complicated the subject matter* the more likely the parties are to want to enshrine their contract in some written document prepared by their solicitors. There is no binding contract unless a formal contract is duly executed, whether the parties provide for this expressly or impliedly.

(ii) Nevertheless, if the parties' intentions have changed so that the need for an executed written agreement is expressly or impliedly *waived* or if a party is *estopped* from relying on his or her non-execution of the document, there is a valid contract. The courts are more likely to so find if *all the essential or important terms have been agreed and substantial work has been done.*

(iii) Where certain terms of economic significance have not been agreed, the parties may be held to have agreed a separate preliminary contract to allow work to begin, although *the more important the un-agreed term, the less likely it is that the parties will have left it for future decision.*

(iv) In the absence of a binding contract, the work done may give rise to a *restitutionary claim for recompense* if the defendant has received an incontrovertible benefit (eg an immediate financial gain or saving of expense) from the claimant's services, where the defendant requested the claimant to provide services or accepted them when offered (having the ability to refuse them), knowing that the services were not being given freely.

(v)   However, no award will be made if the claimant *took the risk* of doing the work in order to obtain and then perform the contract.

2.6.2 Vagueness and incompleteness

Vagueness overlaps with incompleteness since both may leave gaps in the contract that call into question the parties' intention to be bound. As Viscount Maugham said (at 255) in *Scammell and Nephew Ltd v Ouston* (1941): 'In . . . a valid contract the parties must so express themselves that their meaning can be determined with a reasonable degree of certainty . . . [Otherwise] *consensus ad idem* would be a matter of mere conjecture.' The legal question is whether any vagueness can be resolved and any gaps filled *by the court* without further agreement between the parties. The scope of the court's jurisdiction in this exercise is difficult to pin down. Indeed, Macneil describes the attempt to find 'coherent principles' in the uncertainty cases as 'a fool's errand'.[39]

---

[39] 'Biographical Statement' in D Campbell (ed), *The Relational Theory of Contract: Selected Works of Ian Macneil* (Sweet & Maxwell, 2001).

> ### 👤 Pause for reflection
>
> Two reasons can be suggested for the uncertainty of the law on uncertainty.
>
> 1. Whilst the relevant principles can be stated, in practice the crucial distinction between the courts' legitimate interpretation and illegitimate imposition of terms can be a very fine one.
> 2. Judges vary in their views on the extent to which it is desirable or, indeed, possible to cure vagueness in contracts.

2.6.2.1 The bias towards cure

Whilst judges are keen to avoid any suggestion that they are making the contract for the parties, in practice they show a great **willingness to *cure* uncertainty** and uphold contracts. In *Hillas & Co v Arcos* (1932), Lord Tomlin said (at 364) that, 'it is . . . necessary to exclude as impossible all reasonable meanings which would give certainty to the words' before enforcement would be denied. In *Brown v Gould* (1972), Megarry J said (at 58) that this conclusion would only be reached 'if the court is driven to it'. Four reasons support this pro-enforcement stance.

(i) **Imprecision in business practice:** many business people refrain from insisting on precise terms for fear of losing the deal or annoying the other party (see 1.5.3). They hope that no serious problems will arise and that, if they do, amicable and informal solutions can be reached. Lord Wright said: 'Businessmen often record the most important agreements in crude and summary fashion . . . It is . . . the duty of the Court to construe such documents fairly and broadly, without being too astute or subtle in finding defects' (*Hillas v Arcos* at 367).

(ii) **The necessity and difficulty of building in flexibility:** parties may try to agree terms that will allow some flexibility to accommodate market fluctuations and other future unknowns (eg in a contract to supply goods over a ten-year period). Building and civil engineering contracts often contain terms that allow variations in the work to be done, the time for performance, or the price, in view of specific changes. However, it may be impossible to draft a workable and acceptable formula to meet *all* the contingencies that may eventuate and very expensive to try to do so. Courts will strive to fill the gaps and make the arrangement workable in such relational contracts.

(iii) **Protecting expectation and reliance:** courts are reluctant to deny the existence of a contract where the parties clearly act as if they have concluded a contract and have commenced its performance. Lord Denning said that 'when an agreement has been acted upon . . . we ought to imply all reasonable terms' (*F&G Sykes (Wessex) Ltd v Fine Fare Ltd* (1967) at 58; *G Percy Trentham Ltd v Archital Luxfer* (1993) at 27).

(iv) **Unmeritorious pleas of uncertainty:** the courts have little sympathy for parties who seek to escape from contracts for unmeritorious reasons (eg where market fluctuations have made the contract disadvantageous for them because they can sell for more or buy for less elsewhere), particularly if they have already received benefits under them.

> **Pause for reflection**
>
> In 'Objectivity, Subjectivity, and Incomplete Agreements' in J Horder (ed), *Oxford Essays in Jurisprudence* (OUP, 2000) 151, Endicott argues that where contract terms are vague or incomplete (and they are more often than not), the court is justified in imposing rights and duties that have not been agreed to because of the value to contracting parties of a regime in which disputed questions are answered, whether there is a reason for the answer or not. The function of giving an answer, even when reason does not support one answer over another, is an indispensable function of the courts.

2.6.2.2 Overview of the techniques for overcoming uncertainty

Courts fill gaps and resolve vagueness by reference to:

(i)   any previous dealing, customs of the trade, and the standard of reasonableness;

(ii) the technique of severance;

(iii) the nature of the undertaking (to negotiate, or not to negotiate); and

(iv) the workability, or substitutability of any agreed, but defunct, method for ascertaining material terms.

This combination of techniques is reflected in the approach of the UNIDROIT Principles of International Commercial Contracts, the European Draft Common Frame of Reference, and the US Uniform Commercial Code.

However the legal approach is formulated, the courts' stated task is to draw the line between:

- 'construing' a contract and 'making' a contract; or
- upholding a bargain and imposing a bargain on the parties.

The distinction is one of degree and not of kind.

2.6.2.3 Previous dealing, custom, and reasonableness

Steyn LJ said (at 27) in *G Percy Trentham Ltd v Archital Luxfer Ltd* (1993), that where sufficient intention to be bound can be inferred from the *reliance* of the parties on the contract, it will be 'difficult to submit that the contract is void for vagueness or uncertainty. Specifically, the fact that the transaction is executed [performed] makes it easier to imply a term resolving any uncertainty, or, alternatively, it may make it possible to treat a matter not finalised in negotiations as inessential.' Two cases illustrate this liberal approach.

✓ In **Hillas v Arcos**, the parties agreed to buy and sell 22,000 standards of softwood goods 'of fair specification' in 1930. The agreement also gave the buyers an option to buy '100,000 standards for delivery during 1931'. The seller sought to escape the option by alleging that no enforceable meaning could be deduced from the agreed words. The court upheld the option by reference to the parties' previous dealing, the custom of the timber trade, and the standard of reasonableness. The words 'of fair specification' were held to mean a reasonable assortment of timber of the kinds, qualities, and sizes, taking into account the season's output.[40]

✓ In *Foley v Classique Coaches*, F sold some land adjoining his petrol station to C, a bus company, on the basis that C would enter another agreement to buy its petrol from F 'at a price to be agreed by the parties in writing and from time to time': an arbitration clause dealt with any disputes arising out of the pricing agreement. The court enforced the agreement as one to buy fuel at a *reasonable* price. Not only had C bought petrol from F for three years before denying the agreement, but refusal to enforce the petrol agreement would deprive F of part of the price of selling his land (the potential petrol sales).

✓ Where the parties are *silent* as to the price of goods or services supplied, the buyer must pay a reasonable price (Sale of Goods Act 1979, s 8; Supply of Goods and Services Act 1982, s 15(1)).

✗ But these statutes do not apply where the parties are not silent but have stipulated that they will agree the price later. The question is then whether the parties have provided some formula or mechanism for determining the matter (see 2.6.2.6).

While courts adopt a pro-liability stance to uncertainty cases, sometimes they are driven to the conclusion that the uncertainty is *incurable*. For example:

✗ Agreements to sell goods 'on hire-purchase terms' (*Scammell and Nephew v Ouston*) or 'subject to war clause' (*Bishop & Baxter v Anglo-Eastern Trading and Industrial Co Ltd* (1944)) have been denied enforcement for vagueness. The courts could not say which of the many different varieties of such terms the parties intended. Similarly, a contract was denied in *Schweppe v Harper* (2008), where S agreed to seek 'reasonable finance' for H.

✗ *Raffles v Wichelhaus* (1864) is properly situated here. While the parties objectively agreed for goods to be delivered 'ex Peerless from Bombay', it was impossible to say which of the two ships fitting that description the contract referred to (see 2.1.3.3).

✗ In *Baird Textile Holdings Ltd v Marks & Spencer plc* (2002), M&S terminated its arrangement with B, its main supplier of clothing for 30 years. B's claim of an implied contract not to terminate except on reasonable notice of three years was denied because: (i) there were 'no objective criteria by which the court could assess what would be reasonable either as to quantity or price' of goods supplied during the notice period (at [30]); and (ii) it would contradict M&S's deliberate abstention from committing itself to a long-term contract in order to maintain flexibility.

In the absence of a contract, the court may still impose *restitutionary* liability on the recipient of benefits conferred by the other's performance in anticipation

---

[40] Similar implications of reasonableness have been made, eg, to ascertain agreements to pay the 'market value' (*Brown v Gould* (1972)) or for hire to be 'equitably decreased' (*Didymi Corp v Atlantic Lines and Navigation Co Inc* (1988)).

of a contract, if the latter did not take the *risk* that the transaction may not eventuate (see 2.8).

2.6.2.4 Severance

If essential aspects of the transaction are agreed, vague words therein can be severed as meaningless and redundant, and the remaining agreement enforced. This was the conclusion in *Nicolene Ltd v Simmonds* (1953) in relation to the words 'I assume that we are in agreement that the usual conditions of acceptance apply'. Lord Denning (at 551–2) drew a distinction between:

> a clause which is meaningless and a clause which is yet to be agreed . . . In the present case there was nothing yet to be agreed. There was nothing left to further negotiation . . . [The clause in question] was so vague and uncertain as to be incapable of any precise meaning . . . It can be rejected without impairing the sense or reasonableness of the contract as a whole.

If the parties clearly regard themselves as bound (eg by commencing or accepting performance), the law should honour this, lest defaulters search for 'some meaningless clause on which to free ride'.

2.6.2.5 Agreements to (or not to) negotiate

The parties may expressly agree *to* negotiate on a particular matter with a view to reaching agreement, or they may agree *not to* negotiate with third parties over a particular matter. The House of Lords has held that:

✗ agreements to negotiate ('*lock-in*' agreements) are unenforceable for uncertainty;

✓ agreements *not* to negotiate with third parties ('*lock-out*' agreements) are *enforceable* if there is a *time limit* on their duration.

Walford v Miles (1992) contained both. There, the parties agreed that if W provided an assurance from their bank confirming their financial resources to pay M's asking price for his business (a 'comfort letter') M would:

(i)   break off negotiations with any third party and would not consider any other alternative or accept a better offer; and

(ii) would deal exclusively with W with a view to concluding the deal as soon as possible after 25 March.

M continued negotiations with, and eventually sold his business to, a third party. The court awarded damages for misrepresentation to compensate W for his wasted expenses, but held the following.

* Agreements *not* to negotiate with third parties ('lock-out' agreements) are *enforceable* only if there is a *time limit* on their duration (*Pitt v PHH Asset Management Ltd* (1993)), for otherwise it may indirectly impose a duty to negotiate in good faith (*Walford v Miles* at 140).[41]

---

[41] However, Bingham LJ dissenting in the Court of Appeal in *Walford v Miles* favoured the implication of reasonableness to fill any time limit gap.

- An agreement *to negotiate in good faith* such as would put a party in breach if he or she walks away from negotiations without good reason, is unenforceable. Three reasons were given for this conclusion.

(i)   **A contract is about self-interest**: a duty to negotiate in good faith would be 'inherently repugnant to the adversarial position of the parties when involved in negotiations', who are entitled to act self-interestedly (*Walford v Miles* at 138). So long as he or she makes no misrepresentations, a party can withdraw from the negotiations at any time and for any reason. *However*, if the parties have agreed to negotiate in good faith, they have chosen a cooperative, problem-solving mode of negotiation. Agreements to negotiate serve a useful commercial purpose. A party will have the incentive to take the (often considerable) trouble and expense of putting together a proposal if he or she knows that the other party will negotiate in good faith with them. To deny enforcement of the term contradicts the reasonable expectations of the parties.

(ii)   **Difficulty in determining whether breach has occurred**: 'How can a court be expected to decide whether, *subjectively*, a proper reason existed for the termination of negotiations?' (*Walford v Miles* at 138). *However*, this is inconsistent with the court's willingness to enforce an obligation to make 'best endeavours' (recognised in *Walford v Miles*, and applied in *Jet2.com Ltd v Blackpool Airport Ltd* (2012)) and to employ the reasonableness standard in other cases (see 2.6.2.3), when both are also uncertain. The Privy Council in an appeal from Australia *implied* an obligation to use 'reasonable endeavours' to reach agreement. In view of the parties' pre-existing and continuing relationship, Sir Robin Cooke said in *Queensland Electricity Generating Board v New Hope Collieries Pty Ltd* (1989) (at 210):

> their Lordships have no doubt that here, by the agreement, the parties under-took implied primary obligations to make reasonable endeavours to agree on the terms of supply beyond the initial five-year period and, failing agreement and upon proper notice, to do everything reasonably necessary to procure the appointment of an arbitrator. Further, it is implicit in a commercial agreement of this kind that the terms of the new price structure are to be fair and reasonable as between the parties.

In '**Promises to Negotiate in Good Faith**' (2003) 119 *LQR* 357, 363, **Berg** suggests that a duty to negotiate in good faith may require a party to:

- actively commence negotiations and participate in them;
- consider and put forward options;
- not take advantage of the other's known ignorance; and
- not withdraw from negotiations without giving a truthful reason, which should not be wholly unreasonable (in the *Wednesbury* sense (*Associated Provincial Picture Houses v Wednesbury Corp* (1948))), and without giving the other party a reasonable chance to respond.

(iii) **Damages for breach would be impossible to quantify**: Lord Denning said (at 301) in *Courtney & Fairbairn Ltd v Tolaini Brothers (Hotels) Ltd* (1975): 'No court could estimate the damages because no one can tell whether the negotiations would be successful or would fall through: or if successful, what the result would be.' *However*, the Court of Appeal has since found this type of loss ('loss of a chance') to be recoverable in *Allied Maples Group Ltd v Simmons & Simmons* (1995) (see 13.2.5.5).

Pause for reflection

Article II.-3:301 of the European Draft Common Frame of Reference states:

(1) A person is free to negotiate and is not liable for failure to reach an agreement. A person who is engaged in negotiations has a duty to negotiate in accordance with good faith and fair dealing and not to break off negotiations contrary to good faith and fair dealing. This duty may not be excluded or limited by contract. A person who is in breach of the duty is liable for any loss caused to the other party by the breach. It is contrary to good faith and fair dealing, in particular, for a person to enter into or continue negotiations with no real intention of reaching an agreement with the other party.

In *Petromec Inc v Petroleo Brasileiro SA Petrobas* (2005), Longmore LJ said (at [121]): 'I do not consider that *Walford v Miles* binds us to hold that the express obligation to negotiate is completely without legal substance.' He distinguished *Walford* from the present case because the parties' agreement to negotiate in good faith was:

(i) *contained in an otherwise legally enforceable agreement* (in *Walford* there was no concluded agreement at all; everything was 'subject to contract');

(ii) *an express term* 'which is part of a complex agreement drafted by City of London solicitors' (not implied as in *Walford*). Longmore LJ said (at [121]): 'It would be a strong thing to declare unenforceable a clause into which the parties have deliberately and expressly entered . . . To decide that it has "no legal content" . . . would be for the law deliberately to defeat the reasonable expectations of honest men.'

(iii) related only to a particular 'cost to Petromec', which was 'comparatively easy to ascertain . . . If there are any ascertainable losses which arise from a failure to negotiate in good faith, they will likewise be ascertainable with comparative ease' (at [117]–[118]). Likewise, in *Tramtrack Croydon Ltd v London Bus Services Ltd* (2007) the good faith obligation was not abstract but linked to requirements of reasonableness and a mechanism for making the determination. Without these, it would have been 'intrinsically without objective criteria' and contradict the principle in *Walford v Miles* (contrast *BBC Worldwide v Bee Load* (2007) where no machinery supported the assessment of good faith).

(iv) *breached by fraud*—Longmore LJ acknowledged that 'the concept of bringing negotiations to an end in bad faith is somewhat elusive', but said (at [118]):

If fraudulent representations as to the intention to continue negotiations were made, the obligation to negotiate in good faith is likely to fall away as a separate

> obligation; if there was no fraudulent representation, it is perhaps less likely that
> there will have been bad faith in terminating negotiations but it will not be par-
> ticularly difficult to tell whether there was or not.

A requirement of fraud (which is actionable in its own right (see Chapter 5)) would
point to a much narrower duty to negotiate in good faith than Berg suggests.
Consistently, Lord Hope of Craighead has emphasised the **limited role of the principle of good faith in English private law**. He said in *R (European Roma Rights Centre) v
Immigration Officer at Prague Airport* (2004) (at [59]–[60]):

> There are differences between the legal systems as to how extensive and how power-
> ful the penetration of the principle [of good faith] has been. They range from sys-
> tems in the civilian tradition where as a guideline for this contractual behaviour the
> principle is expressly recognised and acted upon, to those of the common law where
> a general obligation to conform to good faith is not recognised . . . The preferred
> approach in England is to avoid any commitment to over-arching principle, in favour
> of piecemeal solutions in response to demonstrated problems of unfairness . . . Good
> faith in Scottish law, as in South African law, is generally an underlying principle of
> an explanatory and legitimating rather than an active or creative nature . . . It is not
> a source of obligation in itself.

In *Emirates Trading Agency v Prime Mineral Exports Private Ltd* (2014), [63]–[64], Teare J
held that a **dispute resolution clause** in an **existing and enforceable contract** which
requires the parties to seek to resolve a dispute by friendly discussions in good faith
and **within a limited period of time** before the dispute may be referred to arbitration
is enforceable because the agreement is:

- not incomplete;
- not uncertain; it has an identifiable standard, namely fair, honest, and genuine
  discussions aimed at resolving a dispute; difficulty of proving a breach in some
  cases should not be confused with a suggestion that the clause lacks certainty;
- not inconsistent with the position of a negotiating party since the parties have
  voluntarily accepted a restriction upon their freedom not to negotiate;
- in the public interest, first the court should enforce freely agreed obligations and,
  second, because it may avoid expensive and time consuming arbitration.

2.6.2.6 The workability of any agreed mechanism for ascertainment

The standard of reasonableness *cannot* be used to fill gaps where the parties *expressly*
agree to agree later. In *May and Butcher v R* (1934), R entered into a written agreement to sell M surplus tentage, explicitly leaving the price and date of payment to 'be
agreed upon from time to time'. Lord Buckmaster said that 'an agreement between
two parties to enter into an agreement in which some critical part of the contract
matter is left undetermined is no contract at all'.

This broad exclusionary approach has been criticised. In *Fletcher Challenge Energy
Ltd v Electricity Corp of New Zealand Ltd* (2002), Blanchard J of the New Zealand Court
of Appeal (at [60]–[61]) confined *May and Butcher* to cases where an 'agreement' omits
an essential term *and* a means of determining such a term. In his view, 'if the Court is

satisfied that the parties intended to be bound, it will strive to find a means of giving effect to that intention by filling the gap'.

Courts are slow to invalidate a contract for uncertainty where *the parties* have agreed **workable criteria** (a formula, objective standard, or machinery, eg arbitration) for resolving the matter left unresolved. If the parties fail to agree or if their designated machinery for ascertainment breaks down, *the court* can step in and apply the agreed formula or standard itself, *unless* the agreed machinery is 'essential'. That is, the failure of the agreed machinery for resolving the uncertainty is *incurable* if the parties only intend to be bound if their stipulated machinery fills the gap.

✓ In *Sudbrook Trading Estate Ltd v Eggleton* (1983), a lease granted the lessees an option to buy the premises at a price to be fixed by two valuers, one nominated by the lessors and the other by the lessees and, in the absence of agreement, by an umpire to be appointed by the valuers. When the lessees sought to exercise the option, the lessors refused to appoint a valuer and claimed that the option clause was void for uncertainty. The House of Lords held that the machinery for appointing the valuers was *subsidiary* (not essential) to the main purpose of ascertaining a fair and reasonable price. Its failure did not prevent the existence of a binding contract. The **court could substitute its own machinery** by ordering an inquiry into the fair value of the premises. Lord Diplock observed (at 479) that it is the court's duty to administer justice and to overrule precedents not 'fit for survival in a civilised system of law'. The option clause should not be flouted by the lessor 'at his own sweet will'. It had induced the lessees' reliance (in entering the lease) and was contained in a long lease that had subsisted for many years.

✓ In *Queensland Electricity Generating Board v New Hope Collieries* (1989), the Privy Council enforced an agreement to supply coal beyond the first five years, although the agreement stated that the price 'shall be agreed by the parties thereto in accordance with clause 8' (setting out the broad criteria to be applied). The long-term agreement also contained a comprehensive arbitration clause. Sir Robin Cooke said (at 210), that in the presence of 'an arbitration or valuation clause in wide enough terms, the Courts accord full weight to their manifest intention to create continuing legal relations. Arguments invoking alleged uncertainty, or alleged inadequacy in the machinery available to the Courts for making contractual rights effective, exert minimal attraction.'

✓ In *MRI Trading AG v Erdenet Mining Corp LLC* (2013) a contract for the sale of goods which left matters, including certain charges and the shipping schedule, to be agreed, was held to be enforceable because it was to be viewed in its wider context. It was one of three contracts entered into pursuant to a settlement agreement between the parties, and on which the parties had acted for over a year. A term was to be implied to the effect that the charges and the shipping schedule were to be reasonable and were to be determined by arbitration in the event of any dispute.

✗ On the other hand, if the stipulated machinery which fails is *essential* (eg if a particular valuer is named because of his or her special skill, knowledge, or personal judgment), there is no contract. In *Gillatt v Sky Television Ltd* (2000), the court held that the stipulation for payment of '55% of the open market value of such shares . . . as determined by an independent chartered accountant' in certain circumstances was essential and not merely a mechanism for determining the *quantum* of payment. There were several different ways of valuing shares in a private company and the parties intended an independent chartered accountant to do it. Since the machinery was only 'broken' because the parties had not bothered to appoint an independent chartered accountant, the court refused to substitute its own assessment.

2.7 Intention to create legal relations

2.7.1 The requirement and its justification

One 'innovation in 19th Century contract law' was to add the requirement of 'intention to create legal relations' to that of contract formation.[42] This translates into two strong presumptions that require clear evidence to rebut, namely, that:

✗ parties do *not* intend to create legal relations in *social* and *domestic* agreements; and

✓ parties *do* intend to create legal relations in *commercial* agreements.

On its face, this invites an inquiry into the *intention of the parties*.

Counterpoint

The view that the requirement of 'intention to create legal relations' is about discerning whether the parties intend to be bound can be criticised as:

1. *superfluous*—an intention to be bound is already required for finding of an offer and an acceptance; and for overcoming uncertainty;

2. *fictitious*—parties will often have given the matter no thought and will have no discernible (ie objective) intention on whether the arrangement entered should invoke legal sanctions; and

3. *inconclusive*—any intentions the parties have are likely to be inconsistent (one party intending the agreement to be legally binding, and the other intending it be morally binding only).

It is now widely accepted that the presumptions of intention to create legal relations are based on *public policy*. Three strands can be isolated.

(i) **Floodgates**: the concern is to avoid swamping the judicial system with social and domestic disputes. As Atkin LJ comments in *Balfour v Balfour* (1919), at 579: 'the small Courts of this country would have to be multiplied one hundredfold if these arrangements were held to result in legal obligations'.

---

[42] A W B Simpson, 'Innovations in Nineteenth Century Contract Law' (1975) 91 *LQR* 247, 263–5.

(ii) **Promoting market transactions**: the presumption in *favour* of an intention to create legal relations in *commercial* contracts is consistent with the view that contract law's primary function is to facilitate transactions between people who may otherwise not deal with each other (see 1.4.6). It makes sense in *this* context to use state coercion (by awarding remedies for breach) to enforce agreements for which informal social sanctions are ineffective.

(iii) **Freedom *from* contract**: the concern is to limit state intrusion in the private lives of its citizens. Atkin LJ said of a wife's action to enforce her husband's promise *(Balfour* at 579):

> Agreements such as these are outside the realm of contracts altogether. The common law does not regulate the form of agreements between spouses . . . The consideration that really obtains for them is that natural love and affection which counts for so little in these cold Courts. The terms may be repudiated, varied or renewed as performance proceeds or as disagreements develop, and the principles of common law . . . find no place in the domestic code . . . In respect of these promises each house is a domain into which the King's writ does not seek to run.

 Pause for reflection

1. In **'Keeping Contract in its Place:** *Balfour v Balfour* **and the Enforceability of Informal Agreements'** (1985) 5 *OJLS* 391, **Hedley** argues that 'intention to create legal relations' is primarily designed to 'keep contract in its place', that is, 'in the commercial sphere and out of domestic cases, *except* where the judges think it has a useful role to play'; in practice, this means that agreements in domestic contexts will only be enforced if one party has already performed their side of the bargain. The real question is whether the contract is executed or executory.

2. In **'Contracting in the Haven:** *Balfour v Balfour Revisited'* in R Halson (ed), *Exploring the Boundaries of Contract* (Dartmouth, 1996) 68, **Freeman** criticises the presumption against the enforceability of family dealings as being out of step with modern developments. *Balfour* (see 2.7.2(i)) concerns a Victorian marriage and emphasises status and obligation. This should now give way to the trend in favour of autonomy and individual choice.

3. But how far should family and social relationships be contractualised? When should agreements be binding in morality and subject to informal social sanctions, and when should they be binding in law and enforceable by state coercion? Contract law should not become involved in private dealings just because the parties wish it to be (see 1.5.1). If two law students sharing a flat agree that their arrangement (for one to cook and the other to clean) should be legally enforceable, the courts are unlikely to award damages for breach. As the Scottish Law Commission[43] has stated: 'it is, in general, right that courts should not enforce entirely social engagements, such as arrangements to play squash or to come to dinner,

➡

---

[43] Scottish Law Commission, *Memorandum No 36 Constitution and Proof of Voluntary Obligations: Formation of Contract*, 10 March 1977, para 72.

> even though the parties themselves may intend to be legally bound thereby'. Contractual regulation of relationships risks reducing them to measurable obligations, shutting out the more open-ended obligations arising from trust and friendship, and subverting the values of the relationship (Collins at 48). For example, any suggestion that parent–child relationships can be defined by contracts and remedied for breach undermines the idea of unconditional love associated with the upbringing of children.

2.7.2 Family and social agreements

(i) Husband and wife

✗ In *Balfour*, a husband and wife returned to England on leave from the husband's employment in Ceylon (now Sri Lanka). The wife remained in England on the doctor's advice and the husband agreed to pay her an allowance of £30 a month until she rejoined him. When the parties formally separated, she sued for the payments. The Court of Appeal denied her claim for lack of consideration (since her love and affection do not count, see 3.1.3.5) and lack of intention to create legal relations because the agreement was made while they were living 'in amity'.

✓ However, the presumption against enforceability does not apply 'when the parties are not living in amity but are separated, or about to separate . . . [t]hey do not rely on honourable understandings. They want everything cut and dried. It may safely be presumed that they intend to create legal relations' (*Merritt v Merritt* (1970) at 1213).

(ii) Pre-nuptial agreements

Until relatively recently pre-nuptial and post-nuptial agreements (agreements that determine the financial consequences of divorce where no divorce was actually planned) were void as a matter of contract law.[44] They were deemed contrary to public policy, due to their potential to encourage or make it easier for parties to divorce. However, in *Radmacher v Granatino* (2010), by a majority of 8:1 the Supreme Court held that in future (at [75]):

> the court should give effect to a nuptial agreement that is freely entered into by each party with a full appreciation of its implications unless in the circumstances prevailing it would not be fair to hold the parties to their agreement.

In practice, once it is shown that the agreement was freely entered into, there is a rebuttable presumption that the agreement is enforceable. It will be up to the party seeking to avoid the agreement to prove that it would be unfair to give effect to it. The Supreme Court was keen to downplay this change since the 'fairness' of holding the parties to their agreement on divorce requires consideration of a far wider range of factors than those which would vitiate a contract (see Part IV). For instance, it will include the parties' emotional state at the time of their agreement, and also their age, maturity, and relationship history (at [72]).

---

[44] *Cocksedge v Cocksedge* (1844) 14 Sim 244, 13 LJ Ch 384.

> **Pause for reflection**
>
> In 'Ante-Nuptial Agreements: Fairness, Equality and Presumptions' (2011) 127 *LQR* 335, Herring, Harris, and George note that the Matrimonial Causes Act 1973 stipulates the factors a court should take into account in deciding on the parties' property distribution on divorce, with the first consideration being the interests of the child. Until *Radmacher*, the courts had refused to allow the parties to restrict the exercise of their discretion. Yet, as Lady Hale points out in her strong dissenting judgment, the majority had done exactly that. As the only specialist family lawyer, and only woman, in the Supreme Court, Lady Hale notes that the traditional view of marriage as a *status* (at [132]) means: 'First, the parties are not entirely free to determine all its legal consequences for themselves . . . Secondly, their marriage also has legal consequences for other people and for the state.' If couples can contract out of the court's redistributive powers on divorce then marriage ceases to have any particular legal meaning. Its legal effect depends substantially on the agreement of the parties. Herring, Harris, and George comment (at 338–9):
>
> > Does it really matter if marriage is now a contract? It does. Intimate relationships, especially those involving children, create inequalities in the parties' economic position. Through the obligations of support which marriage creates, the state has sought to provide some protection from the risks faced by those entering intimate relationships . . . [In general, they] combat gender discrimination and prevent exploitation of the wife's labour. Yet in *Radmacher,* the Supreme Court tells us that the couple can agree to bypass this protection. This is remarkable. There are few, if any, other areas of law where a person can engage in gender discrimination because the other person has consented to the treatment . . . Lady Hale was brave indeed to be explicit about the gendered nature of this decision.
>
> The Law Commission has recommended that couples should be able to decide in advance how they want to deal with their financial assets in the event of a divorce and therefore where there is a 'qualifying nuptial agreement', this should be enforceable by the court.[45] Qualifying nuptial agreements must:
>
> - meet the financial needs of the couple;
> - meet any financial responsibilities to children;
> - be informed by financial disclosure by both spouses;
> - be attended to by independent legal advice for both parties.

(iii) Parents and children

✗ In **Jones v Padavatton** (1969), a mother bought a house for her daughter to live in and maintain herself from the proceeds of letting the other rooms, and the daughter agreed to give up her secretarial work in Washington to read for the Bar in London. Six years later, the daughter had still not passed the course. The parties fell out; the daughter resisted the mother's claim for possession of the house

---

[45] Law Commission report, *Matrimonial Property Needs and Agreements* (Law Com No 343, 2014).

by claiming a contractual entitlement to remain. The Court of Appeal found no enforceable contract because: (i) there was no intention to create legal relations, since the parties were on good terms when the arrangement was made; and (ii) the terms of the arrangement were too vague, particularly as to its duration.

✗ Similarly, it was said in *Fleming v Beeves* (1994) (at 389) that a parent's promise to pay an allowance while the child is at university normally creates a moral, but not a legal, obligation.

(iv) Social agreements

✗ The same presumption against enforcement applies to social arrangements. An agreement to meet for a movie, a walk, or a meal is unenforceable; likewise, arrangements to share petrol costs on a journey (*Coward v Motor Insurer's Bureau* (1963)), and to participate in a golf club competition (*Lens v Devonshire Club* (1914)).

✗ *Hadley v Kemp* (1999) involved the pop group Spandau Ballet. K, a member of the group, was credited as the author of all the group's songs but he shared the income from this with other members of the group and their manager. When K discontinued the payments, they claimed damages for breach of contract. The court found no enforceable contract. The evidence showed that the relationship between the members of the band was not simply one of business (at 624):

> The members of the band had known each other since their schooldays. They have all stressed how at the time they were a close-knit group of friends who were in company with each other constantly. They had formed themselves into a band not just for the business purpose of making money (though they certainly wanted to do that, and rightly so), but also because they loved what they were doing . . . I am not persuaded that the plaintiffs have established that [K's] decision to share his publishing income, and his statement to the band about it, were made with an intention to create legal relations.

(v) Rebutting the presumption

The strong presumption *against* enforcement in family and social agreements is said to be rebuttable by clear evidence of contrary intention. Since the presumption is policy-based rather than intention-based, and since it will often be impossible to find a common intention, it is unsurprising that the courts usually refer to policy considerations in deciding whether the presumption is rebutted. Two stand out.

(i) **Reliance**: courts are more willing to find intention to be bound where one party has *detrimentally relied* upon the agreement.

✓ In **Parker v Clark** (1960), the Cs (an elderly couple) and the Ps (a couple who were 20 years their junior) agreed that if the Ps sold their cottage and came to live with the Cs, sharing their household expenses, Mr C would leave them a portion of his estate. When the couples fell out, the Ps left on C's demand and successfully claimed damages for breach of contract. Devlin J (at 293–4) said that C could not really have supposed 'that the law would leave him at liberty, if he so chose, to tell [the Ps] when they arrived that he had changed his mind, that they could take their furniture away, and that he was indifferent whether they found any-where else to live or not'.

✓ In *John Sadler v George Reynolds* (2005), R agreed that S should ghostwrite R's auto-biography but then contracted for someone else to do it. Slade QC dismissed R's argument that no contract emerged from his meetings with S, which were 'some-where between an obviously commercial transaction and a social exchange' (at [56]). R knew that S was an experienced journalist who made money from ghost-writing and met S in that context. Moreover, S had relied on an express term of the agreement by negotiating a publishing deal.

(ii) The agreement is incidental to the parties' relationship or symbolic of its end-ing, rather than a manifestation of it.

✓ In *Snelling v Snelling* (1973), an agreement between three brothers in relation to the running of the family company, of which they were directors, was held to be enforceable. The same conclusion applies to agreements in respect of a husband and wife's separation.

2.7.3 Commercial agreements

✓ Commercial agreements attract a strong presumption that the parties *do* intend to create legal relations. In *Esso Petroleum Ltd v Commissioners of Customs and Excise* (1976), Esso offered to give away a World Cup coin for every minimum purchase of four gallons of petrol. In deciding whether the coins were subject to tax, the House of Lords concluded that an intention to create legal relations *did* attach to the supply of coins. Lord Simon of Glaisdale reasoned (at 5–6) that the transaction took place in a business setting and *contemplated large commercial advantage to Esso from the scheme*.

✓ In *Edwards v Skyways Ltd* (1964), the court held that an employer's promise to pay a sum to employees made redundant was contractually enforceable, although it was described as 'ex gratia'.

The presumption of enforceability is **rebutted** in two notable instances.

(i) **Collective agreements between employers and trade unions** are conclu-sively presumed *not* to have been intended to create legal relations unless they are in writing and expressly provide to the contrary (*Ford Motor Co Ltd v AEF* (1969), now embodied in **section 179 of the Trade Union and Labour Relations (Consolidation) Act 1992**). The policy is presumably to encourage consensus and discourage resort to courts when parties need to continue to work with each other.

(ii) **Agreements expressed to be without intention to create legal relations**, such as transactions made 'subject to contract', letters of intent, letters of comfort, and honour clauses, are generally unenforceable (see 2.6.1).

✓ In *Rose and Frank Co v JR Crompton and Bros Ltd* (1925), R was appointed C's sole agents in 1913. The agreement was extended to 1920, but C terminated without notice in 1919. The court of first instance found the presumption of enforceability rebutted by the clear 'honour clause' in the agreement, which stated that:

> This arrangement is not entered into . . . as a formal or legal agreement, and shall not be subject to legal jurisdiction in the Law Courts . . . but it is only a definite expression and record of the purpose and intention of the three parties concerned, to which they each honourably pledged themselves, with the fullest confidence—based on past business with each other—that it will be carried through by each of the three parties with mutual loyalty and friendly cooperation.

✗ In the Court of Appeal (1923), Scrutton LJ (at 288) saw 'no reason why, even in business matters, the parties should not intend to rely on each other's good faith and honour, and to exclude all idea of settling disputes by any outside intervention', so long as this is clearly expressed.

✗ In **Kleinwort Benson Ltd v Malaysia Mining Corp Berhad** (1989), K agreed to provide a £10 million credit facility to M's subsidiary company. M refused to guarantee the debt but gave K a **comfort letter** stating that 'it is our policy to ensure that the business of [our subsidiary company] is at all times in a position to meet its liabilities to you under the above arrangements'. The subsidiary ceased to trade when its debts to K reached £10 million. K sued M on the basis that the comfort letter contained a contractual undertaking. The Court of Appeal held that the letter was simply an honest representation of M's policy at the time that the statement was made (see 5.1.2.3). M did not promise to stick by this policy in the future.

However, Lloyd QC warned in *ERDC Group v Brunel University* [2006] (at [27]) that:

> Letters of intent come in all sorts of forms. Some are merely expressions of hope; others are firmer but make it clear that no legal consequences ensue; others presage a contract and may be tantamount to an agreement 'subject to contract'; others are contracts falling short of the full-blown contract that is contemplated; others are in reality that contract in all but name. There can therefore be no prior assumptions, such as looking to see if words such as 'letter of intent' have or have not been used. The phrase 'letter of intent' is not a term of art. Its meaning and effect end on the circumstances of each case.

The discussion at 2.6.1 is relevant here.

Diagram 2C gives an overview of the rules of offer and acceptance. The diagram raises the issues in the chronological order that they are likely to arise in practice. It should provide a useful summary for revision.

Diagram 2C Overview of contract formation

Look on
the Online
Resource
Centre to
view this
figure as a
PowerPoint®
presentation

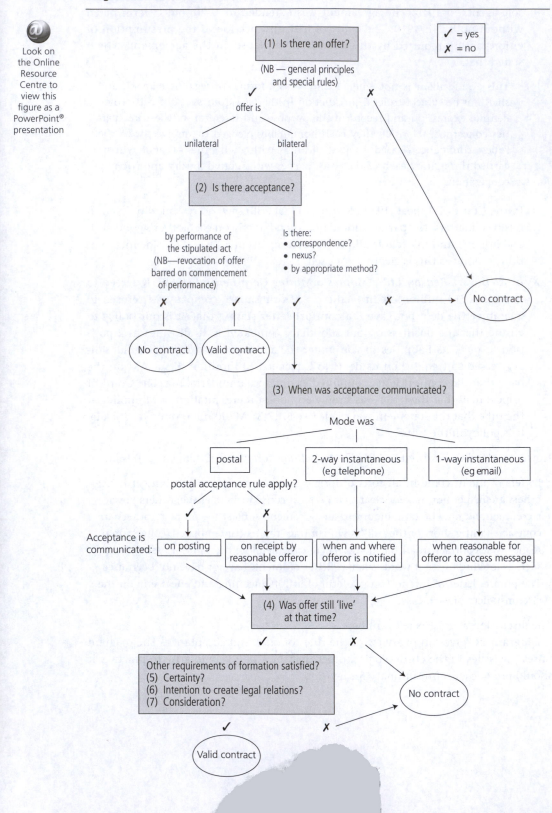

2.8 **Restitution for benefits conferred in anticipation of contracts that do not materialise**

Instead of, or in addition to, liberalising the rules on contract formation, it may be more realistic to admit that sometimes no liability arises in *contract* but may arise under other heads, to reverse *unjust enrichment*. Some cases that have been squeezed into an offer and acceptance format are instances of courts *imposing contracts* as a remedial device to achieve a just solution to what is essentially a non-contractual problem. Stretching the reach of contract law was understandable in a period when courts were slow to recognise induced reliance and unjust enrichment as a basis of liability, but this approach should be abandoned now that courts are more willing to recognise such liability in the context of pre-contractual negotiations (see 1.6.2). This would increase transparency and yield more appropriate remedies.

A restitutionary analysis *was* adopted in ***British Steel Corp v Cleveland Bridge and Engineering Co Ltd*** (1984). B entered into negotiations to manufacture steel nodes for C. C sent B a *letter of intent* stating their intention to place an order for the steel nodes on C's standard terms and requested B to commence work 'pending the preparation and issuing to you of the official form of subcontract'. In the end, no formal contract was agreed; C refused to pay after the final node was delivered. B argued that there was *no contract* and sued for the reasonable value of its work (known as a *quantum meruit* claim). C argued that there *was* a contract and counterclaimed for damages for breach by B (late delivery and delivery out of sequence), which exceeded the contract price. Goff J (at 511) held that:

✗ (i) There was *no contract* because no agreement was reached on price and other essential matters. He said that 'in the vast majority of business transactions, particularly those of substantial size, the price will indeed be an essential term'. This denied C's substantial counterclaim for breach.

✓ (ii) B's claim in *unjust enrichment* was allowed. Goff J (at 511) said:

> Both parties confidently expected a formal contract to eventuate. In these circumstances, to expedite performance under that anticipated contract, one requested the other to commence the contract work, and the other complied with that request. If thereafter, as anticipated, a contract was entered into, the work done as requested will be treated as having been performed under that contract; if, contrary to the expectation, no contract was entered into, then the performance of the work is not referable to any contract the terms of which can be ascertained, and the law simply imposes an obligation on the party who made the request to pay a reasonable sum for such work as has been done pursuant to that request, such an obligation sounding . . . in restitution.

✓ In *Yeoman's Row Management Ltd v James Cobbe* (2008), a property developer orally agreed to buy property 'subject to contract'. The developer spent substantial time and money in obtaining planning permission pursuant to the agreement, but the owner subsequently refused to enter into a binding contract. The developer was awarded a *quantum meruit* payment for his services in obtaining the planning permission.

✗ However, restitutionary awards are inappropriate if the court concludes that the pre-contractual work was done *at the risk of* the performing party. This is likely to be the case where the parties' agreement is expressly 'subject to contract' (see 2.6.1) or where the work done is of questionable value to the other party. Accordingly, no restitutionary award was made in *Regalian Properties plc v London Docklands Development Corp* (1995), where the work involved architectural and other professional fees paid in preparation for a proposed land development, which was abandoned.

 Pause for reflection

The unjust enrichment approach can be problematic when the benefit conferred deviates from that requested. While the performer is protected, the recipient may be left without redress for delayed or defective performance.[46] In *British Steel Corp v Cleveland Bridge and Engineering*, it was held that the delivery of the nodes out of sequence did not diminish the enrichment to the recipient. However, it should be open to a recipient to argue to the contrary.[47]

THIS CHAPTER IN ESSENCE

online resource centre

The key areas and core topics in this chapter are summarised in an easy-to-use list, ideal for revision purposes, on the Online Resource Centre at http://www.oxfordtextbooks.co.uk/orc/chenwishart5e/. Links to websites relevant to the topics covered and any updates to the chapter can also be found on the Online Resource Centre.

QUESTIONS

1 Ada makes Bob a written offer to sell her house to Bob for £20,000. Ada in fact intended to sell for £200,000. Bob accepts immediately. Can he enforce the agreement? What further facts would you need to know?

2 'The distinction between an offer and an invitation to treat is based on the intention of the party making the communication.' To what extent is this true?

3 How does, and how should, the law deal with problems arising from the 'battle of forms'?

4 Should the postal acceptance rule apply to modern methods of communication such as email?

5 'The requirement of "intention to create legal relations" is a misnomer.' Discuss.

---

[46] E McKendrick, 'The Battle of the Forms and the Law of Restitution' (1988) 8 *OJLS* 197, 212; S Ball, 'Work Carried Out in Pursuance of Letters of Intent—Contract or Restitution?' (1983) 99 *LQR* 572.

[47] Either *objectively* (see *Crown House Engineering Ltd v Amec Projects Ltd* (1990)), or as a result of 'subjective devaluation' (ie that the value of the non-conforming performance is less than the objective value *to the recipient*). See P Birks, *An Introduction to the Law of Restitution* (Clarendon Press, 1985) 109–17.

6 'While the rules on contract formation purport to be an elaboration of the requirements of establishing consensus between the parties, an analysis of the rules themselves and their application suggests that other factors also play a role.' Discuss.

7 Conan offers to sell his computer for £300 'first come, first served, email me or text me'. Dan sends the first response by email. Eve texts her response a few hours later saying 'would you accept £250?' Conan sees the text first, then reads his emails but neglects to read Dan's email because the subject line was blank. Conan texts back to Eve 'Yours for £280 unless I hear otherwise within 24 hours'. A day later he reads Dan's message. Advise Conan.

 For hints on how to answer these questions, please see the Online Resource Centre at http://www.oxfordtextbooks.co.uk/orc/chenwishart5e/

KEY FURTHER READING

Chen-Wishart, M (2009), 'Objectivity and Mistake: The Oxymoron of *Smith v Hughes*' in J Neyers, R Bronough, and S G A Pitel (eds), *Exploring Contract Law* (Hart) 341.

Endicott, T (2000), 'Objectivity, Subjectivity, and Incomplete Agreements' in J Horder (ed), *Oxford Essays in Jurisprudence* (OUP) 151.

Gardner, S (1992), 'Trashing with Trollope: A Deconstruction of the Postal Rules in Contract', 12 *OJLS* 170.

Hedley, S (1985), 'Keeping Contract in its Place: *Balfour v Balfour* and the Enforceability of Informal Agreements', 5 *OJLS* 391.

Hill, S (2001), 'Flogging a Dead Horse—The Postal Acceptance Rule and E-mail', 17 *JCL* 151.

McLauchlan, D (1998), 'Rethinking Agreement to Agree', 18 *NZULR* 77.

Nolan, D (2010), 'Offer and Acceptance in the Electronic Age' in A Burrows and E Peel (eds), *Contract Formation and Parties* (OUP) 61.

Rawlings, R (1979), 'The Battle of the Forms', 42 *MLR* 715.

Simpson, A W B (1975), 'Innovation in Nineteenth Century Contract Law', 91 *LQR* 247.

Simpson, A W B (1995), 'Quackery and Contract Law: *Carlill v. Carbolic Smoke Ball Co* (1893)' in *Leading Cases in the Common Law* (Clarendon Press) 259.

3

Enforceability: consideration, formalities, promissory estoppel

'Will the law enforce the agreement?'

English law does not enforce all promises; it will not even enforce all agreements. While offer, acceptance, certainty, and intention to create legal relations are all necessary, they are not sufficient to make a contract legally enforceable; an additional element is required. This is most commonly satisfied by the presence of so-called 'consideration'. To be enforceable, an *informal* agreement must comprise an exchange in which each party treats his or her own performance (or promise of performance) as the **price of the other's performance** (or promise of performance). Consideration is the 'agreed equivalent and inducing cause of the promise'.[1] If consideration is lacking, English law will enforce *formal* promises or agreements (complying with particular formalities, eg where the promise is contained in a deed (see 3.2)). In qualifying circumstances, English law also permits some enforcement of promises that induce the promisee's reliance via the doctrine of promissory estoppel (see 3.3). Thus, *A*'s undertaking to *B* is enforceable by *B* if:

(i) *B* has 'paid for' it;

(ii) it is embodied in the necessary formal instrument; or

(iii) *B* has relied on *A*'s undertaking and it would be unconscionable for *A* to go back on it.

The questions to be considered in this chapter are the following.

(i) What are the requirements of consideration, formalities, and promissory estoppel?

(ii) What is the justification for each test of enforceability?

(iii) Are the rules and scope of each doctrine satisfactory? If not, how should each be developed?

Diagram 3A gives an overview of the enforceability of undertakings.

---

[1] K Llewellyn, 'What Price Contract?' (1930) 40 *Yale LJ* 704, 742.

Diagram 3A Overview: the enforceability of undertakings

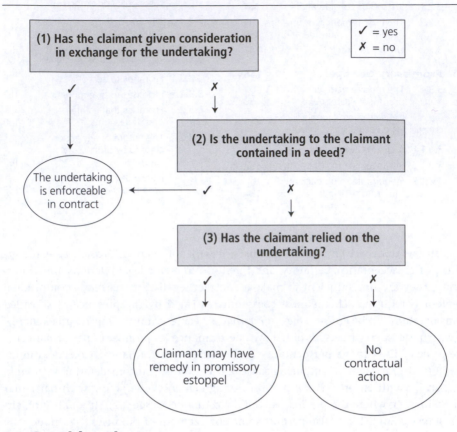

3.1 **Consideration**

'I paid for your promised performance'

3.1.1 **The basic idea and its justification**

The basic idea of the consideration requirement is that in order to *acquire the right* to enforce another's undertaking, a party must undertake to give, or actually give, something stipulated by the other as the price for his or her undertaking. Thus, *X*'s undertaking X** is enforceable by *Y*, if *Y* has given a reciprocal performance or undertaking of Y**, stipulated by *X* as the price for X**. My promise of a laptop for your promise of £1,000 is enforceable by either of us; each promise is supported by consideration from the other.

The enforcement of agreements supported by consideration prioritises bargains over gifts. Why should this be so?

(i) **Consideration as evidence of the existence and seriousness of the undertaking**: it is often suggested that consideration merely performs an evidentiary and cautionary function,[2] analogous to that performed by formality requirements (see 3.2).

---

[2] L Fuller, 'Consideration and Form' (1941) 31 *Columbia L Rev* 799; *Williams v Roffey Brothers* (1991) at 18; R Flannigan, 'Privity—The End of an Era (Error)' (1987) 103 *LQR* 564, 586–7; S Smith, *Contract Theory*

Baragwanath J of the New Zealand Court of Appeal said in *Antons Trawling Co Ltd v Smith* (2003) at [93] that: 'The importance of consideration is as a valuable signal that the parties intend to be bound by their agreement, rather than an end in itself.' On this view, consideration is *unnecessary* if a party's serious intention to be bound can be proved in other ways.

Counterpoint

Although consideration *may* perform an evidentiary function (eg nominal consideration, see 3.1.3.4), its role cannot be reduced to this: (i) even if there is consideration, an oral agreement may be very difficult to prove and an undertaking can be made impulsively without any intention to be bound, (eg 'You can have my house if you sing me a song'); and (ii) even if there is an abundance of evidence that the promisor intends to be bound, his or her informal undertaking is unenforceable if it is not supported by consideration.

(ii) **Welfare maximisation**: the enforcement of bargains is consistent with efficiency theories that interpret contract law rules as being aimed at *welfare maximisation* (see 1.4.3). Since exchanges tend to transfer property or services to those who value them most highly, the consideration requirement is the best indicator of value-maximising transactions. In contrast, donative promises (unsupported by a reciprocal promise or performance) are said to be 'sterile'.[3] However, this is easily challenged; donative promises *may* be efficient (eg a gift from rich grandparents to the needy student grandchild) and exchanges may *not* be (eg the buyer who mistakenly overvalues the property).

(iii) **Reciprocity—the intuitive justice of exchange**: the enforcement of bargains reflects the idea of *reciprocity*. Reciprocation is the norm between equals in most social interactions. This is even clearer outside the social context; it symbolises an ideal of fairness, because it distinguishes *trading* from *taking*, and *bargains* from instances of *exploitation*. Popular sentiment favours the enforcement of promises involving some quid pro quo;[4] a promise ought to be enforced because it is the promisor's payment for getting something that he or she desires. Conversely, the promisee, having paid for the promise, has a more compelling reason to enforce the promise than one who has not paid. This is reinforced by the following.

- **The expectation measure of damages**: the bargain model explains the *extent* of liability for breach of contract. The expectation measure, the distinctive feature of a contractual action, gives the promisee the value of the promised

---

(OUP, 2004) 216–17; Law Commission, *Privity of Contract: Contracts for the Benefit of Third Parties* (Law Com Consultation Paper 121, 1991) para 2.9.

[3] Conversely, R Posner, *Economic Analysis of Law* (8th edn, Aspen, 2014) ch 4; R Posner, 'Gratuitous Promises in Economics and Law' (1977) 6 *JLS* 411; M Eisenberg, 'Donative Promises' (1979) 47 *U Chi L Rev* 1.

[4] E Patterson 'An Apology for Consideration' (1958) 58 *Columbia L Rev* 929, 946–7.

performance (see 13.2), *because* he or she has given the agreed equivalence of that performance.

- Other jurisdictions enforce substantially all agreements that would comply with our test of bargain and most legal systems treat gifts (gratuitous promises) differently.[5] It is often said that abolition of consideration would bring English law more into line with civil legal systems, but this does not withstand closer scrutiny. While French and German law *appear* to enforce a much wider range of promises than English law, in practice they draw essentially the *same* line between gratuitous undertakings and reciprocal undertakings.[6] Civil law enforces gratuitous promises, *but* subjects them to a stringent formality requirement except for 'synallagmatic' contracts (ie bilateral reciprocal undertakings; these do not require formalities).[7] English law requires consideration unless gratuitous promises satisfy formality requirements. They amount to largely the same thing, as Zimmermann notes:[8]

> [T]o define the scope of donation, the German Code is using here, under negative auspices, what has traditionally been, in a positive version, the essential test for the enforcement of promises in the English common law; the absence of any agreed-upon recompense characterizes donations in Germany, the presence of bargain consideration provides the normal reason for enforcing a promise in England.

Stevens notes how widespread the idea of reciprocity is in private law:[9]

> That a party who has provided consideration is more deserving than one who has not is reflected in a number of rules of English law unrelated to contract formation. The force behind consideration is found in the equitable maxim that 'equity will not assist the volunteer'. Bare promises made by way of deed are therefore not susceptible to the equitable remedy of specific performance . . . a deed which has been mistakenly entered into is also much easier to set aside than a contract which has been made for good consideration. Similarly the protection afforded to a *bona fide* purchaser for value without notice of a prior proprietary interest both at law and in equity is not extended to a party who is merely a donee. Further, whether consideration has been provided is relevant in deciding whether a transaction can be set aside upon one party's insolvency. In none of these areas is consideration fulfilling the role played by a requirement of form.

(iv) **Marking the boundary of appropriate legal involvement**: the consideration requirement draws the line between *public* enforceable transactions and *private*

---

[5] J Dawson, *Gifts and Promises: Continental and American Law Compared* (Yale University Press, 1980) 223; K Zweigert and H Kötz, *Introduction to Comparative Law* (3rd edn, Clarendon Press, 1998) 392, 395, and 397; O Lando and H Beale, *Principles of European Contract Law* (Kluwer, 2000) 130–3, 158.

[6] J Dawson, *Gifts and Promises: Continental and American Law Compared* (Yale University Press, 1980); Arthur T von Mehren, 'Civil Law Analogous to Consideration: An Exercise in Comparative Analysis' (1959) 72 *Harvard L Rev* 1009.

[7] §§ 320–6 of the German Civil Code (BGB); Art 1102 of the French Civil Code (*Code civil*).

[8] R Zimmermann, *The Law of Obligations* (OUP, 1996) 504–5.

[9] R Stevens, 'The Contracts (Rights of Third Parties) Act 1999' (2004) 120 *LQR* 292, 322.

unenforceable agreements, a line further reinforced by the presumption against the enforcement of domestic and social agreements (see 2.7). Legal enforcement is unnecessary and inappropriate in the social domain within which we readily make arrangements with friends and family in whom we have a degree of trust, backed up by social or moral sanctions. It is also the context in which gratuitous promises are most likely to occur. Gifts are expressions of the value of *altruism*: their intrinsic value is destroyed if the donor is compelled to give the gift. They are, therefore, regarded as private arrangements, which can be broken only on pain of moral, social, or non-legal sanctions. In contrast, we cannot readily 'do deals' with strangers; here, contract law bridges the gap in trust and provides sanctions to facilitate reciprocal undertakings that further the purposes of both parties.

The **consideration** doctrine has met with increasing criticism and hostility. Some of the difficulties with the consideration doctrine arise from the requirements of nexus and value. Where X undertakes X** in exchange for Y undertaking Y**:

(i) there must be the necessary **nexus** (connection, see 3.1.2) between—

   • the parties X and Y; and

   • the undertakings X** and Y** (each should be induced by and be the price for the other).

(ii) X** and Y** must constitute **value in the eye of the law** (see 3.1.3).

3.1.2 **The requirement of nexus**

3.1.2.1 Consideration must move from the claimant

The traditional view is that the consideration doctrine deals with two questions, namely:

(i) *Which* undertakings are enforceable? Answer: those which have been paid for.

(ii) *Who* can enforce the undertaking? Answer: the party who has paid for it. This is often expressed as a requirement that 'consideration must move from the promisee'. *You* can enforce my undertaking to you because you have performed or promised to perform your undertaking. However, consideration need not move *to* the promisor. You can stipulate that my performance goes to a third party rather than to you.

   • The corollary is that a party who has not provided consideration for a promise cannot enforce it. Thus, a third party cannot enforce my undertaking because you (not the third party) have provided the consideration for it. This is the basis of the **privity rule** (see 4.1), which bars a third party from suing on a contract made for his or her benefit.

   • The Contract (Rights of Third Parties) Act 1999 separates the two questions posed above ('*which* promises are enforceable?' and '*who* can enforce?'). Whilst promises continue to be enforceable only if they are supported by consideration, the Act dispenses with the requirement that consideration must move from the claimant. Hence, a third party can enforce a contract made for his or her benefit even if he or she gives no consideration for it (see 4.1.4). Thus, the consideration requirement is relaxed (or undermined).

3.1.2.2 Consideration must be requested by the promisor

Consideration, broadly defined as conferring a benefit or obviating a disbenefit (or detriment), and must be given *in return for* (ie in order to 'buy') the promise to be enforced. There is no consideration if the promisee incurs a detriment or confers a benefit merely in *reliance on*, rather than *in return for*, the promise. In *Combe v Combe* (1951), a husband promised to pay his wife £100 a year on their divorce. The wife sought to enforce the promise, arguing that she gave consideration for it by not applying for maintenance. The Court of Appeal rejected this because the husband did *not request* her to do this. Her forbearance *resulted from* his promise to pay but was not given *in return for it*.

However, the court *was* prepared to *imply a request* of forbearance in **Alliance Bank v Broom** (1864). B promised to provide some security for its debt to A. When A sued to enforce this, B argued that A gave no consideration for it. The court enforced the undertaking because while B did not expressly ask A to forbear from suing B to recover the debt, the court implied such a request.

 Pause for reflection

These cases show that courts have considerable leeway in deciding whether to imply a request by the promisor and so treat the promisee's reliance or conferral of benefit as consideration. What explains the difference in approach?[10] A request may have been more readily implied in *Alliance Bank v Broom* because a bank is much more likely to institute proceedings than a wife. Moreover, justice did not demand that a request be implied in *Combe* since the wife's income exceeded her husband's and she had delayed six years before initiating action.[11]

3.1.2.3 Past consideration is not good consideration

Since consideration must be given *in response to* (in return or as payment for) the promise, it cannot logically be given or done *before* the other's promise was made. If it is, the law regards the promise as a gratuitous and unenforceable response to the promisee's earlier gift.

Consideration may be past because of the following.

(i) *It has already been given for a reciprocal promise and cannot buy additional promises from the same promisor*: If I promise to pay you £5 for one book, I cannot rely on the same £5 to enforce your later promise to give me an additional book. In *Roscorla v Thomas* (1842), R purchased a horse from T. T's *subsequent* assurance to R that the horse was sound and free from vice was unenforceable because the only possible consideration for it was the price already payable under the original contract and that consideration was past.

---

[10] See A Goodhart, 'Unilateral Contracts' (1951) 67 *LQR* 456.
[11] See 'Consideration: A Restatement' in P S Atiyah, *Essays on Contract* (Clarendon Press, 1986) 179, 232 and Atiyah, 147.

(ii) *Its performance predates the promise sought to be enforced*: in **Eastwood v Kenyon** (1840), a young girl's guardian raised a loan to educate her and improve her marriage prospects. After her marriage, her husband promised to pay off the loan, but the guardian was unable to enforce this promise because his consideration (in bringing up and financing the girl) was past. His actions were not requested by the promisor and could not have been performed in response to the later promise. The husband's moral obligation to pay could not be converted into a legal obligation by his promise.

The courts look at the actual sequence of events, rather than the contractual words. Thus, in *Re McArdle* (1951), consideration was held to be past because, although the promise was made 'in consideration of your carrying out' certain work, the work was completed *before* the promise was made: it was not something yet to be performed.

However, the past consideration rule can operate harshly in some circumstances, and **the exact order of events is not decisive** if the court is satisfied that the promisor's promise and the promisee's past actions are, in fact, part of the *same overall transaction*. This is the gist of the *major exception* to the past consideration rule, the doctrine of **implied assumpsit**. An early example is *Lampleigh v Brathwait* (1615), where B (sentenced to death) asked L to obtain a pardon from King James I. L was successful. B's subsequent promise to pay £1,000 to L was held to be enforceable.

In **Pao On v Lau Yiu Long** (1980), the Privy Council opined that a claimant must show that:

(i)   he performed the act at the promisor's *request*;

(ii) it was clearly understood (implied) at the time of the request that he *would be rewarded* for the act; and

(iii) the eventual promise is one which *would have been enforceable* if it had been made at the time of the act.

In short, where I ask you to do something (Y**) which you do, and I thereafter promise you X**, the court could imply an understanding at the time of my request that you would be paid for doing Y**. If so, my later promise of X** can be 'backdated' to the time of my request as consideration for your performance of Y**, which in turn becomes valid consideration for my 'backdated' promise. This reasoning was applied in *Pao On v Lau Yiu Long*. The parties agreed to exchange shares in their companies. P also agreed not to sell 60% of the shares it received for a year to avoid triggering a fall in their value. In exchange, L agreed to *buy back* those shares at $2.50 each by the end of the year. When P realised that this was an inferior deal if the value of the shares rose beyond $2.50, P refused to proceed with the contract unless L agreed to give a *guarantee by way of indemnity* (ie L would only buy back *if* the shares fell below $2.50). As it turned out, this modification did not increase L's liability because of a dramatic fall in the value of the shares. Nevertheless, L refused to honour *either* scheme of protection for P, alleging the buy-back to be non-existent and the indemnity to be unenforceable for lack of consideration and voidable for duress. The court found no duress (see 8.4.2) and that P's promise not to sell the shares for a year was valid consideration because it was given at L's request with the common intention that L should protect P against a drop in value. This intention survived through the cancellation of the buy-back agreement. L's subsequent promise may be regarded either as *evidence* of the amount payable (as in *In re Casey's Patents* (1892)), or as a new agreement in the nature of a *compromise* settling the amount payable (as in *Horton v Horton (No 2)* (1961)).

Parliament has also mitigated the rigours of the past consideration rule by providing that a pre-existing debt or liability is good consideration for a bill of exchange (Bills of Exchange Act 1882, s 27(1)(b)), and that a debt is deemed to have accrued on and not before the date of the debtor's acknowledgement of the debt (Limitation Act 1980, s 27(5)).

 Pause for reflection

The liability here may be better understood as arising in *unjust enrichment* (see 1.6.2), rather than contract. The promisor has requested and received the benefit of the promisee's performance: the benefit was at the promisee's expense and was unjustly so (the promisor knew that the promisee was not acting gratuitously). This analysis would allow the remedy to be measured by the *objective value* of the benefit received, rather than by the amount *promised* as it is now.

3.1.3 **The requirement of 'value'**

What inclusionary and *exclusionary* rules define the boundaries of valuable consideration? **Diagram 3B** gives an overview and summary of our discussion.

I provides the starting point: the **inner shaded circle** shows the varied and unstable formulations of consideration.

II adds the expansionist tendencies resulting from the principle that consideration *need not be adequate*. The left side of the diagram shows that valuable consideration includes: *nominal* benefits, *compromises* or *forbearances* of claim, and some *intangible* benefits.

III shows how each expansionary tendency can be 'pushed back' (or contained) by the general qualification that consideration must be 'something which is of some value in the eye of the law' (*Thomas v Thomas* (1842) at 859), and so disqualifying certain promises as good consideration.

The **right side** of the diagram addresses the troublesome issue of whether performance of, or promises to perform, a *pre-existing duty* amounts to valuable consideration. The answer is broadly:

✓ 'yes' if the pre-existing contractual duty is owed to a *third party* (see 3.1.4.2);

✗ 'no' if it is *imposed by public law* (see 3.1.4.1).

? If it is already *owed to the other party* in contract:

    ✓ a promise of 'the same' is valuable consideration to enforce a counter-promise to pay 'more' if it confers a 'practical benefit';

    ✗ a promise to perform 'less' than owed is not good consideration for a counter-promise to pay the 'same', even if it confers a practical benefit on the latter.

These are now discussed in greater detail.

Diagram 3B What counts as valuable consideration?

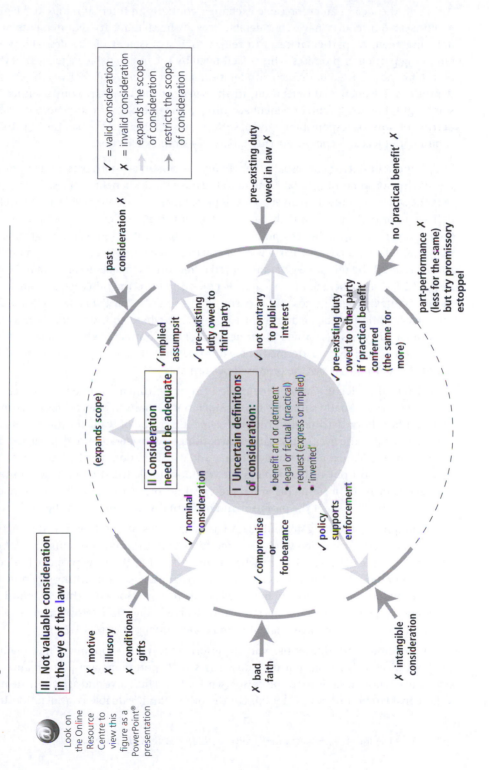

3.1.3.1 The definitions of valuable consideration

Although the idea of an enforceable exchange 'contains an internal rigour and logic' (Collins at 66), courts have considerable leeway in shaping its requirements and applying them to particular cases to reflect their assessment of the desirability of enforcing particular promises. This is facilitated by the unavoidable vagueness in the abstract concepts used to define consideration. *Currie v Misa* (1875) gives the classic definition: 'a valuable consideration, in the sense of the law, may consist either in some right, interest, profit, or benefit accruing to the one party, or some forbearance, detriment, loss, or responsibility given, suffered, or undertaken by the other' (at 162). A number of features complicate this apparently simple definition.

(i) **Benefit or detriment**: usually, benefit *and* detriment are both present. For example, paying for something is a detriment to the buyer and a benefit to the seller; it renders the seller's promise to deliver goods or perform a service enforceable. Conversely, delivering or performing something is a detriment to the seller and a benefit to the buyer, and renders the buyer's promise to pay enforceable. However, an agreement may entail detriment to one party *without* apparent benefit to the other (eg a promise to pay a sum if the promisee gives up her job to retrain, as in *Jones v Padavatton* (1969) (see 2.7.2)); or may benefit one party *without* detriment to the other (eg a promise to perform an existing duty to a third party, as in *Pao On v Lau Yiu Long* (see 3.1.4.2)). Moreover, while benefit or detriment are apparent where consideration is *executed* (ie when a party has performed his or her part of the contract). Where consideration is *executory* (ie yet to be performed), benefit or detriment can only be understood in terms of the *right to enforce* the promised performance.

(ii) **Factual or legal**: *factual* benefit received or detriment suffered, as perceived by the *parties*, is usually sufficient for consideration. However, the courts sometimes insist on benefit or detriment in the *legal sense*; it must be of 'value in the eye of the *law*' and not just the eyes of the parties. Accordingly, consideration may be denied in the presence of factual benefit or detriment, and consideration may be found in their absence. The most obvious example is the traditional rule that the promisee confers no legal value by performing his or her pre-existing contractual duty, however much this may factually benefit the promisor and be factually detrimental to the promisee.

(iii) **Request**: according to Smith: 'All that is necessary is that the defendant should, expressly or impliedly, ask for something in return for his promise, an act or a promise by the offeree. If he gets what he has asked for, then the promise is given for consideration.'[12] *Value is subjective* and, if a party requests something, then he or she must value, and be factually benefited by, its receipt. However, this can blur the distinctions between the *value* question and the *nexus* question, between consideration and motive, and between bargains and conditional gifts (see 3.1.2.2).

(iv) **Tangible and intangible value**: performance with economic value readily qualifies as consideration. But difficulty arises with non-monetary performance of doubtful economic value to the promisor (see 3.1.3.5). Thus, love and affection are not valid consideration (*Bret v JS* (1600)). On the other hand, valuable consideration has

---

[12] J Smith, 'The Law of Contract—Alive or Dead?' (1979) 13 *The Law Teacher* 73, 77.

been found for an uncle's promise to pay a sum on the event of his nephew's marriage to a particular person (*Shadwell v Shadwell* (1860)), and for a man's promise to pay a sum if the mother of his child promised that the child would be 'well looked after and happy' (*Ward v Byham* (1956)) (see 3.1.4.1).

 (v) **Good reason for enforcement**: in '**Consideration in Contract: A Fundamental Restatement**' (1971) (reprinted with revisions in response to Treitel's criticism) in Atiyah, *Essays in Contract* (Clarendon Press, 1986) 179, **Atiyah** argues on the basis of the law actually applied in the courts that 'consideration' is used in a wider sense than simply bargain (at 181–2):

> When the courts found a sufficient reason for enforcing a promise they enforced it; and when they found that for one reason or another it was undesirable to enforce a promise, they did not enforce it. It seems highly probable that when the courts first used the word 'consideration' they meant no more than that there was a 'reason' for the enforcement of a promise.

 (vi) '**Invented' consideration**: in '**Consideration: A Critical Analysis of Professor Atiyah's Fundamental Restatement**' (1976) 50 *Australian LJ* 439, **Treitel** argues for the traditional view of bargain consideration and against Atiyah's 'good reasons' thesis. However, he also emphasises the flexibility of bargain consideration and the possibility of English courts 'inventing' consideration, by treating an act or forbearance as valid consideration, although it was not the promisor's purpose to obtain it (as in *Chappell v Nestlé* (1960), see 3.1.3.4) and although there is no prejudice to the promisee (*Shadwell v Shadwell*, see 3.1.4.2).

 Pause for reflection

The consideration doctrine is a moving target. The different definitions yield different pictures of the scope of valuable consideration (factual/legal; requested/invented; tangible/intangible). Each conception can be contradicted by another; a set of facts may yield valid consideration on one conception but not on another. By moving between the different conceptions of value, courts have considerable latitude in determining whether to find consideration (or not), and hence whether to enforce a promise (or not). But, we need to go beyond bemoaning the instability at the heart of the consideration doctrine and identify the factors which influence the finding of consideration.

3.1.3.2 The pros and cons of enforcement

The **pro-enforcement factors** push out the boundaries of enforceable promises, as illustrated in **Diagram 3B II**. They include the desirability of:

 (i) recognising performance *actually bargained for* (ie desired) when there is some technical obstacle to its qualifying as consideration (eg by the devices of nominal or 'invented' consideration in *Chappell v Nestlé* (see 3.1.3.4), and of 'practical benefit' in *Williams v Roffey Brothers* (see 3.1.5.3));

(ii)   recognising the *subjectivity* of values and respecting the parties' *intention* (eg via nominal consideration (see 3.1.2.2 and 3.1.3.4));

(iii)   protecting the promisee's *reliance* (eg forbearance to sue (see 3.1.3.6));

(iv)   preventing the promisor's enrichment at the promisee's expense (eg the exception to the past consideration rule (see 3.1.2.3));

(v)   encouraging *finality* in dispute resolution (eg compromises and forbearances (see 3.1.3.6)); and

(vi)   imposing responsibility otherwise regarded as *just* (eg *Ward v Byham* (see 3.1.4.1)).

Anti-enforcement factors that restrain the scope of enforceable promises (**III in Diagram 3B**) include the undesirability of enforcing:

(i)   *gifts* and other transactions in the *private* domain, because the law's involvement may do more harm than good (eg the invalidity of mere motive and intangible benefits (see 3.1.3.5));

(ii)   *wholly one-sided* 'bargains' (eg illusory consideration (see 3.1.3.5)); and

(iii)   prevention of *extortion or corruption* (eg the invalidity of promises to perform an existing duty (see 3.1.4.1 and 3.1.4.3)).

3.1.3.3 Consideration need not be adequate

Imbalance of exchange does not offend the doctrine of consideration. A promise is enforceable as long as *something* valuable in the eye of the law is exchanged for it; the values exchanged need not be equivalent. There is valid consideration where:

✓ you buy a house in central London worth £3 million for £20; or

✓ you exchange a painting by Claude Monet worth £10 million for a warm coat, even on a scorching day.

The central premise, that it is for the parties to determine what they value and how much they value it, fits closely with the free-market philosophy underlying efficiency theories of contract law (see 1.4.3). As Posner said:[13] 'Courts have no comparative advantage in determining at what price goods should be sold. On the contrary, in all but very exceptional cases, negotiation between buyer and seller is the more reliable method of determining a price at which exchange is mutually beneficial.'

◄◄ Counterpoint

The rule that consideration need not be adequate can be misleading. Although we can easily grasp the idea of subjective and idiosyncratic valuation of benefits (eg the rich paying vast sums for a trivial item on a whim), this cannot often explain cases involving a glaring disparity between the values exchanged. A contract supported by consideration can still be set aside for a host of *vitiating factors* (eg misrepresentation, duress, or undue influence (see Part IV)) or its ➡

---

[13]   R Posner, *Economic Analysis of Law* (10th edn, Aspen, 2014) 100–1.

➡️

contents may be supplemented by *implied terms* or partially invalidated because of unfairness (see Part V). In these cases, the presence of serious inadequacy of consideration will usually be the major, although not the sole, factor.

3.1.3.4 Trivial and nominal consideration

The most trifling benefit or detriment can constitute valid consideration. Lord Somervell said in **Chappell v Nestlé** (at 114) that: 'A contracting party can stipulate for what consideration he chooses. A peppercorn does not cease to be good consideration if it is established that the promisee does not like pepper and will throw away the corn.' For example, good consideration was found where:

✓ a promisee briefly lent two boilers to the promisor for weighing, in exchange for the promise to return the boilers in the same condition (*Bainbridge v Firmstone* (1838));

✓ a promisee surrendered a document that was thought to be a guarantee but was actually worthless, in exchange for a promise to pay certain bills (*Haigh v Brooks* (1839));

✓ a promisee supplied three wrappers from the promisor's chocolate bars, in exchange for a promised gramophone record (*Chappell v Nestlé*).

In these cases, *factual benefit* to the promisor and *factual detriment* to the promisee are doubtful. Atiyah argues that the promise in *Nestlé* was enforceable without consideration in the bargain sense since: 'it would be ridiculous to assert that the sending or the receipt of the wrappers necessarily involved an actual detriment to the sender or a benefit to the defendants'.[14] Indeed, the promisor insisted that the wrappers were worthless and thrown away on receipt. Treitel bridges the gap with his concept of 'invented' consideration and by emphasising that consideration need not be adequate; there is 'no doctrinal difficulty in holding that a piece of paper or some act of forbearance of very small value can constitute consideration'.[15]

👤 **Pause for reflection**

1. *Chappell v Nestlé* makes better sense when seen in its broader context. The case arose *not* because a customer was trying to enforce the promise to give a gramophone record for the chocolate wrappers, but because the owners of the copyright sought an injunction to prevent the promisor's infringement of their copyright (by failing to pay them a percentage of the profits of the sales that the wrappers represented). The court's conclusion that the wrappers constituted valid consideration is understandable because of their value in Nestlé's marketing strategy (obviously going beyond the intrinsic value of the wrappers themselves). It makes sense then that Nestlé should not retain the whole benefit of their enhanced sales, without

➡️

---

[14] P S Atiyah, 'Consideration: A Restatement' in *Atiyah's Essays on Contract* (Clarendon Press, 1986) 193.
[15] G Treitel, 'Consideration: A Critical Analysis of Professor Atiyah's Fundamental Restatement' (1974) 50 *Australian LJ* 439, 440.

➡ paying the owners of the copyright in the music. To recognise the bargain in *Chappell v Nestlé* (the gramophone record for the enhanced sales), the court overcame the apparent absence of factual benefit or detriment in the wrappers by reference to the *request* conception of value.

2. The converse is illustrated in *Lipkin Gorman v Karpnale Ltd* (1991), a case famous for recognising the principle of unjust enrichment in English law. It is of interest to us here for its *denial of consideration*. C (a solicitor) stole £150,000 from his firm's client account, which he then lost through gambling at the Playboy Club. On the firm's claim for this sum, the club argued that it was protected because it had given consideration for the sum. Since gaming and wagering contracts were void under the Gaming Act 1845, the club argued that its consideration took the form of the *gaming chips* it gave to C in exchange for the money. The House of Lords disagreed, saying that 'the chips themselves were worthless' (at 561, but then, so were the wrappers in *Chappell v Nestlé*) and were not regarded by the parties as valuable in themselves, but merely as a 'convenient mechanism for facilitating gambling' (at 575, but the wrappers were an equally convenient mechanism for facilitating marketing). The concern to protect the victims of the solicitor's theft led the House of Lords to deny that the gambling chips constituted consideration for the money, which the club was then required to return to the firm.

   In *Spreadex Ltd v Cochrane* (2012) EWHC 1290 (Comm) C applied to open an account online with S, a spread-betting bookmaker. When C left his computer at his girlfriend's house for two days, her young son made numerous trades which put his account substantially in debit. Although C had clicked 'Agree' to S's terms which included the following: 'You will be deemed to have authorized all trading under your account number', he was not bound. No valid contract between C and S pre-existed to make C liable on these unauthorised trades because S reserved the right to refuse any bet, to remove its online service, and to close the customer's account at any time; hence S gave no consideration. The provision of an online interactive platform was simply a more modern equivalent of a readiness to contract by phone. It merely facilitated the making of ad hoc contracts in the form of individual trades.

3. The rule that consideration need not be adequate can allow form to triumph over substance. Gratuitous promises are enforceable if they are 'dressed up' as bargains (eg a peppercorn for £5,000). Here, the doctrine of consideration does not serve its main purpose of distinguishing gratuitous promises from bargains. As Atiyah observes: 'a promise for nominal consideration is just about the clearest possible indication that the promisor intended his promise seriously and intended to give the promisee a legally enforceable right'.[16] Since compliance with *formalities* (eg deeds) also makes a promise enforceable (see 3.2), the law clearly has no objection to the enforceability of gratuitous promises per se. It is only *informal* gratuitous promises that are not enforceable; the nominal consideration device is thus analogous to invoking formalities to make gratuitous promises binding.

There are **two limits** to the nominal consideration device.

(i) The promise is unenforceable if the consideration alleged is incontrovertibly less than the promise sought to be enforced, as a matter of arithmetic. For example, I cannot enforce your promise to pay £500 in exchange for my paying you £1. However,

---

[16] P S Atiyah, 'Consideration: A Restatement' in *Atiyah's Essays on Contract* (Clarendon Press, 1986) 194.

the exchange of *specific* money (bearing a certain date or in a certain currency), or payment at an *earlier time* in exchange for a sum of greater face value, is enforceable.

(ii) The contractual right obtained by giving nominal consideration is less secure, if not negated, in certain circumstances. For example, specific performance of the promise will not be ordered, and the promise will not be enforced if it would prejudice third party interests (Law of Property Act 1925, s 205(1)(xxi)).

3.1.3.5 Motive and other consideration valueless in law

Although consideration need not be adequate, it must have some *minimum content*. A promisor will always have a motive (reason) for making a promise, but his or her promise is only enforceable if his or her motive can be construed as that of *obtaining something* valuable in the eye of the law from the promisee.

(i) Motive

Consideration requires at least the *form* of a present or future *exchange*. The promisor's mere wish to confer a benefit is unenforceable, since nothing comes back the other way *in exchange* for it. Thus, *mere motive* is not good consideration. This is another reason why past consideration is not good consideration (see 3.1.2.3); it is merely the motive for the promise. In **Thomas v Thomas** (1842), a testator expressed his intention to let his widow have his house for the rest of her life. After his death, his executors promised to carry out the testator's desire if the widow paid £1 per annum towards the ground rent and kept the house in repair. The court held that while the testator's wish was merely the *motive* for the transaction, the widow's promise to pay rent and make repairs were of value in the eye of the law as consideration for the executor's promise.

(ii) Conditional gifts

The promisee's satisfaction of the qualifying *condition* for a promise is not good consideration, unless that condition was *requested* as the *price* for the promise. If the promise is to confer a benefit on the happening of an event that is *independent* of the promisee's action, there is only an unenforceable conditional gift (eg 'I'll pay you £20 if it rains tomorrow'). But if the condition consists of some action by the promisee, it is likely to be regarded as good consideration. For example:

- ✓ sending in chocolate wrappers in *Chappell v Nestlé*;
- ✓ purchasing four gallons of petrol to get a coin depicting a World Cup footballer in *Esso Petroleum Co Ltd v Customs and Excise Commissioners* (1976);
- ✓ buying the smoke ball, using it as directed, and catching influenza in *Carlill v Carbolic Smoke Ball* (1893).

(iii) Intangible benefits

The line between gratuitous promises and bargains is reinforced by the rule that intangible benefits are not consideration in the 'eye of the law'. Thus, the following were held to be unenforceable:

- ✓ a father's promise made in consideration of a son's 'natural love and affection' (*Bret v JS* (1600));

✓ a father's promise in exchange for his son's promise not to annoy the father with complaints (*White v Bluett* (1853));

✗ a customer's promise to pay the builder's demand 'in order to maintain an amicable relationship' (*North Ocean Shipping Co v Hyundai Construction Co (The Atlantic Baron)* (1979)).

However, the intangibility of the benefit promised poses no insurmountable obstacle if the courts think it just to enforce the reciprocal promise:

✓ a woman's promise to behave 'with sobriety, and in a respectable, orderly, and virtuous manner' and not to act in such a way as to bring on herself or her former husband 'hate, contempt, or ridicule' in exchange for an allowance from him (*Dunton v Dunton* (1892));

✓ a mother's promise to see that her child is 'well looked after and happy' in exchange for the father's promise to pay towards her upkeep (*Ward v Byham* (1956), see 3.1.4.1).

The intangible benefit may arise from the promise to *refrain* from some activity.

✓ In the controversial American case of ***Hamer v Sidaway*** (1891), a promise to pay a nephew a sum of money if he refrained from 'drinking liquor, using tobacco, swearing and playing cards or billiards for money' until he was 21 was enforced. The court reasoned that the nephew gave consideration by forgoing his legal right to engage in such activities. However, it could equally be said that the son in *White v Bluett* refrained from perfectly lawful conduct, yet Pollock CB said that the son had 'no right to complain' to his father (it was the father's decision how he wanted to distribute his property). It may be relevant that the conduct forgone in *White v Bluett* (not to complain) is less deserving of reward than that in *Hamer* (not to drink, smoke, or gamble). But this cannot explain the next case.

✓ In ***Pitt v PHH Asset Management Ltd*** (1993), PHH accepted P's bid of £200,000 for a cottage 'subject to contract', but withdrew the next day when B (a third party) made a higher offer. PHH's subsequent promise to sell the cottage to P for £200,000 and not to consider other offers for the property (a 'lock-out' agreement, see 2.6.2.5) was held to be enforceable because P gave good consideration by promising to:

(i) exchange contracts within two weeks of receiving the draft contract;

(ii) refrain from telling B that he was no longer interested in the property to induce B to lower her offer to PHH; and

(iii) withdraw his threat to seek an injunction restraining the sale to B.

Whilst (i) is clearly good consideration, (ii) and (iii) are questionable as such since they amount to recognising value in being free of a nuisance. Since Peter Gibson LJ held that P's threat to claim an injunction lacked substance, accepting (iii) as valid consideration contradicts the rule that no consideration is provided by compromising a claim that is made in bad faith (see 3.1.3.6).

> ### 👤 Pause for reflection
>
> 1. *Pitt v PHH* suggests that, where the benefit of avoiding a 'nuisance' consists of avoiding litigation, the policies supporting the settlement of disputes incline the courts towards finding consideration even if the promise could amount to 'illegitimate pressure' under the duress doctrine (see 8.1.2 and 8.4). Peter Gibson LJ said (at 332): 'I accept that the threat of an injunction only had a nuisance value in that I cannot see how the plaintiff could have succeeded in any claim. Nevertheless, that nuisance was something which the defendant was freed from.' However, it is arguable that the promisee's conduct amounted to exploitation by abuse of the legal process and should be denied recognition as consideration. If you pay me not to harm you, your not being harmed is clearly a benefit to you, but this should not constitute value in the eye of the law.
>
> 2. The general rule that intangible benefits are not valid consideration is justifiable because of their *uncertainty* and the impossibility of *enforcement* (how do you compel someone to give 'love and affection', or quantify its monetary worth in damages?).
>
> 3. However, when courts consider it desirable to do so, they may find consideration in intangible benefits resulting from measurable conduct via:
>   - the concept of request (although this may be practically indistinguishable from desire or mere motive); or
>   - the idea of forbearance from lawful action.

(iv) Illusory consideration

Although the law will tolerate a considerable variation between the values exchanged in deference to individual choice, it draws the line where the recipient will *inevitably* get nothing, nothing which is enforceable, or nothing more than he or she would have received anyway. Consideration may be illusory and of no value in the eye of the law in the following cases.

(i) **Impossibility**: where, at the time of contract formation, the promisee's performance is known by both parties to be physically or legally impossible, 'the parties could not be supposed to have so contracted' (*Clifford (Lord) v Watts* (1870) at 588); if the impossibility of performance is unknown to the parties, the contract may be void for mistake (see 6.2.2).

(ii) **Discretionary promises**: where a party promises to do something 'if I still feel like it when the time comes'. Whilst promises are *effectively* discretionary if they are accompanied by a clause excluding all liability for breach (eg where the promise 'to do X' is cancelled out by the term 'but I am not liable if I don't do X'), legislation may simply render such exemptions ineffective, leaving the substantive promises binding without qualification (see 11.4 and 11.5).

(iii) **Un-induced performance by the promisee**: 'it is no consideration to refrain from a course of action which it was never intended to pursue' (*Arrale v Costain Civil Engineering Ltd* (1976) at 106); if the promisor could show that the nephew in *Hamer v Sidaway* never intended to drink, smoke, or gamble, the nephew could not have enforced his uncle's promise to pay him for refraining. However, the contrary was held in *Pitt v Jones* (2007). J sought an emergency shareholders' meeting to approve the sale of his shares. To encourage P to give approval, J said he would persuade the purchaser to buy P's shares at the same price in six months' time, failing which J would pay for P's shares himself. Although P never considered refusing approval for J's proposed sale, Lady Justice Smith held (at [18]) that:

> [T]here was so clear a chronological link between the respondent's offer of the undertaking and the appellants' willingness to sign the documents that the natural inference to draw was that the two were directly connected. I would hold that the appellants' cooperation was given in return for the respondent's undertaking . . . notwithstanding the fact that the appellants did not con- sciously realise that by signing the documents they were subjecting themselves to a detriment and were giving consideration for the respondent's undertaking.

3.1.3.6 Compromise and forbearance to sue

Where *X* has a legal claim against *Y*, *X* may provide consideration for *Y*'s promise if *X*:

- **forbears from suing** on his or her claim—here, *Y* concedes *X*'s claim and *X* agrees not to enforce it for a specified time or at all (eg a creditor gives a debtor extra time to pay or extinguishes the debt); or

- **compromises** his or her claim—here, *Y* does not concede *X*'s claim but *X* agrees to abandon his or her claim (eg where the parties agree to settle their differences).

✓ **Where *X*'s claim is valid in law**, his or her compromise or forbearance is clearly good consideration for *Y*'s reciprocal promise. Where the *duration* of forbear- ance is unspecified, an implication of reasonable time will be made (*Payne v Wilson* (1827)). Forbearance is only consideration if it is *requested* by the promisor. However, a court may be prepared to *imply a request* where the promisee's actual forbearance (ie detriment) is not merely in reliance on, but also *in return for*, the other party's promise (see 3.1.2.2).

✓ **Where *X*'s claim is *doubtful* in law**, his or her compromise or forbearance is still good consideration (*Haigh v Brooks* (1839)).

✗ **If *X* *knows* that his claim is *invalid***, his or her compromise or forbearance is not valid consideration. As Tindal CJ said (at 564) in *Wade v Simeon* (1846): 'It is almost *contra bonos mores* [against good conscience], and certainly contrary to all the principles of natural justice, that a man should institute proceedings against another, when he is conscious that he has no good cause of action.' In practice, the more unreasonable his or her claim, the more likely it is to be inferred that he or she has no honest belief in its validity.

✓ **If *X*'s claim is *invalid* in law, but made in *good faith and on reasonable grounds***, he or she gives good consideration (*Cook v Wright* (1861) at 569). Cockburn CJ explains in *Callisher v Bischoffsheim* (1870) at 452:

> Every day a compromise is effected on the ground that the party making it has a chance of succeeding in it, and if he *bona fide* believes he has a fair chance of

success, he has a reasonable ground for suing, and his forbearance to sue will constitute a good consideration. When such a person forbears to sue he gives up what he believes to be a right of action, and the other party gets an advantage, and, instead of being annoyed with an action, he escapes from the vexations incident to it . . . It would be another matter if a person made a claim which he knew to be unfounded, and, by a compromise, derived an advantage under it: in that case his conduct would be fraudulent.

As long as a party forbears or compromises a claim which is not 'vexatious or frivolous, he gives up something of value. It is a mistake to suppose it is not an advantage . . . to be able to litigate his claim even if it turns out to be wrong' (*Miles v New Zealand Alford Estates Co* (1886) at 291).

 Pause for reflection

If a party's claim is *in fact* invalid, compromising or forbearing from suing on it entails no factual detriment to that party and confers no factual benefit on the other party. However, recognising legal value in *X*'s forbearance or compromise of an honest but mistaken claim is supportable as: (i) encouraging settlements (or 'finality in disputes') and (ii) conferring factual benefit on the promisor in being rid of the nuisance of litigation.

3.1.4 **Pre-existing duties**

The consideration doctrine attracts particular attention where *X* promises to do something that *X* was already legally bound to do (ie it is the subject of *X*'s pre-existing duty). Has *X* given good consideration? The traditional answer depends on whether *X*'s pre-existing duty was imposed:

(i)   by the general law;

(ii) by a contract with a third party; or

(iii) by an existing contract with the promisor.

The orthodox position is that, while (ii) is good consideration, (i) and (iii) are not. **Diagram** 3C summarises the pro-enforcement and anti-enforcement policies in each category, and the legal techniques used to implement them.

3.1.4.1 **Pre-existing duties imposed by public law**

The general rule is that a promise to perform (or the performance) of an existing public duty is no consideration for a reciprocal promise. There is no value in the eye of the law even if there is undoubted factual value to the recipient. The concern is to prevent opportunistic exploitation. It would be highly undesirable to allow public officials to extract benefits in return for the performance of their existing legal duties (eg requesting payment for the attendance of an ambulance or fire brigade). It may also taint impartiality and probity in the administration

Diagram 3C Consideration and pre-existing duties

Pre-existing duty:	(i) In law	(ii) To a third party	(iii) In contract to the other party
Pro-enforcement policies	1. Promisor undertakes new liability. 2. Promisee receives factual or additional benefit.	1. Promisor undertakes new liability. 2. Promisee receives factual benefit.	1. Practical benefit to promisor of avoiding worse alternatives. 2. Promote cooperation. 3. Economic efficiency. 4. Quasi-frustration: prevent harshness to promisee.
Legal basis for enforcement	• Promisor receives and promisee undertakes something 'extra', ie *legal benefit*.	• *Presence of legal benefit*.	• finding *legal benefit*, • finding '*practical benefit*', • replacement with *new contract*, • *compromise* of claim.
Anti-enforcement policies	1. Risk of bribery, extortion, corruption in public life.	1. Merely gratuitous promise.	1. Risk of extortion, duress. 2. Promisee undertakes no new liability. 3. Promisor obtaining no new benefit. 4. Protect the sanctity of original contract.
Legal basis for non-enforcement	• *Finding no legal benefit or detriment*.	• *Mere motive*.	• *Finding no legal benefit or detriment*. • *Precedent against enforcement*.

of justice and in government (eg judges or politicians receiving payments to take certain actions).

✗ In *Collins v Godefroy* (1831), G's promise to pay if C gave evidence at G's trial was held to be unenforceable, since C had already been subpoenaed to give evidence at the trial.

✓ However, where enforcement would *not* undermine such public policies, courts can circumvent the general bar by 'finding' that *more* was promised than was strictly owed under the pre-existing legal duty. Thus, in *Glasbrook Bros v Glamorgan CC* (1925), mine owners, fearful of violence during a strike, agreed to pay the police £2,200 for protection. The court enforced the payment because the police had provided stronger protection than they had judged necessary. These cases now come under section 25(1) of the Police Act 1996, which allows claims for 'special police services'. In *West Yorkshire Police Authority v Reading Festival Ltd* (2006), Scott Baker LJ said (at [66]) that the services to be paid for will either 'have been asked for but will be beyond what the police consider necessary to meet their public duty obligations, or they are services which, if the police do not provide them, the asker will have to provide them from his own or other resources.'

✓ In **Ward v Byham**, the father of an illegitimate child promised to pay the child's mother £1 per week provided that the child was 'well looked after and happy'. The father argued that the mother had provided no consideration because she was simply performing her existing legal duty (at the time, the father of an illegitimate child had no corresponding legal duty of support). The majority of the Court of Appeal found that the mother had promised to do *more* than was required under her legal duty by promising to keep the child 'happy'. The fact that natural love and affection are not generally sufficient consideration (see 3.1.3.5(iii)) did not prevent the court from enforcing what was, otherwise, regarded as an appropriate payment.

Lord Denning attacked the general rule head-on in *Ward v Byham*. He found that although there was no *legal* detriment to the mother, there was *factual benefit to the promisor*. The father was benefited by the mother's promise just as if a third party without a legal duty had promised to look after the child for payment. This is how *Ward v Byham* was interpreted by Glidewell LJ in *Williams v Roffey*.

 Pause for reflection

The current rule against the promise or performance of pre-existing public duties being valid consideration is over-inclusive. It denies both the practical and indeed *legal benefit* that such promises can confer on the recipients (for they would acquire a new right), and the *legal detriment* to the promisors (they are now liable to the promisees, aside from any liability for breaching the public duty). In *Williams v Williams* (1957), Lord Denning said (at 151) that 'a promise to perform an existing duty is, I think, sufficient consideration to support a promise, so long as there is nothing in the transaction which is contrary to the public interest'. In practice, where enforcement is judged desirable and not contrary to the public interest (as in *Ward v Byham*), this can be achieved by finding: that *more* was being promised or done than was previously required or, more controversially, that it conferred a *'practical benefit'*.

3.1.4.2 Pre-existing contractual duties owed to a third party

The performance (or promise to perform) an existing contractual duty owed to a third party is generally regarded as good consideration. The promisee obtains the desired performance or a directly enforceable obligation, and the promisor undertake a new liability that is quite independent from that owed to the third party. The policies therefore support enforcement.

✓ In **Shadwell v Shadwell** (1860) an uncle promised £150 yearly to his nephew until the nephew's income as a Chancery barrister reached 600 guineas (1 guinea being £1.05). This was held to be enforceable because the nephew provided consideration by marrying Ellen Nicholl, which he was already contractually bound to her to do.

This conclusion is not obvious; the value of the marriage to the uncle is, at most, intangible or sentimental, and unlikely to be accompanied by contractual intent. At most, it is a conditional gift. While the decision is easier to understand as a desirable family arrangement in 1860, it was relied upon as authority for the enforceability of promises supported by performance of a pre-existing duty to a third party in:

✓ *Scotson v Pegg* (1861), where P's promise for S's delivery of coal was held to be enforceable, although S was already contractually obliged to do so for a third party; and

✓ *Pao On v Lau Yiu Long,* where the House of Lords affirmed that the *mere promise* of performing the duty owed to a third party is good consideration (see 3.1.2.3).

3.1.4.3 Pre-existing duties owed to the other party

The most common modern-day consideration problem involves the performance of (or promise to perform) a pre-existing duty already contractually owed to the other party. For example, *A* agrees to pay *B* £3,000 to paint their house; subsequently *A* agrees to pay an additional £1,000 to *B* for the same job. In contrast to the previous categories, *A* (the promisor) obtains no new enforceable right over and above their existing entitlement (for *B* to paint his or her house). The traditional position is that *B*'s promise of 'the same' is not good consideration for *A*'s promise to pay more. This was overturned by *Williams v Roffey* where the promise to perform a pre-existing contractual duty was recognised as conferring 'practical benefit' on the party promising to pay more for it (see 3.1.5.3). The far-reaching implications of this case must be put in the wider context of the role of consideration in contract modifications generally.

3.1.5 **Contract modifications**

In general, contract parties can make an enforceable agreement to end (sometimes called 'rescind' or 'discharge') or vary their contract, so long as this is supported by *consideration.*

3.1.5.1 Agreements to end the contract

✓ Where *both parties* owe outstanding obligations to (and so have outstanding rights against) each other, each party provides consideration for the release from his or her own obligation by releasing the other party from theirs.

✗ If *only one party* promises to give up their contractual rights, this is 'entirely unilateral and unsupported by any consideration' (*Collin v Duke of Westminster* (1985) at 598). Thus, if I *have outstanding obligations* to you but you have no outstanding obligation to me (you have completed your performance), your promise to release me from my obligations is unsupported by consideration; I must give you something extra to enforce your promise.

3.1.5.2 Agreements to modify the contract

This may take a number of forms.

(i) **End the existing contract and make a new contract**: the existing contract can be ended by satisfying the requirements of consideration, followed by a *new contract* on different terms in relation to the same subject matter. In the American case of *Watkins & Sons Inc v Carrig* (1941), the parties entered a contract for W to excavate a cellar for C at a fixed price. After discovering solid rock in the excavation site, W obtained C's agreement to pay eight times the original contract price. C later refused to pay, arguing an absence of consideration. The trial judge disagreed. He held that the original contract was abandoned (when each party gave up their rights to sue the other) and replaced by a new agreement.

(ii) **Modification supported by consideration on both sides**: a modification is enforceable if *each* party gives consideration by conferring a new benefit or assuming a new burden. The mere possibility that either party *may* benefit or be prejudiced by the new arrangement is enough (*WJ Alan & Co Ltd v El Nasr Export & Import Co* (1972)). For example, a change in the currency of future contractual payments may benefit or prejudice either party depending on currency fluctuations.

(iii) Modifications that can only benefit one contracting party:

- the promisor agrees to *pay more for the same* performance originally contracted for (the promisee gives 'the same for more').

- the promisor agrees to *accept less* in satisfaction of the performance originally contracted for (the promisee gives 'less for the same').

As we will see, the traditional position that these are *unenforceable* for want of consideration has effectively been reversed. But difficulties remain.

3.1.5.3 *'The same for more'*: pre-existing contractual duty owed to the other party

(i) The traditional *Stilk v Myrick* rule—no consideration

Whether a promise of 'more for the same' is enforceable depends on whether the promisee's reciprocal promise of 'the same for more' is valid consideration. The traditional answer given by **Stilk v Myrick** (1809) is 'no'. There, two of the 11 seamen deserted during a voyage and the master agreed to share the deserters' wages with the remainder of the crew if they would work the ship back to London. S could not enforce the master's promise. Two reports give different reasons.

- In Campbell's report, S's claim failed because he gave **no consideration** for the master's promise: he was already contractually obliged to sail the ship home. This reasoning would bar *all* claims for additional payments supported by the performance or a promise to perform a pre-existing contract. This version was accepted as English law in *North Ocean Shipping Co v Hyundai Construction Co (The Atlantic Baron)*.

- In the Espinasse report, S's claim failed on the narrower ground of policy: namely, the concern to **prevent duress**—the possibility of sailors on the high seas making *extortionate demands* upon their masters as the price for bringing the ship safely back to the home port. On this rationale, absence of consideration does not necessarily bar enforcement of promises to pay more. The question is one of duress. The focus on this version was renewed in *Williams v Roffey*.

(ii) Traditional 'exceptions' to the traditional rule

A promise to pay more *is* enforceable if one of the following occurs.

- ✓ The promisee gives *something 'more'* than he or she was obliged to under the original contract, as in **Hartley v Ponsonby** (1857). The desertion of 17 out of

36 crew, leaving only four or five able seamen, was held to entitle the remaining crew to refuse to continue with the original contract. Thus, in agreeing to continue with the voyage, the remaining crew did *more* than they were obliged to do and so gave consideration for the promise of more pay. This would explain the *outcome* in the American case of *Watkins & Sons Inc v Carrig* (see 3.1.5.2(i)).

✓ *The parties agree to end the existing contract and make a new contract* on different terms relating to the same subject matter (eg *Watkins & Sons v Carrig*, see 3.1.5.2). In *Williams v Roffey*, Purchas LJ (at 20) rejected 'the attractive invitation' to follow *Watkins*.

✓ A *compromise* is entered into, where there is any dispute about the parties' obligations (see 3.1.3.6). The scope of this is potentially very wide.

(iii) *Williams v Roffey Brothers*—practical benefit is valid consideration

RB contracted to refurbish 27 flats, subcontracting the carpentry work to W for £20,000. W finished nine flats, but was at risk of not finishing the rest because of financial problems, arising partly from underpricing the original job and partly from W's deficient supervision of his workers. Realising this and mindful of its potential liability to its main employer, RB promised to pay W an additional £575 on the timely completion of each of the remaining 18 flats (totalling £10,300). W substantially completed eight more flats, but RB did not pay the sums promised, so W discontinued work and sued for £10,847. RB engaged other carpenters to complete the job and incurred a week's time penalty under the main contract. RB argued that W gave no consideration for the additional sums promised. The Court of Appeal affirmed the lower court's decision in W's favour, but only awarded W £3,500, not W's expectation of around £10,300 (see (vi)).

Glidewell LJ concluded (at 15–16) that:

(i) if A has entered into a contract with B to do work for, or to supply goods or services to, B in return for payment by B; and (ii) at some stage before A has completely performed his obligations under the contract, B has reason to doubt whether A will, or will be able to, complete his side of the bargain; and (iii) B thereupon promises A an additional payment in return for A's promise to perform his contractual obligations on time; and (iv) *as a result of giving his promise, B obtains in practice a benefit, or obviates a disbenefit*; and (v) *B's promise is not given as a result of economic duress or fraud on the part of A*; then (vi) the benefit to B is capable of being consideration for B's promise, so that the promise will be legally binding (emphasis added).

In essence, *Williams v Roffey* stands for two propositions.

(i) *Consideration*, in the bargain sense, is *still necessary* to enforce promises of more for the same. But, the case enlarged the scope of consideration to include any *practical* benefit moving to the promisor. Contrary to *Stilk v Myrick, legal* benefits (rights) or detriments (obligations) additional to those contained in the existing contract are unnecessary.

(ii) Any concerns about the promisee applying improper pressure to induce the promisor's agreement to pay more should be dealt with by the doctrine of *economic duress*.

(iv) The scope of practical benefit

What is the nature and scope of the additional 'practical benefit' flowing from promises of the same, which now counts as valid consideration to enforce the reciprocal promise to pay more? The Court in *Williams v Roffey* identifies four practical benefits to RB:

(i) W's continued performance;

(ii) avoiding the trouble and expense of obtaining a substitute;

(iii) avoiding the penalty payment for late performance under the main contract; and

(iv) RB's promise to pay more only as each flat was completed gave W the incentive to perform in a more orderly manner; this allowed RB to coordinate its other subcontractors more effectively and efficiently towards timely completion of the main contract.

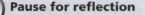 **Pause for reflection**

1. The first three practical benefits confer *nothing more* than was already promised under the original contract. The value of W's reassurance of performance (like promises to love, be good, or not to complain) is the comfort it gives to RB; it is intangible and, like things of sentimental value, is generally regarded as insufficient consideration (see 3.1.3.5).

2. Actual performance can only be construed as something *additional* if the law were to regard a contractual *promise* to perform as less valuable than its *actual* performance. This reflects the Holmesian idea[17] that a contract party has an option to perform, or to pay damages and not perform. Thus, Purchas LJ said in *Williams v Roffey* (at 23) that it was open to W to be in deliberate breach of the contract in order to 'cut his losses' commercially. On the one hand, it is objectionable to allow a party to 'create' consideration by first threatening breach, and then promising not to. It shows disrespect for the very idea of contract as creating binding obligations, and makes a contract no more than a starting point for further negotiation.[18]

3. On the other hand, *Stilk v Myrick* is based on the fiction that a contract right is the same as contractual performance. The unpalatable truth is that there is no straightforward equivalence between the two. Contract law itself does not take such an elevated view of contractual obligations. Many rules are inconsistent with the protection of a claimant's performance interest (see eg Chapters 12–14). We bargain for performance, but we get a more fragile right in remedial terms. The law's starting point is that 'the essence of contract is performance. Contracts are made in order to be performed'.[19] But this is balanced against countervailing policies such as the concerns to: prevent undue harshness to the contract-breaker; avoid waste; promote finality in dispute resolution; and ➡

---

[17] O W Holmes, *The Common Law* (Little, Brown, 1881) 298.

[18] P Birks, 'The Travails of Duress' [1990] *LMCLQ* 342, 346.

[19] D Friedmann, 'The Performance Interest in Contract Damages' (1995) 111 *LQR* 628, 629. C Webb, 'Performance and Compensation: An Analysis of Contract Damages and Contractual Obligation' (2006) 26 *OJLS* 41.

→

terminate hostile relationships. This requires compromises which entail deviations from the starting point.

4. A common misunderstanding is that W gave additional *legal* benefit by performing in a more orderly way. However, this benefit to RB was merely *consequential* on RB's timetable for the *additional* sums; there was no change to payments under the *original* contract. W did not *promise* it and RB only obtained the *chance* (not the assurance) of a more desirable sequence of performance; it could not have enforced this order of performance. There was no legal benefit, but only practical benefit. Practical benefit in the form of a *chance* of receiving an actual benefit was accepted as consideration in *Anangel Atlas Compania Naviera v Ishikawajima-Harima Heavy Industries Co Ltd* (1990). I-H, a ship-builder, was faced with a serious slump in the shipping industry: many buyers were threatening cancellation, seeking delays in delivery, and price reductions. I-H promised various concessions if A would accept the timely delivery of a hull as A had already contracted to do. Hirst J found consideration for the concessions in the practical benefit to I-H of *the chance* that *other buyers* would follow A's example of due acceptance and be deterred from breach. This benefit was *not promised* by A but merely hoped for by I-H; and the benefit, if it were to eventuate, would have come from third parties, not A.

5. In 'Consideration: Practical Benefit and the Emperor's New Clothes' in J Beatson and D Friedmann (eds), *Good Faith and Fault in Contract Law* (OUP, 1995) 123, I argued that the notion of 'practical benefit' as merely the 're-promise' of a pre-existing contractual duty confers no additional enforceable benefit, and thus is illusory. Some enforcement of contract modifications is desirable in an unpredictable world, but this is better addressed by developing the more flexible equitable doctrine of promissory estoppel.

6. In 'A Bird in the Hand: Consideration and Promissory Estoppel' in A Burrows and E Peel (eds), *Contract Formation and Parties* (OUP, 2010) 89, I argue:

   (i)   for a narrower concept of practical benefit: if we accept that a bird in the hand is worth two in the bush, then the idea that the *receipt* of (even part-) performance confers a benefit over and above the *right* to performance, and can be exchanged for something from the recipient, is consistent with the core idea of consideration as bargain;

   (ii) implementing this by replacing the bilateral contract analysis in *Williams v Roffey* with a unilateral contract analysis (the promisor is only bound if the stipulated performance is actually received); and

   (iii) adopting a more nuanced approach to the circumstances when revocation of this unilateral offer should be permitted prior to the promisee's actual completion. This is preferable to the particular version of promissory estoppel advanced in *Collier v Wright* (see 3.3.2.2).

(v) How far does 'practical benefit' apply?

The recognition of 'practical benefit' as valuable consideration can logically extend beyond contract modification to *contract formation*, and include the *chance of* making a contract or some other un-promised benefit, or the chance of avoiding some nuisance or other harm threatened by the promisee. Such an extension would dilute the consideration requirement to the point of extinction. What were previously regarded as *illusory consideration, bad faith compromise or forbearance, merely gratuitous options,* or *promises to perform an existing legal duty* could now support the enforcement of reciprocal promises. The same applies to *past consideration* if it consists of an executory (unperformed) promise (see 3.1.2.3). Likewise, the concept of 'practical benefit' can logically be extended from promises of 'the same for more' to promises of 'less for the same'. However, the Court of Appeal in *Re Selectmove Ltd* (1995) refused to do this (see 3.1.5.4).

(vi) What *rights* are obtained by 'practical benefit'? The measure of recovery

It is often overlooked that, in *Williams v Roffey*, the practical benefit did *not* buy W (the builder) an *expectation* interest in RB's promise to pay more. It was RB's breach (by failing to make due payment) that entitled W to terminate his performance before completion. On a *contract* action, W *should* have got his full expectation (around £10,300). However, the court awarded only £3,500, based *explicitly* on the extent of W's performance up to the point of RB's breach (*Williams v Roffey* at 7), that is, on W's *reliance*. This is consistent with the unilateral contract analysis I advocate earlier.

On the other side, if RB had not breached and W simply failed to complete despite re-promising to do so, RB's expectation would derive no *more* protection from having been purchased twice. Indeed, a promisor in such a situation would be worse off! For example, you promise to pay me £5,000 for a job and later promise an additional £3,000 (total £8,000); despite this, I still do not do the job, and the cost of substitute performance is £10,000. Your contract damages should be: the cost of substitute performance *minus* your saved costs from not having to pay me. Is your saved cost £5,000 or £8,000? If your promise to pay more is contractually enforceable, then the answer is £8,000. That would make you *worse off* than if you had not tried to salvage the situation.

> **Pause for reflection**
>
> The injustice of this is recognised by the Ontario Law Reform Commission. In such an instance, the appropriate deduction is the *original sum* promised, and not the greater sum of the variation, because 'it would be an implicit understanding between the parties that failure to comply with the terms of the new agreement would revive the old one'.[20] The additional promise is only enforceable *on the promisee's performance*. This is a unilateral contract analysis (on the revocation of such unilateral offers, see 2.3.5.2).

(vii) The current status of *Stilk*

The Court in *Williams v Roffey* was adamant that it had not overruled *Stilk v Myrick* but only 'refined' and 'limited' it. It explains the outcome in *Stilk v Myrick* in terms of preventing even the chance of duress, but this does not explain why a different outcome was arrived at in *Williams v Roffey*. The two cases are obviously analogous: if

---

[20] Ontario Law Reform Commission, 'Report on the Amendment of the Law of Contract' (No 82, 1987) 12–13 discussing the promise to accept part-performance.

RB received practical benefit from W's promise to complete performance, so must the master of the ship have received benefit from S's promise to work the ship back home. In substance, while *Williams v Roffey* affirms the *need* for fresh consideration to enforce an additional promise, it *has* overruled *Stilk v Myrick* as to what *counts* as fresh consideration. In **South Caribbean Trading Ltd v Trafigura Beheer BV** (2005), Coleman J recognises that *Stilk v Myrick* requires legal benefit while *Williams v Roffey* says that practical benefit will do. He made clear that he would not have followed *Williams v Roffey* but for it being binding on him (not having 'yet' been declared 'wrongly decided' by the House of Lords, at [108]). *Williams v Roffey* is followed in *Attrill v Dresdner Kleinwort Ltd* (2011 and 2013). There, an employer undertook to establish a guaranteed minimum bonus pool for certain employees, but then argued that this was unenforceable for want of consideration. It was unnecessary to decide on the matter but the Court of Appeal found that the purpose of the undertaking 'was to retain their staff [during the financial crisis]. The evidence suggests that it was largely successful. The continued work of the employee is, at least arguably, adequate consideration for the establishment of the guaranteed minimum bonus pool' (2011) at [35], and (2013) at [95]).

(viii) Consideration and duress
Before *Williams v Roffey*, the issue of improper pressure in inducing one-sided contract modifications did not arise because *Stilk v Myrick* automatically barred such modifications for lack of consideration. The more expansionist approach to consideration in *Williams v Roffey* is coupled with the call to control improper pressure via the doctrine of economic duress. In *The Alev* (1989), Hobhouse J said (at 147): 'Now that there is a properly developed doctrine of the avoidance of contracts on the grounds of economic duress, there is no warrant for the Court to fail to recognise the existence of some consideration even though it may be insignificant and even though there may have been no mutual bargain in any realistic use of that phrase.'

 Pause for reflection

Duress rests on the finding that there is: (i) an 'illegitimate threat' by one party that (ii) leaves the other party with 'no practicable alternative' but to submit (*Universe Tankships Inc of Monrovia v International Transport Workers Federation* (1983), (see 8.4.3)). What is given by recognising 'practical benefit' seems liable to be taken away by the economic duress doctrine. There is debate over the proper scope of economic duress, but its potential for invalidating one-sided modifications is obvious.

1. Illegitimate pressure can include a threatened breach of contract, which can be *implied*; this could cover facts analogous to *Williams v Roffey*. A promisee who is aware of the promisor's need for completion can make known the unlikelihood of his or her timely completion and passively wait for, rather than actively demand, extra payment.

2. The doctrines of consideration and of economic duress are likely to operate on the *same facts* to yield *different conclusions* on the question of enforceability. The reasons for finding

➡

➡️

'practical benefit' to the promisor (eg to avoid the problems consequent on breach) are the *very same* reasons for finding duress, because the promisor had 'no practicable alternative' but to agree (ie to avoid the problems consequent on breach).

3. Likewise, Coleman J's approach in *South Caribbean Trading v Trafigura* (2005) in widening the notion of invalidating duress, could totally negate the effect of recognising practical benefit. He held that the promisee who threatens not to perform an existing duty *cannot* rely on the benefit that his or her performance would confer on the promisor, because their threat is 'analogous to economic duress' if the threat is not based on an argument that the promisee was discharged from its original obligation (at [108]). That is, *any unjustified* express or implied threat of non-performance disqualifies the promisee from relying on 'practical benefit'. If the promisee's non-performance is *justified*, any subsequent promise to pay more is enforceable anyway as a legitimate compromise of his or her claim.

3.1.5.4 *'Less for the same'*: part-performance

(i) The rule in *Foakes v Beer*

Instead of you promising to *pay more* for the contractual performance I already owe you, you may promise to *accept less* than is already due from me. For example, you lend me £100 but, when I plead inability to pay, you agree to accept £70 instead. Does my promise to pay less constitute 'practical benefit' enabling me to enforce your promise to accept less in discharge of my entire debt? And, if I do not pay the £70, can you claim the original £100 I owe, or only the £70 you agreed to accept? If I can enforce your new promise, you could only claim £70. However, the **general rule** is that a promise to accept part-payment of a debt in discharge of the whole debt is unenforceable for want of consideration. The general rule is traceable to *Pinnel's Case* (1602), and was upheld by the House of Lords in *Foakes v Beer* (1884), where B's promise to abandon her claim to interest on F's debt to her was held to be unenforceable for want of consideration. B was not barred from claiming the interest.

> ### 🧍 Pause for reflection
>
> In *Some Landmarks of 20th Century Contract Law* (OUP, 2002) 24–6, Treitel defends *Foakes v Beer*. He points out that, when B promised F more time to pay the principal debt, the issue of interest was not discussed and B was probably 'tricked into making a promise which, on its true construction, had an effect not intended by her' (ie she only intended to give extra time to pay, but *not* to forgo interest on late payments). Whatever the faults of *Foakes*, the actual outcome 'does not seem to be unjust. What seems to have happened was that Dr Foakes' solicitor dug a technical trap for Mrs Beer and the House of Lords arranged an equally technical rescue', by relying on the rule that part-payment is not good consideration to discharge the whole.

(ii) Traditional exceptions to the rule in *Foakes*

Your promise to accept less than is due from me is enforceable if:

✓ I give *something additional* for the dispensation granted by you (eg I agree to pay earlier, at a different place, or in a different currency). Part-payment cannot discharge the whole debt 'but the gift of a horse, hawk, or robe, &c., in satisfaction is good, for . . . [they] might be more beneficial to the plaintiff than the money . . . or otherwise the plaintiff would not have accepted it in satisfaction' (*Pinnel's Case*). The odd result is that my debt of £100 can be discharged for a peppercorn, but not for £70;

✓ I dispute your claim and the modification amounts to a *compromise* of your claim;

✓ your claim is *unliquidated* (unquantified) and the new agreement merely fixes the sum I owe;

✓ the promise is made to third parties (eg you agree to accept less from a third party in exchange for not suing me). This exception is necessary to support a *composition among creditors*, for where a composition has been agreed, it would be a fraud on other creditors for you, having promised to take less and received it, then to sue me for the balance. Moreover, I (the debtor) will have rearranged my affairs in reliance on such compositions. I may now be able to enforce such a composition under the Contracts (Rights of Third Parties) Act 1999 (see 4.1.3).

(iii) Practical benefit is *not* good consideration for promise to accept less

Although a promise of part-performance confers no *legal* benefit, the creditor may obtain *practical benefit* by the receipt of the part-performance. A bird in the hand is worth two in the bush. In *Foakes v Beer* (at 622), Lord Blackburn noted his:

> conviction that all men of business, whether merchants or tradesmen, do every day recognise and act on the ground that prompt payment of a part of their demand may be more beneficial to them than it would be to insist on their rights and enforce payment of the whole. Even where the debtor is perfectly solvent, and sure to pay at last, this is often so. Where the credit of the debtor is doubtful it must be more so.

In *Collier v P & M J Wright (Holdings) Ltd* (2008), Arden LJ said (at [3]) that, while the rule in *Pinnel's Case* 'may sound like a good result in terms of creditor protection, the consequence is . . . [that it] makes it difficult to enter into compromises of claims, which it can often be commercially beneficial for both parties to do'.

If promises of 'the same for more' confer a practical benefit amounting to valid consideration, so should promises of 'less for the same'. Yet this logic was rejected in **Re Selectmove Ltd**. The Revenue applied for an order for the compulsory winding up of a company that owed arrears in taxes. The company argued that the debt was not yet due since the Revenue had agreed to let the company defer payment. In exchange, the Revenue would receive the practical benefit of 'recover[ing] more from not enforcing its debt against the company which was known to be in financial difficulties, than from putting the company into liquidation'. Peter Gibson LJ (at 481) recognised that any creditor accepting less for the same 'will no doubt always see a practical benefit to himself in doing so'. But, he refused to recognise this as valid consideration because the House of Lords in *Foakes v Beer* declined to do so after expressly considering this argument. To treat 'practical benefit' as consideration here would leave *Foakes v Beer* without any application. This could only be done by the House of Lords, 'or more appropriately, by Parliament after consideration by the Law Commission'. It cannot be done by reference to the Court of Appeal decision in *Williams v Roffey* which did not expressly consider this issue.

However, a ship-builder's promise to accept a *reduced* price was enforced in *Anangel Atlas* (see 3.1.5.3(iv)), because the buyer, by duly accepting delivery of the ship, increased *the chance* that other buyers would follow suit and be deterred from breach, a practical benefit to the builder. The Supreme Court of New South Wales, in *Musumeci v Winadell Pty Ltd* (1995), also applied *Williams v Roffey* to enforce 'less for the same' modifications. Santow J found no distinction between 'the same for more' modifications and 'less for the same' modifications.

(iv) The remedial conundrum

To extend *Williams v Roffey* to 'less for the same' modifications would raise a remedial conundrum analogous to that identified in enforcing modifications of 'the same for more' (see 3.1.5.3(vii)). If 'less for the same' modifications were *contractually* enforceable, it would logically *reduce* the claim of the party agreeing to accept less, even if the other party fails to pay the lesser sum agreed. If you promise to accept £70 in discharge of my debt of £100 in the *hope* of *actually getting* £70, but *I still do not pay*, and your claim is confined to £70, you are worse off than if you had not bothered to salvage the situation at all. The *Sixth Interim Report on the Statute of Frauds and the Doctrine of Consideration*[21] recommends (at para 35) that 'the greater obligation can be discharged either by a promise to pay a lesser sum or by actual payment of it, but that if the new agreement is not performed then the original obligation shall revive'.[22]

(v) The problem of pressure

The traditional rules in *Stilk v Myrick* and *Foakes v Beer* can counter a promisee's use of pressure to 'get more' or 'do less'. If *Williams v Roffey* were extended to counteract *Foakes v Beer*, the focus for controlling the enforceability of such modifications would again shift to economic duress. However, Treitel[23] warns that economic duress 'may not go far enough'. The justice of the outcome in *Foakes v Beer* (because the creditor was tricked) may not be achievable even by an expanded concept of duress.

3.1.5.5 The roles of consideration and promissory estoppel in modifications

In the absence of consideration, contract parties may seek to enforce promises on other grounds. The doctrine of promissory estoppel allows the limited enforcement of relieving (ie 'less for the same') promises that induce reliance, in qualifying circumstances (see fuller discussion at 3.3). The doctrine undoubtedly undermines the rule in *Foakes v Beer*. However, it does so by reference to a wide-ranging assessment of events leading up to, and even after, the modification, and allows flexibility in the remedial response. For example, in **D&C Builders v Rees** (1966), R owed D&C £482 for building works but, knowing D&C were in 'desperate financial straits', R offered

---

[21] Law Revision Committee (Cmd 5449, 1937).
[22] The Ontario Law Reform Commission (n 20; 10, 12–13) favours the actual performance option.
[23] G Treitel, *Some Landmarks of Twentieth Century Contract Law* (OUP, 2002) 24–6, 45–6.

£300 in full settlement or 'nothing'. D&C eventually accepted this but later sued for the balance. Based on *Foakes v Beer*, the majority of the Court of Appeal refused to recognise the alleged settlement. The court also rejected the plea of promissory estoppel because it was not inequitable for D&C to go back on its promise to accept less because R 'really behaved very badly'. R misled D&C as to her own financial position and used D&C's financial difficulties to intimidate D&C into accepting a lower sum in discharge of the entire debt (at 626).

Re Selectmove shows how events *subsequent* to the modification can also be taken into account. Peter Gibson LJ rejected the claim of promissory estoppel because 'it was not inequitable or unfair' to go back on that agreement since 'the company failed to honour its [lesser] promise'. That is, since the promisee failed to actually perform his reduced obligations, the promisor could revert to its original rights. However, the Court of Appeal's decision in *Collier v P & M J Wright (Holdings) Ltd* (2008) would severely reduce this flexibility by artificially widening the scope of promissory estoppel (see 3.3.2.2 and 3.3.2.3).

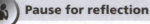 **Pause for reflection**

1. To a significant extent, the doctrines of consideration, promissory estoppel, and duress operate in the same territory. The scope of each affects the other. For example, expanding the scope of consideration (which should logically confer *full* enforcement of promises) will reduce the need to invoke promissory estoppel (which confers only enforcement, as justice requires), and vice versa. Further, expanding the scope of duress undermines the effect of expanding the scope of consideration.

2. If the *Williams v Roffey* notion of 'practical benefit' includes mere re-promises to perform, the discretion to take account of all the circumstances and remedial flexibility under promissory estoppel becomes redundant. The promisee who succeeds on consideration obtains a stronger right than under promissory estoppel. Likewise, flexibility would be lost by the hardening of promissory estoppel in the new shape outlined in *Collier v Wright*. The preferable approaches are:

   (i) via the unilateral contract analysis, so that the promise is unenforceable until the promisee's performance is actually completed; or

   (ii) via the traditional promissory estoppel approach extended to adding promises: Russell LJ said (*Williams v Roffey* at 17) that he 'would have welcomed the development of argument . . . on the basis that there was . . . an estoppel' to prevent the promisor from going back on this promise to pay *more*.

3.1.6 **Consideration: an assessment**

We have noted the increasing criticisms of and hostility towards the consideration doctrine for being:

   (i)   inconsistent with the intention of the parties;

   (ii) over-inclusive, in enforcing some non-bargains as bargains;

Diagram 3D Consideration: reform suggestions

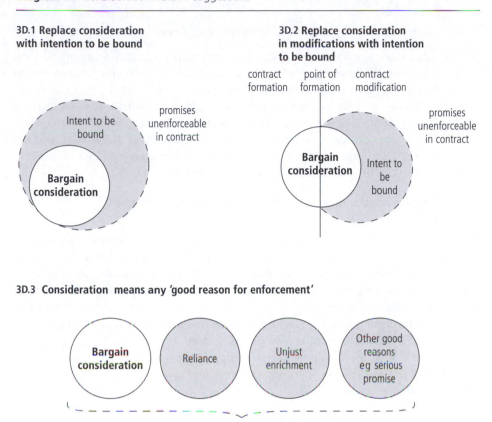

3D.1 Replace consideration with intention to be bound

Intent to be bound

Bargain consideration

promises unenforceable in contract

3D.2 Replace consideration in modifications with intention to be bound

contract formation point of formation contract modification

Bargain consideration

Intent to be bound

promises unenforceable in contract

3D.3 Consideration means any 'good reason for enforcement'

Bargain consideration

Reliance

Unjust enrichment

Other good reasons eg serious promise

'consideration'
But questionable that contract remedies are appropriate

3D.4 Retain bargain consideration but give due recognition to non-contractual sources of liability. Remedies as appropriate

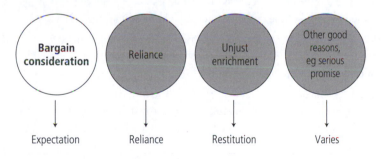

Bargain consideration

Reliance

Unjust enrichment

Other good reasons, eg serious promise

Expectation

Reliance

Restitution

Varies

(iii) under-inclusive, in failing to enforce some undertakings that deserve enforcement; and

(iv) overly technical, artificial, and internally incoherent.

This yields a picture of a doctrine plagued by uncertainty and inconsistency, flowing from the court's ability to manipulate the abstract concept of 'value' in response to the perceived intention, reliance, pressure, and fairness factors of the particular case. Lord Goff observed in *White v Jones* (1995) that: 'our law of contract is widely seen as deficient in the sense that it is perceived to be hampered by the presence of an unnecessary doctrine of consideration' (at 262–3). The Law Commission has identified the consideration doctrine as a suitable topic for a future separate review.[24] Some possibilities for reform can be identified and assessed (see **Diagram 3D**).

3.1.6.1 Replace consideration completely with a test of intention (Diagram 3D.1)

Williams v Roffey signals a shift away from the bargain view of contract towards one based on the *intention of the parties*. Russell LJ said in *Williams v Roffey* (at 18): 'consideration there must still be but, in my judgment, the courts nowadays should be more ready to find its existence so as to reflect the intention of the parties to the contract where the bargaining powers are not unequal'. On this view, consideration is simply *evidence* of the primary question about the intention of the parties (see 3.1.1(i)).[25] This is reinforced by the new emphasis on duress. Indeed, in *Gay Choon Ing v Loh Sze Ti Terence Peter* (2009), the Singapore Court of Appeal raises the spectre of replacing consideration with the doctrines of economic duress, undue influence, unconscionability, and promissory estoppel.

◀ Counterpoint

1. *Lack of 'fit'*: the consideration doctrine is not reducible to its evidentiary and cautionary functions, as supporters of its abolition assert (see 3.1.1(i)). An informal (not contained in a deed) undertaking unsupported by consideration is unenforceable even if there is undoubted evidence of the promisor's intention to be bound (see 3.2).

2. The function of the *vitiating factors*, discussed in Part IV, is also not solely that of determining the presence of contractual intention, and the vitiating factors cannot replace the functions performed by consideration.[26]

3. *Authority*: the abolition of consideration is unlikely to be judicially sanctioned anytime soon. Lord Steyn expresses the prevailing attitude:[27] 'I have no radical proposals for the wholesale review of the doctrine of consideration. I am not persuaded that it is necessary. And great

→

---

[24] Law Commission, *Privity of Contract: Contracts for the Benefit of Third Parties* (Law Com No 242, Cm 3329, 1996).

[25] L Fuller, 'Consideration and Form' (1941) 41 *Columbia L Rev* 799, 800–6.

[26] M Chen-Wishart, 'Consideration and Serious Intention' [2009] *SJLS* 434.

[27] J Steyn, 'Contract Law: Fulfilling the Reasonable Expectations of Honest Men' (1997) 113 *LQR* 433, 437.

➡️

legal changes should only be embarked on when they are truly necessary . . . On balance it seems to me that in modern practice the restrictive influence of consideration has markedly receded in importance.'

4. *Normatively questionable*: the idea that the law should enforce all seriously made promises is normatively questionable. It is doubtful that many would choose to live in a world in which they were 'bound by every promise, no matter how foolish, without any chance of letting increased wisdom undo past foolishness. Certainly, some freedom to change one's mind is necessary for free intercourse between those who lack omniscience.'[28] If we are concerned to uphold the autonomous intention of a party, why should we not take equally seriously that party's subsequent abandonment of his or her initial choice? Why privilege the latter when both are equally serious expressions of his or her will?

5. *Alternative*? The obvious alternative to the consideration requirement is the requirement of *intention to create legal relations*. But this is no panacea.

   (i) We have seen that the requirement under that name is more about limiting legal involvement in private affairs than about any genuine or systematic search for the parties' intentions (see 2.7).

   (ii) It is not obvious that such an elastic criterion as the parties' intentions will be any easier to apply, or any less susceptible to judicial manipulation, than bargain consideration itself.

   (iii) Even if an intention to be bound can be proved, this simply begs the follow-on question: bound to *what* legal effect? What rights or liabilities were intended to be transferred, created, waived, or suspended by the promisor? Was the transfer intended to be absolute or conditional?

3.1.6.2 Replace consideration in contract modifications with a test of intention (Diagram 3D.2)

A more modest reform is to do away with the need for consideration in contract modifications, leaving consideration as a requirement only at the formation of the original contract.[29] Reiter argues against 'the illogicality of equating modifying with originating promises' because:[30]

insofar as consideration serves to exclude gratuitous promise, it is of little assistance in the context of on-going, arms-length, commercial transactions where it is utterly fictional to describe what has been conceded as a gift, and in which there ought to be a strong presumption that good commercial 'considerations' underlie any seemingly detrimental modification.

§ 2-209(1) of the US *Uniform Commercial Code* dispenses with the consideration requirement for contract modifications. In *Antons Trawling Co Ltd v Smith* (2003), the New Zealand Court of Appeal said that promises of more for the same should be enforceable

---

[28] Morris R. Cohen, 'The Basis of Contract' (1933) 46 *Harvard L Rev* 553, 572.

[29] B Coote, 'Consideration and Benefit in Fact and in Law' (1990) 2 *JCL* 23; F M B Reynolds and G Treitel, 'Consideration for the Modification of Contract' (1965) 7 *Malaysian L Rev* 1.

[30] B Reiter, 'Courts, Consideration and Common Sense' (1977) 27 *UTLJ* 439, 507.

in the absence of contrary 'policy reasons'. The policy qualification, applied flexibly, could perform the same function as the wide-ranging inquiry under the promissory estoppel doctrine. In *Teat v Willcocks* (2013) the New Zealand Court of Appeal held that no consideration was required for a contract variation that is voluntarily agreed.

⏩ Counterpoint

1. Insofar as the justification is based on the centrality of the *parties' intentions*, the same counterpoints as given at 3.1.6.1 apply.

2. Insofar as the consideration doctrine supports the distinction between gifts and bargains, there is a *lack of internal coherence* in making the distinction vital at formation, but not at modification. Why should one have to give consideration to enforce a reciprocal promise to pay £100, but not to enforce a promise to pay £100 *more*?

3. The scope of 'policy reasons' that would render modifications unenforceable is uncertain.

3.1.6.3 Consideration includes any 'good reason for enforcement' (Diagram 3D.3)

In **'Consideration in Contract: A Fundamental Restatement'** (1971) reprinted with revisions in response to Treitel's criticism in P S Atiyah, *Essays in Contract* (Clarendon Press, 1986) 179, **Atiyah** argues for a fundamental restatement of the consideration doctrine based on an analysis of the law as actually enforced in the courts. He concludes that 'consideration' is used in a wider sense than simply bargain (at 181–2):

> When the courts found a sufficient reason for enforcing a promise they enforced it; and when they found that for one reason or another it was undesirable to enforce a promise, they did not enforce it. It seems highly probable that when the courts first used the word 'consideration' they meant no more than that there was a 'reason' for the enforcement of a promise.

This *pluralistic interpretation* of consideration concedes that the courts have always, though inconsistently, adopted a functional approach to the finding of bargain consideration (they manipulate the rules or resort to avoidance devices to achieve just results). Better to openly admit that the finding of consideration merely signifies the conclusion that rather than explaining why, a promise is enforceable. Significantly, Atiyah regards promissory estoppel, which protects reasonable reliance on a promise, not as an exception to consideration but as another 'consideration' supporting enforcement.

⏩ Counterpoint

An expansion into *non-bargain criteria for enforcement* necessitates enormous compromises of the fundamentals of contract law, which will weaken rather than strengthen its internal coherence. There is an enormous difference between exceptional deviations because of

➡

➡

countervailing policies, and an approach that invites all-comers. At its most basic, contract orthodoxy sets a threshold of enforceability based on bargain consideration, is restrictive of the scope of excuses for non-performance (see Part IV), and normally enforces to the full extent the promisee's expectations. Expanding the basis for enforcement will require appropriate adjustments. The demands of justice will vary with: (i) the particular *context* (whether commercial, consumer, charitable, family, and so on); (ii) the particular *reason* for enforcement (whether bargain, reliance suffered, benefit received, fulfilment of family responsibilities, and so on); and (iii) any excuses pleaded (eg non-disclosure, subsequent conduct, or change of circumstances). Moreover, if enforcement is to be divorced from exchange, it is not obvious what the proper remedial response should be. As Waddams observes (at [22]): 'There seems little point in arguing strenuously for the use of a single word [consideration] for all enforceable promises if an immediate division is to be required between fully enforceable promises and promises that are only partially enforceable.'

3.1.6.4 Retain bargain consideration whilst recognising other good reasons for non-contractual enforcement (Diagram 3D.4)

To support the retention of bargain enforcement is not to deny that non-bargain promises may also be legally relevant. As Treitel points out, 'contract does not exhaust the category of statements which are actionable or otherwise capable of having legal effects'.[31] Consistently, Waddams (at [22]) supports 'continuing the present usage of reserving "consideration" for bargains leading to fully enforceable contracts and to recognise that though some promises may be enforceable without consideration, the full "normal" panoply of contract remedies, in particular damages measured by the value of the promised performance, may not always be appropriate'.

Pause for reflection

Consideration in the bargain sense requires that something which counts in law should be given in exchange for a promise in order to make that promise enforceable in a *contractual* action. Whilst there have always been exceptional examples of non-bargain enforcement via contract, bargain provides the overwhelming, and commercially most important, explanation of contractual liability. Moreover, preserving a distinct category for bargain transactions serves two important functions:

- it gives the party seeking to enforce the promise a compelling *justification*, because he or she has given an enforceable agreed exchange for that promise;

- at the *remedial* end, it provides the basis for determining the *extent* of liability on the promise. The distinctive feature of a contractual action, the expectation measure, gives the promisee the value of the promised performance because he or she has given the agreed

➡

---

[31] G Treitel, 'Consideration: A Critical Analysis of Professor Atiyah's Fundamental Restatement' (1976) 50 *Australian LJ* 439, 441.

➜ equivalence of that performance. Other reasons set out at 3.1.1 reinforce the importance of bargain consideration.

While non-bargain policies have also influenced the development of the consideration doctrine (see 3.1.3.2), to sweep them all under the label of 'consideration' sacrifices too much in the orderly development and understanding of the law of enforceable promises. To open consideration to 'all-comers' dilutes the distinctiveness of a contractual action.

3.2 **Formalities**

'You went through the ceremony'

The law may require certain contracts be made in a stipulated way, usually by some requirement of writing and witnessing. Failure to comply with these requirements renders the contract unenforceable. The stipulated formalities may be in *addition to*, or *instead of*, the requirement of consideration.

3.2.1 **Instead of consideration**

Gratuitous promises are enforceable *without consideration* if they are contained in a *deed*. Thus, the deed is commonly used to make donations to charities because its enforceability enables the charities to claim the income tax paid on the promised sum by the donor. For a document to constitute a deed, **section 1(2)–(3) of the Law of Property (Miscellaneous Provisions) Act 1989** requires that it:

(i)   is clear on its face that it is intended to be a deed by the person making it; and

(ii) is validly executed as a deed by that person; that is, the document must be:

  • signed either by him or her (attested by one witness) or at his or her direction (requiring two witnesses); *and*

  • delivered as a deed by him or her or an authorised person on his or her behalf.

A deed is enforceable without consideration, but specific performance will not be awarded.

 Pause for reflection

1. Treitel states (at para 3–170) that '[t]he binding force of such a promise does not depend on contract at all'. Insofar as we see deeds as part of contract law, it simply shows that contract law is not exclusively concerned with the enforcement of bargains. Deeds allow people to commit themselves *formally* to gratuitous promises. In any case, parties who want to make gratuitous promises enforceable can cast them in the *form* of bargains for nominal consideration (see 3.1.3.4).

➜

→

2. The specified formality performs an **evidentiary and a cautionary function**. Requiring someone to go through a 'ceremony' impresses on him or her the significance of what they are doing; gives him or her a final opportunity to reflect on its wisdom; and operates as a check against impulsive action. The law is not against gifts; it just refuses to enforce *informal* gifts.

3. Absent formalities and consideration, a gratuitous promise, if executed (carried out), will not be reversed unless it is tainted by some vitiating factor.

3.2.2 The requirement of formalities in addition to consideration

The general rule is that contracts supported by consideration can be made in any form and evidenced by any means. However, some contracts require compliance with formalities, in addition to consideration. They are generally contracts which are particularly important or potentially one-sided, or where one party belongs to a vulnerable group warranting special protection.

The **stipulated formalities** may require that a particular type of contract be made:

(i) *by deed*: eg a lease for more than three years (Law of Property Act 1925, s 52(1));

(ii) *in a particular documentary format*: for example, most contracts for the sale or disposition of an interest in land (Law of Property (Miscellaneous Provisions) Act 1989, s 2); regulated consumer credit contracts, such as hire purchases, must be made in the **form prescribed by government regulations**, setting out all the express terms, and giving notice of the debtor's right to cancel during the **'cooling off' period** and other specified information; the contract must be **signed** by both parties and a **copy** given to the debtor (Consumer Credit Act 1974, ss 60–4; see also 1.7.3 and *Wilson v First County Trust Ltd (No 2)* (2003)); or

(iii) *evidenced in writing*: for example, contracts of *guarantee* (Statute of Frauds Act 1677, s 4).

Formalities requirements perform **three main functions**.

(i) *The cautionary function*: this is particularly important in one-sided (eg guarantee) or traditionally important (eg land) transactions. In *Ruddick v Ormston* (2005), R sought specific performance of an alleged contract to buy O's flat. O offered to sell his house directly to R without valuation for £25,000. R realised at once that O's asking price was significantly less than its worth, so R immediately signed, and got O to sign a hastily drawn up agreement on two diary pages (one stating that O would sell to R for £25,000 and the other that R would buy O's flat for £25,000). O refused to proceed with the sale when he realised that his flat was worth £65,000. The court refused specific performance because these signed pages did not comply with section 2(1) of the Law of Property (Miscellaneous Provisions) Act 1989. The contract was unenforceable without the need to consider whether it was also unconscionable (see 9.4).

(ii) *The evidentiary function*: formalities provide evidence of, and minimise disputes over, the existence and content of the alleged contract. Thus, commercial contracts are often reduced to writing, even though it is unnecessary to do so. Formalities also provide a marker for the parties engaged in lengthy negotiations to signify the point at which negotiations turn into a binding contract.

(iii) *The protective function*: Parliament affords protection in certain types of contracts to the party which typically has the weaker bargaining power (eg the tenant, employee, consumer borrower, and guarantor) by ensuring that he or she receives a written record of the agreement, in clear language, and, in certain cases (eg consumer credit, timeshare, and package holidays), allowing him or her to escape the contract within the 'cooling off' period.

Formalities requirements raise a number of **problems**.

(i) Formalities requirements can be *inconvenient, mysterious, and inaccessible* to ordinary people.

(ii) There is *inconsistency as to the types of contracts affected*: the evidentiary, cautionary, and protective functions of formalities are performed in a piecemeal and unsystematic way. It is impossible to explain why certain contracts require formalities while other similar contracts do not. This leads to the next difficulty.

(iii) Formalities can generate much litigation over the *jurisdictional question*; that is, whether the disputed contract comes within the class of contracts which must comply with the formalities. For example, contracts of *guarantee* must be evidenced in writing, but not the functionally similar contracts of *indemnity*, and the difficulty in distinguishing them has 'raised many hair-splitting distinctions of exactly that kind which brings the law into hatred, ridicule and contempt by the public' (*Yeoman Credit Ltd v Latter* (1961) at 835).

(iv) *Inconsistency in the formalities required*: it is not apparent why some contracts must be in the form of a deed, some must actually be in writing, and others need only be evidenced in writing.

(v) Dispute can also arise over *how to satisfy the formalities requirements*: for example, the simple requirement of a signature has required much judicial elucidation. Treitel (at 5–021) concludes that: 'A party need not sign his full name: initials will do. The signature may be printed, and may be in any part of the document, not necessarily at the bottom. It may be put on the document before the contract was made so long as it is "recognised" at the time of contracting.' In *Mercury Tax Group v HMRC* (2008) Underhill J held that the substitution of the signature pages from an earlier to a later draft of an agreement that included substantially different terms did not satisfy the requirements of section 2 of the Law of Property (Miscellaneous Provisions) Act 1989, although it was said to be normal commercial practice to obtain a client's signature to a draft and subsequently transfer it to the final document. In other circumstances, even a complete signature will not suffice. In *Francis F Berndes v Others* (2011) the parties had both signed a document in which the defendant declared a willingness to sell the property. However, the High Court held that the letter did not identify the purchaser and failed to incorporate the obligation to purchase the property in compliance with section 2 of the Act.

(vi) *Non-compliance* with formality requirements renders the contract void or unenforceable; this can *cause hardship*. In *Actionstrength Ltd v International Glass Engineering* (2003), the House of Lords (at [6]) denied enforcement to an oral contract of guarantee, but with regret because of the harsh consequences, particularly since this 'was not a bargain struck between inexperienced people, liable to misunderstand what they were doing . . . These were not small men in need of paternalist protection'. Moreover, it was doubtful that the parties appreciated that their agreement would be construed as a guarantee. In *Pitt v Jones* (2007), an unmeritorious party escaped his obligations because he gave a guarantee to minority shareholders which he refused to put in writing as was required by section 4 of the Statute of Frauds 1677. The agreement was therefore unenforceable. Lady Justice Smith (at [39]) reached this conclusion 'with some reluctance'. Her Ladyship saw much merit in the claimants' position and found the defendant's stance 'most unattractive'.

This potential injustice caused to a party who has detrimentally relied on the validity of an unenforceable contract was historically mitigated by the *doctrine of part performance*. It made a non-complying contract enforceable if one party had induced or knowingly allowed the other party to alter his or her position on the faith of the contract; it was considered a fraud to rely on the formalities requirements (*Wakeham v MacKenzie* (1968)). Unsurprisingly, the doctrine was perceived to undermine the formalities requirements. **The Law of Property (Miscellaneous Provisions) Act 1989** swung the pendulum firmly the other way. It requires contracts for the sale or other disposition of an interest in land to be '*made* in writing' and not merely '*evidenced* in writing'. Non-compliance with the Act means that *no contract comes into existence* to be partly performed; the doctrine of part-performance has nothing to apply to. However, section 2(5) of the 1989 Act specifically preserves 'the creation or operation of resulting, implied or constructive trusts' (ie proprietary solutions) to mitigate the potential injustice of the formalities requirements. On the one hand, there is a stronger emphasis on certainty; in *Yaxley v Gotts* (2000) Robert Walker LJ said (at 175) that the 1989 Act:

> [c]an be seen as embodying Parliament's conclusion, in the general public interest, that the need for certainty as to the formation of contracts of this type must in general outweigh the disappointment of those who make informal bargains in ignorance of the statutory requirement. If an estoppel would have the effect of enforcing a void contract and subverting Parliament's purpose it may have to yield to the statutory law which confronts it, except so far as the statute's saving for a constructive trust provides a means of reconciliation of the apparent conflict.

Conversely, Beldam LJ stated (at 193) that the 'social policy of simplifying conveyancing by requiring the certainty of a written document' does not mean 'that unconscionable conduct or equitable fraud should be allowed to prevail'.

3.2.3 **Online contracts**

In response to the increasing prevalence of online contracting, Article 9 of the EC Directive on Electronic Commerce (2000/31/EC) requires Member States not to create obstacles to the creation of contracts by electronic means. Section 8 of the Electronic Communications Act 2000 empowers the relevant minister to modify existing legislation to authorise the use of electronic communications to comply with formalities requirements. The Law Commission regards this as unnecessary since electronic communications will generally satisfy such requirements.[32] Indeed, in *Golden Ocean Group v Salgaocar Mining Industries* (2011), Christopher Clarke J held that an agreement concluded by a long sequence of emails satisfied the writing requirements of section 4 of the Statute of Frauds Act 1677.

However, given the cautionary and protective functions of formalities, it would be undesirable to allow electronic contracts to be made too easily. In *Caton v Caton* (1867) the House of Lords held (at 139) that, to constitute a signature, a name must be inserted 'in such a manner as to have the effect of "authenticating the instrument" or "so as to govern the whole agreement"'. In *Pereira Fernandes SA v Mehta* (2006), Judge Pelling QC held that an email sent by M's staff (at M's request) offering to guarantee his company's debt and accepted orally by the creditor satisfied the memorandum, but not the signature, requirement of section 4 of the Statute of Frauds 1677. M's email address was automatically inserted by the Internet Service Provider and his name did not appear in the body of the email. It is 'a clear example of the inclusion of a name which is incidental . . . Its appearance divorced from the main body of the text of the message emphasises this to be so . . . To conclude . . . [otherwise would] have widespread and wholly unintended legal and commercial effects' (at [30]). Thus (at [27]):

> a party can sign a document . . . by using his full name or his last name prefixed by some or all of his initials or using his initials, and possibly by using a pseudonym or a combination of letters and numbers . . . providing always that whatever was used was inserted into the document in order to give, and with the intention of giving, authenticity to it. Its inclusion must have been intended as a signature for these purposes.

A Scottish Law Commission report (*Review of Contract Law, Report on Formation of Contract: Execution in Counterpart* (Scot Law Com No 231, 2013)) concludes that an electronic document repository would be a very useful development in the practice of Scottish law and proposes changes, some of which are aimed at facilitating the use of electronic media to form contracts.

3.3 **Promissory estoppel**

'Your undertaking induced my reliance'

In a contractual setting, one party can say or do something that induces the other to act to its detriment. Undertakings that induce *reliance* may be enforceable via the doctrine of promissory estoppel (also known as 'equitable estoppel'), *even absent consideration or formality*. Promissory estoppel is one application of the broader equitable principle of estoppel which is 'a principle of justice and of equity',[33] one which is

---

[32] *Electronic Commerce: Formal Requirements in Commercial Contracts* (2001), para 3.43.
[33] Lord Denning in *Moorgate Mercantile Co Ltd v Twitchings* (1976) at 241.

'perhaps the most powerful and flexible instrument to be found in any system of court jurisprudence'.[34] Cooke gives a taste of the varieties of estoppel.

- 'If your bank pays money into your account by mistake, it may be estopped from telling you later that it is not yours and demanding repayment—but only if it has assured you that the money is yours, and you have relied on that by spending the money.' This is **estoppel by representation** (see 3.3.2.1).

- 'The parties to a commercial deal might agree: "we'll treat clause 2 as meaning such-and-such"; if they go ahead with the deal on that basis, they have to abide by that agreement if the construction of the document is disputed later.' This is **estoppel by convention** (see 3.3.2.3 (i)).

- A son who invites his elderly mother to build and live in a 'granny flat' on his land may be prevented from ejecting her when relations sour. This is **proprietary estoppel** (see 3.3.2.3(i)).

- 'A landlord might reassure his or her tenant: "I will not insist that you pay for the roof repairs, even though your lease obliges you to do so"; he or she may then be estopped from going back on that promise and demanding payment.' This is **promissory estoppel**.

Although liability under this doctrine arises in the contractual context, it is a matter of debate whether the liability generated is *contractual* or *tortious* in nature. The source of the debate is the apparent lack of fit between its justification and its remedial response. Promissory estoppel is based on the protection of *reliance*, yet its effect is often to hold the promisor to his or her promise, thus protecting the promisee's **expectation**. Birks supports this contractual view:[35] 'The word "stop" in the middle [of estoppel] gives a clue. The French original means "bung" or "stopper" . . . As a wine bottle is corked, so one is restricted or shut up. In short, one is bound . . . In most estoppels the thing in question is an undertaking, and in equitable [or promissory] estoppel it is an undertaking as to the future or, in short, a promise.' Likewise, Cooke explains that: 'Estoppel is a mechanism for enforcing **consistency**; when I have said or done something that leads you to believe in a particular state of affairs, I may be obliged to stand by what I have said or done, even though I am not contractually bound to do so.'[36] On this view, estoppel is an *alternative* (to consideration) to the *contractual* enforcement of undertakings. In **'Estoppel and the Protection of Expectation'** (1997) 17 *LS* 258, **Cooke** argues that proprietary and promissory estoppel are and should be aimed at fulfilling expectation unless this would be inappropriate or there is unjust enrichment. Protection of reliance would confuse and emasculate the law of estoppel, conflict with the law of contract, and is an inappropriate way to supplement the doctrine of consideration. In **'The Remedial Discretion in Proprietary Estoppel'** (1999) 115 *LQR* 353, **Gardner** concedes that the presumptive remedy in proprietary estoppel cases is expectation based, but notes that this may be varied to take account

---

[34] Lord Wright in *Canada and Dominion Sugar Co Ltd v Canadian National (West Indies) Steamships Ltd* (1947) at 55.

[35] P Birks, 'Equity in the Modern Law: An Exercise in Taxonomy' (1996) 26 *UWALR* 1, 21–2.

[36] E Cooke, *The Modern Law of Estoppel* (OUP, 2000) 1–2.

of the parties' misbehaviour. However, Gardner argues that the true explanation is that the remedy is based on a notion of what the parties' respective property rights *ought* to be given the nature of their *family* obligations, and that these might be more satisfactorily dealt with if they were treated explicitly upon that basis.

The competing view is that estoppel is **reliance**-based because of: (i) the basic rationale; (ii) the nature of its requirements; and (iii) its *potential* for less than contractual enforcement. These are discussed below.

3.3.1 The requirements of promissory estoppel

The foundation for the modern development of promissory estoppel was laid by the House of Lords in **Hughes v Metropolitan Railway Co** (1877). H, the landlord, gave notice to M, the tenant, requiring M to carry out certain repairs within six months. M asked whether H wished to purchase M's interest in the premises and suggested that repairs be deferred pending negotiations. The House of Lords gave M relief against forfeiture for failing to make the repairs within the original time frame because H's conduct had induced M to believe that the time period would stop 'running' during the negotiations. Thus, the six months only ran from the point that negotiations broke down. To allow H to enforce his original rights would be inequitable, although their Lordships found that H had 'no intention here to take advantage of, to lay a trap for, or to lull into false security those with whom he was dealing' (at 448; ie there was no bad faith).

Hughes was applied by Denning J in *Central London Property Ltd v High Trees House Ltd* (1947). C let a block of flats in London to H on a 99-year lease for £2,500 per year. In 1940, the outbreak of war and the evacuation of people from London meant that H could not sublet enough of the flats to cover the rent. C agreed to accept half the rent. In 1945, when the war ended, the property market returned to normal and the flats were fully let. C requested H to resume paying the original rent, but H refused. Denning J held that C was entitled to demand the entire rent *from the date of their notice* in 1945. That is, had C sought it, C would have been estopped (prevented) from claiming *back payment* of the rent forgone between 1940 and 1945.

The **requirements** of promissory estoppel are that:

(i) *A* makes a clear promise to *B*;

(ii) *B* acts in reliance on it; and

(iii) it would be inequitable for *A* to resile from the promise.

The **effect** of promissory estoppel is:

(iv) generally suspensory and not extinctive (ie it only extinguishes *A*'s entitlement up to the end of *A*'s reasonable notice to *B* of *A*'s intention to resume his or her rights, but not *A*'s future entitlements unless justice demands);

(v) the application of promissory estoppel is generally **restricted** to relieving promises. It can only prevent *A* from fully enforcing his or her previous rights against *B*; it cannot confer new or additional rights on *B*. Thus, the doctrine is said to act defensively, not offensively; it is a 'shield, but not as a sword'.

Diagram 3E compares promissory estoppel with consideration. In contrast to promissory estoppel, the presence of consideration makes the promise *fully* enforceable, *irrespective* of reliance, the justice of enforcement, and whether the promise relieves from some pre-existing obligation or confers new or additional rights.

How do the consideration and promissory estoppel doctrines interact? We have noted that:

- both doctrines broadly answer the same question (ie the enforceability of promises), so that their relationship depends on their relative *scope*;
- the scope of *consideration* is potentially very wide because its definitions are many and unstable, and the courts have considerable latitude in determining whether it is present;
- the wider the scope and effect of *promissory estoppel*, the more likely it is to challenge consideration as the key determinant of enforcement. The key lies in the answer to two questions, namely:

   (i) Is and should the *effect* of promissory estoppel be contractual (in enforcing the *full* expectation, as consideration does; if so, promissory estoppel directly undermines consideration) or merely reliance based (3.3.1.4)?

   (ii) To which *types of promises* can promissory estoppel apply: only relieving promises (as currently prescribed), or should it be extended to promises which create or add new rights (this would impinge more directly on consideration, see 3.3.3)?

Diagram 3E Comparison of promissory estoppel and consideration

A. Promissory estoppel	B. Consideration
(1) Clear promise	**Clear promise**
(2) Reliance (or change of position) by promisee; need not be requested but must be foreseeable by or known to promisor.	Promisee must have given **consideration** which may consist of requested reliance. Promise enforceable **without reliance**.
(3) Inequitable to resile: by reference to (1), (2) above and subsequent events.	**Irrelevant** short of vitiating factors (see Part III) with high thresholds.
(4) Suspensory and not extinctive: ie promisee may not be awarded full expectation; the promisor can resume his original rights on giving reasonable notice to the extent that the promisee can resume his original position.	Enforcement of **full expectation** (ie can be extinctive).
(5) Shield not sword: only operates as a defence to enforce promises to accept less. Cannot create or add new rights. ***Is reform desirable to allow the creation or addition of new rights?***	**Shield and sword:** can operate as defence to enforce promises to accept less and to create or add new rights.

3.3.1.1 A clear relieving promise

First, there must be a clear and unequivocal promise which indicates the promisor's intention not to insist on his or her strict legal rights against the promisee (*Woodhouse v Nigerian Produce Marketing Co Ltd* (1974)). As *Hughes* demonstrates, the promise need not be express but may be *implied* from the circumstances. No estoppel arises if the language is qualified or imprecise (eg a statement made 'without prejudice': *IMT Shipping v Chansung Shipping Co* (2009)). Silence or inaction in the face of a breach will not normally estop a party from suing on the breach. A party does not lose his or her rights simply because he or she has failed throughout to insist upon strict performance.[37] In *Legione v Hately* (1982), the statement: 'I think that'll be alright, but I'll have to get instructions' did not amount to a promise that an extension would be given.

3.3.1.2 Reliance: change of position

Second, the promisee must have *relied* on the promise or representation. This is conventionally understood as requiring *detrimental*[38] reliance in the sense that, if the promise is revoked, the promisee will be *worse off* than he or she was before the promise was made. Harm to the promisee is the main reason why it may be inequitable for the promisor to resile (see 3.3.1.3). In *Hughes v Metropolitan Railway Co*, we saw that the tenant relied on the landlord's implied promise to 'stop the clock' during negotiations by not carrying out timely repairs. If the landlord could renege on his promise, the tenant's failure to make timely repairs would have resulted in the forfeiture of its lease.

It is rather more difficult to find detrimental reliance in *High Trees*, where the landlord simply promised to accept half the rent; indeed, none was identified in the decision. Nevertheless, analogous to the defence of *change of position* in the law of unjust enrichment, where a promisee has, or can be presumed to have, committed him or herself to a course of action which he or she would not otherwise have adopted, such that he or she would be prejudiced if the promisor were to resile from the promise, this is sufficient for reliance (*The Post Chaser* (1982) at 701). The lessee's reliance in *High Trees* can be seen to take the form of 'loss of opportunity' to rearrange its financial affairs by renegotiating the lease, seeking alternative finance, or declaring itself bankrupt. Reliance can also take the form of dissipating the money saved by paying other expenses. In a very real sense, the lessee is worse off in having to find five years of back rent immediately (£7,910) than if it had budgeted on the basis of paying the full rent from the start. The nub is the promisee's *inability to resume his or her original position* due to the reliance.

The corollary is that, if he or she *can* resume their original position, or can resume their liability on reasonable notice (as in *High Trees*), there is no inequity in resiling from the promise either completely or for the future, as the case may be. Notice serves to halt reliance. In *The Post Chaser*, the sellers of palm-oil delayed in handing over certain documents in breach of contract. The buyer waived this breach, but then rejected the oil when its sub-buyer rejected it. The seller's claim for damages against the buyer failed because it was not inequitable for the buyer to enforce its original right since the seller was not prejudiced by it.

---

[37] *Société Italo-Belge pour le Commerce et l'Industrie SA v Palm & Vegetable Oils (Malaysia) Sdn Bhd (The Post Chaser)* (1982) at 700.

[38] Eg *United Overseas Bank Ltd v Jiwani* (1976).

A radical departure is signalled by *Collier v P & M J Wright (Holdings) Ltd* (2008). There, C was jointly liable for a debt to W with two former business partners. W told C to pay his one-third and said he would pursue the other debtors for their share. On the partners' bankruptcy, W sued C for the whole sum. The Court of Appeal found a triable issue on promissory estoppel, but only by heavily diluting its requirements. In particular, it held that:

- C's 'reliance' can be satisfied by making part-payment of his debt,
- *that* reliance makes it inequitable for W to resile from his promise, and
- the effect is to extinguish W's rights altogether.

Arden LJ concluded (at [42]) that if:

(1) a debtor offers to pay part only of the amount he owes; (2) the creditor voluntarily accepts that offer, and (3) in reliance on the creditor's acceptance the debtor pays that part of the amount he owes in full, the creditor will, by virtue of the doctrine of promissory estoppel, be bound to accept that sum in full and final satisfaction of the whole debt. For him to resile will of itself be inequitable. In addition, in these circumstances, the promissory estoppel has the effect of extinguishing the creditor's right to the balance of the debt. This part of our law originated in the brilliant obiter dictum of Denning J in the *High Trees* case [1947] KB 130. To a significant degree it achieves in practical terms the recommendation of the Law Revision Committee chaired by Lord Wright MR in 1937.

Strictly speaking, the Court of Appeal only held that there was a *triable issue* on promissory estoppel; unfortunately, Arden LJ's approach has not been tested on the facts at full trial; the case was probably settled.

👤 Pause for reflection

1. Arden LJ found reliance, although she noted (at [19]) that the lower court found it 'difficult to see any sufficient relevant alteration of position on the part of Mr Collier, rendering it inequitable for the creditor now to resile from its alleged promise'. Neither C's continuing to make the payments that he was already making, nor his 'wild speculation' that he could otherwise have pursued the other creditors amounted 'to anything rendering it unconscionable on the part of the creditor now to pursue Mr Collier for the full amount of the debt'. Indeed, her Ladyship agreed (at [36]) that 'there is no evidence that Mr Collier's position now is in any material respect different from that immediately before the agreement was made'.

2. Longmore LJ was less than enthusiastic in his endorsement of this position. Although he conceded that *D&C Builders Ltd v Rees* (1966) could be interpreted in this way, he thought that there was 'much to be said on the other side'. He said that if this position is sustained courts should be slow to find a promise to forgo rights in the first place (at [47], [48]).

3. *D&C Builders Ltd v Rees* (1966) is rather weak precedent for the proposition in *Collier v Wright*. Promissory estoppel did *not* apply on the facts. All three judges applied *Foakes v Beer*. The fact that part-payment was actually made did not, on the facts, make the modification enforceable.

3.3.1.3 Inequitable to go back on the promise

The third requirement of promissory estoppel is that it must be 'inequitable' for the promisor to go back on his or her promise. This is usually, but not always, satisfied by the promisee's reliance (change of position). But inequity is an *independent* requirement and considers other factors such as the following.

(i) The *time lag* before the promisor asserts his or her original right and the degree of *prejudice to the promisee*: there was no inequity in resiling in *The Post Chaser* where the promisor reasserted its legal right just two days later and the promisee *could be restored* to its original position.

(ii) The *circumstances surrounding the relieving promise*: there was no inequity in resiling in *D&C Builders v Rees*, because the promisee had extracted the promise to accept a lesser sum by threatening non-payment in bad faith.

(iii) Events *subsequent to the making of the promise*: in *Williams v Stern* (1879), a creditor promised a debtor extra time to pay before he exercised his right to seize the debtor's furniture, but he reneged when he heard that the debtor's landlord was about to seize the same assets for unpaid rent. The creditor's conduct was not inequitable. Similarly, if *A* excuses *B* from part of his or her obligations for a particular reason (eg because of labour shortages or price rise of raw materials), it may not be inequitable for *A* to renege if a subsequent change of circumstances eliminates the reason for the promise, at least if *A* gives sufficient notice. Recall *Re Selectmove*, where a company challenged an order for its compulsory winding up on the petition of the Revenue, to which the company owed arrears and taxes. The company argued that the Revenue had given it extra time to pay. However, the court found that since the company had failed to pay the instalments even with extra time, it was not inequitable or unfair for the Revenue to demand immediate payment of all the arrears, and to present a winding-up petition to enforce the debt.

3.3.1.4 The extent of enforcement: suspensory or extinctive?

The effect of promissory estoppel is generally said to be suspensory and not extinctive of the promisor's original rights; the promisor may, on giving due notice, assert his or her original rights (***Tool Metal Manufacturing Co Ltd v Tungsten Electric Co Ltd*** (1955)). In other words, the relief contained in the relieving promise may be *temporary* or may be terminated by notice, *if* the promisee can resume his or her original position. The corollary is that promissory estoppel can *extinguish* part or all of the promisor's existing rights if the promisee cannot resume his or her position (***Ajayi v RT Briscoe (Nigeria) Ltd*** (1964) at 1330).

The real issue is not whether promissory estoppel suspends or extinguishes the original right, but rather what is necessary to ensure that the promisee is not prejudiced by his or her reliance on the promise. This may require:

- total extinction of the original right—in *Hughes v Metropolitan Railway Co*, the landlord's implied promise was merely to suspend his right to *timely* repairs (ie stop time running) during their negotiations, and *this* right *was* extinguished because it was impossible for the tenant to wind the clock back;

- partial extinction of the original right—in *High Trees*, the lessors were permitted to revert to the full rent on giving reasonable notice, but would not have been entitled to demand the rent waived up to that point. The right to those payments *was* extinguished; or
- no effect to be given to the promise—in *The Post Chaser*, the promisee could resume its original position.

The potential for the promisor to reassert his or her original rights under promissory estoppel shows that it is not primarily an instrument for the enforcement of a promise, but one for preventing injustice to the promisee by protecting reasonable reliance.

3.3.2 The types of promise subject to promissory estoppel

English law treats promissory estoppel as a '**shield but not a sword**'. It only applies where there is *a pre-existing contractual or other legal relationship* between the parties, and one party promises to give up some of his or her rights under that relationship. Promissory estoppel operates *defensively* (to prevent the promisor from enforcing the original rights he or she has relinquished); it cannot operate *offensively* (to give the promisee an action for more than his or her original rights as in the *Williams v Roffey* situation, or a *new* cause of action where the parties have no pre-existing legal relationship). In short, promissory estoppel:

✓ *can* enforce promises of '*same for less*';

✗ *cannot* enforce promises of '*more for the same*'; and

✗ *cannot* create *new* legal rights independent of the parties' pre-existing legal relationship.

Although courts have permitted *claimants*, rather than defendants, to appeal to promissory estoppel, so that it can be said to operate as a sword,[39] it only does so to prevent the defendant *promisor* from relying on a defence which (but for his or her promise not to rely on it) would have defeated the promisee's claim (eg the defence that the promisee's claim is time-barred, or satisfied). The crucial point is that the claimant promisee's cause of action arises *independently* of the promise being enforced by promissory estoppel.

The reason for these restrictions is to *avoid undermining consideration as the primary test of contractual liability*. If a promise could be enforced simply because of the promisee's reliance, this would blow a great hole in the boundary of contractual liability put up by the doctrine of consideration. Lord Denning said in *Combe v Combe* (at 220) that 'the doctrine of consideration is too firmly fixed to be overthrown by a side wind'.

Diagram 3F helps map the roles of consideration and promissory estoppel in the enforcement of contract modifications.

---

[39] See R Halson, 'The Offensive Limits of Promissory Estoppel' [1999] *LMCLQ* 256, 259–61.

Diagram 3F Contract modifications: the role of consideration and promissory estoppel

| | | ✓ is operative |
| | | ✗ is inoperative |

Enforceability of	Via consideration?	Via promissory estoppel?
(1) Promises to accept less	(1a) ✓ Legal benefit ✗ Practical benefit	(1b) ✓
(2) Promises to give more	(2a) ✓ Legal benefit ✓ Practical benefit	(2b) ✗

3.3.2.1 Promises to accept less

A agrees to build ten shelves for *B* by a certain date for £5,000. Subsequently, *A* says that he or she will have difficulty performing on time, and *B* allows *A* to deliver only seven shelves for the same price (this relieving promise is represented by **(1)** in Diagram 3F).

Relieving or 'subtracting' promises are enforceable only if supported by **consideration (1a)** in the form of *legal* (but not practical) benefit or detriment. But absent consideration, a relieving promise may, via **promissory estoppel (1b)**, operate as a *defence* against the promisor's enforcement of his or her original rights. Here, promissory estoppel *cuts back* the promisor's original rights. *Hughes v Metropolitan Railway Co* and *High Trees* are ready examples of the defensive function of promissory estoppel.

Promissory estoppel appears to contradict the rule in *Foakes v Beer* that promises to accept the same for less are unenforceable for want of legal consideration. Indeed, in *Collier v Wright*, Arden LJ approves Denning J's statement (in *High Trees* at 135) that 'the logical consequence' of promissory estoppel 'is that a promise to accept a smaller sum in discharge of a larger sum, if acted upon, is binding notwithstanding the absence of consideration'. However, the apparent contradiction disappears if it is understood that consideration yields the *full* enforcement of the subtracting promise (*permanently extinguishing* the promisor's original rights), while promissory estoppel should only reduce the promisor's original rights when it would be inequitable for the promisor to renege on his or her promise and *to the extent necessary to protect the promisee's reliance*. The defensive function of promissory estoppel is mirrored in two related doctrines.

(i) Someone who makes a representation of an *existing fact* which induces another's *detrimental reliance* is permanently prevented from proving facts contrary to his or her representation, by the doctrine of **estoppel by representation**. In *Avon CC v Howlett* (1983), A could not recover a mistaken payment to an employee H because of its representation to H that he was entitled to the money and H had spent the money in reliance upon the representation. The estoppel operated as a 'shield' to defeat a claim which would otherwise have succeeded.

(ii) The doctrine of **waiver** applies to statements of *intention* to forgo the speaker's strict legal rights against the addressee. In **WJ Alan & Co Ltd v El Nasr Export and Import Co** (1972), a contract for the sale of coffee required payment by irrevocable letter of credit. A non-conforming letter of credit was provided but the seller did not complain and drew on the credit. The Court of Appeal held that the seller had waived its strict legal rights, where waiver is practically indistinguishable from promissory estoppel. Lord Denning said (at 623) in *Charles Rickards Ltd v Oppenheim* (1950) that: 'Whether it be called waiver or forbearance on his part, or an agreed variation or substituted performance, does not matter . . . It is a particular application of the principle . . . in *Central London Property Trust Ltd v High Trees House Ltd*.' In *Brikom Investments Ltd v Carr* (1979), Lord Denning applied promissory estoppel, whilst Roskill and Cumming-Bruce LJJ treated the case as one of waiver; all agreed that the promise not to enforce certain terms of the lease should be enforced. Waiver also operates as a shield and not a sword, but its effect (like promissory estoppel) could enable an independent claim to succeed which would otherwise fail. For example, in *Hickman v Haynes* (1875) the buyer of goods asked the seller to delay delivery but then refused to accept the goods claiming that the seller had breached by late delivery. The court allowed the seller's damages claim against the buyer because the buyer had waived his right to demand timely delivery and could not subsequently reassert it without giving reasonable notice.

3.3.2.2 Promises to give more

A agrees to build ten shelves for *B* by a certain date for £5,000. Subsequently, *A* says he or she cannot complete the job for the agreed price and *B* agrees to pay him or her an extra £1,000.

Diagram 3F row **(2)** shows that the law adopts an inconsistent approach to that applied to subtracting promises (to accept less for the same, see 3.3.2.1):

- adding promises are enforceable if supported by **consideration**, in the sense of legal or *practical* benefit (*Williams v Roffey*, see 3.1.5.3). Recall that only *legal* benefit is sufficient to enforce subtracting promises (*Foakes v Beer* at 3.1.5.4, and compare **(1a)** with **(2a)** in **Diagram 3F**);

- adding promises *cannot* be enforced via **promissory estoppel** (*Williams v Roffey* at 17–18), while subtracting promises *can* (compare **(1b)** with **(2b)** in **Diagram 3F**).

In short, while promissory estoppel can enforce *subtracting promises*, practical benefit cannot and, while practical benefit can enforce *adding promises*, promissory estoppel cannot.

Pause for reflection

1. *Consistency and justice*: there is no logical justification for the law's inconsistent approach. There is no functional difference between a promise to 'pay more' or to 'accept less' than under the pre-existing contract. In both cases, the promisor is getting *proportionately* 'less' than his or her original entitlement, and the promisee is getting 'more'. If the promisee's reliance on subtracting promises is worthy of protection, so should his or her reliance on adding promises. It should not matter whether the promise is the claimant or the defendant. In *Williams v Roffey*, Russell LJ said (at 17) that he 'would have welcomed' an estoppel argument to the effect that it would be unconscionable to allow the defendants to renege on their promise. However, the expansion of consideration to include practical benefit removes the incentive to extend promissory estoppel in this way.

2. *Transparency, flexibility, and accuracy*: promissory estoppel permits greater transparency, flexibility, and accuracy in balancing the competing policies than the notion of practical benefit as consideration.

    (i) Promissory estoppel can openly assess *whether* a modifying promise should be enforced by reference to the circumstances prompting the parties' renegotiation, the promisee's conduct in inducing the modification (any pressure applied or tricks played), the reasonableness of the modification, and any subsequent change in the circumstances of the parties. *In contrast*, the doctrine of consideration asks whether the promisor obtained a practical benefit and, if so, whether duress taints the transaction.

    (ii) Promissory estoppel can determine the *extent* of appropriate enforcement of the modifying promise to protect the promisee's change of position in reliance on the promise. *In contrast*, consideration and duress yield an all-or-nothing response—once consideration is found, adding promises are *fully* enforceable (at least in theory, for, as we saw, the actual award in *Williams v Roffey* seemed to be based on the extent of the promisee's actual performance, and hence to resemble the reliance-based response of promissory estoppel) (see 3.1.5.3(vi)). But, if duress is found, the promise is totally unenforceable.

3.3.2.3 Promises that create or add more rights

If there is a good case for extending the operation of promissory estoppel from subtracting promises to adding promises, should promissory estoppel also be able to enforce an entirely new cause of action in the absence of a pre-existing legal relationship between the parties? Recall **Combe v Combe**, where a husband promised, but did not pay, his wife £100 a year upon divorce. She claimed the arrears after six years, pointing to her reliance on the promise by not applying for maintenance payments. The court held that: (i) the wife's reliance was not requested by the husband and so was not good consideration (see 3.1.2.2); and (ii) promissory estoppel did not apply because it could not create new causes of action where none existed before. This avoids undermining consideration as the primary test of contractual liability. However, if the nub of promissory estoppel is the promisor's unconscionability (in inducing the promisee's reliance on his or her promise and then reneging on it), it should not matter whether or not there is a pre-existing legal relationship between the parties.

Three reasons support the expansion of promissory estoppel to *create* new causes of action.

(i) Other estoppels can create new causes of action

Where the parties to a transaction have acted upon a common assumption (of fact or of law, whether resulting from mistake or misrepresentation), **estoppel by convention** prevents either party from denying that common assumption.

> ✓ In *Amalgamated Investment and Property Co v Texas Commerce International Bank Ltd* (1982), T's subsidiary made loans to A's subsidiary. T and A contracted on the common assumption that A was guaranteeing *that* loan; in fact, the wording of the guarantee only covered loans made *by* T itself (of which there were none). A's liquidators unsuccessfully sought a declaration that A had no such liability. A was estopped from denying that the guarantee was for the loan by T's subsidiary. On the facts, T used the estoppel as a shield to A's claim for a declaration; however, Lord Denning (and arguably Brandon LJ) held that T could have *sued on the guarantee* to recover the sum (ie creating a cause of action). Anyway, since the guarantee did not literally cover the relevant loan, in substance T's right to the sum (whether claiming or keeping it) was founded on estoppel. Brandon LJ stated (at 131–2) that while no one can 'found a cause of action on an estoppel, he may, as a result of being able to rely on an estoppel, succeed on a cause of action on which, without being able to rely on that estoppel, he would necessarily have failed'. The qualification can swallow the rule.

Proprietary estoppel can found a cause of action. The typical scenario is that *A* the landowner 'stands by' ('acquiescence'), while *B* incurs detriment in reliance on *A*'s promise that he or she has, or will get, an interest in *A*'s land.

> ✓ In *Pascoe v Turner* (1979), P and T lived together for some years. When P left T for another woman, he told T that the house and everything in it was hers. After T spent £230 on repairs, P sued for possession of the house. T successfully counterclaimed for a declaration that the house and its contents were hers. Although T gave no consideration for P's promise, she had acted to her detriment in reliance on his promise and this created a *new* cause of action. The decision goes beyond reversing unjust enrichment; the promisee's claim was not limited to the value of her work (a *quantum meruit*). She received the whole promise.

> ✓ Where it succeeds, proprietary estoppel does not always enforce the promise in full. More limited relief may be granted. In *Inwards v Baker* (1965), the promisee (who was induced by his father to build a bungalow on his father's land, but the land was left to another on the father's death) was simply allowed to stay on the property for as long as he wished.

> ✓ In *Crabb v Arun DC* (1976), A promised C, an adjoining landowner, a second right of way from a portion of A's land and erected gates for two access points. In reliance on this, C sold the portion of his land with the existing access, but A closed off the second access point, thereby locking in the land that C retained.

A demanded £3,000 from C for the access. The Court of Appeal held that it would be inequitable to allow A to renege on its promise when this had induced C's detrimental reliance. Since A's conduct had 'sterilised' C's land for several years, the court granted the right of way without payment but said that, in an appropriate case, the promisee would be required to pay its fair value.

Promissory estoppel can also assist the promisee as claimant in that it may prevent the promisor from relying on a defence that would, but for the promise, have been available to him or her: for example, the defence that a claim which the promisee has made against him or her is time-barred (*Nippon Yusen Kaisha v Pacifica Navegacion SA (The Ion)* (1980)).

(ii) Differences in restriction unprincipled

It is difficult to justify the inconsistent answers to the questions of whether estoppel can create a cause of action and what the appropriate remedy should be. There have been calls to unify the various estoppels.[40] However, it has also been cautioned that the differences are established as a matter of authority and reflect the different contexts in which they are applied.[41] Lord Goff, in *Johnson v Gore Wood & Co (A Firm)* (2001) at 100, was 'inclined to think that the many circumstances capable of giving rise to an estoppel cannot be accommodated within a single formula'. Nevertheless, he acknowledged that 'it is unconscionability which provides the link between them'.

 Pause for reflection

If there is an overarching principle linking different estoppels,[42] then a piecemeal approach seems difficult to justify. The appeal to *precedent* is an assertion that the differences 'just *are*'. The appeal to *contextual* differences does not explain why reliance on promises conferring interests in *land* can create a cause of action, but reliance on *other* promises cannot. Whilst the promisee's reliance on promises relating to land may enrich the promisor, it does not invariably do so. Moreover, although it is arguable that land warrants special treatment because of its historical importance as a form of wealth, this would tend to point to the need for very strict guidelines to transfer rights in land (recall the formalities requirements) and not rest merely on reliance. Different manifestations of a common principle should not be allowed to ossify into different rules detached from the principle from which they were derived.

---

[40] Eg Lord Denning in *Amalgamated Investment & Property Co v Texas Commerce International Bank Ltd* at 122 and Oliver J in *Taylor Fashions Ltd v Liverpool Victoria Trustees* (1982) at 151–2.

[41] Lord Steyn said in *Republic of India v Indian Steamship Co Ltd (No 2)* (1997) at 830 that: 'to restate the law in terms of an overarching principle might tend to blur the necessarily separate requirements, and distinct terrain of application'. Mance LJ said in *Baird Textile Holdings v Marks & Spencer* at [84] that: 'not only are we bound in this court by previous authority on the scope of particular types of estoppel, but it seems to me inherent in the doctrine's very flexibility that it may take different shapes to fit the context of different fields'.

[42] In *Taylor Fashions Ltd v Liverpool Victoria Trustees* Oliver J said at 151–2 that the question is: 'whether . . . it would be unconscionable for a party to be permitted to deny that which, knowingly or unknowingly, he has allowed or encouraged another to assume to his detriment'.

(iii) Promissory estoppel and consideration rest on different bases
The most convincing reason for preventing promissory estoppel from creating a new cause of action is to avoid a direct clash with the requirement of consideration. However, there is no clash if we recognise that consideration and promissory estoppel are two distinct types of liability.

- **Consideration** yields a contractual cause of action for the enforcement of the promisee's *full expectation*.

- **Promissory estoppel** seeks to *avoid the detriment* arising from the promisee's reliance on the promise, if it would be inequitable for the promisor to renege.

This distinction is highlighted by the High Court of Australia in **Waltons Stores (Interstate) Ltd v Maher** (1988) (see also *Commonwealth of Australia v Verwayen* (1990)). M entered into negotiations to lease land to W for a major construction project. The plan required M to demolish the existing building on the site and erect a new building to W's specifications. Solicitors were instructed to prepare the formal documents. W's solicitors told M's solicitors that 'we believe that approval will be forthcoming. We shall let you know tomorrow if any amendments are not agreed to'. M signed the requisite documents, which were forwarded to W's solicitors for execution and exchange (to satisfy the formality requirement). Believing that they would shortly exchange and complete and because W's timetable required urgent action, M began demolishing the building on his land. Meanwhile, W had second thoughts and instructed their solicitors to 'go slow', although they knew that M had commenced work on the site. After two months, when M had completed a substantial amount of the work, W informed M of their intention to withdraw from the project. The court held that W was estopped from denying the existence of a contract. It rejected W's argument that since the parties had *no pre-existing legal relationship*, there was nothing for promissory estoppel to relieve from. Thus, **in Australia, promissory estoppel *can* create a cause of action**; it can act as a sword. But *Waltons Stores v Maher* makes it clear that enforcement via promissory estoppel rests on the 'creation or encouragement by the party estopped in the other party of an assumption *that a contract will come into existence* or a promise will be performed and that the other party relied on that assumption to his detriment to the knowledge of the first party' (at 406, emphasis added). The emphasised part is highlighted by Mance LJ in **Baird Textile Holdings v Marks & Spencer** (2002) at [98], who offers a more limited interpretation of *Waltons Stores v Maher* as a case involving:

> complete agreement on the terms of the lease. The agreement was merely unenforceable for want of compliance with the statute. It may be arguable that recognition of an estoppel here would not be to use estoppel 'as giving a cause of action in itself', and it would certainly not be to undermine the necessity of consideration. Rather, it would preclude the potential lessee from raising a collateral objection to the binding nature of the agreed lease.

On this view, promissory estoppel only bridges the gap in formalities and not in consideration. It entails no conflict with the consideration doctrine.

> ### Pause for reflection
>
> The Australian doctrine has been criticised for its uncertain scope. The doctrine is also difficult to reconcile with a number of fundamental principles of English law, such as that informal gratuitous promises (even if relied on) are unenforceable and that there is no right to damages for a wholly innocent non-contractual misrepresentation (see 5.2.1.1). In 'The Offensive Limits of Promissory Estoppel' [1999] *LMCLQ* 256, Halson argues that promissory estoppel should *not* create a new cause of action because:
>
> (i)   it would create uncertainty and conflict with contractual actions;
>
> (ii) it wrongly assumes that the disparate estoppel doctrines share a common purpose; in fact they have distinct policy objectives; and
>
> (iii) promissory estoppel has been developed particularly in the context of contract modifications, and this expertise and experience will be wasted if promissory estoppel is merged in a wider doctrine of estoppel.

3.3.2.4 The nature of any action created by promissory estoppel

If promissory estoppel could *create new actions*, the liability it generates can be classified as follows.

(i) **Contractual**: this is consonant with Atiyah's[43] pluralistic interpretation of 'consideration' encompassing any good reasons for contractual enforcement (see 3.1.6.3). Birks' analysis also locates liability in contract (see 3.3.1). He states that '[t]here is no other kind of unconscionable behaviour involved other than that which consists in failing to honour one's promises'.[44] *However*, it can be countered that the unconscionability is located in the promisor's *knowledge* that his or her conduct will induce the promisee's detrimental reliance. Moreover, *Waltons Stores v Maher* stresses that the *aim* is not to enforce the promise but, rather, to *avoid the detriment* occasioned by the promisee's reliance on the promise, although sometimes this will require full enforcement of the promise as in *Walton Stores* itself.

(ii) The preferable view is that promissory estoppel is most closely aligned to the law of **wrongs** (torts). The focus is on the promisor's reprehensible conduct which causes *harm* to the promisee. This view is consistent with the references to 'unconscionability' in the cases and the academic literature. Promissory estoppel is analogous to misrepresentation, which attracts reliance damages. Even an innocent misrepresentation puts the representor under a duty to correct the representee if he or she becomes aware of its falsity before contract formation. He or she cannot stand by while the representee detrimentally relies on their misrepresentation (see 5.1.3.2).

If the wrongdoing view implies a *reliance-based* response, how do we explain the cases that seem to enforce the promisee's *expectations*? In *Waltons Stores v Maher*, damages were awarded on the basis that the promisor was estopped from going back on the promise

---

[43] P S Atiyah, 'Consideration: A Restatement' in *Essays on Contract* (Clarendon Press, 1986) at 179.

[44] P Birks, 'Equity in the Modern Law: An Exercise in Taxonomy' (1996) 26 *UWALR* 1, 64.

that the contract would be completed (in effect, the expectation measure). One view is that expectation is, and should be, the normal remedy. The preferable view is that the *extent* of enforcement must follow from the *reasons* for enforcement. In **'Reliance and Expectation in the Estoppel Remedies'** (1998) 18 *LS* 360, **Robertson** argues that the expectation is sometimes awarded because that is the only way of fully protecting the promisee's *reliance* interest (which includes the loss of opportunity to make other contracts). Thus, the expectation measure is sometimes the best proxy for the reliance measure. This is readily understandable in *Waltons Stores*, when reliance comprises demolishing one's own building and erecting another to the promisor's specifications. The crucial point is that, on the wrong-doing-hence-reliance-damages view, if the expectation greatly exceeds the reliance, there is scope to award *less than the expectation* (see the Australian decision in *Giumelli v Giumelli* (1999) at [43]–[45]). This very possibility distinguishes promissory estoppel from consideration. Acceptance of the wrong-doing view of promissory estoppel eliminates any necessary conflict with the doctrine of consideration. The source of liability and the remedial response are different.

3.3.3 Future development of promissory estoppel

Currently, promissory estoppel can only relieve a party from his or her pre-existing obligations. Its operation can be extended in three ways.

(i) Extension to promises to comply with formalities

The narrowest extension is to promises to comply with *formalities* requirements in respect of an agreement *supported by consideration*, as per Mance LJ in *Baird Textile Holdings v Marks & Spencer* (2002). Here, promissory estoppel only bridges the gap in formalities requirements and not in consideration, which is still necessary.

(ii) Extension to promises to give more

A wider extension is to cover contract modifications that *add* to the promisee's rights. On this view, promissory estoppel *can* fill a consideration gap, but only in contract modifications. The latter qualification can be criticised: the underlying problem of unconscionability may be present, whether the promise relates to the formation or the modification of a contract, and whether it relates to rights in land or other subject matter.

(iii) Extension to the creation of new actions

The widest option is to follow the more expansive interpretation of *Waltons Stores v Maher*, and allow promissory estoppel to create new causes of action (in addition to enforcing the promises in options (i) and (ii)). Spence[45] persuasively argues in favour of a 'duty to ensure the reliability of induced assumptions'. To recognise such a duty would be a radical departure from the current law. It would take an unusually bold House of Lords to sweep aside *Combe v Combe* in favour of *Waltons Stores v Maher*. If it is minded to do so, the concern not to undermine consideration can be met by the following.

  (i) **Clarifying the requirements of promissory estoppel**: a clear and firm threshold should be maintained, for the lower the threshold, the closer we get to simply

---

[45] M Spence, *Protecting Reliance: the Emergent Doctrine of Equitable Estoppel* (Hart Publishing, 1999) 2–3.

saying that promises are enforceable without consideration. This is precisely the criticism of *Collier v Wright*—that by accepting part-performance as sufficient reliance which inevitably makes the promisor's resiling inequitable, it has gone too far.

(ii) **Emphasising the reliance basis of enforcement**: the crux of the distinction between consideration and estoppel is the potential difference in the *remedial response*—between enforcement of the full expectation and enforcement as necessary to negate detrimental reliance. This distinction should be more consciously acknowledged. Promissory estoppel should not be over-generous to the promisee: his or her expectation should only be protected when, exceptionally, it is the only way of protecting his or her reliance (as in *Crabb v Arun*). In contrast, *consideration buys* the *full* enforcement of the expectation.

If the distinct basis of promissory estoppel is accurately expressed in the requirements triggering the cause of action and the remedial response, its extension will not make consideration redundant. Promissory estoppel, as a route to a fundamentally different remedy, will merely *supplement* and not usurp consideration. Promissory estoppel is *contractual* in the sense that it arises in the context of contract formation or modification, but is *non-contractual* in nature; it does not, and should not, automatically lead to the full enforcement of promises. The current orthodoxy that promissory estoppel merely suspends and does not extinguish the promisor's original rights reinforces the logic that the doctrine confers *softer protection* on the promisee than bargain consideration. Promissory estoppel and consideration enforce promises for different reasons, and so will enforce them to a different extent.

THIS CHAPTER IN ESSENCE

The key areas and core topics in this chapter are summarised in an easy-to-use list, ideal for revision purposes, on the Online Resource Centre at http://www.oxfordtextbooks.co.uk/orc/chenwishart5e/. Links to websites relevant to the topics covered and any updates to the chapter can also be found on the Online Resource Centre.

QUESTIONS

1 Ivan agrees to build an elaborate stage and 20 kiosks for Jo's concert on 1 January for £25,000. Progress is worryingly slow. Ivan informs Jo that this is due to a severe labour shortage. Jo agrees to (a) increase his payment to £30,000 to enable Ivan to attract workers; and (b) reduce the number of kiosks to 15. For extraneous reasons, the labour supply improves rapidly; Ivan attracts enough workers without paying more. Jo decides that she really will need all 20 kiosks. Is Jo entitled to 20 kiosks? How much must Jo pay?

2 'The presence of consideration is a sufficient but not a necessary reason for treating a promise as binding. The outer boundaries of consideration are uncertain.' Is this true? What other good reasons, if any, might there be?

3 Advise the Law Commission whether reform of the consideration doctrine is necessary or desirable, outlining any suggestions you have for reform.

4 'It is vital that promissory estoppel remains a shield and not a sword to prevent it from outflanking the requirement of consideration.' Discuss.

5 What is the relationship between the doctrines of promissory estoppel and of consideration? What should it be?

 For hints on how to answer these questions, please see the Online Resource Centre at http://www.oxfordtextbooks.co.uk/orc/chenwishart5e/

KEY FURTHER READING

Atiyah, P S (1986), 'Consideration: A Restatement' in P S Atiyah, *Essays in Contract* (Clarendon Press) 179.

Barnes, M (2011), 'Estoppels as Swords', *LMCLQ* 372.

Chen-Wishart, M (1995), 'Consideration: Practical Benefit and the Emperor's New Clothes' in J Beatson and D Friedmann (eds), *Good Faith and Fault in Contract Law* (OUP) 123.

Chen-Wishart, M (2010), 'A Bird in the Hand: Consideration and Promissory Estoppel' in A Burrows and E Peel (eds), *Contract Formation and Parties* (OUP) 89.

Chen-Wishart, M (2013), 'In Defence of Consideration', 13 *OUCLJ* 209.

Cooke, E (1997), 'Estoppel and the Protection of Expectations', 17 *LS* 258.

Halson, R (1999), 'The Offensive Limits of Promissory Estoppel', *LMCLQ* 256.

Kötz, H, and Flessner, A (1997), *European Contract Law Volume One: Formation, Validity and Contents of Contracts; Contracts and Third Parties* (OUP) chs 4–5.

Treitel, G (1976), 'Consideration: A Critical Analysis of Professor Atiyah's Fundamental Restatement', 50 *Australian LJ* 439.

PART III

Privity

'Who can enforce and who is bound by the contract?'

INTRODUCTION

In Chapters 2 and 3 we examined how a contract is formed. Here we ask: whose legal position can be affected by a contract? A contract clearly alters the rights and liabilities of the contract parties: they are said to be privy to the contract. But what about someone who is not a contract party, a so-called 'third party' to the contract (hereafter 'TP')?

(i) Can a TP have *obligations* imposed on him or her by other people's contracts?

(ii) Can a TP *acquire enforceable rights* under other people's contracts?

At common law, the answer to both questions is 'no': only the contract parties can be entitled or bound by the contract; only they can sue and be sued on it. This is known as 'privity of contract'.

- The rule that contract parties *cannot impose obligations* on TPs is relatively obvious and uncontroversial, although not without exceptions (see 4.2). Such liability as there is focuses on the *wrongfulness* of a TP who knowingly interferes with the parties' *proprietary* rights acquired by a contract; such rights 'run with the property' and so are enforceable in kind and against everyone.

- The rule *against* conferring *enforceable* benefits or immunities on TPs is more controversial since it seems to: (i) contradict the contract parties' freedom to confer such benefits, and (ii) defeat the TP's reasonable expectation of such a right. The rule was always subject to numerous exceptions and avoidance devices, making this area of the law complicated and technical prior to the Contracts (Rights of Third Parties) Act 1999 (hereafter 'the 1999 Act'). This Act added a 'general and wide-ranging exception',[1] conferring enforceable rights on TPs. However, it has brought its own practical and conceptual difficulties. For example, the 1999 Act:
  - challenges some fundamental tenets of contract law, such as that claimants in contract actions must be *promisees* who have given *consideration*, and that damages compensate for the *promisee's loss*;

---

[1] Law Commission, *Privity of Contract: Contracts for the Benefit of Third Parties* (Law Com No 242, Cm 3329, 1996) at paras 5.16, 13.2.

- raises uncertainty as to the scope of the qualifying test for TP enforcement, and the circumstances when the contract parties are barred from changing their contract; and

- raises the question about *the relative priority of rights* where conflict arises between the interests of the TP and either (or both) of the contract parties.

The key question is 'whose loss is it?' when a contract conferring a benefit on a TP is breached by the promisor (is it the promisee or the TP)? The tensions in this area of the law arise out of our ambivalence over the answer to this question.

4

Privity

'Who can enforce and who is bound by the contract?'

The questions to be addressed are the following.

(i) What are the arguments *for*, and *against*, the general rule that only contract parties can sue on a contract?

(ii) What rights of enforcement does the Contracts (Rights of Third Parties) Act 1999 confer on a TP?

(iii) What is the impact of the 1999 Act on the requirement that a contract claimant must have given *consideration*?

(iv) To what extent can *a promisee* enforce a contract for the benefit of a TP?

(v) Aside from the 1999 Act, what legal avenues exist for *TPs to enforce* promises made for their benefit?

(vi) When and how does a contract *bind TPs*?

4.1 **Conferring benefits on third parties**

4.1.1 **The general rule**

The orthodox rule is that a party seeking to enforce a contractual promise must:

(i) be the promisee (ie the offeree who accepted the promise contained in the offer); *and*

(ii) have provided consideration for that promise.

Thus, in a contract where *A* promises *B* to give *C* £500 in exchange for *B*'s promise to paint *A*'s car, *C* cannot enforce *A*'s promise to pay him or her £500; *C* is not the promisee, nor has he or she given any consideration (see **Diagram 4A.1**).

The rule was established in ***Tweddle v Atkinson*** (1861). The fathers of an engaged couple contracted to pay a sum to the husband after the marriage. The court held that the husband could not enforce the contract against his wife's father even though the contract expressly stated that he could. Blackburn J said (at 764) that: 'in general no action can be maintained upon a promise, unless the consideration moves from the party to whom it is made' (see **Diagram 4A.2**).

The House of Lords in ***Dunlop Pneumatic Tyre Co Ltd v Selfridge*** (1915) agreed. Dunlop operated a price-fixing ring by selling tyres to a dealer (Dew) on terms that Dew: (i) would not sell below Dunlop's list price; and (ii) would obtain a written undertaking from anyone to whom they sold Dunlop products that they would not sell below Dunlop's list price. S bought Dunlop products from Dew, but sold them below Dunlop's list price. The court denied Dunlop's claim for an injunction and damages against S to enforce the price-fixing contract. Dew, and not Dunlop, had provided consideration for S's promise (see **Diagram 4A.3**). Viscount Haldane LC said that 'only a person who is a party to a contract can sue on it'. Dunlop could not enforce the promise for two separate reasons:

(i) Dunlop was not a party to the contract between Dew and S, and

(ii) Dunlop gave no consideration for S's promise as to selling price.

Diagram 4A Contracts for the benefit of third parties: illustrations

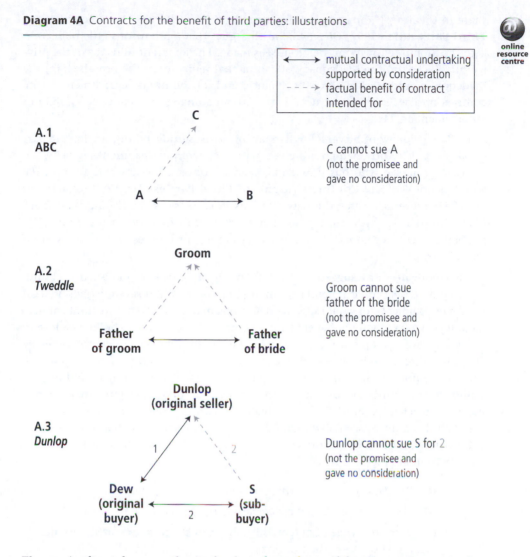

online
resource
centre

	mutual contractual undertaking supported by consideration
	factual benefit of contract intended for

A.1
ABC

C

A ⟷ B

C cannot sue A
(not the promisee and
gave no consideration)

A.2
Tweddle

Groom

**Father
of groom** ⟷ **Father
of bride**

Groom cannot sue
father of the bride
(not the promisee and
gave no consideration)

A.3
Dunlop

**Dunlop
(original seller)**

1   2

**Dew
(original
buyer)** ⟷ **S
(sub-
buyer)**
2

Dunlop cannot sue S for 2
(not the promisee and
gave no consideration)

The case is often taken as authority for the independence of the two requirements: that a contract claimant must: (i) be the promisee; *and* (ii) have given consideration for the promise.

4.1.2 Justifications for the privity rule

The privity rule follows logically from the definition of, and reasons for enforcing, a contract.

(i) **Exclusivity:** if contractual liability derives from voluntary undertaking (see 1.4.1), it follows that only a person to whom the undertaking is addressed (the promisee) can enforce it. Contractual rights and duties *are personal* to those who create them. Collins (at 314) analogises it to a marriage in which the associated rights and duties remain personal to those who create them: TPs cannot claim the right to share in them. In **'Contracts for the Benefit of Third Parties: In Defence of the Third Party Rule'** (1997) *OJLS* 645, **Smith** argues that a promisor's only obligation is to the promisee to whom the promise is made. The apparent injustice of the privity rule lies in: (a) the inadequacy of contractual remedies to the promisee; (b) the inadequate protection of the TP's reliance; and (c) the unjust enrichment of the contract-breaker. Each can be dealt with without going so far as to confer a right of enforcement on TP.

(ii) **The priority of buyers**: English law prioritises undertakings which are part of *bargains* over those which are given without reciprocal payment (eg gifts, see 4.1.1). A promisee who has provided consideration is more deserving than a TP who has not. In **'The Contracts (Rights of Third Parties) Act 1999'** (2004) 120 *LQR* 292, **Stevens** refutes the Law Commission's reasons for the Act and identifies some difficulties. He argues that there is no justification for giving TPs the right to enforce contracts because they are not promisees and have given no consideration.

(iii) **Floodgates**: any suggestion that the privity rule can be abolished is absurd. Without it, *anyone* could potentially enforce *any* contract; a position which no legal system or commentator would support. The problem remains even if we limit enforcement to TPs who rely on or benefit from a contract. If a contract to build a motorway beside a village is not performed, it seems oppressive to allow the builder to be sued by all those living or buying houses in the village in the anticipation of a rise in property values. The privity rule limits both liability for others' disappointment and responsibility for the fulfilment of others' *expectations*. Traditionally, contractual enforcement is restricted to: (a) parties to a bargain; (b) parties to a deed; and (c) promisees who have been unconscionably induced to rely on a promise, as **Diagram 4B** shows at **I**. However, the line can be drawn more widely. The 1999 Act expands the range of liability from **I** to include:

- **II** (TPs *expressly given the right to sue* in the contract); and
- **III** (TPs on whom *the contract purports to confer a benefit*).
- However, the range of potential liability can be stretched further to include **IV** (TPs who *rely* on the contract),
- **V** (TPs who would have benefited incidentally from contractual performance); and
- **VI** (TPs who would *benefit indirectly* from contractual performance), each raising the question of what the appropriate remedial response should be.

In **'Privity Reform in England'** (2000) 15 *LQR* 43, **Kincaid** argues that the Act departs from the underlying philosophy of civil liability. Hitherto, 'If P is to single out D from the mass of the population and seek the coercive power of the state to force D to realise P's interests, the state (the law) has required P to show that they have both participated in a relationship which justifies making D responsible to P.' In contrast, the 1999 Act amounts to an 'abdication of the law's duty to define justice between

Diagram 4B Who can sue on a promise? What for?

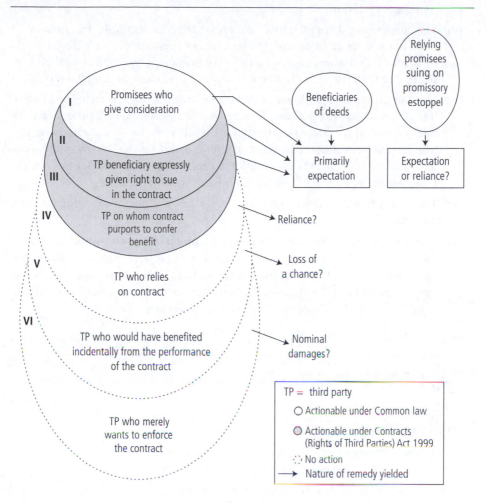

parties. The new law is equivalent to the law's saying "Justice is whatever you, the parties, say it is".'

4.1.3 **Contracts (Rights of Third Parties) Act 1999**

4.1.3.1 Reasons for the Act

The Contracts (Rights of Third Parties) Act 1999 lays down a wide-ranging exception to the privity rule. In *Privity of Contract: Contracts for the Benefit of Third Parties* (Law Com No 242, Cm 3329, 1996), paras 3.1–3.28, hereafter 'Report 242', the Law Commission sets out its **criticisms of the privity rule**, which also operate as its justifications for reform.

(i)   The privity rule **defeats the intention of the contracting parties** by preventing TPs from suing when the contract parties intend them to be able to sue.

(ii) The rule is **unjust to TPs** because it defeats their: (a) expectation interest; and (b) reliance interest.

(iii) The rule creates **difficulty in commercial life**:[2] for example, in *insurance* (*A* takes out insurance from *B* for *C*'s benefit); in *construction* (*A* employs *B* to do work for *C*); and where contract parties try to exempt the liability of their sub-contractor (*A* agrees that *B*'s subcontractor *C* can exclude or limit liability to *A*).

(iv) The rule creates a **legal 'black hole'**[3] into which contractual rights and liabilities simply disappear because: (a) the contract party (the promisee) can sue but can obtain no effective remedy for breach since he or she suffers no loss (the factual benefit being directed to the TP); and (b) the TP who suffers the 'loss' cannot sue. There is the additional problem of **unjust enrichment** if the promisor has already received the promisee's performance.

(v) The **'exceptions'** to the privity rule (see 4.1.6) are piecemeal, complex, and uncertain.

(vi) The **'rule has been abrogated throughout much of the common law world**, including the United States, New Zealand, and parts of Australia'. Moreover, 'the legal systems of most of the **Member States of the European Union** recognise and enforce the rights of TP beneficiaries under contracts' (see Arts II.-9:301–II.-303 of the European Draft Common Frame of Reference).

Pause for reflection

To what extent does the Act address the Law Commission's criticisms of the privity rule?

The privity reform receives support from:

- N Andrews, 'Strangers to Justice No Longer: The Reversal of the Privity Rule under the Contracts (Rights of Third Parties) Act 1999' (2001) 60 *CLJ* 353;

- R Flannigan, 'Privity—the End of an Era (Error)' (1987) 103 *LQR* 564;

- C MacMillan, 'A Birthday Present for Lord Denning: the Contracts (Rights of Third Parties) Act 1999' (2000) 63 *MLR* 721.

The reform is criticised in:

- P Kincaid, 'Privity Reform in England' (2000) 15 *LQR* 43;

- S Smith, 'Contracts for the Benefit of Third Parties: In Defence of the Third-Party Rule' (1997) 7 *OJLS* 643; and

- R Stevens, 'The Contracts (Rights of Third Parties) Act 1999' (2004) 120 *LQR* 292.

---

[2] See A S Burrows, 'The Contracts (Rights of Third Parties) Act 1999 and Its Implications for Commercial Contracts' [2000] *LMCLQ* 540, 553.

[3] D Wallace, 'Third Party Damage: No Legal Black Hole?' (1999) 115 *LQR* 394; *McAlpine v Panatown* at 534 (Lord Clyde).

Diagram 4C Third party action under the Contracts (Rights of Third Parties) Act 1999

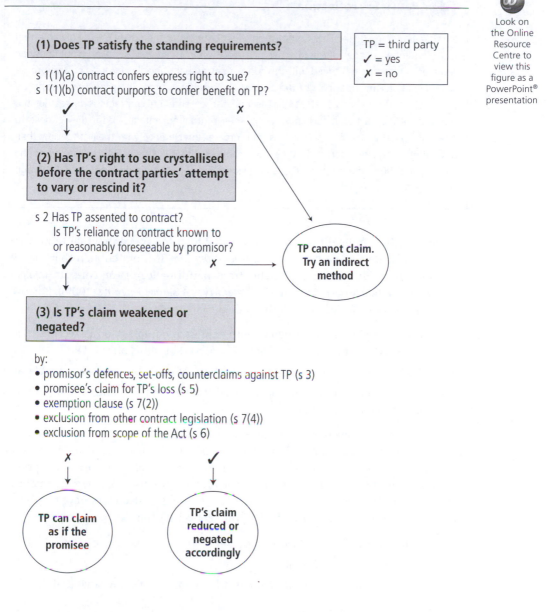

4.1.3.2 The test of enforceability by a third party

The Contracts (Rights of Third Parties) Act 1999 sets out the qualifying conditions for a TP to enforce a contractual term as if he or she were the promisee (see **Diagram 4C**). A deed is treated as a contract for the purposes of the 1999 Act (*Prudential Assurance Company Ltd v Ayres* (2007) at [27]).

Section 1(1)(a) allows a TP to enforce a contractual term where the contract '*expressly provides that he may*'. **Section 1(6)** recognises that the term enforced may take the form of an exclusion or limitation of the TP's liability.

> **Pause for reflection**
>
> Section 1(1)(a) meets the Law Commission's first criticism of the privity rule by giving effect to the intention of the contract parties. The decision in *Tweddle v Atkinson* would now be reversed. This can be squared with orthodox contractual principles by treating the promisor's liability to the TP as *part of the promisor's consideration* for the promisee's reciprocal promise. As Collins states (at 314): 'The purpose of entering contracts is to restrict the freedom of the parties in certain ways for their mutual advantage, and if they choose to give a legal right to a third person this is no greater interference with their autonomy than any other term of the contract.' Where *A* promises *B* that if *B* paints *A*'s house, he or she will pay *C* £100 (enforceable by *C*), *A*'s consideration for *B*'s painting is to pay *C* £100 *and* to allow *C* to sue on it.

Section 1(1)(b) is quite different. It allows a TP to enforce a contractual term where the contract merely *'purports to confer a benefit on him'*. It is not enough that the TP's position will obtain incidental benefits from performance of the contract (*Dolphin Maritime & Aviation Services Ltd v Sveriges Angfartygs Assurans Forening* (2009)). Burrows[4] offers three reasons for section 1(1)(b):

- contractual rights are contained in both express and implied terms; section 1(1)(b) recognises the contract parties' *implied* conferral of rights on the TP;
- section 1(1)(a) would not cover many situations where TP actions are desirable; and
- section 1(1)(a) will only be invoked in well-drafted contracts and TP action should be recognised beyond these.

The presumption in favour of TP enforcement is said to be a 'strong one'.[5] The burden of proof is on the promisor to show that 'the parties did not intend the term to be enforceable by the third party' (s 1(2)), as where, for example, the contract expressly says so, or expressly prohibits assignment without the promisor's consent (as in *Linden Gardens Trust Ltd v Lenesta Sludge Disposals Ltd* (1994)). Decided cases have confirmed the wide scope and relative ease of satisfying section 1(1)(b):

- ✓ *Nisshin Shipping Co Ltd v Cleaves & Co Ltd* (2003);
- ✓ *The Laemthong Glory* (2005);
- ✓ *Great Eastern Shipping Co Ltd v Far East Chartering Ltd (The Jag Ravi)* (2012).

Section 1(1)(b) may apply even if:

- benefiting TP is not the contract's predominant purpose;
- other parties are also benefited (*Prudential Insurance v Ayres* (2007));
- TP has an existing, alternative right of action (*Nisshin Shipping*).

---

[4] A S Burrows, 'The Contracts (Rights of Third Parties) Act 1999 and Its Implications for Commercial Contracts' [2000] *LMCLQ* 540, 542–6.

[5] A S Burrows, 'Reforming Privity of Contract: Law Commission Report No 242' [1996] *LMCLQ* 467, 473.

However, under both tests in section 1(1), **section 1(3)** requires the TP to be *expressly* identified in the contract 'by name, as a member of a class or as answering a particular description, but need not be in existence when the contract is entered into'. This 'simply does not allow a process of construction or implication' in identifying TP (*Avraamides v Colwill* (2006) at [20]).

⏩ Counterpoint

Arguably, section 1(1)(b) goes too far in permitting TP enforcement where the contract merely 'purports to confer a benefit' on him or her:

1. *Uncertain*: when does a contract, which 'purports to confer a benefit' on a TP, raise a rebuttable presumption that the contract parties intend him or her to be able to sue for the benefit?

   ✓ *Beswick v Beswick* (1968, see 4.1.5.1) is clearly within the scope of section 1(1)(b); the widow would now be able to sue in her own right.

   ✗ Incidental benefits to the TP from the promisor's performance clearly fall outside the scope of section 1(1)(b), as where *B* employs *A* to cut down a tree which obstructs *B*'s light and view; the fact that *A*'s performance would also benefit *B*'s neighbour, *C*, is irrelevant since the contract does not purport to confer a benefit on *C*.

   ? However, the Law Commission's view that *White v Jones* (1995) also falls outside section 1(1)(b) is puzzling. What is the difference between:

   ✗ a father who *employs a solicitor* to change his will in favour of his daughter (which the Law Commission regards as outside section 1(1)(b), barring the daughter's enforcement: paras 7.20, 7.25, and 7.48), and

   ✓ a father who employs a builder to add an extension to his daughter's house (which the Law Commission regards as entitling the daughter to sue under section 1(1)(b) (para 7.39))?

The Law Commission's answer is that drafting the will only enables the *father* to confer the benefit; the solicitor does not *directly* confer the benefit itself. However, it can equally be said that the builder is simply enabling the *father* to confer the benefit, whilst the solicitor, by amending the will, is conferring a benefit on the daughter.

2. *Over-inclusive*: TP enforcement under section 1(1)(b) entails three leaps from the original rationale of giving effect to the parties' express intention to allow TP action.

   (i) The view that such intentions may be implied is unobjectionable.

   (ii) The Act presumes this implied intention when the contract 'purports to confer a benefit on a third party'. This formulation replaces the tighter earlier formulations of an 'intention to create a legally enforceable obligation on the third party', in addition to an intention to benefit the TP (Consultation Paper 121, 1991, para 5.10). The two formulations are not interchangeable. Just because I contract for my daughter to receive music lessons does not automatically imply that I want her to be able to sue for them and keep the damages without accounting to me.

➡

➤ (iii) The crux is that where a contract is *silent* on whether the parties intend to allow the TP to sue, the *default position* is that there *will* be a strong presumption that they so intend, rebuttable only by positive evidence to the contrary (s 1(2)). In practice, this reverses the burden of proof: once the TP shows that the contract purports to benefit him or her, it is up to the promisor to positively show that the parties did not so intend.

The argument can be made that this still respects the contract parties' intention since they can 'contract out' (ie state in the contract that the TP should not be able to sue). But it is no justification *for* a default position to say that the parties can say they *don't* want it, *if* they knew about it. Many, perhaps most, parties not legally advised would be ignorant of it.

3. *Wrong solution?* It is arguable that contract law should uphold the parties' intentions *not* by conferring actions on TPs but, rather, by ensuring effective remedies to promisees (an important theme of Chapters 13 and 14). Where the promisor fails to perform, only the promisee's expectation is defeated. As Stevens observes, if 'the promisor wishes to comply with his original promise all he needs to do is keep it'.[6] Traditionally, upholding 'the intention of the parties' translates, on breach, into protection of the *promisee*'s expectation. Insofar as the promisee's remedies against the promisor are inadequate (see 4.1.5), the logical response is to strengthen those remedies, rather than allow TPs to sue the promisor. The Law Commission prefers the latter course because the promisee (i) may be *unable to sue*, being dead, sick, away, or unable to finance the claim or (ii) may *not want to sue* (Report 242, para 3.4).

The circumstances in (i) can affect *any* right-holder, yet rights are not thereby standardly transferred to others. As for (ii), this seems to contradict the concern to protect the promisee's intention. Atiyah points out (at 360) that the promisee will usually be closely related to the TP beneficiary and his or her reasons for conferring the benefit in the first place will usually prompt him or her to sue on their own initiative, or at least lend his or her name to the TP's action (as an insured does to an insurer). If the promisee chooses not to do so, it undermines their intention to allow the TP to sue.

4. *Creating the potential for double liability*: the 1999 Act assumes that loss from breach resides solely with the TP and makes *no provision for the promisee's recovery for his or her own loss*. Thus, **section 5** reduces a TP's claim only if the promisee has already recovered a sum in respect of the *TP's* loss (although it does not require the promisee to account for this sum to the TP) or for his or her own expense in making good *that* loss. The TP's claim is *not* reduced if the promisee recovers in respect of his or her *own* loss (see 4.1.5.3). Say you contract for me to make a particularly meaningful gift for your friend (a ring you design). I breach by making a different and less valuable ring which your friend nevertheless likes and keeps. Your friend can sue for the difference in value between the ring ordered and the one delivered, but it is arguable on the basis of the 'broad ground' in *Alfred McAlpine Construction Ltd v Panatown Ltd* (2001) (see 13.2.4.4) that *you* can also claim damages for your *own loss*, namely your inability to give the gift you intended and paid for. The 1999 Act exposes the promisor to liability to both the promisee and the TP.

[6] R Stevens, 'The Contracts (Rights of Third Parties) Act 1999' (2004) 120 *LQR* 292, 293.

4.1.3.3 Variation and rescission by the contract parties

Section 2 of the 1999 Act attempts to reconcile the potential conflict between the *contract parties'* ability to modify their contract and *the TP's* reliance on or expectation from the original contract. It does so by *setting out when contract parties are barred from extinguishing or altering the rights of a TP qualifying under section 1 without his or her consent*. Namely, where (s 2(1)):

   (i)   the TP has communicated his or her *assent* to the promisor (by words or conduct; communications sent by post or other means; takes effect when it is *received*);

   (ii) the promisor *knows* of the TP's actual *reliance* on the term; or

   (iii) the promisor can *reasonably foresee* the TP's actual *reliance*;

unless the contract parties *expressly* state (s 2(3)):

   (a) that they can rescind or vary the contract without the TP's consent; or

   (b) the specific circumstances (other than those spelt out in s 2(1)) in which the TP's consent is required.

Courts have limited residual discretion to authorise variation or discharge (on such terms as seems appropriate, including payment of *compensation* to the TP, s 2(6)) where:

- the parties cannot contact the TP to get his or her consent (s 2(4)(a));
- the TP is mentally incapable of consenting (s 2(4)(b)); or
- the parties are uncertain whether the TP has relied and so whether the latter's consent is required (s 2(5)).

◀▶ Counterpoint

The *default presumption* that the contract parties intend to forgo their usual right to vary or rescind their contract, *unless* they *expressly* say otherwise, is open to criticism:

1. *Inadequate respect for the parties' intention*: the cumulative effect of presuming that the contract parties (i) intend to allow TP action under section 1(1)(b), and (ii) do *not* intend to retain their power to vary or rescind the contract tilts the balance too far in favour of protecting the TP. To permit TP rights (which may be *imputed* by operation of a strong legal presumption) to trump the contract parties' *express* agreement to vary or rescind their contract undermines the Law Commission's stated primary aim of giving effect to the contract parties' intentions. Why should the parties' *past* intention be 'protected' at the expense of their present intention? Again, it is no justification for this default position to say that parties who know of the presumption can 'contract out' of (vary) it.

2. *Doubtful legitimacy of the TP's claim*: why should TPs be protected? Contract law is not generally concerned to prevent disappointment. Even promises which generate foreseeable expectations in (or reliance by) *promisees* are not enforceable without consideration, formalities, or promissory estoppel (see Chapter 3). There is no justification for

➡

➡

treating TPs who are *not promisees* more favourably than gratuitous promisees. As Coote[7] observes: 'The fact that a gift is less or other than what was hoped for by the recipient does not by itself constitute loss or damages in the legal sense of those words. Even expenditure on repairing the defect is merely by way of augmentation or improvement of the benefit as received.' Likewise, there is no justification for treating the TP who has relied on the contract more favourably than promissory estoppel claimants. The latter must be promisees, can only access the remedy 'as justice requires' (usually on the reliance measure), and are vulnerable to the promisor reneging if that would not be inequitable. In contrast, the TP beneficiary need not be the promisee, can obtain the expectation, and is not subject to the promisor reneging when it would not be inequitable to do so.

3. *Remedy is too generous*: why should the TP's expectations be protected, as opposed to his or her reliance? Say I contract for you to landscape *X*'s garden, but then change my mind (I have fallen on hard times or fallen out with *X*). You are busy and therefore happy to call the deal off. The 1999 Act prevents us from rescinding or varying the benefit to *X* once he or she has said 'I accept' or has relied on the gift (eg bought new plants) where we know of or can reasonably foresee that reliance. *X*'s remedy against you under the 1999 Act is the expectation measure, even if his or her reliance falls far short of this.

4.1.3.4 The third party's claim

The 1999 Act only treats the TP *as if he or she were a party to the contract* for the specified purposes outlined in:

- section 1(5), relating to the TP's available remedies;
- section 3(4), relating to the certain defences available to the promisor.

A qualifying TP can enforce a contractual term and claim 'any remedy that would have been available to him or her in an action for breach of contract if they had been a party to the contract (the rules relating to damages, injunctions, specific performance and other relief shall apply accordingly)' (s 1(5)). The remedy of termination is excluded on the basis that it is not a judicial remedy and because it 'may be contrary to the promisee's wishes or interests' (Report 242, para 3.33). Since the TP's rights are *derivative* from the promisee's, the starting point is that his or her claim replicates the promisee's; the promisor is liable to the same extent as if they were sued by the promisee. Subject to *express* agreement to the *contrary*, section 3(2) allows the promisor to rely on any defences or set-offs that would have been available against the promisee (eg misrepresentation). However, **the promisor may incur *greater* liability to a TP than to the promisee** in three respects.

(i) The promisor can only rely on an otherwise effective **defence or set-off** where it arises 'from or in connection with the contract *and is relevant to the term*' sought to be enforced by the TP (s 3(2)(a)).

(ii) The promisor cannot bring any **counterclaim** against the promisee into the calculation. This is superficially justifiable on the basis that no 'burden' can be imposed

---

[7] B Coote, 'The Performance Interest, *Panatown*, and the Problem of Loss' (2001) 117 *LQR* 81, 93.

on the TP (they should not end up being potentially liable to the promisor). However, it is inconsistent with the derivative nature of the TP's claim. The simple solution should have been to allow a counterclaim to reduce the TP's claim to zero.

(iii) The promisor may be exposed to **double liability** since section 5 (which reduces a TP's claim if the promisee has recovered a sum in respect of TP's loss) does not reduce a TP's claim if the promisee recovers in respect of *his or her own loss* under the common law (see 4.1.5.3).

The promisor's position against the TP is *stronger* than against the promisee (ie the TP's position is weaker than the promisee's) in four respects.

(i) The promisor can rely on any **defences**, **set-offs**, or **counterclaims** (not arising from the contract) that would have been available had the TP been a party to the contract (eg if the TP had induced the contract by misrepresentation or owes the promisor money) (s 3(4)).

(ii) The TP only receives very limited protection from **UCTA**:

- ✓ section 2(1) of UCTA applies to *invalidate* an exemption of the promisor's liability for negligence causing TP's death or personal injury (s 7(2));
- ✓ section 2(2) of UCTA does *not* apply so that an exemption of liability for other loss to the TP resulting from the promisor's negligence is *valid* (s 7(2));
- ✗ section 3 of UCTA does not apply so that an exemption of liability for the TP's loss resulting from the promisor's breach is *valid*. The requirement of reasonableness under section 3 of UCTA would not apply where the claimant is a third party beneficiary (s 7(4)).

Thus, an exemption clause is effective against a TP action when it may be invalid against the promisee.

Pause for reflection

On the one hand, this can be criticised because the unreasonableness targeted by UCTA might equally arise in the context of contracts for the benefit of TPs (eg you contract for me to repair your parents' roof and my breach causes damage to their property). Conversely, it can be supported for respecting the parties' intentions. Moreover, it is unclear how the 'reasonableness test', designed to apply as to the contract parties, should be applied to TP beneficiaries. The Law Commission saw it as raising complex policy issues going beyond those involved in reforming the doctrine of privity (Report 242, para 13.10(vii) and (viii)).

(iii) The TP is not treated as a contract party 'for the purposes of any other Act' (s 7(4)). Thus, the TP cannot appeal to the Law Reform (Frustrated Contracts) Act 1943 (Chapter 7), the Misrepresentation Act 1967 (Chapter 5), or the Unfair Contract Terms Act 1977 (Chapter 11).

(iv) Certain types of contract are excluded from the scope of the 1999 Act, barring TPs from suing on them (eg bills of exchange, promissory notes or other negotiable instruments, carriage of goods, bills of lading, company and partnership agreements, and employment contracts).

4.1.4 Consideration, privity, and the 1999 Act

The *impact* of the 1999 Act on the doctrine of consideration depends on how we see the *relationship* between the privity rule and the doctrine of consideration. The traditional analysis is that the consideration doctrine answers two questions.

(i) '*Which* promises are enforceable?' Answer: those which have been paid for.

(ii) '*Who* can enforce the promise?' Answer: the promisee who has paid for it.

A party can only enforce a promise if he or she: (1) has given consideration for the promise, and (2) is the promisee. On this view, the privity rule is merely the flipside of the consideration doctrine and cannot be reformed without reforming ('undermining', 'creating an exception to', or 'distorting') the consideration doctrine. The 1999 Act does not expressly dispense with (1) or (2) but, by allowing a party to sue who conforms with neither, it implicitly recognises an *exception to each requirement*; otherwise, the reform would be rendered pointless.

The alternative view is that the consideration doctrine *only* addresses question (1), not question (2).[8] It is only concerned with *which* promises are potentially enforceable; it serves *notice to the promisor* that the law will only hold him or her liable if he or she has been paid for it. The question of *who* can enforce promises supported by consideration is a completely separate issue. As long as consideration is provided by *someone*, a party who *otherwise qualifies* can sue without providing consideration. In this way, *exchange* can be maintained as a pre-condition of enforceability, while not limiting enforcement to those providing the exchange. On this view, while the 1999 Act clearly contradicts (2) (that the claimant be the promisee), it does not contradict (1) since consideration is still provided by the promisee. *The Act merely adds to the categories of persons who can sue*, the list now including:

✓ promisees who provide consideration;

✓ joint promisees; and

✓ TPs qualifying under the 1999 Act.

Authorities relied upon for the separation are:

- Viscount Haldane's judgment in *Dunlop Pneumatic Tyre Co*; and
- the joint promisee doctrine suggested by the High Court of Australia in ***Coulls v Bagot's Executor & Trustee Co Ltd*** (1967). There, B gave A the right to quarry in exchange for A paying £5 and royalties to B and C (his wife). When B died, the majority barred C's claim against A, but said obiter, that if the contract had been by A to pay B and C as joint promisees, C would be entitled to sue although she provided no consideration.

---

[8] Collins (at 308); R Flannigan, 'Privity—The End of an Era (Error)' (1987) 103 *LQR* 564.

The 1999 Act undermines the importance of the consideration requirement. Indeed, the Law Commission suggests that the doctrine of consideration may be a 'suitable topic for a future separate review' (Report 242, para 6.17).

⏩⏪ Counterpoint

1. All the judges in *Dunlop Pneumatic Tyre Co* (except Lord Parmoor) based their decisions on the absence of consideration, as did the court in *Tweddle*, so that these two leading cases can be seen as straightforward applications of the traditional view of consideration (fusing the *which* and *who* questions).

2. In **'Consideration and the Joint Promisee'** (1978) 37 *CLJ* 301, **Coote** strongly supports Windeyer J's dissenting view in *Coulls v Bagot* that C was not merely a promisee, but also gave consideration, not by actually providing the quarry but by her 'accountability in law should her husband have defaulted' (at 311). Providing consideration means *being liable for it* as opposed to *actually performing it*. Windeyer J said (at 493) that where A makes a promise to B and C jointly, the requirement of consideration does not require consideration to be 'furnished by them separately. It means a consideration given on behalf of them all, and therefore moving from all of them . . . as between [the promisor and the promisees] it matters not how they [the promisees] were able to provide the price of his promise to them.'

3. The consideration doctrine links the question of *which* promises are enforceable with that of *who* can enforce. Merely being a promisee confers no right to sue on a promise; it is the provision of consideration which entitles the provider to sue on an informal contract. Moreover, since consideration is by definition something given *in return for* the promise (usually *at the promisor's request*), the provider of good consideration will therefore be the promisee. To say that a person is not a party to the contract is just to say that he or she is not one of the reciprocating promisors. This explains the rule that 'consideration must move *from the promisee*' (see 3.1.2.1). Thus, reforming (2) (requiring the claimant to be the promisee) while leaving (1) in place (requiring the claimant to give consideration) would negate the reform.

4. A party who has 'paid for' a promise is more deserving of the law's assistance (see 3.1.1) than a TP who has not 'paid for' nor been promised anything.

4.1.5 Enforcement by the promisee

The claims available to the promisee and the TP aside from the 1999 Act are set out in **Diagram 4D**. They are important because they:

- continue to be available;
- undermine the criticism of the privity rule based on the piecemeal, complex, and uncertain nature of the exceptions since the 1999 Act leaves them intact; and
- challenge the legal 'black hole' argument in support of the Act (ie that the promisee who can sue obtains no effective remedy).

Diagram 4D Overview of promisee and third party actions

Where A undertakes a contractual obligation to B to perform for C's benefit:

B (promisee) can claim:	C (third party) can claim:

1. *Specific performance*
2. *Damages for C's loss*
  • Trust
  • Agency
  • Bailment
  • Subrogation
  • Social or domestic contexts
  • The *Albazero* exception
3. **Damages for B's own loss**
	1. As a *principal* in a *contract* with A via:
	  • Agency
	  • Collateral contract
	2. As a victim of A's *tort*
	3. As a beneficiary of a *trust* of the promise
	4. As an *assignee* from B
	5. Via the rules on *negotiable instruments*
	6. Via *statutory exceptions* (other than 7.)
	7. Via the **Contracts (Rights of Third Parties) Act 1999**

4.1.5.1 Specific performance

The promisee can ask the court to compel the promisor to perform his or her promise (ie claim specific performance, injunction, or a stay of proceedings, see 14.2). These remedies compel the promisor to benefit the TP as he or she contracted to do, so that the interests of the promisee and the TP are satisfied simultaneously. In **Beswick v Beswick** (1968), an elderly man sold his business to his nephew in exchange for the nephew's agreement, inter alia, to pay an annuity of £5 a week to his wife after his death. The House of Lords awarded specific performance to compel the nephew to pay. However, the widow could only sue because she was the *administratrix* (representative) *of her husband's estate*; she could not have sued simply as a beneficiary. The court rejected the nephew's argument that she could only obtain nominal damages because the breach caused no loss to his uncle's estate. Such a result 'would be grossly unjust' (at 73), particularly since the nephew had 'received the whole benefit of the contract and it is a matter of conscience for the court to see that he now performs his part of it' (at 89).

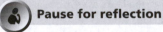

Pause for reflection

Specific performance is the most obvious and efficient way to meet the interests of the promisee and the TP while also preventing the unjust enrichment of the promisor. *Tweddle v Atkinson* could have been resolved in this way *if* the promisee (the groom's father) had performed his own obligation (which he had not) and sought specific performance. The remedy avoids the problems of locating and quantifying the loss, particularly as the promisee's own loss is traditionally regarded as nominal (although Lord Pearce casts doubt on this in *Beswick*) and he is barred from suing for another's loss. Moreover, awarding specific performance in these contracts is consistent with the main qualification for the remedy: that damages are inadequate to compensate for the loss (see 14.2.1.2). If specific performance were systematically awarded in such cases, there would be no legal 'black hole'.

If the relevant promise was to *refrain from suing* the TP, the promisee could ask the court to exercise its discretion to stay the proceedings against the TP, where the promisee has a *sufficient interest* in doing so. In **Snelling v Snelling** (1973), a family company was indebted to three brothers who were directors of the company. The brothers agreed that any of them resigning from the company would forfeit his debt (benefiting the company). When the claimant resigned, his brothers could prevent him from suing the company to recover his money because of their interest in the family company.

4.1.5.2 Damages for the loss of the third party

The House of Lords in **Alfred McAlpine Construction Ltd v Panatown Ltd** (2001) affirms the orthodox position that a promisee cannot sue for a TP's loss of expectation. Lord Millett said (at 581):

> It is inherent in the concept of compensation that only the person who has suffered the loss is entitled to have it made good by compensation. Compensation for a TP's loss is a contradiction in terms. It is impossible on any logical basis to justify the recovery of compensatory damages by a person who has not suffered the loss in respect of which they are awarded unless he is accountable for them to the person who has.

Lord Goff highlights the difficulty with this position (at 547):

> a wealthy man who lives in a village decides to carry out at his own expense major repairs to, or renovation or even construction of, the village hall, and himself enters into a contract with a local builder to carry out the work to the existing building which belongs to another, for example to trustees, or to the parish council.

What can the wealthy man do if the builder breaches?

A number of avenues exist for a **promisee to sue on behalf of the TP**, *handing over any damages to the TP*. The first three commercially important avenues involve technical qualifying conditions and require an understanding of the relationships of bailment, trust, and agency. They are merely listed here.

(i) A promisee who is also a **bailee** in respect of the subject matter of the promise can recover for damage to the bailor's goods even though he or she is not liable to the bailor for the damage.

(ii) A promisee who is also a **trustee** in respect of the subject matter of the promise can recover damages for the beneficiary's loss flowing from breach (the beneficiary can also sue in his or her own right, see 4.1.6.3).

(iii) A promisee who is also an **agent** in respect of the subject matter of the promise can recover damages for the loss suffered by his or her principal (the principal can also sue in his or her own right, see 4.1.6.1).

(iv) **Quasi-agency in domestic and social situations** may also entitle the promisee to sue on behalf of TP beneficiaries. In *Jackson v Horizon Holidays Ltd* (1975), J booked a holiday for himself, his wife, and his sons for £1,200. The substandard accommodation, food, amenities, and facilities were in breach of contract and caused distress and inconvenience for the whole family. The Court of Appeal upheld the award of £1,100 in damages to J. James LJ took the view that the sum was awarded *solely for J's loss* and not that of his family. But Lord Denning MR felt that this would make the award excessive and explained it in terms of compensation for the loss suffered by *the whole family*. Denning's interpretation was disapproved by the House of Lords in **Woodar Investment Development Ltd v Wimpey Construction UK Ltd** (1980). There, purchasers of land agreed to pay £850,000 to the vendor and £150,000 to a TP on completion of the contract. The House of Lords found no repudiation by the purchaser, so that the question of whether the vendors could sue for the sum payable to the TP did not arise, but their Lordships (at 283) preferred James LJ's explanation of *Jackson v Horizon Holidays* 'as a broad decision on the measure of damages' or as 'an example of a type of contract—examples of which are persons contracting for family holidays, ordering meals in restaurants for a party, hiring a taxi for a group—calling for special treatment'.

(v) The most important exception for our purposes is '**The Albazero exception**' (*Albacruz v Albazero* (1977)) which allows the promisee to recover damages for the TP's loss, *held in trust for* the TP. Originally, the claim applied to *loss or damage* to goods in contracts of carriage by sea where the parties contemplated that the promisee would *transfer* the *ownership* of the goods, carried by the promisor, to the TP after the contract's formation but before its performance. From this narrow beginning, the scope of the exception has broadened considerably:

(a) the original requirement of damage to or loss of property in carriage by sea contracts was extended to allow claims for incomplete or defective performance (ie from claims of being 'worse off' to not being 'better off') in building contracts (in *Linden Gardens* (1994));

(b) the original requirement of a contemplated transfer of ownership from the promisee to the TP was abolished to allow recovery without such a transfer (see **Darlington BC v Wiltshire Northern Ltd** (1995) where the promisee never owned the property in question).

As Lord Millett (*McAlpine v Panatown* at 585) observes, the second step 'uncouples the rule from . . . the grounds which originally sustained it'. Nevertheless, it continues to be necessary to show that the TP:

- is *identifiable* at the time of contract formation as *likely to suffer damage* on breach (*Rolls-Royce Power Engineering plc v Ricardo Consulting Engineers Ltd* (2003)); and

- has no claim of its own against the promisor (the TP in *Panatown could* claim against the promisor under their 'duty of care deed' so the *Albazero* exception did not cover the situation, see 13.2.4.4(iv)).

Pause for reflection

1. In sum, the cases suggest that a promisee may recover loss on behalf of a TP where: (i) the contract parties intend to benefit an identifiable TP; and (ii) the TP acquires no contractual rights against the promisor. If that is so, no legal 'black hole' exists in Lord Goff's example. The philanthropist can sue on behalf of the TP beneficiary.

➡

➡

2. However, the width of *The Albazero* exception is of questionable legitimacy. As Lord Millett observes in *Panatown* (at 585), to apply the exception in the absence of an anticipated transfer of ownership 'uncouples the rule from . . . the grounds which originally sustained it'.

3. Moreover, the promisee's duty to account to the TP may be objectionable if it *changes the type of the benefit obtained* by the TP. A promisee who intends to give a specific non-monetary benefit should not be compelled to hand over money instead. In Lord Goff's example, if the philanthropist is accountable to the parish council, there is nothing to stop the latter spending the money in some way unintended by the donor.

4.1.5.3 Damages for the promisee's own loss

Can the promisee recover for his or her own loss so that he or she need not hand over any damages awarded to the TP? The traditional approach is to deny any compensable loss on the promisee's part in contracts to benefit TPs. Three exceptions are arguable (see 13.2.4.4).

(i) The promisee can claim if he or she suffers **direct pecuniary loss**, as where breach results in his or her own obligation to the TP not being discharged or brings him or her under a legal or factual obligation to the TP. In Lord Goff's example, the philanthropist could claim if he or she cured the breach themselves or was likely to do so (*Panatown* at 533, 574; see also *Radford v de Froberville* (1977) where the promisee landlord erected the fence himself for the benefit of his tenants).

(ii) Absent direct pecuniary loss, the promisee *may* have a claim for substantial damages under the '**broad ground**' in *Panatown*. The decision on the '*narrow ground*' (ie on *The Albazero* exception) was that it was inapplicable since the 'duty of care deed' gave the TP a direct action against the promisor. But the promisee also claimed damages *in its own right* for *not receiving the promised performance* (this is the 'broad ground'). The claim failed on the facts although controversy surrounds the precise *ratio* of the case (see 13.2.4.4).

 Pause for reflection

1. It is strongly arguable that the *loss belongs to the promisee*, although supporters of TP actions are highly critical of such an approach.[9] Allowing the promisee to recover substantial damages in his or her own right eliminates the 'black hole' and the need for direct TP action.

2. The possibility of a TP claim creates the risk of *double liability* for the promisor if he or she is sued by both parties for their own loss since section 5 of the 1999 Act only reduces the TP's claim if the promisee has already claimed for the TP's loss.

➡

---

[9] A S Burrows, 'No Damages for a Third Party's Loss' (2001) 1 *OUCLJ* 107, 112; N Andrews, 'Strangers to Justice No Longer: The Reversal of the Privity Rule under the Contracts (Rights of Third Parties) Act 1999' (2001) 60 *CLJ* 353, 377.

➡

3. If the promisee and the TP both sue on their own behalf for the same breach, *how should their claims be prioritised*? The Act is silent. In *Panatown*, Lord Millett (at 595) suggests that payment to either will *pro tanto* discharge the liability to both, but also that the promisee's action should be stayed until the court is assured that the TP is content for it to proceed (ie it should be either 'first come, first served', or the TP should have the 'first bite'). In contrast, Lord Goff saw the promisee's claim as principal and the TP's claim as derivative so that satisfaction of the former eliminates the TP's loss. This interpretation is preferable since it allows the promisee to retain control over whether and what benefit is conferred on the TP.

4. Although section 4 of the 1999 Act states that the availability of TP actions does 'not affect any right of the promisee to enforce any term of the contract', in practice it will stifle the *promisee's claim* whether in his or her own right or on behalf of the TP (Report 242, para 11.17).

(iii) The promisee's claim may be for his or her own **loss of amenity**; that is, his or her loss of satisfaction (enjoyment, peace of mind, or freedom from distress, see 13.2.4.1) from the promisor's failure to confer the benefit on the TP. This is consistent with James LJ's judgment in *Jackson v Horizon Holidays* and supported by the House of Lords in *Woodar*. If the law is willing to compensate a promisee for the loss of satisfaction in knowing that the pool he is safely diving into is 7 feet 6 inches deep whereas it is really only 6 feet deep (*Ruxley v Forsyth* (1996) approved in *Panatown*), the law should also be willing to compensate a promisee for the loss of satisfaction in failing to confer a specific benefit on the TP (eg a new roof for his or her elderly parents' house). The first requirement for loss of amenity claims, namely that the promisee's non-pecuniary purpose should be distinct, important, and communicated to the promisor, will be relatively easy to meet where the contract is for a TP's benefit. The second requirement, that damages should take account of 'reasonableness', requires courts to determine *why* the promisee wants performance, *whether* and *how much* he or she still wants it, and the proportionality between the cost of cure on the one hand, and the contractual price, the benefits already conferred, and the additional benefit to be derived from cure, on the other.

4.1.6 **Getting around the privity rule: third party enforcement aside from the 1999 Act**

Numerous common law techniques allow TPs to circumvent the privity rule and sue the promisor. They are retained by the 1999 Act. Some are not true exceptions to the privity rule, although they are often labelled as such (refer back to **Diagram 4D**). The first three operate by **promoting the TP into a 'first' party** with a direct right to sue as:

(i)   a promisee in a separate *contract* with the promisor (via agency or collateral contract (see 10.3.2));

(ii) a party to whom the promisor owes a duty of care in *tort*; or

(iii) a beneficiary of a *trust* of the promise.

Other devices are **genuine exceptions**, namely:

   (iv) assignment;

   (v) negotiable instruments; and

   (vi) statutory exceptions.

4.1.6.1 Contractual devices

(i) Agency

An agent is someone who acts on behalf of his or her principal. Where *A* makes a contract with *B* who acts on behalf of *C*, *C* is not really a TP but is a contract party in his or her own right. *C* can therefore sue on the contract without contravening the privity rule. Where *C* is a *disclosed* principal, *A* knows that *C* is really the other party to the contract. The difficulty arises where *C* is an *undisclosed* principal. In that case, both *B* and *C* can sue *A* and be sued by *A*, and *A* can appeal to any defences he or she may have against *B* in an action with *C*. Reynolds observes that: 'it is difficult to deny that the undisclosed principal is really a TP intervening on a contract which he or she did not make.'[10] It seems anomalous that an undisclosed principal can sue while a TP who is expressly intended by the parties to be able to sue is barred. See **Diagram 4E.1**.

(ii) Collateral contract

A party can also enforce the benefit of a promise if the court is prepared to find (or create) a collateral contract between him or her and the promisor. For example, in *Shanklin Pier Ltd v Detel Products Ltd* (1951), D told S that its paint was suitable for painting S's pier and would last for seven to ten years. S then instructed its contractor to buy and use D's paint, which turned out to be less durable than stated. S successfully sued D on the basis of a collateral contract between them: D's promise on the paint's durability was supported by S's consideration in directing its contractor to buy paint from D. See **Diagram 4E.2**.

Diagram 4E.1–9 Indirect third party enforcement **Diagram 4E.1** Agency

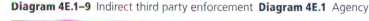

agent principal

A ⟷ (B) C

C can sue *A* as a principal.

⟷ mutual contractual undertaking
- - → factual benefit of contract in contention intended for

Diagram 4E.2 Collateral contract: *Shanklin*

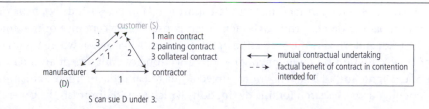

customer (S)

3   1 2

1 main contract
2 painting contract
3 collateral contract

manufacturer ⟷ contractor
(D)   1

⟷ mutual contractual undertaking
- - → factual benefit of contract in contention intended for

S can sue *D* under 3.

---

[10] F M B Reynolds, M Graziadei, and W Bowstead, *Bowstead and Reynolds on Agency* (19th edn, Sweet & Maxwell, 2012) para 8-071.

Diagram 4E.3 Exemption clause: *Eurymedon*

Look on the Online Resource Centre to view this figure as a PowerPoint® presentation

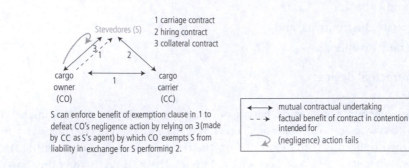

(iii) Exemption of third parties from liability
See **Diagram 4E.3**.

Section 1(6) of the 1999 Act allows qualifying TPs to benefit from exclusion or limitation clauses. Prior to this, courts combined the agency and collateral contract devices to do the same job, typically protecting *S* (the stevedore) working for *CC* (the cargo carrier), against a claim by *CO* (the cargo owner or shipper) where *CO* had agreed to exempt *CC* from liability. This protection had fluctuated as the balance between protecting *A* as the victim of negligence and holding *A* to the agreed contractual risk allocation was struck in different ways. An initial use of the doctrine of vicarious immunity[11] (*Midland Silicones Ltd v Scrutton's Ltd* (1962)) was later reversed (*New Zealand Shipping Co Ltd v A M Satterthwaite & Co Ltd (The Eurymedon)* (1975); *Port Jackson Stevedoring Pty Ltd v Salmond & Spraggon (Australia) Pty Ltd (The New York Star)* (1981)). But the pendulum swung back again via an **agency–collateral contract analysis**.

The template (known as a *Himalaya clause*, after the name of a ship in *Adler v Dixon* (1955)) was set out by Lord Reid in *Midland Silicones Ltd v Scrutton's Ltd* (1962) (at 474). Accordingly, the contract (a 'bill of lading' in carriage of goods by sea) must stipulate that:

- *CC* acts as *S*'s *agent*;

- when concluding a *collateral* contract with *CO*;

- in which *CO* exempts *S* from liability in exchange for *S*'s *consideration* of (i) performing (on a *unilateral* contractual analysis)[12] or (ii) agreeing to perform (on a *bilateral* contractual analysis) services in relation to the cargo which *S* already owes under a contract with *CC*.

However, this collateral contract may still fall short (eg *S* damages goods *before* he or she starts unloading (ie performing the act which constitutes acceptance of the unilateral contract and triggers the protection of the exemption clause), or where *S* is unaware of the exemption on commencing performance (one cannot accept an offer of which one is ignorant)). Lord Wilberforce urged a relaxed approach: 'their Lordships would not encourage, a search for fine distinctions which would diminish the general

---

[11] In *Elder Dempster & Co v Paterson & Zochonis & Co Ltd* (1924).
[12] This avoids *S* being in breach if he or she validly terminates his or her contract with *CO*.

applicability, in the light of established commercial practice, of the principle' (*The New York Star* (1980) at 144).

> ### Pause for reflection
>
> The common law could have avoided these contortions and achieved the same result as section 1(6) of the 1999 Act via the doctrine of vicarious immunity. Despite its rejection in *Midland Silicones*, the doctrine has substantive force. If we accept the doctrine of vicarious liability (making the employer liable for his or her employee's tort) why should we not also accept the idea of vicarious immunity (allowing the employee to enjoy the same immunity in tort as his or her employer contracts for). As Beale, Bishop, and Furmston[13] point out, it seems anomalous that the employer or principal's contract covers the stevedore against liability for trespass in handling the shipper's goods, but cannot protect him or her from liability for negligent handling. A TP can also benefit from an exemption clause via tort reasoning (see 4.1.6.2 question (2)).

4.1.6.2 Tort of negligence

Two questions arise here.

(1) Can a contract *confer a tortious action* on the TP against a contract party?

(2) Can a contract negate *the TP*'s tortious liability to a contract party?

(1) The first translates into the question of whether *A*'s breach of his or her contractual duty owed to *B* might also amount to a breach of *A*'s duty of care owed to *C* (the TP), entitling *C* to sue *A* in negligence (see **Diagram 4E.4**). *C*'s claim is relatively straightforward where the loss involves physical injury or property damage.

However, courts are far more reluctant to impose liability where the loss is *purely economic* mainly because of the concern to avoid indeterminate liability. This is reflected in the very narrow scope of the **promisor's duty of care** in such cases.

✓ A controversial decision *allowing* a TP claim for pure economic loss is *Junior Books v Veitchi Co Ltd* (1983), represented in **Diagram 4E.5**. J employed a main contractor (MC) to build a factory, who subcontracted the flooring to V (J is thus a TP to the latter contract). When the floor was laid defectively, J did not sue his

Diagram 4E.4 Negligence causing physical injury or property damage

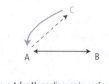

C can sue A for A's negligence in performing main contract but ie normally no action for pure economic loss as A owes C no duty of care.

◄────►	mutual contractual undertaking
‐ ‐ ►	factual benefit of contract in contention intended for
────►	(negligence) action against

ook on
e Online
esource
entre to
ew this
ure as a
verPoint®
sentation

[13] H Beale, W Bishop, and M Furmston, *Contract: Cases and Materials* (5th edn, Butterworths, 2007) 1157.

Look on the Online Resource Centre to view this figure as a PowerPoint® presentation

Diagram 4E.5 Exceptional negligence claim for pure economic loss: *Junior Books*

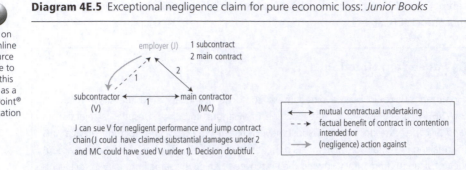

J can sue V for negligent performance and jump contract chain (J could have claimed substantial damages under 2 and MC could have sued V under 1). Decision doubtful.

Diagram 4E.6 Exceptional negligence claim for pure economic loss: *White v Jones*

Look on the Online Resource Centre to view this figure as a PowerPoint® presentation

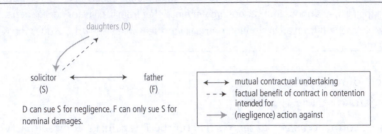

D can sue S for negligence. F can only sue S for nominal damages.

main contractor but sued V directly. The House of Lords allowed the claim on the questionable assumption that V *assumed a responsibility* towards J, despite the contractual structure which made V directly responsible to MC, and MC to J. *Junior Books* is now regarded as an anomalous case on negligence liability for pure economic loss and has been confined to its own facts.

White v Jones (see **Diagram 4E.6**) is a more widely accepted decision allowing indirect enforcement of a contract via a negligence action by a TP. A solicitor's negligent preparation of a will deprived each of the intended beneficiaries of £9,000. By a bare majority of 3:2 the House of Lords allowed the beneficiaries to claim the intended legacies from the solicitor. Their Lordships recognised that this contradicted the privity rule, but thought it necessary to do practical justice (at 221, 224) and avoid the legal 'black hole'. Since the testator's estate could not seek specific performance (it is too late), nor claim more than nominal damages, the solicitor would get away with it unless he was held liable to the beneficiaries in tort.

The case is confined to wills and does not apply to gifts made during the donor's lifetime since the donor can choose whether to rectify the solicitor's negligence.

✗ The general approach, signalled by *Simaan General Contracting Co v Pilkington Glass Ltd (No 2)* (1988), is that a party only assumes contractual liability to his or her immediate contractual partner and is not liable in tort to more remote parties further removed in the contractual chain.

Where a TP can sue in negligence, this is distinctive from (usually *more restrictive* than) any available contractual action (eg via agency, collateral contract, or the 1999 Act).

(i)   The TP must be owed a *duty of care* in respect of: (a) the conduct representing the contractual performance; and (b) the nature of the loss incurred.

(ii) The promisor must *breach this duty*, and the *standard* of liability in negligence (carelessness) is usually lower than his or her contractual liability (usually strict).

(iii) The *measure of damages* differs in principle; a *contract* action protects the claimant's expectation while a *tort* action protects the claimant's reliance. In *Muirhead v Industrial Tank Specialties Ltd* (1986), M sued I, suppliers of a defective motor in a pump which was used to run M's lobster farm. Although M had no contractual relationship with I, M succeeded in his claim for: (a) physical loss (the dead lobsters); and (b) economic loss consequential on this (the loss of profits on these lobsters); but *not* in respect of (c) his pure economic loss (the general loss of profits from the installation of the pump) which is normally considered the subject of contract actions. In *White v Jones*, the damages awarded in tort were indistinguishable from those in contract because, in the will-making context, the only measure of damages which imposes meaningful liability on the negligent solicitor is the value of the benefit not received (strictly speaking, the legatees suffered no reliance loss).

(2) Can *A's contract with B negate C's tortious liability to A*? This revisits, *via tort reasoning*, the question of whether C can benefit from an exemption of liability contained in the contract of others (see 4.1.6.1(iii)). The short answer is 'yes'; whether the loss involved is physical (*Norwich CC v Harvey* (1989)) or purely economic (*Hedley Byrne v Heller* (1964)). Where A agrees with B to exempt B's subcontractor C from tortious liability, this may negate *any duty of care* that C would otherwise owe A.

Thus in *Norwich*, represented in **Diagram 4E.7**, N contracted with X for an extension to a swimming pool accepting the risk (ie exempting liability) for loss or damage by fire and agreeing to maintain adequate insurance cover. The same exemption was contained in X's contract with H to provide the roofing. When the property was extensively damaged due to the negligence of H's employee, the Court of Appeal denied N's claim against H for negligence because H owed N no duty of care. May LJ observed (at 837) that the mere absence of privity between N (the employer) and H (the subcontractor) should not prevent H from relying on the clear basis that all the parties contracted in relation to fire damage, even if it was caused by negligence.

4.1.6.3 Trust of the contractual right

A TP has a direct action against the promisor if the court construes the promisee as holding his or her contractual right to sue the promisor on *trust* for the TP. As the

Diagram 4E.7 Exemption clause: *Norwich*

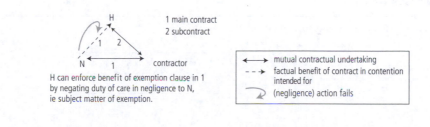

H can enforce benefit of exemption clause in 1 by negating duty of care in negligence to N, ie subject matter of exemption.

1 main contract
2 subcontract

→ mutual contractual undertaking
--→ factual benefit of contract in contention intended for
↻ (negligence) action fails

beneficiary of the trust, the TP acquires *a property* right enforceable against the promissor. For example, if *A* promises a sum to *C* in exchange for *B*'s transfer of a benefit to *A*, *C* can sue *A* for the sum if the trust device can be invoked (*Les Affreteurs Reunis v Walford* (1919)). Once a trust is recognised it is irrevocable; the TP's rights crystallise and the contract parties cannot change their minds. The courts' insistence on robust evidence of the parties' intention to create a trust restricts the utility of this device in circumventing the privity rule. The Court of Appeal refused to adopt a liberal approach in *Re Schebsman* (1944). Where S agreed to the termination of his contract in exchange for six instalments payable to himself and, on his death, to his wife and daughter, the court found no evidence that the parties intended to create a trust in favour of the widow and daughter. Lord Greene MR said (at 89): 'To interpret this contract as creating a trust would, in my judgement, be to disregard the dividing line between the case of a trust and the simple case of contract made between two persons for the benefit of a third.' See **Diagram 4E.8**.

4.1.6.4 Assignment

Although contract parties cannot confer a directly enforceable benefit on the TP, the promisee can subsequently *assign* his or her contractual rights to the TP (see **Diagram 4E.9**). For example, if *A* makes an enforceable promise to *B* to pay *B* a sum of money, *B* can assign the benefit of that promise to *C*, enabling *C* to enforce the promise against *A*. The assignee takes the benefit 'subject to equities' and is therefore vulnerable to all the promisor's defences against the promisee/assignor. One party can assign his or her right without the other party's consent *unless*:

✗ the contract forbids such assignment;

✗ the assignee has no genuine or commercial interest in taking the assignment; or

✗ the relationship between the contract parties is personal (eg where contractual performance involves personal skill). The rights against the promisor should only be assignable where it makes no difference to the promisor for whom he

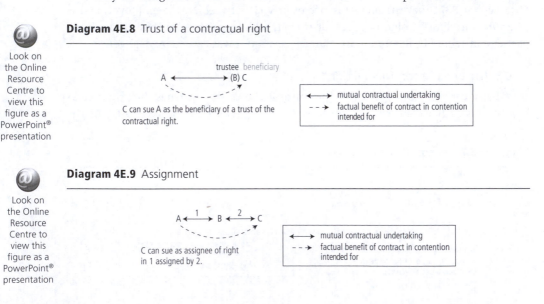

Diagram 4E.8 Trust of a contractual right

trustee beneficiary
A ←————→ (B) C

C can sue A as the beneficiary of a trust of the contractual right.

←——→ mutual contractual undertaking
--→ factual benefit of contract in contention intended for

Diagram 4E.9 Assignment

A ←—1—→ B ←—2—→ C

C can sue as assignee of right in 1 assigned by 2.

←——→ mutual contractual undertaking
--→ factual benefit of contract in contention intended for

Look on the Online Resource Centre to view this figure as a PowerPoint® presentation

Look on the Online Resource Centre to view this figure as a PowerPoint® presentation

or she performs (*Tolhurst v Associated Portland Cement Manufacturers Ltd* (1902) at 668).

The courts are keen to ensure that 'there should if at all possible be a real remedy which directs recovery from the defendant towards the party which has suffered the loss' (*Technotrade Ltd v Larkstore Ltd* (2006) at [83]).

4.1.6.5 Negotiable instruments

The best known example of a negotiable instrument is the cheque. The writer of the cheque (the drawer) instructs the bank (the drawee) to pay a specified sum to the named TP (the payee). The TP is better off than the assignee because he or she takes free from any defects in the title of the prior parties: the cheque gives him or her the secure right to demand payment.

4.1.6.6 Statutory exceptions

Legislation has made inroads into the privity doctrine to regulate three important TP relationships. The most obvious is that of insurance, where policies often confer benefits on someone other than the insured. TP beneficiaries can sue directly for the contractual benefit under the:

- Married Women's Property Act 1882: under section 11 a husband or wife (or children) can sue in respect of the spouse's (or parent's) life insurance policy;
- Marine Insurance Act 1906: under section 14(2) a party with an interest in the subject matter (eg mortgagee or consignee) may insure it on behalf of another interested party; and
- Road Traffic Act 1988: under section 148(7) a TP can sue the insurer directly in respect of the insured's liability to the TP covered by the policy.

4.2 Imposing burdens on third parties

The 1999 Act does not change the widely accepted rule that contract parties cannot, via their contract, impose burdens (obligations, liabilities) on TPs. The rule prevents contract parties from:

(i) imposing positive burdens on TPs (ie to do something); and

(ii) depriving TPs of some right or restricting their freedom of action (ie *not* to do something).

The general rule is subject to a small number of exceptions to which we turn.

4.2.1 Inducing breach of contract

Tort law imposes an obligation on TPs not to intentionally or recklessly induce one party to breach its contract (eg a publisher should not induce *A* to disclose confidential information in breach of *A*'s contract with *B*). In *OBG v Allan* (2007), Lord Hoffmann said that there must be an actual breach of the relevant contract (it is not enough to have merely 'interfered' with the performance of the contract). Moreover, the TP must know that it is inducing a breach of contract (it is not enough that the act procured by the TP does in fact amount to a breach). To do so would incur liability to the innocent contract party for the **tort of inducing or procuring breach of contract**. In *Lumley v Gye* (1853), L (a theatre owner) engaged a famous singer W to sing only at his theatre for a set time. G, a rival theatre owner, persuaded W to break her contract with L by promising more pay. L successfully claimed damages against G for causing him loss by inducing W to break her contract.

 Pause for reflection

This conclusion is not obvious. After all, it was W who chose to break her contract and L could equally have sued her for his loss. However, in the context of rival 'bidders' for a particular skill, the court seems to have attributed greater mischief to the TP's enticement than the contract party's succumbing to the enticement.

Likewise, a TP can be liable if he or she acquires property with knowledge of a contract affecting it and his or her acquisition or use of the property is inconsistent with that contract. In *BMTA v Salvadori* (1949), B bought a car and undertook to A not to resell it for a year without first offering it to A. When C bought the car from B with notice of the undertaking, C was liable to A for wrongful interference with A's contractual right.

4.2.2 Sub-bailment contracts

Where *C* (the bailor) entrusts property to *A* (the bailee) for *A* to hold for or at the direction of *C*, and *A* then entrusts the property to *B* (the sub-bailee), *C* is bound by the terms of the sub-bailment between *A* and *B* to which he or she has consented, whether expressly or impliedly (*Morris v Martin & Sons Ltd* (1965)). Thus, where *C* entrusts a mink stole to *A* (a furrier) for cleaning and, with *C*'s consent, *A* sends the mink to *B* (a specialist cleaner), *C* is bound by the exemption clause in the sub-bailment contract.

4.2.3 Restrictions on property acquired

Where *A* makes contract (1) with *B* regarding the use of *B*'s property, and *B* then transfers the property to *C* via transaction (2), is *C* bound by the terms of contract (1)? The policy arguments are those of free trade (buyers should be free from strings which might be attached to their purchases) versus the security of proprietary rights acquired (which should be enforceable against anyone).

4.2.3.1 Respect for proprietary rights

Where *A* has acquired *a proprietary interest* from contract (1) with *B* (eg the contract may create a lien, a lease, an equitable proprietary interest, or a constructive trust which 'runs with' the property). *A*'s proprietary rights attach to the property (which may physically remain with *B*) and can prejudice the rights of TPs *C* who later acquire the property from *B*. For example, covenants contained in leases bind the successors in title of both the landlord and the tenant, and contractual rights which are specifically enforceable vest an equitable proprietary right in *A*. Thereafter, in the eyes of equity, *C* can only take the property from *B* subject to *A*'s proprietary interest.

4.2.3.2 A wider principle?

Is there a broader principle which operates in the absence of recognised proprietary interests, simply on the basis of the TP's *knowledge* of the vendor's contractual obligations towards the claimant in respect of the property acquired (ie *C* has notice of *B*'s contract with *A*)? The answer which has evolved is: 'no, but not always'.

The first step was taken in a case on **restrictive covenants attached to land**. In *Tulk v Moxhay* (1848), T sold land subject to a restrictive covenant that the land should be preserved in its existing condition and not be built upon. A number of conveyances later, M acquired the land with notice of the restrictive covenant but sought to build on the land. T was awarded an injunction to restrain the proposed building. The basis for the decision was M's *notice of the covenant at the time of purchase*.

But subsequent cases have narrowed the interpretation of *Tulk* by emphasising the *additional* requirement that the covenant must have been for the benefit of neighbouring land owned by the party enforcing the restrictive covenant (*London CC v Allen* (1914)). That is, *C* is only bound by a restrictive covenant in respect of land acquired from *B* if, at the time of the purchase:

- *C* knows of the restrictive covenant in favour of *A*; and

- *A* owns the adjoining land which could benefit from the covenant.

A's right to prevent *C*'s inconsistent use is described as an 'equitable interest' (*Re Nisbet and Potts' Contract* (1905)). Thus, the analysis is not so much that *C* is bound because of his or her *notice* of *A*'s right, but because the restrictive covenant agreed between *A* and *B* is promoted to the status of *a proprietary* right.

The proprietary analysis has also been used when *C* acquires something from *B* and **undertakes to honour** *A*'s contractual rights against *B* in respect of the acquisition; *C* will be restrained from acting unconscionably by exercising his or her legal right to treat the property as his or her own regardless of *A*'s rights. The restraint has been referred to as a *constructive trust* (*Binions v Evans* (1972); *Ashburn Anstalt v Arnold* (1989)).

Despite the narrowing of *Tulk* along proprietary lines, the case was relied upon in *De Mattos v Gibson* (1858) to introduce a **general principle** that equity will protect the original promisee's *contractual right* in respect of the property transferred by imposing restrictions on the TP who has acquired the property with *knowledge* of those rights. Knight Bruce LJ said (at 282):

> Reason and justice seem to prescribe that, at least as a general rule, where a man, by gift or purchase, acquires property from another, with knowledge of a previous contract, lawfully and for valuable consideration made by him with a third person, to use and employ the property for a particular purpose in a specified manner, the acquirer

shall not to the material damage of the third person, in opposition to the contract and inconsistently with it, use and employ the property in a manner not allowable to the giver or seller.

This principle from *De Mattos* was applied by the Privy Council in **Lord Strathcona Co Ltd v Dominion Coal Co Ltd** (1926) to restrain S (the purchaser of a ship) from using the ship in a manner inconsistent with the time charter which was made by a previous owner with D and which S *knew of and agreed to respect*. S was said to be 'plainly in the position of a constructive trustee with obligations which a Court of equity will not allow him to violate' (at 125). The decision has attracted much adverse criticism (*Clore v Theatrical Properties* (1936); *Greenhalgh v Mallard* (1943)).

(i) The emphasis in the restrictive covenant cases subsequent to *Tulk* on the *claimant's ownership of adjacent land* capable of benefiting from an injunction against the TP undermines the general principle stated in *De Mattos* in reliance on *Tulk*.

(ii) A proprietary analysis along the line of *De Mattos* is *too wide*:

- it would substantially outflank the privity rule against imposing burdens on TPs;

- the use of proprietary reasoning (the constructive trust) would tend to suggest the expansion of TP liability: (a) to cases of mere *constructive notice* (which is normally enough to bar TPs from appeal to the bona fide purchaser for value defence in proprietary claims); and (b) beyond the mere award of an injunction to restrain TP actions which contradict the claimant's rights (eg to an award of account of profits or a reasonable user fee or equitable compensation).

Port Line Ltd v Ben Line Steamers Ltd (1958) refused to follow *Lord Strathcona Co*, regarding it as contrary to principle. However, the *De Mattos* principle was confirmed although narrowed by Browne-Wilkinson J (at 572–5) in **Swiss Bank Corp v Lloyds Bank Ltd** (1979): *A* can obtain an injunction to prevent *C* from dealing with property in such a way as to cause *B* to breach his or her contract with *A* if:

(i) *C* had *actual knowledge* of the contract between *A* and *B* when he or she acquired the property (constructive knowledge is insufficient); *and*

(ii) it is still possible for *B* to perform the contract (if not, it is *B*'s conduct (not *C*'s) which undermines *A*'s right).

The cases can be rationalised along the following lines.

- The actual decision in *De Mattos* to deny an injunction is explicable on point (ii). D chartered a ship from C who subsequently charged the ship to G who knew of the charterparty. G sought to sell the ship prior to the completion of the charterparty. D's application for an injunction against G was refused because, although G knew of the charterparty, C could not complete the charterparty due to its financial difficulties. Thus, G's proposed action did not interfere with D's contractual rights.

- *Lord Strathcona Co* is explicable in terms of the proprietary right generated by C's *undertaking* in its contract with B to *respect A's right* in relation to the property acquired.

- The refusal to grant an injunction in *Port Line* is explicable on point (i) (since C did not have sufficient knowledge of A's right), and because A was not merely seeking an injunction but claimed the compensation C received when the ship was requisitioned.

Although the *existence* of this exception to the rule against imposing restrictions on a TP's use of property acquired is established, the *basis of the exception* remains clouded by talk of constructive trusts. The equitable proprietary reasoning is insecure given the criticisms and qualifications mentioned previously. The preferable explanation is that *De Mattos* and *Lord Strathcona Co* represent the *equitable counterpart to the tort of knowing interference with contractual rights (Port Line Ltd* (at 55) and *Swiss Bank* (at 574)). Thus, a TP may, exceptionally, be bound by the contract of others where his or her conduct amounts to unconscionable conduct in exercising his or her legal right in respect of property acquired in a manner inconsistent with the claimant's right, where he or she had **undertaken to honour the claimant's right** when they acquired the property.

THIS CHAPTER IN ESSENCE

online resource centre

The key areas and core topics in this chapter are summarised in an easy-to-use list, ideal for revision purposes, on the Online Resource Centre at http://www.oxfordtextbooks.co.uk/orc/chenwishart5e/. Links to websites relevant to the topics covered and any updates to the chapter can also be found on the Online Resource Centre.

QUESTIONS

1 'The Contracts (Rights of Third Parties) Act 1999 was necessary to counter the legal "black hole" created by the privity doctrine.' Discuss.

2 'The Contracts (Rights of Third Parties) Act 1999 has brought as many problems as it has solved.' Discuss.

3 What is the effect of the Contracts (Rights of Third Parties) Act 1999 on the requirement of consideration?

4 Pat and Quentin agree that they would each pay Rose half of the cost of a 'round the world' holiday when she finishes her law exams. Rose is delighted. Subsequently, Pat and Quentin refuse to pay because they disapprove of Rose's new lifestyle. Can Rose sue?

5 Sam pays Toby £5,000 to make alterations to his daughter Una's business premises to prepare it for a major marketing event. Toby limits his liability for breach to £500. Toby botches the job and parts of the ceiling fall down during Una's presentation, injuring Una. Una has also suffered: (a) damage to her premises; and (b) loss of profits she would have made from the event. Advise Sam and Una.

 For hints on how to answer these questions, please see the Online Resource Centre at http://www.oxfordtextbooks.co.uk/orc/chenwishart5e/

KEY FURTHER READING

Andrews, N (2001), 'Strangers to Justice No Longer: The Reversal of the Privity Rule under the Contracts (Rights of Third Parties) Act 1999', 60 *CLJ* 353.

Burrows, A S (2000), 'The Contracts (Rights of Third Parties) Act 1999 and its Implications for Commercial Contracts', *LMCLQ* 540.

Flannigan, R (1987), 'Privity—The End of an Era (Error)', 103 *LQR* 564.

Kincaid, P (2000), 'Privity Reform in England', 15 *LQR* 43.

Law Commission (UK) (1996), *Privity of Contract: Contracts for the Benefit of Third Parties* (Law Com No 242, Cm 3329).

MacMillan, C (2000), 'A Birthday Present for Lord Denning: The Contracts (Rights of Third Parties) Act 1999', 63 *MLR* 721.

Roe, T (2000), 'Contractual Intention Under Section 1(1)(b) and Section 1(2) of the Contracts (Rights of Third Parties) Act 1999', 63 *MLR* 887.

Smith, S (1997), 'Contracts for the Benefit of Third Parties: In Defence of the Third Party Rule', 7 *OJLS* 643.

Stevens, R (2004), 'The Contracts (Rights of Third Parties) Act 1999', 120 *LQR* 292.

PART IV

'Vitiating' factors

'Can I get out of this contract?'

INTRODUCTION

Even if an agreement satisfies the test of formation discussed in Part II, its enforceability is not guaranteed. It may still be avoided if there is a good reason for releasing one party from it. This question is logically prior to that of ascertaining the *contents* of the contract (Part V) since that question only arises if an initially valid contract cannot be set aside.

Good reasons for releasing party A from the contract are:

(i) Party *B*'s *improper behaviour* in inducing *A*'s consent to the contract;

(ii) *A*'s *impaired consent* due to deficiencies in *A*'s knowledge or judgment;

(iii) an unforeseeable *change of circumstances* that radically alters the significance (point) of the contract; or

(iv) the *unfairness of the contract* in the sense of a marked imbalance in values exchanged.

On the classical model of contract law, the law's legitimate concern is confined to ensuring that the bargain was fairly negotiated, not with whether the outcome was fair (see 1.3.5). Policing *procedural* fairness is permitted, while policing *substantive* fairness is not. Procedural fairness has two aspects. On one side, it looks to the *blameworthiness of the defendant* (the party seeking to enforce the contract, (i) above): has he or she lied to, coerced, or otherwise taken advantage of the claimant (ie the party seeking to escape the contract)? On the other side, it looks to the *quality of the claimant's consent* which may be adversely affected by his or her incapacity or some less serious 'bargaining disability' making him or her more vulnerable to exploitation or serious mistakes ((ii) above). In addition, despite judicial insistence that substantive unfairness is irrelevant to the validity of a contract, the latter plays an important, often covert, role in vitiating contracts ((iv) above). Lastly, a contract may be brought to an end ('frustrated') by a radical change of circumstances after formation ((iii) above).

These situations are regulated to different degrees by the doctrines to be discussed in this part:

Chapter 5   Misrepresentation and non-disclosure

Chapter 6   Mistaken assumptions

Chapter 7   Frustration

Chapter 8   Duress

Chapter 9   Undue influence, non-commercial guarantees, unconscionable bargains, and the desirability of a general doctrine on unfairness. This chapter also contains a brief introduction to the incapacity doctrine, which is more fully discussed in Additional Chapter 1 which is available on the Online Resource Centre.

The doctrine of frustration is discussed here because the *reason* for allowing the claimant to escape closely resembles the mistake doctrines, although its *effect* is to discharge an initially valid contract, rather than to wipe away the contract from the beginning. These doctrines are collectively described as 'vitiating factors', but they affect the status of contracts in different ways. As we will see, they may render the affected contracts void, voidable, unenforceable, or discharged, as the **Introductory Diagram** shows. It is enough to note for now that:

- most vitiating factors render a contract *voidable* at the option of the claimant (he or she can elect to 'rescind' or 'affirm');

- but the mistake doctrine may render the contract *void* from the beginning (there is no choice); and

- the frustration doctrine *automatically discharges* both parties from performance irrespective of their wishes, but only from the time of the radical change of circumstances.

Part IV Introductory Diagram: The effect of 'vitiating' factors

	valid	void	voidable	discharge	unenforceable
Misrepresentation			✓		
Mistake		✓	✓ (?)		
Frustration				✓	
Duress			✓		
Incapacity	✓	✓	✓		✓
Undue influence			✓		
Improvident guarantees			✓		
Unconscionable bargains			✓		
Illegal contracts	✓	✓			✓

The questions for consideration are the following.

(i)   In *practice*, what must a claimant prove under each of these doctrines to escape the contract? To what extent do the burdens of proof relate to the defendant's blameworthy behaviour, the claimant's defective consent, or the fairness of the outcome?

(ii) On the *theoretical* level, what do the answers to the first question tell us about the *reasons* for judicial intervention? What is the law's role in controlling procedural and substantive unfairness? What is the *justification* for each vitiating factor?

(iii) Is the current piecemeal approach of English law to the problem of unfairness satisfactory? Would it be desirable to adopt a general principle against contractual unfairness? If so, what would be the specifics of such a doctrine?

In addition, in **consumer transactions**, the European Unfair Commercial Practices Directive[1] requires Member States to prohibit, and to provide 'adequate and effective' means to combat, unfair commercial practices; these include misleading and aggressive practices (defined as the use of harassment, coercion, or undue influence). The Directive and the Regulations passed to implement it[2] criminalise such unfair commercial practices. The **Consumer Protection (Amendment) Regulations 2014** (SI 2014/870) now allow consumers to seek redress where misleading[3] or aggressive practices by businesses have caused them to enter the contract or to make payments for goods or services (including digital content). The new remedies available are:

- a right to *unwind the contract* and receive a full refund;[4] or

- a right to a *discount* of 25, 50, 75, or 100% in respect of past or future payments due depending on the seriousness of the incident;

- in either case, the consumer can *claim damages* for: (i) consequential financial loss; and/or (ii) alarm, distress, or physical inconvenience or discomfort, *unless* the trader can show that it used due diligence.

This right now exists alongside common law actions in misrepresentation and duress, which are complex and little used by consumers. Nevertheless, to avoid duplication of claims under the Misrepresentation Act 1967, section 2(4) of the 1967 Act (inserted by reg 5 of the 2014 Regulations) removes any entitlement to damages under section 2(1) where a consumer has a right to redress under Part 4A of the Consumer Protection from Unfair Trading Regulations 2008 in respect of the conduct constituting the misrepresentation.

---

[1] Directive 2005/29 on unfair commercial practices [2005] OJ L149/22.

[2] The Consumer Protection from Unfair Trading Regulations 2008 (SI 2008/1277), reg 29; Business Protection from Misleading Marketing Regulations 2008 (SI 2008/1276), reg 29.

[3] No right to bring a claim arises where there has been a misleading omission.

[4] Assuming the product has not been fully consumed, and the consumer rejects it within 90 days of the later of the date of the contract or of its delivery or supply, and any goods supplied are made available for collection by the trader.

5

Misrepresentation and non-disclosure

'You misled me'

Consistent with an adversarial model of contract negotiation, English law recognises no general duty of good faith. The parties need not disclose important matters about the transaction to each other, nor make reasonable efforts to reach agreement. There is no liability for such omissions. However, contract parties should not make false statements to induce the other party's consent to the contract. This is regulated by the law on misrepresentation. This law is complicated by two factors. First, its rules are a patchwork of common law, equity, and statute. Second, it must be put in the context of related doctrines that deal with the same general problem (of disappointed expectations), but yield different legal responses. For example, proof of misrepresentation allows the claimant to get out of a contract and even claim money, but other causes of action (eg mistake or breach of contract) may also be possible and may give, perhaps, better remedies. The legal adviser must navigate around these related doctrines to find the most advantageous cause of action. The questions addressed in this chapter are:

(i)   What must the claimant prove in an action for misrepresentation?

(ii)   What liability is there, if any, for non-disclosure?

(iii)   When can the claimant get out of the contract?

(iv)   How is any compensation to the claimant measured?

(v)   To what extent can a party exclude or limit his or her liability for making a misrepresentation?

(vi)   What justifications underlie the remedies for misrepresentation?

(vii)   Is the current law on misrepresentation satisfactory? If not, how might it be developed in the future?

5.1 **What is an actionable misrepresentation?**

In brief, an actionable misrepresentation is:

(i)   an unambiguous false statement of existing fact;,

(ii)   made to the claimant;

(iii)   which induces him or her to enter the contract.

If these requirements are satisfied, the claimant can **rescind the contract** subject to the bars (see 5.3.2). But, if he or she *also* (or *instead*) wants to claim **damages** to compensate him or her for the loss suffered from entering the contract, an *additional* element is required:

(iv) **the misrepresentation must have been made with** *the requisite state of mind*. A misrepresentation that is made honestly and on reasonable grounds will yield no damages.

Before examining these requirements in more detail, we need to mention two preliminary issues with important analytical and remedial consequences. **Diagram 5A** shows how different *classifications* of the statements made yield different *remedies* if the statements turn out to be false.

Starting at the left side, **(1)** the first question is: 'Did the statement complained of induce the *claimant into a contract with the misrepresentor?*' This being a text on contract law, our discussion will focus on this scenario. In this situation, the next question relates to the *status* of the false statement, for this determines **(3)** the remedies available, and **(4)** the law applicable to any exemptions of liability.

- If the statement is a *term inside* the contract, its falsity gives the claimant an action for breach of *contract* (see Part VI), and any term exempting liability is subject to particular legislative control (see Chapter 11).

- If it is a *representation outside* the contract, the claimant has access to the advantageous action for damages under the Misrepresentation Act 1967 (hereafter 'the 1967 Act'), and any term exempting liability is subject to control by the 1967 Act itself. Although the pre-existing tort and equity actions continue to be available, the claimant will have no incentive to resort to them.

- If it is a mere 'puff', it has no legal effect; the claimant has no action.

Diagram 5A The remedial significance of classifying statements

Look on the Online Resource Centre to view this figure as a PowerPoint® presentation

MA Misrepresentation Act 1967			**(3) Claimant/addressee's potential remedies**			**(4) Effect of exclusion or limitation of liability**
			Damages	**Get out of contract**	**Performance**	
(1) Contract is made with the maker of statement. The statement is:	**A term of the contract** ↑ incorpo-ration | s 1(a) ↓ MA		Expectation measure	Termination	Specific performance	Subject to s3 Unfair Contract Terms Act 1977 and r5 Unfair Terms in Consumer Contracts Regulations 1999
	A representation		Fraud measure s 2(1) MA	Rescission	No term to breach	Subject to s3 MA and UTCCR
	A mere 'puff' without legal effect		No	No		
(2) No contract is made with the maker of the statement. The statement is made:	Fraudulently		Fraud measure	No contract to escape	No contract to perform	Subject to s2 Unfair Contract Terms Act 1977
	Negligently		Negligence measure			
	Innocently		No			

If the statement does not induce a contract with the addressee (2) (eg where *A*'s misrepresentation induces *B* to contract with *C*, as in *Hedley Byrne v Heller* (1964)), the claimant cannot resort to the 1967 Act, but must rely on the common law tort actions of fraudulent or negligent misrepresentation and the equitable action for innocent misrepresentation.

5.1.1 Representations and terms

5.1.1.1 The remedial importance of the distinction

If an untrue statement induces a contract with the maker of the statement, the remedies available depend on whether the statement is a term *inside* the contract or a representation *outside* the contract.

- A **term** is an enforceable contractual undertaking to do (or refrain from doing) something, or to guarantee the truth of something. Where a term is breached, the remedies are, broadly speaking, *'forward looking'*. The innocent party can claim damages aimed at putting him or her in the position they would have been in if the contract had been performed. They may also have a claim for specific performance to compel the contract-breaker's performance, or be able to end (terminate) the contract for a sufficiently serious breach (see Part VI).

- A **representation** is a statement which asserts the truth of a given state of affairs and invites reliance upon it, but it does not *give an enforceable guarantee of its truth*. If it is actionable, the remedial response is, broadly speaking, *'backward looking'*. The claimant may be able to get out of (rescind) the contract and/or claim damages aimed at putting him or her in the position they would have been in had they not relied on the representation (ie not entered the contract).[5] This is represented by the columns of (3) on **Diagram 5A** (see also **Diagram 10A**).

A party may be able to prove that the statement made to him or her is *both* a misrepresentation and a contractual term, for a statement that induces the contract *may* also be incorporated as a, usually written, term of the contract:

- The claimant will prefer to rely on the statement's *contractual* status if his or her remedies for breach are better than his or her remedies for misrepresentation (eg if the preference is for specific performance, expectation damages, or termination) or if rescission for misrepresentation is barred (see 5.3.2).

- Exceptionally, a party will prefer the remedies for *misrepresentation* (eg where he or she cannot meet the high threshold of termination for breach (see 12.2.2), but *can* meet the lower threshold for rescission for misrepresentation).

- **Diagram 5B** compares the measure of damages yielded by the different actions depending on whether the claimant made a good bargain or a bad bargain. Here, C pays £50,000 for goods that turn out to be worth only £30,000 because D's statement was untrue:

---

[5] The distinction between contractual damages for loss of bargain and tortious damages for reliance losses is blurred where reliance damages for *fraud* include the *'loss of opportunity'* to make another similar contract, see 5.2.1.2(ii).

Diagram 5B Good bargain, bad bargain, and measure of damages

	Contract measure	Tort measure
Good bargain: C pays £50,000 for value of £70,000	**£ 40,000 =** £70,000 – £30,000	**£20,000 =** £50,000 – £30,000
Bad bargain: C pays £80,000 for value of £70,000	**£ 40,000 =** £70,000 – £30,000	**£50,000 =** £80,000[2] – £30,000

- If C has made *a good bargain* (eg the goods would be worth £70,000 *if the statement had been true*), C will prefer the contractual measure of damages, and so rely on the statement being a contractual term.[6]

- Conversely, if C has made a *bad bargain* (eg C has paid £80,000 for goods which would be worth £70,000 *if the statement was true*), C would prefer to go 'backwards' (and get out of the contract) rather than 'forwards' (and enforce his or her contractual expectation). C will prefer to rely on the statement being a misrepresentation.

- The term-or-representation distinction is also important if the claimant wants to **get out of the contract**. Ironically, it is easier to end the contract for misrepresentation than for breach; *any* misrepresentation entitles the claimant to rescind the contract, while only a *serious* breach (see 12.2.2) allows the claimant to terminate the contract. Before the 1967 Act, if a statement was both a misrepresentation and a contract term, the latter status took priority so that the claimant lost his or her right to rescind the contract for any misrepresentation irrespective of seriousness. He or she could only get out of the contract if the breach was a serious one. This anomaly is remedied by **section 1(a)** of the 1967 Act, which gives the representee the *option* of treating the statement as a misrepresentation and claiming rescission *even* if it was incorporated into the contract as a term. However, this solution generates its own inconsistencies. For, while a party cannot terminate for breach of a minor term, he or she *can* terminate if the term also happens to be a misrepresentation: he or she can escape a bad bargain (by rescinding it) for a relatively trivial breach. This possibility is, in turn, met by **section 2(2)** of the 1967 Act, which empowers courts to *deny rescission* by reference to equitable considerations (see 5.3.2.6). The reforms of the 1967 Act to the remedies for misrepresentation (narrowing the right to rescission and expanding the right to damages) have reduced the practical importance of the term–representation distinction, although the distinction remains fundamental in principle.

---

[6] Although it is arguable that the claimant's over-payment is not caused by the misrepresentation, the 'fiction of fraud' (see 5.2.1.2) allows the court to assume that the claimant would not have contracted at all without the misrepresentation, and so should be fully restored by damages. The claimant would certainly recover the sum on rescission.

5.1.1.2 How is the representation–term distinction made?

The distinction is said to be based on the **intention** of the parties as objectively manifested by their words and conduct (*Heilbut, Symons & Co v Buckleton* (1913); *Oscar Chess Ltd v Williams* (1957)). However, the parties will often, in truth, have no intention at all on the matter, for, as Atiyah (at 180) observes, such intention would virtually require the parties to appreciate the legal distinction between a term and a representation. Moreover, even if the parties thought about the matter, their intentions are likely to differ. The real question is not whether the maker of the statement *has* agreed to *bear contractual* responsibility for the truth of the statement, but whether he or she *should*. The courts are guided by the following criteria, although none is said to be decisive (*Heilbut, Symons & Co v Buckleton* at 50–1).

(i) **Importance of the truth of the statement**: the more important the statement is to the representee, the more likely it is to be a term. In *Bannerman v White* (1861), W was expressly assured that the hops on sale had not been treated with sulphur, after saying that they would not even bother asking the price if they had. In fact, sulphur was used on a small portion of the hops. The statement was held to be a *term* of the contract. In *Couchman v Hill* (1947), the seller's reply to the buyer's question that the heifer being auctioned was 'not in calf', was held to be a *term* of the contract because the seller knew that the buyer would not have been interested otherwise. The heifer suffered a miscarriage and died within two months of its purchase.

(ii) **Special knowledge**: a court is more likely to find a term if the maker of the statement has special skill or knowledge in the subject matter of the statement, or is in a better position to ascertain, or bears more responsibility for ascertaining, the accuracy of the statement than the other party. Accordingly:

✓ a *term* was found in **Dick Bentley Productions Ltd v Harold Smith (Motors) Ltd** (1965) where a car dealer made a false statement to a private buyer about the mileage of the car since its engine replacement ('20,000 miles', when actually 100,000 miles). The dealer, being 'in a position to know, or at least find out the history of the car . . . stated a fact that should be within his own knowledge';

✗ in contrast, no breach of term but only a *misrepresentation* was found in **Oscar Chess Ltd v Williams** (1957) where a private seller (without any special knowledge) stated the model of the car he was selling to a car dealer as 1948 (relying on the car's log book which had been altered by the previous owner) when it was actually a less valuable 1939 model. It was held that the car dealer was in at least as good a position to discover the car's true age as the private seller.

(iii) **Request to verify**: a statement is unlikely to be a term if the maker of the statement tells the other party not to rely solely on the statement but to verify its truth. A *representation* was found in *Ecay v Godfrey* (1947) where a seller stated that the boat was sound but advised the buyer to have it surveyed. However, a *term* was found in *Schawel v Reade* (1913) where the seller said to the buyer: 'You need not look for anything; the horse is perfectly sound. If there was anything wrong with this horse, I should tell you.'

(iv) **Initiation or merely passing on**: in *Routledge v McKay* (1954), Lord Denning explains that *where* a motor car is sold second-hand from one person to another in succession and each seller in the chain is passing on information about the year the car was made by relying on a false entry in the registration book by some remote seller, the statement would be treated as a representation and not a term. The seller, unless he or she is the person who altered the registration book, is not the originator of the false statement, but a mere innocent passer-on (as in *Oscar Chess*).

(v) **Formal recording**: a contract may be oral, but if it is recorded in writing, the presumption is that the document records the complete terms (*Heilbut Symons v Buckleton* at 37, 42, and 47; this is the 'parole evidence rule', see 10.3.1) and anything not included therein is a representation. Nevertheless, the court may, although it is slow to, find a statement outside the document to be a binding *collateral* term or contract (see 10.3.2).

 Pause for reflection

The relevant factors point to concerns beyond the stated one of the parties' intention in making the term–representation distinction. They suggest that courts are also concerned to protect the addressee's reasonable expectations induced by the statement, and to determine whether the maker of the statement *should* reasonably bear the responsibility for that expectation, even if he or she has not actually agreed to bear it. Certain statutes simply declare that particular statements should always be treated as terms. For example, by virtue of the Package Travel, Package Holidays and Package Tours Regulations 1992, any statements in travel brochures detailing holidays and tours are regarded as contractual terms.

5.1.2 **Statements of fact and other statements**

A representation outside the contract, to be actionable, must be an unambiguous, false statement of existing *fact* or *law*. **Diagram 5C** gives an overview of actionable statements and non-disclosures. Express statements of fact and law are clearly included. Statements of *intention, opinion, law*, or '*puffs*', although not prima facie statements of fact, may be found to contain *implied* statements of fact. Even *omissions* (silence) are actionable if there was an independent duty to disclose the omitted information.

5.1.2.1 **Statements of fact**

Statements of fact can be made by words or by conduct. In *Walters v Morgan* (1861), Campbell LC said (at 724) that, whilst simple reticence is not actionable, 'a nod or a wink, or a shake of the head, or a smile from the purchaser intended to induce the vendor to believe the existence of a non-existing fact, which might influence the price of the subject to be sold' is actionable. In *Spice Girls Ltd v Aprilia World Service BV* (2002) the band, the Spice Girls, made a contract to promote the defendant's motorcycles on 6 May 1998. One member left the band three weeks later causing considerable loss to the defendant. The Court of Appeal held that the Spice Girls had made

Diagram 5C Identifying actionable statements and omissions

The objectionable conduct:	Legal category:	Test of actionability:	Actionable as:
ACTS words or conduct amounting to statements of:	Fact	If statement is false If the statement is true but: • misleading • falsified before contract formation	Misrepresentation
	Intention	If there is a false *implied* statement of fact that the representor: • is honest, or • has a reasonable basis for the statement	
	Opinion		
	'Puffs'		
OMISSIONS	Contract *uberrimae fidei*	If there is a duty to disclose the fact withheld	Actionable non-disclosure
	Fiduciary relationship		Breach of fiduciary duty
	Doctrines indirectly relieving non-disclosure (6.1.3.4)	Different tests according to the doctrine invoked	Different remedies according to the doctrine invoked

a misrepresentation by conduct since all five members participated in a commercial photo shoot, and supplied logos, images, and designs when they knew that one member was to leave.

5.1.2.2 Statements of law

The traditional rule that a statement of law cannot give rise to an actionable misrepresentation (*Beesly v Hallwood Estates* (1960)) was always subject to numerous and rather complicated exceptions and avoidances.[7] These exceptions have been superseded by the House of Lords' *abolition of the law–fact distinction* in the context of mistaken payments (*Kleinwort Benson Ltd v Lincoln CC* (1999)); such payments are now recoverable whether they were made under a mistake of fact or of law. The law on misrepresentation, which is really the law on *induced* mistakes, has followed suit. In *Pankhania v Hackney LBC* (2002), Rex Tedd QC explains (at [57]):

> when the principles of mistake and misrepresentation are set side-by-side, there is a stronger case for granting relief against a party who has induced a mistaken belief as to law in another, than against one who has merely made the same mistake

---

[7] Eg statements of foreign law have always been treated as statements of fact and it can be notoriously difficult to decide whether a statement is one of law or of fact (*André* & *Cie SA v Ets Michel Blanc & Fils* (1979)).

himself . . . The survival of the 'misrepresentation of law' rule following the demise of the 'mistake of law' rule would be no more than a quixotic anachronism.

5.1.2.3 Statements of intention

A statement about the speaker's intention is not *in itself* a statement of fact, nor necessarily (although it may be) a contractual undertaking. A statement of intention is *actionable* if:

(i) it is a **term** of the contract (see 5.1.1 and 10.2); or

(ii) it is **dishonest**: a statement of intention *always* implies a statement of fact to the effect that it reflects the speaker's state of mind. If it is honest, there is no misrepresentation. The representor is entitled to change his or her mind and his or her failure to carry out their stated intention is not actionable (*Wales v Wadham* (1977)).

✗ In *Kleinwort Benson Ltd v Malaysia Mining Corp Berhad* (1989), M refused to guarantee the debt of its subsidiary company to K, but gave K a 'letter of comfort' stating 'it is our policy to ensure that the business of [our subsidiary company] is at all times in a position to meet its liabilities to you under the above arrangements'. When K sued M alleging the comfort letter to be a contractual undertaking, the court held that the letter was simply an honest *representation* of M's policy at the time that the statement was made. M did not promise to stick by this policy in the future (at 2.7.3).

✓ A statement *is* actionable if the representor was dishonest. In **Edgington v Fitzmaurice** (1885), company directors issued a prospectus inviting subscriptions for debentures which said that it was raising money to develop and expand the business; in fact, the money was used to repay existing company debts. Denman J held (at 483) the directors liable for deceit, explaining that:

> the state of a man's mind is as much a fact as the state of his digestion. It is true that it is very difficult to prove what the state of a man's mind at a particular time is, but if it can be ascertained it is as much a fact as anything else. A misrepresentation as to the state of a man's mind is, therefore, a misstatement of fact.

5.1.2.4 Statements of opinion

Statements of opinion or belief are not statements of fact and are not actionable just because they turn out to be inaccurate. However, such statements may be *actionable* if they concern the following.

(i) They are **dishonest**: like statements of intention, dishonesty in asserting an opinion not genuinely held is *always* a misstatement of fact (ie regarding the state of his or her opinion). The same applies if the speaker could not honestly hold the opinion he or she asserts, given the facts known to them. This shades into the second exception.

(ii) There is **no reasonable ground**: *if* the representor is in a better position than the representee to know the truth, the court may *imply* a statement of fact that the representor has reasonable ground for his or her opinion, making him liable if he or she does not (*Brown v Raphael* (1958)). In *Smith v Land and House Property Corp* (1884), Bowen LJ said (at 15):

where the facts are equally well known to both parties, what one of them says to the other is frequently nothing but an expression of opinion . . . But if the facts are not equally known to both sides, then a statement of opinion by the one who knows the facts best involves very often a statement of a material fact, for he impliedly states that he knows facts which justify his opinion.

However, a speaker *without* greater knowledge than the representee who offers an honest opinion makes no actionable misrepresentation. In ***Bisset v Wilkinson*** (1927), the vendor of a farm in New Zealand told the prospective buyer that he thought the land could carry 2,000 sheep. Both parties knew that the land was untried as a sheep farm and so were in the same position to form an opinion on this. The court held the vendor's statement to be an honest opinion that did not imply that he knew facts justifying it. The same was concluded in *Humming Bird Motors Ltd v Hobbs* (1986), where a private seller of a car said that he believed the odometer reading to be correct, since he had no way of knowing whether or not it was correct.

(iii) They are a **contractual term**: a statement of intention may in fact be an actionable term of the contract. An opinion made by one having superior knowledge and experience may also amount to a contractual *term* to the effect that care and skill had been exercised in giving the opinion. But, in practice, the damages available for breach of such a term confer no remedial advantages over a claim for misrepresentation; in both cases, damages are measured by reference to the addressee's loss flowing from the speaker's lack of skill and care in making the statement. In ***Esso Petroleum Ltd v Mardon*** (1976), M was induced to lease a petrol station then under construction by E's statement that the estimated future annual turnover was 200,000 gallons per year. E reaffirmed this estimate after the local authority refused planning permission for the original layout, and the station was eventually built with more restricted access. In fact, the change reduced the annual turnover to 78,000 gallons. M incurred considerable losses from operating the station and successfully claimed for damages for negligent misrepresentation and breach of contract.

5.1.2.5 'Puffs'

Vague and exaggerated laudatory statements about the subject matter of the contract may amount to neither terms nor representations because it would be *unreasonable to rely* on them. Advertising slogans which claim, for example, that a brand of petrol will put 'a tiger in your tank' or that a deodorant will make you totally irresistible to the opposite sex, are not statements that a reasonable person would take literally. In *Dimmock v Hallett* (1866), it was held that a statement that land was 'fertile and improvable' would only exceptionally be considered an actionable misrepresentation.

However, the more resemblance the statement bears to a statement of **opinion**, the more likely it will be found to contain an implied statement of fact. It is a matter of degree. In ***Smith v Land and House Property Corp***, a purchaser was allowed to rescind the contract for misrepresentation where the vendor of property told him that it was 'let to a most desirable tenant', when the vendor knew that the rent had been hard to extract and was in arrears. The vendor's dishonest and unreasonable statement was vague, but the buyer was entitled to rely on it because the vendor had knowledge not available to the buyer. In addition, the context and specificity of the statement may also elevate a statement to the status of a **term**. In *Carlill v Carbolic Smoke Ball Co* (1893), the court rejected the seller's claim that its advertisement was a mere puff (see 2.2.2.2). It stated that £100 would be paid to anyone 'who contracts the increasing epidemic influenza, colds, or any disease by taking cold, after having used the ball three times daily for two weeks according to the printed directions', adding that £1,000 had been deposited with the Alliance Bank 'showing our sincerity in the matter'.

Pause for reflection

To summarise: the key question is whether, having regard to all the circumstances, it is reasonable *for the representee to rely* on the statement made and, on the other side, for the statement maker to be answerable for the representee's loss incurred by such reliance. The simple answer that it is only reasonable to rely on statements of *fact* is subject to qualifications. Not only is the old bar against actions for misrepresentations of law now dissolved, courts can construct *implied* statements of fact out of statements of intention and opinions taking into account:

- the importance of the statement;
- the context in which it is made (social, professional, or commercial); and
- the relative expertise and knowledge of the parties.

The last factor is also important in distinguishing: (i) an actionable misrepresentation from an unactionable one; *and* (ii) terms from representations (see 5.1.1.2). This is unsurprising when the questions are essentially the same; that is, whether and to what extent the maker of the statement should take responsibility for its accuracy.

5.1.3 Silence

5.1.3.1 No general duty of disclosure

During contractual negotiations, a party need not say anything; but anything he or she *does* say should at least be honest. Contract law responds to *active* misrepresentations; at common law there is generally no liability for omissions; that is, for silence or non-disclosure, even if it relates to important facts that the silent party knows or should know that the other party is ignorant of or mistaken about (*Keates v Cadogan* (1851)). Blackburn J said (at 607) in *Smith v Hughes* (1871):

> if the vendor was aware that the purchaser thought that the article possessed that quality, and would not have entered into the contract unless he had so thought, still the purchaser is bound, . . . a mere abstinence from disabusing the purchaser of that impression is not fraud or deceit; for, whatever may be the case in a court of morals, there is no legal obligation on the vendor to inform the purchaser that he is under a mistake, not induced by the act of the vendor.

Consistently, the 1967 Act only applies where the defendant *makes* a positive representation, and not where he or she is completely silent on the matter (***Banque Keyser Ullman SA v Skandia (UK) Insurance Co Ltd*** (1990) at 790).

Pause for reflection

Non-disclosure raises the problem of *informational asymmetry* between the parties; the party with less information will undoubtedly come off worse in the contract. Four arguments support the general denial of liability for non-disclosure.

1. *Incentive to invest:* since accurate information enhances the efficiency of the market system, the law should give parties the incentive to acquire such information. This means that a knowledgeable party must generally be allowed to take advantage of a less knowledgeable party. If an oil company has invested heavily in research to identify land holding possible oil reserves, it should not have to share its information in negotiations to buy this land. To require disclosure would discourage investment in the acquisition of such information. This overlaps with the second justification.

2. *Permissible self-interest*: parties are under no obligation to help one another (see 1.3.6).

3. *No liability for omissions*: the common law does not generally impose liability for mere non-feasance or pure omissions (*Smith v Littlewoods* (1987) at 271).

4. *Uncertainty and floodgates*: if a duty of disclosure were recognised, it would be very difficult to determine when the duty arises and what its precise contents were (no one can be expected to disclose everything which may influence the other party's judgment).

On the other hand, blanket immunity for non-disclosure could result in sharp practice and unacceptable advantage-taking. The need for economic investment in skill and knowledge will only justify so much and the picture of robust self-interest is not always appropriate. Where one party knows that the other is relying on his or her skill, knowledge, and judgment, economic arguments carry less weight and uncertainty (or floodgates) arguments are less compelling.

English law contrasts sharply with the position in the **European Draft Common Frame of Reference**. Article II.-3:101 recognises a general duty of disclosure which applies to *all* business and consumer contracts, with the latter attracting a higher duty. The business is liable for any loss caused to the other party by its failure to disclose even if no contract is concluded (Art II.-3:109(3)).

Nevertheless, English law can protect the less knowledgeable party by:

(i)   extending the catchment of actionable misrepresentations;

(ii) imposing a duty to disclose where the parties are in special relationships; and

(iii) invoking other doctrines which can meet the problem of non-disclosure indirectly.

5.1.3.2 Extending the scope of actionable misrepresentation

The court can *imply*, from what the defendant *has said*, other statements that, if false, may be actionable.

(i) Change of facts: *falsification by later events*

A statement of fact is *deemed to be continuing*, so that a change of circumstances prior to the conclusion of the contract can convert what was a true statement into an actionable misrepresentation, *unless* the representor corrects it (ie makes disclosure: *Shankland & Co v Robinson and Co* (1920)). In **With v O'Flanagan** (1936) the vendor of a medical practice correctly represented its value as £2,000 at the start of negotiations. However, the practice was almost worthless by the time the sale was concluded five months later because of the vendor's supervening ill health. The sale was rescinded for misrepresentation. The decision effectively imposes an obligation on the vendor to disclose a change of circumstances, which would almost certainly put off the purchaser, either completely or on the original terms.

Must the representor know of the change of circumstances? It seems only reasonable to expect the representor to disclose changes known to him or her (Romer LJ in *With v O'Flanagan* (at 586) suggests that the rule is so confined).[8] However, to require knowledge amounts to imposing liability only for fraud and this contradicts the general position that even non-fraudulent misrepresentations are actionable. Lord Wright MR does not specifically require knowledge. Unhelpfully, Clauson J agreed with both his brethren.

Does the continuing representation rule apply to statements of intention? Here, the representor will invariably know of the falsifying change of circumstances (ie his or her own change of mind), unless he or she has forgotten their original statement. *Trail v Baring* (1864) requires the representor to disclose his or her change of intentions before the conclusion of the contract. However, *Wales v Wadham* does not. Here, the wife told her husband that she had religious objections to remarriage after divorce; this resulted in her obtaining a more generous divorce settlement on the basis that she would remain single. The court upheld the settlement, although the wife had secretly agreed to marry another prior to the conclusion of the settlement. *Wales v Wadham* has been approved in *Livesey v Jenkins* (1985).[9]

> ◆◀ **Counterpoint**
>
> The result in *Wales v Wadham* is objectionable. While it is arguable that intention statements only imply an honest reflection of the representor's state of mind *at the time of speaking*, the power of such statements to induce contracts clearly rests on the representee's assumption that they, like other statements of fact, hold good, at least up to the formation of the contract.

(ii) 'Half-truths': *representations that only give part of the picture*

A party who chooses to say something may be liable although what he or she says is *literally true*, if he or she omits important qualifications that *distort* the representee's assessment of the proper *weight* to be attached to the statement. The representor

---

[8] Lord Dunedin supports this view in *Shankland v Robinson* (1920) at 101.

[9] Although it was held that a duty of disclosure was owed *to the court* making a family settlement order, breach of which entitled the other party to set the agreement aside.

fails to make clear that implications which are likely to be drawn cannot in fact be drawn. He or she is 'economical with the truth', 'paints a misleading picture', tells a 'half-truth', or implies that the material facts omitted do not exist. For example:

✓ in *Nottingham Patent Brick and Tile Co v Butler* (1886), the vendor's solicitor said that he did not know of any restrictive covenants affecting the land under nego-tiation, but failed to add that this was because he had not bothered to check. The purchaser was entitled to rescind the contract;

✓ in *Clinicare Ltd v Orchard Homes & Developments Ltd* (2004), the prospective land-lord (O) stated, in response to the prospective tenant's (C) inquiry, that it was unaware of the property being affected by dry rot. In fact, O's surveyor had advised further investigation to determine the true extent of the dry rot that had been discovered. O dealt with the obvious dry rot but made no further investigation. O was liable for misrepresentation because its better position to discover the dry rot (which was hidden by O's refurbishment) implied that rea-sonable steps had been taken to see whether dry rot existed;

✓ regulation 5 of the Consumer Protection from Unfair Trading Regulations 2008 (SI 2008/1277) and section 20 of the Consumer Protection Act 1987 make it an offence for a business party to give misleading information about the subject matter of the contract. This protects unsophisticated and credulous consumers who are likely to be misled by 'sales talk' even if what is said is strictly true.

5.1.3.3 Exceptions to the no-liability rule based on special relationships

The law recognises some exceptions to the no-liability rule where the model of 'stran-gers bargaining at arm's length' is inappropriate.

(i) Contracts *uberrimae fidei*: contracts of utmost good faith
In cases within this category, the material facts lie within the exclusive knowledge of one party and failure to disclose them makes the contract voidable. The *content* of the duty of disclosure varies with the type of contract in question.

• Historically, in contracts of **insurance**, the insured has a duty to disclose[10] all facts which a reasonable or prudent insurer would regard as material to the risk assessment (*Pan Atlantic Insurance Co Ltd v Pine Top Insurance Co* (1995); Marine Insurance Act 1906, s 18(2)). Failure to disclose (eg a serious medical condition in a life insurance contract) will entitle the insurer to avoid the contract and deny claims under it. This duty can operate oppressively since it assumes that the insured knows what information affects the insurer's estimation of risk.

  (i) The Consumer Insurance (Disclosure and Representations) Act 2012 has abolished the consumer's duty to volunteer material facts. Instead, con-sumers must take reasonable care to answer their insurer's questions fully and accurately. If the consumer's misrepresentation was honest and rea-sonable, the insurer must pay the claim; if it was careless, the insurer has a compensatory remedy based upon what the insurer would have done had the consumer taken care to answer the question accurately; and if it was

---

[10] The insurer also has duty to disclose: *Banque Financière de la Cité v Westgate Insurance Co Ltd* (1990).

deliberate or reckless, the insurer can decline all claims, and retain the premiums, unless there was a good reason why they should be returned.

(ii) The Law Commission[11] has recommended that replacing businesses' duty of disclosure with a duty of fair presentation based on developments in case law, covering what should be disclosed and the form of disclosure; encouraging insurers to take a more active role; and providing a regime of proportionate remedies in the event of breach by the policyholder based on what the insurer would have done if it had received a fair presentation.

- Other types of contracts call for some measure of disclosure, although they may not all be *uberrimae fidei* in the strict sense. These include contracts of partnership, contracts to subscribe to company shares, family settlements, and contracts of guarantee.

It is arguable that these instances can be generalised into a duty of disclosure whenever one party has knowledge which is inaccessible to the other.

(ii) Fiduciary relationships

Broadly speaking, fiduciary relationships arise where *A* entrusts *B* to perform a specific job, or to hold or control *A*'s property, or *A* trusts in, depends on, or is committed to *B* (see undue influence at 9.2). Where *B* abuses *A*'s trust to obtain an advantage at *A*'s expense, *B* 'will not be permitted to retain the advantage, although the transaction could not have been impeached if no such confidential relation had existed' (*Tate v Williamson* (1866) at 61). Where such a relationship exists, the objections to a disclosure duty based on the need to give incentives to acquire knowledge, to allow self-interested behaviour, and the concern about floodgates largely disappear. The *scope* of fiduciary relationships is potentially very broad.[12] The *content* of the duty (eg to make particular disclosures, to avoid a conflict of interests, to give disinterested advice, or to suggest independent advice), and the appropriate *remedies* for breach (eg rescission, account of profits made, or liability for equitable compensation) will vary with the precise nature of the fiduciary relationship.

5.1.3.4 Indirect techniques of giving relief for non-disclosure

Other, seemingly unrelated, contract rules and doctrines can effectively impose a duty of disclosure on the knowing party seeking to enforce the contract or particular terms. The law protects ignorant parties by giving the knowing party incentives to disclose (mainly the *terms* of the contract) in a number of situations.

(i) Where *A* knows of *B*'s **mistake as to the *terms* of the contract**, the contract is void. To ensure the enforceability of the contract on *A*'s terms, *A* must correct *B*'s mistake (see 2.1.3).

(ii) If *A* has exploited *B*'s disability (including ignorance of the value of the contract's subject matter) to extract a grossly unfair exchange it may be set aside as an **unconscionable bargain** (eg *Ayres v Hazelgrove* (1984) and see 9.4).

---

[11] Law Commission, *Insurance Contract Law: Business Disclosure; Warranties; Insurers' Remedies for Fraudulent Claims; and Late Payment* (Law Com No 353, July 2014).

[12] P Finn, *Fiduciary Obligations* (Law Book Co, 1977) 201 describes a fiduciary as 'simply, someone who undertakes to act for or on behalf of another in some particular matter' whether requested or not, whether gratuitously or for payment. Similar descriptions have been used judicially.

(iii) **Non-commercial guarantees** are only enforceable if lenders ensure that guarantors are independently advised of the material features of the contract (see 9.3).

(iv) **Onerous or unusual terms** in an unsigned document purporting to bind a party are only enforceable if that party had reasonable notice of the terms (see 10.3).

(v) There are numerous **statutory duties of disclosure** designed to mitigate the effects of inequality of bargaining power between consumers (generally less knowledgeable, expert, and experienced about the subject matter of the contract) and traders.[13] Traders may commit an offence or be unable to enforce particular terms unless they present the terms in legible, plain English, follow a particular set of words (eg in consumer credit), or highlight them by colour, size, or position on the page. Consumers may have to be provided with copies of the contract or 'cooling off' periods during which they can cancel.

(vi) While there is no general duty to rescue others from harm,[14] a **duty of care** arising between parties in a 'special relationship' may impose a tortious duty to disclose information relevant to the contract (*Banque Keyser Ullman SA v Skandia (UK) Insurance Co Ltd* (1990) at 794).

(vii) The use of **implied terms** (see 10.4) is arguably the most effective technique for protecting the parties' reasonable expectations. Rather than requiring A to disclose *deviations* from B's reasonable expectation, implied terms make these expectations contractually enforceable unless A discloses deviations. Moreover, A may be barred from excluding these implied terms (eg the Unfair Contract Terms Act 1977, s 6; see 11.4.3). While the categories of contracts requiring disclosure are regarded as closed and generally arise only where relevant facts are known, implied terms are not so confined. Moreover, implied terms are ostensibly justified by the parties' implied intentions, whereas disclosure obligations are derived from less easily justified factors external to the parties' intentions.

 Pause for reflection

These apparently isolated and discrete common law and statutory rules are unified by the policy of protecting contract parties from informational asymmetry and inequality of bargaining power.[17] This policy could guide the courts when they are considering possible extensions of disclosure requirements in the common law.[18] Still, duties of disclosure can only do so much. There is no guarantee that weaker parties such as consumers will understand or even read the often vast amount of information provided; nor, if they did, that they could negotiate any change in their favour. This explains the statutory controls of contractual fairness discussed in Chapter 11.

---

[13] Eg the Mail Order Transactions (Information) Order 1976 (SI 1976/1812); the Business Advertisements (Disclosure) Order 1977 (SI 1977/1918) requires advertisements by businesses to reveal their true identity; see also the Package Travel, Package Holidays and Package Tours Regulations 1992 (SI 1992/3288), regs 7–8; and the Medicines Act 1968, ss 85(2), 95(4)(a), and 96.

[14] *Yuen Kun-Yeu v AG of Hong Kong* (1988) at 192.

5.1.4 **Made to the claimant**

Statements can travel along a chain as they are repeated (from *A* to *B* to *C* to *D* and so on). It would be unfair to impose liability on the original representor for every subsequent representee's reliance on his or her statement. Thus, an actionable misrepresentation must have been addressed either to the claimant directly, or to a third party with the intention that it be passed on to the claimant (*Smith v Eric S Bush* (1990)), who may be a member of the public at large (*Andrews v Mockford* (1896)). Beyond these, the misrepresentation is regarded as 'spent' (*Gross v Lewis Hillman Ltd* (1970) at 461). In cases of indirect communication, the 1967 Act only applies to *A*'s misrepresentation communicated via *B* to *C* if it induces *C* to contract with *A*; otherwise, *C*'s actions lie in the torts of deceit or negligent misrepresentation.

5.1.5 **Inducement and materiality**

5.1.5.1 Inducement

The claimant must prove that the misrepresentation *induced* (caused) him or her to enter into the contract. The standard of *causation* required is low and easily satisfied. It is enough if the misrepresentation was *an* inducement actively present in the claimant's mind; that is, it need only be *'one of' his or her reasons* for entering into the contract, it need not be the 'but for' reason, let alone 'the', 'the predominant', or 'the sole' reason for his or her agreement (*Edgington v Fitzmaurice*). Thus, it is no bar that the claimant had other reasons for entering into the contract or that he or she might have entered into the contract anyway without the misrepresentation (*Re Leeds Bank* (1887)). Indeed, the Court of Appeal held that where the representation is material, it is for the representor to show that the representee was not induced by it to enter the transaction (*Vahey v Kenyon* (2013) at [19]).

Inducement is strongly inferable from the *materiality* (or importance) of the misrepresentation (see 5.1.5.2). As Jessel MR said: 'if a man has a material misstatement made to him which may, from its nature, induce him to enter into the contract, it is an inference that he is induced to enter into the contract by it. You need not prove it affirmatively' (*Mathias v Yetts* (1882) at 502).

The fact that the claimant could have, but did not, *verify the accuracy of the representation* will not ordinarily bar his or her claim. In ***Redgrave v Hurd*** (1881), the prospective buyer queried the seller's statement about the turnover of the solicitor's practice but he declined an invitation to examine further documents. Baggallay LJ said (at 22–3) that the seller should not blame the buyer for trusting him: '[t]he representation once made relieves the party from an investigation . . . [Ordinarily], the mere fact that he does not avail himself of the opportunity of testing the accuracy of the representation made to him will not enable the opposing party to succeed'.

However, the scope of *Redgrave v Hurd* has been confined by *Smith v Bush* so that, if it would be *reasonable* for a representee to take an opportunity to discover the truth (or unreasonable for him or her to rely on the representation), his or her claim in *negligent* misrepresentation will fail; the position should, *a fortiori*, be the same where the misrepresentation is *wholly innocent*. Aside from this, a failure to verify may reduce a representee's damages for *contributory negligence* (see 5.2.1.2).

✗ In *Peekay Intermark Ltd v ANZ Banking Group Ltd* (2006), the Court of Appeal found that P was not induced to invest by ANZ's misrepresentation as to the nature of the investment. ANZ's agent gave only a 'rough and ready' description of it and P's agent was an experienced investor who could have had no doubt of the need for a definitive and detailed description of the 'product' from the contract documents. Indeed, P's agent had agreed 'as per the attached document' to ANZ and had signed a Risk Disclosure Statement stating that he had read and understood the document. Thus, P was induced to sign the documents, not by ANZ's misrepresentation, but by its own assumption that the contractual document corresponded with ANZ's representation.

✗ In *Kyle Bay Ltd v Underwriters* (2007), K, the insured, carelessly relied on U's erroneous statement about the basis for calculating an insurance claim without checking the policy itself. The Court of Appeal held that U only gave its opinion and did not make a representation of fact. K's agent was professionally qualified and experienced and must be taken to have a copy of the policy. It was open to the trial judge to find that K's agent was not induced to enter the contract by U's statement, but simply decided to proceed on its own assumption that U's contention was correct.

There will not be the requisite inducement if the claimant: is *unaware* of the representation (*Horsfall v Thomas* (1862));[15] *knows* that the representation is untrue (*Cooper v Tamms* (1988)); is *unaffected* by the representation because he or she relies on other information (*Atwood v Small* (1863)); or regards it as *unimportant* (*Smith v Chadwick* (1884)), although the line between this and the rule that the representation need only be *one* of the reasons inducing the contract will be a fine one. In *JEB Fasteners v Marks Bloom and Co* (1983), the court denied J's claim for damages for M's negligent preparation of the accounts of a company J was taking over; J did not rely on these accounts but proceeded with the takeover because it wished to secure the services of two of its directors.

5.1.5.2 Materiality

The immateriality (ie unimportance of the matter stated) of the misrepresentation will not defeat a claim if the representor was fraudulent (*Smith v Kay* (1859)), or knows or ought to know that his or her statement will influence the claimant (*Nicholas v Thompson* (1924); *Goff v Gauthier* (1991)). Otherwise, there is disagreement[16] over whether the materiality requirement:

• simply functions as *evidence of inducement*; if the misrepresentation is material (ie would induce a reasonable person to enter the contract), inducement is presumed and the onus is on the misrepresentor to show no reliance by the claimant; if it is *not* material, the claimant must prove affirmatively that he or she *was* induced into the contract (*Museprime Properties Ltd v Adhill Properties Ltd* (1991) at 124); or

---

[15] Where the seller tried to conceal a defect in the cannon to be sold by inserting the metal plug into a weak spot but the buyer never examined it.

[16] Eg the requirement is questioned in *Chitty* at para 6-040, and not mentioned in *Anson's* at 305; but asserted by Treitel at para 9-016.

- is *separate* from the inducement requirements (*Smith v Chadwick* at 196), making materiality an *objective* requirement which filters out trivial statements that could not have influenced the judgment of a reasonable person, analogous to the exclusion of 'mere puffs' as actionable.

5.2 **Money awards for misrepresentation**

An actionable misrepresentation gives the representee access to two principal remedies:

• *rescission* (setting aside the contract): broadly speaking, *every* misrepresentation (fraudulent, negligent, or innocent) allows the representee to rescind the contract subject to the bars to rescission (see 5.3.2);

• *damages* (compensating the claimant for loss incurred by entering the contract): the claimant succeeds under section 2(1) of the 1967 Act *unless* the *misrepresentor* can show that he or she honestly *and* had reasonable grounds to believe in the accuracy of his or her statement (if the misrepresentor *can*, the representation is not actionable). This is represented by **column I** in **Diagram 5D**. The diagram gives an overview of the *types* of money claims available for a false statement.

The relatively simple picture presented by section 2(1) is complicated by two factors.

(i)   Section 2(1) of the 1967 Act widens the test for actionable misrepresentations, but links the *measure* of damages to the common law action for *deceit*, necessitating reference to the common law actions (**column II**).

(ii)   Other money claims may be available for the false statement instead of (or in addition to) any section 2(1) claim. Thus, we need to put section 2(1) claims (column I) in the context of related claims which yield monetary awards:

- **column III**: for **breach** where the statement is classified as a contractual term (expectation damages are available irrespective of the speaker's state of mind);

- **column IV**: which **implements rescission** (also available irrespective of the speaker's state of mind); and

- **column V**: **instead of rescission** (only available for non-fraudulent misrepresentation).

5.2.1 **Damages under section 2(1) Misrepresentation Act 1967**

To start with a discussion of the common law claims existing before the 1967 Act (fraudulent, negligent, and innocent misrepresentation), and only *then to* examine the section 2(1) claim, may mislead readers as to the relative importance of the four causes of action. While the common law claims continue to be available where the misrepresentation has induced a contract between *A* the representee

Look on the Online Resource Centre to view this figure as a PowerPoint® presentation

Diagram 5D Money claims for misrepresentation

				✓ = actionable ✗ = not actionable	
I. S 2 (1) Misrepresentation Act (reliance damages 'fiction of fraud')	**II. Misrepresentation at Common law** (reliance damages)	**III. Breach of term** (expectation damages)	**IV. Restitution & indemnity** (getting back)	**V. S 2(2) Misrepresentation Act** (damages in lieu of rescission for non-fraudulent misrepresentation)	
✓ If the representor cannot prove **honest and reasonable belief**. Damages as for fraud (but, may be reduced for contributory negligence if action for negligent misrepresentation co-exists)	✓ **Fraudulent** problems of proof but 'fraud measure (no remoteness limit, no reduction for contributory negligence)	✓ If the false statement is classified as a term, irrespective of maker's state of mind	✓ For all types of misrepresentations if rescission is allowed	✗ Fraudulent misrepresentation	
	✓ **Negligent** problems of proof, more 'limited' reliance measure (remoteness limit, reduction for contributory negligence)			✓ Non-fraudulent misrepresentation if rescission is denied	
✓ The *representee* cannot show he is *honest and reasonable* but *neither can the representee* prove fraud or negligence	✗ **Innocent** if *representee* cannot show fraud or negligence*				
✗ **'Purely' innocent** if *representor* can prove honest and reasonable belief*	✗				

* The distinction between an 'innocent misrepresentation' at common law and an unactionable misrepresentation under section 2(1) Misrepresentation Act, called a 'purely' innocent misrepresentation, is further explained at 5.2.1.1(iv).

and *B* the representor, the common law claims are 'out-gunned' by the section 2(1) action which:

- lowers the qualifying threshold; and
- yields the most generous measure of damages via the so-called 'fiction of fraud'.

Only where no contract results between *A* and *B*, must *B* resort to the common law actions. In the contractual context, this can occur where:

- *A*'s misrepresentation induces *B* into a contract with *C*, as in *Hedley Byrne v Heller*; or

- *A*'s misrepresentation induces *B* into a contract with *A*, but the contract is void, as for mistake (eg mistake of identity or *non est factum*, see 6.4) or illegality (see Additional Chapter 2 available on the Online Resource Centre).

5.2.1.1 Lowering the qualifying threshold: comparing fraudulent, negligent, and section 2(1) misrepresentation

Section 2(1) of the 1967 Act prescribes:

(i)   the *measure of damages*: a representor is liable for damages *as if he or she* had made a fraudulent misrepresentation *even though* 'the misrepresentation was *not* made fraudulently' (this is known as the 'fiction of fraud',[17] see 5.2.1.2); and

(ii) the *qualifying threshold*: the representor is liable *unless* 'he proves that he had reasonable ground to believe and did believe up to the time the contract was made that the facts represented were true'.

Thus, in order to *qualify* for the fraud measure of damages, a claimant under section 2(1) need not show fraud; he or she only needs to show that the representor made a false statement of fact or law (express or implied) which induced him or her into the contract with the representor. It is then for the *representor* to show that he or she *honestly* believed on *reasonable* grounds that his or her statement was true when he or she made it. This **reversal of the burden of proof** regarding the representor's state of mind is a radical departure from the common law actions where the burden of proof remains with the representee. This *pro-representee* move is aimed at eliminating the obstacles of proof in the common law actions for fraudulent and negligent misrepresentations to which we turn.

(i) Fraudulent misrepresentation (deceit)

To succeed in common law deceit, the *representee* must prove that the representor made the false statement (*Derry v Peek* (1889)):

(i)   knowingly;

(ii) without belief in its truth (including knowing that he or she is ignorant of its truth); or

(iii) recklessly; careless of whether it be true or false, even if his or her motive is worthy (*Polhill v Walter* (1832)). Acting unreasonably is not enough; what is required is gross carelessness justifying an inference of fraud (*Angus v Clifford* (1891)). Thus, fraud was rejected in *Derry v Peek* where the representee bought shares in a company, relying on claims in its prospectus that the company was entitled to use steam power to run its trams. The company honestly believed this, although it had still to obtain permission which was later denied. The

---

[17] P S Atiyah and G Treitel, 'The Misrepresentation Act 1967' (1967) 30 *MLR* 369, 372–5.

House of Lords held that the directors were not liable merely because they had acted unreasonably in failing to check the truth of the statement.

The difficulty of proving fraud has meant few successful claims. In contrast, a section 2(1) claimant can access the generous deceit measure of damages (see 5.2.1.2) unless the *representor* proves his or her honesty and reasonableness in making the statement.

(ii) Negligent misrepresentation

Until 1964, *Derry v Peek* was thought to rule out liability for negligent misrepresentations (statements made carelessly or without reasonable grounds for believing their truth), apart from when the parties are in a fiduciary relationship (*Nocton v Lord Ashburton* (1914)). ***Hedley Byrne v Heller*** recognised other *'special relationships'* that can trigger a duty to take care in making statements. In that case, HB sought assurances from H bank about the financial health of a third party with whom HB proposed to contract. H bank gave a negligent assurance that the third party was 'considered good for its ordinary business transactions', and HB proceeded with the contract, suffering loss when the third party breached its obligations. HB's claim for negligent misrepresentation would have succeeded but for H bank's stipulation that its assurance was given 'without responsibility'.

Hedley Byrne v Heller widened the scope of damages-yielding misrepresentations, but the measure of damages for negligence is *less generous* than for deceit because it is vulnerable to *two reductions* from which deceit claims are immune.

- The rule on *remoteness of damages* limits damages to losses that the representor could reasonably foresee as flowing from the misrepresentation (*Overseas Tankship (UK) Ltd v Morts Dock & Engineering Co Ltd (The Wagon Mound (No 1))* (1961)).

- Damages are further reducible by reference to the representee's *contributory negligence* (Law Reform (Contributory Negligence) Act 1945, s 1; *Gran Gelato Ltd v Richcliff (Group) Ltd*).

Since section 2(1) of the 1967 Act invokes the 'fiction of fraud', it would also seem to be immune from these reductions (see 5.2.1.2).

The scope of actionable negligent misrepresentation has undergone considerable expansion but is subject to uncertain limits. The uncertainty arises, in large part, from the concern to restrain liability in an already overstretched legal system. After all, carelessness is less blameworthy than deliberate falsehood, and careless *words* can travel far and trigger widespread and purely economic losses, the latter being considered less worthy of protection than physical injuries or damage to property. Thus, liability is confined by the requirement that the claimant be in a *'special relationship'* with the representor such that the latter owes him or her a duty to take reasonable care in making the statement. The uncertainty of the notion of 'special relationship' is reflected in the instability, vagueness, and variety of the formulations put forward by their Lordships in *Hedley Byrne v Heller* itself ('reliance', 'assumption of responsibility', 'undertaking' (at 486, 502–3, 514, 528–9)). One of the main achievements of the 1967 Act is to dispense with the need to prove a special relationship where a misrepresentation *induces the representee to contract with the representor*.

(iii) Misrepresentation under section 2(1)

Section 2(1) not only eliminates the need to prove a special relationship with the representor, it also dispenses with the need to prove the representor's negligence at all. Once the representee shows that:

✓ the representor made a false statement, which

✓ induced him or her into a contract with the representor,

he or she is entitled to the most generous measure of damages (as for fraud), *unless* the representor can prove his or her honesty and reasonableness in making the statement.

The impact of section 2(1) can be seen in **Howard Marine and Dredging Co v A Ogden & Sons** (1978). H's manager misrepresented the carrying capacity of two barges being hired out to O as 1,600 tonnes. O refused to pay on discovering, six months later, that they could only carry 1,055 tonnes. H sued for the hire charges and O counterclaimed for £600,000 lost due to the lower carrying capacity. The Court of Appeal accepted H's honesty in making the statement and two of the three judges thought there was probably no liability even for common law negligent misrepresentation. But H was liable (as for fraud) under section 2(1) because H did not have reasonable grounds for its belief. H could not explain why it was reasonable to disregard the ships' documents containing the accurate figures, in favour of the figures in the Lloyd's register.

(iv) Innocent misrepresentation

At common law, *no damages* are available for 'innocent misrepresentation' because no tort (wrong) is committed. The only remedies were rescission and indemnity (see 5.2.2). The court could circumvent this by classifying the false statement as a *term* of the contract (see 5.1.1 and 10.3.2) and awarding expectation damages for breach (eg *De Lassalle v Guildford* (1901). However, there is less need to do this as the category of 'innocent misrepresentation' has dwindled. **Prior to** *Hedley Byrne v Heller*, the category included all 'non-fraudulent' misrepresentations because damages were only available for fraud. **After** *Hedley Byrne v Heller*, it describes any misrepresentation that the representee cannot prove was made fraudulently or negligently. **The 1967 Act** further reduces the category. The reversal of the burden of proof means that a misrepresentation, which is 'innocent' at common law (because the *representee* cannot prove fraud or negligence), may still attract liability under section 2(1) if the *representor* cannot show his or her honesty and reasonableness in making the statement. Only if the representor can prove otherwise is his or her representation '*innocent*'. We can call this 'purely innocent' misrepresentation to signal its different scope from common law 'innocent' misrepresentation law).

(v) Non-disclosure

Section 2(1) does not apply to *pure non-disclosures* (see 5.1.3.3) since an *active misrepresentation* is required under the Act (*Banque Financière de la Cité SA v Westgate Insurance Co* (1989) at 1003–4).

Pause for reflection

1. The scope of section 2(1) includes: (i) common law fraud; (ii) common law negligent misrepresentations; and (iii) some misrepresentations which would be regarded as 'innocent'
   under the common law. Only *'purely innocent'* misrepresentations and non-disclosure
   cases fall outside the scope of section 2(1).
2. The 'fiction of fraud' under section 2(1) when applied to statements of *opinion and
   intention* would seem to make such statements actionable per se, unless the representor can prove his or her honesty and reasonable basis. If that is right, *Bisset v Wilkinson*
   (discussed at 5.1.2.4) would be decided differently under the 1967 Act, for it would be
   insufficient that the representor gave his or her opinion honestly and without any special
   expertise, he or she would have to *prove* the honesty and reasonableness for his or her
   opinion.

5.2.1.2 The remedial advantage of a section 2(1) claim: the fiction of fraud

A complex body of law governs the award of damages for misrepresentation. It is now
settled that:

(i) **The basic measure of damages** under the 1967 Act (as with common law fraudulent or negligent misrepresentations) is the tortious or **reliance** measure (*Royscot
Trust Ltd v Rogerson* (1991); *Sharneyford Supplies Ltd v Edge Barrington Black and Co* (1987)
at 323) and not the contractual measure as some initially suggested (eg Lord Denning
in *Gosling v Anderson* (1972), *Jarvis v Swan's Tours* (1973)). The reliance measure aims to
protect the representee's *status quo interest* by putting him or her, as far as money can
do, in the position he or she would have been in had the misrepresentation *not been
made* (ie the contract not entered).

(ii) **The starting point** is that the representee can recover for:

- *reduction in property value at the time of contracting*: where the representee is
  induced to buy some property, he or she is entitled to the difference between
  the price paid and the market value of the property at the time the contract was
  entered; and

- *consequential losses*: the representee can recover damages for other 'out of pocket'
  losses such as for personal injury, loss of or damage to property, and wasted
  expenses.

(iii) **The 'fiction of fraud'**: the generous common law measure for fraud applies to
claims under section 2(1); the representor is liable for damages *as if* he or she was fraudulent *even though* he or she was not (*Royscot Trust v Rogerson*). This has been criticised
for yielding an unjustifiably favourable measure of damages where the representor was
merely negligent or simply unable to prove that he or she was not negligent. We will first
examine the remedial advantages conferred by the fiction of fraud and then assess the
criticisms of the fiction. **Diagram 5E** gives an overview of the advantages of the fraud
measure over the negligence measure at common law and the extent to which the section 2(1) claims mimic the fraud measure.

Diagram 5E The remedial advantages of the 'fiction of fraud'

	Fraud	s 2(1)	Negligence
			✓ = yes ✗ = no
1. Proof of causation	✗	✗	✓
2. Remoteness limit	✗	✗	✓
3. Claim for devaluation of property *after* contract formation	✓	✓	✗
4. Claim for loss of opportunity	✓	✓	✗
5. Reduction of claim for contributory negligence	✗	✗ (Unless concurrent action in negligence)	✓
6. Exemplary damages	✓	✓	✗
7. Limitation of claim	6 years from *discovery*	may not mimic fraud (?)	6 years from *making of statement*

Doyle v Olby (Ironmongers) Ltd (1969) and *Smith New Court Securities Ltd v Scrimgeour Vickers (Asset Management) Ltd* (1997) set out the main principles in assessing damages for fraud.

1. ***Causation***: in cases of fraud, damages are calculated on the *assumption* that the representee would not have entered the contract 'but for' the misrepresentation, hence he or she can claim *all* their losses from *entering* the contract. This position is mimicked by section 2(1) claims.[18] In contrast, in cases of *negligent* misrepresentation, it *is* relevant that the representee might have entered the contract anyway, even if on different terms, since this affects the causal connection between the misrepresentation and the loss claimed (*South Australia Asset Management Corp v York Montague Ltd* (1997) at 218).

2. ***No remoteness limit***: whilst damages for negligent misrepresentation are limited to that which was in the reasonable contemplation of (foreseeable by) the other party (ie not too remote), damages for deceit are not so limited; the claimant can recover *all* losses flowing from the fraud, even if they were unforeseeable by the representor.

3. ***Existing flaws and loss in value after contractual formation***: we noted that the representee is entitled to the difference between the price paid and the market value of the property *at the time the purchase was made*. In cases of fraud, the House of Lords in **Smith New Court v Scrimgeour Vickers** (at 267, 284) held that the representee can

---

[18] *Downs v Chappell* (1997); *Smith New Court Securities v Scrimgeour Vickers* at 284–5; *Avon Insurance plc v Swire Fraser* (2001).

also claim for falls in the value of the property *after* contract formation if: 'either (a) the misrepresentation has continued to operate after the date of the acquisition of the asset so as to induce the plaintiff to retain the asset or (b) the circumstances of the case are such that the plaintiff is, by reason of the fraud, locked into the property'. SV's fraudulent misrepresentation about the presence of rival bidders induced SNCS to buy shares for £23 million when the market price at the time was £21.8 million. In addition to the difference between them, the House of Lords also allowed SNCS's claim for:

- loss due to *'existing flaws'* in the property: the subsequent discovery of an unconnected and unknown fraud in the company meant that the value of the shares at the time of the contract (had the fraud been known) was only £12.25 million. The House of Lords (at 279) drew an analogy with someone who is fraudulently induced to buy an already diseased racehorse which later dies; he or she can recover the entire price paid;[19]

- loss due to being *'locked into' the property*: since it was not commercially feasible for SNCS to resell the shares immediately on discovering the fraud, it suffered further losses from a general fall in the share market. The shares were eventually sold for £11.75 million.

In short:

£23.00 million = Price paid

£21.80 million = Devaluation due to fraud

£12.25 million = Further devaluation due to existing flaw

£11.75 million = Price sold (further devaluation due to being locked into property)

Damages = £23 million – £11.75 million = **£11.25 million**

SNCS's full compensation for all its losses is justified by 'considerations of morality and deterrence', which do not apply where the misrepresentation is negligent (*South Australia Asset Management v York Montague*).

4. *Loss of opportunity*: in principle, damages for fraud are different from damages for breach of contract but, in practice, the two measures can yield the same sum if reliance loss includes 'loss of opportunity' to make another similarly profitable contract.[20]

The idea is that *if* the representee had not been induced into the contract with the representor, he or she would have invested it in *another* similar profit-making contract. Therefore, to restore him or her to the position that they would have been in had they not entered *this* contract, damages must include the loss of profits that he or she would have made from entering *another* similar contract not tainted by misrepresentation. The representee can even recover loss to reflect the fact that, but for the misrepresentation, he or she would have made a more profitable contract (ie on better terms) with the representor (*Clef Aquitaine SARL v Laporte Materials Ltd* (2001)). This

---

[19] *Naughten v O'Callaghan* (1990).

[20] This reasoning led Fuller and Perdue, in 'The Reliance Interest in Contract Damages' (1936) 46 *Yale LJ* 52, 60 to argue that contract damages are in fact merely a surrogate for the more justifiable reliance (tortious) damages; see 1.4.2 and 5.1.1.1.

is theoretically distinct from the contract measure (which puts the representee in the position he or she would be in if the statement was *true*) but the practical difference is invisible because the contract measure is used to *quantify* the measure of the loss of opportunity. Sedley J conceded that 'loss of opportunity' 'mimic[s] reasoning more familiar in contract' (*Clef Aquitaine* at 513). In *East v Maurer* (1991), E was induced to buy a hairdressing business for £20,000 by M's fraudulent misrepresentation that he had no intention of working regularly in another hairdressing salon in the same town. In fact, M did so and many of his clients followed him, resulting in significant trading losses to E, who eventually sold the business for £5,000. The court awarded E:

- the difference between what E paid and what he received;

- E's wasted expenditure, for example in trying to improve the business; *and*

- £10,000 representing the loss of profits which E would have made from buying another similar hairdressing business. In quantifying this, the court (at 468) referred to the profit that the salon actually purchased would have made *if the representation had been true*.

In *4Eng Ltd v Harper* (2007), H sold 4Eng a company with fraudulent practices, which subsequently went into liquidation. 4Eng's damages included its loss of opportunity to acquire another company, T, in which it was seriously considering investing at the time it acquired H's company. David Richards J held (at [46]) that, in a deceit claim, 'a loss is too remote only if it is not in the eyes of the law directly caused by a defendant's deceit'. On the balance of probabilities, the judge found that 4Eng would have bought T had it not been for H's fraudulent misrepresentations, and awarded substantial damages to reflect lost capital value and profits.

5. *Contributory negligence*: while damages for *negligent* misrepresentation can be reduced if the loss was partly the representee's fault (Law Reform (Contributory Negligence) Act 1945, s 1), damages for fraud are immune from this reduction (*Alliance & Leicester BS v Edgestop Ltd* (1993)). The 'fiction of fraud' points to section 2(1) claims being likewise immune. However, in *Gran Gelato v Richcliff (Group)*, Nicholls VC held (at 573–4) that contributory negligence *can* bite 'where there are concurrent claims . . . in negligence in tort and under the Act of 1967'. Ironically, it would be the *representor* who would have the incentive to argue that he or she owes and has breached a tortious duty of care against the representee in order to bring the latter's contributory negligence into account.

6. *Exemplary damages*: it is arguable that exemplary damages may now be available for fraudulent misrepresentation (see 13.2.1).

The generosity of the **'fiction of fraud'** measure of damages has attracted some **criticism**.

- **Liability versus measure**: it has been argued that the 'fiction of fraud' should only be used to establish *liability* and not the *measure* of damages.[21] Also, that

---

[21] R Hooley, 'Damages and the Misrepresentation Act 1967' (1991) 107 *LQR* 547; R Taylor, 'Expectation, Reliance and Misrepresentation' (1982) 45 *MLR* 139, 141; J Stuart-Smith QC, 'Recovery of Damages after Misrepresentation' (2000) 150 *NLJ* 865–6.

while *Royscot Trust v Rogerson* expressly supports the fiction of fraud, the case did not actually turn on this point since the loss claimed *was* foreseeable and would have been recoverable without the fiction. *However*, the fraud measure is supported by the literal wording of section 2(1) and by the Law Reform Committee Report.[22]

- **Section 2(1) claims do not track deceit claims exactly**: first, there is the potential, albeit small, for *contributory negligence* to bite in section 2(1) claims. Second, dicta in *Garden Neptune Shipping Ltd v Occidental World Wide Investment Corp* (1990) at 335 suggest that the extended **limitation period** for fraud (six years from the discovery of the fraud rather than from the making of the statement, see 13.2.5.7) may *not* apply under section 2(1).

- **'Fools should not be treated as if they were rogues'**.[23] This is the most forceful criticism. It is widely thought to be undesirable and unjustifiable to treat non-fraudulent misrepresentors as if they were fraudulent. Further, section 2(1) is said to be out of step with modern developments. It is the product of the Law Reform Committee's report, published in 1962 when it was not thought to be the 'general function of the civil law to grade the damages which an injured person may recover in accordance with the moral guilt of the defendant'.[24] In **'Deceit, Damages and the Misrepresentation Act 1967, s2(1)'** (1992) *LMCLQ* 40, **Brown and Chandler** argue that it is unlikely that the legislature really intended unintentional misrepresentation to attract the same moral opprobrium as deceit, and section 2(2) signals the legislature's intention to differentiate between them.

Since 1962, the law *has* come to reflect the relative degree of moral fault in damages awards (eg *The Wagon Mound (No 1)*, tying liability to foreseeability, and *Hedley Byrne v Heller*, recognising lesser liability for negligent misrepresentation than for deceit). Section 2(1) is out of line with this approach. The House of Lords in *Smith New Court Securities v Scrimgeour Vickers* notes the 'trenchant academic criticisms' of the fiction of fraud. It declined to comment on the correctness of *Royscot Trust v Rogerson* while questioning whether 'the rather loose wording of the statute compels the court to treat a person who was morally innocent as if he was guilty of fraud when it comes to the measure of damages' (at 283, 267). Rix J also expresses considerable scepticism and suggests that courts may be inclined not to find a misrepresentation at all to avoid having to award fraud-like damages (*Avon Insurance v Swire* (2001) at 576, 633).

---

[22] Law Reform Committee, *Innocent Misrepresentation* (10th Report, Cmnd 1782, 1962); and see *F&B Entertainments Ltd v Leisure Enterprises Ltd* (1976) at 461, where Walton J, a member of the Law Reform Committee, indicates that the deceit measure was intended by the Committee.

[23] *Anson's* at 327; A Fairest, 'Misrepresentation and the Act of 1967' (1967) 25 *CLJ* 239, 244; R Hooley, 'Damages and the Misrepresentation Act 1967' (1991) 107 *LQR* 547, 549–51; cf P S Atiyah and G Treitel, 'The Misrepresentation Act 1967' (1967) 30 *MLR* 369, 373; J Cartwright, *Unequal Bargaining: A Study of Vitiating Factors in the Formation of Contracts* (Clarendon Press, 1991) 131–2.

[24] Law Reform Committee, *Innocent Misrepresentation* (10th Report, Cmnd 1782, 1962) para 22.

> ### ⏪⏩ Counterpoint
>
> The arguments do not all go one way. The *representee*'s position must also be weighed in the balance. The aim of the 1967 Act was to *simplify and enhance protection* for the victims of contract-inducing misrepresentations by lowering the qualifying conditions for damages *in tandem with* awarding the most advantageous measure of damages.[25] Dispensing the representee from proving fraud or negligence but still awarding fraud damages straightforwardly achieves simplification and greater protection for the representee. If the default measure for section 2(1) claims is the negligence measure, the representee would revert to the position of having to prove fraud to access the fraud damages, so undermining the aims of the 1967 Act. Moreover, the fraud measure merely compensates the representee for his or her *provable* losses and this does not seem inherently unjust.

5.2.2 Other money claims: expectation damages, restitution, and indemnity

Aside from section 2(1) damages, facts supporting an actionable misrepresentation may yield other money claims, as **Diagram 5D, columns III–V** show. An understanding that they rest on different bases and yield potentially different measures of damages will enable a claimant to decide which claim, or combination of claims, is most advantageous in his or her circumstances. The possible claims are the following.

(i) **Damages on the contract measure** (see 5.2.1.2) where the representation is incorporated as a term of the contract.

(ii) **Restitution on rescission** (see 5.3): where the contract is rescinded for misrepresentation the representor must return any benefit (money or, more controversially, non-money) received under the contract as part of the mutual giving-back required for rescission.

(iii) **Indemnity on rescission** of any costs incurred in discharging legal obligations *necessitated* by the (now rescinded) contract. These costs are part of the 'price' the representee pays for the contract, which the representor should 'give back' on the contract's rescission. In *Newbigging v Adam* (1887), N successfully rescinded a partnership agreement which he was induced to enter into by A's innocent misrepresentation. N recovered the purchase price under the contract *and* an indemnity against the liabilities he might have incurred while a partner. Since rescission is prima facie available for all types of misrepresentations, so are restitution and indemnity.

(iv) **Damages in lieu of rescission** made available by section 2(2) of the 1967 Act if the court exercises its discretion to bar rescission (see 5.3.3).

---

[25] A Fairest, 'Misrepresentation and the Act of 1967' (1967) 25 *CLJ* 239, 243–4; Law Reform Committee, *Innocent Misrepresentation* (10th Report, Cmnd 1782, 1962) para 22; J Cartwright, *Unequal Bargaining: A Study of Vitiating Factors in the Formation of Contracts* (Clarendon Press, 1991) 131–2.

Care must be taken to distinguish reliance damages, restitution, and indemnity, which all claim to restore the representee to his or her 'pre-contractual' position:

- **restitution** returns to the representee what he or she paid under the contract and an **indemnity** compensates him or her for the additional costs and liabilities directly imposed on them by the contract;

- **reliance damages** are potentially wider than rescission-related claims. They include consequential loss from entering the contract that does not enrich the misrepresentor (eg personal injury, damaged goods, and wasted expenditure), and loss of opportunity where fraud is present (see 5.2.1.2(iii)(4)). These are not available where a misrepresentation is *innocent* under the common law or 'purely innocent' under the 1967 Act, although a representee can claim restitution and indemnity on rescission.

These differences are illustrated by ***Whittington v Seale-Hayne*** (1900). W was induced to lease premises for breeding prize poultry by S's innocent misrepresentation that the premises were in good sanitary condition. In fact, the water supply was contaminated. W's manager became sick and the poultry died. The court allowed rescission of the lease and indemnity-based recovery for what was spent on rent, rates, and the replacement of drains which had been required by the local authority, since these expenses were incurred in meeting 'obligations created by the contract' (the seller would have been liable for them had he kept the property). However, W could not recover for the lost stock and profits or the manager's medical expenses. These reliance losses would now be available under section 2(1) of the Act unless S could prove its honesty and reasonableness in making the statement.

5.2.3 **Combination of claims**

Any item of loss can only be claimed once (*Archer v Brown* (1984)). The rule of thumb is that a claimant must choose between going 'forwards' and 'backwards'; he or she cannot do both at the same time. Thus, claimants *can*:

- go 'backwards' and claim restitution and indemnity on rescission (or damages in lieu of rescission) in addition to reliance (excluding devaluation of the property), aggravated, and exemplary damages. Section 2(3) expressly permits claims under both section 2(1) and section 2(2), although in calculating the former account should be taken of the latter; or

- go 'forwards' and claim remedies for breach of contract.

Claimants *cannot*:

- ✗ simultaneously go *forwards* and *backwards* by claiming expectation damages and either reliance damages or rescission; or

- ✗ go *backwards in money and in kind* by claiming rescission *and* either damages in lieu of rescission or devaluation of the property acquired under the contract.

5.3 **Rescission for misrepresentation**

5.3.1 **What is rescission?**

(i) **The effect**: rescission operates to *set aside the contract*; it is conditional on mutual restoration of any benefits received under it; each party gives back and gets back. The aim is to prevent unjust enrichment (*MacKenzie v Royal Bank of Canada* (1934) and see 5.3.2.5).

(ii) **Availability**: rescission is available for *all* types of misrepresentations, subject to the 'bars' discussed in the following section.

(iii) **How and when**? Rescission is only effective once it is *communicated* to the other party. The timing is important if the representee wants to recover property transferred under the voidable contract. If *A* transfers property to *B* pursuant to a contract induced by *B*'s misrepresentation, and *B* then sells that property to *C, A* can only recover the property from *C* if he or she rescinds his or her contract with *B before B* passes the property to *C* (see 6.4.1.1). Rescission may be a judicial remedy (awarded by the courts) or a self-help remedy (effected by the representee's *own action*). In the former case, rescission is *communicated* when the representee resists a claim for specific performance by counterclaiming for rescission, or when the representee applies directly to the court to set aside the contract. In the latter case, rescission is *communicated* when the representee notifies the representor. However, a representee may be able to rescind by taking all possible steps to recover the goods, without actually notifying the representor. In *Car and Universal Finance Co Ltd v Caldwell* (1965), C was fraudulently induced to sell his car in return for a bad cheque. The buyer disappeared and C immediately sought assistance from the police and the Automobile Association. *Subsequently*, the buyer sold the car to CUF. Since it would be unfair to insist that the representee actually notify an absconding fraudster, it was held that C had effectively rescinded the contract by his actions, thereby revesting title to the car in himself and preventing CUF from acquiring effective title thereafter. C could recover the car from CUF. This outcome is harsh for the third party buying property from the fraudster in good faith, and the Law Reform Committee has recommended that such a purchaser should acquire a good title (*Transfer of Title to Chattels* (12th Report (Cmnd 2958, 1966) at para 16)).

(iv) **Rescission vs termination**: students sometimes confuse the *rescission* of voidable contracts (eg those induced by misrepresentation and other vitiating factors in Part IV) with the *termination* of valid but breached contracts (Chapter 12). This is unsurprising since some courts and texts refer to both as 'rescission' (as recognised in *Photo Production Ltd v Securicor Transport Ltd* (1980) at 844). Both bring a contract to an end but they are quite distinct (*Johnson v Agnew* (1979) at 492).

- *Rescission* of contracts for misrepresentation (and other vitiating factors such as duress, undue influence) is often described as 'rescission *ab initio*' (the contract is set aside *from the beginning*). Although property rights *can* pass under a voidable contract up to the time of rescission, *as against the other contract party* (here, the misrepresentor), rescission nullifies the contract prospectively *and* retrospectively. Any obligations yet to be performed are cancelled and any benefits transferred are treated as if they were never due and so must be returned. The representee's right of election as to whether to rescind or affirm did not include a middle course of affirming the transaction only to the extent of the misrepresentation; there can be no partial rescission (*Potter v Dyer* (2011)).

- *Termination* of contracts for *breach*, on the other hand, recognises an undoubtedly valid contract between the parties. In limited circumstances (see 12.2), the contract may be terminated by the innocent party, thereby dispensing both parties from *further* performance of their primary obligations. In their place is substituted the contract-breaker's liability to remedy the breach. Termination is therefore only prospective; it is 'rescission *de futuro*' (for the future). Anything transferred under the contract up to the point of termination is generally not recoverable by the claimant (he or she cannot go 'backwards', but see 13.4) but is taken into account in calculating his or her damages, which are designed to take him or her 'forwards' to their expectation position (*Photo Production v Securicor Transport* at 844–5, 849–50).

5.3.2 The 'bars' to rescission

Misrepresentation makes a contract voidable. Unlike void contracts, the right to set aside voidable contracts is not absolute: it can be lost or 'barred'. The 1967 Act removes two pre-existing bars to rescission and adds one, making the final list: (i) affirmation; (ii) lapse of time; (iii) third party rights; (iv) impossibility of mutual restitution; and (v) inequity. **Diagram 5F** gives an overview of their effect on the different types of misrepresentation. It shows that the bars may be lowered or removed where there is fraud.

5.3.2.1 Removal of bars by section 1 Misrepresentation Act 1967

We saw that **section 1(a)** of the 1967 Act preserves the representee's right to rescission even if the representation becomes incorporated as a term of the contract (see 5.1.1.1). This creates a potential problem because rescission would deprive the representee of his or her former right to contractual damages (since one cannot go 'backwards' and 'forwards'). Where a claimant's contractual damages exceed his or her reliance damages (ie he or she made a good bargain), the court must decide whether his or her refusal to continue with the contract amounts to rescission (limiting him or her to reliance damages) or termination (preserving their right to expectation damages). Another complication is that the claimant may not qualify for termination (since it is only available for 'serious' breaches, see 12.2.3). Thus, a claimant may find that he or she has unwittingly rescinded the contract (eg by returning defective items), thereby extinguished his or her rights to superior contractual damages. In **'Misrepresentation Act 1967'** (1967) 30 *MLR* 369, **Atiyah and Treitel** argue that the Act has failed to simplify the law in a number of respects including section 1(a); they also cite section 3. They are also critical of the 'fiction of fraud', although they approve the discretion to bar rescission under section 2(2).

Diagram 5F How the bars to rescission apply to different types of misrepresentation

		✓ = yes
		✗ = no

'Bars'	Fraudulent	Negligent	Innocent
1. Affirmation	✓	✓	✓
2. Lapse of time	✗	✓	✓
3. Third party rights	✓	✓	✓
4. Impossibility of mutual rescission	✓ but less stringent	✓	✓
5. Inequity under s 2(2) Misrepresentation Act	✗	✓	✓

Section 1(b) removes the former bar to rescission where contracts for the sale of property induced by non-fraudulent misrepresentations have been *performed* (*Angel v Jay* (1911)).[26] While this bar served the interests of security of receipts and certainty of contracts, it often operated unjustly because it may be impossible to discover the truth before the property is transferred.

5.3.2.2 Affirmation

Misrepresentation only makes a contract voidable, and not absolutely void. The claimant can elect to rescind or affirm the contract.

(i) Affirmation requires **knowledge** of the facts giving rise to the right to rescind. However, a representee without the relevant knowledge may be *estopped* from denying affirmation if the representor has detrimentally relied on the representee's unequivocal conduct indicating his or her intention to affirm (*Peyman v Lanjani* (1985) at 486–8).

(ii) Affirmation can be **express** or **implied from conduct**. Thus, rescission has been barred where, after discovering the misrepresentation, the claimant continues using the goods bought (*United Shoe Machinery Co of Canada v Brunet* (1909)), accepts dividends, votes at meetings, attempts to sell the shares bought (*Scholey v Central Rly Co of Venezuela* (1867)), or continues to reside and pay rent on premises leased (*Kennard v Ashman* (1894)). However, the mere use of property, or delay in rescinding, in order to verify the suspicion of misrepresentation does not amount to an affirmation (*Long v Lloyd* (1958)). The court will take into account the nature of the contract, any lapse of time, any change of position by the representor in reliance on the absence of protest by the representee, and whether third parties have been affected (*Clough v London & NW Rly* (1871) at 34, 35; *BCCI (In Liquidation) v Ali (No 1)* (1999) at 1023).

---

[26] Although the scope of the former rule was uncertain it being unclear whether sale of goods contracts came under this rule: *Leaf v International Galleries* (1950).

(iii) Affirmation is very similar to acquiescence and estoppel. The claimant may be estopped from rescinding the contract where it has led the defendant, by unequivocal statements or actions, to believe that it intends to affirm the contract, and the defendant **has acted on this to its prejudice**. The claimant can be estopped even where they do not know the facts or his or her rights. It is 'inequitable' for the claimant to rely on her right because of the defendant's detrimental reliance (*Habib Bank Ltd v Nasira Tufail* (2006)).

5.3.2.3 Lapse of time

Where the misrepresentation is **fraudulent**, lapse of time *cannot* bar rescission whilst the representee remains ignorant of the misrepresentation (*Armstrong v Jackson* (1917) at 830). With **non-fraudulent** misrepresentations, a representee who fails to rescind the contract within a *reasonable* time of discovering the truth may be held to have affirmed the contract (*Clough v London & NW Rly* (1871)). But even if the representee remains ignorant of the non-fraudulent misrepresentation, a substantial passage of time *may* bar rescission (ie lapse of time operates either as evidence of affirmation or as an independent bar). In *Leaf v International Galleries* (1950), L was induced to buy a picture of Salisbury Cathedral by I's innocent misrepresentation that it was painted by the famous artist Constable. L only discovered this was false when he tried to sell the picture some five years later. Nevertheless, L's claim to rescind the contract was denied due to lapse of time. Jenkins LJ said (at 92) that contracts 'cannot be kept open and subject to the possibility of rescission indefinitely'. Moreover, the statement as to the identity of the painter was held to be a term, for the breach of which L could have claimed expectation damages, although he did not do so.

5.3.2.4 Third party rights

Rescission will be barred if, in the meantime, an innocent third party has given consideration to acquire an interest in the subject matter of the contract (*White v Garden* (1851)). For example, rescission of a contract for shares is barred once the company goes into liquidation, since this fixes the creditors' rights to share in the company's assets. This bar promotes the general interest in the security of transactions. The *voidable* status of contracts tainted by misrepresentations (and most other vitiating factors) means that the contract's ability to transfer rights is effective until the contract is rescinded. It follows that a bona fide third party who acquires property rights for value before the contract is rescinded is protected (see 5.3.1(iii) and 6.4.1.1). Moreover, if a third party has acquired property rights in the subject matter of the contract, it is obviously impossible for the *representor* to return the precise property to the representee as part of rescission; the representee can only include the value of the property in his or her reliance claim against the representor.

5.3.2.5 Impossibility of mutual restitution

Rescission involves the 'giving back and taking back of the obligations which the contract has created, as well as the giving back and the taking back of the advantages' (*Newbigging v Adam* (1886) at 595). Executory (unperformed) contracts pose no problems since rescission just cancels both parties' contractual obligations. But where the contract is partially or wholly executed (performed), rescission is barred if it is impossible to return the benefits transferred under the contract. In practice, this is the *main bar to rescission* because English law treats rescission as a *proprietary* rather than a personal remedy. This means that, money aside, what must be restored is the *exact* thing received. So, rescission has been barred where return in kind:

- to the *representee* was never possible, as with services (*Boyd & Forrest v Glasgow & South Western Railway* (1915)); or has become impossible, as where the property is substantially dissipated through use, consumption, or selling on to a third party (*White v Garden* (1851)); and

- to the *representor* is not substantially possible, as where the claimant bought a mine and sought to rescind after it had been worked out (*Vigers v Pike* (1842)).

This bar has shown some signs of relaxation by allowing monetary substitution.

- In *O'Sullivan v Management Agency & Music Ltd* (1985), a pop singer rescinded the contract with his manager. The latter had to account for their profits, but were given credit for their skill and labour in promoting the singer and significantly contributing to his success (9.2.5.1).

- In *Erlanger v New Sombrero Phosphate Co* (1878) at 1278–9, the court emphasised its *equitable* jurisdiction to give rescission 'whenever, by the exercise of its powers, it can do what is practically just [eg by giving an *account of profits* made from use of the property and making *allowances* for deterioration of the property] though it cannot restore the parties precisely to the state they were in before the contract'.

- *Fraud* increases the courts' willingness to make adjustments to allow rescission. In *Spence v Crawford* (1939) at 288–9, Lord Wright said:

  > The court will be less ready to pull a transaction to pieces where the defendant is innocent, whereas in the case of fraud the Court will exercise its jurisdiction to the full in order, if possible, to prevent the defendant from enjoying the benefit of his fraud at the expense of the innocent plaintiff. But restoration is essential to the idea of restitution . . . the court can go a long way in ordering restitution if the *substantial identity of the subject-matter of the contract remains* (emphasis added).

However, by requiring 'substantial' (even if not precise) restitution, the bar retains much of its force. Thus, even in a fraud case, Lord Browne-Wilkinson thought it necessary to say that shares, which had been sold on to third parties, could be 'returned' *if* the representee could buy and return 'other, identical, shares' on the market (*Smith New Court Securities Ltd v Scrimgeour Vickers* at 262). By implication, the shares could not simply be returned in money's worth.

◆◆ Counterpoint

Impossibility of precise return in kind by either party should not bar rescission. If English law is prepared to make small money adjustments to *supplement* a representee's return of substantially subsisting property, then it should be prepared to make big money adjustments, even to the extent of wholly *substituting* for benefits which could never, or can no longer, be returned in kind. The same applies to the representor's restitutionary liability. The current insistence

➡

> ➡
>
> on substantial restitution can give rise to unfair results. If rescission is barred, the admittedly unfair contract remains enforceable (even by a party guilty of fraud or duress). The representee has no claim for damages if the misrepresentation is purely innocent, and may become liable in damages for breach of this unfair contract (even if specific performance can be resisted). The requirement of substantial mutual restitution is further discredited when we consider that the object of rescission is not, strictly speaking, to restore the parties to their pre-contractual position (*MacKenzie v Royal Bank of Canada* (1934)). Rather, it is to prevent the claimant from being unjustly enriched at the other's expense by keeping the benefits received while getting back their own 'payment' for that benefit (*Bouygues Offshore v Owner of the M/T Tigr Ultisol Transport Contractors* (1996) at 1–59). A fairer solution is to recognise that benefits received can always be given back, by money substitution if not in kind.

5.3.2.6 Inequity: section 2(2) Misrepresentation Act 1967

Where the misrepresentation is *non-fraudulent* (ie negligent, innocent, or purely innocent), section 2(2) empowers courts to deny rescission (or reinstate an already rescinded contract), awarding the claimant damages in lieu (see 5.3.3), where 'it would be equitable to do so, having regard to the nature of the misrepresentation and the loss that would be caused by it if the contract were upheld, as well as to the loss that rescission would cause to the other party'. The motivation for section 2(2) is *pro-representor*.[27] We noted the anomaly that while termination is only available for a *serious* breach of contract, rescission is prima facie available for *any* and even trivial misrepresentation. The 1967 Act irons out this anomaly in two moves:

(i) section 1(a) *liberalises* access to rescission (preserving the representee's right to rescind even if the representation is incorporated only as a warranty (less 'serious' term) of the contract, see 5.3.2.1);

(ii) section 2(2) *restricts* access to rescission by giving courts the discretion to protect a non-fraudulent representor from being deprived of his or her entire bargain for a relatively trivial misrepresentation and to prevent the representee from escaping a bad bargain. In return (or in consolation), the representee is awarded damages.

William Sindall plc v Cambridgeshire CC (1994) illustrates the operation of section 2(2). W bought land for development from C for over £5 million in 1988. In 1990, W discovered that a sewer buried under the land would prevent its proposed development unless the sewer could be rerouted. W's claim of misrepresentation failed, but Hoffmann LJ expressed the view that, even if it had succeeded, the court would have barred rescission under section 2(2) because of:

• the relatively *minor impact* on the buyer if rescission is denied—it would only cost £18,000 to rectify the problem, and was unlikely to interfere seriously with the development or resale value of the property;

• the relative *unimportance of the representation* in the *context* of a £5 million sale;

---

[27] Law Reform Committee, *Innocent Misrepresentation* (10th Report, Cmnd 1782, 1952) paras 11, 12; A Fairest, 'Misrepresentation and the Act of 1967' (1967) 25 *CLJ* 239, 245.

- the colossal loss to the seller if rescission is allowed—the seller would have recovered land now worth less than £2 million due to a general fall in land values while having to repay the buyer about £8 million (purchase price plus interest).

5.3.3 **Section 2(2) Misrepresentation Act 1967: damages in lieu of rescission**

5.3.3.1 Measure of damages

If rescission is barred under section 2(2), what is the measure of the 'damages in lieu'?

✗ Section 2(2) damages cannot simply replicate section 2(1) reliance damages; that would deprive section 2(2) of any effect and would make nonsense of section 2(3), which recognises the possibility of concurrent claims under both and requires section 2(1) awards to take account of any section 2(2) awards.

✗ Although the words 'in lieu of rescission' suggest that the measure should be the *money's worth of actual rescission* of the contract, this cannot be right. In *William Sindall*, it would totally undermine the reason for denying rescission (ie to prevent the hardship to the representor of being deprived of the whole bargain because of some minor misrepresentation) if the representor were then required to pay £6 million in lieu to compensate the representee for not getting rescission.

The move is towards measuring damages in lieu of rescission on the basis that the misrepresentation is a term of the contract that has been breached, although the representor has not promised the truth of the statement. In the Court of Appeal, Evans LJ in *William Sindall* (at 1037) held that the correct measure is the difference in value between what the representee believed they were acquiring and what they in fact acquired. Likewise, Hoffmann LJ (at 1045) said that section 2(2) is 'concerned with damage caused by the property not being what it was represented to be'.

👤 **Pause for reflection**

1. Section 6(1)(a) of the New Zealand Contractual Remedies Act 1979 entitles a misrepresentee to damages 'in the same manner and to the same extent as if the representation were a term of the contract that has been broken'.

2. The 'measure under section 2(2) may be either: (i) the diminution of value (difference between the contract price and any reduction in the actual value of the property due to the *misrepresentation); or (ii) the cost of correcting the defect (Evans LJ in William* Sindall at 1045). Alternative (ii) will be preferable if the property is worth no less because of the misrepresentation.

3. Section 2(2) damages should not cover consequential reliance losses (which belong under s 2(1)), or consequential losses of expectation (which belong properly in a breach of contract claim).

4. In 'Damages in Lieu of Rescission for Misrepresentation' (1995) 111 *LQR* 60, Beale argues that it is undesirable and unprincipled to measure damages under section 2(2) by the contract measure (ie 2(ii) above) because no promise has been given in respect of the statement. Only the tort measure (2(i) above) is justifiable.

5.3.3.2 Availability of section 2(2) damages

(i) Despite a previous decision to the contrary (*Thomas Witter Ltd v TBP Industries* (1996)), **Govt of Zanzibar v British Aerospace (Lancaster House) Ltd** (2000) has confirmed that the representee must have a good claim for rescission to be eligible for damages 'in lieu of' rescission; **rescission cannot be barred**, he or she must have something of value to 'trade in' for the damages. This accords with the Law Reform Committee's position (10th Report, Cmnd 1782, 1962 at para 27) and the clear wording of the subsection.

(ii) Section 2(2) is **not an independent route to previously unavailable damages**; the representee can only obtain damages 'in lieu' where he or she has *sought* but been *denied rescission* by the court. A rational representee will only seek rescission (ie to go backwards) if that will make him or her better off than leaving the contract on foot (ie when he or she has made a bad bargain). This is the facts in *William Sindall* where the property purchased dramatically plunged in value. But, bearing in mind the *pro-representor thrust* of section 2(2), this is precisely the situation when rescission is likely to be barred and a *less advantageous* award of damages in lieu substituted. True, the representee will get a previously unavailable *monetary* award, but only by trading in a *more valuable* remedy which would have yielded more money or money's worth.

5.4 **Exemption of liability for misrepresentation**

At common law, a party **cannot exclude or restrict liability for his or her own fraud** (*S Pearson & Son v Dublin Corp* (1907)). But the contract may also attempt to limit or exclude liability for non-fraudulent misrepresentations via the following.

(i) Terms that exempt liability for misrepresentation.

(ii) **'No representation' or 'no reliance' clauses**: these seek to prevent the claimant from establishing one of the requirements of an actionable misrepresentation by agreement to a state of affairs that may not actually be true; that is, that the defendant did not make or that the claimant did not rely upon any representations.

(iii) **Entire agreement clauses**: these clauses state that the written contract constitutes the 'entire agreement' between them. They prevent the claimant from arguing that the defendant's statement amounted to a collateral term or contract, which the defendant has breached.

The effectiveness of such clauses depends on their construction and on statutory provisions.

5.4.1 **Construction**

To avoid liability for misrepresentation, the relevant clause must be interpreted (or 'construed') to cover one of the three aims identified in 5.4. In *AXA Sun Life v Campbell Martin*, a term, referred to as an 'Entire Agreement' clause, stated: 'This Agreement . . . constitute the entire agreement and understanding between you and us in relation to the subject matter thereof . . . [It] shall supersede any prior promises, agreements, representations, undertakings or implications whether made orally or in writing . . .'.

This clearly excluded any collateral terms (at [34]). But does it also operate as a no-representation clause?

The court warned that issues of construction would always turn upon the precise wording of the clause. Rix LJ held (at [94]) that an exclusion of liability for misrepresentation must be clearly stated either by express exclusions of liability, or by no-representation or no-reliance clauses; otherwise, talk of the contract superseding prior 'representations' will not by itself absolve the defendant of misrepresentation. On the facts, the clause was ineffective as a no-representation clause because, inter alia, (at [80]–[82]): the word 'representations' was 'completely sandwiched between words of contractual import'; that is, the surrounding clauses were concerned with the scope of the contractual agreement, whereas the effect of misrepresentations is quite distinct.

5.4.2 **Evidential and contractual estoppel**

Until recently, courts have denied effect to 'no-representation' and 'no-reliance' clauses by treating them as representations rather than as contractual terms. In *Lowe v Lombank* (1960), affirmed in subsequent cases (eg *Watford Electronics v Sanderson* (2001)), the Court of Appeal held that the parties could not contractually agree upon a state of affairs (eg the absence of representations) that both parties knew did not really exist. Consequently, the defendant in a misrepresentation claim would need to establish an 'evidential estoppel' by showing (amongst other things) that he or she believed in the truth of the no-reliance clause.

However, *Springwell Navigation Corp v JP Morgan* (2010) reversed this in practice. The Court of Appeal held (affirming *Peekay Intermark v ANZ Banking* (2006)) that there is nothing in principle to prevent parties from *contractually* agreeing upon the existence of a fictitious state of affairs (at [143]). Aikens LJ said that such clauses give rise to a 'contractual estoppel', which *prevents* the claimant in a misrepresentation action from alleging facts inconsistent with the contractual agreement (eg that representations were made or that the claimant relied upon them). This approach is affirmed by the Court of Appeal in *AXA Sun Life Services v Campbell Martin* (2011) (at [93]). The label 'contractual estoppel' seems misleading since the ground bears very little family resemblance to the other doctrines of estoppel (see 3.3); in particular, the defendant need not show that it would be unconscionable for the other party to resile from the agreed state of affairs (at [177]). In truth, these are simply contractual terms.

5.4.3 **Statutory controls**

Even if a term seeking to exempt liability is properly incorporated (see 10.3.3) and construed to cover the situation (see 5.4.2), it is still subject to various statutory tests of validity.

5.4.3.1 Section 3 Misrepresentation Act 1967

According to this section, a term which excludes or restricts *liability* or the available *remedies* for misrepresentation 'shall be of no effect except insofar as it satisfies the requirement of **reasonableness** as stated in section 11(1) of the Unfair Contract Terms Act 1977'. Two questions arise.

- First, does the clause come within the scope of section 3; that is, does it exclude or restrict liability or the available remedies for misrepresentation?
- Second, if so, does it satisfy the requirement of reasonableness?

Although the **scope of section 3** seems to cover only terms *excluding liability* for a misrepresentation (and not terms denying the existence of a misrepresentation at all), the distinction is one of substance (effect) rather than merely of form (literal wording). Nevertheless, the authorities are inconsistent:

✗ In *Springwell Navigation* the Court of Appeal held that a party's agreement that it had made its decision to contract independently, without relying on the other party, and that it was fully familiar with the risks, created a contractual estoppel to the effect that any statement by other would amount to merely one of opinion (at [173]) and were not within section 3.

✓ However, a sentence in the same paragraph stating that the other party would not be liable for any loss unless it was caused by gross negligence or wilful misconduct was within section 3 (at [181]).

✓ Aikens LJ said that a statement that '. . .no representation or warranty, express or implied, is or will be made' by the relevant party 'is more difficult to classify'; but he was inclined to treat it as falling within section 3 (at [181]–[182]). In *AXA Sun Life v Campbell Martin*, Stanley Burnton LJ held (obiter) that any contrary view would be 'too formalistic', adding that the matter should be looked at 'sensibly and practically' (at [51]).

Pause for reflection

In favour of the enforceability of 'no-representation' and 'no-reliance' clauses (and so exemption from section 3 of the Misrepresentation Act), are the following.

✓ *Freedom of contract*: in *Springwell*, Aikens LJ said (at [143]): 'If A and B enter into a contract then, unless there is some principle of law or statute to the contrary, they are entitled to agree what they like. Unless *Lowe & Lombank* is authority to the contrary, there is no legal principle that states that parties cannot agree to assume that a certain state of affairs is the case at the time the contract is concluded or has been so in the past, even if that is not the case, so that the contract is made upon the basis that the present or past facts are as stated and agreed by the parties.'

✓ *Certainty*: as Moore-Bick LJ explained in *Peekay* (at [56]):

There is no reason in principle why parties to a contract should not agree that a certain state of affairs should form the basis for the transaction, whether it be the case or not. For example, it may be desirable to settle a disagreement as to an existing state of affairs in order to establish a clear basis for the contract itself and its subsequent performance. Where parties express an agreement of that kind in a contractual document neither can subsequently

➡

➡️ deny the existence of the facts and matters upon which they have agreed, at least so far as concerns those aspects of their relationship to which the agreement was directed. The contract itself gives rise to an estoppel.

✗ Against the enforceability of 'no-representation' and 'no-reliance' clauses the concern is that of *unfairness and lack of consent*: here, the parties' bargaining power is important. In *Raiffeisen Zentralbank Osterreich AG v Royal Bank of Scotland* (2010) Christopher Clarke J said (at [314]–[315]) that:

> . . . If sophisticated commercial parties agree, in terms of which they are both aware, to regulate their future relationship by prescribing the basis on which they will be dealing with each other and what representations they are or are not making, a suitably drafted clause may properly be regarded as establishing that no representations (or none other than honest belief) are being made or are intended to be relied on. Such parties are capable of distinguishing between statements which are to be treated as representations on which the recipient is entitled to rely, and statements which do not have that character, and should be allowed to agree among themselves into which category any given statement may fall.
>
> Per contra, to tell the man in the street that the car you are selling him is perfect and then agree that the basis of your contract is that no representations have been made or relied on, may be nothing more than an attempt retrospectively to alter the character and effect of what has gone before, and in substance an attempt to exclude or restrict liability.

Ultimately, the question is whether a misrepresentation was made; if the evidence, including the clause, shows that the representee did not rely on a misrepresentation, then section 3 does not apply. But if the contract *was* induced by misrepresentation, section 3 applies, and its effect cannot be excluded (*Cremdean v Nash* (1977)). As Toulson J said in *IFE Fund SA v Goldman Sachs International* (2006) (at [68]–[69]):

> If a seller of a car said to a buyer 'I have serviced the car since it was new, it has had only one owner and the clock reading is accurate', those statements would be representations, and they would still have that character even if the seller added the words 'but those statements are not representations on which you can rely' . . . If, however, the seller of the car said 'The clock reading is 20,000 miles, but I have no knowledge whether the reading is true or false', the position would be different, because the qualifying words could not fairly be regarded as an attempt to exclude liability for a false representation arising from the first half of the sentence.

In sum:

✓ **exclusions of liability or of an otherwise available remedy for misrepresentation** are within the scope of section 3 (*Walker v Boyle* (1982));

? **'no-representation' or 'no-reliance' clauses** may be within the scope of section 3;

✗ **entire agreement clauses** which merely prevent the finding of any collateral term or contract relating to the subject matter of the main agreement are *outside* the scope of section 3 (*Watford Electronics v Sanderson* (2001) at [40]).

The **reasonableness requirement** is determined in accordance with section 11 of UCTA (see 11.4.6.2 for a full explanation of this test). In contrast to exemptions for breach, courts seem relatively willing to uphold exemptions for misrepresentation. For example, in *Cleaver v Schyde Investments* (2011) Etherton LJ said (at [38]):

> . . . there is nothing self-evidently offensive, in terms of reasonableness and fairness, in a contractual term which restricts a purchaser's right to rescind the contract in the event of the vendor's misrepresentation to cases of fraud or recklessness or where the property differs substantially in quantity, quality or tenure from what the purchaser had been led to expect, and to confine the purchaser to damages in all other cases. That is a perfectly rational and commercially justifiable apportionment of risk in the interests of certainty and the avoidance of litigation. While each case turns on its own particular facts, the argument in favour of upholding such a provision as a matter of the commercial autonomy of the contracting parties is particularly strong where, as here, (1) the term has a long history, (2) it is a well established feature of property transactions, (3) it is endorsed by the leading professional body for qualified conveyancers, (4) both sides are represented by solicitors, and (5) the parties (through their solicitors) have negotiated variations of other provisions in the standard form.

Likewise, in *Lloyd v Browning* (2013) liability was excluded where the seller had misrepresented the extent of planning permission, which reduced the value of the farmland sold by £55,000. A clause in the contract stipulated that the buyer had entered the agreement solely on the basis of his inspection, and had not been induced by any statement made by the seller except for written responses to pre-contractual inquiries. The Court of Appeal approved the general purpose behind such clauses: to achieve certainty and to forestall disputes that could lead to contested issues of fact. The court also endorsed the approach of *FoodCo UK LLP (t/a Muffin Break) v Henry Boot Developments Ltd* (2010) on the reasonableness assessment of such clauses under section 11 of UCTA. In this case, the term was reasonable (see [34]–[36], [39]–[42]):

- each side was legally advised and the buyer had also instructed architects and planning consultants;
- the law required contracts for a sale of land to be in one contractual document signed by both parties;
- the clause was not of the 'take-it-or-leave-it' type sometimes imposed in small print in consumer agreements. It was a special condition agreed by both parties' lawyers, with equal negotiating positions;
- the term was used by the regional law society and in common use;
- crucially, had the buyers wished to rely on an oral statement, they could have made a written pre-contractual inquiry and relied upon the written response. The planning consultant's report had indicated potential problems and the buyers could have made inquiries to establish the planning position.

Similar considerations were decisive in upholding the term in *AXA* (at [59]–[63]).

Ironically, once exemptions are interpreted as not covering fraud, more exemptions are likely to satisfy the reasonableness requirement and be effective against claimants (*Govt of Zanzibar v British Aerospace* (at 2346–7)).

5.4.3.2 The Unfair Terms in Consumer Contracts Regulations 1999

UTCCR applies a requirement of fairness to all non-core non-negotiated terms in consumer contracts (see 11.5 for a full explanation). Two points suffice here.

(i) The test of 'unfairness' under UTCCR and the test of 'reasonableness' under UCTA are unlikely to yield different results in the context of a clause attempting to avoid liability for misrepresentation.

(ii) Although entire agreement clauses fall outside the scope of section 3 of the Misrepresentation Act 1967, they will nevertheless fall inside the control of UTCCR. They are indicatively unfair under Schedule 2, paragraph 1(n).

5.5 **The justification for remedying misrepresentations**

Rescission and damages for **fraudulent or negligent** misrepresentations are readily explicable in terms of preventing the representor from profiting from his or her own *wrong* and ensuring that he or she compensates for the loss they have caused. The wider scope of liability under **section 2(1)** of the Misrepresentation Act 1967 can be explained by the concern to raise the *standard of care* in pre-contractual negotiations: someone who makes statements to induce another to contract with him or her should take care to ensure that he or she does so honestly and on reasonable grounds, *and* can show that they have done so.

Something beyond the representor's wrongdoing or lack of care is required to explain *rescission for* purely **innocent** misrepresentations. Although Jessel MR (*Redgrave v Hurd* at 13) refers to the innocent misrepresentor's 'moral delinquency' in enforcing a beneficial contract obtained by a statement 'which he knows *now* to be false', this sort of constructive unconscientiousness (after the fact) is unhelpful in pinpointing the exact reason for invalidating the contract. Why, otherwise, does it not apply equally to widen the very narrow scope of operative mistake and frustration?

 Pause for reflection

It is helpful to understand misrepresentations as induced mistakes, invoking the rationale of the claimant's defective consent (see 6.2.3.3), rather than the misrepresentor's unconscientiousness. Nevertheless, the analogy with mistake is not exact. The explanation for the significantly wider scope of relief for misrepresentation than for mistake (see 6.2.4 and 6.2.5) may lie in the parties' respective degrees of responsibility for the mistakes and in the seriousness of the mistake. Thus, while spontaneous un-induced mistakes only operate if they are catastrophic (but then trigger the very serious consequence of voidness), a party's mistake induced by the other's misrepresentation is always operative (but only renders the contract voidable subject to various bars and adjustments). But, this suggests that a very serious misrepresentation should also be able to void the contract, for the defendant who has induced the claimant's mistake should not be better off than one who has not.

THIS CHAPTER IN ESSENCE

online
resource
centre

The key areas and core topics in this chapter are summarised in an easy-to-use list, ideal for revision purposes, on the Online Resource Centre at http://www.oxfordtextbooks.co.uk/orc/ chenwishart5e/. Links to websites relevant to the topics covered and any updates to the chapter can also be found on the Online Resource Centre.

QUESTIONS

1 How can you tell whether a pre-contractual statement is: (a) a term; (b) an actionable misrepresentation; or (c) a puff? Why does it matter?

2 Explain (giving examples) the difference between:

(a) damages for breach of contract;
(b) damages for misrepresentation; and
(c) money claims related to rescission.

3 When is, and when should, rescission be available for misrepresentation?

4 To what extent can a party exclude or restrict liability for misrepresentation?

5 Did the Misrepresentation Act 1967 improve the law on misrepresentation?

6 Katie wants to set up an ostrich farm and discusses with Leo the possibility of buying Leo's flock. Leo says:

You take them as they are. Get them checked if you like, but I'm an old hand and I say they're in the peak of health. I saw an article yesterday that said you'll get a 500% return. If you go ahead, my restaurant chain will be your best customer.

Katie buys Leo's ostriches. Advise Katie on the following facts:
(i) no orders were ever placed by Leo's restaurants;

(ii) 25% of the birds were sick at the time of purchase and died shortly after;

(iii) the article Leo mentioned is two years old; more recent and available market research shows declining consumer demand for ostrich meat; Katie can only sell the remaining flock at a loss.

 For hints on how to answer these questions, please see the Online Resource Centre at http://www.oxfordtextbooks.co.uk/orc/chenwishart5e/

KEY FURTHER READING

See generally, Cartwright, J (2006), *Misrepresentation* (2nd edn, Sweet & Maxwell).

Atiyah, P S, and Treitel, G (1967), 'Misrepresentation Act 1967', 30 *MLR* 369.

Beale, H (1995), 'Damages in Lieu of Rescission for Misrepresentation', 111 *LQR* 60.

Brown, I, and Chandler, A (1992), 'Deceit, Damages and the Misrepresentation Act 1967, s 2(1)', *LMCLQ* 40.

Hooley, R (1991), 'Damages and the Misrepresentation Act 1967', 107 *LQR* 547.

6

Mistaken assumptions

'I should not be bound as things really were'

Mistake is a common occurrence in daily life. In Chapter 2, at 2.1, we examined mistakes as to the *terms* of the contract in the context of the objective test of intentions. Here, we discuss mistakes that affect a party's *reasons* for entering a contract. If a party would not have entered the contract had he or she known the true state of facts, he or she can realistically complain that they should not have to take the normal responsibility for their apparent consent. On the other hand, the objective test of intentions renders mistakes (other than known mistakes as to terms) irrelevant to the validity of contracts. This chapter explores how contract law balances these competing norms. It should be read in tandem with Chapter 7 on frustration. The two doctrines are closely related:

- if a contract party's assumption deviates from the state of things *at the time of formation* (eg you buy a ticket to a gig which has already been cancelled), this is a 'present' mistake and is regulated by the doctrine of **mistake**;

- if a contract party's assumption deviates from the state of things *as they turned out to be* due to a subsequent and unexpected change of circumstances (eg you buy a ticket to a gig, but it is cancelled when the venue is later destroyed by fire), this can be called a 'future' mistake and is the subject of the doctrine of **frustration**.

Diagram 6A shows the mistake doctrine in the context of related doctrines.

Recent judicial recognition of the common ground between mistaken assumptions and frustration has reduced the importance of this *temporal* distinction (see 7.1.1).

The main questions to be addressed in this chapter are the following.

(i)   *When can a claimant* escape a contract on the ground of his or her mistaken assumption about the relevant facts?

(ii)   What *remedies* are available for such mistakes?

Diagram 6A Mistake and related doctrines

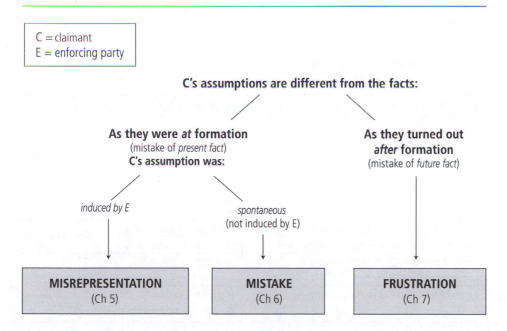

(iii) What is the *justification* for any relief?

(iv) Is the current law *satisfactory*? How might it be *developed*?

6.1 **Preliminary points**

The law on mistake is notoriously difficult to stabilise. Three factors contribute to its complexity. First, situations where parties enter contracts under mistake can be decided by doctrines other than that of mistake, as **Diagram 6B** illustrates (eg *induced* mistakes are the subject of the law on misrepresentation, and concerns about the *unfair results* of mistake may trigger the doctrines of unconscionability or undue influence).

Second, the law of mistake is riddled with very difficult **distinctions**, some of which have only superficial logic and which can cut across each other. The following are examples.

- *Mistakes as to terms/mistaken assumptions as to background fact*: the distinction lies in the difference between saying 'I did not mean to buy that guitar' and 'I *did* mean to buy it, but only because I mistakenly thought it once belonged to Elvis'. The former raises the problem of contract formation (see 2.1.3); the latter raises the problem of vitiation of a prima facie valid contract. The distinction is analogous to that between terms and representations. However, the difference can reduce to vanishing point when the mistaken assumption relates to some *quality of the contract's subject matter*. How should the distinction be drawn between a claimant who says 'I thought the guitar belonged to Elvis' (no relief), and one who says 'I thought you were *promising* that the guitar belonged to Elvis' (relief if mistake known by the other party)?

- *Common law* and *equity* impose different thresholds, and grant different forms of relief.

Diagram 6B Mistake and applicable legal doctrines

Nature of mistake	Applicable law
I did not intend to agree to *that*	Objectivity and mistake as to terms (2.1.3) Uncertainty (2.6) Implied terms (10.4) Incorporation (10.3.3) Rectification (6.6) Interpretation (10.5)
You *induced* my mistaken assumption	Misrepresentation (Ch 5)
You took *unfair advantage* of my mistake	Unconscionability (9.4)
We did not *anticipate* the *change of circumstances*	Frustration (Ch 7)
I thought our agreement was *permitted*	Illegality (Additional Chapter 2 available on the Online Resource Centre)

- *'Classes' of mistaken assumptions*: different types of mistake attract different assumptions about their legal effect (eg common mistakes as to the *existence or ownership* of the contractual subject matter are thought to *void* the contract, but common mistakes as to the *quality* of the subject matter do *not*). However, these mistakes are not mutually exclusive (ie the same mistake may be described in different ways and attract inconsistent assumptions).

Third, the **seriousness** of the mistaken assumptions necessary for relief to be granted is notoriously difficult to stabilise. The mistake must be 'fundamental', and 'go to the root' or 'basis' or 'identity' of the contract.

The final preliminary point is that the traditional bar against relief for contracts tainted by **mistakes of law** was abolished in *Brennan v Bolt Burdon* (2004). Hence, any references in texts and judgments to 'mistakes of fact' should now be read to include mistakes of law. However, a mistake of law does not include a compromise of claim (see 3.1.3.6) that is based on a view of the law which turns out to have been 'mistaken' because it is subsequently overruled. In *Kleinwort Benson Ltd v Lincoln CC* (1999), Sedley LJ (at [64]) said: 'a shift in the law cannot be allowed to undo a compromise of litigation entered into in the knowledge of how the law now stood and of the fact—for it always is a fact—that it might not remain so'; each party *takes the risk* that their view of the law might turn out to be wrong (at [31], [39]).

Diagram 6C gives an overview of the law on mistake. The shaded areas are discussed in this chapter as follows.

6.2 Common (shared) mistake at common law

6.2.1 General principles

The doctrine on shared mistaken assumptions is variously called *'mistaken assumption'*, 'motivation mistake', or more opaquely 'mutual mistake' or 'common mistake'. The leading cases on the modern law are *Bell v Lever Brothers Ltd* (1932) and *Great Peace Shipping v Tsavliris Salvage (International) Ltd* (2002). Both denied relief for mistake. In *Bell v Lever Brothers*, L paid £50,000 to terminate the employment of two employees as part of its corporate reorganisation. Unknown to L, the employees had breached their contracts by speculating in cocoa on their own account, entitling L to dismiss them without compensation. On discovering this, L sought the return of the £50,000 for fraud. When this failed, L relied on the alternative ground of mistake. The jury found that L would never have paid if they had known the truth, and that the employees did not have their breach in mind so that they were also 'mistaken' in believing that their employment contracts were only terminable by agreement. The House of Lords recognised the jurisdiction to void a contract for common mistaken assumption, but held by a majority of 3:2 that the mistake here was, on the facts, *not* sufficiently fundamental to void the contract (see further 6.2.6). The majority judgments, whilst reaching the same outcome, were sufficiently different to generate subsequent controversy over what the case actually stands for.

In *Great Peace v Tsavliris* (2002), T agreed to provide salvage services to the ship the *Cape Providence* (CP), which had suffered serious structural damage in the South Indian

Diagram 6C Overview of relief for mistake

	✓ Relief available ? Relief uncertain

	Unilateral	Common (shared)
Mistake of TERM inside the contract (Formation)	✓ **Common law** if: (i) no objective offer and acceptance ('snapping up' or misleading offer, 2.1.3) (ii) latent ambiguity (2.1.3.3)	✓ **Equity:** rectification of written contract (6.6)
	(iii) fundamental mistaken identity (6.4.1) (iv) fundamental mistake about the nature of the document (*non est factum*, 6.4.2) ✓**Equity** if: less fundamental but still serious and other party unconscionable or otherwise more blameworthy (6.5)	
Mistaken assumptions inducing the contract (Vitiation)	✓Action in misrepresentation if mistake is induced (Ch 5)	✓ **Common law** if: fundamental (6.2) *Bell v Lever* ? **Equity** if: less fundamental but still serious (rejected by *Great Peace*) (6.3) ✓ If mistake induced by one party then rescission for *innocent* misrepresentation (Ch 5)

Ocean and was in imminent danger of going down with her crew and cargo. Since the tug that T proposed to use was some five days away, T looked for merchant vessels in the vicinity which could evacuate the crew of the CP in the meantime if necessary. Relying on information from a third party that one vessel, the *Great Peace* (GP), was about **35 miles** away from the CP, T hired the GP for a minimum of five days to divert to the CP as back-up pending the arrival of the tug. In fact, the GP was **400 miles** away; another vessel was substantially nearer to the CP. T refused to pay the hire for the GP claiming that the contract was (i) void for common mistake (ie that the GP was 'in close proximity' to the CP) under *Bell v Lever Brothers*, or (ii) voidable for mistake in equity under *Solle v Butcher* (1950) (see 6.3.1). The Court of Appeal rejected both grounds. After careful evaluation of the precedents, Phillips MR set out the conditions for voiding a contract on the ground of common mistake at common law (at [76]):

(i) there must be a common assumption as to the existence of a state of affairs; (ii) there must be no warranty by either party that that state of affairs exists; (iii) the non-existence of the state of affairs must not be attributable to the fault of either party; (iv) the non-existence of the state of affairs must render performance of the contract impossible; (v) the state of affairs may be the existence, or a vital attribute, of the consideration to be provided or circumstances which must subsist if performance of the contractual adventure is to be possible.

This can be summarised as a three-step inquiry represented by **Diagram 6D**. A claimant can only void a contract by showing that:

(i) **construction**: the risk of the mistake was not allocated to either party;

(ii) **fault**: he or she was not at fault (eg by making a very unreasonable mistake or inducing the other party's mistake);

(iii) **fundamentality**: the mistaken common assumption was so serious as to make performance 'impossible'.

Diagram 6D Common mistake at common law: a three-step approach

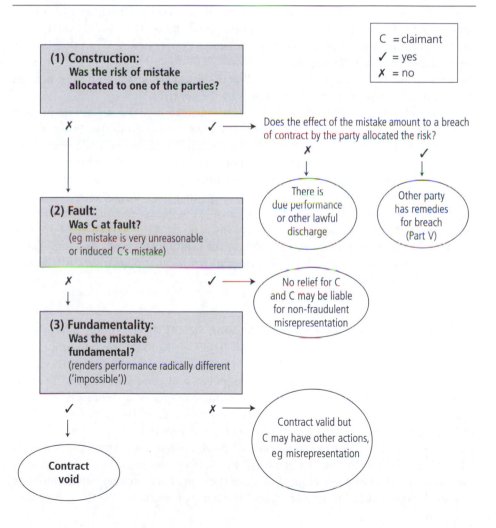

This approach mirrors that adopted by Steyn J in *Associated Japanese Bank (International) Ltd v Crédit du Nord SA* (1989) which was generally approved in *Great Peace v Tsavliris*.

6.2.2 **The contractual allocation of risk: construction**

The question is whether the contract has: (i) allocated the risk of mistake to either party; or (ii) provided, expressly or impliedly, that the contract's existence is contingent on the existence of an assumed state of affairs (see 12.2.2.1). If the answer is 'yes', then what the contract says governs the situation. Only if the contract is 'silent on the point' can the mistake doctrine apply.

6.2.2.1 Risk allocation to either party

Courts will usually find that one or other party has assumed the risk of the *ordinary uncertainties* existing at the time of contract formation by reference to the contract itself and to the rules of general law (*William Sindall plc v Cambridgeshire CC* (1994) at 1035). In that case, the party to whom the risk is allocated must perform his or her contractual obligations or be liable for its non-performance. No relief is available for the mistake. The general principle of *caveat emptor* ('buyer beware') in sale of goods law and the rule that sellers or lessors of land do not impliedly warrant the fitness of the land for any particular purpose mean that the risk of any mistake on these matters is *impliedly* allocated to the buyers or lessors by the contract.

But, the seller may be held to bear the risk of the mistake. In ***McRae v Commonwealth Disposals Commission*** (1951), CDC invited tenders for 'an oil tanker lying on the Jourmand Reef . . . said to contain oil'. M tendered successfully and embarked on an expensive expedition to salvage the vessel but, amazingly, neither the tanker nor the Jourmand Reef existed. M successfully claimed damages for breach of contract. The High Court of Australia rejected CDC's argument that the contract was void due to the parties' common mistake as to the existence of the subject matter. The court held (at 410) that 'the only proper construction of the contract is that it included a promise by the Commission that there was a tanker in the position specified'. Any impossibility of performance did not relieve CDC from its contractual obligations: it triggered CDC's liability for breach.

6.2.2.2 Fault

In *Associated Japanese Bank v Crédit du Nord*, Steyn J stated (at 268, approved in *Great Peace v Tsavliris*) that: 'a party cannot be allowed to rely on a common mistake where the mistake consists of a belief which is entertained by him without any reasonable grounds for such belief' because 'policy and good sense dictate that the positive rules regarding common mistake should be so qualified'. Moreover, no relief is available if a party contracts 'with minimal knowledge of the facts to which the mistake relates but is content that it is a good speculative risk'. Thus, another reason for the decision in *McRae v Commonwealth Disposals Commission* is that a party cannot rely on a mistake which 'consists of a belief which is, on the one hand, entertained by him without any reasonable ground, and, on the other hand, deliberately induced by him in the mind of the other party' (at 408). Induced mistakes give the representee an action for misrepresentation. The claimant's carelessness inclined the court against relief in *Kyle Bay Ltd v Underwriters* (2006). K compromised its insurance claim for £100,000 less than it was entitled to based on U's mistaken calculation and without checking its own policy. Jonathan Hirst QC refused to void the compromise, concluding that it was simply 'a rather poor deal' for K.

6.2.2.3 Condition precedent

Rather than allocating the risk of the mistake to one or other party, the contract may provide, expressly or impliedly, that the parties' obligations will only arise if an assumed state of affairs is true, so that no obligations arise if this 'condition precedent' is not satisfied. In *Associated Japanese Bank v Crédit du Nord*, a fraudster purported to sell to, and then lease back from, AJB four machines which did not actually exist. CN was sued as the fraudster's guarantor on the fraudster's bankruptcy. The Court of Appeal held that since the guarantee stipulated that the machines could only be substituted with CN's consent, this amounted to an *express* condition precedent that the guarantee was for the lease of *existing* machines. Alternatively, the court was prepared to *imply* such a condition from all the facts (see further 6.2.5.4).

6.2.3 Justifications for the mistake doctrine

Risk allocation in the contract (or construction) will deal with many claims of mistake. The question is whether construction of the contract can deal with all problems in this area, leaving no room for the operation of a doctrine of mistake. On this, opinions diverge.

6.2.3.1 The implied terms analysis

Those denying the need for a mistake jurisdiction at common law include:

- **Slade, 'The Myth of Mistake in the English Law of Contract'** (1954) 70 *LS* 385;
- **Atiyah and Bennion, 'Mistake in the Construction of Contracts'** (1961) 24 *MLR* 421; and
- **Smith, 'Contract—Mistake, Frustration and Implied Terms'** (1994) 110 *LQR* 400.

These authors argue that all problems of contractual mistake can be dealt with by the law on contract formation (because there is no offer and acceptance), or implied terms (specifically, the 'implied condition precedent' that no contract comes into effect if the parties' common assumption is incorrect). Questions about 'mistake' are really questions about the *risk allocation* for mistake and the answers, they argue, can *always* be found in the contract interpreted in its context. So, when contracts are voided, this is the result of something that the *parties themselves* have agreed, albeit impliedly; it is not *imposed* by the law. There is no room left for the operation of a distinct doctrine of mistake. Moreover, this is the *right* approach because of the policies against relief for mistakes. Namely:

- the concern that a mistake doctrine would provide an open-ended excuse to escape bad bargains and undermine the contractual risk allocation;

- the need to promote certainty by upholding the parties' objective intention; and
- the need to reward research and knowledge in a free-market system, so that knowledgeable parties must generally be allowed to take advantage of less knowledgeable (mistaken) parties.

McRae v Commonwealth Disposals Commission was reasoned solely on contractual construction.

▶◀ Counterpoint

The implied terms analysis is sometimes realistic, as in *Associated Japanese Bank*. But, the view that it provides a complete explanation for *all* cases where contracts are voided for mistake can be criticised:

(i) *Contradicted by weight of authority*: Lord Atkins said in *Bell v Lever Brothers* (at 224–5) that the 'implied condition precedent' reasoning is merely an 'alternative mode of expressing the result of a mutual [ie common][1] mistake'; it is only a synonym for common mistake. The general judicial consensus is that an independent mistake doctrine *does* exist and only operates *after* construction has exhausted the contract's ability to determine the consequences of the mistake.[2] Mistake only kicks in to sort out the mess once the contract runs out.

(ii) *Odd reasoning*: there is something distinctly odd in saying that a contract is void (a nullity *from the beginning*) because an implied term *inside* that void contract says so: the contract 'self-destructs' before coming into being.

(iii) *Uncertain*: the concept of an implied condition precedent tells us little about *when* such a condition (the 'self-destruct' instruction) will be implied.

(iv) *Over-inclusive*: an implied conditions precedent need not be limited to very serious (fundamental) mistakes.

(v) *Unrealistic*: the implied terms story of mistake necessitates the fiction that contract parties have agreed what should happen in a state of affairs that is completely *different* from the one they both believed existed at formation. In truth, it is usually impossible to say in any meaningful, non-attributive, way what *the parties* would have wanted in the event of catastrophic mistake. It is certainly unlikely that they would have been happy for the contract to simply fall away regardless of what gains and losses may have been accrued under it. The implied terms view of mistake was rejected in *Great Peace v Tsavliris* (at [73]) as 'unrealistic'. Rather, '[t]he avoidance of contract on the ground of common mistake results from a rule of law'.

---

[1] Confusingly, the expression 'mutual mistake' is sometimes used to describe shared or common mistake.

[2] *Associated Japanese Bank (International) Ltd v Crédit du Nord SA* at 268; *William Sindall v Cambridgeshire CC* at 1035; *Grains & Fourrages SA v Huyton* (1997); *Bank of Credit and Commerce International SA (in liquidation) v Ali* (1999) at 1020.

6.2.3.2 Impossibility of performance

In *Great Peace v Tsavliris*, mistake is said to operate 'if it transpires that one or both of the parties have agreed to do something which it is impossible to perform' (at [73]). Lords Atkin and Thankerton in *Bell v Lever Brothers* support the impossibility justification by reference to the frustration doctrine. In *Great Peace* the court recognises (at [61]) that 'consideration of the development of the law of frustration assists with the analysis of the law of common mistake'. The frustration doctrine allows the law not to recognise the *continued existence* of a contract which has *become* impossible to perform. The basic idea is illustrated in *Taylor v Caldwell* (1863), in which a music hall hired for concerts for four nights was burnt down before the first. The court excused performance since it depended on the continued existence of the music hall. If the music hall was already, unknown to either party, destroyed *at the time* the contract was made, the impossibility of performance would be resolved by the mistake doctrine.

Since physical impossibility is neither necessary nor sufficient, **what does the mistake doctrine mean by 'impossibility of performance'?** Performance was physically impossible in *McRae v Commonwealth Disposals Commission* but the contract was not voided for mistake because the risk of that impossibility was allocated to the seller. On the other hand, performance may be perfectly possible, yet the contract may be void for mistake if the *'substance'* of the contract is deemed to be 'impossible' to achieve. That is, if the significance/meaning/point of the, even physically *possible*, performance in the *actual* state of affairs is radically different from that supposed by the parties at formation then the contract is void (*Great Peace v Tsavliris* at [63]). In other words, mistake is operative if it results in the non-existence of a state of affairs assumed by both parties as going to the foundation (or the 'substance', 'root', 'essence', or 'basis') of the contract. In *Great Peace* Lord Phillips MR ([68], [74]) approved Vaughan Williams LJ's view (at 749) in *Krell v Henry* (1903) that:

> you first have to ascertain, not necessarily from the terms of the contract, but, if required, from necessary inferences, drawn from surrounding circumstances recognised by both contracting parties, what is *the substance of the contract*, and then to ask the question whether that substantial contract needs for its foundation the assumption of the existence of a particular state of things. If it does, this will limit the operation of the general words [ie qualify the obligation], and in such a case, if the contract becomes impossible of performance by reason of the *non-existence of the state of things assumed by both parties as the foundation of the contract*, there will be no breach of the contract thus limited (emphasis added).

Why should the law care about 'impossibility' of performance when the non-performing party can always be sued for breach? In the High Court, Toulson J (*Great Peace v Tsavliris* at [119]–[120], affirmed by the Court of Appeal at [155]–[157]) rejected any suggestion that the mistake doctrine is aimed at avoiding the injustice resulting from mistake because this would put 'palm tree justice in place of party autonomy', when concerns to avoid injustice are adequately dealt with by other doctrines such as fraud, misrepresentation, and undue influence.

6.2.3.3 Consent nullified

The defective consent rationale ultimately offers the best explanation for the mistake doctrine. As Lord Atkin said in *Bell v Lever Brothers* (at 217): 'If mistake operates at all it operates so as to negative or in some cases to nullify consent.' Four reasons support this.

(i) **Impossibility, essential context, and lack of consent**: physical impossibility of performance is neither necessary nor sufficient to void a contract for mistake. The test of 'impossibility of performance' is shorthand for saying that the parties' *consent* is vitiated if the falsification of their *essential assumption* about the context of the contract makes performance of the *substance* (its purpose and not just its literal terms) *impossible* (*Bell v Lever Brothers* at 208 and 226).

(ii) **Meaningful consent**: however, effective consent to a contract does not require knowing consent to every *detail* of the content (hence, eg, the objective test of intention, the parties must, as a minimum, actually consent (be correct about) to the 'gist' or 'core' or 'substance' of what they have undertaken; they must at least be in the right 'ball park'). You need not have actually agreed every rule of the club to be bound by them, but you must at least have joined the right club. This explains why only mistakes which fatally undermine the 'root' or 'substance' or 'essence' or 'basis' or 'foundation' of the contract void the contract. Only such mistakes negate commitment to the contract.

(iii) **Threshold of consent is fixed by the law**: the defective consent view explains why the effect of fundamental mistake is rightly regarded as being imposed by the *law* rather than agreed by the *parties*. The law proceeds on the basis that the objective consent giving rise to prima facie contractual liability at formation can be negated by a catastrophic mistake going to the root or substance of the contract; it negates the justification for enforcement.

(iv) **Explains the effect of voidness**: the 'no consent' view explains why contracts tainted by mistake are *void* (of no effect from the beginning), rather than voidable (good until the claimant rescinds) as with most vitiating factors.

 Pause for reflection

The stark effect of voidness has its drawbacks.

1. *Innocent third party purchasers* are not protected against claims by the mistaken party for the return of property transferred under the void contract (since ownership does not generally pass under a void contract, see 6.4.1.1).
2. Benefits transferred under the void contract must be returned but there is *no mechanism for taking account of losses sustained* in the performance of the contract *which does not end up as a benefit in the other's hands* (in contrast there is some allowance for loss apportionment where contracts are discharged for frustration (see 7.6)).

These problems prompted Lord Denning to develop the *equitable* doctrine of common mistake to access more flexible remedies including rescission on terms (see 6.3).

6.2.4 **Actionable common mistake at common law**

An actionable common mistake at common law must be: (i) shared; and (ii) of fundamental importance.

6.2.4.1 Mistake must be shared

The reason for this requirement would be obvious on the 'implied terms' explanation of mistake: a condition precedent can only be *implied* if *both* parties regarded the mistaken assumption as fundamental to the contract. However, the requirement is not obvious on the 'no consent' view, since a catastrophic mistake by only *one* of the parties should void the contract. Indeed, some *unilateral* mistakes, even if unknown to the other party, can void contracts, as the law on mistaken identity and *non est factum* show (see 6.4). The explanation for requiring the mistake to be shared is pragmatic. The concern to uphold contractual certainty and avoid giving contract parties an easy escape route necessitates a very narrow scope for operative mistakes. Seen in this light, the requirement that the mistake be shared:

(i) serves an *evidentiary function* by: (a) corroborating the claimant's assertion of mistake; and (b) showing the importance of the mistake; shared assumptions are more likely to relate to the *essential substance* of the contract;

(ii) shows that the enforcing party's expectations are not reasonable since it is *also* tainted by catastrophic mistake. Voiding the contract in such circumstances deprives him or her of benefits (including unexpected windfalls) which are *unworthy of protection* because he or she could not reasonably have expected them when they entered the contract.

6.2.4.2 Mistake must be fundamental

The question is whether there is a sufficient degree of *disparity* between performance of the contract in the *mistaken* state of affairs, and its performance in the *actual* state of affairs, that consent to the contract can be regarded as nullified.

6.2.5 **Illustrations of operative mistaken assumptions**

Operative mistake must relate to 'the existence, or a vital attribute, of the consideration to be provided or circumstances which must subsist if performance of the contractual adventure is to be possible' (*Great Peace v Tsavliris* (at [76])). This yields the traditional categories of common mistake:

(i)   mistake as to the *existence* of the subject matter;

(ii)   mistakenly acquiring one's *own property*;

(iii)   mistake as to the *essential quality* of the thing contracted for; and

(iv)   mistake as to an *essential background assumption*.

It is important to emphasise that this is not a list of *qualifying* 'impossibilities', but merely *illustrations* of mistakes which *can* (but not necessarily will) so undermine the substance of the contract as to negate the apparent consent given to it. Relief may not be granted just because a case seems to come within one of the categories.

6.2.5.1 Mistake as to the existence of the subject matter

The non-existence of the subject matter of the contract which is mistakenly thought to exist (*res extincta*) will normally negate the essential *purpose* of a contract or the *means* for achieving it. This is the most widely accepted example of operative common mistake. Lord Atkin said that: 'the agreement of A and B to purchase a specific article is void if in fact the article had perished before the date of sale . . . a consent to transfer or take delivery of something nonexistent is deemed useless, the consent is nullified' (*Bell v Lever Brothers* at 217). The same should apply if the subject matter had never existed (unless the risk was allocated), as in *McRae v Commonwealth Disposals Commission*.

Subsequent cases have regarded *Couturier v Hastie* (1856) as the leading case of *res extincta*. It involved the sale of corn which was in transit from Salonica to England. The cargo had deteriorated and already been sold on *before* the date of the sale, but the seller sued for the price, claiming that the buyer had bought not the corn itself but the rights derived from the shipping documents, so that the risk of the non-existence of the corn was allocated to the buyer. The House of Lords disagreed. Analogous to the *McRae* case, it held, *as a matter of construction*, that the contract was for the sale of *existing* cargo (the corn itself) and not for cargo whether existing or not (the buyer was not taking a gamble, in the nature of a 'lucky dip'). The risk of mistake as to existence of the corn was allocated to the seller; its non-existence meant that there was a '**total failure of consideration**' (complete non-performance) by the seller, so that the buyer did not have to pay. The House of Lords never actually mentioned 'mistake' in its reasoning. However, the ground of 'total failure of consideration' (see 13.3) can mask operative mistake. In *Strickland v Turner* (1852), S bought and paid for an annuity on the life of a man who, unknown to both parties, was already dead. S recovered the purchase price for total failure of consideration. Since the ground only allows the claimant not to pay or to recover payments made, it will not apply if the *buyer* sues for the seller's non-delivery, and neither party is allocated the risk of non-existence. Only then will the question of mistake arise.

Section 6 of the Sale of Goods Act 1979 stipulates that: 'Where there is a contract for the sale of specific goods, and the goods without the knowledge of the seller have perished at the time when the contract is made, the contract is void.' This is narrower than the common law approach because: (i) it only applies to specific goods *that once existed* but then perished; and (ii) unlike many other sections of the Act, section 6 is not expressly subject to contrary intention and therefore seems to apply irrespective of the parties' risk allocation. Section 6 should be reformed to cover goods that never existed and to allow parties to opt out of having their contract automatically voided.

6.2.5.2 Mistakenly acquiring one's own property

Where the parties contract to transfer some interest in property that, unknown to either, already belongs to the buyer (*res sua*), the contract is void. It is not only senseless to buy one's own property, but 'such a transfer is impossible' (*Bell v Lever Brothers* at 218). In *Cooper v Phibbs* (1867), C agreed to lease a fishery from P but, unknown to both parties, P had no title while C was already tenant for life of the fishery; the lease was set aside. Although the proceedings were brought in equity (making the contract *voidable*) to allow an award for the improvements P made to the fishery, the House of

Lords in *Bell* said that 'the common law would have ruled the contract void for mistake' (*Great Peace* at [118]). This category is often called 'mistake as to title', but this is too broad since it would also cover mistakes as to the *seller*'s title. This risk is allocated to the seller by section 12 of the Sale of Goods Act 1979 by an implied term that the seller warrants (guarantees) his or her title to the property sold and is therefore liable for breach if this is untrue.

6.2.5.3 Mistake as to an essential quality of the subject matter

In both of the previous categories (non-existence of the subject matter or buying one's own property), performance of the contract is physically impossible. This is not necessarily so with the next two categories (mistakes as to the quality and as to background assumptions). Here, 'impossibility' of performance is measured by the *extent of deviation from the 'substance of the contract'* which is, in turn, determined by the parties' common purpose (in the broadest sense of what they thought they were contracting about). What is required is a mistake about 'the existence of some quality which makes the thing without the quality *essentially different* from the thing as it was believed to be' (*Bell v Lever Brothers* at 218, 227). The enormity of the difference required is captured in the distinction between:

✗ mistakes as to 'quality' (or attributes), which will not void the contract; and

✓ mistakes as to 'substance' (or 'essence' or 'vital quality'), which will.

However, the application of the distinction has given rise to much *uncertainty* and *inconsistency*. **Diagram 6E** gives a summary of some cases.

(i) Examples of inoperative mistakes as to quality

The courts have emphasised the narrowness of the scope of mistakes void for mistake as to quality because of the 'paramount importance that contracts should be observed' (*Bell v Lever Brothers* at 224). Relief will only be given in 'unexpected and

Diagram 6E Mistakes as to quality: an overview of some cases

✗ (i) Inoperative mistakes as to **quality**	✗ (ii) Inoperative mistakes as to **substance**	✓ (iii) Operative mistakes as to **substance**
✗ shares in a company with a lucrative contract when contract *ultra vires* (*Kennedy v Panama*); ✗ old oats when new oats (*Smith v Hughes*); ✗ 1948 model of car when 1939 (*Oscar Chess v Williams*); ✗ pure kapok when inferior product (*Harrison v Bunten*); ✗ sound horse when unsound horse (example given in *Bell*).	✗ picture by Constable when not (*Leaf v International Galleries*); ✗ rental of 'new' dwelling house when not (*Solle v Butcher*); ✗ 'horse beans' when 'feveroles' (*Rose v Pim*).	✓ racehorse when carthorse (example given in *Bell*). ✓ table napkins of Charles I when Georgian (*Nicholson and Venn v Smith Marriott*); ✓ sterile cow when pregnant cow (*Sherwood v Walker, US*); ✓ building land when building permit was unobtainable (*Alessio v Jovica, Canada*); ✓ prefabricated cottage when not conforming with building regulations (*Frazer v Dalgety, NZ*).

wholly exceptional' situations (*Associated Japanese Bank v Crédit du Nord* at 268). It is not enough that the mistake was causative (ie the claimant would not have entered this contract but for the mistake) or that it will result in unexpected hardship to one or advantage to the other. Hence, mistakes as to the quality of the subject matter will not generally void contracts of sale. The claimant will only be protected if there are stipulations in the contract expressly[3] or impliedly[4] warranting the *quality* to be as believed. The mistakes made were not sufficiently fundamental:

✗ in *Kennedy v Panama, New Zealand, and Australian Royal Mail Co Ltd* (1867), the claimant purchased shares in a company in reliance on the company's prospectus saying that money was being raised to fulfil a lucrative contract which turned out to be ultra vires, triggering a plunge in the value of the shares (no damages for innocent misrepresentation at common law but equity would have allowed rescission);

✗ in *Smith v Hughes* (1871), the claimant purchased oats believing them to be 'old' oats, only having use for such, when they were in fact 'new' oats (the mistake was neither fundamental nor shared, see 2.1.3.1);

✗ in *Oscar Chess Ltd v Williams* (1957), the claimant purchased a car which both believed to be a 1948 model when it was in fact a less valuable 1939 model;

✗ in *Bell v Lever Brothers* Lord Atkin (at 224) said that the purchase of an unsound horse believed to be sound still gives the buyer the substance of what was bargained for;

✓ on the other hand, Greer LJ (at 597), in the Court of Appeal said that the contract for the sale of a racehorse *would* be void if it turned out to be a carthorse.

(ii) Examples of inoperative mistakes as to *substance*
Difficulty arises because relief has been denied in some cases although the mistake appears to go to the substance (or the identity) of the subject matter. However, it is notable that in all three cases, the claimant had alternative avenues of relief:

✗ in *Leaf v International Galleries*,[5] the claimant bought a picture which both parties mistakenly believed was painted by the famous artist Constable (the court held that the claimant could have obtained damages for breach but he chose not to do so, hence the case was really decided on construction (risk allocation), analogous to *McRae v Commonwealth Disposals Commission*, see 6.2.2.1);

✗ in *Solle v Butcher*, the parties entered a lease for £250 of rent per year mistakenly believing that the property had undergone sufficient renovations to qualify as a 'new' dwelling house, thus evading the £140 limit imposed by the Rent Acts (but equity allowed rescission on terms that the landlord give the tenant the option of staying on at the higher rent, see 6.3);

✗ in *Frederick E Rose (London) Ltd v William H Pim Junior & Co Ltd* (1953), the parties contracted for 'horse beans' mistakenly believing these were 'feveroles', which

---

[3] *Gompertz v Barlett* (1853).
[4] Eg the Sales of Goods Act 1979, s 12 (title); s 13 (correspondence with description); s 14 (quality and fitness for purpose); s 15 (sale by sample).
[5] This result was foretold in *Bell v Lever Brothers* at 224.

the buyer needed to meet its customer's order. In fact 'feveroles' were an entirely different sort of bean although they could also be described as 'horse beans' (rescission would have been allowed for innocent misrepresentation).

(iii) Examples of operative mistakes as to quality

The following contracts of sale *were* voided for fundamental mistake as to quality:

✓ in the US case of *Sherwood v Walker* (1887), a cow ('Rose of Abalone the II'), believed to be sterile, was sold for beef for about $80 when it was actually in calf and worth at least $750;

✓ in the Canadian case of *Alessio v Jovica* (1974), land zoned as building land was bought but no building permit could be obtained because it lacked sewage facilities;

✓ in the New Zealand case of *Frazer v Dalgety & Co Ltd* (1953), a prefabricated 'cottage' was bought, but could never be erected because it did not conform to the building regulations;

✓ in the English case of *Nicholson and Venn v Smith Marriott* (1947), the buyer successfully sued for damages for breach when he purchased table napkins described as 'the authentic property of Charles I' for £787 10s when they were in fact Georgian and worth only £105. The court suggested, somewhat inconsistently with awarding contract damages, that the contract could have been voided for mistake.

Pause for reflection

1. These cases are unlikely to convince a modern court, three being from other jurisdictions and the last being decidedly unconvincing as well as internally inconsistent, since the contract must have been valid for it to be breached and contract damages awarded.

2. The supposed distinction between 'substance' and 'quality' (or 'identity' vs 'attribute') is quite illusory. The 'substance' or 'identity' of a thing must be comprised of its various qualities or attributes.

3. Treitel suggests (at para 8-019) asking 'the parties, immediately after they made the contract, what its subject matter was. If, in spite of the mistake, they would give the right answer [eg 'car' rather than '1948 model of car'] the contract is valid.' This test is consistent with the no consent view of mistake and provides a helpful starting point. The difficulty is that contract parties might reasonably describe the subject matter of their contract in various ways, and relief should not hang on the *degree of specificity* with which they happen to describe that subject matter: whether 'cow' or 'barren cow', 'table linen' or 'Charles I's table linen'. Moreover, it would not explain *Leaf v International Galleries*; the buyer would certainly have said he was buying 'a Constable' and not simply 'a picture'. Further, in *Bell v Lever Brothers* Lord Thankerton (at 236) emphasises the *objective* quality of the test: it must have 'either appeared *on the face of the contract* that the matter as to which the mistake existed was an essential and integral element of the subject matter of the contract, or it was an inevitable inference from the *nature of the contract* that all the parties so regarded it' (emphasis added). The parties' belief at a greater level of detail is irrelevant.

6.2.5.4 Other mistaken fundamental assumptions

The parties may make a mistake about other background assumptions fundamental to the essential point of the contract. They are 'circumstances which must subsist if performance of the contractual adventure is to be possible' (*Great Peace v Tsavliris* at [76]). Their Lordships said, in *Bell v Lever Brothers* (at 225–6, 236), that 'whenever it is to be inferred from the terms of the contract or its surrounding circumstances that the consensus has been reached upon the basis of a particular factual assumption, and that assumption is not true, the contract is avoided'. For example:

✓ in *Gallaway v Gallaway* (1914), a separation deed was voided because the parties thought they were validly married but they were not. This mistake destroyed the very point of the deed;

✓ in *Scott v Coulson* (1903), a life insurance policy was sold for £460 on the assumption that the insured was alive. In fact, the aptly named insured (Death) was dead, increasing the value of the policy to its full surrender value of £777;

✓ in *Sheikh Brothers Ltd v Ochsner* (1957), S granted O a licence to cut and manufacture all sisal grown on their estate in exchange for O's payment and delivery of 50 tons of sisal per month. However, the estate was incapable of yielding this quantity of sisal so *performance of the contract was physically impossible*. The Privy Council, relying on *Bell v Lever Brothers* to interpret and apply the Indian Contract Act 1872, voided the contract because 'both the parties to an agreement are under a mistake as to a matter of fact essential to the agreement'.

Pause for reflection

Physical impossibility of performance does not, in itself, void contracts; people are normally responsible for the obligations they have undertaken and will be liable for breach if performance is impossible. The contract was only voided in *Sheikh Brothers v Ochsner* because it was held (at 146–7) to be in the nature of a joint venture to exploit the sisal on the land and entered *on the basis* that the area was *capable* of producing an average of 50 tons a month throughout the term of the contract. That being so, is the decision really based on implied condition precedent and not mistake?

✓ in **Griffith v Brymer** (1903), a contract for 'hire of a room *to see the coronation procession of King Edward VII*' (not just 'a room hire') was made when the procession was already cancelled. The contract was voided although its performance was perfectly possible. The falsification of their common and fundamental assumption that the event would take place made the *substance* of the contract impossible to achieve;

✓ in **Great Peace v Tsavliris**, the contract's *purpose* remained constant but the mistaken assumption undermined the *means* for achieving it. The question was whether the GP was actually so far away from T's distressed ship 'at the time of the contract as to defeat the contractual purpose [to provide escort and standby services for five days until the rescue tug arrived]—or in other words to turn it into something essentially different from that for which the parties had bargained? This is a question of fact and degree' (in the High Court at [56]). The court concluded that although the parties believed that the GP was 35 miles (three hours' sailing) away, rather than actually 400 miles (39 hours' sailing) away, this did not defeat the parties' common assumption that it could still act as a backup. This was reinforced by T's failure to cancel the agreement on discovering the mistake until they found and hired a nearer vessel to assist. Significantly, Toulson J (High Court at [55]) said that, if there was five days' sailing distance between the ships, the contract *would be void* since its purpose would be unachievable;

✗ in **Bell v Lever Brothers**, the court upheld the contract to terminate a valid employment contract when it was really voidable. Lord Atkin (at 223–4) explains that: 'The contract released is the identical contract in both cases, and the party paying for release gets exactly what he bargains for.' Analogously, he said that there would be no remedy where a purchaser of a roadside garage was unaware that a decision had already been taken to construct a bypass road which would divert substantially all the traffic from passing his garage.

Pause for reflection

1. *Inconsistency with other cases*: the denial of relief in *Bell v Lever Brothers* sits uneasily with the relief granted in other cases also involving contracts purporting to deal with related contracts that were mistakenly believed to be valid.

   ✓ In *Magee v Pennine Insurance Co Ltd* (1969), P agreed to pay M £385 on a motor insurance policy that was in fact invalid. The agreement was not void at common law but was *voidable in equity*. The Court of Appeal in *Great Peace* held that *Magee* was only reconcilable with *Bell v Lever Brothers* by postulating that there are two categories of 'mistake' one rendering contracts *void at law* and one rendering them *voidable in equity* (at [153]). Since the latter is rejected in *Great Peace* (see 6.3.2), *Magee v Pennine Insurance* must now be regarded as wrongly decided.

   ✓ In *Associated Japanese Bank v Crédit du Nord*, a *guarantee* of a lease of machines was *voided* because the non-existence of the machines made the lease voidable for fraud. Since the subject matter of the guarantee contract was not the non-existent machinery but the *lease* which, while voidable, undoubtedly existed, Steyn J's analogy (at 269) with the *res extincta* cases is questionable. The closer analogy is to *Bell v Lever Brothers* (which also involved a contract dealing with a voidable contract thought to be valid), but no relief was given there.

2. *Payment not unfair*: it was judicially noted in *Bell v Lever Brothers* that the employers were anxious to facilitate smooth and urgent corporate reorganisation and might have agreed the severance package even knowing the truth (*Bell v Lever Brothers* at 236, 181, and *Associated Japanese Bank* at 267). In '**How Temptation Led to Mistake: An Explanation of *Bell v Lever Bros Ltd*'** (2003) 119 *LQR* 625, **MacMillan** offers a different explanation for the outcome in terms of: (i) the absence of fraud; (ii) the outstanding service given by the

➡

➔

> employees who had been 'most efficient, devoted, strenuous, and successful' on behalf of the company; (iii) the fairly minor nature of their breaches of duty which had yielded relatively small gains; and (iv) the harshness of depriving them of £50,000 (*Bell v Lever Brothers* at 173). It is arguable that relief was denied not *because* the mistake was insufficiently fundamental or causative; rather, the mistake was held to be insufficiently fundamental *so that* the employees could keep their severance payments, which were fair in the circumstances.
>
> 3. *Discretion in categorising the mistake made*: the mistake in *Bell v Lever Brothers* was treated as a mistake as to the quality of the subject matter, which does not generally void the contract. However, in **'Contracts—Mistake, Frustration and Implied Terms'** (1994) *LQR* 400, **Smith** points out (at 414) that the mistake could also have been described as one which *is* generally regarded as voiding contracts, namely:
>
>   ✓ *res sua* (the employer was buying the right to terminate an employment contract which it already had); or
>
>   ✓ *res extincta* (the employees were selling their right to continued employment which was non-existent).

6.2.6 **The effect of common mistake**

Operative common mistake at common law voids the contract for all purposes. This means that property rights will not pass under it and innocent third parties who purchase that property are left unprotected from action by the original mistaken transferor to recover the property. This contrasts with the more flexible *equitable* remedies of: *rescission* which can protect third party bona fide purchasers; *refusal of specific performance* for unilateral mistake; and *rectification* of the contract.

The Court of Appeal in *Great Peace v Tsavliris* (at [76], [162]) recognised the desirability of greater remedial flexibility in cases of common mistake at common law analogous to that available in cases of frustration (the Law Reform (Frustrated Contracts) Act 1943 allows courts more scope to fine-tune the effects of frustration, see 7.6.2).

6.3 **Common mistake at equity**

6.3.1 **Rescission (on terms)**

Until recently, the judgment of Denning LJ in *Solle v Butcher* was authority for an *equitable* doctrine of common law mistake that conferred a *wider scope* of relief and *greater remedial flexibility*. In *Associated Japanese Bank v Crédit du Nord*, Steyn J said (at 266–7): 'Equity will give relief against common mistake in cases where the common law will not, and it provides more flexible remedies including the power to set aside the contract on terms.'

In **Solle v Butcher**, the parties agreed a £250 yearly rental when they were, in fact, subject to a £140 limit under the Rent Act unless a 'notice of increase' was served. This was not done due to a common mistake about the status of the property. The court granted the landlord rescission of the lease but on the terms that he offered the tenant a new lease for £250. Similarly, in *Grist v Bailey* (1967), a house was sold for £850 on the mistaken common assumption that a protected tenant was in occupation when in fact the tenant had died before the sale; this increased the value of the property to £2,250. Although the risk of such a mistake is generally allocated to the seller, the sale was rescinded in equity on the terms that the seller offers the buyer the option of buying it at the 'proper vacant possession price' (at 543).

6.3.2 Rejection of the jurisdiction

The Court of Appeal in *Great Peace v Tsavliris* (at [158]), agreeing with Toulson J at first instance, rejected an equitable jurisdiction that would set aside contracts not void at common law. Four reasons can be identified.

(i) **Contradiction of *Bell v Lever Brothers***: *Solle v Butcher* represents 'a significant extension of any jurisdiction exercised up to that point and one that was not readily reconcilable with the result in *Bell v Lever*'. *Solle v Butcher* did not so much supplement or mitigate the common law, as outflank and contradict it (at [130]).

(ii) **Lack of precedent**: there was no clear authority for a more expansive equitable jurisdiction either before or in *Bell v Lever Brothers* itself (at [111]–[118]). *Solle v Butcher* had relied heavily on *Cooper v Phibbs* (see 6.2.5.2), but the case was not authority for a lower threshold since it involved mistakenly acquiring one's own property, which would have voided the contract at common law. Neither is *Cooper v Phibbs* authority for greater remedial flexibility in setting aside contracts 'on such terms as the court thinks fit'. The restitutionary remedy ordered there (rescission subject to a lien in favour of the mistaken lessor) merely recognised the latter's improvements to the fishery in the mistaken belief that it was his and ensured that the party recovering the property was not unjustly enriched (at [129]). Denning LJ's suggestion in *Solle v Butcher* that the House of Lords in *Bell v Lever Brothers* had overlooked existing equitable principles relieving mistakes was unrealistic (at [126]).

(iii) **Uncertainty**: the scope of the more expansive equitable jurisdiction is also said to require 'fundamental' mistakes (*Solle v Butcher* at 693), although they must logically be less 'fundamental' than those required at common law. Subsequent cases applying *Solle v Butcher* have not identified 'the test of mistake that gives rise to the equitable jurisdiction to rescind in a manner that distinguishes this from the test of a mistake that renders a contract void in law' (at [153]).

(iv) **Illegitimacy**: the equitable jurisdiction is largely motivated by the desire to avoid unjust outcomes. In essence, Denning LJ in *Solle v Butcher* (at 671) supported the landlord's claim 'that it is unfair' for the tenant to pay £140 for the remaining five years of the lease when the market rent is £250. The Court of Appeal supported Toulson J's view (at [119]–[125]) that it was not the court's role to dissolve or vary contracts thought to be harsh on the basis of so-called equitable principles. Such considerations were properly considered under other existing equitable doctrines such as fraud, misrepresentation, and undue influence (at [155]–[157]). Some of the post-*Solle v Butcher* cases were dismissed as muddled, confused, and failing to take account of contractual allocations of risk.[6]

---

[6] *Grist v Bailey* and *Laurence v Lexcourt Holdings* in *William Sindall v Cambridgeshire CC* at 1035.

6.3.3 **The future of equitable common mistake**

In practice, the Court of Appeal's abolition of equitable common mistake seems secure since a litigant will now be reluctant to argue the point and, as *Great Peace v Tsavliris* noted, decisions in lower courts present no clear resistance to the demise of *Solle v Butcher*.

> **◆◆◆** **Counterpoint**
>
> 1. *Uncertainty*: whilst the scope of equitable mistake is admittedly uncertain, the scope of common law mistake is itself highly unstable. In *Chwee Kin Keong v Digilandmall.com Pte Ltd* (2005), the Singapore Court of Appeal regarded the view that equitable intervention would create unacceptable uncertainty as exaggerated (at [81]) and affirmed the continued existence of an equitable jurisdiction for mistake after *Great Peace*.
>
> 2. *Authority*: the existence of equitable common mistake is accepted by a number of decisions after *Solle v Butcher*, including Court of Appeal decisions.[7] Steyn J in *Associated Japanese Bank v Crédit du Nord* regarded the interacting set of rules as 'an entirely satisfactory state of the law'. In '***Great Peace* and Precedent**' (2003) 119 *LQR* 180, **Midwinter** points out that since the mistake in *Great Peace* was insufficiently serious to qualify even for equitable relief, it was unnecessary to decide on the validity of the doctrine. As a matter of precedent, *Solle v Butcher* should have been regarded as binding on both the High Court and the Court of Appeal in *Great Peace*.
>
> 3. *The relevance of fairness*: considerations of fairness permeate contract law; it is present in common law mistake as instanced by the accounts of *Bell v Lever Brothers* itself The denial of relief in *Great Peace* can also be regarded as fair in the context of a commercial contract which had been relied upon. Indeed, it is arguable that the owners of the *Great Peace* made no mistake at all. Reynolds observes that they merely believed, 'correctly, that the salvors had reason to believe that the *Great Peace* was the nearest ship'.[8] The case for relief is stronger in non-commercial or consumer cases. Deserving cases driven out of mistake are likely to find their way into other vitiating factors.
>
> 4. *Proportionality of legal response*: it would be perfectly rational to have a system where serious mistakes void contracts, and less serious mistakes merely render contracts voidable, whether the mistakes are induced or not.[9] Moreover, it seems odd that an innocent misrepresentation will only render contracts voidable whilst a common mistake induced by an innocent misrepresentation will render the contract either void or valid (all-or-nothing).
>
> 5. *Judicial vs legislative development*: the Court of Appeal's rejection of the equitable jurisdiction (evolved to introduce remedial flexibility) is accompanied by a simultaneous call for the introduction of legislation analogous to the Law Reform (Frustrated Contracts) Act 1943 to give greater remedial flexibility. As Reynolds observes, 'It is not clear why a statute (hardly
>
> ➡

---

[7] *Rose v Pim* (1953); *Grist v Bailey* (1967); *Magee v Pennine Insurance* (1969); *Laurence v Lexcourt Holdings* (1978); *William Sindall v Cambridgeshire CC* (1994); *Nutt v Reed* (1999); *Clarion v National Provident Institution* (2000); *West Sussex Properties v Chichester DC* (2000).

[8] F M B Reynolds, 'Reconsider the Contract Textbook' (2003) 119 *LQR* 177, 178.

[9] See A S Burrows, 'We Do This at Common Law and That at Equity' (2002) 22 *OJLS* 1, 5–6.

→

an item of priority for law reformers) would do any better than a careful judicial interpretation of Lord Denning's doctrine, which is after all but a slight extension of lines of existing
equity cases on misrepresentation and unconscionability in general.'[10]

6. *Remedial flexibility*: the Court of Appeal's call for greater flexibility is odd in the context
of its denial of equitable mistake, because if a mistake is not sufficiently fundamental to
void the contract, it is *valid* and cannot be the subject of '*remedial* flexibility'. The Court of
Appeal must be read as supporting a wider *scope* (lowering the threshold) for relievable
mistake *and* wider discretion to tailor appropriate remedies (beyond voiding contracts).
While the law of frustration is held up as the example to follow, it is questionable (see
7.6.2–7.6.4) that the Law Reform (Frustrated Contracts) Act 1943 permits sufficient remedial flexibility (it only allows restitution and limited loss apportionment). In comparison, in
German law a party making a unilateral mistake can set aside the contract on compensating the other party who does not know of the mistake (§ 122 of the German Civil Code
(BGB)). The New Zealand Contractual Mistakes Act 1977 confers on the court a wide discretion to grant relief including cancellation, validation, or variation of the contract and the
awarding of restitution or compensation.

6.4 **Unilateral mistake at common law**

Aside from mistake as to terms (see 2.1.3), two types of unilateral mistake can void
contracts at common law: mistake as to the *identity* of the other party and mistake as
to the *nature* of the document.

6.4.1 **Mistake as to identity**

6.4.1.1 The nature of the problem

The typical problem arises where *A* makes an apparent contract with *B* believing *B*
to be *C*; *A* passes property to *B* under this contract, which *B* then passes on to *D* in a
subsequent transaction before *B* disappears or is not worth suing. Can *A* recover his
or her property from *D*?

$$A \rightarrow B(C) \rightarrow D$$

The legal response to this question is beset by 'illogical and sometimes barely perceptible distinctions' (*Shogun Finance Ltd v Hudson* (2002) at [11] and (2003) at [141]).
Two factors have contributed to this picture. First, several different doctrines with
distinct lines of reasoning are inconsistently applied to the problem. Second, a failure
to clearly identify and respond to the relevant issues. In *two-party cases*, *B*'s fraud or
knowledge that *A* only intends to contract with someone else is usually enough to
deny *B* the contract. However, *three-party cases* raise different issues. The law must

---

[10] F M B Reynolds, 'Reconsider the Contract Textbook' (2003) 119 *LQR* 177, 179.

allocate the risk of *B*'s fraud between *A* and *D*. However, the public interest in protecting the security of transactions is largely suppressed by an overly technical approach in deciding whether *B*'s transaction with *A* is void or voidable. The three options are illustrated in **Diagram 6F**.

Diagram 6F.1: where the *A–B* **transaction is *void***, no legal title passes with the physical transfer of the property to *B*; *B* then cannot pass title to *D* (since *B* can give no better title than he or she has). The *legal title* to the property remains with *A*, allowing *A* to recover the property from *D*, who is left unprotected.

Diagram 6F.2: where the *A–B* **transaction is *voidable***, the contract is valid *until A rescinds it*. Until then, *B* obtains good legal title from *A* and can validly pass it on to *D*. *D* is protected if he or she obtains title before *A* rescinds, and if *D* is a 'bona fide purchaser for value' (ie *D* gave consideration for the property in ignorance of the defect in *B*'s title). *A* cannot recover the property from *D*; *A*'s only action is against *B* for reliance damages, if *B* can be found and is worth suing.

Diagram 6F.3: if *A* rescinds the voidable contract *before B* transfers the property to *D* as a bona fide purchaser, this revests title to the property in *A* from that point in time. *D* cannot subsequently obtain legal title from *B*, although he or she obtains physical possession of it. *A* can then recover the property from *D*.

6.4.1.2 Identity vs attributes

The general rule is that a mistake as to the identity of the other party will only void a contract if it goes to the other party's 'identity' as opposed to merely the 'attributes' (eg as to solvency, character, or social position). This is analogous to the troublesome distinction between common mistakes that go to the 'substance', as opposed to merely the 'qualities', of the subject matter of the contract. The problem is that the identity of a person or a contract's subject matter is an accumulation of their respective attributes

Diagram 6F Void and voidable contracts in three-party cases

Look on the Online Resource Centre to view this figure as a PowerPoint® presentation

———→ physical transfer of property
- - - -→ transfer of title to the property

1 If contract between A and B is void, A can recover property from D

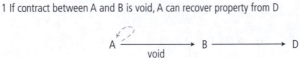

A ————→ B ————————→ D
     void

2 If contract between A and B is voidable and A rescinds *after* B transfers to D, A cannot recover property from D if D is a good faith purchaser

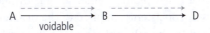

A - - - - - → B - - - - - → D
     voidable

3 If contract between A and B is voidable and A rescinds *before* B transfers to D, A can recover property from D even if D is a good faith purchaser

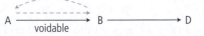

A ————→ B ————————→ D
     voidable

or qualities. Moreover, just as a 'mere' quality may be so *essential* that its absence voids the contract in common mistake, the same goes for a person's attributes. Four sometimes contradictory 'rules' guide the courts in making the identity–attribute distinction: (i) objectivity; (ii) written contracts; (iii) non-existence of the identity assumed; and (iv) face-to-face dealings.

6.4.1.3 Objectivity: you cannot accept someone else's offer

The objective test of formation prevents a party from accepting an offer that he or she knows was not intended to be made to him or her. In **Bolton v Jones** (1857), J sent a written order for some goods to Brocklehurst, with whom J had previously dealt and against whom he could set-off (deduct) sums that Brocklehurst owed him. Bolton took over Brocklehurst's business and filled out J's order without disclosing the change of ownership. The court held that J need not pay since Bolton could not accept an offer that he *must have known* was not addressed to him. Likewise, there would be no valid contract if the offeror knows that the offeree has accepted an offer reasonably believing it came from someone else. However, this assumes that the identity of the other contract party is *vital* to the claimant (*Ingram v Little* (1961) at 57; *Lewis v Averay* (1972) at 209). Otherwise, mistake as to identity is irrelevant to formation. For example, retailers are not generally concerned about the identity of the shopper, or the auctioneer with the identity of the bidder (*Dennant v Skinner* (1948)).

6.4.1.4 Written contracts

Where a contract is reduced to writing, it can only be between the persons *named in a written contract as the parties* to the contract. In **Cundy v Lindsay** (1878), L received an order for goods from Blenkarn of '37 Wood Street, Cheapside', who had forged the signature of Blenkiron & Co of 123 Wood Street, with whom L had previously dealt. L sent the goods to Blenkarn, who sold them on to C. The House of Lords voided the contract for L's mistake of identity: L only made a contract with the party identified in the writing (ie Blenkiron & Co). C had to return the goods to L. The decision was applied by the House of Lords in **Shogun Finance v Hudson** (2003). S sold a car on hire purchase to R, a fraudster posing as 'Mr Patel', after checking the credit rating of Mr Patel, whose driving licence R produced. R then sold on to H. The House of Lords allowed S to recover the car from H because the buyer's identity named in the agreement was crucially important to S; therefore there was no valid contract between S and R. H could not rely on section 27 of the Hire Purchase Act 1964 (which protects a good faith third party who buys a car from the 'debtor' under a 'hire purchase agreement' before the debtor has acquired legal title to the car) because R was not such a 'debtor'.

> ### Pause for reflection
>
> 1. The decision in *Shogun* can cut across the rules that a contract is only voidable (not void) for mistaken identity where: (i) the mistaken identity is non-existent; and (ii) the contract is concluded by face-to-face dealings (see 6.4.1.5 and 6.4.1.6).
>
> ➡

➡

2. Lord Millett, dissenting, reasoned that the contract should only be voidable for misrepresentation rather than void for mistake because there should be a presumption that a party intends to deal with the person with whom he or she is *physically dealing* (ie R). Moreover, whether the parties deal face to face *or in writing*, a contract should come into being if there is a *sufficient correlation* between the offer and the acceptance (at [81] and see Lord Nicholls at [36]). A good faith third party should be protected if he or she buys the property before the original owner rescinds the contract. Accordingly, the minority regard *Cundy v Lindsay* as wrongly decided.

4. MacMillan explains *Cundy v Lindsay* as the result of 19th-century criminal law.[11] It was assumed that 'convictions of the rogue for obtaining goods by false pretences necessarily meant that the contract was void', and the Larceny Act 1861 allowed the original owner to recover their goods from innocent third party buyers as long as they prosecuted the felon to conviction. Since these no longer apply, there is no sound basis for the decision in *Cundy*.

6.4.1.5 Non-existence of the identity assumed

A's mistake as to *B*'s identity will only void their contract if *A* mistook *B* for another existing and identifiable party, *C*. If *A* merely believes that *B* is *C* who is *non-existent* or unidentifiable, the contract is only voidable. In ***King's Norton Metal Co Ltd v Edridge, Merrett & Co Ltd*** (1897), K sent goods in response to an order from the fictitious 'Hallam & Co' written on headed stationery with a picture of a large factory and a list of overseas depots. The fraudster then sold the goods to E. Although the contract was in writing, the contract was only *voidable* for fraud because K intended to contract with the writer of the letter, being mistaken only as to his attributes; namely, solvency and respectability. The contract was not *void* for K's mistake that it was contracting with 'Hallam & Co' because 'Hallam & Co' was non-existent. 'If it could have been shown that there was a separate entity called Hallam & Co . . . then the case might have come within the decision in *Cundy v Lindsay*' (at 99).

It is difficult to see why *A* and *D*'s rights should depend on whether *A* mistook *B* for another *real* entity or not. Furthermore, why was it not enough in *King's Norton* that K believed that 'Hallam & Co' existed, when it did not?

This supposed rule is subject to two exceptions, which require impossible distinctions to be drawn.

(i) A contract may be voided if *A* makes the additional mistake that *C* exists, even if *C* does not exist. But is there a meaningful difference between *A* believing '*B* to be not *B*', and by implication someone else, and *A* believing '*B* to be *C*, mistakenly believing that *C* exists'? After all, in *Lake v Simmons* (1927), the mistress of a wealthy customer, a widower, purchased some items from L, and then persuaded L to let her take away valuable pearl necklaces for her 'husband's approval'. L's loss was only insured if no

---

[11] C MacMillan, 'Rogues, Swindlers and Cheats: The Development of Mistake of Identity in English Contract Law' (2005) 63 *CLJ* 711, 743.

valid contract was made with the mistress. The court so found although she was posing as a non-existent wife.

(ii) It is enough to void a contract when *A* merely believes that *B* who pretends to be *C* was not *B* (whether *C* exists or not), as long as there is an *implied term* that *B* is not *B* (*Said v Butt* (1920)), as where:

- an offer is made only to persons fitting particular descriptions which excludes *B* (eg 'current students of a particular university', or being 'over 18 years' to buy alcohol); or

- *B* may know from previous dealings that *A* is unwilling to contract with them (eg *B* is barred from a pub or a soccer match).

If the rationale is merely that *B* cannot accept an offer known not to be meant for them, then why did this not apply in *King's Norton Metal* when the fraudster must have known that K had no intention of contracting with him?

6.4.1.6 Face-to-face dealings

Where the parties deal with each other face to face (*inter praesentes*), the law presumes that each intends to deal with the 'person present, and identified by sight and hearing'. The contract is only **voidable** and bona fide third party purchasers who obtain title before the contract is rescinded are protected. In ***Phillips v Brooks Ltd*** (1919), a fraudster selected some jewellery in P's shop and wrote a cheque for £3,000 saying 'I am Sir George Bullough', a person of good credit known by reputation to P. P used a directory to check the address the fraudster had given and accepted the cheque. The fraudster then pledged the jewellery to B for £350. P's mistake did not prevent the property passing to B. It was held that P *intended to sell to the person present in the shop* even though P believed that person was Sir George Bullough, an identifiable and existing third party.

The decision is difficult to reconcile with *Lake v Simmons* and *Ingram v Little*. In both cases, it could equally be said that the claimant intended to contract with the party before them. In ***Ingram v Little*** (1961), a fraudster calling himself Hutchinson offered to buy the Ingram sisters' car, offering payment by cheque. On their insistence for cash, he gave his initials and address and described himself as a respectable businessman. The sisters did not know of this person, but ascertained his existence and address from the telephone directory. They then accepted the cheque which was dishonoured. Meanwhile, the fraudster sold the car to L. The Court of Appeal held that the original sale was **void** and the sisters could recover their car from L. Their checking of the telephone directory *rebutted the presumption* that they intended to deal with the person in front of them: they only intended to deal with Hutchinson.

Ingram was criticised in *Lewis v Averay* (1972) (at 206, 208), where structurally identical facts only made the contract **voidable**. A fraudster posing as a well-known actor Richard Green offered to buy L's car with a cheque. When L refused to let the car go until the cheque cleared, the fraudster produced an officially stamped pass to Pinewood Studios in RG's name but bearing the fraudster's photograph. L then let the fraudster take the car which was sold on to A. The cheque was dishonoured. The court held that L intended to contract with the person before him, so that property validly passed to A via the fraudster; L could not recover his car.

The different results reached in *Phillips v Brooks* and *Lewis v Averay* on one side (contracts only voidable) and in *Lake v Simmons* and *Ingram v Little* on the other (contracts void) are impossible to reconcile. All the sellers (other than in *Lake*) took steps to check the alleged identity of the buyers: there is no difference between the merits of the respective sellers' claims. The conflict seems now to have been resolved in favour of **voidability** *unless the contract is in writing*. The House of Lords held in *Shogun Finance v Hudson* that the presumption against a contract being void for mistaken identity in face-to-face dealings is a strong one (at [22], [27], [69], [170], and [187]). Indeed, two of their Lordships even doubted the possibility of rebutting this presumption (at [37], [67]), although Lord Walker (at [187]) was prepared to accept it in wholly exceptional cases (eg where the fraudster impersonates a person known to the mistaken party whose senses are impaired). Nevertheless, despite the *face-to-face dealing* on the facts of *Shogun*, the majority of their Lordships sidestepped this presumption. The fact that S's written contract was with Mr Patel trumped S's face-to-face dealing with R. The contract was void.

Counterpoint

The law's approach in asking whether the original contract is void or voidable bears no relationship to the real problem before the court in three-party cases; that is, how to balance the interests of innocent purchasers (*D*) who deal with the apparent owners of goods (*B*), with the interests of (*A*) innocent sellers who are duped into parting with their goods. Why should *D*'s rights depend on the particular way that *B* defrauds *A* (ie making *A* think *B* was '*C*' or just 'not *B*'; in person or in writing)? If such irrelevant criteria are adopted it is unsurprising that the law becomes complex and incoherent. The crucial point is that it is *A* who assesses the risk and decides whether to sell on credit. This makes *A* better able to self-protect than *D* and so should take the risk of mistake. The increase in identity theft (eg credit card fraud) underlines the importance of reform. Three alternative approaches can be suggested:

1. *Good faith third party purchasers fully protected if they obtain title before rescission*: the Law Reform Committee recommends that mistaken identity in sale of goods contracts should only be regarded as rendering the contract voidable ('Transfer of Title to Chattels' (12th Report (Cmnd 2958, 1966) at para 15)).

2. *Loss sharing*: Devlin LJ dissenting in *Ingram v Little* (at 73–4) suggested loss sharing between the two innocent parties according to the *comparative negligence* of each. This mitigates the 'all-or-nothing' result of the void-voidable approach, but substitutes it with the uncertainty of assessing what counts as loss and how it should be apportioned. Loss apportionment on the basis of fault (contributory negligence) is still generally avoided by the common law.

3. *Protection of third party change of position*: the law of unjust enrichment allows recovery of mistaken transfers subject to the defence of change of position. This defence protects the recipient's innocent expenditure in reliance on the security of his or her receipt by offsetting that sum against that which must be returned. Accordingly, *A* should be able to

➡

> recover the property (or its value) on condition that he or she compensates *D* for the price *D* paid for the property (or deducts this from the value returned). If *D* acquired the goods at undervalue, *A* could recover the value of the goods exceeding the price *D* paid. In *Phillips v Brooks*, the third party would be compensated for the £350 paid, but the original seller would recover the jewellery worth almost ten times that. This solution balances the equities between two innocent parties.

6.4.2 Fundamental mistake about the nature of the document: *non est factum*

6.4.2.1 The nature of the problem

The importance of ensuring the certainty and security of transactions means that a person is normally bound by his or her signature to a contractual document irrespective of his or her knowledge or understanding of its contents (see 10.3.3.1). The doctrine of *non est factum* ('this is not my deed') is an exception which can void a contract and any transfers of rights under it. The doctrine recognises that in wholly exceptional circumstances (eg where the signer is blind or illiterate, and the nature or effect of the document is misrepresented to them) the interest of certainty may be outweighed by the concern for justice and the importance of ensuring a minimum of meaningful consent to the contract. However, in deference to certainty and security, the thresholds of the seriousness of the mistake made and the impairment of the claimant are set very high.

Non est factum raises similar issues to mistaken identity. In **two-party cases**, where *A* signs or executes a document being mistaken as to its real nature and effect, relief is available without resort to *non est factum* (*Lloyds Bank plc v Waterhouse* (1991) at 184–5, 190–1) as a *misrepresentation*, if *B*'s misrepresentation has induced *A*'s mistake or there is no contract, if *B* knows of *A*'s mistake as to terms or has negligently induced *A*'s mistake (2.1.3.1 and 2.1.3.2). *B*'s unconscientious conduct or knowledge entitles *A* to some remedy, even if *A* has been careless.

The case for *A*'s relief is much weaker in **three-party** cases. The situation can arise where *B*'s misrepresentation:

- induces *A* into a contract, *A* then transfers rights to *B*, which *B* then transfers to *D*; or

- induces *A* to contract with *C* who is ignorant of *B*'s misrepresentation (eg *United Dominion's Trust v Western* (1976)).

As with mistaken identity cases, *A*'s catastrophic mistake as to the nature of the signed document must be balanced against protection of the third party good faith purchaser (*C*) who relies on the document. As with mistaken identity, the law resolves such cases by reference to the void–voidable distinction.

6.4.2.2 How serious must the mistake be?

The House of Lords requires a '*fundamental*' or '*essential*' or '*radical*' or '*very substantial*' or '*serious*' difference between the nature of the actual document and the document as it is believed to be (*Saunders v Anglia Building Society*, affirming *Gaillie v Lee* (1969)). The difference is one of *degree* rather than of kind: it must be determined by the 'difference in practical result', rather than 'difference in legal character' (at 1017). Like common mistake, instances of operative *non est factum* are rare. For example, in *Foster v Mackinnon* (1869) M was induced to endorse a bill of exchange by a misrepresentation that it was a guarantee like one he had previously signed.

Non est factum was *rejected* where *the purpose of the contract is not fundamentally undermined*. In **Saunders v Anglia Building Society**, S (a 78-year-old widow) wanted to help her nephew raise money on the security of her house, provided she could remain there for life. She signed a document without reading it, having broken her glasses, when she was told that it was a deed of gift to her nephew. She actually signed a sale of her house to her nephew's friend (he purported to be raising money in his own name for the nephew's benefit because the latter wanted to avoid his wife's maintenance claim). The friend mortgaged the house to A but kept the money it raised. Although a gift to her nephew seems fundamentally different from a sale to his friend, the court held that it was not: her purpose of assisting her nephew by raising money on her house would have been achieved by the actual sale had the nephew's friend paid up. Again, no relief is available if *there is no positive mistake but mere ignorance*. In *Gillman v Gillman* (1946), a woman signed a separation deed in ignorance of its true nature, but without any positive idea of what she was signing. One should not sign something if one has no idea of its contents.

6.4.2.3 Who qualifies for relief?

In *Saunders v Anglia Building Society* (at 1016), it was held that *non est factum* cannot normally be relied upon by literate persons of full capacity. It applies to 'those who are permanently or temporarily unable through no fault of their own to have without explanation any real understanding of the purport of a particular document, whether that be from defective education, illness or innate incapacity', or from being tricked. A claimant who is relevantly disadvantaged must still take such care as could be expected of them. He or she is disqualified if they do not. This was an alternative basis for denying relief to the widow in *Saunders v Anglia Building Society*. It was held that while she might not have understood all its complexities, she could at least have checked the identity of the transferee. This carelessness may explain why she also failed to void the contract for mistaken identity. The requirement of care disqualifies a claimant who signs a document in blank leaving another to fill in the details (*United Dominion's Trust Ltd v Western*).

In **two-party cases**, the claimant's carelessness is irrelevant (*Peterlin v Cullen* (1975) at 360; *Bradley West Solicitors Nominee Co Ltd v Keenen* (1994) at 118): it cannot lie in the fraudster's mouth to say that the claimant should not have been taken in, and the fraudster should not profit from their own wrong. In **three-party cases** where the contest is between two innocent parties, the claimant's carelessness is directly relevant to the question of who should bear the loss. The policies encouraging responsibility in contractual formation and protecting reasonable reliance on signatures would allocate the risk to the claimant whose mistaken and careless signature initiated the disastrous train of events, rather than the innocent third party who has merely acted in reliance on the signed document.

6.5 **Unilateral mistake at equity**

There are some cases giving relief in equitable mistake where one party has made a mistake about the terms of the contract when it would be unconscionable for the other party to take advantage of it. Since most of these cases can be decided on other, more established, grounds and, given the Court of Appeal's rejection of an equitable mistake doctrine, this category has receded in importance. For example, the courts have allowed rescission if *B*'s misrepresentation has induced *A*'s mistake.[12] Relief for equitable mistake has also been given in *Torrance v Bolton* (1872), where the seller had advertised property for sale as an 'absolute freehold reversion' but qualified this at the auction by orally disclosing its encumbrance by four mortgages; this went unheard by the deaf purchaser who made the successful bid (see also *Denny v Hancock* (1870) and *Malins v Freeman* (1837)). Insofar as these relate to *mistake as to terms*, this is the equitable analogue of misleading offers instanced by *Scriven v Hindley* (see 2.1.3.2), although it is unclear why these contracts are merely voidable rather than void. The same comment can be made of the equitable analogue of *Hartog v Shields* (see 2.1.3.1). In *Webster v Cecil* (1861), C mistakenly offered to sell land for £1,250 when he intended to say £2,250. C informed W of his mistake immediately after W accepted it. The mistake must have been obvious to W because C had previously refused to sell for £2,000.

The courts will generally deny relief where a mistake was entirely the product of the mistaken party's own *carelessness*, as in *Tamplin v James* (1880), where J bid for some property believing it to be more extensive than it was, even though plans of the lot were on exhibition at the auction (see also *Riverlate Properties Ltd v Paul* (1975)). A mistake as to the effect or the commercial consequences of the contract is not enough (*Clarion Ltd v National Provident Institution* (2000) at 1898–9).

6.6 **Mistake in recording the contract: rectification**

Parties who wrongly record their agreement (eg the amount of the rent or the area of land to be sold) can apply for rectification to make the contract conform to their actual agreement.

6.6.1 **What must be proved?**

Lord Hoffmann approved the following conditions for allowing rectification (*Chartbrook Ltd v Persimmon Homes Ltd* (2009) at [74]).

(i)   The parties had a common continuing intention up to the execution of the instrument to be rectified, whether or not amounting to an agreement, in respect of a particular matter in the instrument.

---

[12] *May v Platt* (1900) at 623; *Redbridge LBC v Robinson Rentals* (1969) at 1131; *Riverlate Properties Ltd v Paul* (1975) at 140–1, 145.

(ii) There was an **outwards expression of accord**: the test is objective. However, this may require 'refinement as different and more complex factual situations' arise for adjudication (*Daventry DC v Daventry & District Housing Ltd* (2011) at [104]).

(iii) By mistake, the instrument did not reflect that common intention.

    ✓ In *Joscelyne v Nissen* (1970), the daughter's agreement to purchase her father's business was rectified in line with the parties' continuing common intention that the daughter should pay all his household expenses, although the written agreement was silent on it and no prior contract existed on this issue.

    ✓ In *Munt v Beasley* (2006), rectification was allowed where both parties understood that the lease included the loft as stated in B's agent's particulars of sale although not in the actual lease. Four years after the lessee started a loft conversion, the Court of Appeal denied B's claim for trespass and breach of covenant. Mummery LJ (at [36]) noted 'the trend in recent cases to treat the expression "outward expression of accord" more as an evidential factor rather than a strict legal requirement in all cases of rectification'. This is particularly so 'where the party resisting rectification has in fact admitted . . . that his true state of belief when he entered into the transaction was the same as that of the other party and there was therefore a continuing common intention which, by mistake, was not given effect in the relevant legal document'.

Nevertheless, the mistake must be in the *recording* of the contract and not in the *making* of it. Thus, *rectification is not available* if there is:

(i) any confusion over what was agreed (*Cambro Contractors Ltd v John Kennelly Sales* (1994));

(ii) merely an *omission* to deal with some matter (*Kemp v Neptune Concrete* (1989) at 377, 379–80);

(iii) *no literal disparity* between the terms used in the parties' agreement and the document purporting to record it. Thus, rectification was denied in *Frederick E Rose v William H Pim Junior* where the parties entered an oral agreement for 'horse beans', later recorded in a written agreement, although both parties mistook them for 'feveroles' (the seller's innocent misrepresentation would have allowed rescission but the buyer wanted rectification so that he could claim expectation damages). But rectification would have been available if the parties had *expressly* agreed the meaning of particular words *in the written contract*; that is, that 'horse beans' meant 'feveroles' (*London Weekend Television v Paris and Griffith* (1969); *Joscelyne v Nissen* at 98);

(iv) *no shared mistake*, only unilateral mistake; a party is not mistaken if he or she is indifferent to the relevant matter (*Riverlate Properties v Paul* at 140).

6.6.2 **Rectification and interpretation**

To some extent, rectification has been overtaken by Lord Hoffmann's more relaxed approach to the interpretation of contract (see 10.5). In particular, he said that if the court concludes that 'the parties must . . . have used the wrong words or syntax' or 'that something must have gone wrong with the language, the law does not require judges to attribute to the parties an intention which they plainly could not have had'. In *Cherry Tree Investments Ltd v Landmain Ltd* (2012) at [62], Arden LJ described this as a process of 'corrective interpretation'. Burrows has argued that this renders the rectification doctrine largely superfluous ('**Construction and Rectification**' in A Burrows and E Peel (eds), *Contract Terms* (OUP, 2007) 77). However, Lewison LJ said that 'there is still a useful role for rectification to play' (*Cherry Tree* at [98]). In particular, he said (at [132]) that the court cannot, by the process of interpretation, insert whole clauses that the parties have mistakenly failed to include. This is especially so when it relates to a legal charge, which is a public document on a public register upon which third parties are expected to rely to obtain an accurate picture of the state of the title to the land. In *Daventry DC v Daventry & District Housing Ltd* (2011) at [198], Lord Neuberger MR observed three differences between interpretation and rectification:

(i) prior negotiations are admissible in a rectification claim, but not generally for interpretation;

(ii) some subjective evidence of intention or understanding is normally required in a rectification claim since the claimant must show that he or she made the relevant mistake when they entered into the contract;

(iii) rectification is an equitable remedy and therefore is subject to somewhat different rules from interpretation (eg it is discretionary).

6.6.3 **Rectification for unilateral mistake**

Rectification may be allowed for a **unilateral mistake** in recording the contract if it would be **inequitable** for the unmistaken party to object because they:

(i) actually knew of the mistake and of the mistaken party's real intentions (*Thomas Bates & Sons Ltd v Wyndhams Ltd* (1981) at 515–61, 520–1; *Commission for the New Towns v Cooper* (1995) 277–80);[13]

(ii) failed to draw the mistaken party's attention to the mistake, or made 'false and misleading statements' to divert the other from discovering the mistake (*Commission for the New Towns v Cooper* at 280); *and*

(iii) the mistake results in benefit to the unmistaken party or detriment to the mistaken party.

The contract may be enforced on the mistaken party's understanding.

---

[13] Actual knowledge includes wilfully shutting one's eyes to the obvious, or wilfully and recklessly failing to make such inquiries as an honest and reasonable person would have made.

Pause for reflection

In **'The "Drastic" Remedy of Rectification for Unilateral Mistake'** (2008) 124 *LQR* 608, **McLauchlan** argues that rectification for unilateral mistake is simply the objective test of contract formation in action. Rectification will be allowed where *A* leads *B* into believing that *A* is agreeing at *B*'s terms (see 2.1.2.1). Otherwise, there is no contract at all. This also overlaps with the principles of contextual interpretation when something is thought to have 'gone wrong with the language' (see 10.5.2).

THIS CHAPTER IN ESSENCE

online
resource
centre

The key areas and core topics in this chapter are summarised in an easy-to-use list, ideal for revision purposes, on the Online Resource Centre at http://www.oxfordtextbooks.co.uk/orc/chenwishart5e/. Links to websites relevant to the topics covered and any updates to the chapter can also be found on the Online Resource Centre.

QUESTIONS

1 'There is no doctrine of mistake; there is only the parties' contractual risk allocation.' Discuss.

2 'It is impossible to explain a doctrine of mistaken assumptions whilst also insisting on an objective approach to contractual formation.' Discuss.

3 'It is irrational to recognise an equitable jurisdiction to relieve for common mistake co-existing with a common law jurisdiction to do the same. *Solle v Butcher* is inconsistent with *Bell v Lever Brothers*. One of them must go.' Discuss.

4 '[T]here is scope for legislation to give greater flexibility to our law of mistake than the common law allows' (*Great Peace v Tsavliris*). Do you agree? How might greater flexibility be achieved?

5 The law on mistaken identity is beset by 'illogical and sometimes barely perceptible distinctions'. Are matters clearer after *Shogun Finance Ltd v Hudson*?

6 Max, who bears a striking resemblance to a well-known pop star, walks into Nina's jewellery shop and selects an expensive diamond ring priced at £50,000. He says to Nina, 'I've forgotten my credit card, but you know who I am and that I'm good for it.' Nina is overawed and says 'yes, of course'. She allows Max to take the ring after Max signs a sale agreement. Max sells the ring to Otis for £2,000. Max cannot now be found. Advise Nina.

 For hints on how to answer these questions, please see the Online Resource Centre at http://www.oxfordtextbooks.co.uk/orc/chenwishart5e/

KEY FURTHER READING

Atiyah, P S, and Bennion, F (1961), 'Mistake in the Construction of Contracts', 24 *MLR* 421.

Chen-Wishart, M (2009), 'Objectivity and Mistake: The Oxymoron of *Smith v Hughes*' in J Neyers, R Bronough, and S G A Pitel (eds), *Exploring Contract Law* (Hart Publishing) 341.

MacMillan, C (2003), 'How Temptation Led to Mistake: An Explanation of *Bell v Lever Bros. Ltd*', 119 *LQR* 625.

McMeel, G (2006), 'Interpretation and Mistake in Contract Law: "The Fox Knows Many Things . . . "', *LMCLQ* 49.

Slade, C (1954), 'The Myth of Mistake in the English Law of Contract', 70 *LQR* 385.

Smith, J (1994), 'Contract—Mistake, Frustration and Implied Terms', 110 *LQR* 400.

Stevens, R (2007), 'Objectivity, Mistake and the Parol Evidence Rule' in A Burrows and E Peel (eds), *Contract Terms* (OUP) 101.

7

Frustration

'I should not be bound as things have turned out'

7.1 **Introduction**

If a high-rise office block is destroyed by an earthquake just before you complete its renovation, must the building owner still pay you? Can you be sued for failure to complete? The absurdity of a positive answer in either case is assumed by the doctrine of frustration. In *National Carriers Ltd v Panalpina (Northern) Ltd* (1981), Lord Simon said (at 700):

> Frustration of a contract takes place when there supervenes an event (without default of either party and for which the contract makes no sufficient provision) which so significantly changes the nature (not merely the expense or onerousness) of the outstanding contractual rights and/or obligations from what the parties could reasonably have contemplated at the time of its execution that it would be unjust to hold them to the literal sense of its stipulations in the new circumstances.

The doctrine excuses parties from further contractual performance when unforeseen events, *subsequent* to contract formation, make performance *illegal, impossible*, or *radically different* from the obligations the parties undertook at formation. Any obligations accruing before the frustrating event remain binding, but *neither party can be sued for* failure to perform outstanding obligations (they are extinguished). Thus, frustration is a defence to an action for breach of contract. As with the mistake doctrine (Chapter 6), the frustration doctrine is extremely narrow because of the concern to uphold contractual certainty and the parties' risk allocation. It is not enough that the change of circumstances makes performance more onerous or less advantageous for one of the parties. Contracts will only be discharged in the most exceptional cases. The main questions to be considered are the following.

(i) What is the relationship between the doctrines of *frustration* and of *mistake*?

(ii) What is the *justification* for the frustration doctrine?

(iii) What must be *proved* to frustrate a contract?

(iv) What is the *effect* of frustration?

(v) Is the current law on frustration *satisfactory*? If not, how might it be developed?

7.1.1 **Frustration and mistake**

The doctrines of frustration and common (ie shared) mistaken assumption (see 6.2) deal with essentially the *same* problem, namely how the law should respond when the parties' assumptions are, or turn out to be, radically different from those which the parties assumed when they entered the contract. Three points support this analysis.

(i) **Only difference in timing**: if the parties' common assumption is false *at* contract formation, the law treats this as a mistake; if their common assumption is falsified *after* contract formation, the law treats this as a case of frustration (see **Diagram 7A**). This temporal difference affects *when* the contract loses its binding force. Mistake sets the contract aside from the beginning (*ab initio*; although voidable contracts can pass property to third parties before they are rescinded). In contrast, frustration *discharges* an otherwise valid contract (discharging future performance) on the occurrence of the frustrating event. Mistake and frustration are essentially similar doctrines:

- the parties' mistake concerns an *existing* or a *future* non-term assumption;
- the assumption *is* or *has become* different from that supposed at formation; and
- both doctrines can be justified in terms of risk allocation, implied terms, impossibility of performance, or deficiency of consent (see 7.2).

The European Draft Common Frame of Reference enables the court to modify the contract not only where an 'exceptional change of circumstances [has] occurred after the time when the obligation was incurred' (Art III.-1:110(3)) (ie frustration) but also where 'both parties have made the same mistake' (Art II.-8:203(3)) at formation.

(ii) Two coronation cases:

- in ***Krell v Henry*** (1903), a flat overlooking Pall Mall was rented out for the purpose of watching the coronation procession pass by. The contract was **frustrated** when the king fell ill and the coronation was cancelled. The common assumption that the coronation would take place was falsified *after* formation;
- in ***Griffith v Brymer*** (1903), a similar contract was made at 11 am but the decision to cancel the procession for the king's illness had already been made an hour earlier. The contract was voided for **mistake** as made upon a 'missupposition of the state of facts which went to the whole root of the matter'.

Any apparent difference between these cases disappears when it is realised that the mistake in *Krell v Henry* could easily be described as relating to the state of the king's health at the time of contract formation. The legal response should not depend on whether the parties made their contract five minutes before or five minutes after the first appearance of the symptoms, the diagnosis of the disease, the advice to postpone, the king's decision to accept the advice, or the announcement of the cancellation itself.

(iii) **Judicial recognition of similarity**: many cases have noted the similarity between frustration and common mistake.[1] Most recently, the Court of Appeal assimilated the two doctrines under the formulation of *'impossibility of performance'* (*Great Peace Shipping Ltd v Tsavliris Salvage (International) Ltd* (2002) at [62]–[73]). One doctrine can cater for both situations. **Diagram 7A** shows that the test for relief is reducible to a three-step inquiry (mirroring that for mistake in Diagram 6D).

(1) **Construction**: was the risk of the change of circumstances expressly or impliedly allocated to one of the parties?

(2) **Fault**: was the frustration self-induced?

---

[1] *Associated Japanese Bank (International) Ltd v Crédit du Nord SA* (1989) at 264 ('related areas'); *William Sindall plc v Cambridgeshire CC* (1994) at 1039 ('same concept'); *Grains & Fourrages SA v Huyton* (1997) at 630 ('analogous concepts'); cf *Joseph Constantine Steamship Line v Imperial Smelting Corp Ltd* (1942) at 186 ('different juristic concepts').

Diagram 7A Frustration: the three-step approach

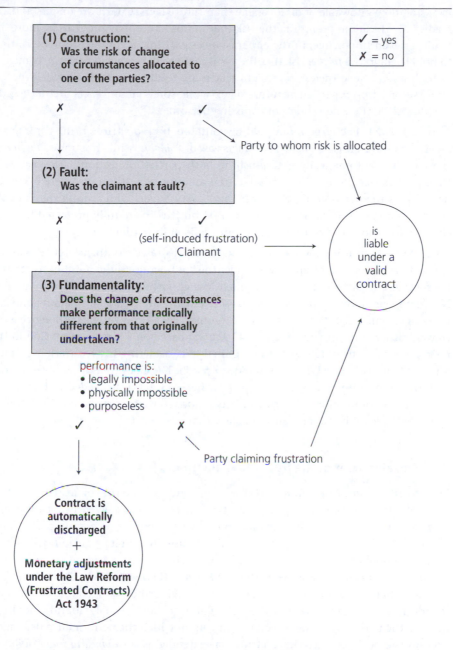

(3) **Fundamentality**: did the new circumstances render the obligation to perform radically or fundamentally different from that originally undertaken?

Three main differences between mistake and frustration can be identified.

(i) **Scope**: the scope of frustration is wider than that for mistake; events amounting to frustration may not be sufficient to warrant relief for mistake. *However*, the difference is one of degree and not of kind, and rests on the intuition that present facts are more knowable or discoverable than future facts. Courts are understandably readier to allocate to promisors the risk that performance may prove to be more difficult, or even impossible, in the circumstances existing *at* contract formation, than to hold them to the *further* risk that they will *continue* to be able to perform 'come hell or high water'. Nevertheless, some future facts are readily knowable (eg when the sun will rise or set on a particular future date), while some present facts are not (eg the cure for AIDS, the whereabouts of a missing person).

(ii) **Contract discharged, not void or voidable**: both doctrines bring contracts to an end. However, mistake makes contracts *void* or *voidable*, while frustration *discharges* the contract, automatically extinguishing both parties' obligations, irrespective of their wishes (see 7.6.1). This can affect the amount of restitution ordered (see (iii) below) and the position of good faith third party buyers who acquire rights in the subject matter of the contract (see 6.4.1.1). Third parties are fully protected irrespective of frustration since the contract is fully valid at formation.

(iii) **Monetary adjustments**: the Law Reform (Frustrated Contracts) Act 1943 allows courts to adjust the gains and losses under the contract up to the point of frustration (to reverse enrichment and allow limited loss apportionment, see 7.6.3 and 7.6.4). No analogous statutory power exists to sort out the aftermath of operative mistake (although some restitution is available at common law). However, this difference is fortuitous rather than principled. The 1943 Act was based on a Law Revision Committee report whose terms of reference were limited to considering the frustration problem arising from *Chandler v Webster* (1904) (see 7.6.2.2). The Court of Appeal in *Great Peace v Tsavliris* recognised (at [162]) that, just as the 1943 Act 'was needed to temper the effect of the common law doctrine of frustration, so there is scope for legislation to give greater flexibility to our law of mistake than the common law allows'.

7.1.2 Development of the frustration doctrine

Prior to 1863, **Paradine v Jane** (1647) was authority for the rule of absolute contractual liability (the *'no excuses'* rule). Accordingly, the court rejected J's plea for relief from paying rent when an enemy invasion drove him out of the premises. The Court said (at 27): 'if the lessee covenants to repair a house, though it be burnt by lightning, or thrown down by enemies, yet he ought to repair it'.

This extreme position was overturned by **Taylor v Caldwell** (1863). There, C hired to T a music hall and gardens for concerts on four nights and was sued for breach when the music hall burnt down before the first night. Blackburn J (at 839) found C not liable because the perishing of the person or thing upon which the performance depended, excuses the performance. The doctrine was extended *beyond physical impossibility* to cases, like the coronation cases, where performance, although literally possible, 'had become something radically different from that which the parties contemplated when it was concluded' (*Great Peace v Tsavliris* at [63]); this has also been called 'failure of adventure' or 'impracticability'. In **Jackson v The Union Marine Insurance Co Ltd** (1874), J's ship was chartered to proceed from Liverpool, load a cargo of iron rails, and continue to San Francisco. The contract was frustrated when the voyage was delayed for over six months, because the ship was stranded before loading the cargo. The court held that 'a voyage undertaken after the ship was sufficiently repaired would have been a different voyage . . . different as a different adventure' (at 141); the delay was so substantial that it destroyed the *commercial sense* of the original transaction.

7.2 **Justification**

As with mistake, the basis for the frustration doctrine has been controversial. The main explanations put forward are:

(i)   implied terms;

(ii) just and reasonable solution; and

(iii) lack of consent to a radical change in the obligations assumed at formation.

Analogous to the mistake doctrine, explanation (iii), ultimately rooted in lack of consent, yields the best 'fit' with the three-step inquiry of frustration.

7.2.1 **Implied terms**

Taylor v Caldwell justified the doctrine on the basis of an implied term to the effect that the contract will come to an end on the occurrence of the event that actually occurred. In *FA Tamplin Steamship Co Ltd v Anglo-Mexican Petroleum Products Co Ltd* (1916), Earl Loreburn said (at 404) the relevant question is: 'Were the altered conditions such that, had [the parties] thought of them, they would have taken their chance of them, or such that as sensible men they would have said, "if that happens, of course, it is all over between us"?' On this view, the contract is discharged because that is what *the parties* have provided for *in* the contract and not because the court has imposed a solution from *outside* the contract; 'the law is only doing what the parties really (though subconsciously) meant to do themselves' (*Hirji Mulji v Cheong Yue SS Co Ltd* (1926) at 504).

⏩⏪ Counterpoint

The attraction of this theory is its apparent respect for freedom of contract and the will of the contract parties. However, it is open to strong criticisms:

1. *Can agreement be implied about an unforeseeable event?* Lord Radcliffe observes in *Davis Contractors Ltd v Fareham UDC* (1956) (at 728) that: 'there is something of a logical difficulty in seeing how the parties could even impliedly have provided for something which *ex hypothesi they* neither expected nor foresaw'. As Lord Sands (at 597) elaborates (in *James Scott & Sons Ltd v Del Sel* (1922)): 'A tiger has escaped from a travelling menagerie. The milk girl fails to deliver the milk. Possibly the milkman may be exonerated from any breach of contract; but, even so, it would seem hardly reasonable to base that exoneration on the ground that "tiger days excepted" must be held as if written into the milk contract.'

➡

➡

2. *Would the parties have agreed?* Even if the parties *had* contemplated the supervening event, they are unlikely to have agreed that the contract should simply cease to bind the parties, leaving losses and gains to lie where they fall. Lord Wright observes: 'On the contrary, they would almost certainly on the one side or the other have sought to introduce reservations or qualifications or compensations' (*Denny, Mott & Dickson Ltd v Fraser (James B) & Co Ltd* (1944) at 275). This is confirmed by the widespread use of *force majeure* clauses (see 7.4.1) where the *parties* (not the frustration doctrine) stipulate the fate of the contract and the gains made and losses suffered in its performance on the occurrence of various contingencies.

3. *Courts can override the parties' attempt to continue the contract*: the implied terms rationale sits uncomfortably with cases where contracts are frustrated despite the parties expressly *agreeing otherwise* (see 7.4.2). Thus, a contract was discharged for frustration on a change of law although the parties expressly provided that their obligations should only be postponed (*Ertel Bieber & Co v Rio Tinto Co Ltd* (1918); and see 7.3.1).

These difficulties led the courts to move the *source* of implied terms from the *actual* contract parties to *fictional reasonable* contract parties. Lord Watson said: 'the meaning of the contract must be taken to be, not what the parties did intend (for they had neither thought nor intention regarding it), but that which the parties, as fair and reasonable men, would presumably have agreed upon' (*Dahl v Nelson, Donkin & Co Ltd* (1881) at 59). As Lord Radcliffe famously observes (at 728) in *Davis Contractors v Fareham*:

> By this time it might seem that the parties themselves have become so far disembodied spirits that their actual persons should be allowed to rest in peace. In their place there rises the figure of the fair and reasonable man. And the spokesman of the fair and reasonable man, who represents after all no more than the anthropomorphic conception of justice, is and must be the court itself.

In truth, the contract is discharged by *operation of the law*; the outcome is imposed on, rather than intended by, the parties.

7.2.2 **Just and reasonable solution**

The frustration doctrine has also been explained as 'a device, by which the rules as to absolute contracts are reconciled with a special exception which justice demands' (*Hirji Mulji v Cheong Yue SS* at 510).[2] This view acknowledges that discharge by frustration is imposed *by the courts*. Lord Wright said:[3] 'The truth is that the Court . . . decides on the question in accordance with what seems just and reasonable in its eyes.' Similarly, Bingham LJ in *J Lauritzen AS v Wijsmuller BV (The Super Servant Two)* (1990) at 8 said that the frustration doctrine:

> was evolved to mitigate the rigour of the common law's insistence on literal performance of absolute promises. The object of the doctrine was to give effect to the

---

[2] And see *Joseph Constantine Steamship Line Ltd v Imperial Smelting Corp Ltd* (1942) at 186; *British Movietonews v London and District Cinemas* (1951) at 200; *Shell UK v Lostock Garage* (1977) at 487.

[3] R Wright, *Legal Essays and Addresses* (CUP, 1939) 259; *Denny, Mott & Dickson Ltd v Fraser (James B) & Co Ltd* (1944) at 274–6.

demands of justice, to achieve a just and reasonable result, to do what is reasonable and fair, as an expedient to escape from injustice where such would result from enforcement of a contract in its literal terms after a significant change in circumstances.

Counterpoint

1. *Inconsistent with other judicial statements*: the House of Lords has denied any broad judicial discretion to release parties from contracts whenever a change of circumstances makes the contract significantly more onerous or less advantageous than first anticipated (*British Movietonews Ltd v London and District Cinemas Ltd* (1952)). Nevertheless, it would be difficult to disagree with Rix LJ in *The Sea Angel* (2007), when he said that justice 'is a relevant factor which underlies all and provides the ultimate rationale of the doctrine' (at [132]). It is a 'reality check' to test the result obtained by other factors.

2. *Inconsistent with drastic response*: the concern with justice and reasonableness does not explain why contracts are *automatically discharged* rather than, for example, modified to make them more just and reasonable.

7.2.3 Radical change in the obligations: lack of consent

There is now general agreement[4] that the appropriate test for frustration is that of 'radical change in the obligations undertaken' as set out by Lord Radcliffe (at 729) in *Davis Contractors v Fareham*:

> Frustration occurs whenever the law recognises that without default of either party a contractual obligation has become incapable of being performed because the circumstances in which performance is called for would render it a thing radically different from that which was undertaken by the contract. *Non haec in foedera veni*. It was not this that I promised to do.

Lack of consent is the rationale. It is distinguishable from the 'just and reasonable' rationale, which presumes the parties' consent to the absolute obligations from which *the court* gives relief in the new circumstances. It is distinguishable from the 'implied terms' rationale, which pretends that *the parties* themselves have consented to end the contract in the new circumstances. The 'radical change' test assumes that the parties only consent to perform in a limited (although wide) range of circumstances; thus, when events radically change the circumstances taking them *outside* that range, **consent runs out.**

- 'The question is whether the contract made is, on its true construction, wide enough to apply to the new situation: if not, the contract is at an end' (*Davis Contractors v Fareham* at 721).

---

[4] *Tsakiroglou & Co Ltd v Noblee Thorl GmbH* (1962) at 131; *Pioneer Shipping Ltd v BTP Tioxide* (1982) at 744, 745, 751–2; *Paal & Co A/S v Partenreederei Hannah Blumenthal* (1983) at 909, 918; *Nationals Carrier Ltd v Panalpina (Northern) Ltd* (1981) at 688, 700, 717.

- The change of circumstances must be 'fundamental enough to transmute the job the contractors had undertaken into a job of a different kind, which the contract did not contemplate and to which it could not apply' (*Sir Lindsay Parkinson & Co Ltd v Commissioners of Works* (1949) at 667).

- '[If] consideration of the terms of the contract, in the light of the circumstances existing when it was made, shows that they *never agreed to be bound in a fundamentally different situation* which has now unexpectedly emerged, the contract ceases to bind at that point—not because the court in its discretion thinks it just and reasonable to qualify the terms of the contract, but because *on its true construction it does not apply in that situation*' (*British Movietonews v London & District Cinemas* at 185, emphasis added).

The lack of consent rationale, underlying the 'radical change of obligations' test, is consistent with *other judicial formulations* of frustration which 'shade into one another' (*National Carriers v Panalpina* (1981) at 687–8, 703).

(i) The *construction approach*: the range of circumstances to which the obligations attach must be construed from the contract (*Davis Contractors v Fareham* at 720–1, 729).

(ii) *Disappearance of the foundation of the contract*: in *Krell v Henry*, Vaughan Williams LJ defined the foundation as 'rooms to view the coronation procession' which was destroyed when the procession was cancelled (see also *FA Tamplin Steamship v Anglo-Mexican Petroleum Products* at 406–47).

(iii) *Impossibility of performance*: in *Great Peace v Tsavliris*, Lord Phillips MR (at [62]–[73]), while not objecting to the 'radical difference' formulation, preferred the *'impossibility of performance'* formulation. He approved (at [68]) Vaughan Williams LJ's statement in *Krell v Henry* (at 749) which merges the 'construction', 'foundation', and 'impossibility' approaches:

> You first have to ascertain, not necessarily from the terms of contract, but, if required, from necessary inferences, drawn from surrounding circumstances recognised by both contracting parties, what is the substance of the contract, and then to ask the question whether that substantial contract needs for its foundation the assumption of the existence of a particular state of things. If it does, this will limit the operation of the general words, and in such a case, if the contract becomes impossible of performance by reason of the non-existence of the state of things assumed by both parties as the foundation of the contract, there will be no breach.

7.2.4 **Total failure of consideration**

The House of Lords has rejected the explanation for frustration based on *total failure of consideration*. This is a ground for recovering money paid when the defendant breaches the contract by total non-performance (see 13.3). It can apply only if the frustrating circumstances *totally* obstruct one party's performance (*National Carriers v Panalpina* at 687, 702). But this rationale does not explain why a party incurs no contractual liability for its failure of consideration.

We will now examine the three stages of the frustration inquiry set out in **Diagram 7A**, starting with the changes of circumstances that are fundamental enough to trigger the frustration doctrine.

7.3 **Frustrating circumstances**

Diagram 7A shows that subject to the risk allocation contained in the contract (see 7.4) and the claimant's 'fault' (see 7.5), frustration will only be found if literal performance in the changed circumstances would amount to the performance of a fundamentally or radically different obligation from that originally undertaken. So, a court must: **first**, construe the contract terms 'in the light of the nature of the contract and of the relevant surrounding circumstances when the contract was made' to determine *the scope of the original rights and obligations* (*Davis Contractors v Fareham* at 720); and, **second**, compare this with a literal enforcement of the obligations in the *new circumstances* to see whether it is radically or fundamentally different from the original rights and obligation (*Tsakiroglou & Co Ltd v Noblee Thorl GmbH* at 115, 118, and 123).

'[W]hether a supervening event is a frustrating event or not is, in a wide variety of cases, a question of degree' (*National Carriers v Panalpina* at 688). A contract for the carriage of ice would be frustrated by a shorter delay than one for the carriage of iron rails (*Jackson v Union Marine Insurance Co* at 146). Frustration is not lightly invoked to relieve parties from the consequences of bad bargains. Hardship, inconvenience, or material loss is insufficient. The question is whether the new circumstances make 'performance . . . fundamentally different in a commercial sense' (*Tsakiroglou v Noblee Thorl* at 119; *The Nema* at 752). In *The Sea Angel* (2007), Rix LJ concedes that the circumstances of frustration 'can be so various as to defy rule making' and advocates a 'multi-factorial approach' (at [111]), taking into account: 'the terms of the contract itself, its matrix or context, the parties' knowledge, expectations, assumptions and contemplations, in particular as to risk, as at the time of contract, at any rate so far as these can be ascribed mutually and objectively, and then the nature of the supervening event, and the parties' reasonable and objectively ascertainable calculations as to the possibilities of future performance in the new circumstances'.

The scope of frustrating circumstances can only be understood by reference to decided cases. The following overlapping categories give a sense of the shape and size of the doctrine:

(i)   legal impossibility;

(ii) physical impossibility; and

(iii) impossibility of purpose.

The catastrophic destruction of the Twin Towers in New York on 11 September 2001 would frustrate any contract to provide cleaning services on the premises; performance would be illegal (entry being barred), physically impossible, and purposeless.

7.3.1 **Legal impossibility**

Contractual performance is sometimes made legally impossible by a change in the *law*, or by a change of *circumstances* triggering the operation of pre-existing law. The law may:

(i) **prohibit the performance undertaken in the contract**: For example,

- trading with the enemy (*Fibrosa Spolka Akcyjna v Fairbairn Lawson Combe Barbour Ltd* (1943)); or

- continuing with a project (*Metropolitan Water Board v Dick Kerr & Co Ltd* (1918), a certain type of trading (*Denny, Mott & Dickson v Fraser*), or an employment (*Reilly v R* (1934)).

(ii) **deprive a party of control over the subject matter of the contract**: as where land (*Baily v De Crespigny* (1869)), ships (*Bank Line Ltd v Arthur Capel & Co* (1919)), or oil fields (*BP Exploration Co (Libya) Ltd v Hunt (No 2)* (1979)) are compulsorily acquired by the state.

In this category, the *public policy* underlying the illegality *trumps the parties' express provisions*. Thus, a prohibition against trading with enemy aliens will frustrate a contract between residents of warring countries even if their contract only postpones their obligations until the cessation of hostilities (*Ertel Bieber v Rio Tinto* (1918)).

Aside from trading with the enemy, a supervening law (or fact triggering the application of existing law) will only frustrate a contract if it makes a **radical difference to the contractual obligations originally undertaken** and not if it merely delays or hinder its operation in part. Again, it is a matter of degree.

- ✓ A contract to build a reservoir in six years was halted when the government ordered the builders to cease work and remove and sell their plant. Although the contract provided for extensions of time 'whatsoever and howsoever occasioned', this was held not to apply because the interruption was of such a character and likely to last so long as to fundamentally change the obligations undertaken; the builder 'is not bound to submit to an aleatory [ie random] bargain to which he has not agreed' (*Metropolitan Water Board v Dick Kerr* at 128).

- ✗ A 99-year lease was not frustrated by government restrictions on building since the lease still had over 90 years to run and 'the length of the interruption so caused is presumably a small fraction of the whole term' (*Cricklewood Property and Investment Trust Ltd v Leighton's Investment Trust Ltd* (1945) at 231–2).

- ✗ In *FA Tamplin Steamship v Anglo-Mexican Petroleum Products*, a ship chartered for five years was requisitioned by the government after two years and altered for use as a troopship. The dispute was over who should get the substantial compensation from the Crown. The ship-owner claimed the sum arguing the frustration of the charterparty. The House of Lords agreed with the charterer's claim for the sum because there was no frustration; the charterparty expressly permitted the charterer to sublet the ship on Admiralty or other service and there remained many months when the ship might still be free for commercial use.

7.3.2 **Physical impossibility**

The clearest case of frustration occurs when the supervening event makes performance physically impossible (usually only for one party, the other being still able to perform by paying money). However:

(i) **Impossibility of performance is *insufficient***: even a wholly unforeseen catastrophe will not excuse a party if the construction (risk allocation) of the contract shows that he or she has undertaken to pay damages anyway. There is a difference between misjudgment and wholly unforeseen events; 'a man may undertake to do that which turns out to be impossible, and yet he may still be bound by his agreement' (*Taylor v Caldwell* at 833).

(ii) **Impossibility of performance is *unnecessary***: legal impossibility and impossibility of purpose (see 7.3.1 and 7.3.3) may frustrate contracts although they are still *physically* possible to perform. Moreover, supervening events may result in *partial* impossibility or simply make the contract more onerous or time-consuming to perform. Whether they frustrate the contract is a question of *degree*. Courts are particularly unwilling to allow *commercial* parties to escape bad bargains or risks against which they could reasonably be expected to provide for.

Frustration cases can be divided into: (a) death or incapacity in personal service contracts; (b) destruction of the subject matter of the contract; (c) failure of supplies; and (d) delay and hardship.

7.3.2.1 Death or incapacity in personal service contracts

A contract of personal service is frustrated if the death or incapacitating illness of one party renders its performance impossible or radically different. Contracts have been frustrated where the performing party:

✓ dies (*Stubbs v Holywell Railway Co* (1867); *Condor v The Barron Knights Ltd* (1966); *Whincup v Hughes* (1871));

✓ is *interned, conscripted*, or *imprisoned* for all or the substantial remainder of the contract's duration; although in the case of imprisonment only the employer can frustrate the contract; the employee is barred since it is their fault (ie frustration is self-induced, see 7.5) (*Horlock v Beal* (1916); *Morgan v Manser* (1948); *FC Shepherd & Co v Jerrom* (1987));

✓ is *incapacitated by illness*: in *Notcutt v Universal Equipment Co* (1986), an employment contract was frustrated when an employee suffered a heart attack after which he would never work again. Illness will not necessarily frustrate a contract of employment. The question is one of degree; namely, whether the employee's incapacity or likely incapacity is such that 'further performance of his obligations in the future would either be impossible or would be a thing radically different from that undertaken by him and accepted by the employer under the agreed terms of this employment' (*Marshall v Harland & Wolff Ltd* (1972) at 903–5). Relevant considerations include: the *terms* of the contract; the *nature* and *duration* of the employment and of the *illness*; the period of past service; and the prospect of recovery. In *Atwal v Rochester* (2010), the court found a building contract to be frustrated when the builder suffered a heart attack and was advised by his doctors permanently to cease work midway through the project. The builder was a sole trader and had been chosen 'because he was known to the family and had built up a personal relationship of trust' (at [32]).

The contract is not necessarily frustrated by death or incapacity if *performance is not of a personal character*:

✗ in *Phillips v Alhambra Palace Co Ltd* (1901), a contract between performers and music hall proprietors was not frustrated by the death of one of the proprietors.

7.3.2.2 Destruction of the subject matter

Destruction of something necessary for contractual performance may frustrate the contract. Destruction by fire is a ready example (*Taylor v Caldwell* discussed earlier, and *Appleby v Myers* (1867) where the contract was to supply and install machinery in a factory and fire destroyed the factory including the machinery). The courts have suggested that *leases* (see further 7.3.3.2) could, wholly exceptionally, be frustrated by the *literal disappearance of the premises*, as where 'some vast convulsion of nature swallowed up the property altogether, or buried it in the depths of the sea [eg a tsunami]' (*Cricklewood v Leightons* at 229) or if an upper floor flat were totally destroyed by fire or earthquake (*National Carriers v Panalpina* at 690).

Where the subject matter is only **partially destroyed**, frustration is a matter of degree.

✓ In *Asfar v Blundell* (1895), a cargo of dates was submerged for two days and so affected by water sewage as to become 'for business purposes something else' (at 128), although it could still be distilled into spirit and sold for £2,400.

✓ In *Jackson v Union Marine Insurance Co*, a charterparty was frustrated when, on the first day, the ship ran aground and was not refloated and repaired for seven months. The damage occasioned such delay that it amounted to 'practical commercial destruction'; performance after such delay would be of no use to the charterer.

All this is subject to the *contractual allocation of risks* for the supervening destruction of the subject matter (see 7.4). After all, very little is physically impossible to replace today if one puts in enough money and effort. The music hall and the factory can be rebuilt; that being so, physical destruction cases overlap with cases of delay and increased costs discussed at 7.3.2.4.

7.3.2.3 Failure or disruption of supplies

Section 7 of the Sale of Goods Act 1979 provides: 'Where there is an agreement to sell specific goods and subsequently the goods, without any fault on the part of the seller or buyer, perish before the risk passes to the buyer, the agreement is avoided.' '**Specific goods**' are goods identified and agreed on at the time the contract is made (otherwise it is impossible to tell whether 'they' have perished).

Contracts for **unascertained goods** are rarely frustrated because, subject to physical or legal impossibility, the *source of supply is normally at the supplier's risk*. He or she can always find an alternative source, albeit at greater cost and inconvenience. Consistently, where a particular source was only intended by *one* of the parties, failure of that source will not frustrate the contract (*Blackburn Bobbin Co Ltd v TW Allen Ltd* (1918)). For instance, in *CTI Group Inc v Transclear SA* (2008), C planned to export a cargo of cement to Mexico to try to break a cartel operated by Cemex. C contracted to buy from T who could not perform because of Cemex's influence. Frustration was not found because the source of the cement, which failed, was not agreed. But a contract may be frustrated if the source of supply was intended by *both* parties and it fails without the fault of either party, for example where:

✓ a potato crop grown on land specified in the contract fails through drought or disease (*Howell v Coupland* (1876)); or

✓ importation of the goods from a particular place has become impossible due to war, natural disasters, or prohibition of export *(Re Badische Co Ltd* (1921) at 381–3).

Where the commonly intended source **partially fails**, a term will be implied requiring the supplier to deliver the smaller quantity available. He or she is relieved only to the extent of the deficiency (see 7.5.3 Pause for reflection, point 4). In *Sainsbury v Street* (1972), S agreed to sell Sainsbury's 275 tons of barley grown on Street's farm, but the yield was only 140 tons, which Street sold to a third party. The court held that Sainsbury should have the option of requiring S to deliver the tonnage actually produced. Otherwise, in times of failing crops the supplier could disregard his or her contracts and profit from rising prices by selling elsewhere.

🧑 Pause for reflection

Although partial excuse for non-performance was justified by reference to *implied terms* in *Sainsbury v Street* (see also *Howell v Coupland*) rather than to any wider doctrine of 'partial frustration', the solution draws from the same basis as frustration. It permits a more flexible response by, in effect, *varying the contract* (see further 7.7), rather than automatically discharging it. By analogy, where a supplier makes a *number of contracts* intending to satisfy them from a supply which partly fails, a *pro rata division* is the fair response, but if partial performance is impossible because the supply cannot be sensibly divided (eg ships or hotel rooms) then allocation along the lines of '*first come, first served*' can be justified, frustrating the rest (see further 7.5.3).

7.3.2.4 Delay and hardship

Few contracts are 'impossible' to perform; it all depends on the state of technology and the amount of trouble and expense a party can be expected to go to. The United States prefers the terminology of 'impracticality' (Uniform Commercial Code, § 2-615). The Second Restatement of the Law of Contracts, § 261, refers to 'extreme and unreasonable difficulty, expense, injury or loss' to one of the parties. These terms suggest a wider scope of frustrating circumstances than under English law where it is not enough that performance has become commercially unreasonable; a radical change in the obligations originally undertaken is required. However, in practice, the line will be difficult to draw.

Delay and hardship have many potential causes. **Charterparties** may be affected by the ship being:

- stranded (*Jackson v Union Marine Insurance Co Ltd*);
- requisitioned (*FA Tamplin Steamship v Anglo-American Petroleum Products*);
- seized (*WJ Tatem v Gamboa* (1939); *The Adelfa* (1988)); or
- detained (*Embiricos v Reid (Sydney) & Co* (1914)).

They may also be affected by strikes (*Budgett & Co v Binnington & Co* (1891)), or the closure of intended routes (*Tsakiroglou v Noblee Thorl; The Eugenia* (1962)).

Building contracts may be affected by:

- shortages of labour and materials (*Davis Contractors v Fareham*); or
- wartime restrictions (*Metropolitan Water Board v Dick Kerr*).

The focus is not the *cause* of the delay or hardship, but the *effect* it has on the *performance* of the obligations undertaken (*The Nema* at 754). Do they fall outside what the parties could reasonably contemplate at the time of contracting? Three factors are particularly significant to a finding of frustration:

(i) The increased difficulty of performance is caused by a new and unforeseeable event and is not merely within the commercial risks undertaken

✗ In **Davis Contractors v Fareham** D agreed to build 78 houses for F. The work took almost three times longer and cost £17,000 more than was planned because of serious labour shortages and difficulties in obtaining building supplies. D completed performance but argued that the contract was frustrated so that they were not confined to the contract price but could claim an extra £17,000 on a *quantum meruit* (a reasonable price in the absence of a contract). The House of Lords rejected this since:

    (i)   by agreeing a fixed price, D took the risk of increased costs and delay;

    (ii) the difficulties were clearly foreseeable and D could have provided for them in the contract; and

    (iii) although D's performance was significantly more onerous, it was *not radically different* from that originally undertaken.

✗ Lord Radcliffe (at 729) said: 'it is not hardship or inconvenience or material loss itself which calls the principle of frustration into play. There must be as well such a change in the significance of the obligation that the thing undertaken would, if performed, be a different thing from that contracted for'. Thus, frustration will not avail where building contracts encounter delays or disruptions in the supply of labour or materials, or where rising prices eat into the builder's expected profit. As Lord Reid said (at 724), although 'the delay was greater in degree than was to be expected . . . [i]t was not caused by any new and unforeseeable factor or event: the job proved to be more onerous but it never became a job of a different kind from that contemplated in the contract.'

✗ *Inflation* and *fluctuations in the value of currencies* will not normally frustrate the contract, although fluctuations of a wholly astronomical order may do so.[5]

✗ *Severe economic crises* will not normally frustrate the contract. In *Tandrin Aviation v Aero Toy Store* (2010), the court rejected the defendant's submission that the 'unanticipated, unforeseeable and cataclysmic downward spiral of the world's financial markets' was sufficient to constitute a *force majeure* event (see 7.4.1), nor would it amount to frustration (at [50]).

✗ In *The Sea Angel* (2007), a 20-day charter of a vessel to a salvor to transport oil from a casualty which had caused a major pollution incident was not frustrated where before redelivery the vessel was unlawfully detained for three months by port authorities. Comparing the probable length of the delay with the unexpired duration of the charter is not decisive. Here, the purpose of the charter had been performed and the risk of detention by local authorities due to concerns about pollution was foreseeable by the salvage industry and provided for by the charter. Unlike cases frustrated by a major conflict where one cannot negotiate or litigate one's way out, the instant case was one of 'wait and see'; only if commercial negotiation failed, would there be frustration.

✗ *Bad weather conditions* which delayed the unloading of the cargo by four days did not frustrate the contract in *Thiis v Byers* (1876). Since the charterer was given a number of days for unloading, he must 'take the risk of any ordinary vicissitudes'; he was liable for demurrage. The same generally applies where delays in loading or unloading are caused by *strikes* (*Budgett & Co v Binnington & Co* (1891)). However, a prolonged strike may exceptionally frustrate the charterparty because of the operation of the following two factors.

(ii) Parties are entitled to know where they stand

A party can claim frustration through delay *before* the expiry of the time for performance since parties should be able to rearrange their affairs in response to the event and not be left in suspense. In *The Nema*, Lord Roskill said (at 752, see also *National Carriers v Panalpina* at 706; *Bank Line v Arthur Capel* at 454):

> it is often necessary to wait upon events in order to see whether the delay already suffered and the prospects of further delay from that cause, will make any ultimate performance of the relevant contractual obligations 'radically different' . . . from that which was undertaken by the contract. But, as has often been said, businessmen must not be required to await events too long. They are entitled to know where they stand. Whether or not the delay is such as to bring about frustration must be a question to be determined by an informed judgment based upon all the evidence of what has occurred and what is likely thereafter to occur. Often it will be a question of degree whether the effect of delay suffered, and likely to be suffered, will be such as to bring about frustration of the particular adventure in question.

---

[5] *Multiservice Bookbinding Ltd v Marden* (1979); *British Movietonews v London and District Cinemas* (1952) at 185; *Davis Contractors Ltd v Fareham* at 724; *National Carriers v Panalpina* at 712.

Lord Roskill recognised that judgments may differ on what is ultimately a question of law, and said that appeal courts should be slow to interfere with a lower tribunal's finding on this issue.

✓ In *The Nema*, a ship was chartered for seven consecutive voyages between April and December 1979. After the first voyage, strikes beginning on 6 June grounded *The Nema*. On 3 October, an arbitrator (later upheld by the House of Lords) decided that the contract was frustrated although the strike ended two days later.

✓ In *Embiricos v Reid*, a charterparty for a voyage through the Dardanelles was frustrated on the outbreak of war between Greece and Turkey when it was thought that the Dardanelles would be closed for the entire length of the charterparty, although it was actually opened for a period during which the contract could have been performed.

(iii) Performance in the new circumstances radically alters the original rights and obligations

Three categories can be isolated.

First, if it is clear from the terms or nature of the contract that it was to be performed *only at a specified time or within a specified period*, subsequent delayed performance may be of *no use to the recipient* and so frustrate the contract. Thus:

✓ in *Jackson v Union Marine Insurance Ltd*, a seven-month delay in a charterparty, according to which a ship was to sail 'with all possible despatch' to load a cargo at Newport for San Francisco, frustrated the contract. The court held that a voyage after the delay would be a 'different voyage' from the one undertaken, as it would be an autumn rather than a spring voyage which was crucial in the context of the contract.

Second, performance after the delay may be radically different because it would occur in a *radically altered market*.

✓ In *Acetylene Corp of Great Britain v Canada Carbide Co* (1921), a shipment of goods sold was delayed for three years by wartime requisitioning. The contract was held to be frustrated because the market conditions had radically changed in that time.

✓ In **Metropolitan Water Board v Dick Kerr** (see 7.4.1), wartime restrictions delayed indefinitely the performance of a contract to build a reservoir two years into the six-year contract period. The House of Lords frustrated the contract since the project was so disrupted that enforcement of performance would not be to maintain the original contract but to substitute a different contract. As Lord Parmoor (at 139) said:

> It is not necessary to say that the works are not physically possible, or could not practically be carried out as a business adventure, at a subsequent date. I agree that the probability of hardship to one side or the other is not a matter of material consideration, but it is quite a different matter when there is an indefinite and indeterminate liability which might impose on either party an unforeseen burden totally foreign to the ordinary incidents in a contract of this character . . . [Performance] at some future period . . . will be under a different contract

based on changed considerations. All the prices will have to be fixed in reference to different conditions, and the time over which the work will be carried on will be wholly different.

✓ In *Bank Line Ltd v Arthur Capel & Co Ltd* (1919), a charterparty to start in April for 12 months was frustrated when the ship was requisitioned until September. Later performance would be, 'as a matter of business a totally different thing', mainly because the hire rates had increased enormously over the short period.

Third, a contract may be frustrated when the contemplated *means* of performance is made impossible by a supervening event when: (i) it is the *only* method of complying with the contract; or (ii) the alternative means radically alters the obligations undertaken.

✓ In *Nicholl & Knight v Ashton Etridge & Co* (1901), a contract for the sale of goods 'to be shipped per steamship Orlando from Alexandria during . . . January' was frustrated when the ship ran aground and could not reach Alexandria in January.

✓ In *Codelfa Construction Pty Ltd v SRA (NSW)* (1982), a contract to excavate tunnels within 130 weeks was frustrated when the means contemplated by both parties to enable timely completion was prohibited by an injunction preventing work from 10 pm to 6 am.

✗ In *The Eugenia* (1964), a charterparty between Genoa and India (normally through the Suez Canal) was not frustrated by the blocking of the canal during the Anglo-French invasion of Egypt in 1956, although the alternative route, via the Cape of Good Hope, increased the journey time from 108 to 138 days. The difference was not sufficiently radical since '[t]he cargo was such as not to be affected by this delay and there was no evidence that the early arrival of the cargo in India was of particular importance' (at 243).

✗ In *Tsakiroglou v Noblee Thorl*, no frustration was found although alternative performance via the Cape of Good Hope (rather than the stipulated one through the Suez Canal) was *three times* longer and far costlier. The House of Lords held that the contract was not commercially or fundamentally different because: the route of delivery is normally irrelevant to the buyer of goods; the goods were not perishable; there was no date fixed for delivery; and there was no shortage of available shipping carrying goods via the Cape. Thus, a contract is not frustrated if the alternative means of performance does not fundamentally differ from the intended means, even if it was *stipulated in the contract* (at 112, applied in *The Captain George K* (1970)).

7.3.3 **Impossibility of purpose**

A contract may be frustrated although performance of the contract is not illegal, impossible, or more onerous. Rather, the recipient of the performance claims that the supervening event has so undermined the *purpose* of the contract for him or her that they should not be required to accept or pay for it. The obvious danger with such a category is its potential width and the danger of allowing claimants to escape bad bargains; its existence has attracted criticism (eg *Blackburn Bobbin v TW Allen* at 542). Two factors severely limit its scope.

(i) The purpose which has become impossible to achieve must be *common to both parties* and have expressly or impliedly, 'been assumed by the parties to be the foundation or basis of the contract' (*Krell v Henry* at 749). The frustrated purposes of only one party will not suffice (*Congimex Companhia Geral de Comercio Importadora and E Expordarora SARL v Tradax Export SA* (1983) at 253). It will generally be difficult for a claimant to establish that his or her purpose, even if obvious, was shared by the other party.

(ii) The common purpose must be thwarted to a *very high degree*.

7.3.3.1 Non-occurrence of an event

Very exceptionally, the *non-occurrence of an event* which constitutes the basis of the contract can frustrate a contract.

✓ In *Krell v Henry*, a contract to hire rooms to see the passing coronation was frustrated when the coronation was cancelled, because the hire was 'for the purpose of seeing the Royal procession' and not simply 'an agreement to let and take the rooms' (at 750). This was inferred from the position of the flat, the flat owner's advertisement for windows to view the royal coronation, and the unusual hire terms (an enhanced price charged for two days excluding nights). Clearly, *the more detailed the description of the common contractual purpose, the more likely that a supervening event will frustrate it*.

✗ It was said in *Krell v Henry* (at 750) that there would be no frustration if a contract to hire a cab to go to Epsom on Derby Day at an enhanced price was made pointless when the races are cancelled. The purpose is only that of the hirer; 'the cab had no special qualifications for the purpose which led to the selection of the cab for this particular occasion. Any other cab would have done as well'.

✗ Frustration was rejected in *Herne Bay Steamboat v Hutton* (1903) where HBS hired out a pleasure boat to be put 'at Mr Hutton's disposal' and 'for the purpose of viewing the naval review and for a day's cruise around the fleet'. Although the naval review was cancelled along with the coronation, the Court of Appeal (at 689, 690, 692) regarded H's venture to charge passengers for the cruise as his own and at his own risk. By analogy to a cab hire, 'although the object of the hirer might be stated, that statement would not make the object any the less a matter for the hirer alone, and would not directly affect the person who was letting out the vehicle for hire' (at 691). Moreover, H's purpose was not entirely thwarted; he could still 'cruise round the fleet. The fleet was there'.

7.3.3.2 Leases and sales of land

It was once thought that **leases** could not be frustrated since a lease is more than a contract and vests an estate in land (a proprietary interest) which remains even if a supervening event negates the purpose of the lease. However, the House of Lords (at

692, 697) in *National Carriers v Panalpina* accepts that leases can, in principle, be frustrated (*short-term leases* with a *closely prescribed purpose*), although 'hardly ever'.

✗ In **National Carriers v Panalpina**, a ten-year lease of a warehouse covenanted for use only as a warehouse for the lessee's business was not frustrated although, five years into the lease, the local authority closed the street giving the only vehicular access to the warehouse for 20 months. The length of the unexpired term (more than three years) was a 'potent factor' in the court's decision (at 706); suggesting that the lease would have been frustrated had the prohibition been permanent.

✗ A 99-year building lease would not be frustrated by wartime building restrictions imposed when it still had 90 years to run and the war was likely to last for only a fraction of that term (*Cricklewood v Leightons*).

Frustration is more likely if commercial premises are let for a *short term*, for *one principal purpose known to the lessor*, that purpose gives the premises its substantial *value*, and the supervening event defeats that purpose for a *substantial proportion* of the lease (*National Carriers v Panalpina* at 702).

✓ In the US, leases restricting the use of premises to that of a drinking saloon were held to be frustrated when that use was outlawed.[6]

✓ In *Denny, Mott & Dickson v Fraser*, an agreement to lease a timber yard to allow the parties to perform their contract was frustrated when wartime regulations prohibited the performance.

✓ Leases may also be frustrated by catastrophic events which physically destroy the leased premises (see 7.3.2.2).

Frustration of **sales of land** is even rarer than frustration of leases, since the risk of destruction, damage, or changes to the land's uses is usually borne by the purchaser as the equitable owner in the period between the making and completion of the contract (when they become the legal owner).

✗ A contract is not frustrated if between the formation and completion of the contract the land is compulsorily purchased (*Hillingdon Estates Co v Stonefield Estates Ltd* (1952); *E Johnson & Co (Barbados) Ltd v NSR Ltd* (1997)).

✗ In *Amalgamated Investment & Property Ltd v John Walker & Sons Ltd* (1977), J advertised a site as suitable for redevelopment and A made clear that they were buying the property for this purpose. Shortly after the contract was made, the building was listed as a place of special architectural and historical interest. This inhibited redevelopment and reduced the property value from £1.7 million to about £200,000. The Court of Appeal rejected A's claim of frustration because there was no warranty that the property could be redeveloped, and the risk that the property might be listed was one that all buyers of property assumed. Performance was not radically different from what was undertaken by the contract. This is something of a retreat from *Krell v Henry*, since the property seems to have been bought and sold *for redevelopment*.

---

[6] See G Treitel, *Frustration and Force Majeure* (Sweet & Maxwell, 1994) at paras 7-021, 11-017.

7.4 **Construction of the contract**

Faced with a defence of frustration to a claim for breach, the court must decide whether the contract, on its proper construction, has *positively* allocated the risk of the supervening events. Only if the contract has *not* expressly or impliedly provided for what should happen in the new circumstances can the frustration doctrine step in to determine whether the parties are absolved from liability for non-performance.

7.4.1 **Express provision: *force majeure* and hardship clauses**

The uncertainties and rigidity of the frustration doctrine have made many contracting parties wary of leaving it to the courts. Rather, *they* stipulate in the contract what should happen in certain eventualities (known as *force majeure, hardship,* or *intervener* clauses). Parties can frequently anticipate, in more or less general terms, occurrences that will disturb the equilibrium of their contract to an unacceptable degree. Inserting clauses to deal with such eventualities increases certainty; it lets parties know where they stand, and allows them to depart from the default rules provided by the frustration doctrine. They can specify:

(i) the **circumstances** excusing further performance of the contract (these may be wider or narrower than the scope of frustrating circumstances), for example acts of God or of war, strikes, riots, breakdown of machinery, currency fluctuation, or increased costs; and

(ii) the **consequences** of the triggering circumstance (beyond the consequences of frustration, being automatic discharge and statutory remedies, see 7.6), for example provision for delay or suspension of performance, conferring rights of cancellation on one or both parties, requiring submission to arbitration, disciplinary procedures or good faith renegotiation between the parties,[7] or triggering a price-escalation clause.

The parties' express provision for a supervening event **must still be interpreted by the courts** to determine whether they actually cover the supervening event in a 'full and complete' way (*Bank Line v Arthur Capel* at 455). The courts have taken a restrictive approach to the interpretation of such clauses to avoid unfair outcomes, analogous to their *contra proferentem* interpretation of very wide clauses excluding or limiting liability for breach (see 10.6.3); likewise, this is done in the name of the parties' *presumed* intention. For example:

✓ Frustration was found in *Metropolitan Water Board v Dick Kerr* for prolonged delay, although a clause in the contract provided for an extension of time in the event of delay '*whatsoever and howsoever occasioned*'. This was held (at

---

[7] This is distinguishable from *Walford v Miles* (1992) where the existence of the contract depended on good faith negotiation (see 2.6.2.5). It is closer to *Petromec Inc v Petroleo Brasileiro SA Petrobas* (2005) where within an otherwise legally enforceable commercial agreement, the good faith negotiation related to certain specific costs which are 'ascertainable with comparative ease'.

126) *not* to cover the situation when the government stopped the work and required the plant to be sold because the disruption and delay ensuing 'could not possibly have been in the contemplation of the parties to the contract when it was made'. Thus, although the clause clearly covered the situation, it was very narrowly interpreted to exclude the situation and so absolve the builder from liability. Asquith LJ said (*Sir Lindsay Parkinson v Commissioners of Works* at 665) that a delay clause suspending the contract does *not* 'apply where the delay was so abnormal, so pre-emptive, as to fall outside what the parties could possibly have contemplated.' Thus, 'delay' 'has been read as limited to normal, moderate delay, and as not extending to an interruption so differing in degree and magnitude from anything which could have been contemplated as to differ from it in kind'. Events will be excluded from the parties' provision if it renders further performance of the contract 'unthinkable' (*The Playa Larga* (1983) at 189).

✓ In *Staffordshire Area Health Authority v South Staffordshire Waterworks Co* (1978), a contract was made in 1929 for the supply of water for 7 pence per 1,000 gallons '*at all times hereafter*'. Lord Denning MR held that the contract ceased to bind the parties 50 years later when, in a fundamentally different context, it cost 20 times more to supply the water. Although the Court of Appeal disagreed with this reasoning, it arrived at the same result by *implying a term* that the contract was terminable by the supplier on reasonable notice.

On the other hand, the court adopted a rather literal interpretation of the *force majeure* term in a charterparty, so that charterers were not allowed to put the vessel off-hire from when it was seized by pirates (*Cosco Bulk Carrier Co Ltd v Team-Up Owning Co Ltd (The Saldanha)* (2010)). This was justified by reference to the great importance of certainty in commercial law and the fact that under a typical time charterparty, hire was payable continuously unless charterers could bring themselves within any exceptions, the onus being on the charterers to do so.

Pause for reflection

In 'Force Majeure and Frustration—Their Relationship and a Comparative Assessment' in McKendrick (ed), *Force Majeure and Frustration in Contract* (2nd edn, LLP, 1995) 33, McKendrick argues that more extensive judicial powers to rewrite contracts would cause uncertainty. He notes the increasing use of *force majeure* clauses, particularly in international standard form contracts, and the 'self-help' they represent in supplementing the narrowness and overcoming the uncertainties of the frustration doctrine, although they may add to transactions costs.

7.4.2 Implied allocations of risk: foresight

The court can infer from the parties' silence that they have *impliedly* allocated the risk of the supervening event to the performing party (ie frustration would not excuse non-performance). The *type of transaction* may be generally understood as *allocating a particular risk*. For example:

- a long-term lease or a sale of property generally allocates almost all risks to the lessor/buyer; a short-term lease for a specific purpose allocates fewer (see 7.3.3.2);
- a building contract allocates to the builder the risk that the soil conditions and the cost and availability of labour and materials will make performance more onerous than anticipated (*Davis Contractors v Fareham*), but *not* that subsequent legislation will make it illegal;
- fluctuations in prices or the value of currencies will not normally frustrate the contract (*Davis Contractors v Fareham* at 724, but Lord Reid reserved his position on fluctuations of a wholly astronomical order).

How foreseeable must the supervening event be to oust the frustration doctrine?

The narrowness of the doctrine is often justified on the basis that it should only cover unforeseeable events for which the parties could not be expected to provide. However, this point should not be taken too far; foreseeability is a matter of degree. Anything is foreseeable if you are paranoid enough. Provision for every foreseeable contingency would be enormously costly and ultimately wasteful since most will never happen. Hence, parties should be able to rely on the law for a default solution. It is a question of construction whether the parties' silence, despite foreseeing the risk, should be taken to mean:

(i) that the contract *remains binding* irrespective of the change of circumstances (ousting the frustration doctrine, eg *Walton Harvey Ltd v Walker & Homfrays Ltd* (1931)); or

(ii) that the fate of the contract should be *left to 'the lawyers to sort it out'*, by reference to the frustration doctrine (*The Eugenia* at 234).

The first inference (ousting frustration) should only be drawn where the *degree of foreseeability is very high*. The event or its consequences must be one which any person of ordinary intelligence would regard as likely to occur and, moreover, one which is foreseeable *in some detail*. The courts will not allow frustration to be ousted easily. In *The Eugenia*, Lord Denning explains (at 239):

It has frequently been said that the doctrine of frustration only applies when the new situation is 'unforeseen' or 'unexpected' or 'uncontemplated', as if that were an essential feature. But it is not so. The only thing that is essential is that the parties should have made no provision for it in their contract . . . cases have occurred where the parties have foreseen the danger ahead, and yet made no provision for it in the contract.

Thus, frustration was found in *WJ Tatem Ltd v Gamboa* (1939) where G chartered from T a steamship for 30 days to evacuate refugees from the Spanish Civil War. A daily rate of hire was payable until the ship's return and would only cease if the ship went 'missing'. Halfway through the charter period the ship was seized and not returned for about two months. T's claim for the daily hire rate during that entire period was denied because the contract was frustrated on the ship's seizure. Although it was foreseeable that the ship might be seized (inferable from the very high rate of hire), it was not foreseeable that the ship would be detained for so long after the hire period (at 135).

7.5 Fault: self-induced frustration

Even if the supervening event is sufficiently fundamental and its risk not allocated by the contract to one of the parties, frustration is barred if the claimant's own deliberate or negligent conduct has brought about the alleged frustrating event. This is not 'something altogether outside the control of the parties' (*Denmark Productions Ltd v Boscabel Productions Ltd* (1969) at 836); the claimant remains liable for breach. It is up to the party suing for breach to prove that the event was self-induced (*Joseph Constantine SS Line v Imperial Smelting Corp Ltd* (1942)). In *The Super Servant Two*, Hobhouse J set out three such categories: breach of contract, anticipatory breach of contract, and power to elect.

7.5.1 Breach of contract

A party cannot plead frustration if he or she has contributed to the alleged frustrating event by conduct amounting to a breach of the contract. Thus, a charterer who ordered a ship into a war zone where she was then detained (*The Eugenia*), and a carrier whose ship was unseaworthy causing delays which then made the journey impossible to complete because of the supervening outbreak of war (*Monarch SS Co v A/B Karlshamns Oljefabriker* (1949)), could not frustrate the contract; each remained liable for breach.

7.5.2 Anticipatory breach of contract

A party is also disqualified from claiming frustration if their deliberate, voluntary, or negligent conduct has the effect of disabling them from performance of the contract, analogous to anticipatory breach by the party's own act (*The Super Servant Two* at 10 and in the High Court (1989) at 155). The issue is one of *control*; the test is whether the claimant had the *means and opportunity to prevent* the alleged frustrating event from occurring, but nevertheless caused or permitted it to occur. As Lord Russell said: 'The possible varieties are infinite, and can range from the criminality of the scuttler who opens the sea-cocks and sinks his ship, to the thoughtlessness of the prima donna who sits in a draught and loses her voice.' However, not 'every destruction of corpus for which a contractor can be said, to some extent or in some sense, to be responsible, necessarily' excludes frustration for being self-induced (*Joseph Constantine v Imperial Smelting Corp* at 179); it is a matter of degree. If one party is disqualified by their self-induced frustration, the other party can still rely on the otherwise frustrating event. In *FC Shepherd v Jerrom* (1987), J's detention in borstal for 39 weeks prevented his performance of his apprenticeship. However, his employer could rely upon this as frustrating the contract to counter J's claim for unfair dismissal.

7.5.3 **Power to elect**

Where a party enters into a number of contracts and an external event *partially* destroys his or her supplies so that they cannot satisfy all their contracts, he or she must *choose* which contracts to allocate remaining supplies to, and which to leave unperformed. The very fact that a party has *exercised a choice* not to perform a certain contract bars the frustration of that contract; his or her choice breaks the chain of causation between the external event and his or her inability to perform. In contrast, frustration is permitted if: (i) the outside event *completely* destroys a party's supplies; or (ii) he or she had specified only one mode of performance or allocated a specific supply to a particular contract, and that becomes impossible to perform due to the outside event.

In *Maritime National Fish v Ocean Trawlers* (1935), M chartered a trawler for otter trawling from O. M applied for five licences but received only three, which they allocated to other trawlers (including two of their own), and sought to frustrate the contract with O. The Privy Council held M liable to O for the hire because the reason for O's trawler not being usable for otter trawling was M's own election. The contract with O would have been possible to perform if M had allocated a licence to O's trawler.

But partial destruction may make it impossible to perform all of one's contracts. In *The Super Servant Two*, W agreed to transport L's drilling rig between 20 June and 20 August using, *at its option*, either *The Super Servant One* or *The Super Servant Two*. W internally allocated the latter to this contract and committed *The Super Servant One* to other contracts. Prior to performance, *The Super Servant Two* sank. The Court of Appeal rejected W's claim of frustration because it was W's own election not to use the remaining ship (*The Super Servant One*) that led to its non-performance, and not the sinking of *The Super Servant Two*. The court also justified allocating the risk of partial failure of supplies to the carrier because 'it is within the promisor's control how many contracts he enters into' (at first instance (1989) at 158). In the end, the carrier was excused under the *force majeure* clause in the contract which covered certain events, including 'perils or dangers and accidents of the sea'.

Two objections can be raised.

(i) If frustration is barred because the claimant has chosen to enter a contract or could have provided for the frustrating event, then we are back to absolute liability because this reasoning logically swallows up the rationale for frustration. The same goes for the reasoning that it is always open to the parties to make express provision for supervening events.

(ii) W's power to allocate *The Super Servant One* to its contract with L is entirely *theoretical* since the ship was already allocated to other jobs. Thus, a party can only *guard against the finding of self-induced frustration* by:

- eliminating any choice by expressly allocating specific supplies to particular contracts; or
- including a suitable *force majeure* clause.

> ### Pause for reflection
>
> *The Super Servant Two* can be criticised for leaving a seller or supplier of goods in an impossible position where their source partially fails due to an unforeseen event. He or she cannot perform all of his or her contracts, but because they can perform *some*, they will not be able to frustrate *any*; merely choosing *which* contract not to perform breaks the chain of causation with the supervening event. The rationale of the frustration doctrine should permit a party not at fault to frustrate only *some* of their contracts where a supervening event makes it impossible for him or her to perform them all. Four arguments support this contention:
>
> 1. *Conclusion unnecessary*: the Court of Appeal in *The Super Servant Two* said (at 10, 13) that *Maritime National Fish v Ocean Trawlers* obliged it to find frustration barred by any 'election'. However, while it was possible in *Maritime National Fish* for the claimant to perform *all* of its contracts despite the partial failure of supplies, this was impossible in *The Super Servant Two*. Strictly speaking, *Maritime National Fish* only bars frustration where a party has a genuine choice *whether* to perform all his or her contracts and chooses not to; it does not apply where a party's only choice is as to *which* of his or her contracts will be left unperformed.
>
> 2. *Existence of choice is not inconsistent with discharge*: the presence of choice was also said to bar frustration because choice is inconsistent with the automatic discharge effected by frustration (at 9, 14). However, *FC Shepherd v Jerrom* (see 7.5.2) shows that in certain cases only one of the parties can claim; otherwise, the contract remains valid.
>
> 3. *The problem is not choice but favouritism*: the claimant's choice as to which contracts to perform should not eclipse the greater causative potency of the external event which destroys the claimant's ability to perform all his or her contracts, and forces them to choose in the first place. The real objection to the claimant's limited choice is the potential for him or her to give *preferential treatment* to their most profitable contract partners (whether present or prospective). The same objection may underlie the finding in *George Mitchell (Chesterhall) Ltd v Finney Lock Seeds Ltd* (1983) that the wide clause limiting damages for breach of contract to supply seeds was unreasonable under the Unfair Contract Terms Act 1977 because, inter alia, the evidence showed that in practice the seller, at its discretion, often negotiated settlements well beyond that stipulated in the limitation clause (see 11.4.6.2).
>
> 4. *Other solution preferable*: the solution is to eliminate the claimant's choice by requiring them to allocate their remaining supplies fairly. In relation to fungible (ie interchangeable) goods like potatoes or widgets, the supplier could be required to deliver their supplies *rateably* to each contract partner (ie reducing the amount to each in proportion to what was originally contracted for). This would be consistent with the cases on partial failure of supply where *force majeure* or 'prohibition of export' clauses were in place[8] and where they were not[9] (see 7.3.2.3). Suppliers were excused from full performance if they acted fairly and reasonably in allocating their remaining supplies along the lines suggested. Of course, ships, unlike potatoes or widgets, are not capable of rateable division, but the principle is the same. The supplier should be required to perform his or her contracts in the order that the contracts were made or performance required: 'first come, first served'. Indeed,
>
> ➡

[8] *Intertradax SA v Lesieur-Tourteaux SARL* (1978) at 513; *Bremer Handelsgesellschaft v Continental Grain Co* (1983).
[9] *Howell v Coupland* (1876); *Sainsbury Ltd v Street* (1972).

→

it is arguable that the denial of frustration in *The Super Servant Two* is consistent with this approach. One of the two contracts which W, the carrier, chose to perform instead of L's contract was made *after* the contract with L (at 9). Moreover, W only finally allocated *The Super Servant One* to the other contracts after successfully negotiating extra fees with them after the sinking of *The Super Servant Two* (at 13).

7.6 **The effect of frustration**

7.6.1 **Automatic discharge**

A contract is *discharged* for frustration. The consent which initially attaches to the contract at formation 'runs out' on the occurrence of the frustrating event, relieving both parties from further performance (or liability for non-performance). The contract cannot be kept alive or revived at the option of either party; neither can the court keep the contract on foot and adjust the terms to meet the new circumstances (subject to the discussion on partial failure of supply at 7.3.2.3). In *Hirji Mulji v Cheong Yue*, a charterparty was frustrated although the claimant initially confirmed its willingness to continue with the charter after the ship was released from government requisitioning. However, a party responsible for the frustrating event cannot treat him or herself as automatically discharged from the contract, although his or her contract partner can do so (*FC Shepherd v Jerrom*, see 7.5.2).

7.6.2 **Losses and gains under the contract**

7.6.2.1 Overview

Automatic discharge is straightforward where the contract is executory (yet to be performed), but problems arise where the contract is partly executed (performance has begun). Take the example of a contract where A contracts to pay £50,000 for ten performances by B in A's theatre. At the point of frustration:

- A may have actually made some payment (A$) or the payment may be owing (A$ due); A may also have incurred other costs in furtherance of its own contractual performance, for example maintaining the theatre and advertising the performances (A costs);

- B may have given all or just some of the performances (B non-$ benefit) and may also have incurred costs in furtherance of its contractual performance by, for example, hiring actors and making costumes (B costs).

'A$', 'A$ due', and 'B non-$ benefit' represent the extent of contractual *performances actually conferred* or owed under the contract. They are on the plus side of any restitutionary claim under the Law Reform (Frustrated Contracts) Act 1943 (hereafter 'LR(FC)A').

'A costs' and 'B costs' represent the *cost* of performance (which may exceed the value of any benefit conferred on the other party); they are the minus side which can be deducted from each party's restitutionary liability under LR(FC)A.

The law's response to the gains and losses before and after LR(FC)A is summarised in **Diagram 7B**.

Diagram 7B The Law Reform (Frustrated Contracts) Act 1943

Look on the Online Resource Centre to view this figure as a PowerPoint® presentation

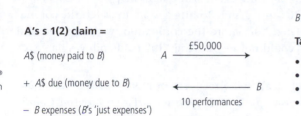

A's s 1(2) claim =

A$ (money paid to B)

+ A$ due (money due to B)

− B expenses (B's 'just expenses')

$A \xrightarrow{\text{£50,000}}$

$B \xleftarrow{\text{10 performances}}$

B's s 1(3) claim =

B non-$ (value of benefit to A)

Taking account of:

- the evaluation in the contract
- the effect of the frustration
- whether A$ received is kept or returned
- A's other performance expenses

	Common law (superseded)	LR(FC)A 1943	Issues under the Act
1. Money paid: A$	A can only recover if total failure of consideration (TFC) from B (*Fibrosa*)	A can recover *without* TFC (**s1 (2)**)	• *Calculation of B's 'just expenses'*
	If so, A can recover entire payment	A's recovery is subject to B's retention of 'just expenses' to reflect B expenses (**s1 (2)**) *Gamerco*	• *B's 'Just expenses' cannot exceed money paid and payable (ie no more than A$ + A$ due)*
2. Money due but unpaid: A$ due	A must still pay this (*Chandler*)	A is only *liable* to the extent that B's 'just expenses' (B expenses) exceed recovery of money paid (A$) (**s1(2)**)	
3. Non-money benefits conferred by B on A: B non-$	B can only recover sums that are 'due' (*Appleby*)	B can claim 'just sum' (**s1 (3)**)= sum not exceeding the benefit conferred on A (B non-$) taking into account: • the effect of frustration on the value of B non-$; • the contract valuation of B's expenses and services (B expenses); • payments from A (A$) subject to s1(2) claim by A; • A's other expenses	• *Stage I: Identification and valuation of benefit received (B non-$)* • *Stage II: Calculation of 'just sum' which cannot exceed B non-$* *BP v Hunt*

7.6.2.2 The common law position

The common law position is superseded by LR(FC)A. But it is important to an understanding of LR(FC)A itself.

(i) Money paid or due:

- originally, any sums paid before the frustrating event were *un*recoverable and any sums *due* before the frustrating event still had to be paid. In *Chandler v Webster* (1904), C paid £100 immediately to hire a room to watch the coronation, £41 being payable later, but before the coronation was cancelled and the contract frustrated. C could not recover the £100 paid and was liable for the £41;

- this position was softened by allowing recovery of money paid for *total failure of consideration* in **Fibrosa Spolka Ackcyjna v Fairbairn Lawson Combe Barbour Ltd** (1943). FSA prepaid £1,000 for the manufacture of machinery. When the contract was frustrated by the outbreak of war, FLCB refused to return the money because they had done considerable work and incurred considerable expenses under the contract. The court allowed recovery of the £1,000. Note that the 'consideration', which had totally failed, is not the consideration required for contract *formation* (this will often just be a *promise* of performance). It is the *performance* of the contract itself; the buyer had received nothing at all. The case still left the law in an *unsatisfactory* state: (a) the requirement of *total failure* barred recovery if the payer has received *any*, even trivial, performance (*Whincup v Hughes* (1871)); and (b) the payee cannot offset their wasted expenses in performance of the contract.

(ii) **Non-money benefits**: prior to LR(FC)A, the value of goods or services conferred under the contract was only recoverable if payment for them was 'due' under the contract *before* the frustrating event. Obligations to pay thereafter, as with all outstanding obligations, are discharged on frustration. In **Appleby v Myers** (1867), a contract to install machinery in M's factory and maintain it for two years, *payment on completion* of the work was frustrated when an accidental fire destroyed the factory and machinery. M recovered nothing for the work already done since payment only fell due on completion (see also *Cutter v Powell* (1795) at 12.2.2.1). This is unjust where the benefit conferred survives the frustrating event.

7.6.2.3 The aims of LR(FC)A

The problems identified under the common law are addressed by LR(FC)A, which regulates the effects of frustrated contracts unless the parties have expressly provided otherwise (s 2(3)). Goff J said (in *BP Exploration Co (Libya) Ltd v Hunt* (1979) at 799) that the 'fundamental principle underlying the Act . . . is prevention of unjust enrichment of either party to the contract at the other's expense' and *not* the apportionment of the loss caused by the frustration of the contract. More broadly, Lawton LJ said in the Court of Appeal that the Act was simply to 'make the operation of the law more fair' (*BP v Hunt* (1981) at 237).

> ◉ **Counterpoint**
>
> 1. The 1943 Act is primarily aimed at reversing unjust enrichment, but this is tempered by *some loss apportionment* to take some account of the recipient's wasted expenses in performance of the contract.
>
> 2. Adjustments to prevent unjust enrichment *and* to apportion loss are justifiable responses to the impact of catastrophic events on innocent parties engaged in a joint enterprise.
>
> 3. In **'Frustration, Restitution and Loss Apportionment'** in A S Burrows (ed), *Essays on the Law of Restitution* (OUP, 1991), **McKendrick** criticises the 1943 Act as inadequately thought through but he approves its emphasis on restitution with only limited loss apportionment allowed. He regards the loss-sharing schemes in other jurisdictions as having gone too far.

7.6.3 **Money paid or payable under LR(FC)A**

Section 1(2) of LR(FC)A:

- allows the payer's claim to recover *payments* made prior to the frustrating event (*A* can claim *A*$);

- relieves the payer from paying *sums due* prior to discharge; and

- empowers the court 'if it considers it just to do so having regard to all the circumstances' to allow the payee to:
  - set off against the sum to be returned; and
  - claim against the sum payable by *A* but not paid,

- the whole or part of his or her *expenses* incurred, before the time of discharge, in or for the purpose of, the performance of the contract (*A*$ + *A*$ due) – B expenses). 'Expenses' include 'such sum as appears to be reasonable in respect of overhead expenses and in respect of any work or services performed personally by the said party' (s 1(4)), including *pre-contract expenses* incurred 'for the purpose of, the performance of the contract'.

(i) **How should the payee's 'just expenses' (*B2*) be calculated?** In *Gamerco SA v ICM/Fair Warning (Agency) Ltd* (1995), represented in **Diagram 7C**, $775,000 was payable by the promoters of a concert of which $412,500 had been paid to the pop group (Guns N' Roses) by the time the concert venue was declared unsafe and the contract frustrated. Both sides had incurred wasted expenses in preparation for the concert (the group $50,000 and the promoters $450,000). How much should be deducted from the promoter's claim under section 1(2) for the sum paid, as 'just expenses', to reflect the group's wasted expenses? Garland J said that the payee had the onus of showing why the discretion should be exercised to reduce its restitutionary liability. He posits three possible approaches.

- ✗ **Total retention**: this allows the payee to offset *all* its wasted expenses, which would reduce the promoter's recovery to $362,500 (ie $412,500 – $50,000). In *BP v Hunt*, Goff J (at 800) supports this on the basis that the Act gave statutory

Diagram 7C Restitution of money paid: deduction of 'just expenses' in *Gamerco*

	Promoter = s 1(2) claimant	**Pop group**
Contractual obligation	Pay $775K	Give performance
Benefit received from the other party prior to frustration	Nothing	$412.5K
Expenses incurred under the contract	$450K	**$50K**

Promoter claims restitution of $412.5K paid. How much should be deducted as the pop group's 'just expenses' for its wasted expenses of $50K?
(a) Total: $412.5K – **$50K** = $362.5K
(b) Equal apportionment: $412.5K – **$25K** = $387.5K
(c) **Broad discretion**: $412.5K – **$0**   = $412.5K

recognition to the defence of *change of position*; that is, the payee can deduct from the sum to be returned (or, claim it against the sum due) the amount spent in reliance on the security of its receipt.

✗ **Equal apportionment**: this offsets half of the payee's wasted expenses, and would reduce the promoter's recovery to $387,500 (ie $412,500 – $25,000).

✓ **Broad discretion**: this is exercised by the court to 'do justice in a situation which the parties had neither contemplated nor provided for, and to mitigate the possible harshness of allowing all loss to lie where it has fallen' (*Gamerco* at 1237).

Garland J thought there was 'no indication in the Act, the authorities, or the relevant literature that the court is obliged to incline either towards total retention or equal division'. Moreover, both these approaches take no account of *the payer*'s wasted expenses. On the facts, Garland J exercised a broad discretion in allowing the promoters to recover the whole of the $412,500 paid *without deduction* to reflect the group's wasted expenses of $50,000. The result seems eminently fair given the promoter's wasted expenses of $450,000.

👤 Pause for reflection

Full loss apportionment would require the pop group to pay the promoter £200,000 (ie (£450,000 – £50,000) divided by 2). But the logic of this would extend to all cases where the contract fails without the fault of either party, as in common mistake (see 6.2.6); it would also have to take into account the reasonableness of the parties' wasted expenses, raising obvious complexities and uncertainties. In '**Frustration, Restitution and the Law Reform (Frustrated Contracts) Act 1943**' [1996] *LMCLQ* 170, **Clark** welcomes the decision as reaching a just result despite the badly drafted Act.

(ii) **What is the ceiling of 'just expenses'?** The sums paid plus any sum due is the *ceiling* of the payee's allowance or claim for 'just expenses'; his or her wasted expenses in *excess* of that figure are not recoverable. Changing the facts of *Gamerco v ICM* a little:

- if the group's wasted expenses were $1,000,000, it would only have been able to offset up to $775,000 of that, being the sum due from the promoter;
- the group cannot recover any of its expenses if no sums were paid by or due from the promoter at the time of frustration.

Ideally, a party should secure a large *pre-payment* from the other party against which to offset its wasted expenses in the event of frustration. The party who has not done so is treated as if he or she has assumed the risk of loss from performance prior to frustration, although this contradicts the idea that frustration is an unforeseeable event for which neither party has assumed the risk. The only alternative is for that party to make a section 1(3) *claim* if his or her expenditure has *benefited* the other party.

7.6.4 **Non-money benefits under the Act**

Diagram 7B shows that **section 1(3)** of the Act allows *B* to claim a 'just sum' where *B's* contractual performance before discharge confers a 'valuable benefit' on *A* other than money to which section 1(2) would apply. The 'just sum' cannot exceed the value of the benefit conferred *on A* (*B* non-$) and should be fixed having regard to all the circumstances of the case and, in particular:

(i)   the amount of any expenses incurred before the time of discharge by the benefited party (*A*) in, or for the purpose of, the performance of the contract, including any sums paid or payable by him or her to any other party in pursuance of the contract and retained or recoverable by that party under the last foregoing subsection, and

(ii) the effect, in relation to the said benefit, of the circumstances giving rise to the frustration of the contract.

In **BP v Hunt**, Goff J broke down such claims to two stages:

Stage I: identifying and valuing the benefit (*B* non-$), and

Stage II: assessing the 'just sum'.

7.6.4.1 **Stage I: identification and valuation of the benefits conferred**

The starting point is to assess the objective (or market) value of the benefits conferred.

- Where *B* transfers *goods* to *A*, the benefit is easily identifiable.
- The situation is more complicated where *B* performs *services*. The services may be intended to yield an *end product* (eg a building or a manuscript) or not (eg transportation, surveying, entertainment, or a holiday). Goff J (at 801–2) said that 'benefit' under the Act will usually denote the end product of services rather than the services themselves, although a small service may create a very valuable end product while lengthy service may create a worthless product.

- However, he acknowledged (at 803) that in cases of *'pure' services*, which are never intended to produce end products, the 'benefit' must be the value of the services themselves. There are no difficulties where *A* receives *completed* performance with an *objective value* from *B*'s services whether they produce an end product or not. Where such services have *no objective value* (such as *B*'s redecoration of a room already in good decorative order to *A*'s appalling taste), its value to *A* must lie in *A*'s request and preparedness to pay the contract price for it. Two situations present more difficulties.

(i) **Partial performance**: where *B* has only partially performed before the frustrating event, its precise value to *A* may be problematic. What is *part* of a building, a painting, a play, a haircut, or a voyage worth to the recipient? Even if part performance of services can be objectively valued, the recipient should still be entitled to say 'but it isn't worth that *to me*'. The point is underscored where the contract is 'entire' (ie payment is only due on completion, see 12.2.2.1). This problem, called 'subjective devaluation',[10] is exacerbated in pure services cases and Beatson cautions against confusing restitution of the *benefit* conferred on *A* with compensation for *B*'s *losses* in performing the contract.[11] The better course is to accord any objective value of the partial performance at Stage I, leaving the problem of 'subjective devaluation' to Stage II.

(ii) **Reduction of the benefit by frustrating event**: the frustrating event may reduce or completely destroy the value of the end product of B's goods or services. Goff J interprets this as belonging in the Stage I assessment to reduce or eliminate the benefit transferred against which *B* can offset claim the 'just sum' at Stage II (at 803).

▶◀ Counterpoint

On this reading, the harshness of *Appleby v Myers* (see 7.6.2.2(ii)) remains unchanged by the Act. The preferable approach is to weigh with other factors, at Stage II:

- the 'subjective devaluation' of the claimant's partial performance; and

- the effect of the frustrating event on the benefit conferred in the court's discretionary assessment of the 'just sum'.

This approach is supported by:

- the wording of section 1(3) which defines valuable benefit (at Stage I) as that obtained *'before* the time of discharge'; and

- the placement of section 1(3)(b) as *one of the factors* to be considered in fixing the 'just sum' (at Stage II).

---

[10] P Birks, *An Introduction to the Law of Restitution* (Clarendon Press, 1989) 109–14.
[11] J Beatson, *The Use and Abuse of Unjust Enrichment* (Clarendon Press, 1991) 5–8, 21, 31–9.

7.6.4.2 Stage II: assessment of the 'just sum'

There is little guidance yet on how the court will calculate the 'just sum'. Whilst Goff J confined the aim of the Act to the prevention of unjust enrichment, the Court of Appeal in *BP v Hunt* (1981) preferred a broader discretionary approach. Lawton LJ said (at 238): 'what is just is what the trial judge thinks is just' and an appellate court should not interfere with that assessment 'unless it is so plainly wrong that it cannot be just'. This discretion is confined by five factors:

(i) **Ceiling**: the value of the benefit fixed at Stage I is the *ceiling* or maximum for the 'just sum'.

(ii) **The effect of the frustrating event on the benefit conferred**: section 1(3)(b) requires this to be taken into account here (contrary to Goff J's view, see 7.6.4.1(ii)).

(iii) **Contractual risk allocation**: Goff J said (at 805, 825) that the assessment should be undertaken in a similar way to a *quantum meruit* or a *quantum valebat* claim (ie a claim for the *objective* value of the claimant's goods or services in the absence of a contract), but he also said (at 806) that the *contractual* allocation of risk is an important consideration; he thought it 'likely' that most section 1(3) claims will be limited to a *rateable portion of the contract price*. It makes sense that a claimant should not profit from the frustration (and escape a bad bargain) by being able to claim *more* than he or she would have earned if the contract had run its course (eg where the market price exceeds the contract price).

(iv) **The date of valuation**: this is generally the date of frustration (at 800). However, under section 1(2) and (3), even if money and services were conferred long before that date, no allowance can be made for their time value (ie the recipient's *use* of the benefit conferred before the frustrating event).

(v) **Recipient's expenses**: section 1(3)(a) directs the court to take account of the *recipient's expenses* in, or for the purpose of, the performance of the contract, including sums paid or payable by the recipient under the contract which are retained or recoverable by him or her under section 1(2).

In *BP v Hunt* (1979), BP entered an agreement to explore and develop H's oil concession in Libya. BP was also to make initial 'farm-in' payments of cash and oil to H in exchange for a 50% share in the concession and a portion of the oil discovered until BP had recouped 125% of its initial expenditure. An oil field was discovered and worked from 1967 to 1971 before the contract was frustrated by the Libyan government's expropriation of the concession. BP had only received part of the oil to which it would ultimately be entitled and made a section 1(3) claim. **Diagram 7D** summarises the basis of the award made.

(i) **Stage I: the benefit to Hunt conferred by BP**—Goff J measured this by the *end product* of BP's work in exploring and working the oil field (ie the enhancement of the value of H's share of the concession), rather than the cost to BP of its work. The value of this end product was substantially reduced by the expropriation. H's benefit was identified as half the value of:

(a) H's receipt of oil from the concession; and

(b) the compensation from the Libyan government.

Diagram 7D Claim for non-money performance: calculation of the 'just sum' in *BP v Hunt*

	BP = s1 (3) claimant	*Hunt*
Contractual obligation	To provide: • services in exploring and developing the oil field, 'farm-in' oil + • money	To give BP: • 50% of his concession • 50% of oil output and reimbursement oil to the value of $98 million (=125% of BP's 'farm-in' oil + money)
Benefit received prior to frustration	• 50% of H's concession (now replaced by compensation for confiscation) • oil to the value of **$63 million**	*Stage I: Identification and valuation of benefit received by Hunt* Half the value of: • oil reaped and • compensation for confiscation (= the end product of the increased value of H's 50% concession adjusted by the frustrating event) = half of $170 million = **$85 million**

Stage II: 'just sum' to BP
= reasonable value of BP's work and expenses
= contractual value of performance due from Hunt ($98m) *minus* value of performance received from Hunt ($63m)
= **$35 million**

This amounted to $85 million (ie 50% of $170 million). This is the ceiling of any section 1(3) award. The other half of the value to H was attributable to H's ownership of the concession.

(ii) **Stage II: the just sum due to BP**—Goff J held that the restitutionary award of the just sum is the *reasonable value* of BP's work and expenses conferred on H. He regarded the best evidence of this value as that which the parties themselves fixed, namely, the consideration due to BP (the contract valuation). Thus, the just sum was the value of the contractual performance *due* to BP from H ($98 million) *minus* that already *received* by BP from H ($63 million), being $35 million. This was awarded in full since it came well under the ceiling of $85 million calculated at Stage I. Although the court's task is not to enforce the contract, the contract may provide the best evidence of the value of the claimant's performance when restitution is awarded.

7.7 **Hardship and contract modification: frustration, duress, and consideration**

In practice, a supervening event which makes the contract impossible or more onerous for one party to perform may trigger renegotiation of the contract (usually to pay more or to accept less). Whether the parties are bound by the modified contract brings together questions of frustration, duress, and consideration.

(i) **Frustration**: if the original contract is frustrated then the modified contract is enforceable because there is, strictly speaking, an entirely new contract so that the problems raised by one party paying more or accepting less than under the original contract are sidestepped: the *consideration* doctrine presents no obstacle (see 3.1.5.3 and 3.1.5.4), and neither does *duress* since a threat not to contract is generally legitimate (see 8.6.1). However, a party may escape the modified contract by pleading mistake of law (ie they only renegotiated because they thought the original contract was still binding).

Pause for reflection

This is not the only solution to the problem of exceptional hardship.

1. The contract may include a *force majeure clause* expressly providing for price or other adjustments in particular circumstances of hardship, and may require good faith renegotiation or submission to arbitration (see 7.4.1).

2. In the absence of express provision, the law could require the parties to renegotiate, backed up by judicial modification if renegotiations fail in defined circumstances of hardship. The UNIDROIT Principles of International Commercial Contracts stipulate (at Arts 6.2.1 and 6.2.2) that in such circumstances the parties are bound to enter into *negotiations* with a view to adapting the contract or terminating it. On failure to reach agreement within a reasonable time, either party can resort to the *court* to modify the contract, or to terminate the contract at a date and on terms fixed by the court.

(ii) **No frustration, just hardship**: if the supervening event does not frustrate the contract but merely results in hardship to one of the parties, the enforceability of the renegotiation depends on: (a) whether it is supported by *consideration*; and (b) whether *duress* vitiates the renegotiation. The problems raised by *Williams v Roffey Brothers* (1989) on these issues are discussed at 3.1.5.3.

THIS CHAPTER IN ESSENCE

The key areas and core topics in this chapter are summarised in an easy-to-use list, ideal for revision purposes, on the Online Resource Centre at http://www.oxfordtextbooks.co.uk/orc/chenwishart5e/. Links to websites relevant to the topics covered and any updates to the chapter can also be found on the Online Resource Centre.

online
resource
centre

QUESTIONS

1 'The frustration doctrine is quite distinct from that of mistake; it deals with the ending of a contract and not its formation and its consequences are quite different from that of mistake.' To what extent is, and to what extent should, this be true?

2 A contract is only frustrated when its performance is impossible.' Discuss.

3 You have been asked to advise the Law Commission on the problem raised by *The Super Servant Two*. Should the law on self-induced frustration be reformed? If so, how?

4 What can the parties do about losses suffered in performance of a contract which is discharged for frustration?

5 In February, Paul books Queenie to perform at Paul's concert venue for two weeks in August. In early April, Rex books Queenie to perform for late August. Queenie suffers widely publicised bouts of ill health in March and, in mid-April, she is admitted to hospital with a poor chance of recovery. Paul and Rex book other acts instead.

(i)   Can Paul and Rex get their £500 deposit back from Queenie?
(ii) What if Queenie had spent £400 on new costumes in preparation for her performances?
(iii) What if Queenie recovers completely by the end of July?

 For hints on how to answer these questions, please see the Online Resource Centre at http://www.oxfordtextbooks.co.uk/orc/chenwishart5e/

KEY FURTHER READING

Clark, P (1996), 'Frustration, Restitution and the Law Reform (Frustrated Contracts) Act 1943', *LMCLQ* 170.

McKendrick, E (1991), 'Frustration, Restitution and Loss Apportionment' in A Burrows (ed), *Essays on the Law of Restitution* (OUP) 147.

McKendrick, E (1995), 'Force Majeure and Frustration—Their Relationship and a Comparative Assessment' in E McKendrick (ed), *Force Majeure and Frustration in Contract* (2nd edn, LLP) 33.

Treitel, G (1994), *Frustration and Force Majeure* (Sweet & Maxwell).

8

Duress

'You pressured me'

Contract law has always put limits on the permissible means used to persuade another to enter into a contract. Chapter 5 discusses one such limit, namely misrepresentation. This chapter examines another under the label of duress.

If I force you to sign a contract by putting a gun to your head, the law will refuse to help me enforce that contract: you can call it off at your option, subject to the usual bars to rescission (see 5.3.2), including the requirement of 'substantial' restitution (*Halpern v Halpern* (2006)). There are four categories of actionable duress: whilst the law on duress to the *person* and to *property* is relatively settled, the precise contours of the newer categories of *economic* duress and *lawful act* duress are still unclear. The questions to be addressed are the following.

(i) *What sorts* of pressures are regarded as illegitimate by the law?

(ii) *How much* pressure must the illegitimate threat exert on the other party?

(iii) What is the *justification* for the duress doctrine?

(iv) Is the current law on duress *satisfactory?* If not, how might it be developed in the future?

8.1 **The justification for duress**

8.1.1 **Inadequacy of the overborne will theory**

Although duress was originally explained in terms of the victim's will being overborne and his or her consent vitiated,[1] this is now recognised as inadequate. In **'Economic Duress and the Overborne Will'** (1982) 98 *LQR* 197, **Atiyah** argues that contract law should follow criminal law's rejection of the 'overborne will' theory in *DPP v Lynch* (1975). He points out that a victim of duress submits *knowingly* and *intentionally*. If you tell me to 'hand over £10,000 or be horribly maimed', my decision to hand over the money is *very real* indeed. I *know* what I am agreeing to, I *intend* to agree, and I very much *want* to agree. The real objection is not that I did not consent, but that you induced my consent by illegitimate pressure; the complaint is the nature and acceptability of the choices the victim is left with. In *Lynch*, the House of Lords recognised that duress does not make the victim's actions involuntary, the victim's will is not 'overborne' or destroyed, merely deflected. Lord Simon said of the victim (at 926–38): 'There is still an intention on his part to contract in the apparently consensual terms . . . The contrast is with *non est factum* [where the victim does not know what he is signing, see 6.4.2]. The contract procured by duress is therefore not void: it is voidable.'

On the other hand, actionable duress is not merely about consenting under pressure, however strong. Valid consent does *not require freedom from pressures*. I may have 'no choice' but to agree to the interest rate set by the lender, or to the prices charged for the food, shelter, or clothing that I 'need', but such *ordinary pressures* will not excuse me from my contractual responsibilities. As Lord Wilberforce said (at 121) in *Barton v Armstrong* (1976): 'in life . . . many acts are done under pressure, sometimes overwhelming pressure, so that one can say that the actor had no choice but to act. Absence of choice in this sense does not negate consent in law: for this the pressure must be one of the kind which the law does not regard as legitimate'. In short, duress is not ruled out by knowing and willing consent, but neither is it indicated merely by the presence of (even overwhelming) pressure.

8.1.2 **Illegitimate pressure**

In ***Universe Tankships Inc of Monrovia v International Transport Workers Federation*** (1983), the House of Lords recognised (at 400) that: 'The classic case of duress is . . . not

---

[1] *Occidental Worldwide Investment Corp v Skibs A/S Avanti (The Siboen and The Sibotre)* (1976) at 336; *North Ocean Shipping Co Ltd v Hyundai Construction Co Ltd (The Atlantic Baron)* (1979) at 717, 719; *Pao On v Lau Yiu Long* (1980) at 635; *Barton v Armstrong* (1976) at 121; and see P Birks and N Chin, 'On the Nature of Undue Influence' in J Beatson and D Friedmann (eds), *Good Faith and Fault in Contract Law* (OUP, 1995) 55, 62, 88–9.

the lack of will to submit but the victim's intentional submission arising from the realisation that there is no other practical choice open to him.' If you *distort* my decision-making by introducing an *illegitimate pressure*, which presents me with *no practicable alternative* but to submit to your demands, the law will not expect me to take the normal responsibility for my apparent exercise of will; it will *deem* my consent to be vitiated (Lord Diplock at 384). The illegitimate pressure view of duress explains why:

(i) the enforcing party must be tainted in the sense that he or she has applied, or at least knows of the pressure;

(ii) *duress* makes contracts *voidable* analogous to misrepresentation, and not void like mistake (which focuses on the claimant's lack of consent); and

(iii) the *standard of causation* is less than might be expected on the overborne will theory; the illegitimate pressure need not be the overwhelming cause of the victim's consent to contract to qualify as duress.

8.2 **What must be proved?**

In *Universe Tankships v International Transport Workers*,[2] the House of Lords held that the claimant must show the following.

(i) The **pressure** applied by the enforcing party is illegitimate: this depends on the nature of the *threat* and of the *demand*. If the conduct threatened is independently *unlawful* (ie it would amount to a breach of duty by the enforcing party) the threat is generally regarded as *illegitimate*. Correspondingly, threats of *lawful* conduct are generally treated as *legitimate*, unless they are 'immoral or unconscionable' when coupled with an illegitimate demand; the more unfair the *demand*, the more likely that the threat used to back it up will be regarded as illegitimate.

(ii) The illegitimate pressure induced the claimant to enter the contract. The precise *degree* of causation required varies with the type of duress in question with economic duress posing a particularly difficult category.

(iii) The claimant had no practicable alternative but to submit to the demand. This requirement only applies to claims of economic duress (see 8.4.3).

8.3 **Duress to the person and to property**

8.3.1 **Illegitimate pressure**

If I do (or threaten to do) *violence* to you or to *detain* you (or someone in a close relationship with you) to induce your consent to contract, I have clearly applied illegitimate pressure (*Barton v Armstrong; Duke de Cadaval v Collins* (1836)). *Chitty* (at para 7-012) suggests that 'the threat against even a stranger should be enough if the claimant

---

[2] See also *Dimskal Shipping Co SA v ITWF (The Evia Luck) (No 2)* (1992); *Huyton SA v Peter Cremer GmbH & Co Inc* (1999); *R v Her Majesty's Attorney-General for England and Wales* (2003) at [15]–[16].

genuinely believed that submission is the only way to prevent the stranger from being injured or worse'. The same applies if I threaten to damage, take, or keep your *property* (*Astley v Reynolds* (1731); *Maskell v Horner* (1915)), or your *money* (*Crescendo Management Pty Ltd v Moral Westpac Banking Corp* (1988)).

8.3.2 **Causation**

Threats to the person, by analogy with misrepresentation,[3] need only be *'a'* cause of the victim's decision to contract. It is enough if the threat contributed *in any way* to his or her decision to contract. The claimant need not show that it was *'the'*, the *'clinching'*, the *'predominant'*, or the *'overwhelming'* cause for the contract, or that *'but for'* the threat they would not have entered the contract. It is insufficient for the enforcing party to show that the claimant might, or would, have consented for other reasons, even without the threat: to enforce the contract, he or she must show that the illegitimate pressure had *no effect whatsoever* on the claimant's decision. Any one strand in the hangman's rope is *'a'* reason for the victim's ultimate demise, although the same result would have ensued without that one strand.[4] In **Barton v Armstrong** the parties, both major shareholders in a company, were locked in a bitter power struggle for its control. B claimed that he was induced to buy out A's interests on very generous terms, by A's threats to murder him and his family. The trial judge accepted that A made the threats but denied relief because B's main reason for buying out A was to ensure the company's survival. The Privy Council disagreed, holding that B could succeed if A's threats were merely *a* reason for his decision to enter the contract, and even if he might have done so without the threats. It was up to A to show that the threat had *no influence* on B at all.

In *duress to goods* cases, the claimant must show that the threat was a *'significant cause'* (*Dimskal Shipping Co SA v ITWF* (1992) at 165) of his or her consent to the contract. In practice, this causation requirement is easily met. In **Astley v Reynolds**, R told A that he could not redeem his plate (pawned to R) unless he paid more than twice the legal interest rate. A paid but then successfully recovered the excess payment for duress. The court was prepared to *assume* that A 'might have such an immediate want of his property that [an alternative course of action, eg a tort action for wrongful interference with goods] would not do'. A did not need to actually prove it. **Diagram 8A** summarises the law on duress to the person and to property.

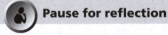 **Pause for reflection**

Duress to the person and to property are such clear contraventions of fair dealing that they are sufficient *in themselves* to justify legal sanction: there is no explicit requirement that the accompanying demand be unfair or improper, although it invariably will be. Indeed, the unfairness of the demand in *Barton v Armstrong* was treated as *evidence of the causation requirement*; that is, that the threat to kill must have had *some* effect on his decision to agree.

---

[3] *Barton v Armstrong* at 118 (Lord Cross).
[4] I am indebted to Professor Robert Stevens for this analogy.

Diagram 8A Summary of duress to the person and to property

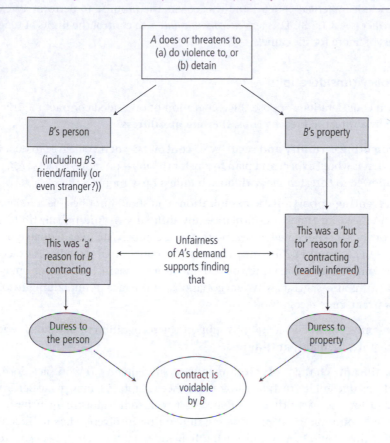

8.4 **Economic duress: threats to breach a contract**

Since *The Siboen and The Sibotre* (1976), the courts have accepted that economic duress may be as coercive and worthy of relief as duress to the person or to property (at 336; *The Atlantic Baron* at 715; *Pao On v Lau Yiu Long* at 635). The most important practical application of economic duress is in the area of one-sided **contract modifications**. That is, where one party threatens to breach an existing contract unless the other agrees to: (i) *pay more* for the original performance; or (ii) *accept less* performance than was originally due. When, if ever, should such renegotiations be enforced? Traditionally, the *doctrine of consideration* (especially the pre-existing duty rule, see 3.1.4) gave the answer: never, since no additional consideration supports the promise to pay more or accept less. However:

- the promissory estoppel doctrine can enforce promises of the 'same for less' in limited circumstances (see 3.1.5.4 and 3.3.2.1), but not if the promisee had applied illegitimate pressure since it would, then, not be inequitable for the promisor to renege on the promise;

* **Williams v Roffey Brothers** (1991) has enlarged the consideration requirement to include 'practical benefit' and this covers the promise to perform an existing contract (see 3.1.5.3). This leaves *economic duress* to control the limits of renegotiations of 'more for the same'.

8.4.1 Policy considerations

Two main considerations oppose the recognition of one-sided contract modifications induced by a threat to breach. Thus, they are **pro-duress**.

(i) **Promoting certainty and security of contracts**: when you agree to do a job for £2,000, that is what I expect and plan to pay for the job—no more, no less. You should not be allowed to threaten me with breach unless I pay more.

(ii) **Preventing opportunistic exploitation**: you should not be able to take advantage of my need for timely performance, my difficulty in finding substitute performance, or the fact the remedial regime may not compensate me adequately for your breach (see 14.2.3 and 14.2.4). The inadequacy of contractual remedies is exacerbated if you become insolvent, making you judgment-proof against any claim I may have. Ironically, this also suggests why renegotiations in the face of impending insolvency *should* warrant some recognition.

Four pro-enforcement considerations support the recognition of one-sided renegotiations; they are, therefore, **anti-duress**.

(i) **Significant change of circumstances** subsequent to contract formation, although insufficient to frustrate the contract (see Chapter 7), may make performance so difficult for one party that he or she must seek some adjustment if he or she is to complete performance. A party facing impending insolvency has no incentive to perform if this would merely exacerbate their indebtedness. Thus, Beatson[5] draws a distinction between:

   ✗ *'threats'*, where the threatening party has a *choice* whether to carry out the threat; and

   ✓ *'warnings'*, where the warning party is simply giving notice of his or her *inevitable* non-performance without renegotiation.

'Threats' are illegitimate, while 'warnings' are not.

(ii) If performance is not viable without renegotiation then, ironically, the concern to **protect the victim** (the recipient of performance) also supports renegotiation. Since, a party in difficulty may be better off breaching a contract to cut his or her losses (recognised in *Williams v Roffey Brothers* at 23), they have no incentive to perform if the law refuses to enforce such renegotiations. The victim could not pay more to ensure that he or she gets performance.

(iii) Reasonable renegotiations to facilitate the completion of contractual performance may be **economically efficient**. In **'The Travails of Duress'** [1990] *LMCLQ* 342,

---

[5] J Beatson, *The Use and Abuse of Unjust Enrichment* (Clarendon Press, 1991) 118–20.

Birks points out that (at 346) it may 'minimise the waste and inconvenience between parties already embarked on a project, and 'bring projects safely to a conclusion without interruptions and unnecessary ill-will.' It may be cheaper overall to pay more to get the job done than to have the whole thing unravel with its consequential waste and hassle. On the other hand, Birks warns against giving contract parties the incentive to bid low in the hope of renegotiating later.

(iv) The values of **cooperation and mutual accommodation** also support contract renegotiations when one party gets into difficulty. This rests on a relational view of contract as an essentially cooperative enterprise in the nature of joint ventures (see 1.3.6).

The courts *have* upheld some renegotiations induced by threats to breach, but they have done so without explicitly weighing these competing policies.

8.4.2 The causation-led approach

A threat to breach an existing contract is a threat of unlawful action since it would breach a legal duty and has generally been treated as illegitimate pressure (see most recently **Kolmar Group AG v Traxpo Enterprises Pty Ltd** (2010) where Clarke J added (at [92]) 'particularly where the defendant must know that it would be in breach if the threat were implemented'). Thus, if any renegotiations so induced are to be upheld, the causation requirement must be raised to prevent a finding of economic duress. In **Huyton v Cremer** (1999), Mance J justified the stronger causal connection required for economic duress on the basis that economic duress is *less serious* than duress to the person or to property.[6] His honour explains (at 636) that the minimum basic test should be the *'but for' test*: 'The illegitimate pressure must have . . . actually caused the making of the agreement, in the sense that it would not otherwise have been made either at all or, at least, in the terms in which it was made. In that sense, the pressure must have been decisive or clinching.' Moreover, he added, the claimant should also show that he or she had *no practicable alternative* but to submit to the demand, although this is not 'an inflexible third essential ingredient' (see further 8.4.3).

In **Pao On v Lau Yiu Long** (1980), Lord Scarman said (at 635) that in deciding whether sufficient causation was present the court should ask whether the victim:

(i)   protested;

(ii) had a *practicable alternative* open to them such as an adequate legal remedy;

(iii) was independently advised; and

(iv) *acted promptly to avoid* the renegotiation.

However, these factors are inconclusive. The victim may not protest because he or she sees no point in it or he or she may not wish to antagonise the coercing party whose performance they need. Knowing that the threat is unlawful does not necessarily increase the victim's realistic options (accepted in *Huyton v Cremer* at 630). Any delay in complaining *after* the renegotiation does not negate the causative effect of

---

[6] Contrast *The Atlantic Baron* at 719, which supports a lower standard of causation.

the illegitimate pressure *at the time* it was agreed, although it may bar rescission for affirmation (see 5.3.2).

The degree of pressure facing the victims does not distinguish the cases where economic duress was found, from those where it was rejected.

✓ In *Atlas Express v Kafco (Importers and Distributors) Ltd* (1989), A, a carrier company, mistakenly under-quoted by a half the price for carrying K's goods to Woolworth's in time for the Christmas sales. On realising its mistake, A refused to make the crucial delivery unless K agreed to double its payment. K agreed, since it was unlikely to find alternative carriers at such short notice and, if no delivery was made, K would have lost its lucrative contract on which the viability of its small business depended.

✓ In *The Atlantic Baron* (1979), H agreed to build a ship for N at a fixed price payable in US dollars. The value of the US currency dropped by 10% and H threatened not to deliver unless N agreed to a 10% increase in the price.

✓ In *B & S Contracts and Design Ltd v Victor Green Publications Ltd* (1984), B agreed to build exhibition stands for V but its workforce, which had been notified of impending redundancies, refused to work unless they received £9,000 in severance pay. V offered £4,500 as advance payment to help B to meet its workers' demand, but B made clear that performance would not proceed unless an *extra* £4,500 was paid. There was no express threat to breach, but the court found an *implied* threat. V agreed because non-performance would have damaged its reputation and exposed it to heavy claims from exhibitors.

✓ In *Adam Opel v Mitras Automotive (UK) Ltd* (2007), AO, a manufacturer of vans, informed M in February 2006 that it would cease to obtain parts from M in August. In response, M demanded certain 'compensation' and an increase in the price of parts to be supplied. AO unsuccessfully sought an injunction against M without notice to M. AO continued to attempt negotiation until it calculated it had only 24 hours' worth of supplies remaining. AO agreed to M's demands when M threatened to cut off supplies because cessation of production would result in severe financial losses and have other adverse knock-on effects. The agreement was set aside for economic duress.

In contrast, economic duress was rejected in the following cases, although, arguably, the victims faced no less pressure to submit.

✗ In *The Siboen and The Sibotre* (1976), charterers of a ship told the ship-owners that they would go into liquidation unless the charter price was significantly reduced. The owners agreed because they were unlikely to find alternative charterers in the state of the market and any rights they had against the charterers would be rendered worthless by their insolvency. The court found no duress, only commercial pressure.

✗ In *Pao On v Lau Yiu Long*, the parties exchanged shares in their companies. In addition, P agreed to delay selling 60% of the shares it received for at least a year to avoid triggering a fall in their value; L agreed to *buy back* those shares at a fixed price at or before the end of the year. When P realised that it would be disadvantaged if the shares rose above the fixed price, he refused to proceed with the contract unless L replaced the buy-back agreement with a *guarantee by way of indemnity* (ie L would only indemnify P if the shares fell below the fixed price). L agreed in order to avoid the delay and loss of public confidence that legal action against P would attract at a critical time in the company's restructuring. Moreover, L believed that the risk entailed in the modification was 'more apparent than real'. When the share price plummeted, L would neither buy back the shares at the fixed price (alleging this arrangement was ended by the modification) nor indemnify P (alleging the modification was voidable for duress). The court found no duress, only commercial pressure, and upheld the agreement to indemnify.

8.4.3 The role of 'no practicable alternative'

The requirement that the victim should have had no practicable alternative but to submit to the threat is an *independent and additional requirement* of duress since it goes to the very essence of the jurisdiction. The House of Lords in *Universe Tankships v International Transport Workers* (at 400) describes the classic case of duress as 'the victim's intentional submission arising from the realisation that there is no other practicable choice open to him'. The US Second Restatement of Contracts describes duress as an improper threat which leaves no reasonable alternative (§ 175(1)). In *Huyton v Cremer*, Mance J said (at 636) that the 'but for' test 'could lead too readily to relief being granted. It would not, for example, cater for the obvious possibility that, although the innocent party would never have acted as he or she did, but for the illegitimate pressure, they nevertheless had a real choice and could, if they had wished, equally well have resisted the pressure and, for example, pursued alternative legal redress.'

✓ In **Adam Opel v Mitras Automotive**, the court rejected M's argument that there was no economic duress because AO *did* have a practical alternative. AO's new supplier was far from ready to begin production and AO could not have obtained alternative supplies elsewhere. While AO had a strong case for an injunction, the court recognised (at [32]), that AO:

> had to take a rapid decision in circumstances where the threat had already become reality. Capitulation would ensure with certainty the restoration of supplies and at a price which, though seen by GMR as extortionate, would be a fraction of the loss which would otherwise be suffered. By contrast, there were serious imponderables about the injunction route ... [AO] were in my view entitled to consider that the outcome would not inevitably be in their favour ... [T]he court's attitude to the grant of a mandatory interim injunction to supply an indeterminate number of units on an indeterminate timetable could not in my view have been assumed.

✗ In **DSND Subsea v Petroleum Geo-Services** (2000), Dyson J recognised 'no practicable alternative' as a separate requirement of duress but found that P did have the practicable alternative of terminating the contract and finding alternative vessels for the job. However, what was arguably most determinative was Dyson

J's finding (at [134]) that D's conduct (part-suspension of the job pending resolution of its concern about P's provision of insurance and indemnities), even if it amounted to breach which coerced P, was 'reasonable behaviour by a contractor acting *bona fide* in a very difficult situation'.

8.4.4 Alternative approaches based on illegitimate pressure

Instead of the problematic causation-led approach to economic duress cases, the focus of the inquiry should switch to the illegitimacy of the pressure applied with the causation requirement stabilised at the level of the '*but for*' standard. Three variants have been suggested.

First, the legitimacy of the threat to breach can be made to depend on the presence or absence of **good faith** or otherwise of the party making the threat.[7] This is consistent with the idea that variations negotiated in bad faith (ie having no honest belief in the reasons advanced for the demand) are unenforceable as a bad-faith compromise (see 3.1.3.6). However, the concept of *good faith* is notoriously unstable. Burrows suggests that[8] a threatened breach of contract should be regarded as illegitimate if aimed at exploiting the claimant's weakness rather than solving financial or other problems of the defendant, but not 'if the threat is a reaction to circumstances that almost constitute frustration . . . [or] if it merely corrects what was always clearly a bad bargain'.

►◄ Counterpoint

1. *Judicial scepticism*: despite its application in *DSND Subsea v Petroleum Geo-Services* (see 8.4.3), Mance J in *Huyton v Cremer* (at 637) describes the good faith approach as 'by no means uncontentious', adding that it is 'difficult to accept that illegitimate pressure applied by a party who believes *bona fide* in his case could never give grounds for relief against an apparent compromise'. Indeed, Judge Wilkie QC has concluded that an *honest but mistaken demand* for immediate payment forcing the claimant to close his bets (crystallising his debt) amounted to economic duress in *Cantor Index Ltd v Shortall* (2002).

2. Failure *to explain the finding of duress in many cases* although good faith was present because the coercing party:

   • badly miscalculated and so underpriced the contract by a half (*Atlas v Kafco*);

   • lost on the real value of the contract price due to currency devaluation (*The Atlantic Baron*);

   • found the cost of performance substantially increased due to industrial action (*B & S Contracts v Victor Green*); or

   • was not paid by a third party while still being obliged to perform (*Vantage Navigation Corp v Suhail & Saud Bahwan Building Materials LLC (The Alev)* (1989)).

   ➤

---

[7] See P Birks, *An Introduction to the Law of Restitution* (Clarendon Press, 1989) 183; *DSND Subsea Ltd v Petroleum Geo-Services ASA* at [131]–[132].

[8] A Burrows, *The Law of Restitution* (3rd edn, OUP, 2010) 233.

3. *Inconsistent with competing policies*: the good faith approach suppresses some important policies, such as responsibility in contract formation and preserving the security and certainty of contracts. A party who deliberately, recklessly, or even mistakenly tenders low to win a job should not necessarily be able to renegotiate a better deal by threatening breach just because it is 'clearly bad' for him or her or has become much more difficult to perform. Short of frustration, contractual obligations are absolute and not discharged by change of circumstances which make performance less profitable or more costly (but see 7.7). The future is inherently uncertain and allocating the risks for such uncertainties (so that parties know where they stand) is the reason why most contracts (not simultaneously performed) are made in the first place.

The second approach is advocated by McKendrick in 'The Further Travails of Duress' in A Burrows and A Rodger (eds), *Mapping the Law: Essays in Memory of Peter Birks* (OUP, 2006) 180. He proposes treating *all* threats to breach as illegitimate pressure, which would only have to be 'a' reason for the claimant's consent. He reasons that: (i) courts should uphold the integrity of the original contract; and (ii) English law does not distinguish between good faith and bad faith threats to breach. This approach is consistent with Coleman J's dicta in *South Caribbean Trading Ltd v Trafigura Beheer BV* (2005) to the effect that the promisee who threatens to breach an existing duty cannot rely on 'practical benefit' as consideration for any extra payment because the threat is 'analogous to economic duress' (see 3.1.5.3(viii)).

 Pause for reflection

Whilst the good faith approach is under-inclusive (it avoids too few renegotiations for duress), McKendrick's approach is over-inclusive and avoids too many renegotiations.

Where the difficulties *threaten the performing party's economic survival so that performance is practically impossible without some renegotiation*, it is appropriate to uphold a reasonable and consensual modification. This suggests a third approach.

- It should be illegitimate pressure for a party to threaten breach if he or she *can* perform without modification; any non-performance would be 'self-induced', analogous to frustration.

- It should be legitimate for a party to renegotiate to his or her advantage if they have *no practicable alternative* but to do so to complete contractual performance.

A party's difficulties in performing must be severe before they can seek renegotiation by intimating the likelihood of breach. It is only then that they have 'no practicable alternative' but to seek negotiation. This approach strikes the right balance between the relevant competing policies.

(i) It *minimises the threat to the sanctity of the original contract* and the risk of exploitation by narrowly confining the scope of permissible renegotiations.

(ii) It protects the *victim's interest in receiving performance* when its substitute right to sue an insolvent party for breach would be worthless.

(iii) It *avoids the economic waste* entailed by breach and encourages cooperation and compromise between parties faced with difficult circumstances.

(iv) It *explains* the *cases*. Economic duress was rejected in *The Siboen and The Sibotre* where charterers said that they would go into liquidation unless the charter price was reduced. The court found only commercial pressure and so no duress. But the real reason may lie in Kerr LJ's observation that renegotiations in such circumstances are common and sensible in the charter market. Similarly, in *Williams v Roffey Brothers*, W's financial difficulty, exacerbated by the initial underpricing of the contract, made timely performance practically impossible. The court upheld R's promise to pay more, observing that 'a main contractor who agrees too low a price with a subcontractor is acting contrary to their own interests. He will never get the job finished without paying more money'.

8.4.5 **The demand**

Recall Lord Scarman's statement (in *Universe Tankships v International Transport Workers* 400–1) that the legitimacy of the pressure depends on the nature of the threat *and* the nature of the *demand*. Similarly, § 176(2) of the US Second Restatement of Contracts asks whether it was commercially reasonable to seek renegotiation *and* whether the *renegotiated terms are fair and equitable*.

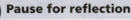 **Pause for reflection**

1. Contrary to the orthodox view that duress is concerned solely with *procedural* unfairness, it is impossible to exclude the *substantive* fairness of the *renegotiated contract* from the assessment. Even where the threatening party has no practicable alternative to renegotiation, he or she should only be allowed to seek such *reasonable* modification as is necessary to give them the incentive to complete their contractual performance. If more is demanded, then he or she *does* have a practicable alternative, namely, to ask for less; their threat is illegitimate.

2. The fairness of the *original contract* may also be relevant: the underprice in the original contract contributed to the courts' assessment in *Williams v Roffey Brothers* that there was no question of duress (at 10). But *Atlas v Kafco* shows that correcting substantive unfairness *alone* will not legitimise a threat to breach. Substantive concerns were also influential in *Pao On v Lau Yiu Long* (at 628) where duress was denied in order to avoid the unfairness of leaving P without the protection that the parties originally intended.

3. In 'Duress, Restitution and Contract Modification' in *The Use and Abuse of Unjust Enrichment* (Clarendon Press, 1990) 95, Beatson suggests that where it is not commercially practicable for a party to continue performance unless the contract is renegotiated, it should not inevitably be viewed as a threat to point that out. Some monitoring of the substantive fairness of the bargain may be inevitable.

8.5 **Other forms of economic duress**

The court will take into account the statutory background in determining whether any threat to the victim's economic interests is illegitimate. Thus, the House of Lords held that a trade union's threat to 'black' a ship (withdraw labour) *could* taint any contract induced by the threat with duress (*Universe Tankships v International Transport Workers* at 383, 397, 400). However, the presence of statutes protecting trade unions from claims for the tort of intimidation may persuade courts not to find duress (at 391, 401).

In *Progress Bulk Carriers Ltd v Tube City IMS LLC* (2012) P chartered its vessel to T. P committed a repudiatory breach when it fixed the vessel to another charterer without informing T. T did not accept that breach as terminating the contract. P admitted its mistake and said that it would provide a substitute and pay full compensation, but only offered T an alternative vessel at a discount on condition that T waived all claims for loss and damage. T had no option but to accept the settlement agreement under protest to avoid further losses. Cooke J held that it was illegitimate for P to produce the 'take it or leave it' offer, having put T into the position it was in by reason of its breach and subsequent conduct (at [18]–[20]). Illegitimate pressure 'can be constituted by conduct which was not in itself unlawful, although it would be an unusual case where that was so, particularly in the commercial context.' A past unlawful act, as well as a threat of a future unlawful act could, in appropriate circumstances, amount to 'illegitimate pressure' (at [30]–[36]).

8.6 **Lawful act duress**

Courts have accepted that the categories of duress are not closed and that a lawful threat may be illegitimate (eg *CTN Cash and Carry v Gallaher Ltd* (1994)), although it must 'at least be *immoral or unconscionable*' (*Alf Vaughan & Co Ltd v Royscot Trust plc* (1999) at 863). The threat may be to the victim's economic interests, reputation, or their concern to protect a loved one. The first step in mapping the uncertain scope of lawful act duress is to put aside the lawful threats which are generally permitted.

8.6.1 **Lawful pressure that is legitimate**

The following lawful threats are generally regarded as legitimate.

(i) Since the **threat not to contract** is implicit in all contractual negotiations, it is difficult to see how it can be objectionable in the absence of a doctrine of inequality of bargaining power or substantive unfairness. Duress was rejected in *Smith v Charlick Ltd* (1923) where the Wheat Board (with a monopoly on selling wheat) threatened to stop trading with S unless S agreed to pay more for the grain than that to which S was already contractually entitled.

(ii) A party's **refusal to waive** an existing contractual obligation is not economic duress (*Alec Lobb Garages Ltd v Total Oil Ltd* (1983)). Duress was denied in

Alf Vaughan v Royscot Trust where A bought cars from R but went into receivership with £34,000 owing under the hire-purchase agreement. R lawfully terminated the contract and threatened to recover the cars (as it was entitled to do) unless £82,000 was paid. A's receivers paid because the cars were necessary for the business to be sold as a going concern.

(iii) A party's **exercise of a right for legitimate purposes** does not amount to duress. In *R v Her Majesty's Attorney-General for England and Wales* (2003), an SAS soldier of the celebrated Bravo Two Zero patrol breached a confidentiality agreement by attempting to publish an account of his experiences. He argued that the agreement was voidable for duress since the Crown threatened to return him from the elite regiment to his regular unit unless he signed it. The Privy Council rejected his claim because the Crown's threat was not only lawful, being within its discretion to transfer soldiers, it was also reasonable, being legitimately concerned to prevent unauthorised disclosures which may threaten the security of its operations and personnel. The threat was lawful and the demand reasonable.

(iv) The law on **compromises of claim** legitimises advantages obtained from threats to sue to enforce an honest, even if mistaken, claim, particularly in a commercial context (see 3.1.3.6). In *CTN Cash and Carry v Gallaher*, G delivered C's order of £17,000 worth of cigarettes to the wrong warehouse. The cigarettes were subsequently stolen before the mistake was rectified. G nevertheless demanded payment from C, honestly but mistakenly believing that they were entitled to do so. G threatened to withdraw C's future credit facility if C did not pay. The Court of Appeal found no duress because G acted in good faith and was entitled to vary the terms of future contracts with C. The court stressed that lawful act duress would not be lightly found in arm's-length commercial dealings where certainty is paramount.

 Pause for reflection

1. In the *commercial* context, the lawfulness of the threat correlates very strongly with the legitimacy of the threat, overriding even clear bad faith as in *Smith v Charlick* and *Alf Vaughan v Royscot Trust*. However, the extraction of a sum which was, in truth, not due in *CTN Cash and Carry* prompted Sir Donald Nicholls VC to comment (at 720) that the outcome seemed unconscionable and to amount to unjust enrichment. The legitimacy of the demand should be relevant to the legitimacy of the pressure since, as Lord Scarman stated (in *Universe Tankships v International Transport Workers* at 400–1), duress can exist 'even if the threat is one of lawful action: whether it does so depends upon the nature of the demand'.

2. Beatson[9] argues that if the objectionable conduct or threat goes beyond the 'wrongful' to encompass the 'illegitimate' (which involves no breach of legal duty), then it is hard not to see economic duress as part of a general doctrine of inequality of bargaining power.

---

[9] 'Duress, Restitution and Contract Modification' in *The Use and Abuse of Unjust Enrichment* (Clarendon Press, 1990) 95.

8.6.2 **Lawful pressure that is illegitimate**

Borrelli, Cornforth Hill, Christensen (Liquidators) v James Ting (2010) is arguably the first case in which lawful act duress has been affirmed by a court. Here, T, the former chairman of Akai Holdings, failed to assist the liquidators in their investigation of Akai's affairs through 'a long process of evasion and prevarication'. T also resorted to forgery and the provision of false evidence to defeat the liquidator's proposed scheme to raise money to investigate T's possible misappropriation and false accounting. T only agreed to withdraw his opposition to the scheme in exchange for the liquidators agreeing not to pursue any claims against him arising out of or in connection with the company. The Privy Council held that:

(i)   economic duress can include unconscionable although lawful action for improper motive;

(ii) T's opposition 'was not made in good faith, but for an improper motive' (at [28]), and was 'unconscionable' (at [32]);

(iii) the liquidators had no reasonable or practical alternative but to make a deal with T, who had them over a barrel (at [31]).

Thus, it would offend justice to allow T to rely on the settlement to prevent the liquidators from suing him (at [33]), or to bar rescission because the parties could not be restored to the position created by T's illegitimate pressure. The settlement was set aside.

In addition three categories of cases can be interpreted as varieties of lawful act duress.

(i) Lord Scarman said in *Universe Tankships v International Transport Workers* (at 401, emphasis added) that: '**Blackmail** is often a demand supported by a threat to do what is lawful, eg to report criminal conduct to the police. In many cases, therefore, "What [one] has to justify is not the threat, but the demand"' (see also *Thorne v Motor Trade Association* (1937) at 806). Blackmail is unlawful under the Theft Act 1968 (s 2(1)).

(ii) Relief in **salvage cases** (involving threats not to rescue life or property on ships in distress unless extortionate terms are agreed) may be considered another long-standing, albeit hidden, example of lawful act duress. In **The Port Caledonia** (1903), two large laden vessels were sheltering from a storm in a harbour when one was dragged dangerously close to the other. The master of a rescue tug demanded '£1,000 or no rope'. This sum was set aside as extortionate and agreed under compulsion; £200 was substituted for the rescue services rendered.

(iii) Cases involving threats to harm the threatened party or their loved ones (by **threatening prosecution (Williams v Bayley** (1866)) **or publication of information** (*Norreys v Zeffert* (1939))) were historically decided as cases of *actual undue influence*. They belong more naturally in the category of lawful act duress.[10] In *Mutual Finance Ltd v John Wetton & Sons Ltd* (1937), Joseph Wetton forged the signatures

---

[10] P Birks and N Chin, 'On the Nature of Undue Influence' in J Beatson and D Friedmann (eds), *Good Faith and Fault in Contract Law* (Clarendon Press, 2005) 51, 63–7.

of his brother Percy and father John, directors of the defendant company, guaranteeing his friend's hire purchase to M. On the friend's default, M threatened to prosecute Joseph unless Percy paid on the guarantee. The court set aside Percy's agreement to honour the guarantee for actual undue influence because M knew that Percy only did so for fear that his father's life would be endangered by the shock of his brother's prosecution.

In a non-commercial context, the question of whether the lawful threat has been used to further a proper purpose is a useful starting point in deciding whether it is illegitimate in the context of duress. However, since the pursuit of profit is prima facie a legitimate purpose in a capitalist society,[11] intervention in commercial contracts induced by lawful threats is difficult to justify. Thus, lawful act duress is unlikely to have significant scope beyond relationships which are deemed by the law to warrant special protection, such as those in need of rescue and those who are dependent on, or otherwise vulnerable to, exploitation by the other party. The doctrines which more directly meet these concerns are examined in Chapter 9.

 Pause for reflection

The crime of blackmail and the public law concept of improper purpose suggest that the pathology in cases where relief has been granted lies in the *mismatch between* the *means* used (the threatened action) and the *ends* sought (the demand made). For example, whilst it is legitimate to publish information, inform the police, or threaten to do these, in support of proper purposes (eg freedom of information or the proper administration of justice), it is improper and so illegitimate to use them to make an unwarranted demand. The threatening party's conduct may be objectionable because he or she has:

1. *no legitimate basis* for the demand (as with blackmail);

2. a legitimate demand but directed *against the wrong party* (ie who does not owe it, as in *Williams v Bayley*, where B threatened to prosecute W's son if W did not pay on his son's forged promissory note); or

3. used *inappropriate means* in support of a legitimate demand; it has been expressed as using 'leverage' which rightly belongs to another, for example, that of:

   • the state in cases of threats to prosecute as in *Williams v Bayley*; and

   • the recipient of the information in cases of threats to inform.

8.6.3 Causation

Whilst the cases recognise the possibility of lawful act duress, there is a notable absence of discussion of the causation element. However, a high level of causation is

---

[11] Consistently, the tort of conspiracy to injure does not require unlawful means but regards increasing profit, market share, or wages as legitimate.

implicit in the cases identified as likely candidates for lawful act duress (blackmail, salvage, and actual undue influence by threats to prosecute or inform). The applicable test here should be the usual one in the law of obligations, the '*but for*' test to be proved by the claimant.

Diagram 8B gives a summary of duress.

Diagram 8B Overview of duress: requirements and policies

	Duress to the PERSON	Duress to PROPERTY	ECONOMIC duress	LAWFUL ACT duress
1. Illegitimate pressure	Unlawful threat	Unlawful threat	Unlawful threat to breach contract *Should it always be illegitimate?*	Immoral or unconscionable threat
– Demand	Generally unwarranted	Generally unwarranted	Generally unwarranted	Generally unwarranted
– Good faith	No mention but unlikely	No mention but unlikely	Relevant but inconclusive	Relevant but inconclusive
2. Causation	'A' cause	'But for' cause, readily inferred	At least 'but for' cause; clinching or decisive cause *Inconsistently applied*	No mention but necessarily implicit to high degree
3. No practicable alternative	No mention	No mention	Formal requirement	No mention but necessarily implicit
Policy considerations	• *Protection of physical integrity* • *Wrongdoers should not profit from own wrong*	• *Protection of property rights* • *Wrongdoers should not profit from own wrong*	• *Promote sanctity of contract* • *Prevent exploitation* **BUT** *modification may be desirable because:* •*Change of circumstances has made performance impossible without it* •*The victim cannot obtain actual performance without it* •*It is economically efficient* •*It encourages cooperation and accommodation in contracts*	• *Prevents lawful but unconscionable conduct* • *Prevents abuse of power* **BUT** *uncertainty in drawing the line*

8.7 **Aggressive commercial practices**

Regulation 7 of the Consumer Protection from Unfair Trading Regulations 2008 (SI 2008/1277) proscribes aggressive commercial practices, and the Consumer Protection (Amendment) Regulations 2014 (2014/870) allows the consumer to seek redress in such cases (see Chapter 5 Introduction). A commercial practice is aggressive if: (i) it significantly impairs (or is likely significantly to impair) the average consumer's freedom of choice or conduct in relation to the product concerned through the use of **harassment**, **coercion**, or **undue influence**; and (ii) it thereby causes or is likely to cause him or her to take a transactional decision that he or she would not have taken otherwise. 'Coercion' includes the use of physical force; and 'undue influence' means exploiting a position of power in relation to the consumer so as to apply pressure, even without using or threatening to use physical force, in a way which significantly limits the consumer's ability to make an informed decision.

THIS CHAPTER IN ESSENCE

online resource centre

The key areas and core topics in this chapter are summarised in an easy-to-use list, ideal for revision purposes, on the Online Resource Centre at http://www.oxfordtextbooks.co.uk/orc/chenwishart5e/. Links to websites relevant to the topics covered and any updates to the chapter can also be found on the Online Resource Centre.

QUESTIONS

1 In February, Samson agrees to make crucial deliveries of Tara's speciality candles for the pre-Christmas trade for £1,000. Samson fails to make a number of deliveries and explains that this is because he had a small heart attack (from which he has recovered but, under doctor's orders, must take it easier) and because petrol prices had increased by 300% because of international events. He tells Tara that unless she agrees to increase the price to £3,000 and reduce the number of deliveries by 40%, the deliveries will not be made. He adds: 'What we agreed just can't be done. I'll go bust or keel over and that's no use to you.' Tara reluctantly agrees as she feels she has no other choice at this late stage. Samson makes the deliveries. Advise Tara.

2 How do the doctrines of economic duress, consideration, promissory estoppel, and frustration apply in the context of one-sided contract modifications?

3 'The current law on economic duress is a mess. It is unclear what pressure and how much pressure is required.' Do you agree?

4 Giving examples, how is the line, and how should it be, drawn between threats of lawful action which are legitimate and those which are illegitimate?

For hints on how to answer these questions, please see the Online Resource Centre at http://www.oxfordtextbooks.co.uk/orc/chenwishart5e/

KEY FURTHER READING

Atiyah, P S (1982), 'Economic Duress and the Overborne Will', 98 *LQR* 197.

Beatson, J (1990), 'Duress, Restitution and Contract Modification' in *The Use and Abuse of Unjust Enrichment* (Clarendon Press) 95.

Birks, P (1990), 'The Travails of Duress', *LMCLQ* 342.

Enonchong, N (2005), *Duress, Undue Influence and Unconscionable Bargains* (Sweet & Maxwell).

Tiplady, D (1983), 'Concepts of Duress', 99 *LQR* 188.

9

Unfairness: undue influence, non-commercial guarantees, unconscionable bargains

'You took advantage of me'

9.1 **Introduction**

In contrast to continental civil systems, English law recognises no general principle controlling unfairness in contracting. Instead, it has developed *piecemeal solutions* to particular problems of unfairness (per Bingham LJ, *Interfoto Picture Library Ltd v Stiletto Visual Programmes Ltd* (1988) at 620–1). We have seen that contracts may be vitiated by doctrines which focus on the **blameworthy conduct** of the enforcing party (**the defendant**), thus:

- *misrepresentation* deals with fraud and induced mistakes (Chapter 5); and
- *duress* deals with illegitimate pressure (Chapter 8).

Other vitiating doctrines focus on **the claimant's defective consent**:

- *mistake* deals with un-induced mistakes (Chapter 6);
- *frustration* deals with radical change of circumstances which fundamentally alters the significance of the contract made (Chapter 7); and

online resource centre

- *incapacity* deals with the most obvious causes of defective consent: youth, mental infirmity, alcohol, or drugs. This is summarised at the end of this chapter and discussed in more detail in Additional Chapter 1 which is available on the Online Resource Centre.

In this chapter, we examine the less obvious cases of impairment and blameworthy inducement which may nevertheless vitiate contracts:

- *undue influence* deals with the abuse of relationships of trust and confidence;
- a doctrine protecting *non-commercial* parties who guarantee another's debts; and
- *unconscionable bargains* which deal with the exploitation of bargaining weaknesses.

These doctrines are difficult to plot in terms of the pathology (unfairness) they seek to remedy. Here, the claimant's *bargaining impairment* may qualify them for relief, although it is not attributable to a present or future mistake, not as clear-cut as minority, or as severe as mental incapacity. Likewise, the defendant may be denied enforcement although he or she has *not acted unlawfully* in procuring the contract but merely 'against conscience'.

Two conflicting ideas wrestle for dominance here: the *fiction of equality* in respect of all adults of sound mind, and the *reality of inequality* which, to some degree, colours every contractual negotiation (see 1.3.3). Neither idea can be fully recognised by the law. To require exact equality of bargaining power would leave no contract standing. But the law is not blind to weaknesses short of recognised incapacities, which impair the ability of parties to negotiate reasonable deals in their own self-interests. Such parties are easier *targets for exploitation* by contracting, without the need for any independently unlawful conduct, misrepresentation, duress, breach of fiduciary obligations, or the like.

The traditional justification for the doctrines which will be discussed in this chapter is firmly anchored in *procedural unfairness*. The doctrines focus on the process of contract formation and are 'content-independent' reasons of invalidity. Namely:

(i)   the *defective consent* of the 'weaker' claimant; or

(ii) the *reprehensible conduct* of the 'stronger' defendant.

On the other hand, *substantive unfairness* will often be the most conspicuous feature of the contracts avoided by these doctrines. This suggests a third justification for invalidity and this is 'content-dependent', namely:

(iii) *relief from improvident transactions* granted to the bargaining impaired.

These justifications overlap. It is often said that 'equity will relieve a party from a contract which he has been induced to make as a result of victimisation. Equity will not relieve a party from a contract on the ground only that there is contractual imbalance not amounting to unconscionable dealing' (**Hart v O'Connor** (1985) at 1018). However, while it will often be very difficult to pinpoint the procedural unfairness being targeted, the improvidence of the transaction to the claimant is usually glaring in cases where relief is granted. The questions to be addressed are the following.

(i)   What is the *justification* for these doctrines?

(ii) What is the *burden of proof* for undue influence, unfair non-commercial guarantees, and unconscionable bargains?

(iii) *In practice*, how is each element of the respective burdens of proof satisfied?

(iv) Is the law *satisfactory*? If not, how might it be developed in the future?

(v)   Should English law adopt a *general principle against unfair contracting*?

9.2 **Undue influence**

Undue influence concerns the *exploitation of a relationship of influence to obtain an undue advantage* (*R v Attorney-General for England and Wales* (2003) at [21]). In *Tate v Williamson* (1866), Lord Chelmsford LC said (at 61):

Wherever two persons stand in such a relation that, while it continues, confidence is necessarily reposed by one, and the influence which naturally grows out of that confidence is possessed by the other, and this confidence is abused, or the influence is exerted to obtain an advantage at the expense of the confiding party, the person so availing himself of his position will not be permitted to retain the advantage, although the transaction could not have been impeached if no such confidential relation had existed.

9.2.1 **Basis of the doctrine**

9.2.1.1 Unconscientious conduct

The dominant view, found in many recent leading cases,[1] including *Royal Bank of Scotland plc v Etridge (No 2)* (2001), is that undue influence is about the defendant's reprehensible conduct in inducing the claimant's agreement to the transaction. Lord Nicholls' leading judgment, with which the other Lordships agreed, explains that the doctrine seeks to (at [6]–[7]):

> ensure that the influence of one person over another is not abused. In everyday life people constantly seek to . . . persuade those with whom they are dealing to enter into transactions, whether great or small. The law has set limits to the means properly employable for this purpose . . . If the intention was produced by an unacceptable means, the law will not permit the transaction to stand. The means used is regarded as an exercise of improper or 'undue' influence, and hence unacceptable, whenever the consent thus procured ought not fairly to be treated as the expression of a person's free will.

▶◀ Counterpoint

1. *Uncertain*: it is seldom clear what the defendant has done wrong.

2. *Unnecessary*: it is unnecessary to find any unconscientious behaviour at all. In *Jennings v Cairns* (2003), Arden LJ said (at [40]) 'the fact that the conduct of the person exercising influence is unimpeachable is not by itself an answer to a claim in undue influence'. This suggests that the real objection lies elsewhere.

3. *Contrary to authority*: the classic case of *Allcard v Skinner* (1887) is inconsistent with an unconscientious conduct rationale.

In *Allcard v Skinner*, a young novice nun took a vow of poverty, chastity, and obedience and gave all her worldly possessions to the Mother Superior of the convent. The rules imposed the most absolute submission by the sisters to the Mother Superior who was to be regarded as the 'voice of God': they could not seek advice outside the sisterhood without her permission. The novice eventually left the sisterhood and sought the return of what remained of her gifts. The undue influence doctrine applies equally to gifts and contracts and the gift here was held to be tainted by presumed undue influence, although the court acquitted the Mother Superior of any active exploitation. She did not act selfishly, preferring her own interests. Indeed, she must have regarded it as in the novice's own best interest to be divested of her worldly goods. Nevertheless, *objectively*, according to the standards of equity, the parties' relationship, and the resulting improvidence of the transaction to the novice, the Mother Superior *failed to do all that she should have to protect the novice's interests* (see 9.2.1.3).

---

[1] Eg *R v Attorney-General for England and Wales* (2003) and *National Commercial Bank (Jamaica) Ltd v Hew* (2003).

At the same time, Lindley LJ (at 184) said that everything she did was 'referable to her own willing submission to the vows she took and to the rules which she approved, and to her own enthusiastic devotion to the life and work of the sister-hood', and (at 178) that nothing justified 'the inference that she was unable to take care of herself or to manage her own affairs'. Bowen LJ (at 189) continued that even 'persons who are under the most complete influence of religious feeling are perfectly free to act upon it in the disposition of their property, and not the less free because they are enthusiasts. Persons of this kind are not dead in law'. This gives a lie to the following justification.

9.2.1.2 Defective consent

In **'On the Nature of Undue Influence'** in J Beatson and D Friedmann (eds), *Good Faith and Fault in Contract Law* (Clarendon Press, 1995), **Birks and Chin** argue that undue influence is concerned with the claimant's defective consent in the sense of their 'excessive' or 'morbid dependency'. He or she 'lacks the capacity for self-management'; their judgment is 'markedly substandard' or 'impaired to an exceptional degree'.

◀▶ Counterpoint

1. *Uncertain and contrary to authority*: it is impossible to draw the line between appropriate and inappropriate levels of dependency. Although Birks and Chin (at 87) suggest that 'the law relieves only an extreme loss of autonomy', something beyond the 99th percentile, since adults of 'widely differing intelligence and personality come under all sorts of different influences, and must be presumed able to cope', the cases do not draw the line so restrictively. *A relationship of influence* is a broad notion and potentially encompasses anyone you love, like, respect, work with, or can be said to have common cause with. It is only when your transaction with that person is disastrously imbalanced against you that the question of undue influence arises.

2. *Unrealistic*: it is unrealistic to say that the novice in *Allcard v Skinner* lacked autonomy or that her consent was 'impaired'. As Lord Nicholls said in *Etridge* (at [6]–[7]), the victim's consent is only *deemed* to be defective *when* the trusted party has acted unacceptably.

3. *Trusting is not pathological*: undue influence claimants (like the former nun) may be naive, romantic or idealistic, trusting, and even altruistic, but they should not be regarded as thereby 'subnormal'. When the nun gave away her worldly possessions, she did not lack autonomy—she *exercised* it. There is nothing intrinsically wrong with the existence or use of influence. As Kekewich J said in *Allcard v Skinner* (at 157–8): 'The law . . . recognises influence as natural and right. Few, if any, men are gifted with characters enabling them to act, or even think, with complete independence of others, which could not largely exist without destroying the foundations of society. But the law requires that influence, however natural and however right, shall not be unduly exercised'.

➡

➡️

4. In 'Undue Influence: *Beyond* Impaired Consent and Wrong-Doing, Towards a Relational Analysis' in A Burrows and A Rodger (eds), *Mapping the Law, Essays in Memory of Peter Birks* (OUP, 2006), I explain why undue influence cannot be explained solely by reference to either the claimant's impaired consent, or the defendant's role in distorting consent.

5. In 'Undue influence: "Impaired Consent" or "Wicked Exploitation"?' (1995) 16 *OJLS* 503, Bigwood argues that Birks and Chin are wrong because impaired consent and exploitation are inseparable. In 'Contracts by Unfair Advantage: From Exploitation to Transactional Neglect' (2005) 25 *OJLS* 65, he argues that the best explanation for some undue influence and unconscionable bargain cases is the defendant's failure to act reasonably on its knowledge of the likelihood of claimant disadvantage.

9.2.1.3 Failure to protect

Allcard v Skinner describes the undue influence doctrine as 'a fetter placed upon the conscience of the [trusted party], and one which arises out of public policy and fair play' (at 190). In *Etridge* (at [9]), undue influence was described in terms of the defendant 'preferring his own interests' and 'failing to protect the claimant's interests'. Here, the language of advantage-taking and victimisation designates an *omission*: a failure by the defendant to protect the claimant's interest as the parties' relationship requires.

> ### 👤 **Pause for reflection**
>
> In 'Undue Influence: Vindicating Relationships of Influence' (2006) 59 *CLP* 231, I set out a relational theory of undue influence. Relationships are vital to our quality of life. Close relationships such as marriage, romance, family, care, and friendship trigger implicit *relational norms* about how people in such relationships treat each other. They determine the appropriate range of *behaviour* and of *outcomes* that are constitutive of (define) the relationship and are implicit in the distinction between 'due' and 'undue' influence. Undue influence targets the unfair outcome procured by the defendant's violations of the implicit *substantive* norm of the parties' relationship of influence by the defendant's acceptance of a benefit, which entails glaring disadvantages to the claimant. It also covers the defendant's violations of the implicit *procedural* norm of the parties' relationship by applying pressure on the claimant to agree, although much less is required than for duress because of the relationship. Given that influence is not bad in itself, it is impossible to tell whether its exercise/effect was 'due' or 'undue' without reference to the fairness of the outcome. An unfair outcome is the 'bad thing' against which the claimant is protected. If the defendant violates these norms, the transaction cannot stand even if he or she has not acted illegitimately to procure the claimant's consent and even if he or she acts in good faith.

9.2.2 **Overview and burden of proof**

9.2.2.1 The *traditional* categories of undue influence

Allcard v Skinner (at 171) sets out two categories of undue influence[2] which, despite the refinements by *Etridge*, remain substantially intact.

(i) **Class 1 Actual undue influence**: where the claimant can prove the defendant's positive application of pressure inducing his or her consent to the contract.

(ii) **Class 2 Presumed undue influence**: from the claimant's proof that:

    (a) he or she was in a 'relationship of trust and confidence' with the defendant:

- **Class 2A** covers specified relationships where the influence is automatically presumed;

- **Class 2B** describes relationships outside Class 2A where the existence of influence must be *proved*;

    (b) the resulting transaction is manifestly disadvantageous to the claimant.

This raises a *presumption of undue influence* which can be rebutted by the defendant's proof that the claimant nevertheless entered the transaction freely (usually by evidence of the presence of independent advice).

9.2.2.2 The restatement by *Etridge*

In *Etridge*, the House of Lords said that too much should not be made of the distinctions between the traditional categories of undue influence, particularly Class 2B. Doing so was apt to lead to error and confusion (at [17], [92], [107], [158]). The old categories did not reflect different bases for intervention, but are merely **different ways of proving *one* category of undue influence**. The **burden of proof** lies on the claimant throughout (at [13], [16], [17]). Lord Clyde (at [93]) said:

> At the end of the day, after trial, there will either be proof of undue influence or that proof will fail and it will be found that there was no undue influence. In the former case, whatever the relationship of the parties and however the influence was exerted, there will be found to have been an actual case of undue influence. In the latter there will be none.

The claimant proves undue influence, either actually or with the benefit of an evidential inference (a presumption), which remained un-rebutted.

9.2.3 **Failure to protect by *overt pressure* (old actual undue influence)**

9.2.3.1 Relational pressure

Once we move the cases dealing with threats to prosecute and to disclose into the category of lawful act duress (see 8.6.2), we are left with cases involving the defendant's

---

[2] See also *Bank of Credit and Commerce International SA v Aboody (BCCI v Aboody)* (1990) at 953; *Barclays Bank v O'Brien* (1994) at 189–90.

overt exploitation of the claimant's relational motivation for consenting. The overt exploitation can take a number of forms.

(i) Threats to abandon

✓ In *Langton v Langton* (1995), the son and daughter-in-law of a man moved in with him after his release from prison for murdering his wife. They knew he feared further institutionalisation and threatened to stop caring for him as his health deteriorated if he did not transfer his property to them.

✓ In *Bank of Scotland v Bennett* (1997), the husband used wounding and insulting language to accuse his wife of disloyalty in contrast to the loyalty of his relatives. He said she would be a 'waste of rations' if she refused to guarantee his business debt and would be splitting up the family. The judge found 'moral blackmail amounting to coercion and victimisation'.

(ii) Excessive control, secrecy, and exclusion of others

✓ In *Morley v Loughan* (1893), M became a member of the 'Exclusive Brethren' and went to live with L in practical seclusion for the last seven years of his life. M was physically frail and L controlled every aspect of his life including his diet and medicines. M placed his entire fortune of £140,000 at L's disposal.

✓ In *Re Killick v Pountney and another* (2000), K had been P's lodger for 40 years (since he was 32). As K's health failed and he entered a nursing home, P took over his possessions and papers. P banned K from contact with his relatives on threat of not allowing him to come home after hospital, which terrified him. K's will provided very generously for P.

(iii) Bullying, confrontation, and harassment

✓ In *Clarke v Prus* (1995), after the elderly C's wife died, he was befriended by the younger P. C gave P gifts totalling £1.9 million over some 20 years. The court held that 'what started out as Mr Clarke's folly . . . finished up as Mrs Prus' victimisation at the end of his life' when her requests turned into increasingly vehement demands made by verbal onslaughts and oppressive harassment.

✓ In *Drew v Daniel* (2005), Daniel coerced his aged aunt to confer a significant benefit on him at the expense of her own son in a distressing and lengthy conversation, coupled by his threat to sue her. He concealed his dealings from her son and her solicitor. Ward LJ found Daniel's conduct 'unacceptable' in view of Drew's vulnerability, naivety in business, and fear of confrontation.

✓ In *Re Craig* (1971), the court *inferred* overt coercion from past dealings. An 84-year-old man hired a companion after his wife's death. Over the next six years he transferred three-quarters of his wealth to her. The court found no direct evidence of pressure but said that 'the amount of the gifts, the circumstances in which they were made, the vulnerability of Mr Craig to pressure by Mrs Middleton [the companion], the evidence of the direct exercise of that pressure on other occasions and for other purposes, the knowledge of Mr Craig and Mrs Middleton of his utter dependence on her, and the whole history of the relationship' persuaded the court (at 121) that the gifts were the product of actual undue influence.

9.2.3.2 Relationship of influence and manifest disadvantage

Proof of actual undue influence is traditionally thought to *dispense* with the need for two elements necessary for the inference (presumption) of undue influence:

(i) the existence of a **relationship of influence** between the parties (because proof of undue pressure is enough, see *Chitty* at para 7-063; *Anson's* at 360); and

(ii) **manifest disadvantage** of the transaction to the claimant; it was held in *CIBC Mortgages v Pitt* (1993) that: 'actual undue influence is a species of fraud . . . A man guilty of fraud is no more entitled to argue that the transaction was beneficial to the person defrauded than is a man who has procured a transaction by misrepresentation' (at 439 and *Chitty* at paras 7-058, 7-062).

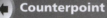 **Counterpoint**

Both these exclusions are questionable.

1. It is the relationship of influence that makes the, otherwise low-level, coercion (harassment, emotional blackmail, or bullying, which would not register on the radar of the duress doctrine) legally relevant.

2. There is a world of difference between a mother pressuring her children to do their homework and her pressuring them to hand over their savings. The outcome colours the determination of whether the pressure applied is 'due' or 'undue'. In *Etridge*, Lord Nicholls (at [12]) affirms the necessity and importance of finding a 'transaction not readily explicable by the parties' relationship' (the preferred formulation to 'manifest disadvantage'); an allegation of undue influence 'is likely to arise only when, in some respect, the transaction was disadvantageous'. Moreover, an unfair outcome is evidence that the pressure, and not something else, induced the claimant's agreement.

9.2.4 **Failure to protect by *omission* (old presumed undue influence)**

9.2.4.1 The burden of proof

This category maps on to the old Class 2 (presumed undue influence). In *Etridge*, Lord Nicholls (at [14]) said:[3]

Proof that the complainant placed trust and confidence in the other party in relation to the management of the complainant's financial affairs, coupled with a transaction which calls for explanation, will normally be sufficient, failing satisfactory evidence to the contrary, to discharge the burden of proof. On proof of these two matters the stage is set for the Court to infer that, in the absence of a satisfactory explanation, the transaction can only have been procured by undue influence. In other words, proof of these two facts is *prima facie* evidence that the defendant abused the influence he acquired in the parties' relationship. He preferred his own

---

[3] See also [16]–[17]; Lord Clyde at [93]; Lord Hobhouse at [104]–[107]; Lord Scott at [156], [161].

interests. He did not behave fairly to the other. So the evidential burden then shifts to him. It is for him to produce evidence to counter the inference which otherwise should be drawn.

The key point is that the presumption raised is not *legal*; this *would* reverse the burden of proof or make the presumption irrebuttable. Rather, the presumption is *evidential*; it merely allows an inference to be drawn, analogous in operation to the doctrine of *res ipsa loquitur* ('the facts speak for themselves'). Talk of 'rebuttal of the presumption' merely refers to a shift of the evidential onus to the defendant to *displace* the **evidential inference** raised by the claimant in the first place; the burden of proof is not reversed. What is needed to counter the inference will depend on the *weight* of the inference; it may prove very difficult, even impossible, to shift on the facts.

The inference is *not* that the defendant has exerted undue pressure on the claimant, but that he or she has **preferred their own interests and failed to safeguard the claimant's**. '[T]he question is whether one party has reposed sufficient trust and confidence in the other' such that the latter owes the former 'an obligation of candour and protection' (at [9]–[10]) which he or she has failed to observe. The answer depends on the nature of the parties' relationship and the fairness of their transaction.

9.2.4.2 Relationship of influence: automatic presumption (old Class 2A)

In *Etridge*, Lord Nicholls explains (at [18]) that: 'The law has adopted a sternly protective attitude towards certain types of relationship in which one party acquires influence over another who is vulnerable and dependent and where, moreover, substantial gifts by the influenced or vulnerable person are not normally to be expected.' Well-known examples falling within this category are:

- doctor and patient;
- solicitor and client;
- parent and child;
- guardian and ward;
- trustee and beneficiary;
- religious adviser and disciple; and
- more controversially, a man and his fiancée although not a husband and wife (*Leeder v Stevens* (2005)).

These relationships trigger an irrebuttable (*legal*) presumption of the existence of a relationship of influence. This must be distinguished sharply from the *evidential* presumption of undue influence which arises when a relationship of influence is coupled with a transaction calling for an explanation.

Pause for reflection

1. In 'The Irrebuttable Presumption of Influence and the Relationship between Fiancé and Fiancée' (2005) 121 *LQR* 567, 569, **Enonchong** observes that this 'leaves the law in a curious position. For, the law would be saying that couples who are engaged to be married ➡

→ repose sufficient trust and confidence in one another but that the trust and confidence somehow evaporate as soon as they are married'. This would also seem to contradict the Supreme Court decision in *Radmacher v Granatino* (2010) that pre-nuptial agreements should be regarded as presumptively enforceable (see 2.7.2).

2. Even in these cases, it should be possible to rebut the presumption of undue influence by specific evidence that *this particular* relationship was *not* one of influence. People are not as obedient and compliant in status relationships as they were when this category was developed. Thus, Lord Clyde's view that Class 2A simply raises a *rebuttable* evidential presumption on very strong facts is preferable (at [93]).

9.2.4.3 Proved relationship of influence (old Class 2B)

Relationships of influence 'tend to arise where someone relies on the guidance or advice of another, where the other is aware of that reliance and where the person upon whom reliance is placed obtains, or may well obtain, a benefit from the transaction or has some other interest in it being concluded' (*Lloyds Bank v Bundy* (1975) at 510–11). The following points can be distilled from the case law.

(i) There is often an element of exclusivity in the relevant relationship. Its essence from the **claimant's side** is an expectation that the defendant will give conscientious advice in the claimant's interest. Therefore, the claimant lets down their guard and may not consciously self-protect or seek outside advice. **The defendant** knows of, and has participated in, the relationship (eg has encouraged or acquiesced in the claimant's reliance and trust), thereby raising an obligation to restrain his or her self-interest and having regard to the claimant's interests when transacting with them.

(ii) It is **unnecessary to prove 'blind, unquestioning trust'** or a **'dominating influence'** (*Tufton v Sperni* (1952)). It is enough that in past dealings the claimant generally reposed trust and confidence in the defendant. Typical examples include:

- a wife and her husband (*BCCI v Aboody* (1990));
- parents and their adult child (*Avon Finance v Bridger* (1985));
- a great-uncle and great-nephew (*Cheese v Thomas* (1994));
- an elderly man and his housekeeper-companion (*Re Craig*);
- a customer and a bank (*Lloyds Bank v Bundy*);
- a pop singer and his manager (*O'Sullivan v Management Agency and Music Ltd* (1985));
- an elderly farmer and his farm manager (*Goldsworthy v Brikell* (1987)); and
- a junior employee and her employer (*Crédit Lyonnais v Burch* (1997)).

(iii) Reliance may be exacerbated by the **claimant's illness or frailty, incompetence, or inexperience** (eg *Re Craig, Goldsworthy v Brikell, Tufton v Sperni*; here, there is an overlap with unconscionable bargains, see 9.4).

(iv) A relationship of influence may even arise in a **one-off dealing**. In *Tufton v Sperni*, T (a convert with no business experience) wanted to set up a centre for Muslim culture in London. S (another Muslim with business expertise) was brought on to the committee overseeing the project. S sold his own house to T for the project at more than twice its market value and reserved numerous privileges including a right to substitute other premises at his complete discretion. The transaction was set aside. Evershed MR (at 523) paints a very wide catchment: '[I]f a number of persons join together for the purpose of furthering some charitable or altruistic objective, it would seem not unreasonable to conclude that in regard to all matters related to that objective, each "necessarily reposes confidence" in the others and each possesses accordingly that "influence which naturally grows out of confidence".'

(v) The **unfairness of the transaction** provides strong evidence of a relationship of influence. Alternatively, substantive unfairness can be seen as narrowing the potential width of 'relationships of influence'. For example, in *Crédit Lyonnais v Burch*, a young junior employee gave a personal guarantee and an unlimited charge on her flat to secure her employer's existing debt to the bank and slightly extend his overdraft facility. Direct evidence of a potentially exploitative relationship of influence with her employer was flimsy: she had worked for him for ten years and sometimes babysat and visited his family in London and Italy. Millett LJ (at 154–5) explains that:

> [T]he mere fact that a transaction is improvident or manifestly disadvantageous to one party is not sufficient by itself to give rise to a presumption that it has been obtained by the exercise of undue influence; but where it is obtained by a party between whom and the complainant there is a relationship like that of employer and junior employee which is easily capable of developing into a relationship of trust and confidence, the nature of the transaction may be sufficient to justify the inference that such a development has taken place; and where the transaction is so extravagantly improvident that it is virtually inexplicable on any other basis, the inference will be readily drawn.

Conversely, no inference will be drawn if an apparently disadvantageous transaction *is* explicable. In *Re Brocklehurst's Estate* (1978), an elderly aristocrat, without independent advice, gave a garage proprietor a 99-year lease of the shooting rights over his estate. This heavily reduced the value of the estate. The court's conclusion that no relationship of trust and confidence existed between the parties coincided with its finding that the gift was a 'spontaneous and independent act' explicable in terms of the friendship between the parties and the donor's desire to deliberately reduce the estate's value before it was inherited by a detested nephew.

9.2.4.4 A transaction calling for explanation

Coupled with a relationship of influence, the unfairness of the transaction operates to raise the inference (or presumption) that the relationship of influence has been *exploited*. It is evidence of the defendant's failure to safeguard the claimant's interests (*Etridge* at [104]).

The requirement, formerly called 'manifest disadvantage', was confirmed in the modern law by *National Westminster Bank plc v Morgan* (1985), it was dispensed with in cases of actual undue influence (*CIBC Mortgages v Pitt*), and its necessity in presumed undue influence cases was questioned (*Barclays Bank v Coleman* (2000)). The House of Lords in *Etridge* affirmed its necessity and importance, although their Lordships criticised the expression 'manifest disadvantage'. The expression is inappropriate in the *husband and wife situation* where, typically, the wife agrees to guarantee or provide security to support a bank's loan to her husband but later claims that she did so because of her husband's undue influence or misrepresentation (see further 9.3; *Etridge* at [26]–[27]). It is an error to treat such guarantees as *always* bad for the wife (because she undertakes an onerous financial obligation while personally receiving nothing in return), or as *never* bad for her (because her fortunes are bound up with her husband's, particularly if his business is the source of the family income). Rather, the inference of undue influence arises when the transaction is 'not readily explicable by the parties' relationship' (at [28]–[29]). Lord Nicholls, relying on Lindley LJ's judgment in *Allcard v Skinner*, justifies the substantive requirement as (at [24]):

> a necessary limitation upon the width of the first prerequisite [the relationship of influence]. It would be absurd for the law to presume that every gift by a child to a parent, or every transaction between a client and their solicitor or between a patient and their doctor, was brought about by undue influence unless the contrary is affirmatively proved. Such a presumption would be too far-reaching . . . The law would be rightly open to ridicule, for transactions such as these are unexceptionable. They do not suggest that something may be amiss. So something more is needed before the law reverses the burden of proof, something which calls for an explanation. When that something more is present, the greater the disadvantage to the vulnerable person, the more cogent must be the explanation before the presumption will be regarded as rebutted.

When does a transaction 'call for explanation'? It must entail a disadvantage that would 'have been obvious as such to any independent and reasonable person who considered the transaction at the time with knowledge of all the relevant facts', and not if it only 'emerges after a fine and close evaluation of its various beneficial and detrimental features' (*BCCI v Aboody* at 965). It is not simply a matter of disproportionate exchange measured against some objective market price. Four relevant considerations can be deduced from the case law.

(i) Impact on the claimant's future autonomy
Transactions entailing such an extreme degree of improvidence that they threaten the claimant's future autonomy will 'call for an explanation'. This is why most undue influence cases involve the loss of the claimant's home or of the vast proportion of the claimant's wealth.

✓ This was arguably the real problem in *Allcard v Skinner*. Describing the novice's gift to the church as 'calling for explanation' is misleading (because it is perfectly explicable by her devotion); it is a shorthand for saying that it is *objectively inappropriate*. The gift substantially undermined her future autonomy because it failed to provide for the contingency that she might later choose a different life and need some resources. Even if it was unobjectionable for the Mother Superior to accept the original gift, her refusal to release the nun (when the parties' assumption at the time it was made had changed) and return what was left of the gift, violated the implicit norms of the relationship.

✓ In *Hammond v Osborn* (2002), H (an elderly and frail man), was befriended by O (a neighbour), who helped him as he became increasingly infirm over 18 months. O claimed that H told her to cash in all his investments (some £300,000 worth) and to keep the proceeds. In finding undue influence, the court emphasised that the sum represented 92% of his liquid assets, while making him liable for capital gains tax of £50,000; H would be unable to meet the costs of his care as he became more infirm.

(ii) Consistency with the nature of the parties' relationship

A relationship of influence does not bar transactions between the parties to it, 'something more is needed before the law reverses the burden of proof . . . the greater the disadvantage to the vulnerable person, the more cogent must be the explanation before the presumption will be regarded as rebutted' (*Etridge* at [24], [28]–[29]). A transaction which is disproportionate to the gratitude, love, or affection evinced by the evolution of the party's relationship will 'call for an explanation'.

✗ *Portman Building Society v Dusangh* (2000) shows that guarantees by parents to support loans to their children, while improvident for the parents, are regarded as unexceptional and 'capable of reasonable explanation on the basis of parental affection'.

✓ In contrast, in finding undue influence in *Crédit Lyonnais v Burch*, Swinton Thomas LJ observed (at 158) that: '[I]t would cause a bank manager to raise his eyebrows more than a little when he was engaged in entering into a contract with a young employee which involved guaranteeing her employer's indebtedness in the sum of £270,000, and mortgaging her home to the bank.'

✓ Recall *Hammond v Osborn*, Ward LJ commented (at [58]) that the gift was: '[W]holly out of proportion to the kindness shown to him. Looking at the matter objectively, it was an irrational decision, not a good one. The very scale of the gift with the disadvantageous consequences that ensued serves only, in my judgment, to heighten the anxiety which founds this presumption, namely that pressure was operating on his mind.'

(iii) Consistency with the claimant's relationship with others

✓ In *Randall v Randall* (2004), the court set aside gifts of land made by an elderly woman to her nephew because, inter alia, they were inconsistent with her desire to protect her beloved donkeys living on part of the land; they made no provision for, or effectively disinherited, other close relatives including the nephew's own mother who lived on part of the land; and they divested her of all the property in the twilight of her life when she would need extra care.

✓ In *Humphreys v Humphreys* (2005), a mother's improvident transfer of her home to her son when she had six other children called for an explanation.

✓ Similarly, in *Pesticcio v Huet* (2004), a man's transfer of his home to his sister was suspicious since it would leave his beloved mother without a home.

(iv) The explicability of any apparent improvidence

Contracts which are not obviously unfair at the time of formation are unobjectionable even if made between people in close relationships. Conversely, transactions which appear very improvident may not be so on closer examination, or may otherwise be satisfactorily explained.

✗ In *National Commercial Bank (Jamaica) Ltd v Hew* (2003), H (a 74-year-old business-man) agreed an overdraft facility of $3 million (for a land development) with C (the branch manager of N bank). The Privy Council found that even assuming a relationship of trust and confidence between H and C, N derived no 'benefits which it would not have sought to obtain from an ordinary arm's-length transaction with a commercial borrower . . . [I]t was not the Bank's responsibility to save Mr Hew from the consequences of embarking upon an unwise project [which was not known to be unwise at the time]'.

✗ In *R v Attorney-General for England and Wales*, the Privy Council accepted that the Army's authority over R gave it considerable influence over R. But, the *reasonableness of R's agreement* not to divulge his activities as a member of the SAS gave rise to no inference that it was obtained by an unfair exploitation of that relationship, even though R lacked independent advice.

✗ Recall that undue influence was denied in *Re Brocklehurst's Estate* where the claimant's gift of a 99-year lease of the shooting rights over his estate was explicable by his desire to reduce its value to his detested nephew who would inherit it.

✗ Similarly, no undue influence was found in *Campbell v Campbell* (1996), where the claimant gave her house to one of her children whom she believed had been imprisoned unjustifiably.

9.2.4.5 Rebutting the presumption

To rebut the evidential presumption of undue influence raised by the claimant's proof of a relationship of influence and a transaction calling for explanation, the defendant must show that the claimant's consent to the transaction was 'full, free and informed' (*Zamet v Hyman* (1961) at 1446). The usual way is by showing that the claimant received adequate independent advice, although this is unnecessary if it can be otherwise proved (*Inche Noriah v Omar* (1929) at 135). The claimant's understanding of the transaction is necessary, but not sufficient. As Lord Nicholls (*Etridge* at [20]) explains:

[A] person may understand fully the implications of a proposed transaction . . . and yet still be acting under the undue influence of another. Proof of outside advice does *not, of itself,* necessarily show that the subsequent completion of the transaction was *free from the exercise of undue influence.* Whether it will be proper to infer that outside advice had an *emancipating effect,* so that the transaction was not brought about by the exercise of undue influence, is a question of fact to be decided having regard to all the evidence in the case (emphasis added).

A weighty piece of evidence in determining whether the inference is rebutted is the extent of unfairness (inexplicability) in the transaction. A court may infer from the degree of disadvantage to the claimant one of the following.

(i) **The claimant's refusal to get or follow independent advice indicates the con-tinuing impact of undue influence**: in *Bank of Montreal v Stuart* (1911), the court (at 137) said of the wife, who was 'absolutely cleaned out' by acting as surety for her husband: 'She says she acted of her own free will . . . and that she would have scorned to consult anyone . . . Her declarations shew how deeprooted and how lasting the influence of her husband was.'

(ii) **Any advice received by the claimant was inadequate**: it failed to emancipate them from the defendant's undue influence. In **Inche Noriah v Omar**, the claimant's gift of land to her nephew was set aside despite her receipt of independent advice because it failed to meet the requirements of *adequacy*. Namely, that it should be: independent; given with knowledge of the claimant's vulnerability and the material aspects of the negotiation; effectively communicated to the claimant; and competent, in only supporting transactions that can sensibly be entered into by a party free of influence.

In *Crédit Lyonnais v Burch* (see 9.2.4.3), the junior employee refused two suggestions from the bank to obtain independent advice. However, Millett LJ (at 156–7) said that the transaction was voidable *even if she had received advice* because while a party is 'normally entitled to assume that the solicitor has discharged his duty and that the claimant has followed his advice . . . he cannot make any such assumption if he knows or ought to know that it is false'. The latter was so here because, in the light of the staggering burden she was assuming, the lender 'must have known that no competent solicitor could advise her to enter into a guarantee in the terms she did'.

(iii) **The claimant did not adequately understand the transaction**: in *Hammond v Osborn*, the Court of Appeal (at [58]) described H's gift as 'an act of generosity wholly out of proportion to the kindness shown to him'. Ward LJ (at [57]) thought it 'inconceivable . . . that the deceased, who was prudently investing for his future, would have saddled himself with a debt he could not pay.'

> **Pause for reflection**
>
> *The proper function of the rebuttal* is to determine whether the defendant had *successfully shifted* his or her obligation to protect the claimant's welfare to a third party (the independent adviser). If so, the paradigm will have changed from a relational to an arm's-length one, leaving the defendant free to deal self-interestedly with the claimant. This makes sense of the requirement of 'adequacy' of the independent advice. *Comprehension* of the transaction is necessary, but not sufficient. The question is whether the advice *emancipated* the claimant from the influences of his or her relationship with the defendant (*Etridge* at [20]). The greater the disadvantage to the vulnerable person, the more he or she needs help, the more cogent must be the explanation: 'The more powerful influence or the weaker patient alike evokes a stronger application of the safeguard' (*Allcard v Skinner* at 157–8).

9.2.5 Rescission for undue influence

9.2.5.1 The bars to rescission

Contracts and gifts tainted by undue influence are voidable and may be rescinded at the claimant's option. The operation of rescission, including its bars, is the same as that applicable for misrepresentation (see 5.3.2). Thus, rescission may be barred by the claimant's *affirmation* of the contract, by *lapse of time* after the cessation of the influence (known as *laches* or acquiescence), if a *third party* acquires an interest in the subject matter of the contract as a good faith purchaser, and if it is impossible to effect *mutual restoration of benefits received* under the transaction.

In *O'Sullivan v Management Agency and Music Ltd* (1985), a *fully performed* contract to manage an inexperienced pop musician was rescinded for presumed undue influence. The manager was required to return the musician's copyright in songs and account for the profit it had made from the agreement. The manager's services which had brought fame and fortune to the musician obviously could not be 'returned' but was recognised by allowing a deduction of a sum from the liability to account for profit. The logic of this approach is to abolish the bar of proprietary mutual restitution. If conversion into money is allowed then, subject to quantification difficulties, *mutual restitution is never impossible*.

9.2.5.2 The defence of change of position

In *Etridge*, Lord Scott (at [144]) said that where undue influence or misrepresentation is established, 'the victim, is entitled, subject to the usual defences of change of position, affirmation, delay etc, to avoid the contract'. The change of position defence, recognised in the law of unjust enrichment, *reduces the claimant's recovery* on rescission to protect a good faith defendant's expenditure in reliance on the security of their receipt. Although the defence has never been overtly applied in a contract case, the decision in **Cheese v Thomas** is an arguable example.[4] C (an 88-year-old man) contributed £43,000 and his great-nephew contributed £40,000 towards the purchase of a home for C to live in for life, but in the nephew's name. The transaction was voidable for undue influence. When the nephew failed to keep up the mortgage payments, the lender forced a mortgagee's sale which realised less than the parties had paid. The court ordered this loss to be borne by both parties in proportion to their contributions. The great-uncle only got back *what was left* of his share. The court exercised its equitable discretion to achieve 'practical justice' because the transaction was in the nature of a *joint venture* (both parties sharing its benefits and the risks), and because the great-nephew was *not morally reprehensible*, having acted with good faith to provide his great-uncle with a home.

This is consistent with dicta in *Allcard v Skinner* (at 177) in that, had the nun not been barred by her delay, the court held that she would have recovered only so much as had not already been spent on the charitable purposes of the convent in which she participated.

9.2.5.3 No partial rescission

In *Glanville v Glanville* (2003) (at [50]), Park J sets out the law: 'relief for undue influence is an all or nothing matter . . . either the [transaction] stands as it is, or it is set aside in its entirety. The judge cannot vary what the claimant did and substitute something else for it.' This led him to reject undue influence. He explains:

In this case I have no power to vary what Mr Glanville did so as to provide Jean [his second wife] with somewhere to live . . . while ensuring that the value of the house

---

[4] M Chen-Wishart, 'Loss Sharing, Undue Influence and Manifest Disadvantage' (1994) 110 *LQR* 173.

passes to Mr Glanville's family [from his first marriage] after Jean's death. If I had the power to do that I believe that it could be achieved, but the law of undue influence does not give me any power to do it . . . [That] leaves me with the choice between depriving her of a home, or leaving the present situation whereby Mr Glanville's family are effectively disinherited so far as the major item on his estate is concerned. There is no middle way.

Partial rescission is further discussed at 9.3.3.

9.3 **Non-commercial guarantees**

9.3.1 **The problem and the policies**

Where a wife is induced to guarantee the debts of her husband (or his company) by the husband's undue influence, misrepresentation, or pressure, can the lender enforce the guarantee against the wife? The question has vexed the courts because the policies for and against enforcement of such guarantees are so finely balanced. The arguments **supporting enforcement** include that: the wife should *take responsibility* for her apparent agreement to the guarantee; she may stand to *benefit* from the loan to her husband, particularly if she is financially dependent on him; it is the husband and *not the lender who has behaved reprehensibly*; and such lending is *socially and economically useful* by unlocking the wealth tied up in the family home for commercial purposes; lenders will be *reluctant to lend* if they lack confidence in the enforceability of their securities.[5]

On the other hand, there are arguments **against enforcement**: the marriage *relationship* provides *scope for abuse* when one party (usually the husband), desperate for finance, may use unconscientious means to induce his or her spouse to guarantee their loan (*Etridge* at [36]); the guarantor is usually *peripheral to the loan negotiations*, often brought in only at the last moment, and so is in no real position to assess the wisdom of her guarantee; *the lender is, or ought to be, aware of the* risk of abuse here; the guarantor's economic interests is linked to, but not identical with, the primary debtor's; *homelessness*, with its attendant social problems for adults and especially children, should be avoided.

9.3.2 **The legal response**

In *Royal Bank of Scotland v Etridge*, the House of Lords clarified the steps laid down in the seminal case of *Barclays Bank v O'Brien*. In this important area, located at the border between the private and commercial spheres, their Lordships tilted the balance towards commercial certainty in favour of the banks. They sought to lay down 'clear, simple and practically operable' minimum requirements which, if followed in the ordinary case without abnormal features, would ensure the enforceability of the

---

[5] In *Etridge* at [34], Lord Nicholls points out that 95% of all businesses in the UK are small businesses responsible for about one-third of all employment and their most important source of finance is bank loans raised by second mortgages on the domestic home.

guarantee (at [2]). An overview is given in **Diagram 9A**. Accordingly, a guarantee is unenforceable if:

(i) some vitiating factor affects the dealing between the guarantor and primary debtor;

(ii) the lender knows that the guarantor is not acting commercially (ie for consideration) and the transaction is for the benefit of the primary debtor; and

(iii) the lender has not taken *reasonable steps* to ensure that the guarantor was properly advised.

9.3.2.1 Vitiation by the primary debtor

The claimant must first show that the guarantee was vitiated by the debtor's misrepresentation, undue influence, or other legal or equitable wrongdoing. However, it is very

Diagram 9A Non-commercial guarantees: the test of enforceability

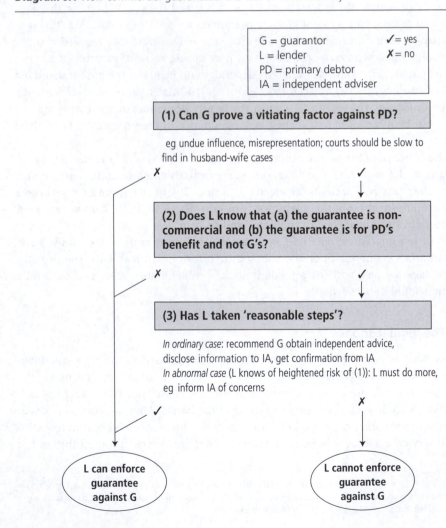

G = guarantor   ✓ = yes
L = lender   ✗ = no
PD = primary debtor
IA = independent adviser

(1) Can G prove a vitiating factor against PD?

eg undue influence, misrepresentation; courts should be slow to find in husband-wife cases

(2) Does L know that (a) the guarantee is non-commercial and (b) the guarantee is for PD's benefit and not G's?

(3) Has L taken 'reasonable steps'?

In ordinary case: recommend G obtain independent advice, disclose information to IA, get confirmation from IA
In abnormal case (L knows of heightened risk of (1)): L must do more, eg inform IA of concerns

L can enforce guarantee against G

L cannot enforce guarantee against G

telling that *Etridge* (at [32]) cautions against being too ready to find this in *husband and wife cases*:

> Statements or conduct by a husband which do not pass beyond the bounds of what may be expected of a reasonable husband in the circumstances should not, without more, be castigated as undue influence. Similarly, when a husband is forecasting the future of his business, and expressing his hopes or fears, a degree of hyperbole may be only natural. Courts should not too readily treat such exaggerations as misstatements.

Lord Nicholls (at [28]–[29]) concedes that, exceptionally, such a transaction may 'call for explanation', but he does not say *when* courts will be prepared to infer that a husband has preferred his own interest and thereby failed to discharge his obligation of candour and fairness to his wife.

Pause for reflection

In *Etridge*, their Lordships said that undue influence is not especially indicated by a wife guaranteeing her husband's debt; it is 'possible but relatively unlikely' ([162], [30]). Rather, her support is the 'natural and admirable consequence of the relationship of a mutually loyal married couple' (at [159]); it is readily explicable in terms of her normal trust and confidence in her husband. But this is precisely why the law is especially vigilant over transactions between those in a relationship of influence.

9.3.2.2 Lender's notice

O'Brien referred to the lender's constructive notice (or being 'put on inquiry') of the debtor's wrongful inducement of the guarantor's agreement to the transaction where it knows that: (i) the debtor–guarantor *relationship* was of a 'sexual or emotional' nature; and (ii) the loan is *for the debtor's benefit*. However, *Etridge* (at [44]) recognises that talk of constructive notice, while convenient in this context, is 'a misnomer'. *Etridge* has established the following.

(i) Since **relationships** of influence are infinitely various and lenders cannot be expected to probe into or evaluate the emotional relationship between debtor and guarantor, 'the only practical way forward' is to require the bank to take reasonable steps 'in every case where the relationship between the surety and the debtor is non-commercial' (at [87]).

(ii) The lender has notice that the transaction is for the debtor's benefit if the guarantee relates to their debts or the debts of their company. This applies even if the guarantor is nominally a shareholder, director, or secretary of the company, since these are not reliable indicators of her real involvement in the conduct of the business (at [48]–[49]). The loan will only be for joint purposes if the guarantor 'is an active participant in managing the company's affairs and is rewarded by remuneration for her work', such that her 'interest and/or involvement is substantive rather than titular'.

But not if the negotiations are conducted by the primary debtor and the guarantor plays no part (*Mahon v FBN Bank* (2011) at [51]).

Knowledge of these two factors alerts the lender to initiate an *administrative procedure* that does not require difficult and sensitive judgment calls.

9.3.2.3 Lender's failure to take reasonable steps

The House of Lords held that, **in the ordinary case**, with no abnormal features, the lender should take 'reasonable steps' to satisfy itself that the guarantor *understands the nature and effect of the transaction*. Lenders have generally refused to provide this information themselves for fear of exposing themselves to allegations of misrepresentation, undue influence, or negligence. The House of Lords accepts (at [79]) that it is enough for lenders to:

(i) *communicate directly with the guarantor*: informing the prospective guarantor that the lender will require a confirmation from a solicitor to the effect that she has been duly advised in order to prevent her from later challenging the guarantee. The solicitor may also act for her husband, or even the lender;

(ii) *disclose the necessary financial information to her solicitor*: ordinarily this includes information about the purpose of the loan, the debtor's current indebtedness and overdraft facility, and the terms of the new loan;

(iii) *obtain a confirmation from her solicitor*: to the effect that she has been advised about the nature and effect of the transaction, in the absence of the primary debtor and, for a sufficient duration to (*Etridge* at [64]–[74] and *Mahon v FBN Bank* at [64]):

(a) explain the *nature and effect of the guarantee* in a meaningful, rather than merely formal, way;

(b) emphasise the *seriousness of the risk* of her being made bankrupt or losing her home;

(c) discuss her financial means, the value of the property being charged, and the availability of other assets out of which repayment may be met; and

(d) state clearly that she has a *choice* whether to proceed and ask whether she wishes to renegotiate particular terms (eg to lower her liability or vary the order of call between various securities).

Failure to obtain this confirmation may render the guarantee unenforceable: *First National Bank plc v Achampong and Owusu* (2003). However, the lender *need not even observe the steps* laid out 'if the surety already knew the details or if the creditor had reason to believe that the surety already knew' (*Etridge* at [189], [95]). The lender is 'safe' as long as it has a solicitor's confirmation. If the *solicitor* giving the confirmation has acted unprofessionally or incompetently, the matter is between the guarantor and the solicitor (at [69]–[74], [77], [115], [173]–[174], [178]–[180]). The lender is protected even if the *solicitor* has a potential *conflict of interest* in also acting for the debtor or the lender in formalising the guarantee; or has been instructed by the lender to advise the guarantor (at [69]–[74], [115], [173]–[174]). Any knowledge acquired by the solicitor, which may raise suspicions, is not generally imputed to the lender (at [77], [115], [180]).

The solicitor 'does not have a duty to satisfy himself of the absence of undue influence' (*Etridge* at [182]). If he or she believes that the transaction is not in the guarantor's best interest, he or she should give advice to that effect but *need not veto it* (by refusing to provide the confirmation certificate), unless it is 'glaringly obvious that the wife is being grievously wronged' (at [61]–[62]) when the solicitor should decline to act (which *would* effectively veto the transaction).

Pause for reflection

This shifts the balance in favour of lenders and against guarantors. The advice is aimed at *informing* the guarantor *rather than emancipating her from undue influence*. Lord Hobhouse (at [111], [115]) observes that the solicitor's advice is often a 'formality or merely served to reinforce the husband's wishes and undermine any scope for the wife to exercise an independent judgment whether to comply. . . . The law has, in order to accommodate the commercial lenders, adopted a fiction which nullifies the equitable principle and deprives vulnerable members of the public of the protection which equity gives them.' Gardner's comment on the Australian decision of *Garcia v National Bank of Australia* is apposite here:[6]

> The clarity . . . of this message is good news for banks, of course . . . [and] even better news for solicitors, one imagines. One might pause, however, over the question whether it truly empowers guarantors. For all its (albeit controversially apt) symbolic value, it may be doubted whether it does. If the debtor asserts that he needs the loan for his business, and a guarantee is required for which there seems to be no other source than his wife or other emotional dependent, it may avail her very little to have it spelled out to her that, if the worst comes to the worst, she may for example lose her home; knowing this may create for her very little or nothing by way of additional choice in the matter.

Etridge does recognise the possibility of the **abnormal or exceptional case**, when the lender may have to take *further steps*. The lender may know facts that indicate the *heightened risk* of undue influence, duress, or misrepresentation by the debtor. These facts may arise from: the lender's past dealings with and knowledge of the parties; the guarantor's conduct that reveals a misunderstanding of the transaction; the debtor's refusal to disclose financial information to the guarantor; or the lender's knowledge or suspicion that the guarantor has not received proper advice (*Etridge* at [57]).

In these exceptional cases, *lenders proceed at their own risk*. The court will determine whether it has taken reasonable steps in response to their heightened suspicion (*Etridge* at [57], [163]). *Appropriate extra steps might include*: insisting on legal advice which is genuinely independent of the debtor or the lender (at [76]–[78], [174], [190]); and informing the debtor's solicitor of any facts giving rise to the lender's heightened suspicion that the guarantor's consent may be improperly obtained (at [79(3)]).

---

[6] S Gardner, 'Wives' Guarantees of their Husbands' Debts' (1999) 115 *LQR* 1, 7–8.

9.3.3 **The remedy**

The primary relief available to guarantors is rescission of the guarantee. The remedy is subject to the usual bars already discussed (see 5.3.2 and 9.2.5.1). Two issues warrant particular mention.

In his summary in *Etridge*, Lord Scott (at [191(7)]) said that the restitutionary defence of change of position, along with other bars, will operate to qualify the claimant's right to rescission. Since bad faith parties are disqualified from the defence, it should only be available (if at all) in 'ordinary' cases when the lender knows no facts that suggest a heightened risk that the guarantor's consent was improperly obtained. More importantly, since the defence operates *by* reducing the claimant's restitution by the amount of the defendant's change of position, it could logically allow lenders to retain a charge for the sum lent to debtors in reliance on the enforceability of the guarantees. This would totally undermine the little protection remaining to guarantors. The defence was not mentioned in *O'Brien* itself and has not been applied.

The courts have no power to award partial rescission. In *TSB Bank plc v Camfield* (1995), a woman was induced by her husband's innocent misrepresentation (that her maximum liability would be £15,000 when it was unlimited) to charge her interest in their home to secure his debts. The charge was voidable because the bank failed to take 'reasonable steps' in the circumstances. At first instance, the charge was partially rescinded to leave a charge of £15,000 because the wife was 'quite prepared to risk' that sum; but the Court of Appeal (at 433, 439) set aside the charge completely saying that rescission 'is an all or nothing process' and the right 'of the representee, not that of the court', so that a court cannot grant 'equitable relief to which terms may be attached'.

▶◀ Counterpoint

The Court of Appeal's inflexible position is open to question. If it is clear that the guarantor would have been prepared to contract on the basis represented, then partial rescission of the charge to uphold her understanding is a logical response to the problem. Her consent to the lower sum represented is not vitiated. In *Vadasz v Pioneer Concrete (SA) Pty Ltd* (1995),[7] the Australian High Court allowed partial rescission on similar facts. Partial rescission is also recognised in the UNIDROIT Principles of International Commercial Law (Art 3.16); and the European Draft Common Frame of Reference (Art II.-7:213).

9.4 **Unconscionable bargains**

9.4.1 **General principles**

The equitable doctrine of unconscionable bargains is distinguishable from *duress* in not requiring the application of illegitimate pressure; it is distinguishable from *undue*

---

[7] See also *Commercial Bank of Australia v Amadio* (1983) where partial rescission was considered but rejected on the facts, and *Scales Trading Ltd v Far Eastern Shipping Co Public Ltd* (1999) at 40–1.

influence in not requiring a relationship of influence between the parties. This colourful doctrine plays out in an array of cases where the sick, the mentally or physically infirm, the drunk, the illiterate, the uneducated, and the incompetent walk on and off stage. It is said to arise 'from the circumstances or conditions of the parties contracting—weakness on one side, usury on the other, or extortion or advantage taken of that weakness . . . it means an unconscientious use of the power arising out of these circumstances and conditions' (*Chesterfield v Janssen* (1751) at 101). This fairly loose and potentially 'run-away' jurisdiction to grant relief is restrained by the stated requirements for relief in the leading modern case of **Boustany v Pigott** (1993).[8]

(i) The claimant must be under an operative *bargaining impairment,* placing it at a serious disadvantage vis-à-vis the other party.

(ii) The defendant must have *exploited* the claimant's weakness in a morally culpable manner.

(iii) The resulting transaction is *manifestly improvident* to the claimant.

(iv) The claimant lacked adequate advice.

For example, contracts were set aside as unconscionable where:

✓ a poor man, entitled to a share of an estate worth £1,700, sold it for 200 guineas (about £210) cash (*Evans v Llewellin* (1787));

✓ two brothers (a plumber's assistant and a laundryman), advised by an inexperienced solicitor also acting for the defendant, sold their reversionary interests at significantly below market value (*Fry v Lane* (1889));

✓ an elderly man, ill and 'intellectually not gifted', sold his property for an inadequate consideration in undue haste and without independent advice (*Clark v Malpas* (1862));

✓ a wife, in the process of divorce, transferred her share in the matrimonial home to her husband without independent advice and for inadequate consideration (**Cresswell v Potter** (1978); *Backhouse v Backhouse* (1978)); and

✓ an 84-year-old widow with senile dementia sold paintings worth £6,000–7,000 for £40 to a young bric-a-brac dealer (*Ayres v Hazelgrove* (1984)).

Pause for reflection

The meaning of 'unconscionable' and its variants can be confusing because it can be used in different senses in different areas of private law. In **'Unconscionability as a Vitiating Factor'** [1995] *LMCLQ* 538, **Bamforth** helpfully distinguishes between unconscionability as:

1. a vitiating factor (as it is discussed in this section);

2. a descriptive label for conduct or transactions which other distinct vitiating factors exist to prevent and as the general policy justification for their existence; and

3. an element of another legal rule.

---

[8] See also *Alec Lobb (Garages) v Total Oil* (1985) at 182–3 and in the Chancery Division (1983) at 94–5.

9.4.2 **Basis of the doctrine**

The usual suspects are present. The older cases emphasise the *impaired consent* of the 'poor and ignorant' claimant (*Fry v Lane*), making the defendant's unconscionable conduct superfluous. The prevailing view now is that **prevention of unconscionable conduct** is the true basis of the jurisdiction. In *Boustany v Pigott*, Lord Templeman (at 303) explains that:

> Unequal bargaining power or objectively unreasonable terms provide no basis for equitable interference in the absence of unconscientious or extortionate abuse of power . . . equity will not provide relief unless the beneficiary is guilty of unconscionable conduct . . . namely that unconscientious advantage has been taken of his disabling condition or circumstances.

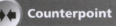 **Counterpoint**

However, the concern to protect vulnerable non-commercial parties from manifest substantive unfairness provides the best explanation for the relief granted.[9] Three arguments support this view.

1. Substantive unfairness is a *necessary condition for relief*; no relief is available without it, even if the procedural unfairness is clear (ie weakness and lack of adequate advice on one side and unconscionable conduct on the other).

2. Substantive unfairness is the *best predictor of unconscionability*; like undue influence, direct evidence of procedural unfairness is usually ambiguous at best, and absent at worst. But they become legally significant in the presence of manifest substantive unfairness. It allows courts to infer that:

   • the claimant *must have* been sufficiently impaired in his or her bargaining ability;

   • the impairment *must have* been known or suspected by the defendant; and

   • the claimant *could not have been adequately* protected by any advice received.

3. Substantive unfairness determines our conception of *procedural unfairness*. It is practically impossible to *define* what impairment, adequate advice, and unconscionable conduct mean or, indeed, why we even *care* about them, if we do not think that a bad deal is a bad thing. It is odd to say that we do *not* care about the reasonableness of a deal but we do care about someone's *ability to make* a reasonable deal. It may not be too much of an exaggeration to say that 'inadequate' advice is advice which fails to save the claimant from a disastrous deal, and unconscionable advantage-taking comprises little more than procuring or accepting the benefit of an extremely one-sided contract at the expense of the claimant. Getting an *obscenely* good deal from such a person, like taking candy from a baby, is hardly a glowing character reference.

---

[9] See further M Chen-Wishart, *Unconscionable Bargains* (Butterworths, 1989).

9.4.3 **What must be proved?**

9.4.3.1 Improvident transaction

Where unconscionability has been concluded, it is often difficult to put your finger on precisely what the defendant has done wrong and why the claimant warrants special protection. But the extreme unfairness of the transaction will usually be clear. Mere undervalue is insufficient it must be overreaching and oppressive or entail such substantial undervalue that it 'shocks the conscience of the court' (***Alec Lobb (Garages) Ltd v Total Oil (Great Britain) Ltd*** (1983) at 94–5).

9.4.3.2 Bargaining impairment

Short of mental incapacity (see Additional Chapter 1 which is available on the Online Resource Centre), what types of bargaining disability of contract parties warrant the special protection of the unconscionability doctrine? The jurisdiction originated in the perceived need to protect expectant heirs who traded their uncertain future expectancies for more certain and immediate gains, often at considerable undervalue (***Earl of Aylesford v Morris*** (1873)). From this, protection was extended to those designated as 'poor and ignorant' (***Fry v Lane***), although the category has been stretched to encompass members 'of the lower income group' and the 'less highly educated' (*Cresswell v Potter* at 257), granting relief to: a telephonist 'in the context of property transactions' (*Cresswell v Potter*); a woman of substantial means who was anxious to 'get a steady and regular income' (*Boustany v Pigott; Ayres v Hazelgrove*); and an intelligent businesswoman of some ability but 'in circumstances of great emotional strain' during a marriage break up (*Backhouse v Backhouse* (1978)).

online
resource
centre

> 👤 **Pause for reflection**
>
> The 'poor and ignorant' formulation is outmoded in a modern welfare state with universal compulsory education. It is time to openly recognise, as in other Commonwealth jurisdictions,[10] and as the English cases accept in practice, that all types of personal and circumstantial weaknesses may adversely affect a party's bargaining power: '[a]mong them are poverty or need of any kind, sickness, age . . . infirmity of body or mind, drunkenness, illiteracy or lack of education, lack of assistance or explanation where . . . [this] is necessary' (*Blomley v Ryan* (1956) at 405, an Australian decision). This emphasis on *personal weakness* excludes the sorts of commercial and economic pressures dealt with by the duress doctrine and goes beyond the relational vulnerabilities addressed by undue influence.
>
> However, 'personal weakness' is ubiquitous and afflicts us all to different degrees from time to time. It lies legally dormant until activated by serious substantive unfairness. Substantive unfairness is relevant: 'firstly as supporting the inference that a position of disadvantage existed, and secondly as tending to show that an unfair use was made of the occasion . . . It
>
> ➡

---

[10] Australia: *Commercial Bank of Australia v Amadio* (1983). Canada: *Paris v Machnik* (1973). New Zealand: *Nichols v Jessup* (1986). US: Uniform Commercial Code, § 2-302.

➜

will almost always . . . [be] "an important ingredient in considering whether a person did exercise any degree of judgement in making a contract, or whether there is a degree of unfairness in accepting the contract"' (*Blomley v Ryan* at 405–6).

9.4.3.3 Unconscionable conduct

Unconscionable conduct is a necessary condition of relief and is the formal justification *for* relief. Lord Templeman said that what is required is that 'one of the parties to [the contract] has imposed the objectionable terms in a morally reprehensible manner . . . in a way which affects his conscience' (*Boustany v Pigott* at 303). However, despite the colourful language often used, actual fraud is unnecessary; *constructive fraud* is enough. The conduct proscribed is that which 'falls below the standards demanded by equity . . . it is victimisation which can consist either of the active extortion of a benefit or the passive acceptance of a benefit in unconscionable circumstances' (Lord Selborne in *Earl of Aylesford v Morris* at 490). The cases have identified a wide range of negotiating conduct as unconscientious; much of it is common and, absent a grossly unfair outcome, inconclusive as to immorality.

- *Active victimisation*[11] includes: taking the initiative in the transaction, haste in concluding it, contributing to a misapprehension without creating it and low-level pressure on the claimant to agree.

- *Passive victimisation* describes the acceptance of a highly advantageous bargain at the expense of a claimant known to be impaired, without 'bring[ing] to the notice of that other party the true nature of the transaction and the need for advice' (*Cresswell v Potter* at 259). Knowledge of impairment may be *constructive*, as where the facts known to the defendant must have indicated the claimant's impairment or put him or her on inquiry (*Ayres v Hazelgrove*).

In **Boustany v Pigott** (1993), P (an elderly woman, described as 'quite slow') leased premises to B for less than one-sixth of the market value (fixed for ten years and with an option to renew at the same price for another ten years). Unconscionable conduct was found on the basis that B, knowing P's affairs were being managed by her cousin G, invited P to a tea party whilst G was away and then 'lavished attention and flattery upon [her]' to secure P's agreement to the lease. B gave P a ride to a solicitor where the transaction was concluded with undue haste and against the solicitor's advice. It seems clear that the harshness of the transaction (rather than just the invitation to tea, the flattery, and the ride) convinced the court of B's moral culpability.

9.4.3.4 Absence of adequate advice

As in undue influence, the absence of adequate independent advice shows that the claimant was not protected by anyone else equal to the task, and that the defendant failed to take adequate steps to meet the claimant's known weakness. Like undue influence, the transaction is not saved simply because:

---

[11] See M Chen-Wishart, *Unconscionable Bargains* (Butterworths, 1989).

- the defendant has recommended independent advice if the claimant's refusal to obtain advice is interpreted by the court as evidence of the seriousness of his or her impairment (eg *Bank of Montreal v Stuart*);

- the claimant has received independent advice if the court concludes (usually from the harshness of the transaction) that the advice was inadequate (eg *Fry v Lane*), or that the severity of the claimant's impairment rendered him or her incapable of benefiting from it (eg *Boustany v Pigott*).

Crédit Lyonnais v Burch (see facts at 9.2.4.3) shows the relationship between a grossly unfair outcome and the independent advice element.[12] Although the bank's solicitor wrote to B twice stressing the unlimited nature of the proposed mortgage, and advising her to seek independent advice, the contract was set aside when B proceeded with the transaction without advice. The court held that it is not enough simply to take reasonable steps to meet the suspicion that the claimant may have been impaired, 'the *result* of the steps which it took must be such as *would* reasonably allay any such suspicion' (emphasis added). The bank should have disclosed the extent of B's potential liability and *insisted*, not merely recommended, that she obtain independent legal advice. Even then the transaction would not stand, for, although it can normally be assumed that the advisers have advised competently and that those advised have understood the advice, this could not be assumed here because C must have known 'that no competent solicitor could advise her to enter into a guarantee in the terms she did' or must have suspected that her impairment has 'cause[d] her to disregard any advice not to do so' (at 155–7).

9.5 Incapacity: a brief summary

The claimant's incapacity to make the contract in question provides a basis for invalidating it. However, the *need to protect* those whose self-protective abilities are impaired to an unacceptable degree must be balanced against the interests of those who have dealt fairly and in good faith with the incapacitated party. Thus, although an incapacitated person is logically *incapable* of giving valid consent (rendering the contract void and of no effect), the legal consequences of incapacity often vary. Recognised categories of personal incapacity are infancy, mental incapacity, and those so affected by drink or drugs as not to know what they are doing.

(i) **Children**: the law adopts a strongly protective attitude to minors. In general, they can enforce their contracts (although not by specific performance), but are not bound by them unless they ratify the contract after reaching 18 years of age. Exceptions have been created to protect those who deal fairly and in good faith with the child and to allow children to enter beneficial contracts:

(a) *contracts for 'necessaries'* are, on the whole, binding if they are beneficial to the child, but not if the terms are harsh or onerous. 'Necessaries' is given a wide meaning;

---

[12] See M Chen-Wishart, 'The *O'Brien* Principle and Substantive Unfairness' (1997) 56 *CLJ* 60.

(b) *contracts beneficial to the child* overall are binding. Examples include: contracts to obtain education, training, employment, medical care, and legal advice;

(c) *contracts involving land, company shares, and partnerships* bind the minor unless he or she repudiates the contract before or within a reasonable time of attaining majority.

A contract not binding on the child may still generate *non-contractual obligations* such as that requiring the child to make restitution of benefits received under section 3(1) of the Minors' Contracts Act 1987.

(ii) **Mental incapacity, drink and drugs**: three categories can be distinguished:

(a) a person lacking capacity under the *Mental Incapacity Act 2005* cannot make a valid contract although he or she remains liable to pay a reasonable price for 'necessaries';

(b) *incapacity due to mental infirmity, drink, and drugs* renders a contract voidable if the claimant can show that his or her incapacity was known to the other party;

(c) *lesser impairments* (short of incapacity) by those who appear sane are subject to the doctrine of unconscionability.

(iii) **Companies and public authorities**: limiting the capacity of such *non-natural persons* is necessary to protect those on whose behalf they act (eg shareholders, lenders, taxpayers):

(a) a *company*'s capacity to contract is limited by its *objects* contained in the memorandum of association. Acts outside its objects are ultra vires (beyond its powers or capacity) and thus void. However, the Companies Act 1985 abolished the ultra vires rule as regards parties who deal in good faith with the company;

(b) *public authorities'* powers are confined by the functions for which they were created. Ultra vires contracts are void. Possible hardship is mitigated by allowing recovery of money paid and property transferred under void contracts unless this would amount to indirect enforcement of the contract.

9.6 **A general doctrine of unfairness?**

9.6.1 **The policy arguments**

Although a general principle against unfairness in contract formation has developed in other common law jurisdictions, such as Australia and the US, under the banner of unconscionability,[13] and in civilian European jurisdictions, under the banner of good faith,[14] this has been resisted by English courts. As Bingham LJ noted (at 439)

---

[13] Australia: *Commercial Bank of Australia Ltd v Amadio* and *Louth v Diprose* (1992); Canada: *Paris v Machnik* (1972); New Zealand: *Nichols v Jessup* (1986); US: Uniform Commercial Code, § 2-302.

[14] H Beale, A Hartkamp, H Kötz, and D Tallon, *Ius Commune Casebooks on Common Law of Europe: Cases, Materials and Text on Contract Law* (Hart Publishing, 2002) 2.2.

in *Interfoto Picture Library v Stiletto Visual Programmes*, whilst English law recognises no 'overriding principle' that parties must act in good faith, it has 'developed piece-meal solutions in response to demonstrated problems of unfairness'. Five overlapping reasons can be identified for this reticence, although each can be countered to some extent.

(i) The common law prefers **cautious incremental extensions** by analogy to existing categories to the recognition of a general broad principle. In *R (European Roma Rights Centre) v Immigration Officer at Prague Airport* (2004), Lord Hope of Craighead emphasised (at [59]–[60]) the limited role of the good faith principle in English private law. In contrast to civilian systems where it is 'expressly recognised and acted upon . . . The preferred approach in England is to avoid any commitment to overarching principle . . . Good faith in Scottish law, as in South African law, is generally an underlying principle of an explanatory and legitimating rather than an active or creative nature . . . It is not a source of obligation in itself.'

Against this must be weighed the desirability of recognising a general principle which highlights the similarities underpinning apparently discrete categories and which identifies inconsistencies or gaps amongst the 'islands of intervention' calling for re-examination (eg *CTN Cash and Carry v Gallaher Ltd* (1994), see 8.6.1(iv)). The analogy is the recognition of the 'neighbourhood principle' underlying the categories of negligence in tort law by *Donoghue v Stevenson* (1932).

(ii) A general doctrine would create an unacceptable degree of **uncertainty** and instability in contractual dealings.

The current picture of piecemeal common law, equitable and legislative interventions, and backward reasoning is hardly certain. The vagaries of this 'list approach' are compounded by the lack of clarity about the basis of some of these doctrines (eg the underlying relief for non-commercial guarantees). Recognition of an overarching class to which the existing species belong will not dispense with the need to carefully identify the different species and chart their particular features.

(iii) It is **not the court's role to redistribute wealth**. Since judicial intervention operates by reversing the transfers of rights or performance under the invalidated contract or term, this can be called *corrective* justice. Semantics aside, it is clear that concern to avoid unfair results cannot be excluded from contract law. Quite the reverse, many rules can be identified which evince concern with fairness in contractual formation, contents, and enforcement.

(iv) It is **Parliament's job to regulate contractual fairness** and not the judiciary's.[15] It is not the court's place to go further than the protection afforded by legislation. However, Beatson observes that 'there are examples of statutory regimes which express a policy from which a principle can be derived being used analogically in developing the common law'.[16] Likewise, Lord Bingham MR said, in relation to the Unfair

---

[15] *National Westminster Bank plc v Morgan* (1985) at 708; *Pao On v Lau Yiu Long* (1980) at 634.
[16] And see J Beatson, 'The Role of Statute in the Development of Common Law Doctrine' (2001) 117 *LQR* 247, 299.

Contract Terms Act 1977, 'the common law could, if the letter of the statute does not apply, treat the clear intention of the legislature expressed in the statute as a platform for invalidating or restricting the operation of an oppressive clause' (*Timeload Ltd v British Telecommunications plc* (1995) at 468).

(v) A general principle against unfairness would **undermine freedom of contract**. Indeed, *Walford v Miles* (1992) expressly rejects any duty to negotiate in good faith (see 2.6.2.5). However, *Walford v Miles* has been criticised and qualified (see 2.6.2.5). Many limits have already been accepted on freedom of contract, including: the vitiating factors, rules *controlling the content of contract* (see Chapter 10), the swathe of *legislative protection* afforded to specific groups such as consumers, tenants, and employees, usually by prohibiting, controlling, or mandating certain terms (rather than setting aside the whole contract—which may disadvantage the weaker party) and by imposing certain procedural safeguards such as requiring 'cooling off' periods during which parties can call off the contract (see Chapter 11) and the rules limiting the parties' ability to agree on remedies (see Chapter 14).

Conceptions of fairness, both procedural and substantive, underpin the rules of English contract law.[17] Steyn LJ said (*First Energy (UK) Ltd v Hungarian International Bank Ltd* (1993) at 196):

> A theme that runs through our law of contract is that the reasonable expectations of honest men must be protected. It is not a rule or a principle of law. It is the objective which has been and still is the principal moulding force of our law of contract. It affords no licence to a Judge to depart from binding precedent. On the other hand, if the *prima facie* solution to a problem runs counter to the reasonable expectations of honest men, this criterion sometimes requires a rigorous re-examination of the problem to ascertain whether the law does indeed compel demonstrable unfairness.

Recognition of a general principle against unfairness would facilitate the rational development of rules which conform to the standards of fair and reasonable people. By giving contracting parties greater security against the risk of opportunism and exploitation, it may also make parties more willing to embark on otherwise risky ventures.

9.6.2 The form and substance of a doctrine of unfairness

How would a general doctrine of unfairness be expressed in the law? One possibility is the doctrine of good faith, which is a key component in the law of contract of other jurisdictions and of international restatements of contract law (eg the German BGB, the French Civil Code, the UNIDROIT Principles of International Commercial Contracts and the European Draft Common Frame of Reference). However, there is *no consistent conception* of the contents of good faith so English courts would have to play an active role in shaping this content. Good faith has entered English law via the

---

[17] See S Waddams, 'Unconscionability in Contracts' (1976) 39 *MLR* 369.

Unfair Terms in Consumer Contracts Regulations 1999, a regulation with European origins (see Chapter 11). Even in this context, the Law Lords do not take a uniform approach: in *DGFT v First National Bank* (2001), Lord Bingham defines good faith as synonymous with 'fair and open dealing' (at [17]), but Lord Steyn rejects '[a]ny purely procedural or even predominantly procedural interpretation of the requirement of good faith' (at [36]–[37]).

A second possibility is the concept of 'unconscionability' which has distinctively common law roots and has found fertile soil outside the UK (eg in the US Uniform Commercial Code, Australia, Canada, and New Zealand).

A third possibility is Lord Denning's doctrine of inequality of bargaining power. Despite its cool judicial reception (Lord Scarman in *Pao On v Lau Yiu Long* and in *National Westminster Bank v Morgan*), the specific components identified by Lord Denning mirror the elements of the unconscionability doctrine. In **Lloyds Bank v Bundy**, Lord Denning (at 339) said after surveying a number of vitiating factors:

> Gathering all together, I would suggest that through all these instances there runs a single thread. They rest on 'inequality of bargaining power'. By virtue of it, the English law gives relief to one who, *without independent advice*, enters into a contract upon *terms which are very unfair* or transfers property for a consideration which is grossly inadequate, when his or her *bargaining power is grievously impaired* by reason of his or her own needs or desires, or by his or her own ignorance or infirmity, coupled with *undue influences or pressures* brought to bear on them by or for the benefit of the other. When I use the word 'undue' I do not mean to suggest that the principle depends on proof of any *wrongdoing* (emphasis added).

The open-textured elements of the doctrines of unconscionability can provide a unifying concept for a number of distinct rules dealt with under different headings, and contribute to a greater consistency in the law by exerting pressure upon incompatible rules. The real challenge is to identify the *contents* of a doctrine against unfairness.

Consistent with the doctrine of unconscionability, the law's concern clusters around three factors.

(i) **Substantive unfairness**: the content of a contract is the key factor in triggering judicial inquiry into the procedural circumstances of the contract and in persuading a court that they are sufficiently deviant to warrant relief. Substantive unfairness includes *severe* deviation from the objective market value, widely conceived social norms or legal norms (eg damages), the claimant's reasonable expectations, or, exceptionally, instances of improvidence or inappropriateness for the claimant in his or her subjective circumstances.

(ii) **Bargaining weakness**: this should also be widely conceived; it includes:

- *personal impairment*: being mentally incompetent or under-aged (incapacity), trust in and dependence on the other party (undue influence), trust and dependence on the primary debtor in guaranteeing his or her debts (non-commercial guarantees), and other, mainly cognitive or personal, vulnerabilities (unconscionable transactions);

- *circumstantial disadvantage*: susceptibility to illegitimate pressures (duress); being in need of rescue (salvage), belonging to a protected class (eg consumers, tenants, employees, debtors).

(iii) **Exploitation of that weakness**: the spectrum runs from duress to the person and fraudulent misrepresentation where 'active victimisation' is clear, through to the 'passive victimisation' where unconscientious behaviour is much less obvious and failure to disclose information or to insist on independent advice is the locus of unconscientiousness. Exploitation may sometimes comprise little more than accepting the benefit of a grotesquely one-sided transaction or particular types of potentially unfair terms in particular circumstances.

The standards set will inevitably be broad and qualitative, rather than detailed and quantitative. The courts must be left to develop the specifics on a case-by-case basis. This is not a simple return to incrementalism. There is a difference **between shaping a discretionary principle through case-by-case adjudication within a defined analytical framework**, and the currently unstructured 'list' approach. The demands of commercial certainty will obviously differ as between contracts made in a *commercial* context and those made in *consumer* or *non-commercial* contexts. Moreover, a **sliding scale** may operate; the stronger one factor is in any case, the less is required of the other two factors.

The controversial issue is whether **substantive unfairness** is a legitimate target for the law. For, while it is generally thought to be legitimate to impose procedural limits, it is generally regarded as illegitimate to proscribe substantive limits. But, no value, even that of freedom of contract, is absolute. Contract power needs to be restrained to preserve maximum freedom for all participants, to protect the practice of contracting, prevent its abuse and make it consistent with widely held notions of social justice.

On such views of contract, there is no particular reason for confining the law's role to the setting of procedural limits. Substantive control of contracts is already widespread once the far-flung instances are collected together. Insofar as the law's role is to support the socially useful activity of contracting, there is no reason why the law should not both inject community standards of fairness into the rules governing how the game of contract should be played *and* place some substantive limits on what can be gained or lost by playing it. The argument of efficiency theorists that judges, not being sophisticated economists, may be wrong on the issue of substantive unfairness,[18] seems spurious in the context of the glaring substantive unfairness involved in the, mostly non-commercial, cases relieved. It is overplayed in view of the wide margin of appreciation which courts will sensibly accord to commercial cases where impairment is, in any case, unlikely to be regarded as operative. In view of the extreme vagueness of 'standards of equity' to which the

---

[18] M Trebilcock, 'The Doctrine of Inequality of Bargaining Power: Post-Benthamite Economics in the House of Lords' (1976) 26 *UTLJ* 359; S Thal, 'The Inequality of Bargaining Power Doctrine: The Problem of Defining Contractual Unfairness' (1988) 8 *OJLS* 17, 25.

courts appeal and of the ambiguity of the *procedural* requirements they generate (eg bargaining impairment and passive victimisation), there seems no particular reason to think that courts are more qualified to lay down procedural limits than substantive ones.

Pause for reflection

1. In '**Contract and Fair Exchange**' in *Essays on Contract* (Clarendon Press, 1986), **Atiyah** challenges the traditional contract dogma that the adequacy of the consideration is immaterial to the validity of a contract. He also cites many examples from different contract law rules where courts are at least partly giving effect to their sense of justice, although they reason in terms of the parties' intentions. Atiyah sees the distinction between procedural and substantive unfairness as unstable because procedures affect outcomes. If there is no such thing as justice in the abstract, there is no such thing as a just procedure in the abstract. Once the law takes an interest in procedures, it must necessarily take an interest in substantive justice. Judicial reluctance to acknowledge the law's concern with substantive unfairness adds complexity to the law and obscures what is actually happening.

2. In '**Undue Influence and Unconscionability: A Rationalization**' (1998) 114 *LQR* 479, **Capper** argues that undue influence should be subsumed into a general doctrine of unconscionability. The basic elements of each are sufficiently similar that they could be merged without many problems. This would solve some present doctrinal problems, and increase the clarity and transparency of the law. In his new general doctrine of unconscionability, transactional imbalance would serve an evidentiary function, while the principal grounds for relief would be relational inequality and unconscionable conduct. The more there was of one feature, the less would be required of another. The new doctrine would be neither specifically plaintiff-sided nor defendant-sided.

THIS CHAPTER IN ESSENCE

online
resource
centre

The key areas and core topics in this chapter are summarised in an easy-to-use list, ideal for revision purposes, on the Online Resource Centre at http://www.oxfordtextbooks.co.uk/orc/chenwishart5e/. Links to websites relevant to the topics covered and any updates to the chapter can also be found on the Online Resource Centre.

QUESTIONS

1 'Undue influence, the doctrine in *Etridge*, and unconscionable bargain address quite different problems; it is impossible and pointless to find one justification for them all.' Discuss.

2 *RBS v Etridge* (2001) has clarified the role of independent advice, manifest disadvantage, and notice in the law on undue influence and non-commercial guarantees.' Discuss.

3 'If a contract is stigmatised as "unfair" it may be unfair in one of two ways. It may be unfair by reason of the unfair manner in which it was brought into existence; a contract induced by undue influence is unfair in this sense. It will be convenient to call this "procedural unfairness". It may also, in some contexts, be described (accurately or inaccurately) as "unfair" by reason of the fact that the terms of the contract are more favourable to one party than to the other . . . it will be convenient to call [this] "contractual imbalance". The two concepts may overlap' (*Hart v O'Connor* (1985)).

How far *does* and how far *should* contract law give relief against either sort of unfairness?

4 Advise the Law Commission on: (i) whether English law should recognise a general doctrine of unfairness in contract formation, and (ii) what such a general doctrine might comprise.

5 Uriah, a retired businessman with a reputation for toughness and independence, dies after a brief but crippling illness. Viv, Uriah's executor, discovers that in the year before his death, Uriah had become friendly with his new gardener Wayne and invited him to move into Uriah's house. Uriah had given Wayne lavish gifts totalling £30,000 and guaranteed a loan of £500,000 to Wayne from Xerxes Bank for an unlimited duration. When Xerxes Bank advised Uriah to get independent advice, Uriah refused saying, 'It's a waste of money, I trust Wayne totally. Anyway, it's only for 6 months.' On Xerxes' insistence Uriah saw Zak, a solicitor who stressed the disadvantageous nature of the guarantee, but Uriah was quite obviously dozing off. Wayne has defaulted on the loan and Xerxes Bank seeks to enforce Uriah's guarantee. Advise Viv.

 For hints on how to answer these questions, please see the Online Resource Centre at http://www.oxfordtextbooks.co.uk/orc/chenwishart5e/

KEY FURTHER READING

Atiyah, P S (1986), 'Contract and Fair Exchange' in P S Atiyah, *Essays on Contract* (Clarendon Press).

Bamforth, N (1995), 'Unconscionability as a Vitiating Factor', *LMCLQ* 538.

Birks, P, and Chin, N (1995), 'On the Nature of Undue Influence' in J Beatson and D Friedmann (eds), *Good Faith and Fault in Contract Law* (Clarendon Press) 57.

Brownsword, R (2000), *Contract Law: Themes for the Twenty-First Century* (Butterworths) at paras 5.3–5.25.

Capper, D (1998), 'Undue Influence and Unconscionability: A Rationalization', 114 *LQR* 479.

Chen-Wishart, M (1997), 'The *O'Brien* Principle and Substantive Unfairness', 56 *CLJ* 60.

Chen-Wishart, M (2006), 'Undue Influence: *Beyond* Impaired Consent and Wrong-Doing, Towards a Relational Analysis' in A Burrows and A Rodger (eds), *Mapping the Law: Essays in Memory of Peter Birks* (OUP) 201.

Chen-Wishart, M (2006), 'Undue Influence: Vindicating Relationships of Influence' 59 *CLP* 231.

Collins, H (2003), *The Law of Contract* (4th edn, LexisNexis) ch 11.

Waddams, S (1976), 'Unconscionability in Contracts', 39 *MLR* 369.

The contents of contracts

*'Precisely what do we owe each other
under the contract?'*

INTRODUCTION

Once the existence of a contract is established by the test of *formation* and its validity is
untainted by the *vitiating factors*, the question arises as to the precise *content* of the parties'
respective rights and obligations under the contract. Part V examines how the law responds
when the parties are in dispute over the enforceability of alleged obligations—'I say you
are bound by *X* and you say you are not'. The traditional answer is that courts identify and
interpret contractual terms *according to the parties' intentions* at formation, no matter how
apparently unfair or unreasonable, unless specific countervailing common law rules or legislation apply. Determining whether an alleged obligation is enforceable is a four-step process
(set out in the **Introductory Diagram**).

(i)   *Identification of terms*: is the alleged obligation a term of the contract or a 'mere' rep-
      resentation? If it is not expressed, can it be implied?

(ii) *Incorporation*: if it is a written term, has the other party had sufficient notice of it to be
      bound by it?

(iii) *Interpretation*: if bound, does the term apply to the event?

(iv) *Invalidity*: if the term applies to the event, is the term nevertheless invalidated or subject
      to variation by statute or common law rules?

The ostensible basis for answering questions (i)–(iii) is the parties' intentions, since courts
do not rewrite bargains. However, contrary to this orthodoxy, numerous techniques give
the courts considerable latitude in controlling unfairness in the contents of contracts. These
techniques are part of the common law's piecemeal solution to specific problems of unfairness. Courts justify them by reference to upholding the parties' 'presumed intentions' or
their 'reasonable expectations', but this can be taken too far. For, in truth, such intentions
and expectations are often *unclear, contradictory*, or *non-existent*—generally, disputes only
reach the courts if both parties genuinely believe their respective interpretations are reasonable. Ultimately, it is for the *courts* to say:

(i)   what, amongst the parties' assurances, are intended to be *inside* the contract and what
      outside (and so determine the term–representation distinction and the question of
      incorporation);

(ii) what may be *added* to the parties' list of express terms (by finding collateral and implied terms);

(iii) what can be *subtracted* from the list (by eg invalidity under the Unfair Contract Terms Act 1977 ('UCTA') or the penalty rule);

(iv) what the terms actually *mean* (by the process of interpretation).

online
resource
centre

The picture of the legal control of the *contents* of contracts is incomplete without at least an aware-ness of the existence of the doctrine which invalidates contracts which are illegal or contrary to public policy. The subject is summarised at 11.8 and more fully discussed in Additional Chapter 2 which is available on the Online Resource Centre.

Part V Introductory Diagram Overview of the legal control of the contents of contracts

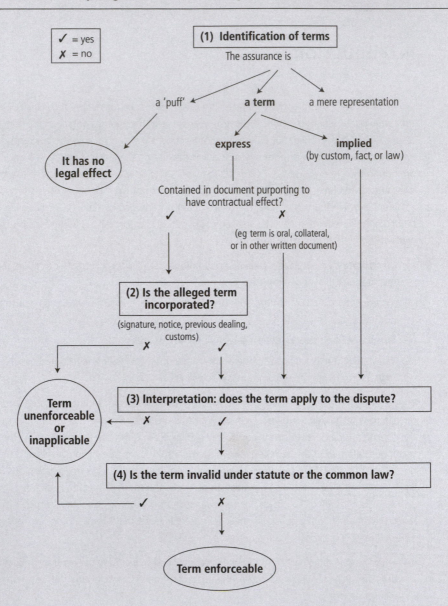

10

Identifying and interpreting contractual terms

'Which assurances are terms inside the contract?'

10.1 **The problem of standard form contracts**

In order to understand judicial action in this area, we should be mindful of the policies in play. On the one hand, are the traditional concerns to promote freedom and certainty of contract (which call for the enforcement of the terms ostensibly agreed). On the other hand, there is the concern to curb the worst excesses of unfairness and exploitation resulting from significant inequality of bargaining power (which calls for enforcement to be denied). Whilst the vitiating factors discussed in Part IV can meet some instances of substantive unfairness, they are usually ineffective against unfair *standard form contracts*. The increasing use of such contracts in the last hundred years has put enormous pressure on traditional contract rules which are premised on the model of individual negotiation between notionally equal parties. In contrast, standard form contracts do not involve 'bargain', 'negotiation', or 'consent' in any meaningful sense (see 1.3.4). They are generally:

- ✓ printed documents containing terms of the contract/clearly purporting to be the contract;
- ✓ put forward by a commercial (the proffering) party who makes many contracts of the same type;
- ✓ presented to the other (the adhering) party explicitly or implicitly on a take-it-or-leave-it basis (the model is closer to an imposition of one party's will than a mutually agreed arrangement; it has been described as 'private legislation' or 'contracts of adhesion'); and
- ✓ signed or accepted by the adhering party who may enter few such contracts.

The **advantages of standard form contracting** are clearly weighted in favour of the proffering party.

(i)   It reduces the proffering party's *transaction costs* in making repeat transactions, increases its profits; in theory this saving is passed onto the adhering party in the form of reduced prices.

(ii)   It allows the senior management in large operations to *maintain control* over the contractual arrangements made by subordinate sales staff.

(iii) It allows the proffering party to *set terms advantageous to itself* by, for example:

  • shrinking its own obligations;

  • inflating the adhering party's obligations;

  • strengthening and facilitating its remedies against the adhering party (see 16.3); and

  • excluding or limiting its own liability.

The danger of exploitation varies with the status of the adhering party. In *Schroeder v Macaulay* (1974), Lord Diplock observes (at 1316) that standard form contracts widely used in **commercial** transactions have generally resulted from extensive prior negotiations and are adopted because they 'facilitate the conduct of trade' (eg bills of lading, charterparties, insurance policies, and contracts of sale in the commodity market).

These contracts will generally be binding because they are used by parties 'whose bargaining power is fairly matched'. But this is not necessarily so even among commercial parties. Thus, the Unfair Contract Terms Act 1977 protects all those contracting on another's standard form from unreasonable *exemption clauses* (see 11.3.2.2), and the Law Commission suggests further extending that protection to micro-businesses (see 11.4.5.4).

Where the adhering party is a **consumer**, the risk of serious unfairness is magnified. Lord Diplock regarded such contracts as 'a classic instance of superior bargaining power' which requires special vigilance on the court's part to see that it has not been abused to drive an unconscionable bargain (*Schroeder v Macaulay* at 1316). Absent a lawyer at their elbow, consumers may not even know of the existence of the fine print, and if they do know, reading will be deterred by the density and length of the fine print, the complicated and unintelligible language, the confusing layout, and the strong social pressure not to appear awkward or confrontational. One study found that even in an environment conducive to reading (the comfort of one's home or office) only one in every 1,000 retail software shoppers clicks on the licence agreement for more than one second. And, those few spent an average of 47.7 seconds[1] on agreements that 'were an average of 74,000-plus words, which is basically the length of the first Harry Potter book'.[2] Lord Reid paints a familiar picture (*Suisse Atlantique Société d'Armement Maritime SA v NV Rotterdamsche Kolen Centrale* (1967) at 406):

> In the ordinary way the customer has no time to read them, and if he did read them he would probably not understand them. And if he did understand and object to any of them, he would generally be told he could take-it-or-leave-it. And if he then went to another supplier the result would be the same. Freedom of contract must surely imply some choice or room for bargaining. At the other extreme is the case where parties are bargaining on terms of equality and a stringent exemption clause is accepted for a *quid pro quo* or other good reason.

The **dangers of standard form contracts** include:

(i) *lack of comprehension ('unfair surprise')*; reading and comprehension is deterred by the context in which the contract is made, the small print (eg tiny grey writing on light grey paper in a hurried transaction or the dense software agreement which must be 'agreed' before your computer can run it), the unintelligible language, the confusing layout, and the strong social pressure not to make a fuss (try reading the paperwork and asking questions next time your signature is required for a loan or a lease);

(ii) *lack of negotiability* due to the inequality of bargaining power; and

(iii) *substantive unfairness* in the serious imbalance of the parties' rights and obligations to the detriment of the adhering party.

[1] This tracked 45,091 households with respect to 66 online software companies. Y Bakos, F Marotta-Wurgler, and D Trossen, 'Does Anyone Read the Fine Print? Testing a Law and Economics Approach to Standard Form Contracts', CELS 4th Annual Conference on Empirical Legal Studies Paper, 2009.

[2] See A Tugend, 'Those Wordy Contracts We All So Quickly Accept', *The New York Times*, 12 July 2013, http://www.nytimes.com/2013/07/13/your-money/novel-length-contracts-online-and-what-they-say.html?pagewanted=1&src=me&_r=1& accessed 3 March 2014.

These concerns are magnified in respect of 'exemption clauses' (terms that exclude or limit the proffering party's liability for breach). They can leave the adhering party with no effective remedy when his or her reasonable expectations arising from the contract are defeated.

We will see that courts can limit the effect of unfair terms by finding:

(i)   a *collateral* or *implied term* in favour of the adhering party that is not contained in the standard form contract;

(ii) that insufficient notice has been given of an *onerous* or *unusual standard term* in an unsigned document to bind the adhering party;

(iii) that the unfair term, *properly interpreted*, is less disadvantageous to the adhering party than first appears; or

(iv) that the unfair term is *unenforceable* under a common law or statutory rule.

These techniques are most commonly applied against *standard form exemption clauses* and many texts discuss them under that heading. However, (i)–(iii) are, in principle, of *general application* and will be so treated here.

10.2 **What are terms?**

We have seen that where one party's expectations from a concluded contract are disappointed, the law's response to that disappointment depends on the *status* accorded to the other party's words or conduct inducing those expectations, whether: (i) a term (sometimes called a 'warranty'); (ii) a representation; or (iii) a 'mere puff'. The remedial significance of the distinction between terms and representations is set out in **Diagram 10A** and discussed at 5.1.1. In any dispute, each party will argue for the status that yields the best remedial result.

10.3 **Express terms**

Contractual terms may be express or implied. *Express terms* are those set out in the contract. *Implied terms* are those which are read into (added to) the contract. Express terms can be in writing or oral or both.

- Where the contract is (i) entirely *oral* or (ii) partly oral and partly written (and the latter is *not in a document purporting to have contractual effect*) the enforceability of statements made between the parties depends on the term–representation distinction (see 5.1.1.2).

- Where a *document purports to contain the terms of the contract*, one question is whether its content can be added to or subtracted from by reference to extrinsic evidence.

10.3.1 **The parole evidence rule**

Contract parties are generally barred from adducing extrinsic (or 'parole') evidence to add to, vary, or contradict a document that purports to record the parties'

Diagram 10A The remedial significance of the terms–representations distinction

	✓ = Remedy available
	✗ = Remedy unavailable

	Damages (getting money)	Ending the contract (getting out)	Specific enforcement (getting performance)
Representation which is false	✓ **Reliance** damages on fraud measure under Misrepresentation Act 1967 *unless* speaker can prove honesty and reasonable basis (see diag 5D) ✓ Restitution on rescission	✓ **Rescission** for any misrepresentation subject to common law and statutory bars	✗ not for misrepresentation
Contractual term (express, collateral, or implied) which is breached	✓ **Expectation** damages for any breach, or ✓ reliance damages not exceeding speculative expectation, or ✓ restitution *if* total failure of consideration, or ✓ account of profits in 'exceptional' cases	**Termination** narrowly available: ✓ breach of a 'condition' ✗ breach of a 'warranty' ✓ breach of an 'innominate' term if consequences serious	✓ **Specific performance** narrowly available

agreement (*Jacobs v Batavia & General Plantations Trust Ltd* (1924)). Contract law accords almost sacred status to such documents; they are regarded as *exclusively* embodying the 'four corners of the contract'. The parole evidence rule ostensibly promotes certainty and predictability and avoids evidential difficulties. However, the long list of *exceptions* to the rule necessitated by the demands of justice and respect for the parties' intention undermines the claims of certainty and predictability. For example, extrinsic evidence can be adduced when it is claimed that the contract:

- is vitiated;
- includes terms *additional* to those contained in the contractual document, whether express (called 'collateral', see 10.3.2) or implied (see 10.4);
- should be *rectified* (see 6.6).

The collective width of the exceptions calls the rule into question since, in practice, it will rarely prevent a party from adducing the sort of evidence that the rule theoretically prohibits. The rule is better understood as an easily rebuttable presumption that a document purporting to be the contract contains the whole contract.

Pause for reflection

1. The reasoning supporting the exceptions to the parole evidence rule (set out in *Allen v Pink* (1838)) is circular. It says that the document is presumed to contain the whole contract, unless the parties did not so intend (such intention requiring extrinsic evidence to prove); that is, the rule applies, unless it does not apply. As Wedderburn[3] comments, this is a 'self-evident tautology' which deprives the rule of most of its effect.

2. Nevertheless, in *Shogun Finance Ltd v Hudson* (2003), the House of Lords held that the parole evidence rule bars extrinsic evidence to support a claim of mistaken identity (see 6.4.1.4). The case undoubtedly strengthens the parole evidence rule although its reasoning is open to question. Is the rule that the contents of the contract must be determined by the contractual document applicable, when the question is *whether* there is a valid contract in the first place?

10.3.2 Collateral terms and collateral contracts

A term (or a contract) may be *collateral* to the main terms (or contract). The existence of collateral terms or contracts is, again, said to depend on the parties' intentions. The test is analogous to that between terms and representations (see 5.1.1.2). However, for the defendant's assurance to amount to a collateral term the claimant must show that the assurance was so important that he or she would not have entered the contract *but for* the assurance.. It is not enough that the statement was *a* cause of the claimant entering the contract (as is the test for misrepresentation). This stronger causal link is understandable since: (i) stronger rights are conferred by collateral terms than by representations, and (ii) because collateral terms may potentially override inconsistent express terms in the contractual document. Phillimore LJ explains (at 183–4, 186) in *Mendelssohn v Normand Ltd* (1970):

> [W]hen a man has made, by word of mouth, a promise or a representation of fact, on which the other party acts by entering into the contract . . . the man is not allowed to repudiate his representation by reference to a printed condition . . . nor is he allowed to go back on his promise by reliance on a written clause . . . The reason is because the oral promise or representation has a decisive influence on the transaction—it is the very thing which induces the other to contract—and it would be most unjust to allow the maker to go back on it. The printed condition is rejected because it is repugnant to the express oral promise or representation . . . Whether you regard that promise as . . . a collateral term of the contract, or whether you regard the contract as being partly oral and partly in writing . . . it seems to me it can make no real difference.

It used to be insisted that a collateral *term* could only add to, but not vary or contradict, the written document.[4] The courts sidestepped this problem by simply finding a whole other collateral *contract* instead (ie a second (unilateral) contract containing

---

[3] K Wedderburn, 'Collateral Contracts' (1959) 17 *CLJ* 58.
[4] *Mann v Nunn* (1874); *Angell v Duke* (1875); *Henderson v Arthur* (1907).

the promise, in consideration of the promisee entering the main contract). It is now accepted that collateral terms and collateral contracts perform the same functions. Namely, the following.

(i) Conferring the **remedial advantages** of an action for breach over that for misrepresentation. Prior to the Misrepresentation Act 1967, the collateral device mitigated the unavailability of damages for non-fraudulent misrepresentations. Even after the Act (widening the availability of such damages), the collateral device is still useful if the claimant prefers the protection of his or her expectation, rather than reliance, interest.

(ii) **Overriding the privity rule**: in **Shanklin Pier Ltd v Detel Products Ltd** (1951), D told S that its paint was suitable for painting S's pier and would last seven to ten years. S then instructed its contractor to buy and use D's paint, which turned out to be less durable than stated. Although S did not buy paint from D directly, S successfully sued D on the basis of a collateral unilateral contract whereby D's promise in relation to the paint was supported by S's consideration in directing its contractor to buy D's paint.

(iii) Overriding inconsistent terms in the main written contract: circumventing the parole evidence rule and so *adding to, varying, or contradicting a contractual document*. For example:

✓ in *City and Westminster Properties (1934) Ltd v Mudd* (1959), a tenant was induced to sign a new lease limiting use of the premises to business purposes by the landlord's oral assurance that the tenant could continue to live on the premises. The landlord was prevented from forfeiting the lease against the tenant for doing so;

✓ in *Harling v Eddy* (1951), a heifer was sold at auction on standard printed conditions that it was 'without warranty'. The seller had enticed a bid by saying that he would guarantee the heifer in every respect. The buyer could claim for breach when the heifer died of tuberculosis three months later;

✓ in *Mendelssohn v Normand Ltd* (1970), M parked in N's garage on terms that N would 'accept no liability for any loss or damage sustained by the vehicle its accessories or contents howsoever caused'. M left the car unlocked on the insistence of N's employee who undertook to lock it for him. M successfully sued for valuables stolen from the car;

✓ in *Curtis v Chemical Cleaning & Dyeing Co Ltd* (1951), C took a wedding dress to CCD for cleaning and was asked to sign a 'receipt' exempting CCD from liability for 'any damage howsoever arising'; C signed after being assured that the exemption only related to beads or sequins on the dress. When the dress was returned badly stained, CCD could not rely on the wide exclusion clause beyond the limited extent stated (at 809);

✓ in *J Evans & Sons (Portsmouth) Ltd v Andrea Merzario Ltd* (1976), the carrier assured the owner of goods that their goods would be shipped *under* deck; the goods were shipped *on* deck and lost overboard. The carrier's oral assurance was treated as a collateral term *qualifying the contractual document* (which gave the carrier complete discretion over the placement of cargo and excluded liability for all but wilful neglect or default) which had been breached.

Entire agreement clauses (also called 'integration' or 'merger' clauses) seek to replicate the parole evidence rule by the parties' express agreement and are enforceable. They state 'that the full contractual terms are to be found in the document containing the clause and not elsewhere, and that, accordingly, any promises or assurances made in the course of the negotiations (which might otherwise have effect as a collateral warranty) shall have no contractual force' (*Inntrepreneur v East Crown Ltd* (2000)). Such clauses thus exclude liability for breach of collateral terms (*SERE Holdings Ltd v Volkswagen Group UK Ltd* (2004)), but may not exclude liability for misrepresentations (see 5.4).

10.3.3 The incorporation of terms

One party may attempt to rely on a term in a document purporting to be the contract which is *unknown and very prejudicial* to the other. The legal question is *not* whether the statement is a term (the nature of the document in which it is contained assumes that it is); rather, it is one of '*incorporation*': whether the term forms part of the contract and so binds the parties. A written term can be 'incorporated' into the contract by:

(i)   signature;

(ii) reasonable notice of the written term; or

(iii) previous dealing or custom.

Only if the term is binding do the subsequent questions of interpretation (see 10.5) and possible invalidity (see Chapter 11) arise.

10.3.3.1 Signed documents

English law attaches enormous significance to signatures. The general rule is that a person is bound by the contents of a contractual document he or she has signed whether or not he or she has read or understood it, and even if they do not know the language in which the contract is expressed (*Parker v South Eastern Railway Co* (1876), *The Luna* (1919)). The potential harshness of this rule is shown by *L'Estrange v Graucob Ltd* (1934). E bought an automatic cigarette vending machine from G which stopped working after a few days. G denied E's claim for breach of an implied term as to fitness for purpose because E had signed an order form which excluded liability for all express and implied and terms and statements. Although the exemption clause was in 'regrettably small print', printed on brown paper, and in an unexpected place, the Court of Appeal held E bound by her signature.

The signature rule is subject to **very narrow exceptions**:

(i)   *non est factum*;

(ii) misrepresentation;

(iii) other vitiating factors such as mistake, undue influence, unconscionability, duress, or incapacity; and

(iv) the non-contractual nature of the signed document: in **Grogan v Robin Meredith Plant Hire** (1996), an oral contract was made for the hire of machinery: the Court of Appeal held that the 'time sheets' signed after the contract commenced could not incorporate the additional terms contained therein. Auld LJ said (at 1131) that it was 'too mechanistic' to treat a signature as invariably binding the signer to its contents irrespective of its nature and the parties' understanding of its purpose and effect. A signature will not bind if the document is only *administrative* in the sense of merely allowing the parties to *implement* their prior agreement.

 Pause for reflection

The signature rule can be criticised.

1. It is unrealistic. In *McCutcheon v David MacBrayne Ltd* (1964), Lord Devlin (at 133) concedes that the rule is premised on a 'world of make-believe which the law has created'. A standard form contract 'is not meant to be read, still less to be understood. Its signature is in truth about as significant as a handshake that marks the formal conclusion of a bargain.'

2. In **'Signature, Consent, and the Rule in** *L'Estrange v Graucob*' (1973) 32 *CLJ* 104, **Spencer** comments that signatures are still treated as if 'some kind of magic operated to take the contract out of the usual rules that governs the formation of contracts'. He argues that a person should not be bound by a signed document if the other party knew of or was responsible for his or her mistake. Waddams agrees. He writes (at [319]):

   > One who signs a written document cannot complain if the other party reasonably relies on the signature as a manifestation of assent to the contents, or ascribes to the words he used their reasonable meaning. But the other side of the same coin is that only a reasonable expectation will be protected. If the party seeking to enforce the document knew or had reason to know of the other's mistake the document should not be enforced.

   This approach was adopted in *Tilden Rent-a-Car Co v Clendenning* (1978). The Ontario Court of Appeal held that a signature is only binding when it is *reasonable* for the enforcing party to believe that it manifests assent to the onerous term sought to be enforced. The court distinguished ordinary *commercial* practice, where a signature can reasonably be taken to manifest assent, from the case of the *hurried, informal, or consumer transaction* with finely printed, unexpected, and harsh clauses 'where the signature by itself does not truly represent an acquiescence to unusual and onerous terms which are inconsistent with the true object of the contract'. In the latter case, 'the party seeking to rely on such terms should not be able to do so in the absence of first having taken reasonable measures to draw such terms to the attention of the other party'. On the facts, the hirer was not bound by a clause making him liable for damage to the car in a wide variety of circumstances far beyond his reasonable expectation because: (i) he had paid extra for 'additional' insurance cover; (ii) it was plain that he did not read nor was expected to read the fine print; and (iii) the speed in completing the transaction was one of the attractions of the service being offered.

3. The European Draft Common Frame of Reference provides that 'terms [supplied by one party and not individually negotiated] are not sufficiently brought to the other party's attention by a mere reference to them in a contract document, *even if that party signs*

   ➔

→

the document' (Art II.-9:103). 'Reasonable steps' must be taken to give notice of standard terms even if they are contained in signed writing.

On the other hand, the signature rule is justifiable on the basis of *certainty, efficiency, administrative convenience*, and ultimately, even the parties' *autonomy*. In reality, the obstacles to giving informed consent to every term in a standard form contract of any complexity is simply insurmountable. A person today who refused to contract without being adequately apprised of the fine print would deny themselves of most means of living in a modern society, or would lead a not very interesting or productive life. The fine print is for all intents and purposes invisible. Given that the parties clearly consent to the main subject matter of the contract, the law treats the signature as a proxy for consent in order to render the contract enforceable. Any unfairness can be mitigated by legal techniques in determining the contents and meaning of the contract as discussed in the following sections.

10.3.3.2 Unsigned documents

In the course of negotiations, a document containing terms may have simply been *delivered* by one party to the other, *displayed* in a notice, or *incorporated by reference* (eg an order form stated to be 'subject to our usual terms'). The proffering party seeking to rely on the terms must have given the other party *adequate notice* of them. The rationale is that *notice* serves to warn the other party what they are letting themselves in for and gives him or her an opportunity to renegotiate or withdraw. The notice must be:

(i) given *at or before* contract formation;

(ii) in a document intended to have *contractual effect*; and

(iii) *reasonable* (ie commensurate with the harshness or unexpectedness of the terms).

In applying these requirements, courts balance the practical convenience and certainty of standard form contracts against the risk that they may contain grossly unfair and unconsented to terms.

(i) **Timing of notice**: the relevant notice must have been given *at or before the time of contract formation*. Notice given thereafter is an impermissible *unilateral* variation of the contract *after* formation. Thus:

✗ an unfair term was not incorporated in **Olley v Marlborough Court Ltd** (1949). O registered and paid at the reception of M's hotel. When he went up to his room, he then saw the notice exempting M from liability for lost or stolen articles. When O's property was stolen because the negligence of M's staff allowed a thief to enter O's room, M was held to be liable for O's loss. Notice of the exemption came too late;

✗ similarly, in *Thornton v Shoe Lane Parking Ltd* (1971), T drove his car into S's multistorey car park, put money into an automatic machine, and was issued with a ticket stated to be 'subject to the conditions of issue as displayed on the premises': these excluded liability for damage and for personal injury.

When T was injured partly due to S's negligence, the court held S liable. S made the offer by holding out the machine as ready to receive the money; the customer accepted when he inserted the money: from that point the customer is 'committed beyond recall'. The notice inside the premises *and the notice on the ticket* came too late.

(ii) **Contractual document or 'mere receipt'?** If a party does not, and cannot reasonably be expected to, know that the document he or she receives contains contractual terms, he or she is not bound by its contents. In *Chapelton v Barry UDC* (1940), B's sign indicated the hire charges for deckchairs. On picking up a deckchair C received a ticket from the attendant, which C put in his pocket unread. When C fell through the defective deckchair and sustained personal injury, the court prevented B from relying on the exclusion clause printed on the back of the ticket because it was contained in a 'mere receipt', which could not reasonably be expected to contain contractual terms. Section 2 of UCTA 1977 now automatically voids exemptions of liability for personal injury caused by negligence (see 11.4.2).

Other examples of non-contractual documents that cannot incorporate terms contained therein are a cheque book cover (*Burnett v Westminster Bank Ltd* (1966)) and a ticket for a public bath house (*Taylor v Glasgow Corp* (1952)). However, commercial or consumer practices may indicate the contractual nature of the document in question. In *Alexander v Railway Executive* (1951), the court noted that 'most people nowadays know that railway companies have conditions subject to which they take articles into their cloakrooms'.

(iii) **Reasonable notice:** in *Parker v SE Railway Co*, P deposited a bag in S's station cloakroom. P received a ticket, which said 'See back'. On the back were printed conditions including one that limited liability for any item to £10. P saw the writing on the ticket, but neither read it nor thought it contained terms. P claimed £24 10s for his lost bag. The Court of Appeal held that the recipient of a ticket is bound if he or she had reasonable notice that the document *contains terms*, even if he or she remains ignorant of the terms. Mellish LJ (at 422) said:

> The railway company . . . must be entitled to make some assumptions respecting the person who deposits luggage with them . . . [, that] he can read, and that he understands the English language, and that he pays such attention to what he is about as may be reasonably expected from a person in such a transaction . . . [if the railway company's action] was sufficient to inform people in general that the ticket contains conditions, I think that a particular plaintiff ought not to be in a better position than other persons on account of his exceptional ignorance or stupidity or carelessness.

Thompson v LM & S Railway Co (1930) shows how little notice may suffice. T bought a railway ticket (for 2s 7d) which stated in 'quite big print and quite legible print', 'for conditions see back'. On the back passengers were referred to the railway timetable for the conditions (which cost 6d). T was illiterate but L successfully relied on an exclusion clause appearing on page 552 of the timetable as having been validly incorporated when L's negligence caused T's personal injury. However, if a party *knows* or should have known that the recipient of the notice is illiterate, more would need to be done to satisfy the notice requirement (*Geier v Kujawa, Weston and Warne*

Bros (Transport) (1970)), and such knowledge may also trigger the unconscionability doctrine (see 9.4).

There was insufficient notice to incorporate a document where:

✗ a ticket made no reference to the existence of conditions on the back (*Henderson v Stevenson* (1875));

✗ a ticket was folded over and the conditions partially obscured by a red ink stamp (*Richardson, Spence & Co Ltd v Rowntree* (1894));

✗ the relevant clause was obscured by a date stamp (*Sugar v London, Midland and Scotland Railway* (1941)); and

✗ reference to terms 'on the back' of a faxed document but the back page was inadvertently not sent (*Poseidon Freight Forwarding Co Ltd v Davies Turner Southern Ltd* (1996)).

Where a party seeks to enforce an **onerous** or **unusual** term, it is *not* enough just to give notice of its *existence*. He or she must show that they took such *additional* reasonable steps to bring their *significance* to the other party's notice. In **Spurling Ltd v Bradshaw** (1956), Denning LJ (at 466) said that 'the more unreasonable a clause is, the greater the notice which must be given of it'. He instanced the exclusion clause in *Thornton v Shoe Lane Parking* (at 170) as being 'so wide and so destructive of rights that the court should not hold any man bound by it unless it is drawn to his attention in the most explicit way . . . In order to give sufficient notice, it would need to be printed in red ink with a red hand pointing to it—or something equally startling'.

This **'red hand'** *rule* has struck down terms *beyond* exemptions of liability. In **Interfoto Picture Library Ltd v Stiletto Visual Programmes Ltd** (1989), S ordered photographic transparencies from Interfoto, which sent 47 transparencies with a delivery note stipulating a 'holding fee' of £5 per day per transparency retained past the stipulated period. S was invoiced for £3,783.50 when they returned the transparencies two weeks late. The Court of Appeal found the term onerous and unusual (the charge was 'high and exorbitant' and 'many times greater than was usual or heard of'); it was unenforceable because Interfoto 'did not do what was necessary to draw this unreasonable and extortionate clause fairly to [S's] attention'. The court substituted a *quantum meruit* award of £3.50 per transparency *per week*, representing their reasonable (market) value.

The orthodox **justification** for the higher level of notice required to incorporate onerous and unusual terms is based on the *presumed intention of the party being bound*. In *Parker v SE Railway Co*, Bramwell LJ (at 428) thought there was 'an implied understanding that there is no condition unreasonable to the knowledge of the party tendering the document and not insisting on its being read'. Similarly, in *Interfoto Picture Library*, Dillon LJ (at 438) observed that the recipient who knows that the document contains terms will 'generally still tend to assume that such conditions are only concerned with ancillary matters of form and are not of importance'.

> ### 👤 Pause for reflection
>
> 1. The increased notice required to incorporate harsh terms allows courts to *control unfair terms* without appearing to do so directly. In theory, a party can incorporate any term, however onerous or unusual, so long as adequate notice of it is given. In practice, the courts' power to determine: (i) whether terms are 'onerous or unusual', and (ii) what amounts to reasonable notice, allows them to invalidate onerous and unusual terms (the print may not be sufficiently large, bold, clear, red, or framed by flashing neon signs).
>
> 2. The term was not enforced in *Interfoto* when there seems little procedural unfairness but significant substantive unfairness. The borrower of the transparencies was a business party and commercial practice would generally impute to the recipient of a delivery note notice of the terms contained therein. In **'The Duty to Give Notice of Unusual Contract Terms'** [1988] *JBL* 375, **Macdonald** concludes that it is impossible to regard the whole of the 'red hand' rule as a logical extension of *Parker*. Rather, as Dillon and Bingham LJJ suggest, the rule represents common law development in response to standard form contracting based on fairness or reasonableness.
>
> 3. Bingham LJ said in *Interfoto v Stiletto* (at 439, 443) of the cases on notice and incorporation:
>
>> At one level they are concerned with a question of pure contractual analysis, whether one party has done enough to give the other notice of the incorporation of the term in the contract. *At another level they are concerned with a somewhat different question, whether it would in all the circumstances be fair (or reasonable) to hold a party bound by any conditions or by a particular condition of an unusual and stringent nature.* . . . [This is] a concept of fair dealing that has very little to do with a conventional analysis of offer and acceptance (emphasis added).
>
> The law's concern with substantive unfairness can be dealt with directly under UCTA and the Unfair Terms in Consumer Contracts Regulations ('UTCCR') (see Chapter 11). Nevertheless, the 'red hand' rule still plays an important role when the unfair term falls outside statutory control (eg a penalty clause disguised as an increased borrowing charge in a business contract, as in *Interfoto*).

10.3.3.3 Previous dealing and custom

In the absence of signature or adequate notice, a term in a printed document may be incorporated by a consistent course of previous dealing between the parties or by the custom of the relevant trade. For example, the challenged term was incorporated in:

- ✓ *Henry Kendall Ltd & Sons v William Lillico & Sons Ltd* (1969); after the parties made an oral contract over the telephone, a document was dispatched containing the challenged exemption which had been consistently used in over 100 transactions between the parties over three years;

- ✓ ***British Crane Hire Corp Ltd v Ipswich Plant Hire Ltd*** (1975); B hired a crane urgently from Ipswich. Ipswich subsequently sent out a printed form. Although the parties had only contracted twice previously on these form, the document was incorporated because: the parties were of equal bargaining power; both were in the crane hire business; and the terms relied upon were habitually used *in the trade*, including by B itself when hiring out;

✓ *Motours Ltd v Euroball (West Kent) Ltd* (2003); M's standard conditions were incorporated by a course of dealing because E's director had previously signed 14 order forms containing M's standard terms over 18 months, although E never read them, they were 'very difficult to read' and not in plain language, and they were never discussed or negotiated between the parties. Nevertheless, the challenged term was struck down under UCTA.

In contrast, the challenged terms were *not* incorporated in:

✗ *McCutcheon v David MacBrayne*; McC's car was lost when McB's ferry sank due to the latter's negligence. McB sought to exclude liability by reference to a risk note, which McC had only signed four times previously when using McB's services, and did not know of its specific contents. This was held not to be sufficiently regular or consistent to incorporate the exemption of liability when McC had not signed on this occasion;

✗ *Hollier v Rambler Motors (AMC) Ltd* (1972); H (a consumer) had signed forms exempting R (a garage) from liability three or four times over five years but had, on this occasion, contracted over the telephone without mentioning the exemption; H's car was damaged by fire due to R's negligence.

10.4 **Implied terms**

In addition to express and incorporated terms, a contract may also contain implied terms. Terms may be implied:

(i)   in *fact* (from the circumstances of the particular contract); or

(ii) in *law* (by statute, common law or custom).

The justifications for implied terms and the test for each type of implication are summarised in **Diagram 10B**. Lord Bingham MR explains that since 'the implication of terms is so potentially intrusive', contract law 'imposes strict constraints on the exercise of this extraordinary power' (*Phillips Electronique Grand Public SA v B Sky B Ltd* (1995) at 481).

10.4.1 **Implication in fact**

Terms may be implied into contracts from the *factual context* to give effect to the parties' *unexpressed intention*. The reasoning is that whether through forgetfulness, lack of time, or bad drafting, the parties have failed to include a term which *they would have done*, had they thought about it, or had the time to draft properly.

Diagram 10 B Overview of implied terms

	Implication in **FACT**	Implication by **LAW** (common law or statute)
Applies to	*Any* specific contract.	Contracts of certain *types* (eg employment, tenancy, sale of goods or services), in particular *trades* or *locality*.
Test for implication of term	✓ Is it necessary for business efficacy? or ✓ Would it satisfy the officious bystander test (reasonableness not enough)? *or* ✓ Is it the meaning which the contract would convey to a reasonable person having all the background knowledge reasonably available to the parties?	Is it: ✓ provided for in statute; *or* ✓ established in precedents; *or* ✓ certain, notorious, accepted as binding, and reasonable? ✓ otherwise reasonably 'necessary' in contracts of that type?
Contra-indications for implication	✗ If inconsistent with express term, unknown to one party, too vague, complicated, or novel or if it is unclear whether the parties would have agreed.	✗ Inconsistent with express term, but NB some implications cannot be excluded in certain situations.
Justifications for implying terms	• presumed intention of the parties; • efficiency of providing default rules; • protection of reasonable expectations; • reasonable and fair risk allocation; • correcting contractual imbalance.	

10.4.1.1 The traditional tests for implication in fact

Two overlapping tests have been put forward, each emphasising the high threshold for implying terms in fact by reference to the requirement of '**necessity**'.

(i) **Business efficacy**: *The Moorcock* (1889) stipulated that the term sought to be implied must be *necessary* to give the transaction such *business efficacy* as the parties must have intended.

(ii) '**Officious bystander**': *Shirlaw v Southern Foundries (1926) Ltd* (1939) held that a term implied in fact 'is something so obvious that it goes without saying; so that, if, while the parties were making their bargain, an officious bystander were to suggest some express provision for it in the agreement, they would testily suppress them with a common "Oh, of course!"'.

A term will not be implied if:

✗ one of the parties is ignorant of the content of the alleged term (*Spring v NASDS* (1956));

✗ it is unclear whether both parties would have agreed to the term (*Luxor (Eastbourne) Ltd v Cooper* (1941));

✗ the parties have entered into a carefully drafted written contract containing detailed terms, raising a strong presumption that this constitutes the complete agreement (*Shell UK Ltd v Lostock Garages Ltd* (1976));

✗ the alleged term is too vague (eg good faith negotiation in *Walford v Miles* (1992); to operate commercial aircraft in *Durham Tees Valley Airport Ltd v BMI Baby Ltd* (2009)) or too complicated (*Ashmore v Corp of Lloyd's (No 2)* (1992));

✗ the contract is a novel or risky one (*Phillips Electronique v BSkyB*); or

✗ it is inconsistent with an express terms (*Duke of Westminster v Guild* (1985)).

10.4.1.2 Implied in fact terms as construction: *AG of Belize v Belize Telecom Ltd*

The Privy Council restated the law in *Attorney-General of Belize v Belize Telecom Ltd* (2009).

(i) Lord Hoffmann emphasised that implying terms in fact is an **exercise in the construction** of the instrument as a whole (at [21], see also Lord Steyn in *Equitable Life Assurance Society v Hyman* (2002) at 459). However, 'that meaning is not necessarily or always what the authors or parties to the document would have intended. It is the meaning which the instrument would convey to a reasonable person having all the background knowledge which would reasonably be available to the audience to whom the instrument is addressed' (at [16]). Lord Hoffmann's view that the process of construction and implying terms in fact are the same has been approved (eg *Jackson v Dear* (2013); *Yam Sen Pte Corp v International Trade Corp* (2013)). In *Stena Line Ltd v Merchant Navy Ratings Pension Fund Trustees Ltd* (2011) at [36], Arden LJ welcomed the development for promoting 'the internal coherence of the law'.

◀◀◀ Counterpoint

1. There is a significant difference between:

• interpreting the words that the parties have expressly agreed by reference to the view of a reasonable person in the parties' position; and

• implying new words into a contract on the basis of necessity; strictly speaking, these words still needs to be interpreted.

2. Collins[5] rejects 'the imperialism of the interpretivists'. He argues that while interpretation deals with a lack of specificity or precision in the words of the contract, implication in fact concerns a reallocation of risk to counter unconscionability (in the sense of taking advantage of an omission to protect against risk in circumstances where this advantage had not been bargained for as part of the consideration).

→

---

[5] In 'Implied Terms: The Foundation in Good Faith and Fair Dealing' (2014) *CLP* 1, 17.

➡

3. Lord Bingham said, in *Philips Electronique Grand Publique SA v BSkyB Ltd* (1995) (at 481) that implied terms serve 'a different and altogether more ambitious undertaking' than interpretation because it requires the 'interpolation of terms to deal with matters for which, ex hypothesi, the parties themselves have made no provision.'

4. A number of cases have recently emphasised that the touchstone for the implication remains necessity rather than reasonableness, and that Lord Hoffmann did not intend to depart from that (*Mediterranean Salvage & Towage Ltd v Seamar Trading & Commerce Inc, The Reborn* (2009) at [15]; *Lomas & Ors v JFB Firth Rixson Inc & Ors* (2012) at [56]–[57]; *Fitzhugh v Fitzhugh* (2012) at [19]–[21]; and see Baroness Hale JSC in *Geys v Société Générale, London Branch* (2012) at [55]).

(ii) The **different stated tests** are not different or cumulative tests. They are 'best regarded . . . as a collection of different ways in which judges have tried to express the central idea that the proposed implied term must spell out what the contract actually means' (*Belize* at [27]) when 'read as a whole against the relevant background' (at [21]). Aikens LJ explains that they are not 'freestanding' tests that must be satisfied (*Crema v Cenkos Securities plc* (2010) at [39]).

Detaching the 'business efficacy' test from the basic process of construction may lead to error because a contract may work perfectly well, since both parties can perform their express obligations, but the consequences would contradict what a reasonable person would understand the contract to mean. This is evident in:

✓ *The Moorcock*: a ship-owner contracted to unload the ship at the defendant's jetty. The ship was damaged when it settled on a hard ridge at low tide. The court implied a term requiring the defendant to take reasonable care to ascertain the safety of the berth, and found the defendant liable for its breach. The real issue was which party should assume the risk of damage to the ship by the river bed: while it was not *necessary* for business efficacy to allocate it one way or the other, it was certainly reasonable and fair to allocate it to the jetty owner;

✓ *Mosvolds Rederi A/S v Food Corp of India* (1982): Steyn J conceded that the alleged implied term was unnecessary for business efficacy, but allowed it because *reasonable* parties would have assented to it if it had been raised.

Likewise, Lord Hoffmann said that the 'officious bystander' test risks (*Belize* at [25]):

diverting attention from the objectivity which informs the whole process of construction into speculation about what the actual parties to the contract . . . would have thought about the proposed implication . . . That . . . is irrelevant. Likewise, it is not necessary that the need for the implied term should be obvious . . . The need for an implied term not infrequently arises when the draftsman of a complicated instrument has omitted to make express provision for some event because he has not fully thought through the contingencies which might arise, even though it is obvious after a careful consideration of the express terms and the background that only one answer would be consistent with the rest of the instrument.

In *Mediterranean Salvage v Seamar Trading (The Reborn)* (2009), while agreeing with Lord Hoffmann, Clarke LJ reverted to the business efficacy test (at [45]) in rejecting the alleged implied term. Rix LJ was largely dismissive of the question of which test to apply (at [48]), and based his rejection of the implied term on the custom of the shipping industry that such terms must generally be expressly stated (at [62]).

(iii) The rule that a term implied in fact **cannot contradict an express term** is subject to a contextual interpretation of the express term itself to **avoid defeating the overriding purpose of the term**.

- In *Attorney-General of Belize v Belize Telecom Ltd*, the articles of association of BT stipulated the election of directors according to particular types and quantity of shareholding. Although they provided that these directors could only be removed on grounds such as lunacy and bankruptcy, the Privy Council implied a term that a director could also be removed when the shareholder with the required shareholding to support his appointment ceased to exist. This is necessary to avoid defeating the overriding purpose of the machinery for appointing directors—to ensure that the board of directors reflected the type and degree of shareholder interests. The decision is not without precedent.

- In *Equitable Life Assurance Society v Hyman* (2002), EL sold retirement annuity policies with guaranteed annuity rates (GARs) between 1957 and 1988. EL's articles of association stated that the amount of any bonus would be 'within the absolute discretion of the directors, whose decision thereon shall be final and conclusive'. However, the House of Lords held that this discretion could not be exercised to override or undermine GARs. The implication was necessary to give effect to the objectively reasonable expectations of the parties. The process 'is one of construction of the agreement as a whole in its commercial setting' (*Banque Bruxelles Lambert SA v Eagle Star Insurance Co Ltd* (1997), at 212). The relevant context included that: the GARs had been 'a good selling point'.

10.4.1.3 Implied limits on the exercise of discretionary power

An agreement may leave a particular matter to be determined by *one of the contracting parties*. This contractual discretion over the rights or liabilities of the other party may be conferred in an unqualified way, using terms such as 'satisfied', 'approved', 'as he thinks fit', or 'in his sole discretion'. Whilst the exercise of discretionary powers by public authorities is constrained by public law concepts, the logic of freedom of contract may suggest that such powers agreed by private parties are unrestricted.[6] However, Leggatt LJ said that: 'where A and B contract with each other to confer a discretion on A, that does not render B subject to A's uninhibited whim' (in *Abu Dhabi National Tanker Co v Product Star Shipping Ltd (The Product Star)* (1993) at 404).

---

[6] J Beatson, 'Public Law Influences in Contract Law' in J Beaton and D Friedmann (eds), *Good Faith and Fault in Contract Law* (OUP, 1995) 263, 265.

Legislation controls such terms in specified circumstances, for example (see Chapter 11):

- in consumer contracts, a term which confers broad discretionary powers on the seller or supplier is presumptively unfair (Unfair Terms in Consumer Contracts Regulations 1999, Sch 2 para 1(j));

- terms purporting to allow a business the discretion of giving *no, only partial*, or *substantially different* performance from that reasonably expected by the other party (a consumer or a business contracting as a consumer or on the other's standard terms) are invalid if they are unreasonable (Unfair Contract Terms Act 1977, s 3(2)(b)).

Judicial control is also long-standing. Courts have long set minimum standards by which even absolute discretionary contractual power must be *exercised*. The Court of Appeal held in *Socimer International Bank Ltd (in liq) v Standard Bank London Ltd* (2008), that such powers must be exercised honestly, in good faith, and not arbitrarily, capriciously, perversely, or irrationally. The focus is procedural (on the decision-making process in the light of the overall purpose and character of the contract) rather than substantive (on the effect or outcome). The overall approach essentially mirrors that employed in the public law context of judicial review of administrative actions, although its application will vary with the different context and purpose for which the contractual power is conferred.[7] For example:

- in *consumer credit* contracts—the lender usually insists on having unilateral power to vary the interest rate in its absolute discretion, subject to notice to the debtor (*Lombard Tricity Finance Ltd v Paton* (1989)). In *Paragon Finance plc v Nash* (2001), the Court of Appeal (at [32]) implied the term that the rate of interest should not be set dishonestly, for an improper purpose, capriciously, or arbitrarily, or in a way in which no reasonable lender, acting reasonably, would do;

- in *employment cases*—in *Horkaluk v Cantor Fitzgerald* (2005), the court rejected the employer's argument that, as the contract expressly provided for a payment to be made as a matter of discretion and not of entitlement, it had no obligation to pay or even consider paying. The court interpreted the provision to require the employer to assess the quantum of payment rationally and fairly, and to pay that to the employee;

- however, the commercial context demands a wide margin of tolerance. In *Paragon Finance plc v Plender* (2005), Parker LJ said (at 120): 'a commercial lender is . . . free to conduct its business in what it genuinely believes to be . . . its best commercial interest'. In *Commerzbank AG v James Keen* (2006), the Court of Appeal rejected K's claim that his employer's decisions in respect of his pay and bonuses were irrational or perverse. Mummery LJ said (at [59]–[60]):

> [T]he Bank has a very wide contractual discretion . . . the burden of establishing that no rational bank in the City would have paid him . . . [as C did here] is a

---

[7] H Collins, 'Discretionary Powers in Contracts' in D Campbell, H Collins, and J Wightman (eds), *Implicit Dimensions of Contracts* (Hart Publishing, 2003) 219; T Daintith, 'Contractual Discretion and Administrative Discretion: A Unified Analysis' (2005) 68 *MLR* 554.

very high one. It would require an overwhelming case to persuade the court to find that the level of a discretionary bonus payment was irrational or perverse in an area where so much must depend on the discretionary judgment of the bank in fluctuating market and labour conditions . . . [Moreover], no independent evidence, expert or otherwise . . . [supported K's] claim of irrationality.

Even a discretion that is required to be exercised in a 'commercially reasonable' manner permits the party exercising it to do so in its own interest in preference to the other party's interest (*Barclays Bank plc v Unicredit Bank AG* (2014)). Longmore LJ reasoned that it was impossible to see how a requirement to have regard to the other party's interests could work in practice. It is hard to see how it would assess what those interests were, let alone weigh those interests in comparison to its own interests. The obligation to act in a commercially reasonable manner would only be breached if it demanded a price way above what it could reasonably anticipate as a reasonable return from the contract. It could be viewed as equivalent to a discretion to which *Wednesbury* principles applied (see [15]–[22]).

10.4.1.4 Implied duty of good faith?

In *Yam Seng v International Trade Corp* (2013), Leggatt J asserted that 'there is nothing novel or foreign to English law in recognizing an implied duty of good faith in the performance of contracts' (at [145]). There, IT granted YS the exclusive right to distribute Manchester United fragrances in parts of the Middle East, Asia, Africa, and Australasia. YS terminated the contract alleging misrepresentation and various breaches of contract, including failing to ship orders promptly, refusing to supply certain products after YS had marketed them, undercutting agreed prices, and attempting to claw back certain distribution rights. Leggatt J found repudiatory breaches of the contract justifying YS's termination and awarded damages for misrepresentation. The primary interest in the case lies in the discussion of why a 'duty of good faith and fair dealing in the performance of the contract' (at [150]) should be implied into the contract; namely, the following.

(i) *Comparative law*: the duty has long been recognised in the United States and some European legal systems; it is gaining ground in other common law jurisdictions, including Scotland. English law's position is 'swimming against the tide' (at [124]–[130]).

(ii) *We already do it*: Leggatt J cites Bingham LJ in *Interfoto v Stiletto* (1989) at 439, 443:

In many civil law systems, and perhaps in most legal systems outside the common law world, the law of obligations recognises and enforces an overriding principle that in making and carrying out contracts parties should act in *good faith*. This does not simply mean that they should not deceive each other, a principle which any legal system must recognise; its effect is perhaps most aptly conveyed by such metaphorical colloquialisms as 'playing fair', 'coming clean' or 'putting one's cards face upwards on the table'. It is in essence a principle of fair and open dealing . . . English law has . . . developed piecemeal solutions in response to demonstrated problems of unfairness.

(iii) *Implied in fact term*: the duty could be implied based on the presumed intention of the parties and the relevant background against which the contract was made, consistent with the *Belize* and *ICS* cases. Relevant background 'includes not only facts known to the parties, but also shared values and norms of behaviour', often taken as read at the time of entering into a contract. '[F]idelity to the parties' bargain' is one of many generally accepted standards of commercial dealing that are central to good faith; contracts cannot expressly provide for every possible event, so their language must be given a reasonable construction which promoted the values and purposes expressed or implicit in the contract (at [132]–[139]). While Leggatt J doubted that English law had reached the stage where it was ready to 'recognise a requirement of good faith as a duty implied by law, even as a default rule, into all commercial contracts', he saw no difficulty 'in implying such a duty in any ordinary commercial contract based on the presumed intention of the parties'.

Leggatt J notes the three main reasons against a duty of good faith in performance (at [123]), namely:

(i) English law's preference for incremental development in response to particular problems over enforcing broad overarching principles;

(ii) English contract law's emphasis on individualism and freedom of contract;

(iii) the concern that such a duty would be too vague and uncertain.

What, then, might constitute the **content** of a duty of good faith and fair dealing in contract performance? Leggatt J observed that English contract law adopts an unsatisfactory 'either-or' approach to duties of good faith, loyalty, and cooperation (at [142]):

• at one extreme, all contract parties can act solely in their own interests subject only to the minimal constraint of fraud or other vitiating factors (see Part III);

• at the other extreme, are situations raising fiduciary duties that require utmost good faith, the avoidance of even the appearance of a conflict of interest, and the placing of the other party's interests ahead of one's own.

This is too crude to capture the full range of the reasonable expectations of honest parties, given the variety and complexity of commercial relationships. There must be an entire spectrum in between the norms of antagonistic self-interest at one end to the demanding obligations of disclosure, and cooperation at the other. Leggatt J identifies one intermediary category of contracts, namely, **'relational' contracts** (eg franchise agreements, long-term distributorship agreements, and some joint venture agreements) involving a longer term relationship to which parties make a substantial commitment that 'may require a high degree of communication, cooperation and predictable performance based on mutual trust and confidence and involve expectations of loyalty' (at [142]).

Indeed, an implied duty of good faith in a relational contract—a hybrid between a joint venture and product distribution agreement—was found in *Bristol Groundschool Ltd v IDC Ltd and others* (2014), at [196]. The test is that of 'conduct that would be regarded as "commercially unacceptable" by reasonable and honest people in the particular context involved; this is the test for dishonesty in *Royal Brunei Airlines Sdn v Tan*'. Richard Spearman QC held that a contract relating to the development of computer-based pilot training materials was a 'relational' contract containing an implied duty of good faith. BG's conduct, in 'hacking' into IDC's computer, showed a disregard for IDC's rights and breached the normally accepted standards of honest conduct, although it did not amount to a repudiatory breach.

(icon) Pause for reflection

Collins, in 'Implied Terms: The Foundation in Good Faith and Fair Dealing' (2014) 27 *CLP* 1, especially 27–34, rejected the duration of contracts as the key variable in the spectrum of good faith obligations since the context of the transaction 'may reveal that the long-term contract was intended to be rigid and binding'. Rather, the 'crucial variable . . . is the point at which the contract falls on the spectrum between market and organization', where:

- 'market' signifies contracts between parties with antagonistic interests in a zero-sum game (ie each seeks to gain at the other's expense); and

- 'organisation' signifies a network of contracts that bind the parties together (eg employment contracts, share ownership, and directorships), where cooperation is required to maximise the joint profits to be distributed according to the contractual formula.

Implied duties of good faith 'should intensify as a contractual arrangement approaches the organizational end of the spectrum'.

In *Compass Group UK and Ireland Ltd v Mid Essex Hospital Services NHS Trust* (2013) Jackson LJ (at [105]) emphasised the absence of a general doctrine of 'good faith' in English contract law, but conceded that a duty of good faith may be implied by *law* as an incident of *certain categories* of contract. On the other hand, while an *express* duty of good faith *in performance* is enforceable (as on the facts of *Mid Essex* itself), such a duty will not be implied in fact. In *Hamsard 3147 Ltd v Boots UK Ltd* (2013), Norris J agreed (at [86]) that *Yam Sen* is not authority for the proposition that parties in commercial contracts may be presumed to intend a general obligation of good faith. He accepted that there 'will generally be an implied term not to do anything to frustrate the purpose of the contract', but not 'that there is to be routinely implied some positive obligation upon a contracting party to subordinate its own commercial interests to those of the other contracting party.'

10.4.2 Implication in law

The House of Lords has distinguished:

- terms implied in *fact*, which are necessary to a particular contract; and

- terms implied in *law*, which prescribe the default rules of a definable category of contractual relationship on the basis of wider considerations

(*Scally v Southern Health & Social Services Board* (1992); *Equitable Life Equitable Life Assurance Society v Hyman* (2000) at 458–9.)

Terms may be implied in law by statute, common law, or custom. Contracts that fall into *certain commonly occurring types* attract their own set of obligations as terms implied in law (either by the courts or by legislation) unless the parties contract out of (ie exclude) them.

10.4.2.1 Examples of terms implied in law

The Sale of Goods Act 1979 implies into **sale of goods** contracts that:

✓ the seller has *title* to sell the goods (s 12(1));

✓ goods sold are *free from charges or encumbrances*, and the buyer will enjoy *quiet possession* of the goods subject to the disclosed or known rights of others before contract formation (ss 12(2), (4), and (5));

✓ goods sold by *description* correspond with their description (s 13(1)) or their *sample* (s 15(2));

✓ goods sold in the course of business are of *satisfactory quality*,[8] unless the buyer's attention has been drawn to, or the buyer's examination ought to reveal, any defect (s 14(2) and (2C)); and

✓ goods sold in the course of business are reasonably *fit for the purpose* that the buyer has made known to the seller (s 14(3)).

Similar terms are implied into *hire-purchase* contracts by the Supply of Goods (Implied Terms) Act 1973, and into contracts for the *supply of goods and services* by the Supply of Goods and Services Act 1982.

It is implied in **employment** contracts that:

✓ the employee will serve diligently, loyally, and with reasonable competence (*Lister v Romford Ice & Cold Storage Co Ltd* (1957));

✓ the employer will not require the employee to act unlawfully (*Gregory v Ford* (1951));

✓ the employer will provide safe premises (*Matthews v Kuwait Bechtel Corp* (1959); Employers' Liability (Defective Equipment) Act 1969), and take reasonable care not to endanger the employee's health (*Johnstone v Bloomsbury Health Authority* (1992)); and

✓ the employer and employee owe each other a duty of trust and confidence (*Malik v Bank of Credit and Commerce Intl* (1997)).

It is implied into **building** contracts that:

✓ the work will be done in a good and workmanlike manner, the builder will use good and proper materials, and the building, once completed, will be reasonably fit for human habitation (*Miller v Cannon Hill Estates Ltd* (1913)).

Terms may be implied by the **custom** of the market, trade, or locality in which the contract is made (custom also plays a role in the incorporation of unsigned documents

---

[8] Ie 'they meet the standard that a reasonable person would regard as satisfactory [on matters including appearance and finish, and freedom from minor defects, safety, and durability] taking account of any description of the goods, the price (if relevant) and all the other relevant circumstances'.

(see 10.3.3.2)) and in interpretation of the contract (see 10.5)). Such terms must be: certain, notorious, recognised as binding, reasonable, and consistent with express terms or nature of the contract (*Cunliffe-Owen v Teather & Greenwood* (1967) at 1438–9). A term may be implied by custom even if it is *unknown* to one or even both parties at contract formation.

Implied-in-law terms provide default rules for a particular kind of contract that will serve to regulate this market transaction for the future. Collins (at 243) observes that 'through the idea of model contracts the courts [can] develop a complete set of terms for a typical contract'.

10.4.2.2 The test for terms implied in law

Although the courts have sometimes said that the test for implication by law is also 'necessity' rather than 'reasonableness',[9] it is clear that 'necessity' here requires something **less stringent** than is required for implication in fact. In ***Liverpool CC v Irwin*** (1977); the House of Lords found that in tenancy agreements, landlords had an implied-in-law obligation to their tenants (in this instance, living on the 9th and 10th floors of L's tower block) to take reasonable care to maintain the common parts of tower blocks they controlled such as the lifts, staircases, lights, and rubbish chutes. However, L had fulfilled this obligation, since it spent more on the repairs than it received in rents. Lord Denning's **reasonableness** approach was firmly rejected by the House of Lords in favour of the **necessity** test. Nevertheless, their Lordships arrived at the same result. Atiyah (at 207) observes that:

> the difference between the judges on this point seems somewhat unreal. . . . It is not *necessary* to have lifts in blocks of flats ten storeys high [indeed high-rise buildings predate the invention of lifts], though it would no doubt be exceedingly inconvenient not to have them. So 'necessary' really seems to mean 'reasonably necessary', and that must mean, 'reasonably necessary having regard to the context and the price'. So in the end there does not seem to be much difference between what is necessary and what is reasonable.

Lord Denning MR returned to his theme in *Shell UK v Lostock Garages* (at 1196):

> These obligations are not founded on the intention of the parties, actual or presumed, but on more general considerations . . . the problem is not to be solved by asking what did the parties intend? . . . [but] by asking: has the law already defined the obligation or the extent of it? If so, let it be followed. If not, look to see what would be reasonable in the general run of such cases . . . and then say what the obligation shall be . . . the obligation is a legal incident of the relationship which is attached by the law.

In *Crossley v Faithful & Gould Holdings Ltd* (2004) at [36], Dyson LJ said that:

> rather than focus on the elusive concept of necessity, it is better to recognise that, to some extent at least, the existence and scope of standardised implied terms raise questions of reasonableness, fairness and the balancing of competing policy considerations.

---

[9] *Liverpool CC v Irwin* (1977) at 254; *Scally v Southern Health and Social Services Board* (1992) at 307.

The Court of Appeal also approved the policy considerations outlined by **Peden** in **'Policy Concerns Behind Implications of Terms in Law'** (2001) 117 *LQR* 459, namely that the courts consider:

✓ whether the proposed term is consistent with the existing law;

✓ how it would affect the parties; and

✓ wider issues of fairness in society.

Peden urges courts to recognise that the underlying idea in all types of implied terms is to maximise the social utility of the relationship; that is, to ensure cooperation between the parties and compliance with society's standards.

Pause for reflection

Collins argues[10] that 'such an open-ended examination of policy considerations is neither appropriate nor necessary'. He posits a two-stage inquiry. First, a court should try to discover a default rule that achieves an efficient allocation of risks as between the parties, since this reduces transaction costs and is likely to have been agreed by the parties had they considered it. Second, the rule should conform to the reasonable expectations of the parties (informed by normal commercial practices, customs, usages, and an understanding of an appropriate commercial balance of obligations); this would avoid the potential risk of granting one or the other an unexpected advantage.

The *imposed* nature of terms implied by law is consistent with the following features of terms implied in law.

(i) Courts often rely exclusively on *precedents* rather than examine the intentions of the parties to the particular contract (*Yeoman Credit Ltd v Apps* (1962)).

(ii) Terms implied-in-law may be very *complex* and so unlikely to have been overlooked because they 'go without saying' (see *Scally v Southern Health and Social Services Board*).

(iii) The parties *cannot agree to exclude* some terms implied by law.

- In *Malik and Mahmud v BCCI*, the House of Lords (at 45) made clear that express terms 'could not affect an implied obligation of mutual trust and confidence'.

- In *Johnstone v Bloomsbury Health Authority* (1992), a junior hospital doctor's contract required him to work up to 88 hours per week. The Court of Appeal held that the employers' power to fix the hours of work was subject to an implied limitation for the health and safety of the doctor and his patients. Stuart-Smith LJ (at 343–6) said that the implied term prevails over the express term since the latter is void under section 2(1) of UCTA as an exclusion of liability for personal injury or death.

---

[10] In 'Implied Terms: The Foundation in Good Faith and Fair Dealing' (2014) *CLP* 1, 24–5.

- Sections 6 and 7 of UCTA makes it *impossible for the parties to contract out of (exclude)* statutory implied terms on sale of goods and services against consumers, and only permits it in *other* contracts if it is reasonable to do so (see 11.4.3). Consumers have the added protection of UTCCR, which invalidates unfair terms.

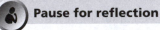

Pause for reflection

The effect of implied terms in sale of goods contracts is to reverse the presumption of *caveat emptor* ('let the buyer beware'). Instead of leaving the buyer unprotected except for any specific undertakings extracted from the trader, sale of goods implied terms assure the buyer of a 'minimum kit' of rights in respect of the goods purchased. The argument that they are necessary to express the parties' presumed intention is unrealistic Here is the clearest example of the implication of terms to protect *reasonable expectations* (specifically that of buyers) and to counter unequal bargaining power.

The court's power to imply terms *by law* is **limited**.

(i) The proposed **implication must fit the generality of contracts of that class** and not only particular instances of it (*Reid v Rush & Tompkins Group plc* (1990)).

(ii) However, courts have considerable latitude in the *level of detail* that they deploy in prescribing the relevant class of contracts. In **Scally v Southern Health and Social Services Board** (1992), a term was implied into a very *narrow subcategory of employment contracts* when some doctors lost out on additional pension entitlements under their employment contracts because they had not known to take certain action. The House of Lords implied a term requiring the employer to take reasonable steps to inform their employees of this right in cases where: (a) a particular term makes a valuable right available to an employee contingent on him or her taking action; (b) the term results from collective bargaining; and (c) the employee cannot reasonably be expected to know of the term without being notified. Freedland observes that: 'There are few if any other situations where this would occur in an employment context.'[11]

Pause for reflection

1. If the classes of contractual relationships may be subdivided into more detailed and numerous categories, so that the terms implied necessarily have a *less general application*, this narrows the distinction between: terms implied *in fact* into *specific* contracts; and terms implied *by law* into contracts of a *recognised type*. It becomes arguable that in respect of

➡

---

[11] M Freedland, 'Individual Contracts of Employment and the Common Law Courts' (1992) 21 *ILJ* 135, 139.

➡️

all contracts the implication of terms is based on the appropriateness of doing so in all the circumstances including: the express agreement; the nature of the contract; the presumed intentions of the parties; the price; the fair and efficient allocation of rights and obligations; and the reasonable expectation of the parties. It is a matter of *degree; policy* considerations once again take centre stage.

2. The overlap between terms implied in law and in fact is well recognised. Cooke P said that implied terms are 'categories or shades in a continuous spectrum', so that 'it may be doubted whether tabulated legalism will ever produce an exhaustive or rigidly discrete classification' (*Vickery v Waitaki Intl Ltd* (1992) at 64). McMeel[12] warns against exaggerating the differences: 'Historically it is likely that all today's implied terms in law commenced as incidents of particular transactions, and then migrated to the sub-category of terms implied in law (once the existence of that classification was made explicit). Today similar journeys are being made.'

3. Any party with sufficient resources will draft express terms to its own advantage. The traditional justification that courts imply terms in order to fill gaps left by the parties, to reduce the parties' transaction costs, and to give effect to their presumed intention is unrealistic. For, the function of contracts is to allocate risks between the parties, so that any 'gap' left by the contract implicitly allocates the risk to the party who suffers the loss. In truth, implied terms serve to reallocate risk away from the party who would otherwise bear the loss. The language of 'gap-filling' merely serves to hide this rewriting of the contractual risk allocation. Terms are often implied to *temper one-sided standard form contracts* and invariably add to the burdens or reduce the benefits of one party. Terms implied by the courts as a matter of law rest on the court's view of the *fair and practical allocation of risks* in particular types of contract. It draws from the same source as duties of care in the tort of negligence. It allows courts 'to equalise the obligations of the parties, even in the teeth of express terms of standard form contracts, and so pursue ideas of fairness' (Collins at 246). Lord Steyn saw *scope for further development of implications by law* and said 'it is tolerably clear that the court may take into account considerations of reasonableness . . . this function of the court is essential in providing a reasonable and fair framework for contracting'.[13]

10.5 Interpretation of terms

Once courts have identified the binding terms of the contract, the next question is what those terms *mean*; in particular, whether and how they apply to the dispute before the court. Lord Goff said, 'the staple diet of the Commercial Court can be summed up in one word—"Construction"'.[14] Given the large number of contractual disputes involving the interpretation of contract terms, the general principles of interpretation assume great practical importance. While the parties are masters of their

---

[12] *The Construction of Contracts* (2nd edn, OUP, 2011) 320.

[13] J Steyn, 'Contract Law: Fulfilling the Reasonable Expectations of Honest Men' (1997) 113 *LQR* 433, 442.

[14] R Goff, 'Commercial Contracts and the Commercial Court' [1984] 1 *LMCLQ* 382, 385.

contracts, it is for the *courts* to determine the meaning of contractual terms. As with other areas of contract law, the usual policies operate in this area, namely:

- the need for certainty and administrability;
- giving effect to the parties' intentions; and
- avoiding unfair results.

Since the meaning of a term depends on the precise words used in the particular context in which the contract was made, precedents are of limited value ('a decision on a different clause in a different context is seldom of much help on a question of construction', *Surrey Heath BC v Lovell Construction Ltd* (1990) at 118). Nevertheless, some broad principles can be stated. Lord Hoffmann summed these up in *Investors Compensation Scheme Ltd v West Bromwich Building Society* (1998) (at 912) with the professed aim of assimilating 'the way in which such documents are interpreted by judges to the common sense principles by which any serious utterance would be interpreted in ordinary life'.

10.5.1 From literal to contextual interpretation

Consistent with the thinking behind the parole evidence rule (see 10.3.1), the traditional method of interpretation adopted a literal stance towards documents embodying an agreement (*Lovell and Christmas Ltd v Wall* (1912)). A contract's meaning was said to be discoverable within the '**four corners**' of the document without reference to extrinsic evidence (*outside* the words of the contractual document). This approach ostensibly aids certainty and administrative efficiency. However, it proceeds on the fiction that words have a 'plain', 'simple', 'ordinary', immutable, or absolute meaning independent of their context. In reality, words take their meaning from the *context* in which they are used. Multiple meanings can be attached to even the simplest of words as a cursory glance at a dictionary shows. For example, an academic who employs a student as a research assistant for the 'summer' will mean a different period of time from a farmer, astronomer, or educational institution using the same words. Thus, courts often have to *choose* between different reasonable meanings, and the factors affecting that choice go beyond purely linguistic ones.

The change in emphasis was signalled in *Prenn v Simmonds* (1971). Lord Wilberforce stated (at 1383–4) that agreements should *not* be seen in isolation 'from the matrix of facts in which they were set and interpreted purely on internal linguistic considerations'. Rather, courts must 'inquire beyond the language and see what the circumstances were with reference to which the words were used, and the object, appearing from the circumstances, which the persons using them had in view'. In *Reardon Smith Line Ltd v Yngvar Hansen-Tangen* (1976), he continued (at 995–7):

> No contracts are made in a vacuum: there is always a setting in which they have to be placed. The nature of what is legitimate to have regard to is usually described as 'the surrounding circumstances' but this phrase is imprecise: it can be illustrated but hardly defined. In a commercial contract it is certainly right that the Court should know the commercial purpose of the contract and this in turn presupposes knowledge

of the genesis of the transaction, the background, the context, the market in which the parties are operating . . . what the Court must do must be to place itself in thought in the same factual matrix as that in which the parties were.

Lord Hoffmann consolidated this development in *Investors Compensation Scheme v West Bromwich* (at 912), setting out some general principles on interpretation. First, the overall aim of interpretation is the 'ascertainment of the meaning which the document would convey to a reasonable person having all the background knowledge which would reasonably have been available to the parties in the situation in which they were at the time of the contract'. This background can be considered even if there is no ambiguity or other problem in the language.

How much contextual information is admissible? Lord Hoffmann's controversial second principle relates to the *scope* of the admissible contextual or background facts in interpreting the contract. He said that 'subject to the requirement that it should have been reasonably available to the parties and to the exception to be mentioned . . . , it includes absolutely anything which would have affected the way in which the language of the document would have been understood by a reasonable man'. Lord Hoffmann's view that 'there is no conceptual limit to what can be regarded as background' seems incontrovertible. It should be a question of the *weight* attached to the evidence rather than of artificially restricting the scope of admissible evidence. In *BCCI v Ali* (2001), Lord Hoffmann explains that he was not 'encouraging a trawl through "background" which could not have made a reasonable person think that the parties must have departed from conventional usage', but only 'anything which a reasonable man would have regarded as *relevant*' (at [39]).

It has been recognised that less weight will be given to the background evidence where the interpretation relates to a standard form contract used in a particular industry (*Re Sigma Finance Corp (in administrative receivership)* (2009)) or to a public document which is available for inspection (*Cherry Tree Investment Ltd v Landmain Ltd* (2012)) because third parties may be prejudiced.

Pause for reflection

In **'How Do the Courts Interpret Commercial Contracts?'** (1999) 58 *CLJ* 303, **Staughton** warns that admitting a larger volume of relevant information:

1. will *increase costs* and prolong litigation;
2. can generate *uncertainty* since multiple and contradictory, but all reasonable, meanings may emerge; and
3. may smack of judicial rewriting of contracts.
4. The contract can end up meaning one thing to the parties aware of the factual matrix and another to *third parties* who can only rely on the wording of the contract.

However, Arden LJ observed that she was 'unaware that the fears expressed . . . have been realized. The powers of case management in the Civil Procedure Rules could obviously be used to keep evidence within its proper bounds' (*Static Control Components (Europe) Ltd v Egan* [2004] at [29]).

10.5.2 **Something must have gone wrong with the language**

Lord Hoffmann emphasises that the aim is to ascertain the meaning of the *person* using the words. These may differ since (at 912–13):

[t]he meaning of words is a matter of dictionaries and grammars; the meaning of the document is what the parties using those words against the relevant background would reasonably have been understood to mean. The background may not merely enable the reasonable man to choose between the possible meanings of words which are ambiguous but even (as occasionally happens in ordinary life) to conclude that the parties must, for whatever reason, have *used the wrong words or syntax* . . .

In that case, 'the law does not require judges to attribute to the parties an intention which they plainly could not have had'. Language that 'flouts business commonsense . . . must be made to yield to business commonsense'. If it is clear that something has gone wrong with the language *and* it is clear what a reasonable person would have understood the parties to have meant, then there is no 'limit to the amount of "red ink" or verbal rearrangement or correction which the court is allowed' (***Chartbrook Ltd v Persimmon Homes Ltd*** (2009) Lord Hoffmann at [25]). In one case, the Court of Appeal rejected both parties' interpretation, but was nevertheless prepared to give meaning to the disputed words. Arden LJ explains that: 'if the agreement is susceptible of an interpretation which will make it enforceable and effective, the court will prefer that interpretation to any interpretation which would result in its being void. The court will also prefer an interpretation which produces a result which the parties are likely to have agreed over an improbable result' (*Anglo Continental Education Group Ltd v Capital Homes (Southern) Ltd* (2009) at [13]).

When will courts conclude that 'something has gone wrong with the language' and **depart from the dictionary meaning of words used?** They can do so where that meaning:

(i) is inconsistent with the parties' intention as evinced by the context (*Chartbrook Ltd v Persimmon Homes*);

(ii) would render the contract ineffective (*Steele v Hoe* (1849)), or inconsistent with the rest of the document (*Watson v Haggit* (1928));

(iii) would not accord with business common sense. In *Rainy Sky SA v Kookmin Bank* (2011), Lord Clarke said that it is only where a term is open to more than one interpretation that it is generally appropriate to adopt that which is most consistent with **business common sense**; however, in *Napier Park European Credit Opportunities Fund Ltd v Harbourmaster Pro-Rata and others* (2014) Lewison LJ explains (at [31]–[33]) that the court should seek to discern the commercial intention and the commercial consequences from the terms of the contract itself, and that fed in to the process of deciding whether a particular word or phrase was in reality clear and unambiguous; where possible, the court should test any interpretation against the commercial consequences. That was part of the iterative exercise of interpretation; it was not merely a safety valve in cases of absurdity;

(iv) would lead to very unfair results. Lord Hoffmann restates what Staughton describes as 'the most important'[15] principle of interpretation; namely, the **presumption against unreasonable results**. Staughton regards this as based on common sense. He cites Lord Reid in *L Schuler AG v Wickman Machine Tool Sales Ltd* (see 12.2.3.2):

> 'The fact that a particular construction leads to a very unreasonable result must be a relevant consideration. The more unreasonable the result the more unlikely it is that the parties can have intended it, and if they do intend it the more necessary it is that they should make that intention abundantly clear.' When speaking to students I tell them that what Lord Reid said there is something which they should learn by heart.

In *Lloyds TSB Foundation for Scotland v Lloyd's Banking Group plc* (2013) Lord Mance confirmed that the proper approach to interpretation is 'contextual and purposive', not 'mechanical'. This is not to say that the mechanics are irrelevant; they are not but 'the value of machinery depends upon its being correctly directed towards the right end.'

On the other hand, courts 'do not easily accept that people have made linguistic mistakes', and they must assume that any lawyers involved would draft on the assumption that words will be given their ordinary, natural, dictionary, or technical meaning. It is not enough to show that a contract is unduly favourable to one party (***Chartbrook Ltd v Persimmon Homes Ltd*** (2009) at [15], [20]). Moreover, 'where the parties have used unambiguous language, the court must apply it' (*Rainy Sky SA v Kookmin Bank* (2011) at [23]). Rix LJ observed (at [110]) that 'judges should not see in *Chartbrook* as an open sesame for reconstructing the parties' contract, but an opportunity to remedy by construction a clear error of language which could not have been intended.' This is acknowledged by Lord Hope in *Aberdeen City Council v Stewart Milne Group Ltd* (2011) at [21]. Consistently, courts have affirmed that 'commercial common sense' should not be elevated to the position of an overriding criterion of construction and that courts should be wary of rewriting the contract to impose a more reasonable solution on the parties (eg *BMA Special Opportunity Hub Fund Ltd v African Minerals Finance Ltd* (2013) at [24]; *Aston Hill Financial Inc v African Minerals Finance Ltd* (2013) at [24]).

Pause for reflection

1. The expansion of the scope of contractual interpretation means that its operation will overlap with that of the doctrines of **rectification** and of **implied terms**. Sir Richard Buxton argues extrajudicially ((2010) 69 *CLJ* 253 at 257) that the process of rectification is virtually identical to Lord Hoffmann's principles of construction in *ICS*. In *Oceanbulk Shipping v TMT Asia* (2010), Lord Clarke cites Buxton's article with approval, commenting that the two are 'closely related' (at [45]). Indeed, in *Cherry Tree Investment Ltd v Landmain Ltd*, Arden LJ describes the modern approach as 'corrective interpretation' (at [62], and see 6.6 on rectification).

→

---

[15] C Staughton, 'How Do the Courts Interpret Commercial Contracts?' (1999) 58 *CLJ* 303, 308.

➡

2. The potential for courts to attribute a different meaning from the natural meaning of clear and unambiguous language, if the context requires, allows a more realistic, more accurate, and fairer approach to ascertaining intentions. In **'Common Sense Principles of Contract Interpretation (and how we've been using them all along)'** (2003) 23 *OJLS* 173, **Kramer** supports Lord Hoffmann's approach as being: based on the 'common sense principles of interpretation', 'the matrix of fact', and 'the parties' reasonable expectations'; versatile and useful concepts with a sound theoretical basis; and reflected elsewhere in the existing law.

Some examples will illustrate the tensions between the literal and purposive approaches to construction.

- In *Pink Floyd Music v EMI Records* (2010), the contract between the rock band Pink Floyd and their record label EMI prohibited EMI from 'unbundling' (selling songs on the band's albums as single tracks). At trial, the judge accepted the reason as that of protecting the 'artistic integrity' of the albums. The question was whether this prohibition on 'unbundling' applies to music sold online. The majority (Lord Neuberger MR and Laws LJ) adopted the purposive approach and answered 'yes'. Lord Neuberger said that 'it seems perverse to imagine that the parties envisaged the integrity of the Albums being rigidly controlled so far as they were physically recorded and distributed, but to have no control whatever over the integrity of digital recordings and distribution' (at [55]). Laws LJ held that where 'the purpose of the provision is clear but the language is equivocal', the contract should be construed 'so as to give effect to its demonstrated purpose' (at [75]). Carnwath LJ, dissenting, concluded that the prohibition on unbundling did not extend to online sales because the definition of 'Records' and 'Album' contained elsewhere in the contract clearly refers to physical items (at [78]). He noted the importance of 'the *prima facie* assumption that the words mean what they say; the dangers of "detailed semantic and syntactical analysis" of a commercial document; and the warning against too readily inferring that something has gone wrong, merely because it appears to result in a "bad bargain" . . .' (at [77]).

- In *ING Bank v Ros Roca* (2011), in which Carnwath LJ refused to depart from the ordinary meaning of the words in a contract for financial services because: (i) nothing had gone wrong with the language; and (ii) the question was not whether the proposed interpretation produced a fairer result, but whether it represented 'the clear alternative interpretation' (at [25]).

- In *Bishops Wholesale Newsagency Ltd v Surridge Dawson Ltd* (2009), the court refused to depart from the ordinary meaning of the contractual words where the parties had been advised by solicitors, there was no doubt about the natural meaning of the words chosen, and no room for inferring an obvious mistake, even though the consequent interpretation seemed unduly favourable to one party.

- *Bashir v Ali* (2011) involved a misdescription of and low reserve for the property auctioned. Nevertheless, the Court of Appeal refused to depart from the clear wording of the auction catalogue, its associated documentation, and the signed contract. This was clear and workable. A good bargain for one of the parties is not enough in itself to depart from the wording of the contract. The contract would only be rectified by construction if, objectively, it was clear what property and terms the seller intended to offer, and that the bidder understood them and intended to bid on that basis. Those requirements could not be satisfied in the instant case.

10.5.3 Inadmissibility of previous negotiations and subsequent conduct

Lord Hoffmann sets out the exclusionary principle that makes legal interpretation *different* from the way we could interpret utterances in ordinary life (at 910): what *cannot* be taken into account in interpreting the contractual document is evidence of the previous negotiations of the parties. Lord Hoffmann recognises that this exclusion undermines the general aim of contextual interpretation, but explains that, since the parties are free to change their bargaining postures, and their positions are unstable until the contract is finalised by formal acceptance of the offer, '[a]ll a court can do is to decide what the final contract means' (*Canterbury Golf International Ltd v Yoshimoto* (2002) at [28]).

However, in *Chartbrook*, Lord Hoffmann conceded that the exclusionary rule did not apply to evidence of negotiations as evidence 'to establish a fact which may be relevant as *background* known to the parties, or to support a claim for rectification or estoppel. These are not exceptions to the rule. They operate outside it.' On the facts, although the contractual words in question made syntactical sense, this 'background' revealed a mistake that needed correction to achieve commercial sense. This was done as an exercise in construction without the need for rectification. Baroness Hale agreed but added (at [99]) that she 'would not have found it quite so easy to reach this conclusion had we not been made aware of the agreement which the parties had reached on this aspect of their bargain during the negotiations which led up to the formal contract'. She saw 'attractions' in the arguments that the exclusionary rule should be reconsidered.

In *Oceanbulk Shipping and Trading SA v TMT Asia Ltd* (2010), the Supreme Court cast further doubt on the exclusionary rule. First, Lord Clarke noted (at [39]) that it may be very difficult to distinguish between material which forms part of the pre-contractual negotiations, which is part of the factual matrix and therefore admissible as an aid to interpretation; and that which is not, and so is inadmissible. Second, Lord Clarke noted (at [44]–[45]) that the width of the principles of construction now encompasses rectification (see 6.6), which *does* allow resort to pre-contractual negotiations. The issue at hand concerned the admissibility of evidence of what was said or written in the course of 'without prejudice' negotiations. The court concluded that it should in principle be admissible both when rectification is sought and 'when the court is considering a submission that the factual matrix relevant to the true construction of a settlement agreement includes evidence of an objective fact communicated in the course of such negotiations'. Nevertheless, Lord Clarke emphasised that his judgment is not 'intended otherwise to encourage the admission of evidence of pre-contractual negotiations' (at [46]).

Schuler AG v Wickman Machine Tool Sales (1973) held that evidence of *conduct subsequent to contract formation* is also inadmissible since, otherwise, the meaning of the contract could change over time.

◄◄ Counterpoint

The exclusionary rules are difficult to justify. In **'Prior Negotiations and Subsequent Conduct—The Next Step Forward for Contractual Interpretation'** (2003) 119 *LQR* 272, **McMeel** rejects both exclusions and argues that the matter should not be one of the weight, and not the admissibility, of the evidence.

Lord Nicholls, writing extrajudicially, in **'My Kingdom for a Horse: The Meaning of Words'** (2005) 101 *LQR* 577, sets out the reasons against the exclusions.

1. *Injustice*: 'Whenever a court is disabled from considering evidence which would assist, the court is to that extent less able to decide how the language of the contract ought fairly to be interpreted' (at 586). It allows 'one party to contend for a meaning he knows was not intended' (at 587). In *Pro Force Recruit Ltd v The Rugby Group Ltd* (2006), Arden LJ agrees (at [57]) that to allow a party to evade the parties' common understanding 'is not, on the face of it, an attractive result'. On the facts, evidence of pre-contractual negotiations was admitted to interpret an 'unusual combination of words' in the contract. Arden LJ (at [57]) remarked that such evidence 'may be admissible for the purposes of interpretation in wider circumstances'. It seems that Lord Hoffmann regards the injustice in the occasional case, as outweighed by the certainty and predictability to be derived from the exclusionary rules (see also *Scottish Widows Fund and Life Assurance Society v BGC International* (2012) at [34]–[35], [70]).

2. *Best evidence*: it would be 'perverse' to 'be barred from having regard to what may be the best evidence of all' (at 583). Evidence of pre-contract negotiations should be 'admissible if they would have influenced the notional reasonable person in his understanding of the meaning the parties intended to convey by the words they used'. A reasonable person with knowledge of the background circumstances minus the negotiations will usually have an incomplete picture of the background to the contract.

3. There are already many '*exceptions*': evidence of previous negotiations is admissible to resolve:

   • questions about the formation of contracts not embodied in a formal contract but made through a course of dealings;

   • claims for misrepresentation or rectification;

   • a plea of estoppel or to show that the contract has been varied (*James Miller & Partners Ltd v Whitworth Street Estates (Manchester) Ltd* (1970));

   • questions on the nature and object of the contract;

   • ambiguity in written documents.

Judges have noted the difficulty in distinguishing such *admissible* evidence from *inadmissible* evidence of the parties' previous negotiating positions.

→

➡

Conduct subsequent to contract formation is already admissible to establish:

- estoppel or variation of the contract (*James Miller v Whitworth Street Estates*);

- the content of an *oral* contract (*Maggs t/a BM Builders (A Firm) v Marsh* (2006) at [26]). Smith LJ said that this will depend on the parties' recollections:

   The accuracy of those recollections may be tested and elucidated by things said and done by the parties or witnesses after the agreement has been concluded.

This exclusionary rule has been departed from in New Zealand (see *Wholesale Distributors Ltd v Gibbons Holdings Ltd* [2007] NZSC 37, [[2008] 1 NZLR 277).

4. *Transparency*: since evidence of the parties' actual intentions often does become known by, and does influence, judges on disputes about interpretation, that should be recognised openly. Lord Nicholls adds (at 588–9): 'As with pre-contract negotiations . . . I suspect that in practice judges from time to time do have regard to post-contract conduct when interpreting contracts . . . Judges are well able to identify, and disregard, self-serving subsequent conduct.'

5. *Uncertainty*: the proper answer to the legitimate concerns about uncertainty and increased costs 'lies in case management and appropriately tight judicial control over the evidence sought to be adduced' (at 588).

6. *Comparative law* (at 586): the exclusions are inconsistent with most other legal systems and international restatements of contract law such as:

- the Vienna Convention on Sale of Goods;

- the UNIDROIT Principles of International and Commercial Contracts; and

- the European Draft Common Frame of Reference.

- The Scottish Law Commission has recently published a comprehensive criticism of the exclusionary rule (*Discussion Paper on Interpretation of Contract* (No 147, 2011) at paras 7.12–7.15), as part of a consultative process into whether Scots law should admit evidence of pre-contractual negotiations.

- Article 5:102 of the Principles of European Contract Law states that 'In interpreting a contract, regard shall be had, in particular, to:

   (a) **the circumstances in which it was concluded, including the preliminary negotiations;**

   (b) **the conduct of the parties, even subsequent to the conclusion of the contract;**

   (c) the nature and purpose of the contract;

   (d) the interpretation which has already been give to similar clauses by the parties and the practices they have established between themselves;

   (e) the meaning commonly given to terms and expressions in the branch of activity concerned and the interpretation similar clauses may already have received;

   (f) usages; and

   (g) **good faith and fair dealing.**

Diagram 10C The scope of admissible evidence in interpreting contracts

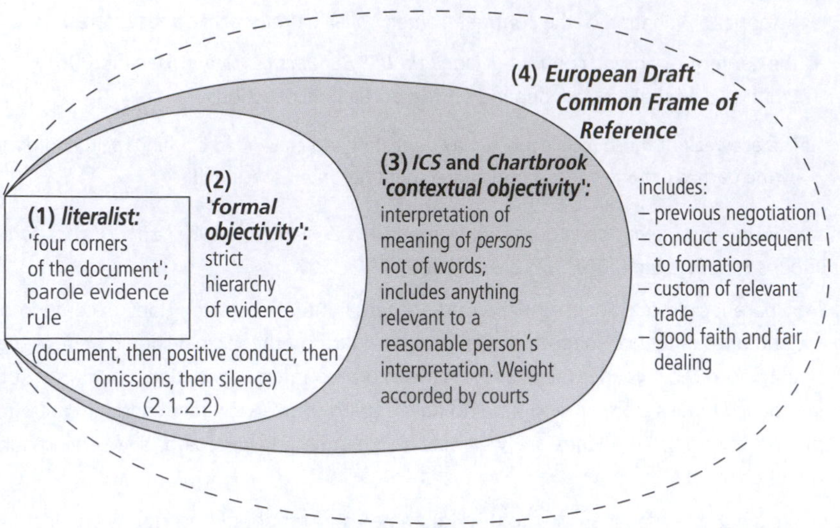

The overall picture is summarised in **Diagram 10C**.

10.6 **Interpretation of exemption clauses**

10.6.1 **Then and now**

Terms that limit or exclude liability for breach of contract ('exemption clauses') can undermine or totally defeat the innocent party's contractual expectations by depriving him or her of compensation for loss caused by the other party's breach. Just as the courts can manipulate the standard of notice required, rendering onerous or unusual terms (often exemptions of liability) unenforceable for lack of incorporation (see 10.3.3.2), they have evolved special rules of interpretation to narrow the coverage of exemption clauses, even if they have been properly incorporated. 'Judicial creativity, bordering on judicial legislation'[16] has sought to prevent contract-breakers from escaping the normal consequences of breach under the 'cover' of exemption clauses. As Lord Denning graphically recounts (in *George Mitchell (Chesterhall) Ltd v Finney Lock Seeds Ltd* (1983) at 296–7):

Faced with this abuse of power—by the strong against the weak—by the use of the small print of the conditions—the judges did what they could to put a curb upon it. They still had before them the idol, 'freedom of contract'. They still knelt down and worshipped it, but they concealed under their cloaks a secret weapon. They used it to stab the idol in the back. This weapon was called 'the true construction of the contract'. They used it with great skill and ingenuity. They used it so as to depart from the natural meaning of the words of the exemption clause and to put upon

---

[16] *BCCI v Ali* (2001) at [60].

them a strained and unnatural construction. In case after case, they said that the words were not strong enough to give the big concern exemption from liability; or that in the circumstances the big concern was not entitled to rely on the exemption clause . . . In short, whenever the wide words—in their natural meaning—would give rise to an unreasonable result, the judges either rejected them as repugnant to the main purpose of the contract, or else cut them down to size in order to produce a reasonable result.

However, legislation such as UCTA and UTCCR (see Chapter 11) have reduced the need 'to go through all kinds of gymnastic contortions to get round' unfair exemption clauses (at 299). In *Photo Production Ltd v Securicor Transport Ltd* (1980), Lord Diplock agrees (at 851) that:

any need for this kind of judicial distortion of the English language has been banished . . . In commercial contracts negotiated between businessmen capable of looking after their own interests and of deciding how risks inherent in the performance of various kinds of contract can be most economically borne (generally by insurance), it is, in my view, wrong to place a strained construction upon words in an exclusion clause which are clear and fairly susceptible of one meaning only.

Thus, Lord Hoffmann declares that '[a]lmost all the old intellectual baggage of "legal" interpretation has been discarded' (*Investors Compensation Scheme* at 912), including the 'artificial rules' relating to the construction of exemption clauses (*BCCI v Ali* (2001) at [62]). This is an overstatement as 'it may be too soon to write the obituary for the old rules',[17] which have been approved by appellate courts. Namely, rules on the interpretation of clauses which:

(i) totally exclude liability;

(ii) merely limit liability;

(iii) exclude or limit liability for negligence; and

(iv) exclude or limit liability for indirect or consequential loss.

These rules show how the common law has sought to respond to perceived problems of unfairness. The law is summarised in **Diagram 10D**.

10.6.2 **Fundamental breach**

In essence, parties were *barred* from relying on clauses which excluded liability for a breach which is fundamental in the sense that it 'goes to the very root' of the contract.

✓ Lord Denning advocated it as a *rule of law* to be applied *irrespective of the parties' intention*; that is, liability for fundamental breach cannot be excluded no matter how widely or clearly it is drawn.[18] This approach was rejected (*Suisse Atlantique Société d'Armement Maritime SA v NV Rotterdamsche Kolen Centrale* (1966)).

---

[17] E McKendrick, 'The Interpretation of Contracts: Lord Hoffmann's Re-Statement' in S Worthington (ed), *Commercial Law and Commercial Practice* (Hart Publishing, 2003) 139, 148.

[18] *Karsales (Harrow) Ltd v Wallis* (1956); *Harbutt's Plasticine Ltd v Wayne Tank Pump Co Ltd* (1971).

Diagram 10D Control of exemption clauses via interpretation

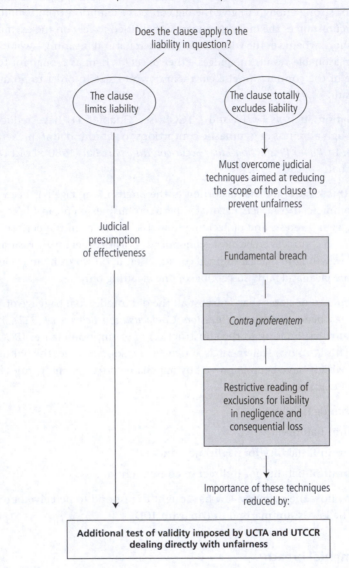

✓ The fundamental breach doctrine is now regarded simply as a *rule of construction* based on the assumption that the *more* unreasonable the result, the *less* likely it is that the parties could have intended it and the court is to interpret the clause as applying to breach. Thus, *very* clear words will be necessary to exclude liability for: (i) breach of terms that go to the root/essential character/purpose of the contract (*Karsales (Harrow) Ltd v Wallis* (1956)), or (ii) a deliberate repudiation of the contract (*Chartbrook Ltd v Persimmon Homes Ltd*). However, such an exclusion is effective if it is clearly set out and fairly susceptible to that interpretation.

In *Photo Production v Securicor Transport*, P engaged S to make periodic security patrols of its factory. During one such visit, S's employee started a fire to keep warm and burnt the factory down. S relied on an exclusion clause which stated that 'under no circumstances' were they to 'be responsible for any injurious act or default by any employee . . . unless [this] . . . could have been foreseen and avoided by the exercise of due diligence'. The House of Lords held the clause effective to shield S from liability. This conclusion was supported by the finding that: (i) no due diligence would have revealed the employee's predilection; (ii) P only paid a small sum for S's service; (iii) the service offered was limited; and (iv) P could have insured more cheaply than S.

However, fundamental breach as a rule of construction still applies. In *Internet Broadcasting Corp Ltd v MAR LLC* (2009), deputy judge Gabriel Moss QC stated that there is 'a strong presumption, against the exemption clause being construed so as to cover **'deliberate, repudiatory breach'** (at [33]). Thus, the defendant's deliberate abandonment of the contract fell outside the scope of the exclusion clause since no reasonable person could have intended it to cover a party walking away. However, Flaux J criticised this reasoning as effectively seeking to 'revive the doctrine of fundamental breach' (*Astrazeneca UK Ltd v Albemarle International Corp* (2011) at [289]); it was 'heterodox and regressive' (at [301]). He rejected the existence of such a presumption. Instead, the question is one of construction, albeit a strict one in the sense that clear words are necessary to exclude liability for a deliberate breach. Nevertheless, in *Kudos Catering (UK) Ltd v Manchester Central Convention Complex Ltd* (2013), the Court of Appeal construed an exclusion clause as covering only defective performance of the contract and not a refusal to perform it or be bound by it. For, otherwise the contract would be 'effectively devoid of contractual content since there is no sanction for non-performance. . . . It is inherently unlikely that the parties intended the clause to have this effect' (at [19]). Tomlinson LJ said that this construction gives effect to 'the presumption that parties do not lightly abandon a remedy for breach of contract afforded them by the general law' (at [28]).

10.6.3 *Contra proferentem*

The doctrine of fundamental breach as a rule of construction is merely an extreme version of *contra proferentem* interpretation. The latter requires **any ambiguity in a contractual term to be construed against the party who introduced it**. It receives legislative recognition in UTCCR (reg 7(2)). Words alleged to shield the contract-breaker from liability are given the *narrowest possible* interpretation, conferring the smallest possible protection from the liability in question. The following are examples.

- ✗ A clause in a contract for the sale of a 'new car' that excludes 'all conditions, warranties and liabilities implied by statute, common law or otherwise' was held not to protect the seller from liability for delivering a *used* car. The clause only covered breach of *implied* conditions and not of an *express* term to deliver a new car (*Andrews Brothers (Bournemouth) Ltd v Singer and Co Ltd* (1934)).

- ✗ In *Beck & Co v Szymanowski & Co* (1924), a contract deemed the sewing cotton delivered complied with the contract, unless the sellers were notified within 14 days of delivery. The buyers complained 18 months later that the cotton received was on average 12 yards short of the stipulated 200 yards long. The

House of Lords found the sellers liable on the basis that the relevant clause only applied to 'goods delivered' while the complaint was of partial non-delivery.

✗   In *BCCI v Ali* (2001), a clause stated that A's settlement of claim against B was 'in full and final settlement of all or any claims whether under statute, common law or in equity of whatsoever nature that exist or may exist and, in particular, all or any claims rights or applications of whatsoever nature that the applicant has or may have or has made or could make in or to the industrial tribunal'. This clause was held not to exclude a claim that *neither party could have been aware of* at the time of the settlement. Lord Nicholls said that courts should be slow to infer that parties have surrendered unknown rights and claims in the absence of clear language. However, since the natural wording seems abundantly clear, Lord Hoffmann's observation (at [61]) is apposite: 'When judges say that "in the absence of clear words" they would be unwilling to construe a document to mean something, they generally mean . . . that the effect of the document is unfair.'

Closely related is the **'peas not beans' rule**, which also echoes the thinking behind fundamental breach. In *Chanter v Hopkins* (1838), Lord Abinger (at 404) explains that: 'If a man offers to buy peas off another, and he sends him beans, he does not perform his contract.' An exemption clause protects from defective performance, not from non-performance. *George Mitchell v Finney Lock Seed* (1983) shows how thin the line is between the two. The seller purported to sell *winter* cabbage seeds, but delivered inferior *autumn* cabbage seeds which produced a useless crop, causing the buyer about £60,000 loss. A term limited the seller's liability to a refund or the replacement of seeds (here, about £200). The Court of Appeal found it to be a case of *non-performance*, while the House of Lords held that it was a case of *defective performance*. Nevertheless, both courts agreed that the clause was invalid for unreasonableness under the Sale of Goods Act (a forerunner of UCTA).

10.6.4 **The limitation–exclusion distinction**

The courts have declared themselves less hostile towards clauses which *limit* rather than totally *exclude* liability for breach on the basis that parties are more likely to agree to limit rather than exclude liability altogether and because limitation clauses play a legitimate role in risk allocation (*Ailsa Craig Fishing Co Ltd v Malvern Fishing Co Ltd* (1983)). **Limitation clauses are therefore presumptively valid.**

◀◀ Counterpoint

1. The distinction is artificial since exclusion clauses may represent legitimate risk allocation (as in *Photo Production v Securicor Transport*, see 10.6.2) while limitation clauses may be so severe as to amount, in substance, to a total exclusion (eg limiting liability to £1).

2. UCTA and UTCCR do not distinguish between their controls of these terms.

→

➡️

3. In *Darlington Futures Ltd v Delco Australia Pty Ltd* (1986), the High Court of Australia rejected the distinction (at 510). In *BHP Petroleum Ltd v British Steel plc* (2000) (at 285) Evans LJ thought it:

> unfortunate if the present authorities cannot be reconciled in the basis that no categorization is necessary and of a general rule that the more extreme the consequences are, in terms of excluding or modifying the liability which would otherwise arise, then the more stringent the Court's approach should be in requiring that the exclusion or limit should be clear and unambiguously expressed.

10.6.5 **Exemptions of negligence liability**

Courts have maintained their hostility towards exclusions of liability for *negligence*. The stated reasons are that it is 'inherently improbable' that the innocent party would have agreed to it, and that parties should not be allowed to hide unfair exemptions behind general words when they are 'shy' of making it explicit for fear of alerting the other party (*EE Caledonia Ltd v Orbit Valve Co Europe plc* (1994) at 1523). UCTA and UTCCR both severely limit the effectiveness of exemptions for negligence (see 11.4.2). But they only apply if the relevant exemption is interpreted as being wide enough to cover the facts in question. In determining this *prior* question, Lord Morton sets out three rules in **Canada Steamship Lines Ltd v The King** (1952) (summarised in **Diagram 10E**).

(i) **Express exemption for negligence**
An exemption clause will only cover negligence liability if it *expressly* exempts such liability; use of words synonymous with negligence may be effective (*Smith v South Wales Switchgear Co Ltd* (1978)). However, even exempting liability for 'loss whatsoever or howsoever occasioned' may *not* be sufficiently express (*Shell Chemicals UK Ltd v P&O Roadtanks Ltd* (1995)).

(ii) **No express exemption for negligence**
Absent express words exempting negligence liability, the question is whether the words used are *wide enough* in their ordinary meaning to cover negligence liability (any doubt being resolved against the party relying on the clause, the *proferens*).

- If *not*, the exemption will not cover negligence liability.
- If so, *and* the clause only *limits* rather than excludes liability, the term is effective (*Ailsa Craig Fishing v Malvern Fishing* and *George Mitchell v Finley Lock Seed*). Examples: 'will not be liable for any accident howsoever caused' (*White v Blackmore* (1972)), 'shall not be liable under any circumstances whatsoever for theft' (*L Harris (Harella) Ltd v Continental Express Ltd & Burn Transit Ltd* (1961)), and excluding liability 'arising from any cause whatsoever' (*Farr (AE) Ltd v Admiralty* (1953)).
- If a clause which is apparently wide enough to cover negligence totally *excludes* liability, another question arises.

Diagram 10E Exemptions from liability in negligence: the *Canada Steamship* rules

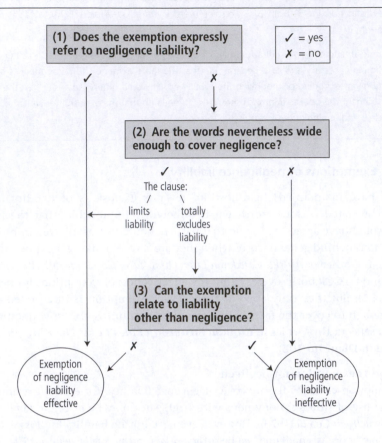

(iii) Can the exemption cover liability other than negligence?

- If *not*, and the contract-breaker's *only* possible liability is for negligence then the exemption is effective. In *Alderslade v Hendon Laundry Ltd* (1945), H negligently lost A's handkerchiefs sent in for cleaning. H could only have been liable for negligent loss and was permitted to rely on a clause limiting liability to 20 times the cleaning charge.

- If the clause *can* apply to liability other than negligence (eg it can also cover strict liability for breach of contract or for breach of statutory duty), it will *only* exempt from the non-negligence liability and *not the negligence liability*. Steyn LJ (in *EE Caledonia Ltd v Orbit Valve Co Europe*, at 244) said that the potential for non-negligence liability should not be so 'fanciful or remote' that the *proferens* cannot be supposed to desire protection from it. However, 'fanciful' interpretation aptly describes *Hollier v Rambler Motors* (1972). R contracted to fix H's car. A term totally excluding liability 'for damage caused by fire to customers' cars' was held not to cover R's negligent damage to H's car by fire because the car could also be so damaged without R's negligence. Since R could not have been liable without negligence, it *does* seem 'fanciful' (because redundant) for R to exclude liability for it. Such a construction deprives the term of any effect although it avoided an unfair result pre-UCTA.

> ## ◄► Counterpoint
>
> The *Canada Steamship* rules are open to criticism.
>
> 1. The rules may *contradict the parties' intentions* if they do intend a clause to exclude both negligence and other liability.
>
> 2. The test applicable where negligence is *not* expressly exempted makes *conflicting demands*, simultaneously requiring the exemption to be drafted *widely* enough to cover negligence but *narrowly* enough to exclude all other possible liability.
>
> 3. These rules were supported in *Caledonia* on the basis that commercial parties are legally advised. However, the possibility of drafting and negotiating around inconvenient rules known only to the legally trained do not justify retaining the rules. They were rejected by the Supreme Court of Victoria in *Schenker & Co (Aust) Pty Ltd v Maplas Equipment and Services Pty Ltd* (1990).

The decision in *Investors Compensation Scheme* has downgraded the *Canada Steamship* rules. While affirming the 'general authority' of the rules, the House of Lords in *HIH Casualty and General Insurance v Chase Manhattan Bank* (2003) said that the court's primary task was to give effect to the intention of the parties. In *Mir Steel UK Ltd v Morris* (2012), the Court of Appeal affirmed that the *Canada Steamship* principles 'should not be applied mechanistically and ought to be regarded as no more than guidelines.' In particular, they do not provide an 'automatic solution' to a particular case. On the facts, the court held that there was no justification for reading the words 'any claim' narrowly to exclude negligence claims. In *National Westminster Bank plc v Utrecht-America Finance Co* (2001), a term excluding liability for negligent *and* even fraudulent non-disclosure was upheld. The contract was between large banks dealing at arm's length and advised by commercial lawyers, and the term was not unfair since it operated both ways. There was no room for applying the *Canada Steamship* rules. Most recently in *Greenwich Millennium Village Ltd v Essex Services Group plc and others* (2014), the Court of Appeal upheld an indemnity clause although the indemnitee should have detected the defects on inspection. Jackson LJ explains that the *Canada Steamship* rules are rules of construction based on the parties' presumed intention. In the context of construction contracts, a failure by the indemnitee to spot defects perpetrated by its contractor should not ordinarily defeat the operation of an indemnity clause, even if that clause failed expressly to encompass damage caused by the negligence of the indemnitee.

10.6.6 **Exemptions for 'indirect and consequential loss'**

Clauses that exclude liability for 'indirect and consequential loss' are also restrictively interpreted. Such exemptions are often used in commercial contracts to confine potential liability for pure economic loss (ie of profit). In *Hotel Services Ltd v Hilton International Hotels (UK) Ltd* (2000), a hotel owner claimed £127,000 for defective 'Robobars', an automated minibar, comprising of the cost of removing and storing them, and of loss of profits. The suppliers were unable to rely on a clause excluding liability for 'any indirect or consequential loss . . . arising from any defect in or failure of the System' because all the losses were held to be 'direct' and outside the scope of the exclusion. Relying on the remoteness test set out in *Hadley v Baxendale* (see 13.2.5.6), the court interpreted 'direct' loss as that arising *naturally* from the breach and 'indirect' or consequential loss as that which was reasonably contemplated in view of *special known facts*. Sedley LJ (at 241) said that if the equipment 'turns out to be unusable and possibly dangerous, it requires no special mutually known fact to establish the immediacy both of the consequent cost of putting it where it can do no harm and—if when in use it was showing a direct profit—of the consequent loss of profit. Such losses are not embraced by the exclusion clause'.

Pause for reflection

This interpretation seems to be inconsistent with the ordinary meaning of 'consequential loss'. All loss of profit is loss *consequential on breach* and this seems clearly covered by a term dealing with 'any indirect or consequential loss'. Rather than distorting this natural meaning, it would be preferable to control unfairness through UCTA or UTCCR.

10.7 **Consumer protection**

The Consumer Contracts (Information, Cancellation and Additional Charges) Regulations 2013 (SI 2013/3134) replaces the previous law on distance selling and doorstep selling. They implement most of the provisions of the EU Consumer Rights Directive (Directive 2011/83/EU). The new rules affecting consumer contracts include:

- ✓ **pre-contract information**: that must be provided to consumers (eg the total costs of the goods/services);

- ✓ **cancellation rights**: for distance and off-premises contracts, the consumer now has 14 days to withdraw from the contract without giving any reasons (known as the 'cancellation right' or 'cooling-off period');

- ✓ **refunds**: if the consumer exercises the cancellation right, the trader must reimburse all payments received from the consumer, including delivery charges, within 14 days;

- ✓ **inertia selling**: a trader will need the consumer's express consent before imposing any additional charges (and will not be entitled to use pre-ticked boxes and the like as evidence of that consent);

- ✓ **new rules on digital content**: traders must provide additional pre-contract information concerning the functionality of the digital content (eg region restrictions) and any information about its compatibility with other hardware or software. Cancellation rights depend on whether the content is downloaded or on a tangible medium.

THIS CHAPTER IN ESSENCE

online resource centre

The key areas and core topics in this chapter are summarised in an easy-to-use list, ideal for revision purposes, on the Online Resource Centre at http://www.oxfordtextbooks.co.uk/orc/chenwishart5e/. Links to websites relevant to the topics covered and any updates to the chapter can also be found on the Online Resource Centre.

QUESTIONS

1 To what extent has the law responded to the problems raised by standard form contracts?

2 'The law on implied terms is very difficult to state; the test for implication is unclear and the categories shade into each other.' Discuss.

3 Adam's advertisement for his airport car hire service states that 'You'll be off in minutes'. Consider the following situations.

(a) Bella is late for a business meeting and she quickly signs Adam's standard form without reading it after Adam tells Bella 'It's all standard stuff.' The car breaks down almost immediately. Bella incurs £150 to get to her meeting. Adam claims £250 for the hire period and £200 for his costs in towing the car back to Adam's premises, as stipulated in the contract. Advise Bella.

(b) As Don is about to drive off, Adam rushes up and hands him the standard form contract but he forgets to ask Don to sign. The brakes in the car fail causing Don to crash; Don's valuable painting is damaged but Adam states that he has excluded all liability in the contract. Advise Don.

(c) Erik is a regular business customer. On this occasion he is not asked to sign Adam's newly revised standard form contract. He returns the car five minutes late. He is told that, as per the contract, that he is now liable to a £300 surcharge for late return. Advise Erik.

4 'Rule one is that the task of the judge when interpreting a written contract is to find the intention of the parties.' Discuss the principles which guide the judge in interpreting contract terms, including exemptions of liability.

5 What evidence is, and what evidence should be, admissible when courts interpret contractual documents?

 For hints on how to answer these questions, please see the Online Resource Centre at http://www.oxfordtextbooks.co.uk/orc/chenwishart5e/

KEY FURTHER READING

Buxton, R (2010), '"Construction" and Rectification after *Chartbrook*', 69 *CLJ* 253.

Clarke, P (1976), 'Notice of Contractual Terms', 35 *CLJ* 51.

Collins, H (2014), 'Implied Terms: The Foundation in Good Faith and Fair Dealing', 27 *CLP* 1.

Gee, S (2001), 'Constructing Contracts with Mistakes in Them', *LMCLQ* 214.

Gee, S (2001), 'The Interpretation of Commercial Contracts', 117 *LQR* 358.

Kramer, K (2003), 'Common Sense Principles of Contract Interpretation (and how we've been using them all along)', 23 *OJLS* 173.

Macdonald, E (1988), 'The Duty to Give Notice of Unusual Contract Terms', *JBL* 375.

McCaughran, J (2011), 'Implied Terms: The Journey of the Man on the Clapham Omnibus', 70 *CLJ* 607.

McKendrick, E (2003), 'The Interpretation of Contracts: Lord Hoffmann's Re-Statement' in S Worthington (ed), *Commercial Law and Commercial Practice* (Hart Publishing) 139.

McMeel, G (1998), 'The Rise of Commercial Construction in Contract Law', *LMCLQ* 382.

McMeel, G (2003), 'Prior Negotiations and Subsequent Conduct—The Next Step Forward for Contractual Interpretation', 119 *LQR* 272.

Lord Nicholls (2005), 'My Kingdom for a Horse: The Meaning of Words', 121 *LQR* 577.

Peden, E (2001), 'Policy Concerns Behind Implications of Terms in Law', 117 *LQR* 459.

Spencer, J (1973), 'Signature, Consent, and the Rule in *L'Estrange v Graucob*', 104 *CLJ* 104.

Staughton, C (1999), 'How Do the Courts Interpret Commercial Contracts?', 58 *CLJ* 303.

11

Direct control over terms

'Can the law refuse to enforce an agreed term?'

11.1 **Introduction**

In Chapter 10, we examined how contractual terms are identified and interpreted. In doing so, courts can exercise some *indirect* control over the contents of contracts. This chapter examines the *direct* controls over the contents of contracts with particular emphasis on the Unfair Contract Terms Act 1977 ('UCTA') and the Unfair Terms in Consumer Contracts Regulations 1999 ('UTCCR'). Put most broadly:

- **UCTA** controls *exemption clauses* (excluding or limiting liability for breach) in favour of consumers and businesses dealing on standard terms by *voiding* them outright or subjecting them to a test of *reasonableness*;

- **UTCCR** invalidates *all unfair non-core terms* (terms not relating to price or main subject matter) which have not been individually negotiated; it only operates in favour of *consumers*.

The **Consumer Rights Bill** ('CRB') was presented to Parliament on 23 January 2014. It streamlines and consolidates over 40 different pieces of consumer legislation including the provisions on consumer protection currently set out in UCTA and UTCCR. The parts of UCTA that relate to business-to-business contracts will remain in force. The wording of UTCCR forms the basis of the unfair terms provisions in the CRB, and will be revoked. Where the provisions of the CRB vary from the existing law, these will be mentioned in the text.

Logically, before we even get to the question of the validity of the challenged term, it must already be determined that the contested statement:

(i) is a *term of the contract* (see 5.1.1 and 10.1–10.2);

(ii) is *incorporated* into the contract (see 10.3); and

(iii) covers the events in question on a proper *construction* (see 10.5).

The availability of direct statutory controls has reduced the need to manipulate these prior steps in order to avoid unfairness, but they are not redundant. If a term is not incorporated or not wide enough to cover the events in question, it does not apply, irrespective of its reasonableness or fairness. These prior questions appear to focus on *procedural* concerns; that is, on flaws in the way the contract was made, or on ascertaining and giving effect to the presumed intention of the parties. Substantive unfairness is said to function merely as evidence of procedural unfairness, although its effect can be decisive (recall the 'red hand' rule: the more onerous or unusual the term, the more notice is required to bind the other party to it).

It is also possible to explain the statutory intervention contained in UCTA and UTCCR in *procedural* terms. The ostensible concerns with 'inequality of bargaining power' leading to 'unfair surprise' (unusual or onerous terms in fine print) and 'lack of negotiability' ('take-it-or-leave-it') can explain the special vigilance shown by the law over standard or non-negotiated terms, especially in consumer contracts. This is reinforced by the *economic efficiency* arguments (see 1.4.3):[1] namely that the incomprehensibility of standard form contracts can leave customers simply shopping for the lowest price, resulting in 'low-cost, harsh terms' contracts. This is inefficient because some customers would prefer 'higher-cost, better terms' contracts. Thus, the statutory controls *correct market imperfections* and encourage businesses to *offer more choice* and so *enhance freedom of contract*.

⏩⏪ Counterpoint

UCTA and UTCCR reveal a direct concern with substantive unfairness, albeit shrouded in the language of protecting the parties' 'reasonable expectations'[2] and 'legitimate interests'[3] or by general references to fair dealing. However, any power to invalidate particular terms (or to imply others) *alters the balance* of the parties' rights and obligations expressly agreed: to strike out an exemption clause makes compulsory obligations which would otherwise have been excluded; to strike out an unfair term relieves a party from observing or being liable for it.

The law seeks to balance its concern to *avoid unfairness* (both procedural and substantive) with the competing demands of *certainty* and *respect for the parties' intentions*. Where the balance is struck bears directly on the relevance and workability of the main distinctions made in this area, namely between:

- consumer contracts and business-to-business contracts;
- standard form contracts and negotiated contracts; and
- exemptions clauses and other clauses.

11.2 The patterns of control

UCTA and UTCCR differ in their history, conception, and structure, but overlap considerably in their coverage.

- **UCTA** is *national* in origin; it evolved from piecemeal legislative control of particular exemption clauses and a Law Commission report.[4] Its name (the Unfair

---

[1] V P Goldberg, 'Institutional Change and the Quasi-Invisible Hand' (1974) 17 *J Law & Economics* 461, 483–4.

[2] J Steyn, 'Contract Law: Fulfilling the Reasonable Expectations of Honest Men' (1997) 113 *LQR* 433.

[3] Council Directive 93/13/EEC on unfair terms in consumer contracts [1993] OJ L95/29, Recital 16.

[4] Law Commissions (joint report), *Exemption Clauses: Second Report* (Law Com No 69, Scot Law Com No 39 (1975)).

Contract Terms Act) is misleading since it gives the courts *no general power* to regulate unfair contractual terms. It only deals with *exemption* and indemnity clauses, by making some of these clauses absolutely invalid and subjecting others to a test of reasonableness. It applies to consumer contracts (whether standard form or not) *and* to many business-to-business contracts (particularly standard form ones).

- **UTCCR** is *European* in origin. It is the national implementation[5] of the Directive on Unfair Terms in Consumer Contracts,[6] largely by 'copying out' the Directive. There was no attempt to dovetail this protection with that of UCTA. UTCCR *only* protects consumers. It subjects *all* non-negotiated and non-core terms to a test of fairness. In contrast to UCTA, the Director-General of Fair Trading ('DGFT') and other qualifying bodies can seek an injunction to prevent the use and enforcement of unfair terms.

The Law Commission observes in its report *Unfair Terms in Contracts* (hereafter 'Report 292'),[7] that we have to come to grips with two overlapping pieces of legislation which differ in their scope, in the concepts, definitions, and terminology employed, and in the way they operate. Simply superimposing UTCCR on UCTA has created a situation of 'nightmarish complexity', a far cry from the aim of simple and 'user-friendly' rules in consumer protection.[8] Take a deep breath! **Diagram 11A** summarises the main differences between UCTA and UTCCR.

Diagram 11B gives a more detailed overview of the patterns of control. It provides a *map* for the rest of the chapter and should be a helpful tool for *revision*. In determining whether and how UCTA and UTCCR apply to any particular situation, the **first column of Diagram 11B** sets out the key questions, namely:

A. What terms are reviewable? (11.4–11.5)

B. Widening the scope of reviewable terms (11.4.5)

C. Against whom? (11.3.1)

D. In favour of whom? (11.3.2)

E. What is the control mechanism? (1.4.6, 11.5.3)

F. Who can bring an action? (11.6)

Thus, row A shows that, whilst **UCTA** applies to the four types of term (1. Indemnities; 2. Exemptions of liability for negligence; 3. for breach of certain statutory implied terms; and 4. for breach of contract), **UTCCR** applies to one very broad class of terms (5. 'non-core' terms), which is wide enough to encompass the previous four categories. These potentially overlapping categories only operate in favour of and against certain parties; are subject to different tests of validity; and are enforceable by different mechanisms.

---

[5] Under the European Communities Act 1972, s 2(2).

[6] Council Directive 93/13/EEC of 5 April 1993 on unfair terms in consumer contracts.

[7] Law Commissions (joint report), *Unfair Terms in Contracts* (Law Com No 292, Cm 6464, Scot Law Com No 199, 2005).

[8] F M B Reynolds, 'Unfair Contract Terms' (1994) 110 *LQR* 1.

Diagram 11A Summary of the main *differences* between UCTA and UTCCR*

	UCTA	UTCCR
1. Type of dealing	Applies to both consumer and business-to-business contracts; applies to certain negligence cases	Applies only to consumer contracts.
2. Consumers	Does not cover certain consumer contracts. Businesses *may* be consumers.	Applies to all consumer contracts. Consumer must be an individual, businesses excluded.
3. Standard form or negotiated	Applies largely where terms are negotiated or in standard form.	Applies only to 'non-negotiated' terms.
4. Types of clauses	Applies only to exemption clauses and consumer indemnities.	Applies to any term other than 'core' terms.
5. 'Blacklist'/ 'grey list'	Gives a small 'blacklist' of terms which are absolutely invalid.	Gives a large 'grey list' of terms which may be regarded as unfair.
6. Review mechanism	Subjects other affected terms to a 'reasonableness' test.	Subjects affected terms to a 'fairness' test.
7. Guidelines	Contains guidelines for applying the reasonableness test.	Contains no detailed guidelines for judging fairness beyond the 'grey list'.
8. Burden of proof	Is on the party seeking to rely on the challenged term to show its reasonableness.	Is on the consumer seeking to challenge the term to show unfairness.
9. Enforcement mechanism and effect	Is enforced by the party seeking to escape the challenged term; the outcome only affects the immediate parties.	Can be enforced by the party seeking to escape the challenged term; other bodies can also act to prevent the use of unfair terms.

* See Law Commission Consultation Paper No 166, paras 2.18–2.19.

We will begin by examining the *parties* affected by comparing UCTA with UCCTA. Then we will look at *which* terms are affected and *how* under UCTA and UTCCR. This chapter will also examine the Law Commission's recommendations for reform. Lastly, we will give an overview of the illegality doctrine and other statutory and direct common law controls over the substantive fairness of contracts.

11.3 **The parties affected and excluded contracts**

11.3.1 **Against whom?**

11.3.1.1 'Business liability' under UCTA

In general, the 'active' sections, that is, sections 2–7 of UCTA (which subject particular terms to review) only apply to *business liability*, leaving private sales outside the

Diagram 11B Overview of UCTA and UTCCR: the patterns of control
(This is the 'map' for the whole discussion in this chapter.)

A. Reviewable Terms:	1. Indemnity clauses (S 4 UCTA)	2. Terms exempting liability for negligence (Ss 2, 5 UCTA)	3. Terms exempting liability for breach of specific statutory implied terms in sale and supply contracts (Ss 6, 7 UCTA)	4. Terms exempting liability for breach of any other term (S 3 UCTA)	5. Non-negotiated 'non-core' term; non-negotiated 'core' term only reviewable if not in plain and intelligible langauge (R 6(2) UTCCR)
B. Who may be prejudiced?	'Business liability' s 1(3)	'Business liability' - may be contractual or non-contractual	'Business liability'	'Business liability'	'Sellers and suppliers'
C. Who are protected? _Consumers_	✓	✓	✓	✓	✓ _[Consumer Rights Bill: extend to negotiated terms]_
Businesses	✗	✓	✓	if dealing on the other's standard written terms	✗
D. The review mechanism	Effective if _reasonable_	Ineffective _outright_ or only effective if _reasonable_	Ineffective _outright_ against consumers; only effective against businesses if _reasonable_	Effective if _reasonable_	Subject to adverse construction if any ambiguity or ineffective if _unfair_. NB: Schedule 2 list of indicatively unfair terms. ***Consumer Rights Bill*: black-list and add to grey-list**
E. The Enforcement mechanism	Contract party	Contract party or victim of negligence	Contract party	Contract party	Contract party, CMA or other qualifying body

control of UCTA (see row C, **Diagram 11B**). Section 1(3) provides that UCTA can only operate against a party incurring liability from:

- conduct in the _course of a business_; or
- the occupation of premises used for _business purposes_ (this relates to 'occupier's liability', generally covered in the tort law syllabus). The occupier is _not_ liable if the other party suffered loss whilst using the premises for '_recreational or educational_' _purposes_, unless it is within the occupier's business purposes to provide access for recreational or educational purposes. This excludes landowners who allow ramblers across their land, but not the 'for-profit' leisure centre.

'Business' also includes *a profession* and the *activities of any government department or local or public authority* (s 14). Thus, the local council operating a school or a leisure centre comes under UCTA's control, although not operating for profit.

11.3.1.2 'Sellers and suppliers' under UTCCR

Instead of 'business' liability regulated by UCTA, UTCCR applies to 'contracts concluded between a seller or a supplier and a consumer' (reg 4(1)). Regulation 3(1) defines a 'seller or supplier' as 'any natural or legal person who, in contracts covered by these Regulations, is acting for purposes relating to his trade, business or profession, whether publicly owned or privately owned'. This covers contracts in relation to goods, services, and land.

Although government departments and local or public authorities are not expressly included in UTCCR (in contrast to UCTA), the Directive[9] makes clear that they come within UTCCR's application. In *R (Khatun and others) v Newham LBC* (2005), the Court of Appeal held that UTCCR applies to contracts made by local authorities pursuant to their statutory duty to house homeless persons (by offering leased accommodation in the private sector). The local authority was a 'seller or supplier' within regulation 3 and homeless persons were 'consumers'.

UTCCR refers to a party acting for purposes 'relating' to business, while UCTA requires action 'in the course of a business'; this semantic difference is unlikely to make any practical difference. The contract need not be integral to the business in question, so long as there is a sufficient connection between the two.

11.3.2 **In favour of whom?**

11.3.2.1 Consumers

Both UCTA and UTCCR protect **consumers** (to different degrees in respect of different types of terms, see 11.4 and 11.5), but their definitions of 'consumer' differ in significant respects.

Regulation 3(1) of UTCCR defines 'consumer' as 'any *natural person* who, in contracts covered by these Regulations, is acting for purposes which are outside his trade, business or profession'. This narrow definition is consistent with the concept of 'consumer' in the European context.[10] Businesses are regarded as broadly capable of looking after their own interests.

Section 12 of UCTA provides that a party is *'dealing as a consumer'* where:

- he or she is not, and is not holding themselves out as, making the contract in the course of business;
- the other party *is* contracting in the course of a business; and

---

[9] Article 2(c) and Recitals 14 and 16 of the Preamble.
[10] *Criminal proceedings against Patrice Di Pinto* (Case C-361/89) [1991] ECR I-1189.

- *if he or she is not an individual*, the contract relates to goods that are *ordinarily supplied for private use or consumption*.[11]

UCTA is *narrower* than UTCCR as it excludes:

- sales by auction or competitive tender; and
- contracts for the sale or supply of goods that are *not* of a type ordinarily supplied for private use or consumption (s 12(1)(c)).

UCTA is *wider* than UTCCR since:

- **UCTA reverses the burden of proof**: it is up to *the business party to prove* that the complainant is *not* a consumer, whilst UTCCR is silent on the point, suggesting that the complainant must prove that he or she *is* a consumer;
- **businesses can use UCTA but not UTCCR**: under UCTA, a company may 'deal as a consumer' if the relevant contract is only incidental to and outside its regular business activity;
  - ✓ in ***R & B Customs Brokers Co Ltd v United Dominions Trust Ltd*** (1988), R&B (a freight forwarding agent) purchased a car for its director's *personal and business use*. When the car roof suffered an irreparable leak leaving the upholstery 'sodden with water, mouldy and evil smelling', R&B successfully challenged the validity of a term excluding implied terms (as to condition or quality or fitness for purpose) because it was 'dealing as a consumer'. Buying cars was *only incidental* to R&B's business activity; it was not *integral* to it, nor was R&B engaged in it with a sufficient *degree of regularity*;
  - ✓ similarly, a company purchase of a Lamborghini car for the use of its managing director was held to be dealing as a consumer in *Feldaroll Foundry plc v Hermes Leasing (London) Ltd* (2004).

In the **Consumer Rights Bill 2014**, the definition of a consumer is narrower than that in UCTA. A consumer is 'an individual acting for purposes that are mainly or wholly outside that individual's trade, business, craft or profession' (s 2(3)). The burden is on the trader to prove that the individual is not a consumer (s 2(4)).

11.3.2.2 Businesses

While businesses are not protected by UTCCR, they *are* protected under UCTA if they **'deal as a consumer'**.

In addition, UCTA also protects businesses *not* **acting as consumers** against unreasonable exemptions of liability for: (i) negligence (s 2); (ii) breach of particular statutory implied terms in contracts for goods or services (ss 6 and 7); and (iii) breach of contract where the business **deals on 'the other's written standard terms of business'** (s 3(1)). The rationale is that even in business-to-business contracts there is a limit to the advantages that can be extracted by superior bargaining power. The substantive limits are primarily fixed by the *nature* and *reasonableness* of the challenged term (see 11.4), but whether the challenged term is reviewable at all may

---

[11] Where the contract is governed by the law of sale of goods or hire purchase, or by UCTA, s 7.

depend on whether it has been *negotiated*. The issue of negotiability arises in both UCTA and UTCCR; since it is an indicator of inequality of bargaining power, we will discuss it here.

11.3.2.3 Standard or non-negotiated terms

Section 3(1) of **UCTA** controls unreasonable exemptions of liability for breach of contract where one party deals as a consumer, *or* on 'the other's written *standard terms of business'*.

(i) This means that UCTA does not apply to contracts which are *oral* or partly written and partly oral.

(ii) Whether written terms are *standard* is matter of 'fact and degree'. Stannard J observes that it would 'emasculate' the Act if it could be evaded simply because it could be shown that the term was occasionally varied or not used. He said (in *Chester Grosvenor Hotel Co Ltd v Alfred McAlpine Management Ltd* (1991) at 113) that standard terms:

> should be so regarded by the party which advances them . . . [who] should habitually contract in those terms. If it contracts also on other terms, it must be determined . . . whether this has occurred so frequently that the terms in question cannot be regarded as standard, and if on any occasion a party has substantially modified its prepared terms, it is a question of fact whether those terms have been so altered that they must be regarded as not having been employed on that occasion.

In *St Albans City & DC v International Computers Ltd* (1996), the Court of Appeal held that a party still 'deals on the other's standard terms' if ostensible negotiations result in *no alteration* to those terms. Nourse LJ (at 491) said: '"deals" means "make a deal", irrespective of any negotiations that may have preceded it'. Parties cannot evade control by going through sham negotiations or regularly changing their standard forms in minor ways.

(iii) Where the parties *deal on model contracts* drafted by a trade or professional association, it is a matter of evidence whether 'the Model Form is invariably or at least usually used by the party in question. It must be shown that either by practice or by express statement a contracting party has adopted a Model Form as his standard terms of business' (*British Fermentation Products Ltd v Compair Reavell* (1999) at 361).

UTCCR can only invalidate unfair non-core terms in consumer contracts that have *'not been individually negotiated'* (reg 5(1)). However:

(i) the challenged term need not be in writing;

(ii) the *burden is on the business* to show that the challenged term *has* been individually negotiated to escape review (reg 5(4)). The fact that a consumer or his or her legal representative has had the opportunity of considering the terms of an agreement does not mean that any individual term has been individually negotiated (*UK Housing Alliance (North West) Ltd v Francis* (2010));

(iii) a term need not be part of the business's usual standard terms as long as it was pre-drafted in advance of the contractual negotiations (reg 5(2)). If a party has put forward a 'pre-formulated standard contract', only the parts that have been individually negotiated are exempt from review (reg 5(3)).

Sellers and suppliers may try to **evade scrutiny**[12] by arguing that: the consumer had the *opportunity* to influence the pre-formulated terms but chose not to; very harsh standard terms were mitigated during negotiations but to a standard format; or the consumer was offered a choice of two or more sets of standard terms (this is one way of showing reasonableness under UCTA). However, courts will look closely at the consumer's *real* ability to influence the substance of the challenged term and will be slow to conclude that it has been individually negotiated.

The **Consumer Bill** extends protection for *consumers* to *all terms* whether negotiated or not in respect of the supply of goods, services, and digital content.

11.3.3 **Excluded contracts**

Schedule 1 to UCTA excludes the following types of contract from its control:

- ✗ contracts of *insurance*;
- ✗ contracts relating to the creation, transfers, or termination of interests in *land*; and
- ✗ contracts creating or transferring *securities* or any right or interest in securities;
- ✗ in *employment* contracts, s 2 of UCTA (referring to the exemptions for negligence) does not apply in favour of employers. Employment contracts also fall outside the ambit of UTCCR since they are not consumer contracts;
- ✗ contracts relating to *intellectual property* rights (patents, trade marks, copyright, and designs);
- ✗ the formation or dissolution of a *company* or its constitution; and
- ✗ *charterparties* and *carriage of goods by sea*.

UTCCR applies to *all consumer contracts* including contracts of insurance, supply of financial services, sale of land, contracts with builders or land developers, consumer mortgages, and leases between business landlords and consumer tenants. Excluded from review are the following.

- ✗ *Terms which reflect 'mandatory statutory or regulatory provisions'* under the law of any Member State of the EU, or in EU legislation having effect in the UK without further enactment (reg 4(2)(a)). This exempts terms of consumer contracts prescribed by legislation (eg terms implied by the Sale of Goods Act 1979, see 10.4.2.1). This is particularly important in the provision of public services where many of the terms are set by legislation.

---

[12] R Bragg, 'Opinion: Implementation of the EC Directive on Unfair Terms in Consumer Contracts' (1994) *Consum LJ* 29.

✗ *Terms which reflect 'the provisions or principles of international conventions* to which the Member States or the Community are party' (reg 4(2)(b)). This excludes terms aimed at complying with conventions in the transport area, notably the Warsaw Convention on International Carriage by Air (1929).

11.4 **Terms controlled by UCTA**

Terms which are reviewable under UCTA and UTCCR are shown in row A of **Diagram 11B. Diagram 11C** gives an overview.

- The **left half of the circle = consumer contracts** (ie one party deals as a consumer whilst the other acts in the course of business):[13] 1* denotes the caveat that the definition of a consumer under UCTA differs from that under UTCCR (see 11.3.2.1).

- The **right half = business contracts** (both parties act in the course of business).

- The **top half of the circle = negotiated terms**.

- The **bottom half =** *non-negotiated* **terms.** 2* denotes the caveat that whilst UCTA refers to 'written standard terms of business', UTCCR refers to terms which are 'not individually negotiated' (see 11.3.2.3).

- The **terms reviewable** under UCTA and UTCCR in *consumer* contracts are shaded in light grey. The terms reviewable under UCTA when in *business* contracts are shaded in dark grey. The broken lines signify the uncertain scope of reviewable terms in the relevant category due to extensions of the definition of 'exemption clauses' (see 11.4.5). 3* denotes that non-negotiated *core* terms are nevertheless reviewable if they are not in plain and intelligible language.

- Current proposals to expand the scope of reviewable terms are represented by the outer arcs.

11.4.1 **Indemnity clauses**

Aside from exemptions clauses, **UCTA** only applies to *indemnity* clauses. Section 4 states that a contract term requiring a person (dealing as a consumer) to *indemnify* (reimburse) the other party in respect of the latter's business liability for negligence or breach of contract, is only enforceable if the term is *reasonable* (see 11.4.6). For example, a firm that hires a car to a consumer may stipulate that the consumer will indemnify the firm against third party claims arising out of the consumer's use of the car. Section 4 offers *no protection to business parties* who agree to indemnify another business party against the latter's liability in negligence (*Thompson v Lohan (Plant Hire) Ltd* (1987) and see further 11.4.5.3). Regulation 5(1) of **UTCCR** gives the same protection to *consumers* where the indemnity clause is not individually negotiated and is unfair.

---

[13] Not where neither party acts in the course of business, the exception being in s 6(4).

Diagram 11C Terms reviewable under UCTA and UTCCR

Look on
the Online
Resource
Centre to
view this
figure as a
PowerPoint®
presentation

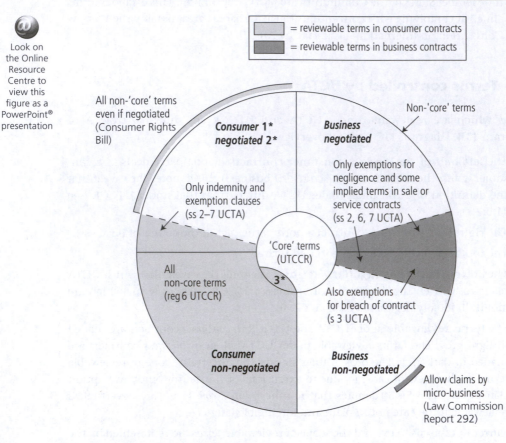

11.4.2 **Exemptions of liability for negligence**

Where contractual terms or non-contractual notices exempt business liability for *negligence*:

- section 2(1) makes an exemption for business liability in respect of *personal injury or death absolutely invalid*; the business party is liable as if the term did not exist;

- section 2(2) subjects to a *test of reasonableness* any exemption for business liability in respect of *loss or damage* other than personal injury or death.

Section 5 makes *absolutely invalid* any exemptions of negligence liability owed by manufacturers or distributors of goods to ultimate consumers (in respect of goods of the type ordinarily supplied for private use or consumption) if they are contained in a **consumer 'guarantee'** (ie a document that appears to confer beneficial rights on the consumer). The ultimate consumer will often have a contract with the manufacturer or distributor since defective goods will usually amount to breach of one of the implied terms under the Sale of Goods Act 1979; any attempted exemptions of such liability against consumers are invalidated under sections 6 and 7 (see 11.4.3).

Other provisions and cases refine the *scope* of the jurisdiction to control exemptions for negligence:

(i) UCTA's operation extends to *notices* exempting negligence liability even absent any contract between the parties (s 1(1)), although not to notices exempting occupiers' liability to *trespassers*;

(ii) UCTA's control cannot be evaded by a business appealing to the defence of *volenti non fit injuria* (ie that the other party voluntarily consented to the risk of injury or loss) simply because the other party agreed to the term or was aware of the notice (s 2(3));

(iii) only terms which 'exclude or restrict' negligence liability to the *victim of the negligence* are reviewable; terms that merely *transfer* liability to a business claimant fall outside section 2 (see 11.4.5.3).

Again, regulation 5(1) of UTCCR replicates the protection to *consumers* where the exemption is *not individually negotiated*. Schedule 2 paragraphs 1(a) and 1(b) list exemption clauses as *indicatively unfair*. UCTA confers potentially stronger protection on consumers by *outright prohibition* of exemptions contained in consumer 'guarantees' and those in respect of liability for death and personal injury.

11.4.3 Exemptions of specific statutory implied terms in sale and supply contracts

We saw in 10.4.2.1 that terms are implied by statute into:

(i) *sale of goods* contracts (by the Sale of Goods Act 1979);

(ii) *hire-purchase* contracts (by the Supply of Goods (Implied Terms) Act 1973); and

(iii) other contracts under which *the possession or ownership of goods passes*, for example hire, barter, or contracts for works and materials such as building contracts (by the Supply of Goods and Services Act 1982).

Section 6 of UCTA controls exemptions of liability for breach of implied terms in contracts of types (i) and (ii). Section 7 controls exemptions in contracts of type (iii). *Any* party can benefit from these sections, although stronger protection is conferred on consumers.

The broad effects, set out in **Diagram 11D**, are:

1. Exemptions of liability for breach of implied terms as to **title** to the goods are *totally invalid* (ss 6(1), 7(3A)).

2. Exemptions of liability for breach of implied terms relating to **quality** (the conformity of the goods with the description or sample, satisfactory quality, and fitness for purpose) are *invalid* against someone *dealing as a consumer* (ss 6(2), 7(2)) and only valid *against others* (not dealing as consumers) if they are *reasonable* (ss 6(3), 7(3)).

3. Exemptions of liability in respect of contracts passing **ownership or possession of goods** are only valid if they are *reasonable* (s 7(4)).

Diagram 11D The operation of sections 6 and 7 UCTA

| | | ✓ = effective |
| | | ✗ = ineffective |

Implied terms as to	Validity of exemptions against those **dealing as consumers**	Validity of exemptions against those **not dealing as consumers**
1. *title* ss 6(1), 7(3A)	✗	✗
2. *quality* ss 6(2) and (3), 7(2) and (3)	✗	✓ if reasonable
3. *right to transfer title or possession or assure quiet possession* s 7(4)	✓ if reasonable	✓ if reasonable

> ### Pause for reflection
>
> The combination of (i) implying terms into certain contracts and then (ii) strictly controlling parties' ability to limit liability for them effectively imposes *mandatory obligations* in these contracts and provides one of the best examples of modern contract law's concern with the substantive fairness of contracts.

11.4.4 Exemptions of liability in contract

Section 3 of UCTA imposes more general control over exemptions of *contractual* liability where one party deals *as a consumer* or *on the other's written standard terms of business*. This covers a very significant number of contracts (consumer and business-to-business).

- **Section 3(2)(a)** prevents a party from enforcing a term which exempts its business liability for breach of contract unless it satisfies the requirement of *reasonableness*.

- **Section 3(2)(b)** extends the reasonableness requirement to terms which purport to allow one party to *substantially vary* or *not to perform* part or all of its contractual obligation (see 11.4.5.4).

11.4.5 What count as reviewable 'exemption clauses' under UCTA?

11.4.5.1 Defensive or duty-defining?

The terminology in UCTA assumes that the function of exemption clauses is *defensive*; they only come into effect after breach of the primary obligations to exclude or limit the contract-breaker's liability for breach. The rival view is that exemption clauses are *duty-defining*; they cut back the *extent* of the primary obligations owed in the first place so that no breach may arise. Both approaches can produce the same outcome. **Diagram 11E** illustrates the example given by **Coote** in ***Exception Clauses*** (Sweet & Maxwell, 1964) at 9.

In a contract to sell a horse promised to be 'sound', a term:

(1) appears *defensive* if it stipulates that 'the seller shall not be liable if the horse is not sound for hunting';

(2) appears *duty-defining* if the seller promises that it is 'sound, except for hunting'.

In (1), the seller who does not provide a horse which is sound for hunting is in breach of his or her undertaking to provide such a horse, but his or her liability is excluded in the contract. In (2), the seller never undertakes to provide a horse sound for hunting in the first place, so there can be no breach of contract if the horse is not sound for hunting. In short, excluding liability for *X* amounts to the same thing as not having an obligation to do *X* at all.

Coote supports the duty-defining view (at 17–18):

Instead of being mere shields to claims based on breach of accrued rights, exception clauses substantively delimit the rights themselves . . . It may seem feasible that the parties should have intended a contractual duty to remain when they excluded liability for its breach, but this is in reality a juristic impossibility. A duty of sorts there may be, but it will be a duty of honour, not a contractual one. It would follow, then, that the current approach to exception clauses is based on a fallacy.

Diagram 11E The function of exemption clauses: defensive or duty-defining?

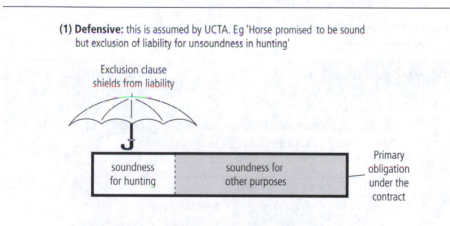

(1) Defensive: this is assumed by UCTA. Eg 'Horse promised to be sound but exclusion of liability for unsoundness in hunting'

Exclusion clause shields from liability

| soundness for hunting | soundness for other purposes | Primary obligation under the contract |

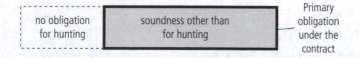

(2) Duty defining: Coote's preferred approach. Eg 'Horse promised to be sound except for hunting'

| no obligation for hunting | soundness other than for hunting | Primary obligation under the contract |

> ### Pause for reflection
>
> Why should UCTA be limited to terms 'excluding or restricting' specified types of liability and not to duty-defining terms in general? One answer is that it allows the law to preserve the appearance of upholding freedom of contract, intervening only in exceptional and clearly prescribed circumstances. UCTA can then be presented as an aspect of the court's legitimate authority to determine the appropriate *remedies for breach*. To openly acknowledge exemption clauses as merely 'disguised duty-defining clauses' would openly challenge the oft-stated position that the law does not control the substantive fairness, and so limit the freedom, of contracts.

Because exemptions of liability can be redrafted into duty-defining terms and because the two may be functionally indistinguishable, UCTA must **counter attempts to evade its control** by expanding the scope of what counts as 'exemption clauses'.

In **Diagram 11F**:

(1) The *three shaded boxes* in the centre represent the exemption clauses expressly controlled by UCTA (those for negligence, breach of statutory implied terms, and breach of contract). These are extended in three ways.

(2) All three *exemptions* are extended to include terms that make claims more difficult to prove.

(3) Exemptions of liability for negligence and breach of statutory implied terms are extended to include duty-defining clauses.

(4) Exemptions of liability for breach of contract are extended to include certain duty-defining clauses by section 3(2)(b).

Diagram 11F Widening the definition of 'exemption clause'

Look on the Online Resource Centre to view this figure as a PowerPoint® presentation

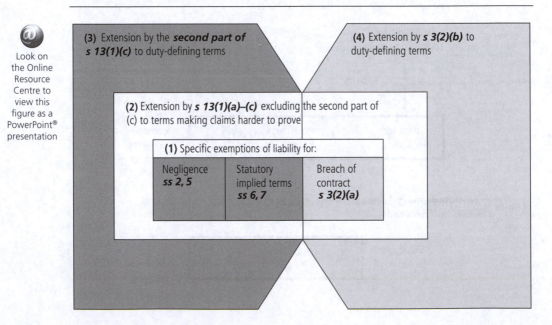

11.4.5.2 Terms that make claims more difficult to prove

Section 13(1) of UCTA brings within the definition of exemption clauses, terms which make it more difficult for the claimant to prove his or her case by:

(a) making the liability or its enforcement subject to *restrictive or onerous conditions* (eg requiring claims to be made within a short time frame or in a specified form);

(b) excluding or restricting any *right or remedy* (eg the right to rescind or terminate the contract), or subjecting the claimant to *prejudicial consequence* if he or she claims any right or remedy (eg withholding payment); and

(c) excluding or restricting *general rules of evidence or procedure* (eg reversing the burden of proof or stating that a customer's signature is conclusive proof that no breach has occurred).

These are mirrored in **UTCCR's** list of indicatively unfair terms in Schedule 2 (eg para 1(m), (n), (o), (q)).

11.4.5.3 Exemptions for negligence and breach of statutory implied terms subject to sections 2, 5–7

The last two lines of **section 13(1)** of UCTA state that: '... sections 2 and 5 to 7 also prevent excluding or restricting liability by reference to terms and notices which *exclude or restrict the relevant obligation or duty*' (emphasis added). However, it is no easy matter to draw the distinction between reviewable and unreviewable clauses which restrict the relevant obligation. For example, what is the nature of a clause which: states that the kitchen utensils sold are unsuitable for non-stick pans; states that a survey only relates to valuation and not structural soundness, or denies the authority of an agent to give undertakings? Are these *really* exemptions of liability dressed up as duty-defining clauses?

A **'but for' test** is supported by *Smith v Eric S Bush* (1989) and *Phillips Products v Hyland* (1987). Accordingly, the question is: would liability arise 'but for' the term in question? This was qualified by Newey J in *Avrora Fine Arts Investment Ltd v Christie, Manson & Woods Ltd* (2012) at [144]; the question is: does the challenged term **attempt to retrospectively alter the character of what has gone before, to rewrite history, or part company with reality?** F purchased a painting represented and warranted to be by a famous Russian artist, which turned out to be untrue. C's conditions of sale provided that each item is sold 'as is'; and that, subject to the limited warranty, no representation, warranty, or guarantee is given on attribution or authenticity. This did not immunise the transaction from UCTA's reasonableness requirement since it *did* part company with reality.

▶◀ Counterpoint

The 'but for' test is *uncertain* and *too* wide.

1. It certainly brings under UCTA's control terms that qualify (restrict, cut back) an obligation or would contradict an implied term. For example, in *Johnstone v Bloomsbury Health Authority* (1992), J (a junior doctor employed by B) was expressly required to work for 40

➡

➔ hours a week and be 'on call' for up to 48 more hours. The court held that this was inconsistent with B's implied obligation not to damage J's health (see 10.4.2.2), and that, if it
defeated this implication, it would be regarded as a clause falling within the final part of
section 13(1) and be invalidated by section 2(1).

2. Taken literally, the 'but for' test swallows up virtually all duty-defining clauses, since all
restrictions on primary duties (whether positive or negative) by definition pre-empt some
primary duties. The test assumes that it is possible to determine the parties' *normative*
rights and obligations independent of the challenged term; any term purporting to under-
cut those is, by definition, an exemption and subject to UCTA.

3. A better approach is to analogise the distinction with that of 'core' and 'non-core' term
in UTCCR (see 11.5.2). In general, only non-core terms fall under UTCCR's prohibition of
unfairness because they are less likely to have come to the consumer's notice and so been
knowingly consented to. In determining whether to contract, the consumer's attention is
generally focused on the core bargain or price; other terms will rarely figure. The same idea
should guide our answer to the scope of UCTA, so that only core terms (relating to the price
or main subject matter of the contract) fall outside its control.

The jurisdictional problem at the heart of UCTA also comes to the fore when deciding whether certain indemnities (outside the scope of s 4) are *really* exemptions of
negligence liability (by virtue of s 13(1)) and so subject to section 2. The short answer
is: 'yes' if the term shifts liability to the *victim* of negligence, but 'no' if it shifts liability to *someone other than the victim* of negligence. The cases highlight the difficult
distinction between terms that define the duty and that exempt liability.

The former is illustrated by ***Phillips Products v Hyland***. P hired a JCB excavator and
driver from H. Condition 8 made the driver *P's employee* and made P responsible for
all claims arising from the driver's operation of the excavator. The driver negligently
crashed the excavator into P's factory wall. H countered P's claim for damages by arguing that condition 8 was outside the control of section 2(2) of UCTA because it did
not exempt liability for breach of duty. It merely restricted H's duty (by shifting it to
P) so that H commits no breach (ie negligence) in the first place. The Court of Appeal
rejected this argument by reference to section 13(1) and the 'but for' test. Slade LJ said
that in considering whether there was negligence liability the court must *ignore* the
clause being relied on to defeat the negligence claim. This liability cannot be transferred to P (the injured party) if it effectively excludes liability to P (at 665).

In contrast, in ***Thompson v Lohan (Plant Hire)***, an identical clause shielded the
defendant from his negligence liability because it was outside the scope of section
13(1) and so *outside* the control of section 2. The facts were identical to *Phillips Products
v Hyland*, except that the driver's negligence caused loss, not to the hirer but to a
third party (it killed Mr Thompson), whose widow had recovered damages from the
hirer. The hirer then sought to recover that payment from the hiring employers. The
court said that the question is not whether the *party relying on the clause* was seeking
to exempt liability (this was plainly so in both cases), but **whether the exemption
excluded liability against the *victim* of the negligence** ('yes' in *Phillips Products*,

Diagram 11G Contrasting *Phillips* and *Thompson*

		C= claimant D = defendant
	Phillips	*Thompson*
Contract	D hires excavator and driver to C	Same
Term	C is responsible for all claims arising in connection with the driver's operation of the excavator	Same
Victim	C	Another party already compensated by C
Does s 13(1) bring term under control of s 2?	✓ Clause seeks to exclude D's liability to the victim (C) for negligence; D *cannot* transfer liability to C unless reasonable	✗ Since clause does not seek to exclude D's liability to the victim for negligence, s 2 is inapplicable, hence applicability of s 13(1) does not even arise; D *can* transfer liability to C even if unreasonable, unless C is a consumer.

but 'no' in *Thompson*). Section 2 only controls clauses which exclude liability to the *victims* of negligence by transferring liability to them. It does not apply to terms that transfer liability to someone other than the victim of negligence. Transfers of liability to consumers who are not the victims of negligence are effective if reasonable (s 4). The contrast between *Phillips Products v Hyland* and *Thompson v Lohan (Plant Hire)* is summarised in **Diagram 11G**.

11.4.5.4 Exemptions for breach of contract

Section 3(2)(a) subjects exclusions or restrictions of liability for breach of contract to the test of reasonableness. The potential for evading this control (by repackaging exemptions for breach of contract as duty-defining terms) is countered by **section 3(2) (b)**. This extends the reasonableness requirement to **terms purporting to reserve to one party the discretion to give no, only partial, or substantially different performance from that reasonably expected** by the other party. If the exemption clause is set aside as unreasonable under section 3(2)(a), then a party's non-, partial, or substantially different performance is not a lawful exercise of discretionary power conferred by the contract, but a breach of contract. An obvious example of this is the holiday contract which allows the provider to substantially vary the accommodation or destination of the holiday, or to cancel the holiday in whole or in part.[14] *Timeload Ltd v British Telecommunications plc* (1995) indicates the potential width of section 3(2) (b). BT's contract to supply services gave BT the right 'at any time' to terminate on one

---

[14] *Anglo-Continental Holidays v Typaldos (London) Ltd* (1967) and see Package Travel, Package Holidays and Package Tours Regulations 1992 (SI 1992/3288): reg 12 requires the organisers to allow consumers to withdraw from the contract if an essential term is altered significantly.

month's notice. T argued that the clause fell under section 3(2)(b); BT answered that T could not expect that which the contract never offered (ie enjoyment of services for an indefinite period). Sir Thomas Bingham MR disagreed (at 468):

> If a customer reasonably expects a service to continue until BT has substantial reason to terminate it, it seems to me at least arguable that a clause purporting to authorise BT to terminate it without reason purports to permit partial or different performance from that which the customer expected.

This term is not only reviewable under section 3(2)(a) of UCTA, but is also indicatively unfair under UTCCR (Sch 2 para 1(j)).

As with section 13, section 3(2)(b) assumes that there is a *normative standard of reasonable expectations* which is ascertainable, independent of the *expectations* defined in the contractual document itself.

 Pause for reflection

1. There is a problem of circularity. It is arguable that the parties' expectations are only reasonable if they are contained *in* the contractual document. To the extent that the two differ, why should the claimant's expectations ever take precedence over what the contract says? Why should the law ignore the challenged clause in determining the claimant's reasonable expectations? Why should only the burdensome terms be ignored when all the terms (whether burdensome or advantageous) make up the whole contract?

2. Section 3(2)(b)(ii) refers to non-performance of part or the whole of a party's *contractual* obligation. This makes sense if that party's discretion to perform is *partial*. However, if his or her discretion is *total* (ie it is entirely up to that party whether to perform), there is effectively no *contractual* obligation to perform at all. Moreover, there is arguably no contract since that party's consideration is illusory.

3. Section 3(2)(b) reinforces Coote's argument that promising much, but then disclaiming liability for not keeping the promise, is the same as promising very little to begin with. Both can deprive the promisee of rights which the promisee reasonably believed the promisor had conferred on them.

4. Again, the distinction between reviewable 'core' and reviewable 'non-core' terms set out in UTCCR (see 11.5.2) should guide our answer to the scope of section 3(2)(b) of UCTA, so that only core terms (relating to the price or main subject matter of the contract) fall outside it and so outside the control of section 3(2)(a) of UCTA.

The Law Commission has suggested[15] extending the current protection to 'micro-businesses'[16] by protecting them from unfair *non-negotiated non-'core' terms*.

---

[15] Law Commissions (joint report), *Unfair Terms in Contracts* (Law Com No 292, Cm 6464, Scot Law Com No 199, 2005).

[16] 'Micro-businesses' are those that: have nine or fewer staff; are not associated with other businesses; do not provide financial services; and make contracts valued at £500,000 or less.

Terms other than those currently regulated by UCTA can obviously be unfair (eg a small business may be required to indemnify the larger business for losses that are not their fault, forfeit deposits, or accept price variations; the larger business may reserve the right to terminate the contract at will, or for only a minor breach, while the small business is bound more rigorously by the contract). A small business may have little more bargaining power than a consumer (eg where it sells all its output to a major carmaker or a supermarket chain, or buys goods or services of relatively low volume or value) and may be just as affected by unfair surprise, lack of comprehension, and lack of choice.

11.4.6 **Control mechanism under UCTA**

11.4.6.1 Outright invalidity

We have seen that UCTA contains a 'blacklist' of terms that are invalid outright. These attempt to exclude or restrict:

(i) business liability for death or personal injury to *anyone* caused by *negligence* (s 2(1));

(ii) business liability for breach of *implied terms as to title* to *anyone* in contracts for sale, hire purchase, or other transfers of property in goods (ss 6(1), 7(3A));

(iii) business liability for breach of the *implied terms as to the description, quality*, etc in contracts for the supply of goods to a party dealing as a *consumer* (ss 6(2), 7(2)); and

(iv) a manufacturer's or distributor's liability in tort to a person injured by *goods proving defective in consumer use* where the exemption is contained in a 'guarantee' of the goods (s 5).

All other terms caught by UCTA are subject to the requirement of *reasonableness* (see 11.4.6.2). Terms coming under UTCCR's control are invalid if *unfair* (see 11.5.3) and Schedule 2 paragraph 1 to UTCCR contains a 'grey list' of terms which are considered indicatively unfair.

The current law is complicated and confusing, with two statutory schemes subjecting the overlapping categories of terms to two differently formulated tests. **Diagram 11H** gives an overview.

11.4.6.2 Review for reasonableness

(i) The time of assessment

Under **UCTA**, the reasonableness of the challenged term should be determined 'having regard to the circumstances which were, or ought reasonably to have been, known to or in the contemplation of the parties when the contract was made' (s 11(1)). Facts arising subsequently, such as the seriousness of the loss or damage actually sustained, are irrelevant, except insofar as they were foreseeable at formation. The same position is adopted in **UTCCR** (reg 6(1)). The justification rests on *certainty* and *predictability*: parties should be able to assess, at the point of contract formation, whether the term will survive the law's review.

Diagram 11H Overview of the reasonableness and fairness tests

	C= complainant ✓ = yes E = enforcing party ✗ = no	
	UCTA	**UTCCR**
Test of validity	**Reasonableness** (see 11.4.6.2)	**No unfairness** (see 11.5.3)
Terms affected	Indemnities and exemptions contracts and certain exemptions in business contracts	All non-negotiated, non-'core' terms and 'core' terms if not in plain and intelligible language
Time of assessment	At formation	At formation
Onus of proof	On E to show term is reasonable.	On C to show term is unfair.
Non-exhaustive factors in assessment of validity	• circumstances at formation; • relative bargaining positions; • alternatives available; • inducement to agree; • C's reasonable notice of the term; • C's reasonable expectations; • whether goods tailored to C's special order; • E's resources to meet any liability; • insurance. (ss 11(1), 11(4), Sch 2 UCTA)	Whether 'contrary to the requirement of good faith, [the term] causes a significant imbalance in the parties' rights and obligations…to the detriment of the consumer.' • circumstances at formation; • relative bargaining power; • inducement to agree; • nature of the subject matter; • whether goods tailored to C's special order; • whether E dealt fairly and equitably with C taking into account C's legitimate interests. (regs 5, 6(1) UTCCR; Recital 16 in EU Directive)
'Blacklist'	✓	✗
'Grey list'	✗	✓ Schedule 2 list of terms which are presumptively unfair.

(ii) The potential width of the exemption

It follows from (i) that the assessment of reasonableness or fairness must be made about the *potential width* of the term and not the actual use made of it (the former may be unreasonable or unfair even if the latter is reasonable and fair). The *wider* the term, the more likely it is to be judged *unreasonable*. A term will be unreasonable if it is susceptible of both reasonable and unreasonable application since, at formation, it is impossible to know which use will be made of it. A court *will not sever the unreasonable part* of a term and leave the rest intact; the *whole* clause is invalidated (*Stewart Gill Ltd v Horatio Myer & Co Ltd* (1992)). Thus, in drafting such clauses, several narrow exemptions would seem preferable over a single all-embracing one so that, if unreasonableness or unfairness is found, it will not taint the entire attempt to evade liability.

(iii) The onus of proof

UCTA puts the onus of proving reasonableness on the business seeking to rely on the term: 'it is for those claiming that a contractual term or notice satisfies the requirement of reasonableness to show that it does' (s 11(5)). This amounts to *a presumption of unreasonableness* unless the contrary is proved.[17] In *Phillips Products v Hyland*, Slade LJ comments (at 668) that section 11(5) takes on 'great significance' when evidence as to the reasonableness of the term or notice is obscure or absent.

(iv) The reasonableness test under UCTA

The nature of the reasonableness test is examined by reference to: the statutory guidelines; its discretionary character; and illustrations of its application.

- **The statutory guidelines**: strictly speaking, three slightly different tests of reasonableness appear in UCTA: the general test in section 11(1); the test applicable to statutory implied terms falling within sections 6 and 7, detailed in Schedule 2; and the test applicable to terms which limit rather than exclude liability referred to in section 11(4). However, the courts have made clear[18] that all the factors mentioned in the various guidelines are applicable to *all* cases in which they appear relevant. Moreover, these factors are neither exhaustive nor determinative; the court may take into account any other relevant circumstances. In practice, therefore, there is *a single test of reasonableness*. The statutory guidelines require consideration of the following.

  (i) *The parties' respective bargaining power, taking into account any alternative means of meeting the customer's requirements.* For example, in *Woodman v Photo Trade Processing Ltd* (1981), a clause limiting liability to the replacement cost of a film was held to be unreasonable. Although it enabled a cheap service to the majority of consumers, it left those whose pictures were of extraordinary value (eg wedding photographs) with no alternative service offering a higher degree of care. However, the mere existence of alternatives will not preclude a finding of unreasonableness if they are oo impractical or expensive (*Smith v Bush* (1989)). In *Air Transworld Ltd v Bombardier Inc* (2012), the

---

[17] Analogous to the de facto presumption of unreasonableness or dishonesty under the Misrepresentation Act 1967, s 2(1), see 5.2.1.

[18] *Rees Hough Ltd v Redland Reinforced Plastics Ltd* (1984) at 151; *Stewart Gill v Horatio Myer* at 608.

court enforced the exclusion of liability where the parties were of equal bargaining power, where the excluding terms are set out in capitals, and where the terms of the warranty were specifically drawn to the purchaser's lawyer's attention.

(ii) Whether the customer received any inducement to accept the term or could have contracted with another without the exemption clause.

(iii) Whether the customer knew or ought reasonably to have known of the existence and extent of the term, having regard, amongst other things, to any custom of the trade and any previous course of dealing between the parties. In *Stag Line Ltd v Tyne Ship Repair Group Ltd (The Zinnia)* (1984), Staughton J (at 222) said that he was inclined to find the exemption clause unreasonable because the print was so small as to be barely legible and 'the draughtsmanship was so convoluted and prolix that one almost need[ed] an LLB to understand them'.

(iv) The reasonableness of conditions imposed on making claims. A term is unreasonable if a breach may not be detectable within the time allowed for making claims (eg in *RW Green v Cade Bros Farms* (1978), three days with respect to the sale of seed potatoes), or if it makes the remedying of defects subject to the customer's return of the product (eg a ship in *Stag Line* (1984)).

(v) Whether the goods were manufactured, processed, or adapted to the customer's special order. If so, it may entail particular risks that make it reasonable for the seller to exempt liability.

(vi) The defendant's resources to meet claims. If the defendant is unable to meet claims, or if the magnitude of the claim is vast in relation to the contract price, the exemption is more likely to be reasonable, although any limitation of the customer's claim to a particular sum requires justification (*Salvage Association v CAP Financial Services Ltd* (1995)). This is related to the next factor.

(vii) *The availability and efficiency of insurance.* The *actual* insurance position of the parties is strictly irrelevant (*Singer Co (UK) Ltd v Tees and Hartlepool Port Authority* (1988) and *The Flamar Pride* (1990)). The question is whether the defendant's exemption of liability is reasonable in view of the *potential availability* of insurance to *either* party, and of their relative *cost*. This guideline aims to protect small businesses that might have inadequate resources to meet or be unable to obtain insurance cover against potential liability. Conversely, it is more likely to be unreasonable for large companies with considerable assets to exempt liability where insurance is available and *affordable*. Thus, in **St Albans City & DC v International Computers** (1995), it was held to be unreasonable for a multinational company with insurance cover of £50 million to limit liability to £100,000. The question is not only one of affordability but also of *efficiency*. In *Photo Production Ltd v Securicor Ltd* (1980), the House of Lords held that the challenged clause excluding liability for a fire which destroyed P's factory would have been reasonable under UCTA since P would already have to insure against fire and S might not have been able to obtain the appropriate insurance, in any case not without passing its cost on to P in higher charges for its security service.

- **The discretionary character of the reasonableness test**: although the statutory guidelines inform the courts' assessment of reasonableness, the discretionary element in the assessment is a broad one since judges may differ in the *weight* they attach to particular factors. Courts must take account of a wide 'range of considerations, put them in the scales on one side or the other, and decide at the end of the day on which side the balance comes down' (*George Mitchell (Chesterhall) Ltd v Finlay Lock Seeds Ltd* (1983) at 816). Nevertheless, the decision of a first instance judge should be treated 'with the utmost respect'; appellate courts should 'refrain from interference with it unless satisfied that it proceeded upon some erroneous principle or was plainly and obviously wrong' (*George Mitchell* at 810). An example is *Watford Electronics Ltd v Sanderson CFL Ltd* (2001) where the first instance judge adopted an incorrect interpretation of the exemption clause and failed to take account of relevant considerations.[19]

- **Illustrations of the reasonableness test**: in *George Mitchell*, G (farmers) bought *winter* cabbage seeds from F but received *autumn* cabbage seeds that produced inferior plants, useless for G's purposes. G sought to recover losses of £61,000 but an exemption clause limited damages to the cost of the seeds (£200). The House of Lords invalidated the clause as unreasonable. The main factors were:

    (i)   the availability and affordability of insurance to the seller;

    (ii) the seller's breach was due to its negligence; and

    (iii) the seller's past practice of settling claims in excess of the limit imposed if it regarded the claims as 'genuine'; this indicated that even F regarded the clause as often inappropriate and unreasonable.

Pause for reflection

Clauses excluding or severely restricting liability give the contract-breaker the option of ignoring the term when it is in the contract-breaker's commercial interest to do so (eg when it is desirable to preserve the goodwill of profitable business customers); this may operate unfairly against smaller customers. Thus, the exemption in *George Mitchell* was objectionable for conferring an *unreasonable remedial discretion* on the contract-breaker, raising the spectre of favouritism. This may also explain why having the power to elect is regarded as self-induced frustration barring relief (see 7.5.3).

---

[19] E Peel, 'Reasonable Exemption Clause' (2001) 117 *LQR* 545.

Recall *Phillips Products v Hyland*, where a term required P (the party hiring a JCB excavator and a driver from H) to indemnify H for any liabilities arising from the driver's operation of the excavator. The effect of the clause was to exclude H's liability to P when the driver's negligence damaged P's buildings (see 11.4.5.3). The term was struck out as unreasonable under section 2(2) of UCTA because:

(i) H was in the business of hiring out, while P only hired such equipment occasionally;

(ii) the hire was for a very short period of time, arranged at short notice, on H's standard form and not negotiated;

(iii) P had little opportunity to arrange insurance cover and would have had to make a special arrangement to insure against an employee's damage to its own property; and

(iv) P had no choice over the driver and no realistic control over how he did the job.

In *Motours Ltd v Euroball (West Kent) Ltd* (2003), telephone services provided by E to M (a travel agency) were partially defective. E sought to exclude liability for all consequential loss howsoever arising. Although it was a commercial bargain between businessmen, the judge found the term unreasonable because:

(i) the exclusion included that for negligence (which could not have been within M's contemplation);

(ii) exclusion clauses were common in the industry so M had little choice;

(iii) the term was not negotiated (the appearance and language of the contract suggests that customers were not expected or encouraged to read it); and

(iv) E had much greater financial strength and bargaining position and could present its terms on a 'take-it-or-leave-it' basis; M was in no position to negotiate.

In *Regus (UK) Ltd v Epcot Solutions Ltd* (2008), R hired serviced office accommodation from E. R sought substantial damages for loss of business due to the faulty air-conditioning. A standard term in the contract excluded any liability for loss of business, profits, anticipated savings, third party claims, or any consequential loss, and loss of or damage to data. The Court of Appeal found this to be *reasonable* under UCTA because:

(i) E could still sue for the defective air-conditioning by reference to the diminution in value of the services promised;

(ii) the exclusion does not cover fraud or wilful, reckless, or malicious damage which would be unreasonable;

(iii) R reasonably limited its liability to the higher of 125% of the fees or £50,000;

(iv) there was no inequality of bargaining power;

(v) R advised its customers to protect themselves by insurance for business losses since this was cheaper than R obtaining liability insurance.

> **Pause for reflection**
>
> 1. In 'The Unfair Contract Terms Act: A Decade of Discretion' (1988) 104 *LQR* 94, **Adams and Brownsword** reviewed the operation of UCTA ten years after it came into operation. They concluded that uncertainty has resulted from appellate courts' view that the determination of the first instance judge on the issue of reasonableness should not be disturbed. They also identified inconsistency in the courts' attitudes towards the appropriate level of intervention in commercial contracts; Lord Wilberforce signalled a 'hands-off' approach in *Photo Production* but this was not heeded in the *George Mitchell* case. They saw the latter approach as interventionist and threatening commercial certainty.
>
> 2. In '**Unfair Contract Terms Act—Thirty Years On**' in A Burrows and E Peel (eds), *Contract Terms* (OUP, 2007) 153, **Macdonald** detects more certainty in the factors taken into account in determining the reasonableness of exemption clauses. She supports the continuing need for UCTA in commercial contracts but argues that courts have been over-inclusive by their broad interpretation of when a business 'deals as a consumer', but under-inclusive in making insufficient use of the extended definition of exemption clauses in section 3(2)(b)(i).
>
> 3. While some of the statutory guidelines relate to *procedural* unfairness (the *way* the contract came about, eg notice and bargaining power), courts can find a term unreasonable under UCTA *solely* because of its *substantive* unfairness. Courts can conclude that an exemption of liability is unreasonable, even if the business has given reasonable notice of it without objection from the customer. Thus, while unreasonableness under UCTA may comprise both procedural and substantive unfairness, it may exceptionally comprise only procedural or only substantive unfairness, to the extent that these are separable. The same can be said of the fairness test under UTCCR, to which we now turn.

11.5 **Terms controlled by UTCCR**

The prohibition of 'unfairness' in regulation 5(1) of UTCCR applies to terms (whether oral or written) in consumer contracts which have 'not have been individually negotiated' (see 11.3.2.3). Implied terms are excluded from UTCCR's protection (*Margaret Baybut v Eccle Riggs Country Park Ltd* (2006)).

Regulation 6(2) states:

Insofar as it is in plain intelligible language, the assessment of fairness of a term shall not relate—

(a) to the definition of the main subject matter of the contract, or

(b) to the adequacy of the price or remuneration, as against the goods or services supplied in exchange.

11.5.1 **The requirement of 'plain and intelligible language'**

Regulation 7(1) of UTCCR requires *all* contractual terms in consumer contracts meet the requirement of 'plain, intelligible language'. This is the first condition of exemption from review. Terms that are not 'plain and intelligible':

(i)   are subject to *contra proferentem* construction (reg 7(2)), duplicating the common law approach to the interpretation of ambiguous terms (see 10.6.3);

(ii) may be subject to review for *unfairness* under regulation 5(1) (see 11.5.2).

In *The Office of Fair Trading v Abbey National* (2008), Andrew Smith J lays down some markers, which were approved by the Court of Appeal (this issue was not appealed).

- Given the consumer protection objective of UTCCR, a very high standard of plainness and intelligibility is required. Absence of ambiguity is not enough, nor that the challenged term is expressed as clearly as is reasonably possible; the typical consumer should be able to understand 'the actual words used . . . [and] how the terms affect the parties' rights and obligations' (at [103], [121]). Even plain, intelligible language may be ambiguous (eg a term which contravenes UCTA but is accompanied by the familiar phrase 'your statutory rights are not affected' is 'plain and intelligible', but may still mislead consumers into believing that it bars redress).

- Relevant considerations include the complexity and legibility of the language, the opportunity to understand it prior to contract formation, the parties' previous contractual dealings, and any non-contractual leaflets and brochures given to consumers at or before contract formation.

On the other hand:

- The standard for assessment used by the European Court of Justice in applying and interpreting European consumer law is that of the 'typical or average consumer' who is 'reasonably well informed and reasonably observant and circumspect' (at [89]) and will 'read and seek to understand the contractual terms in the light of information, advice or explanations in non-contractual material' (at [95]).

Under the **CRB** (s 71), a trader must ensure that a written term of a consumer contract, or a consumer notice, is transparent. If a term of a consumer contract is especially onerous or unusual, the trader must ensure that the term is drawn particularly to the consumer's attention.

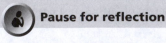 **Pause for reflection**

1. The requirement of 'plain and intelligible language' signals a change in the attitude towards consumer standard form contracts: the orthodox approach of *caveat emptor* ('buyer beware') is replaced by an approach which puts an onus on sellers and suppliers to make their terms transparent to consumers.

➡

> 2. The assumptions about the behaviour of the 'typical or average consumer' seems over-optimistic. Indeed, Kitchin J recognised that the standard of the typical or average consumer must be 'a variable one and must . . . take colour from the context. For example, consumers who are financially sophisticated may be expected to bring to bear a greater understanding of the meaning and implications of the terms of a contract than consumers who are vulnerable as a result of their naivety or credulity' (*OFT v Ashbourne* (2011) at [128]).
>
> 3. Ensuring 'plain intelligible language' is a very limited solution to the problem of unfairness in consumer contracts. The high transaction cost of comprehension (particularly in time), and the lack of negotiability means that consumers will be 'rationally ignorant' when confronted with lengthy and complicated standard form contracts (even if stated in plain intelligible language). This explains why UTCCR goes beyond requiring clear language to providing substantive protection from unfairness.

11.5.2 **Exempted 'core' terms**

Which terms are exempted from review for unfairness (if couched in plain and intelligible language)? The broader the class, the less consumer protection is afforded. *Bankers Insurance Co Ltd v South* (2003) gives a clear example of an exemption under regulation 6(2)(a). B provided holiday insurance to S, which excluded liability for accidents involving S's 'ownership or possession of any . . . motorised waterborne craft'. S was sued for seriously injuring someone whilst driving a jet ski. B was not liable to indemnify S since the clear exclusion clause relates to the *subject matter* of the insurance contract.

On the other side of the line is *DGFT v First National Bank plc* (2001). FNB (the largest independent provider of consumer finance and of loans for home improvements in the UK) used a standard form loan agreement which included a term requiring borrowers who defaulted on the repayment to continue paying interest at the contractual rate until the whole debt was discharged. Thus, even if the court gave extra time for repayment, the borrower remained liable for all interest accruing during that extended period, *over and above* the payments due under the judgment. The House of Lords held that the exclusionary regulation must be interpreted restrictively so as not to undermine the consumer protection objective of UTCCR. Only 'core' terms would escape review. The relevant term was *not exempt* because:

(i) 'core' terms are those 'which define the parties' rights and obligations in the *due* performance of the contract' whereas the challenged term is a *default* provision dealing with what happens if the contract is *breached*;

(ii) the default provisions would not have appeared 'core' *to the consumer*; the average borrower seeking a home improvement loan would not have considered it as an important term in deciding whether to borrow from that lender.

However, the potential for escape from review was significantly widened by the Supreme Court in *Office of Fair Trading v Abbey National plc and others* (2009). This test case was brought by seven banks and one building society (providers of 90% of UK's current accounts) and the Office of Fair Trading ('OFT') to determine whether unarranged overdraft charges (known as 'unpaid item fees', 'guaranteed paid item fees', 'paid item fees', and 'overdraft excess charges') amounting to billions of pounds are subject to UTCCR's fairness requirement. Their Lordships also agreed that regulation 6 must be interpreted restrictively to avoid undue escape from review for unfairness under regulation 5(1). Yet, they *reversed* the High Court and Court of Appeal in holding these charges *exempt* from review under regulation 6(2)(b) because of the following.

(i)   The lower courts had erred in reading 'the adequacy of the price or remuneration, as against the goods or services supplied in exchange' as meaning 'the adequacy of the price or remuneration, as against the *main subject of the contract*'.

(ii)   Regulation 6(2) represents a *compromise between consumer protection and freedom of contract*. The lower courts' reasoning that consumers only consent meaningfully to the 'core' or 'essential' part of the bargain overlooks the purpose of regulation 6(2). **Brandler and Ulmer's** influential article, '**The Community Directive on Unfair Terms in Consumer Contracts: Some Critical Remarks on the Proposal Submitted by the EC Commission**' (1991) 28 *CMLR* 647, 656–7, argue that consumer protection should be achieved by improving transparency which would prevent abuse of power via market forces, rather than by controlling the reasonableness or equivalence of the parties' principal obligations. In '**Good Faith in European Contract Law**' (1994) 14 *OJLS* 229, **Collins** agrees that the meaning of regulation 6(2) is that consumer contracts need not be fair but they must be clear.

(iii)   The Supreme Court saw the issue as one of *construction*. Regulation 6(2) reflect the two sides of any consumer contract: 6(2)(a) what the trader is supplying and 6(2)(b) what the consumer is paying. Neither can be reviewed for fairness. It is not unnatural to say that the charges are part of the payment in exchange for the 'whole package' of services received from the banks. The corollary of accepting a free-if-in-credit account is that charges will be incurred if the account is overdrawn.

(iv)   In any case, Lord Mance said (at [113]) that the construction exercise is 'a matter of objective interpretation for the court . . . having regard to the view which the hypothetical reasonable person would take of its nature and terms'. There is 'no basis for . . . attempting to identify a "typical consumer" or by confining the focus to matters on which it might conjecture that he or she would be likely to focus'.

(v)   The Supreme Court disagreed with the lower courts' conclusions that they are akin to default charges for breach. The charges are not designed to discourage customers from overdrawing on their accounts without prior arrangement; rather, they are an integral part of the banks' charging structure which allows them to offer free-if-in-credit current account services.

(vi)   The Supreme Court rejected the lower courts' view that the charges are not 'the essential element of exchange' because they are only *part* of the price (banks also generate income from consumers' credit balances and interest payments on overdrafts) because the fairness of any part can only be assessed in the context of the whole exchange and that is exempted; there is no principled basis for deciding that some services or prices were more essential to a contract than others; and it is irrelevant that the charges are contingent and only incurred by a minority of customers; words like 'ancillary', 'subordinate', 'incidental', 'non-core', and 'collateral' are unhelpful.

(vii) Even on the lower courts' interpretation, the charges *are* part of the essential bargain because they form over 30% of the banks' revenue stream.

⏴⏵ Counterpoint

1. *Transparency vs fairness*: Lord Mance said (at [113]) that: 'The consumer's protection under the Directive and Regulations is the requirement of transparency . . . That being present, the consumer is to be assumed to be capable of reading the relevant terms and identifying whatever is objectively the price and remuneration under the contract.' *However*, the chief feature of UTCCR is that it goes *beyond* requiring transparency to requiring fairness. The question is: 'of which terms?'

2. *Realism*: the problem for consumers faced with dense-text standard forms is not so much lack of comprehension as the high *transaction cost* of comprehension. The reason why regulation 6(2) only exempts price and subject matter terms (and not *all* terms) which are in 'plain intelligible language' is that consumers know and consent to these core, and logically more transparent, terms of the contracts. Only *these* are justifiably exempted from review for unfairness in the name of freedom of contract. In contrast, there is 'no market in non-core contractual terms'[20] and consumers need protection from unfair un-negotiated and non-core terms.

3. The lower courts' focus on the consumer's reasonable expectations generated from the circumstances and the nature of the contract has clear parallels with: the law on *incorporation* (which requires added notice of onerous and unusual terms in unsigned documents, see 10.3.3.2); and *section 3(2)(b)(i) of UCTA* (which subjects to the reasonableness requirement clauses purporting to allow the business to perform in a 'substantially different' way from what was 'reasonably expected', see 11.4.5.3). They all rest on a distinction between:

   • *terms which the claimant is likely to be well acquainted with* (whether described as 'core', not 'unusual or onerous', or not 'substantially different from what was reasonably expected'); and

   • *terms which are likely to come as nasty surprises*, being 'incidental', 'onerous or unusual', or 'substantially different from what was reasonably expected'.

4. A careful reading of the articles cited by the Supreme Court by Brandler, Ulmer, and Collins actually supports the restrictive interpretation of regulation 6 of the lower courts.[21]

5. *Where to draw the line?* Lord Steyn observed that unless the exemption is interpreted restrictively, it would allow 'the main purpose of the scheme to be frustrated by endless

→

---

[20] S Bright, 'Winning the Battle Against Unfair Terms' (2000) 20 *LS* 331, 352.
[21] M Chen-Wishart, 'Transparency and Fairness in Bank Charges' (2010) 126 *LQR* 157, 161.

> → formalistic arguments as to whether a provision is a definitional or an exclusionary provision' (*First National Bank* at [34]). This mirrors the problematic distinction between 'exemption' and 'duty-defining' clauses under UCTA, since *all* terms can be said to be part of the 'main subject matter' or 'price or remuneration' of the contract. The Supreme Court in *OFT v Abbey* agree that this cannot be the legislative intention. Yet, the tenor of its judgment has the opposite effect.

Since consumers' contractual obligation generally takes the form of paying money, it may well be asked, after *Abbey*: what 'price or remuneration' terms remains under UTCCR's control?

- Some judicial statements in *Abbey* say that *any* term in plain, intelligible language requiring the consumer to pay money may come within the 'price or remuneration' exemption, if it forms part of the trader's revenue stream.

- Other statements suggest that not all payments constitute the 'price or remuneration', in particular, terms on the grey list, including default payments and price-escalation charges (indicatively unfair terms under UTCCR, Sch 2, see para 1(d), (e), (f), (l)). In **Bairstow Eves London Central Ltd v Smith** (2004), the contract court reviewed a default charge that was framed as a price term. It stipulated the estate agent's 'standard commission rate' as 3% but discounted to 1.5% if it was paid within ten working days. A 3% rate would have been uncompetitive and the parties had really negotiated on the basis of 1.5% payable within ten days.

- Some statements say that even price terms can be challenged as unfair, provided the challenge is on grounds *other than* the appropriateness of their amount (at [57], for discussion of what this may comprise, see 11.5.3.3(iii), (iv)).

In *OFT v Ashbourne*, the judge took a narrower view of the exclusion contained in regulation 6(2)(a). The case concerned a series of contracts for gym memberships imposing a minimum membership period on the gym user. Kitchin J held (at [175]) that the assessment excluded by regulation 6(2) relates to 'the meaning or description of the length of the minimum period, the facilities to which the member gains access or the monthly subscription which he has to pay . . . [or] the adequacy of the price as against the facilities provided.'. What is not excluded from review is 'the obligation upon members to pay monthly subscriptions for the minimum period when they have overestimated the use they will make of their memberships and failed to appreciate that unforeseen circumstances may make their continued use of a gym impractical or their memberships unaffordable. Put another way, it relates to the consequences to members of early termination in light of the minimum membership period'.

In the aftermath of these two difficult cases, the Law Commission sought views on, inter alia, the scope of regulation 6(2) (Law Commission and Scottish Law Commission, *Unfair Terms in Consumer Contracts: A New Approach?* (2012)). The upshot is section 64 of the **CRB**, which excludes from assessment of fairness terms that relate to the main subject matter or 'the appropriateness of the price payable under the contract by comparison with the goods, digital content or services supplied under it'. But *only* if it is' transparent and prominent', where:

- '**transparent**' requires the term to be expressed in plain and intelligible language and (where written) is legible;
- '**prominent**' requires it to have been brought to the consumer's attention in such a way that an average consumer would be aware of the term;
- '**average consumer**' means a consumer who is reasonably well-informed, observant, and circumspect.

It remains to be seen whether, in practice, this minimal modification strengthens the consumer protection that was diminished by *Abbey*.

11.5.3 **Review for unfairness**

Regulation 5(1) of UTCCR states that a term 'shall be regarded as unfair if, contrary to the requirement of good faith, it causes a significant imbalance in the parties' rights and obligations arising under the contract, to the detriment of the consumer'. Under section 74 of the **Consumer Rights Bill**, the court has a duty to consider whether a term in the contract is fair even if none of the parties raise that issue, but only if the court considers that it has before it sufficient legal and factual material to enable it to consider the fairness of the term.

11.5.3.1 **The time of assessment and burden of proof**

The test of unfairness under UTCCR, like that of reasonableness under UCTA, is applied 'at the time of conclusion of the contract' (reg 6(1)). Unlike UCTA, UTCCR leaves the burden of proof on the claimant. However, the burden may not be a heavy one. In practice, terms identified in Schedule 2 to UTCCR (see 11.5.3.3(iii)) as indicatively unfair would raise a presumption of unfairness.[22]

11.5.3.2 **The potential width of terms**

As under UCTA, the timing of the assessment points to the judgment being made about the *potential width* of the challenged term rather than the *actual* use made of it. However, Buckley J mitigated the harshness of a broad exemption by *changing the time for assessment* from the time of formation to *the time of breach* (analogous to the intermediate term device, see 12.2.3.1). In *Bankers Insurance Co v South* (2003), a holiday insurance policy required S to report any incidents 'as soon as reasonably possible' and 'immediately upon receipt', forwarding any communication in connection with the claim. Buckley J held these conditions to be *potentially* unfair to consumers under UTCCR (if, eg, any failure is purely technical and does not prejudice the insurer). However, he also recognised the unfairness 'for the insurer to be called upon to indemnify the insured, even as its position has been hopelessly prejudiced by the insured's inactivity'. Buckley J concluded (at [35]) that UTCCR invalidated **the term only to the extent that it operates unfairly**. On the facts, since S's breach had

---

[22] *Treitel*; M Dean, 'Unfair Contract Terms: The European Approach' (1993) 56 *MLR* 581, 587.

resulted in a three-year delay in B investigating the claim, B could fairly rely on the clause to exclude liability to S. Buckley J held this interpretation to be consistent with the objective of UTCCR and with regulation 8(2) which allows the contract to continue 'if it is capable of continuing in existence without the unfair term'.

11.5.3.3 The test of unfairness

The European Court of Justice has held that it is for national courts to determine the fairness of a term (in *Freiburger Kommunalbauten GmbH Baugesellschaft v Hofstetter* (2003)). However, the ECJ will declare a term unfair where it would be unfair on any possible appropriate application of the fairness test (*Oceano Grupo Editorial SA v Murciano Quuitero* (2000)).

The concepts of *'significant imbalance'* and contravention of *'good faith'* in regulation 5(1) are unfamiliar in English contract law. They are often explained in terms of promoting fair and open dealing, preventing unfair surprise, countering the absence of real choice, and preventing substantive unfairness. The nature of the unfairness test must be understood by reference to:

(i)   the statutory guidelines;

(ii) the general test of unfairness itself;

(iii) the list of indicatively unfair terms;

(iv) the House of Lords' application of the tests; and

(v)   the enforcement mechanism.

(i) The statutory guidelines
Regulation 6(1) directs the courts to assess unfairness by 'taking into account the nature of the goods or services for which the contract was concluded and by referring, at the time of conclusion of the contract, to all the circumstances attending the conclusion of the contract and to all the other terms of the contract or of another contract on which it is dependent.' **Recital 16** of the originating Directive requires courts to take into account similar factors as those relevant to the assessment of reasonableness under UCTA. In addition, courts must consider whether the seller or supplier dealt 'fairly and equitably with the other party whose legitimate interests he has to take into account'. Whilst the factors referred to in assessing reasonableness under UCTA and fairness under UTCCR are not identical, there is a high degree of similarity. Moreover, neither list is exhaustive. Any differences between the two tests will not be due to the different language of 'fairness' and 'reasonableness'. Rather, it will come down to the differences in the scope of the two pieces of legislation: the different parties affected, and principally, the different types of terms being tested.

(ii) The general test of unfairness under regulation 5(1)
In *First National Bank*, Lord Steyn (at [37]) approved the view that **significant imbalance** 'obviously directs attention to the substantive unfairness of the contract'.[23] It applies when 'a term is so weighted in favour of the supplier as to tilt the parties' rights and obligations under the contract significantly in his or her favour. This may

---

[23] H Collins, 'Good Faith in European Contract Law' (1994) 14 *OJLS* 229, 249.

be by the granting to the supplier of a beneficial option or discretion or power, or by the imposing on the consumer of a disadvantageous burden or risk or duty' (at [17]).

The requirement of **good faith** is synonymous with 'fair and open dealing'. However, Lord Steyn makes clear (at [36]–[37]) that: 'Any purely procedural or even predominantly procedural interpretation of the requirement of good faith must be rejected . . . there is a large area of overlap between the concepts of good faith and significant imbalance.' On this view, *unfairness can be purely substantive*. This is consistent with the Directive's policy of harmonising the control of standard terms in consumer contracts. Collins[24] explains that it would be wrong to confine good faith to procedural matters since the Directive states that it is the *term*, as opposed to the *negotiating procedures*, which must be in bad faith.

However, Lord Bingham presents contravention of good faith in *procedural* terms (at [17]), and this is accepted in *UK Housing Alliance (North West) Ltd v Francis* (2010). Nevertheless, the extent of overlap with *substantive* unfairness is evident from his description (emphasis added):

> Openness [of dealing] requires that the terms should be expressed fully, clearly and legibly, containing no concealed pitfalls or traps. Appropriate prominence should be given to *terms which might operate disadvantageously* to the customer. Fair dealing requires that the supplier should not, whether deliberately *or unconsciously*, take advantage of the consumer's necessity, indigence, lack of experience, unfamiliarity with the subject matter of the contract, [and] *weak bargaining position* . . . Good faith . . . looks to good standards of commercial morality and practice.

(iii) The indicative list of unfair terms

The Schedule 2 list of indicatively unfair terms 'convincingly demonstrate[s]' that good faith may be breached by substantive unfairness alone (Lord Steyn in *First National Bank* at [36]). Only one of these terms focuses directly on *procedural* unfairness (para 1(i): the consumer's opportunity to know of the term). Even this has an implicit substantive dimension; analogous to unsigned documents, the more unusual or onerous the term, the more notice may be required. Such a term is unobjectionable if it causes no significant imbalance to the consumer.

This list of 17 terms can be grouped into three main types, being those which:

A. defeat consumers' reasonable expectations;

B. give consumers inadequate redress on the trader's breach; or

C. impose unreasonable burdens on consumers.

Column 1 of **Diagram 11I** sets these out. **Column 2** suggests how these terms may count as 'significant imbalance' under regulation 5(1); and **column 3** as 'bad faith' under regulation 5(1) and a 'failure to consider the consumer's interests' under Recital 16 (Directive 93/13/EEC).

Under the **Consumer Rights Bill**, the UCTA bar on exempting liability for death or personal injury and restriction on terms exempting liability for negligence continue to have effect (s 68). Also **blacklisted** are terms that exclude or restrict liability for

---

[24] H Collins, 'Good Faith in European Contract Law' (1994) 14 *OJLS* 229, 250.

Diagram 11I Indicatively unfair terms: the nature of the unfairness

'Grey-list' in Schedule 2 para 1	The test of unfairness	
Nature of the detriment suffered by the consumer – NB: the overlap between categories	**Significant imbalance**: contravening the consumer's 'legitimate interest':	**Contravention of good faith**: the trader has too much power to contravene the consumer's legitimate interest by:

A. Consumers not getting what they reasonably expected due to:
being mislead about the contract
    (n) limiting liability in respect of commitments undertaken by trader's agent or making commitments subject to compliance with formalities
    (i) Binding consumers to terms he had no reasonable opportunity of knowing
the trader having disproportionate power of discretion in performance or of unilateral variation
    (c) binding consumers while trader's performance depends on a condition whose realisation depends on trader's will alone
    (f) allowing trader the discretion to cancel contract but not the consumer
    (g) allowing trader to cancel contract of indeterminate duration without reasonable notice
    (j) allowing trader to vary contract unilaterally
    (k) allowing trader right to change what is supplied
    (m) giving trader right to determine meaning of terms including whether own performance complies with the contract
    (p) allowing trader to assign the consumer's contractual rights and obligations without consumer's agreement where would reduce guarantees for consumer
	• in knowing what was bargained for
	
	• in obtaining the performance reasonably expected
	
	• in a balance of power to influence the life of a contract
		• failing to draw consumer's notice to term
		
		• having too great a power to vary or extinguish its obligations

B. The consumer obtaining no or inadequate redress for loss or damage caused by the supplier
    (a) exclusion or restricting liability for death or injury
    (b) inappropriate exclusion or restriction of contractual liability
    (o) binding consumers where the trader defaults
    (q) restricting the consumer's access to legal rights or remedies
	• in being adequately protected on the trader's breach	• having power to restrict the consumer's access to ordinary remedies

C. consumers having to pay more than reasonably expected or assuming disproportionate burdens
    (d) forfeiture of sums on consumer's cancellation but not vice versa
    (e) disproportionate financial penalty on consumer's breach
    (f) allowing trader to keep sums paid by consumer when the trader cancels
    (h) automatic extension of contract if consumer does not refuse
    (l) allowing the trader to fix price at time of delivery or to increase price
	• in the stability of the obligation owed
	• in fair liability for breach
		• having power to impose additional burdens and to keep or extract disproportionate sums on the consumer's breach

breach of statutory implied terms relating to the sale of goods (s 32), digital content (s 49), and services (s 59).

The **grey list** is listed in Schedule 2 to the Bill and is augmented by the addition of terms which:

- allow the trader to claim disproportionately high early termination charges;

- give the trader discretion to decide the price after the contract has been entered into; and

- give the trader discretion to decide the subject matter after the contract has been entered into.

(iv) Application of the unfairness test

✗ Recall the *First National* case (see 11.5.2), involving a clause in a loan contract that, on the borrower's default, gives the bank the right to all sums due *plus* additional interest at the contractual rate until the date of full repayment. This means that even if the court gives extra time to pay, the borrower who complies with the court order (tailored to meet his or her means) does not pay off, but actually increases, his or her debt. The House of Lords rejected the DGFT's argument that this is unfair because it contravenes the borrower's reasonable expectation, because:

   (i)   although awards of *statutory* interest on judgment debts are prohibited,[25] *contractually agreed* interest is not;

   (ii) it is not up to lenders to inform borrowers of their rights under the Consumer Credit Act 1974 to apply for extra time or a reduction of the interest rate;

   (iii) even if the borrowers' attention had been drawn to the relevant term before contracting, they would *not* have thought it unfair because it merely allows the lender to recover the contractual interest rate until the completion of payment. Against *this baseline*, the term was not unexpected, unbalanced, or detrimental to the consumer.

In *OFT v Abbey*, the House of Lords held that the charges levied by the banks were exempted by regulation 6(2)(b) from review for unfairness (see 11.5.2). Nevertheless, Lord Phillips said (at [57]) that 'it would be open to the OFT to assess the fairness of the price according to other criteria' (ie other than of the price-to-services ratio). His Lordship added that the consumer's reasonable expectations when entering the contract is 'relevant to **whether the *method* of pricing is fair**. It may be open to question whether it is fair to subsidise some customers by levies on others who experience contingencies that they did not foresee when entering into their contracts' (at [79]–[80], emphasis added). In this respect, the House of Lords noted (at [87]) that the 20% of current account customers who incur the relevant charges, generate 30% of the banks' total revenue from current account customers. The remaining 80% who stay in credit only account for 50% of the total revenue (from the banks' use of their funds). Lord Mance commented that the banks 'were engaged in a sort of "reverse Robin Hood exercise"' (at [2]). Lord Walker said that 'Ministers and Parliament may

---

[25] County Court (Interest on Judgment Debts) Order 1991 (SI 1991/1184).

wish to consider the matter further' (at [52]). However, Lady Hale (at [93]) thought the banks' charging structure was not 'necessarily unfair when viewed as a whole'. It is a pity that there is no appeal on this issue.

> ### (👤) Pause for reflection
>
> 1. The observation of Andrew Smith J at first instance is a complete answer to Lady Hale. He said: 'the Directive and the 1999 Regulations are concerned with the fairness of the *individual* contract between the seller or supplier and a particular consumer and are not directly concerned with whether seller or supplier treats fairly consumers *as a body*' (at [415], emphasis added). Thus, good faith and significant imbalance 'to the detriment of the consumer' must be judged on the **micro-level of the individual**; fairness at the macro-level, in the sense that banks may not be over-profiting overall, is irrelevant.
>
> 2. Although regulation 6(2)(a) prevents a direct assessment of substantive unfairness, by exempting the price and main subject matter, regulation 5(1) inevitably requires some assessment of substantive fairness.
>
>   (i) The fairness of non-exempt terms is assessed against *the background of the whole contract* (Recital 19 of Council Directive 93/13/EEC).
>
>   (ii) The law's emphasis on transparency is often put in terms of preventing 'unfair surprise', but surprises are only unfair if they are detrimental in substantive terms; nice surprises are unobjectionable.
>
>   (iii) An unfair term under regulation 5 is knocked out, leaving the rest of the contract binding 'if it is capable of continuing in existence without the unfair term' (reg 8). Thus we can see the exemption of 'core' terms from review as facilitating the continuation of the contract. Substantive unfairness is better remedied by allowing consumers to retain their contracts with the offending terms invalidated (counteracting the 'significant imbalance'), than to strike down the whole contract.

✓ In *OFT v Ashbourne*, Kitchin J granted an injunction to prevent the use of terms in standard form agreements for membership of gym and health clubs specifying minimum membership periods of 24 to 36 months. Such terms were unfair under UTCCR, since they were designed and calculated to take advantage of the naivety and inexperience of the average consumer who overestimates the use he or she would make of gym facilities.

✓ In *Spreadex Ltd v Cochrane* (2012) C opened an account online with S, a spread-betting bookmaker. When C left his computer at his girlfriend's house for two days, her young son made numerous trades which put his account substantially in debit. Under S's pre-trade contract S would assume no obligations and C would have no rights. However, C would be made liable for any unauthorised trade on the account. The result was a significant imbalance in the parties' rights and obligations. Without any limitation on the customer's liability, that imbalance was contrary to good faith and unfair. Also the manner in which S sought to make the customer aware of clause 10(3) was entirely inadequate and a further factor in rendering it an unfair term (at [17]–[21]).

✗ In *West v Finlay & Associates* (2014), W employed F to renovate W's house. The contract limited F's liability 'to the amount that it was reasonable for it to pay having regard to "the contractual responsibilities of other consultants, contractors and specialists appointed by [W]" '. The Court of Appeal concluded no invalidity under **UTCCR** because (at [38]–[39], [48]–[61]):

- while the term was imbalanced against W, was not drawn to W's attention, and was expressed in a way that concealed its dangers, the imbalance was not significant because: (i) the term is prevalent in the industry standard forms; (ii) the clause would be regarded as not unusual in a commercial contract; and (iii) W had the final decision on the future choice of other contractors;

- even if there was significant imbalance, it was not in a manner or to an extent which is contrary to the requirement of good faith because: (i) the term was clearly and openly presented to W; (ii) F did not set out to exploit W; and (iii) the reasonable equality of the parties' bargaining power.

The term was also not invalid under section 11 of **UCTA** on largely the same factors (at [67]):

(i)   W was in an equal bargaining position with F;

(ii) although W received no inducement to agree, they could have renegotiated the term, gone to another architect or protected themselves by some other commercial route (eg insurance);

(iii) W ought reasonably to have known of the term's existence as it was placed prominently in the agreement.

(v) The availability of pre-emptive challenge

Under UTCCR, the DGFT and the 'qualifying bodies' listed in Schedule 1 can apply to courts for injunctions against the *future use* of specific unfair terms (see 11.6.2). Logically, this must be done *without* reference to any procedural unfairness that has occurred or might occur in any particular case. The same argument applies to the Schedule 2 indicatively unfair terms. As Lord Steyn explains, 'inevitably, the primary focus of such a pre-emptive challenge is on issues of substantive unfairness' (*First National Bank* at [33]). Moreover, once an injunction is granted against a particular unfair term (including terms with like effect), its use is prohibited no matter what transparency, notice, or other procedural safeguards surround it.

11.6 **The enforcement mechanism**

11.6.1 **UCTA**

Only a party directly affected can claim under UCTA. Such challenges will rarely be worth the cost in money, time, and general aggravation to ordinary consumers or even small businesses. Even if terms are invalidated under UCTA, nothing prevents their future use. The OFT notes the disturbing frequency with which it has encountered unfair terms which conflict with consumer protection legislation, including UCTA, that have been in place for over 30 years.[26] This may be because businesses are ignorant of their obligations, cannot be bothered to comply, or deliberately seek to deter claims. It is clear that, in consumer contracts, reliance on action by individuals is *wholly inadequate* to vindicate the protection conferred by UCTA.

11.6.2 **UTCCR**

In contrast to UCTA, UTCCR lays down a *dual system* of individual challenges and pre-emptive challenges by appropriate bodies. The result of a successful **individual challenge** mirrors that under UCTA: it makes the offending term unenforceable, but the rest of the contract continues to bind the parties 'if it is capable of continuing in existence without the unfair term' (reg 8(1) and (2)). This enforcement mechanism suffers from the same problems as UCTA (only a handful of consumers have relied on UTCCR) and the impact of any success does not extend beyond the individual consumer.

More importantly, a new enforcement mechanism authorises **pre-emptive challenges** by the Competition and Market's Authority (CMA) and other 'qualifying bodies'.[27] The CMA has primary responsibility for:

- investigating complaints;
- bringing actions, coordinating actions with other qualifying bodies, and monitoring actions;
- disseminating information about the operation of UTCCR; and
- monitoring compliance generally (mainly achieved through the OFT publishing information about: the workings of the OFT; the OFT's views on what is considered potentially unfair for the guidance of traders;[28] the undertakings given by traders to discontinue using particular terms; and any actions taken or pending under UTCCR).

In '**Winning the Battle Against Unfair Contract Terms**' (2000) 20 *LS* 331, **Bright** reports on the effectiveness of the Unfair Contract Terms Unit ('UCTU') in getting traders to change or discontinue the use of unfair terms and contracting practices. This is overwhelmingly achieved by *negotiation* and requiring traders to give informal *undertakings*. The trader has many incentives to cooperate with the UCTU: to give an undertaking and perhaps accept a reduced profit margin will often be less costly than defending a court action; cooperation also avoids bad publicity, is good for its public image, and cultivates a good working relationship with the OFT. The success of this **administrative model of enforcement** is partly attributable to its *proactive approach*

---

[26] OFT, *Unfair Contract Terms*, Bulletin No 2 (1996), 5.

[27] The powers were vested in the these powers were vested in the Office of Fair Trading but this was abolished from March 31, 2014 and its powers under the UTCCR were transferred to the Competition and Markets Authority (CMA).

[28] Eg OFT, *Guidance: Contract Terms For Package Holidays* (5 March 2004).

and the implicit threat of court action if matters are not otherwise satisfactorily resolved. The UCTU will not only investigate the term complained of, but also assess the contract as a whole. It has initiated investigations of whole sectors and liaised with relevant trade associations such as the home improvement industry, vehicle rental, package holidays, and conditions of airline use, achieving notable success in securing the amendment of terms in mobile phone contracts. Actual court action is regarded as the *last resort*. Bright warns that this success of the UCTU will be threatened if courts adopt a less consumer-orientated interpretation of UTCCR.

Under Schedule 3 to the **Consumer Rights Bill**, enforcement of the law on unfair contract terms vests in the Competition and Markets Authority and other regulators.

11.7 **Other statutory and common law control of terms**

Other statutes and common law rules control the *contents* of contracts. A course on general contract law cannot examine these in detail (they are the subject of specialist texts and courses, eg on consumer, employment, or tenancy law). Suffice it to note that their existence and emphasis on avoiding domination and unfairness necessitates an adjustment in the fundamental assumptions of classical contract law that it is not interested in the substance of the contract (see 1.3.5).

11.7.1 **Statutory control of terms**

Aside from UCTA and UTCCR, many other statutes regulate the content of *particular types* of contract. They counter unfairness by, for example:

(i)   invalidating whole or parts of contracts;

(ii) implying terms;

(iii) prohibiting certain terms;

(iv) imposing a notice or 'cooling off' period (a period when consumers can cancel the contract without penalty) requirements; and even

(v)   modifying unfair terms.

The general approach is piecemeal; the trouble hotspots identified affect *most* contracts which ordinary consumers make, for example:

- Consumer Credit Act 2006;
- Financial Services and Markets Act 2000;
- Sale of Goods Act 1979;
- Supply of Goods and Services Act 1982;
- Landlord and Tenant Act 1985;
- Employment Rights Act 1996;
- Consumer Protection Act 1987;
- Defective Premises Act 1972;

- Package Travel, Package Holidays and Package Tours (Amendment) Regulations 1992 (SI 1998/1208); and

- Consumer Protection (Distance Selling) Regulations 2000 (SI 2000/2334).

11.7.2 Common law control of terms

These can be divided into three categories.

(i)   **Indirect controls** can be imposed over the contents of contracts by instrumental applications of other rules to reach just results (ie 'backward reasoning', see 1.2.3 and 2.5.1.4). Some notable examples are the *identification, incorporation*, and *interpretation* of terms, whether express, implied, or collateral (see Chapter 10).

(ii)   **Direct control:** courts are empowered to invalidate certain terms including:

   (a)   *penalty clauses* (exorbitant payments on breach, see 14.3.2);

   (b)   unreasonable *deposits* and *forfeitures* (forfeiture of money already paid on breach, see 14.3.3);

   (c)   exclusion of liability for fraud; and

online resource centre

   (d)   unreasonable *restraints of trade* (restricting a party's liberty to carry on his or her trade in the future, see Additional Chapter 2 which is available on the Online Resource Centre, at 2.1.2.9);

online resource centre

   (e)   the entire contract can be rendered unenforceable for being *illegal* or *contrary to public policy*, although this doctrine is narrowly applied. Discussion of the illegality doctrine (including an examination of restraint of trade) can be found in Additional Chapter 2 which is available on the Online Resource Centre.

(iii)   Varying a term:

   (a)   in **salvage** cases, involving the rescue of life or property on ships in distress (see 8.6.2), courts can substitute more reasonable sums for the extortionate sums agreed;

   (b)   section 2(2) of the Misrepresentation Act 1969 allows courts to award damages in lieu of rescission broadly in circumstances where it would be fair to do so, the damages effectively treating the **misrepresentation** as if it were a term which has been breached (see 5.3.3);

   (c)   in equitable common **mistake** cases (see 6.3), the complainant has been granted *rescission on terms* that he or he gives the other party the option of contracting on fairer terms;

   (d)   courts can award **rectification** of contracts to reflect the parties' true agreement (see 6.6).

11.8 Illegality: a brief summary

One doctrine that overtly controls the contents of contracts and yet is left off the syllabus of most contract law courses, is the so-called 'illegality' doctrine. For reasons of space, a brief summary is offered here. A more detailed discussion is offered in Additional Chapter 2 which is available on the Online Resource Centre.

This represents the most open and direct interference with contract parties' freedom to determine the *substance* of their contracts. It is justified in terms of the law's refusal to support immoral or reprehensible contracts. Courts will generally neither *enforce* an illegal contract nor allow restitution of any money or property transferred under it.

What contracts are illegal or contrary to public policy? Statutes may prohibit the *formation, purpose, or performance* of certain contracts. Examples include prohibitions on the trade of certain weapons and body parts. The categories of **common law illegality** reflect changing social and moral values. They include contracts which:

- commit or further a criminal or civil wrong;

- interfere with the administration of justice;

- oust the jurisdiction of the court, although parties can agree to arbitrate before resorting to the courts;

- prejudice the state, such as trading with the enemy in wartime, and contracts which corrupt public life, like the buying of 'honours';

- prejudice family life, such as contracts to transfer parental rights and duties;

- unduly restrict personal liberty, such as contracts of slavery and 'servile' employment contracts;

- further sexually immoral purposes, such as prostitution; however changes in societal attitudes mean that courts are unlikely to hold with the past refusal to enforce contracts such as to pay rent on premises known to accommodate the promisor's mistress or contracts between unmarried cohabiting couples;

- are in **restraint of trade** (in practice, the most important head of illegality) whereby one party agrees to restrict his or her freedom to trade or conduct his or her profession or business in a particular locality for a specified time. The doctrine applies principally to employment, sales of businesses, and exclusive dealing agreements. Such restraints are invalid to the extent that they are more than is reasonably necessary to protect the legitimate interests of the party imposing the restraint.

What is the effect of illegality? The relevant statute may stipulate the consequence of the illegality (eg impose a penalty or bar enforcement to either or both parties). If not, the court must decide the consequences on the same general principles as apply to common law illegality. The rule of thumb is that courts **will not enforce** contracts which are expressly or impliedly prohibited by statute or contrary to public policy, irrespective of the claimant's good faith. **However**, there are exceptions; for example:

- a *collateral contract* not tainted by illegality may be enforced;

- an innocent claimant may claim damages for *fraudulent misrepresentation*;

- even a bad faith claimant can enforce the contract if: (i) the purpose of the illegality is to protect a class of persons to which the claimant belongs; (ii) the illegality is too remote from the contract; or (iii) the claimant is seeking to enforce a statutory entitlement (eg against unfair dismissal) attaching to the contract;

- a good faith claimant ignorant of the illegal manner in which the other party is performing a legal contract can enforce the contract. Even the offender may enforce if the purpose of the illegality is merely to impose a penalty on the offender rather than to prohibit the contract;

- a contract is enforceable if its illegal part can be severed.

In all these cases, enforcement must not subvert the policies underlying the illegality.

Exceptionally, a party may be able to **claim restitution** of the benefits he or she conferred on the other party under an illegal contract where he or she:

- is less blameworthy than the defendant (eg is a member of the protected class);

- has *withdrawn* from the transaction in time; or

- can establish a legal or equitable *proprietary right* to the property independent of the illegal contract.

11.9 **Control of substantive unfairness**

(i) To what extent does the law control the substance of contracts?

This question is *descriptive* and can be answered by distilling the scope for indirect and direct judicial control of substantive unfairness (a significant imbalance of the rights and obligations under the contract). Although reasonable observers may disagree on the extent of control, it is clear that there is scope on the doctrinal level and evidence at the practical level for arguing that the law *can* and *does* exercise control over the substantive unfairness of contracts. Thus, we have seen that rules have developed to control:

(i) particular *fact situations* or *relationships* that entail a heightened risk of substantive unfairness (eg undue influence, mistake, salvage, consumer contracts, standard form contracts, frustration);

(ii) particular *conduct* likely to induce agreement to unfair terms (eg misrepresentation, duress, and unconscionable conduct);

(iii) particular *terms* likely to contain substantive unfairness (eg clauses exempting liability for breach or stipulating payments or forfeitures on breach); and

(iv) *contracts of certain types* which have attracted a high incidence of substantive unfairness (eg consumer, tenancy, sale of goods, package holidays, non-commercial guarantees).

(ii) Justifications for controlling the substance of contracts

Three justifications can be advanced.

(i) The traditional justification is that substantive unfairness plays an **evidentiary role**. It is merely indirect or corroborative evidence of procedural unfairness (ie one side's defective consent and the other's reprehensible conduct). On such a view, the concern about substantive unfairness is consistent with supporting freedom to contract. However, we have seen that such reasoning can wear thin. It results in the 'finding' of bargaining disabilities and unconscionable conduct in commonplace and unremarkable situations which do not stand out from the norm (see generally Chapter 9) and which only become legally significant when accompanied by glaring substantive unfairness.

(ii) A bolder justification is based on the idea that **freedom of contract is not the only value in contract law and must be balanced against fairness**. It may be necessary to restrain contractual power to *uphold the practice of contracting itself,*[29] *and to shape it according to widely held conceptions of social justice* (see 1.4.6). It is perfectly reasonable for the law to inject community standards of fairness into *both* the rules governing how the 'game' of contract should be played *and* the *substantive* limits on what can be gained or lost by playing it. The argument that judges, not being sophisticated economists, may make mistakes on the issue of substantive unfairness[30] is exaggerated in the context of the manifest unfairness involved in the mainly *non-commercial* cases where relief has been given. Moreover, courts will sensibly give a wide margin of tolerance to *commercial* cases where operative bargaining disability is anyway unlikely to be legally relevant. Given the vagueness of statutory standards like 'reasonableness' and 'fairness' and judicial appeals to the 'standards of equity', there is no particular reason to think that courts are more qualified in laying down procedural limits than substantive ones. In any case, the two overlap significantly and the standard of procedural unfairness required cannot be fixed without reference to the substantive outcome likely to be produced.

(iii) The boldest justification follows on the view that contractual enforcement amounts to '**state subsidisation**'. If we see contract law's control of substantive unfairness in the conventional language of legal 'interference', 'paternalism', 'rewriting the contract for the parties', or 'saving parties from foolish bargains', we insert a bias into the inquiry. It assumes the starting point that parties are free and so entitled to the enforcement of *all* contracts they make; any restrictions would amount to interference with this right/freedom which must be justified. But we can adopt the *different starting point* that sees contract law as a form of state *subsidisation* of a valuable activity, that of enhancing individual autonomy. The institution of contract is a social creation through which the community provides support for the agreements of its members by facilitating them and giving them greater security. That the state is justified in enforcing contracts does not require it to do so in an unqualified way (*always* and in *absolute* terms). Since resources are limited, priorities for action justifiably rest on the worthiness of the project being supported.

On this scheme, the law's refusal to help in enforcing substantively unfair contracts or terms can be understood as the state's refusal to implicate itself in 'that sort of thing',[31] or to support an unworthy activity. Shiffrin[32] speaks of the law's avoidance

---

[29] J Raz, 'Promises in Morality and Law' (1982) 95 *Harvard L Rev* 916.

[30] M Trebilcock, 'The Doctrine of Inequality of Bargaining Power: Post-Benthamite Economics in the House of Lords' (1976) 26 *University of Toronto LJ* 359; S Thal, 'The Inequality of Bargaining Power Doctrine: The Problem of Defining Contractual Unfairness' (1988) 8 *OJLS* 17, 25.

[31] J Raz, *The Morality of Freedom* (Clarendon Press, 1988) ch 14.

[32] S Shiffrin, 'Paternalism, Unconscionability, and Accommodation' (2000) 29 *Philosophy and Public Affairs* 203.

of complicity with exploitation; Dalton[33] refers to the restraint on self-interest necessitated by norms of *decency* and *equality*; Smith[34] argues that contracts at non-normal price disrupt individuals' planning and ability to lead self-directed, autonomous lives.

Problems of uncertainty are bound to arise at the level of application. The most obvious examples are provided by the class of illegal contracts and contracts against public policy (see Additional Chapter 2 which is available on the Online Resource Centre). But more work is needed to elaborate the collective values by which the worthiness of contracts should be measured in a market system which is inevitably based on some level of exploitation of inequality.

online
resource
centre

This general explanation provides a helpful context for understanding the direct and indirect legal control of substantive unfairness manifested in many, if not most, rules of contract law, whether at the level of doctrine or application. It also provides a starting point for understanding the law's reluctance to enforce certain transactions involving controversial subject matter such as trading in babies, child labour, body parts, reproductive services, sex, weapons, and addictive drugs. There is something unsavoury about these, even if there is no procedural unfairness in the way the contracts were created.

THIS CHAPTER IN ESSENCE

online
resource
centre

The key areas and core topics in this chapter are summarised in an easy-to-use list, ideal for revision purposes, on the Online Resource Centre at http://www.oxfordtextbooks.co.uk/orc/chenwishart5e/. Links to websites relevant to the topics covered and any updates to the chapter can also be found on the Online Resource Centre.

QUESTIONS

1 'First appearances suggest that the Unfair Contract Terms Act 1977 only applies to terms that limit or exclude liability, but the reality is far messier, and the Unfair Terms in Consumer Contracts Regulations 1999 just adds to the complexity.' Discuss.

2 'The picture of legislative control of unfair terms is bewildering. Some terms are "blacklisted", some are "grey listed", some must be reasonable and some must not be unfair, whatever they mean. Reform is sorely needed.' Discuss.

3 'To avoid frustrating the purpose of the Unfair Terms in Consumer Contracts Regulations 1999, the scope of unreviewable contractual terms, sometimes called core terms, must be narrowly construed.' Discuss.

4 What amounts to 'unfairness' under the Unfair Terms in Consumer Contracts Regulations 1999?

---

[33] C Dalton, 'An Essay in the Deconstruction of Contract Doctrine' (1985) 94 *Yale LJ* 997, 1024–38.
[34] S Smith, 'In Defence of Substantive Unfairness' (1996) 112 *LQR* 138.

5 Finn, a business, and Gigi, a consumer, each purchase computers, the price payable by six monthly instalments, from Herman, a retailer. Finn and Gigi are handed a document. They do not notice the following terms in very small and faint print.

(i)   All implied terms are excluded.

(ii) Herman's liability is limited to £200 per customer.

(iii) Customers must notify Herman of any complaints within 48 hours of purchase and cannot withhold any monthly payments for whatever reason.

Advise Finn and Gigi who find out a week later that the computers are seriously defective and practically useless.

 For hints on how to answer these questions, please see the Online Resource Centre at http://www.oxfordtextbooks.co.uk/orc/chenwishart5e/

KEY FURTHER READING

Adams, J, and Brownsword, R (1988), 'The Unfair Contract Terms Act: A Decade of Discretion', 104 *LQR* 94.

Bright, S (2000), 'Winning the Battle Against Unfair Contract Terms', 20 *LS* 331.

Chen-Wishart, M, 'Transparency and Fairness in Bank Charges' (2010) 126 *LQR* 157.

Chen-Wishart, M, 'Controlling Unfair Terms: Protecting the Institution of Contract' in L Gullifer and S Vogenauer (eds), *English and European Perspectives on Contract and Commercial Law* (Hart Publishing, 2015) 105–30.

Collins, H (1994), 'Good Faith in European Contract Law', 14 *OJLS* 229.

Coote, B (1964), *Exception Clauses* (Sweet & Maxwell).

Law Commissions (joint report) (2005), *Unfair Terms in Contracts* (Law Com No 292, Cm 6464, Scot Law Com No 199).

Macdonald, E (2002), 'Scope and Fairness of the Unfair Terms in the Consumer Contracts Regulations: Director-General of Fair Trading Versus First National Bank', 65 *MLR* 763.

Macdonald, E (2004), 'Unifying Unfair Terms Legislation', 67 *MLR* 69.

Macdonald, E (2007), 'Unfair Contract Terms Act—Thirty Years On' in A Burrows and E Peel (eds), *Contract Terms* (OUP) 153.

Morgan, P (2010), 'Bank Charges and the Unfair Terms in Consumer Contracts Regulations 1999: The End of the Road for Consumers?', *LMCLQ* 208.

Whittaker, S (2011), 'Unfair Contract Terms, Unfair Prices and Bank Charges', 74 *MLR* 106.

Breach and remedies for breach

'What can I get if you break the contract?'

INTRODUCTION

In Part VI, we examine the end of the life of a contract. A contract may be lawfully brought to an end by:

(i) *full performance*: the overwhelming majority of contracts are discharged by due performance, they are 'spent'; the lawyer's role in these contracts is in drafting the initial contract;

(ii) *agreement*: this is a modification of the original contract and must normally be supported by consideration (see 3.1.5). If neither party has started or finished performance, consideration is provided by each party giving up his or her rights against the other;

(iii) *operation of a term in the contract*: which stipulates that the contract will come to an end on the happening of an event (not amounting to breach), or that one party can serve notice to cancel or terminate the contract under certain conditions (see 12.2.3.2(ii)–(iii));

(iv) *operation of the law*: as where contracts are frustrated (see Chapter 7);

(v) *termination for breach of contract*: the scope of an innocent party's right to terminate the contract for the defendant's breach is discussed in Chapter 12.

Introductory Diagram A gives a brief overview of how contracts may be brought to an end.

Contract parties are entitled to performance in accordance with the terms of the contract (see Part V). Contracts that are made and performed simultaneously (eg buying a bus ticket) require little support from contract law while those involving a time lag between contract formation and performance (eg a building contract) are vitally dependent on contract law's remedial regime. Breach of contract opens the gateway to a *menu of remedies* to innocent parties who meet the qualifying conditions. **Introductory Diagram B** gives an overview of these remedies. The innocent party may claim:

- *termination*: call the contract off (Chapter 12);
- *damages*: obtain monetary compensation for the breach (Chapter 13);

- *specific performance*: compel the contract-breaker to do what he or she undertook in the contract (Chapter 14).

The relationship between these remedies can be complicated. A diagram in Chapter 14 (**Diagram 14A**) suggests an approach to problem questions on remedies for breach.

Part VI Introductory Diagram A: Overview of the end of a contract

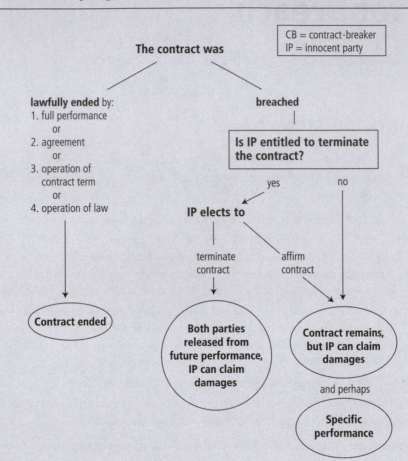

Part VI Introductory Diagram B: Overview of remedies for breach of contract

CB = contract-breaker
IP = innocent party

Remedy	Effect		Availability
IP wants to get out of the contract **Termination** **(ch 12)**	**Termination** discharges both parties from further performance of the primary obligations (but CB has obligation to pay damages).		✓ Renunciation ✓ Impossibility of performance ✓ Actual breach of '*condition*' or serious breach of 'innominate term'.
	IP may elect to **affirm** the contract (12.3) in order to sue for the *agreed price* (14.1)		✗ Not if IP's performance requires CB's cooperation or IP has no 'legitimate interest' in affirming.
IP wants to claim money **Damages** **(ch 13)**	**Expectation** measure		✓ All breaches but subject to limits, eg mitigation and remoteness.
	Reliance measure		✓ All breaches but cannot get more than expectation.
	Restitution measure	Giving *back*	If contract terminated IP can recover: ✓ money paid if total failure of consideration, and ✓ value of non-money performance (*quantum meruit/quantum valebat*).
		Giving *up* profits	If IP would otherwise be inadequately protected, can claim: ✓ compensation for loss of hypothetical bargain, or ✓ account of profits only if IP has special interest in preventing CB from profiting by the breach.
IP wants CB to do what CB promised **Specific remedies** **(ch 14)**	**Specific performance**—of primary obligations (whether (a) to pay money or (b) to confer non-monetary performance)		✓ (a) as debt action ✓ (b) but subject to extensive bars, eg adequacy of damages, constant supervision, personal services, and unfairness.
	Agreed remedies— secondary (remedial) obligations, eg (i) specific performance, (ii) termination, (iii) exemptions of liability, (iv) payments on breach, (v) forfeiture of payments made		✗ (i) cannot fetter court's discretion ✓ (ii), (iii) subject to strict construction ✓ (iv) subject to penalty rule ✓ (v) subject to relief

12

Breach of contract and termination

'You have breached the contract and I want out'

The questions addressed in this chapter are the following.

(i) What is breach of contract and when does it occur?

(ii) What sorts of breach will entitle a claimant to elect whether to end (terminate) the contract?

(iii) What is the effect of terminating a contract?

(iv) When can the claimant insist on continuing with performance when the defendant no longer wants it?

12.1 **Breach of contract**

A party breaches a contract when, *without lawful excuse,* he or she fails to perform any of his or her contractual obligations. The burden of proof is on the claimant alleging breach. The question is whether the claimant has received *exact and precise performance* of the contract from the defendant. For example, in *Re Moore & Co Ltd and Landauer & Co* (1921), a contract to sell 3,000 tins of fruit to be packed in cases of

30 tins was breached when some of the consignment contained cases of 24 tins. This breach entitled the buyer to reject the whole consignment, and get out of the contract although the performance was no less valuable than that promised.

Most contractual obligations are *strict liability*; that is, the promisor guarantees to achieve *a particular state of affairs* (eg to paint a house, to sell goods of satisfactory quality). The contract is breached when performance falls short of this, even if the defendant has done his or her best. However, some contracts stipulate a lesser standard of performance, requiring only the *exercise of reasonable care*, without guaranteeing any particular end result.[1] Liability for contracts of services such as that of a lawyer or doctor will usually be fault-based (*Thake v Maurice* (1986) at 677, 684–7) and can trigger a concurrent duty in tort to take reasonable care (see 1.6.2).

The defendant's breach may be:

- *anticipatory* by (i) **renunciation** (expressly or impliedly refusing to perform) or (ii) **impossibility** (disabling his or herself from performing) *before* performance is due; or

- *actual* by (iii) **failure to perform** *when* performance is due.

The *timing* matters because, where breach is anticipatory, the claimant can immediately sue for remedies, even before the time due for performance.

'Renunciation', 'impossibility', and 'failure of performance' overlap, but each has its own distinctive characteristics (see 12.1.1–12.1.3). They are often called 'grounds of termination' and are collectively known as 'repudiatory breaches' (*Heyman v Darwins Ltd* (1942) at 397). However, they are only repudiatory (entitling the claimant to terminate the contract) when they cross a 'seriousness' threshold (see 12.2.2.2), while they always give rise to claims for damages.

12.1.1 Renunciation ('repudiation')

Renunciation (also called repudiation) **occurs** when one party by *words or conduct* evinces an *intention not to perform* part, or all, of the contract. Absent an express refusal, the question is whether the defendant's acts or omissions would lead a *reasonable person* to conclude that he or she no longer intends to perform his or her contractual obligations (*Universal Cargo Carriers Corp v Citati* (1957) at 436). Renunciation *at* or *after* the time of performance amounts to *actual* breach.

(i) **Timing**: renunciation before the time fixed for performance is often referred to as 'anticipatory breach', suggesting erroneously that breach is 'to come'. In fact, renunciation is itself a breach and, if sufficiently 'serious' (see 12.2.2.2), entitles the claimant to terminate the contract *immediately* and claim damages for the loss of the contract. In **Hochster v De la Tour** (1853), DT employed H to commence work for three months from 1 June but repudiated the contract on 11 May. H could claim damages *immediately* (before 1 June). As Cockburn CJ (at 114) explains in *Frost v Knight* (1872): 'The promisee has an inchoate right to the performance of

---

[1] The Supply of Goods and Services Act 1982, s 13, provides that a person who supplies a service in the course of a business impliedly undertakes to 'carry out the service with reasonable care and skill'.

the bargain, which becomes complete when the time for performance has arrived. In the meantime he has a right to have the contract kept open as a subsisting and effective contract. Its unimpaired and unimpeached efficacy must be essential to his interests.'

Pause for reflection

Awarding damages on termination for breach *before* performance is due may seem objectionable, especially where there is a long interval between termination and the time of performance. It accelerates the defendant's obligations and increases the potential for errors in quantifying damages since that conventionally rests on the market value of the lost performance *at the time of performance*. However, this rule encourages the speedy resolution of broken-down contracts and minimises the claimant's losses by encouraging him or her to terminate the contract immediately and make substitute arrangements, instead of keeping him or herself ready to perform a contract which will inevitably be breached. In long-term contracts with periodic performances, the rule avoids the inefficiency of requiring the claimant to sue as each performance falls due.

(ii) **The extent of renunciation**: where the defendant refuses to perform *all* his or her contractual obligations, the claimant has the undoubted right to terminate the contract. Otherwise, the court must decide whether any *partial* renunciation is sufficiently 'serious' to justify termination (see 12.2.2.2).

(iii) **The relevance of the contract-breaker's mistake or good faith**: a party's words or conduct can amount to renunciation even when they result from an *honest but mistaken view* of his or her contractual rights and obligations. If you and I make a contract, the question is whether your conduct objectively signals to me:

(a) a genuine *dispute about the proper construction of the contract*, when the courts will lean *against* finding renunciation by you; or

(b) an intention not to perform the objective interpretation of the contract, which constitutes renunciation by you.

Where I purports to terminate the contract for your alleged renunciation but get it wrong (ie the court concludes that you did not renounce the contract), my unjustified termination will itself amount to a wrongful repudiation entitling you to terminate (my termination 'gun' turns back on me). This means instead of my being able to claim damages from you, I become liable for damages to you. The distinction between (a) and (b) can be a fine one and the cases are not entirely consistent. No renunciation was found in the following cases.

✗ *Woodar Investment Development Ltd v Wimpey Construction UK Ltd* (1980): the buyer of land honestly but mistakenly purported to exercise a contractual right to terminate the contract; the seller then claimed termination for repudiatory breach and sued for damages. The House of Lords (at

280) denied the seller's claim for, 'far from repudiating the contract, [the buyer was] relying on it and invoking one of its provisions'. Moreover, the seller's letter showed that he knew the buyer was willing to perform the contract if his purported termination was found to have been invalid (at 299).

✗ *Eminence Property v Heaney* (2010): sellers of land purported to terminate the contract on the mistaken basis that the buyer failed to complete on time. The buyer then purported to terminate by arguing that the seller's wrongful termination was itself a repudiatory breach. The Court of Appeal rejected this because 'looking at all the circumstances objectively', the seller's mistake would have been clear to a reasonable buyer, as would the seller's desire that conveyance be completed by the actual date. Thus, the seller had not 'clearly shown an intention to abandon and altogether refuse to perform the contract' (at [61]).

✗ Renunciation was found in ***Federal Commerce and Navigation Co Ltd v Molena Alpha Inc (The Nanfri)*** (1978) where the owner disputed the charterer's deductions from the hire payments. On legal advice, the owner threatened not to issue freight prepaid bills of lading, which would have very serious consequences for the charterer. The House of Lords held that this amounted to a repudiatory breach by the owner entitling the charterer to terminate the contract, although the owner had wanted to maintain the profitable charterparty.

Come the time for performance, a party whose performance deviates from the objectively correct interpretation of the contract will have actually breached the contract irrespective of his or her good faith.

12.1.2 Impossibility of performance

Impossibility of performance is a breach by the party whose act or omission has *disabled him or her from performance*. This is usually more difficult to prove than renunciation. The latter only requires that the defendant's conduct would lead a *reasonable person* to believe that he or she was *not intending to perform*. Impossibility requires the claimant to show, on the balance of probabilities, that the defendant's performance was *impossible in fact* (*Alfred C Toepfer Intl GmbH v Itex Hagrani Export SA* (1993) at 362). The answer may be clear.

✓ For instance, where the defendant sells the subject matter of the contract to a third party (*Bowdell v Parsons* (1808)).

✓ In *Universal Cargo Carriers Corp v Citati* (1957), U chartered a ship to C who agreed to provide the cargo and nominate a berth and a shipper before a certain date. C wanted to perform but had done nothing three days before the due date. This left it so late that performance would inevitably be delayed and this would frustrate the commercial purpose of the contract. The court held that C had not renounced the contract, but its inability to perform entitled U to terminate and find another charterer.

However, impossibility is not made out just because the defendant:

- ✓ declares his or her intention to perform in a way that seems impossible if he or she can also choose to perform by a possible means (*The Vladimir Ilich* (1975) at 329);

- ✓ enters into inconsistent obligations (*Alfred C Toepfer v Itex Hagran*); he or she *may* find an alternative way of successfully performing:

(i) **timing**: impossibility occurring *before* performance is due amounts to anticipatory breach; the contract can be terminated from this point and damages claimed. Impossibility occurring *after* performance is due constitutes actual breach;

(ii) **the extent of impossibility**: as with renunciation, a party is only entitled to terminate the contract if the part which is impossible to perform would amount to a sufficiently 'serious' breach of contract (see 12.2.2.2). Although the test has been compared with that for frustration (*Trade and Transport Inc v Iino Kaiun Kaisha Ltd* (1973) at 221), the analogy is really to *self-induced frustration* since the impossibility of performance does not excuse the defendant;

(iii) **the contract-breaker's good faith is irrelevant**: he or she is liable for the breach that is bound to happen whether due to his or her own acts or omissions, or from circumstances for which he or she bears the risk (*Universal Cargo v Citati* at 441). If neither party bears the risk for the occurrence of circumstances making performance impossible, the issue becomes one of frustration (see Chapter 7).

12.1.3 Failure of performance

The most common type of breach is actual failure of performance when performance becomes due. Failure can take the form of non-, late, or defective performance: all entitle the claimant to sue for damages and, if sufficiently serious, to terminate the contract.

12.2 Termination for breach

Unnecessary confusion can result from the inconsistent use of terminology in this area of law. Contracts that are terminated for breach may be referred to in judgments and academic writings as: 'repudiated', 'rescinded', 'brought to an end', or 'rejected' (in sale of goods). They can all mean the same thing. However, *'rescission for breach'* must be distinguished from 'rescission for vitiating factors' (eg misrepresentation and undue influence). The latter sets aside a contract both *retrospectively and prospectively* (see 5.3) and requires mutual restitution. The former only sets aside the contract prospectively (*de futuro*), and gives the claimant the right to expectation remedies. Again, termination for breach is often expressed as *'discharge by breach'*. But a serious breach merely entitles the claimant to terminate, if he or she so chooses. In contrast, *discharge* by frustration occurs *automatically*.

12.2.1 **The effect of termination**

(i) **Termination discharges** *both* **parties from further performance** of their primary obligations under the contract. But the contract-breaker's unperformed primary obligation is replaced by 'a *secondary* (remedial) obligation to pay monetary compensation' to the claimant for his or her loss (per Lord Diplock, ***Photo Production Ltd v Securicor Transport Ltd*** (1980) at 849). The claimant is also entitled to damages in respect of the breach up to the time of termination.

(ii) **Accrued and other continuing obligations remain enforceable:** since the contract only discharges the parties from future obligations (ie falling due after termination), 'rights are not divested or discharged which have been unconditionally acquired' (*The Dominique* (1989) at 1098). Terms in the terminated contract that specifically relate to the post-termination situation (eg agreed damages (see 14.3)) or restriction of otherwise available remedies for breach (eg requiring arbitration or exempting liability) continue to apply.

(iii) **Claims for restitution:** subject to the bar on double recovery, **the claimant** may elect to sue for:

✓ restitution of any money paid under the contract if there has been *total failure of consideration* from the contract-breaker (see 13.3);

✓ a *quantum meruit* or *quantum valebat* for the reasonable value of goods or services supplied but not yet paid for under the contract (*Planché v Colburn* (1831)).

These restitutionary claims are preferable if the claimant has made a bad bargain. If instead, the claimant sues for expectation damages, any benefits transferred by the defendant are factored into the calculation of the claimant's expectation damages.

On termination, the contract-breaker may only:

✓ recover *part-payments* for goods or land for total failure of consideration (*Dies v British and Intl Mining & Finance Corp Ltd* (1939)), or the contract price earned by performance subject to the entire obligation rule (12.2.2.1 III);

✓ obtain *relief from forfeiture* (*Workers Trust & Merchant Bank Ltd v Dojap Investments Ltd* (1993) and see 14.3.3.1).

 Pause for reflection

The European Draft Common Frame of Reference:

1. does not take an all-or-nothing approach: termination may be in whole or only in part (Art III.-3:506);

2. takes a more even-handed approach to restitution: *mutual* restitution is required except 'to the extent that conforming-performance by one party is met by conforming-performance by the other' (Arts III.-3:510 and III.-3:511). If precise restitution cannot be made, then restitution can be made in money's worth (Art III.-3:312);

3. allows the claimant who *accepts* non-conforming performance to claim a price reduction (Art III.-3:601).

The advantages of termination for the claimant are the following.

(i) Termination is a *self-help remedy*: the claimant can end the contract quickly without the inconvenience and cost of seeking the court's assistance. Rather, it is the contract-breaker who must go to court to challenge the termination.

(ii) Faced with a serious breach, it is often preferable for the claimant to *discontinue his or her own performance* than to continue (eg by paying money), only to claim unsecured damages later (he or she will lose out if the defendant becomes insolvent).

(iii) Termination can *save the claimant from a bad bargain*: he or she might be better off not performing or recovering payments than claiming expectation damages for breach (eg where he or she pays or has promised to pay £10,000 for goods which, by the time of performance, are only worth £6,000) or where his or her losses may not be recoverable as damages (eg where they are too remote, see 13.2.5.6).

However, termination may be disadvantageous to the contract-breaker:

(i) he or she may have incurred *expenses* in performance, which will now be wasted;

(ii) his or her part-performance may have conferred *benefits* on the claimant who may not be liable to make restitution (see 13.3.2);

(iii) he or she may *lose the benefit of a good bargain*, which would amount to a penalty entirely disproportionate to the harm caused by the breach (*Schuler AG v Wickman Machine Tool Sales Ltd* (1974)).

12.2.2 **When is termination allowed?**

Where breach or anticipatory breach is *total*, the claimant can clearly terminate the contract; where it is *partial*, difficult technical questions arise. The answer ostensibly depends on the *status* of the term breached. The rule of thumb is that:

✓ breaches of *'conditions'* allow the claimant to terminate;

✗ breaches of mere *'warranties'* do not.

However, balancing the parties' conflicting interests necessitates a *consequentialist approach*: if the breach has seriously prejudiced the claimant's position, he or she should be able to call the contract off; but, if the defendant has largely performed what was bargained for, substantial justice is done if the contract remains on foot and damages are paid to compensate the claimant for the breach. We will see that the law has moved some way in that direction by recognising the category of *innominate terms*. However, the concern to promote certainty (important for a self-help remedy not requiring resort to the courts) while also avoiding harshness to the defendant has resulted in considerable complexity.

12.2.2.1 Clearing the ground

Treitel, in ' "Conditions" and "Conditions Precedent" ' (1990) 106 *LQR* 185 examines the many senses in which the expression 'condition' is used when determining whether a claimant can withhold his or her own performance. An overview is provided by **Diagram 12A**.

- **Levels I–III** concern the *order* of performance: the claimant may be able to withhold his or her own performance simply because it is 'not their turn yet'.

- **Level IV** concerns the *conformity* of the performance given with the obligations undertaken: here, lack of conformity amounts to breach and the claimant's withholding of his or her own performance, if he or she is entitled, amounts to termination.

Diagram 12A Overview of the claimant's right to withhold performance

Look on the Online Resource Centre to view this figure as a PowerPoint® presentation

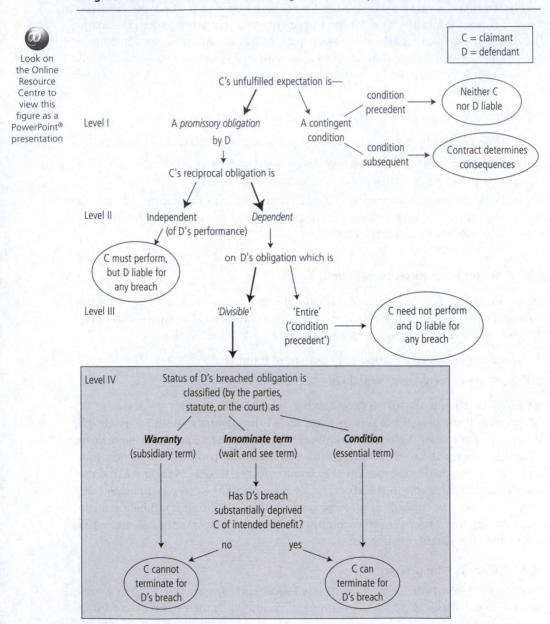

Level I: Contingent or promissory obligation?

At the highest level of generality, 'conditions' may be either contingent or promissory.

- A **contingent condition** is one for which neither party is responsible, but upon which both parties' obligations to perform or keep performing depend. It may be a *condition precedent* (as where contractual performance depends on one party obtaining a licence or planning permission: *Pym v Campbell* (1865)), or a *condition subsequent* (as where continuing performance depends on continued funding from a specified third party: *Brown v Knowsley BC* (1986)). There is no question of breach (and thus, of termination for breach) if the condition precedent fails or the condition subsequent occurs: the obligation to perform the contract simply does not arise (or is discharged). On one interpretation, the mistake doctrine is simply an instance of an implied condition precedent (see 6.2.2.3), and the frustration doctrine, an instance of an implied condition subsequent (see 7.2.1).

- A **promissory condition** refers to something which one party has an *obligation* to bring about. But whether breach of this condition entitles the claimant to terminate the contract depends on whether the promissory condition is 'dependent' or 'independent'.

Level II: Dependent or independent obligation?

- Where the promissory condition undertaken by *A* is **independent** of *B*'s performance, *A* cannot terminate the contract on *B*'s failure to perform (*A* must still perform). For example, a tenant's covenant to pay rent is independent of the landlord's covenant to repair: the tenant cannot withhold payment even if the landlord fails to repair (*Taylor v Webb* (1937)). Since this may leave *A* inadequately protected from *B*'s non-performance, courts are slow to designate an obligation as being 'independent' unless the contract makes this very clear.

- Contractual obligations are normally regarded as being **dependent** (or *interdependent*): each party's obligation to perform is dependent on the other's performance or readiness and willingness to perform.[2]

Level III: 'Entire' or 'divisible' obligation?

Dependent obligations may be 'entire' or 'divisible'.

- An obligation is '**entire**' when it must be *completely* performed *before* the other party is obliged to perform (also called the 'entire contract' rule). For example, where *A* engages *B* to build a conservatory for £40,000, payment on satisfactory completion of the whole (or part-payment for defined parts), *A* need not pay, and *B* cannot sue for part-payment, if *B* fails to complete the whole (or stipulated part). *B* has not fulfilled the condition triggering the payment. *B*'s performance here is sometimes described as a 'condition precedent' to *B*'s right to claim payment (not to be confused with the contingent 'condition precedent' at level I). Making an obligation 'entire' gives *A* great protection from *B*'s non-performance and gives *B* a powerful incentive to complete performance. However, the **potential harshness**

---

[2] Eg the Sale of Goods Act 1979, s 28, regarding the delivery of the goods and payment of the price; the failure of one party discharges the other from performance.

to B is instanced by ***Cutter v Powell*** (1795). C agreed to work on a ship sailing from Jamaica to England for 30 guineas (almost four times the going rate), payment on completion of the voyage. C died just before the journey was completed and his widow was denied recovery of wages for his part-performance. As Sir George Jessel MR (at 545) explained in *Re Hall & Barker* (1878), 'if a shoemaker agrees to make a pair of shoes, he cannot offer you one shoe and ask you to pay one half the price'. The potential harshness of the rule is mitigated in two main ways:

(i) the *doctrine of 'substantial performance'*[3] protects the contract-breaker who has substantially performed his or her obligations. The other party cannot withhold performance but must pay after setting-off (ie deducting) any loss suffered from the incomplete or defective performance. In *Dakin (H) & Co Ltd v Lee* (1916), D agreed to carry out certain repairs on L's premises for £1,500 and did so except in minor respects which would cost £80 to rectify. The court held that D had substantially performed the contract and was entitled to the price less the costs to L of fixing it;

(ii) the part-performing contract-breaker can claim *restitution* for the benefit conferred on and 'accepted' by the other party. Section 30(1) of the Sale of Goods Act 1979 allows a buyer who receives less than the quantity of goods contracted for to reject them or pay the contract rate for them. Alternatively, a part-performer can claim a *quantum meruit* (the market value) if the other party had the *opportunity to reject* but has accepted the benefit. In ***Sumpter v Hedges*** (1898),[4] S agreed to build two houses for H for the lump sum of £565. When S informed H that he could not complete because he had run out of money, H completed the houses himself. S was denied a reasonable remuneration for the work done since H had no option but to accept what was done on his land. However, S could recover the value of the *materials* left behind; H had a choice as to whether to use them.

(👤) Pause for reflection

The requirement of 'acceptance' counters the recipient's right to say that the part-performance received (one shoe as opposed to two) is worth *less* than the reasonable market value or *nothing at all* to them. However, the part-performer may still be able to claim restitution by showing that the recipient was *incontrovertibly benefited* by his or her part-performance, in receiving a *readily realisable financial benefit* or being *saved inevitable expenses*,[5] unless the parties clearly intended the part-performer to bear the risk of non-completion even where he or she has clearly benefited the other party.[6]

---

[3] *Hoenig v Isaacs* (1952).

[4] See B McFarlane and R Stevens, 'In Defence of *Sumpter v Hedges*' (2002) 118 *LQR* 569.

[5] *Hain SS Co Ltd v Tate & Lyle Ltd* (1936) at 358, 367–8, 373; *Procter & Gamble Philippine Manufacturing Corp v Peter Cremer GmbH & Co (The Manilla)* (1988).

[6] Law Commission, *Law of Contract: Pecuniary Restitution on Breach of Contract* (Law Com No 121, 1983), paras 2.66–2.69, 2.73.

• In order to avoid the problems associated with 'entire' obligations, courts lean towards finding obligations to be **'divisible'**. Breach gives the claimant an action for damages, but does not *necessarily* allow him or her to withhold his or her own performance by terminating the contract. Whether it does depends on the status of the term breached.

12.2.2.2 The status of terms: conditions, warranties, and innominate terms

It was once assumed that *every* contractual term could be classified *at the time of formation* as:

• a **condition**: an essential term, the breach of which (a 'repudiatory breach') gives the claimant the right to terminate and claim damages for losses *up to* termination and *beyond* (ie for loss of the bargain); or

• a **warranty**, a non-essential or subsidiary term, the breach of which yields no right to termination; the claimant can only claim damages for losses *up to* the time of the action (but not for loss of the bargain since the contract continues).

In short, the claimant can terminate for breach of a condition, but not for breach of a warranty, irrespective of the seriousness of the *actual consequences* of breach.

If a term is not clearly classified by the parties, statute, or binding precedent (see 12.2.3), it may be difficult to say *at the time of formation* how important a term is, because the consequences of its breach will vary wildly in seriousness, depending on the precise circumstances of the breach (*Bentsen v Taylor, Sons & Co* (1893) at 281). The judicial solution was to recognise a new category of '*wait and see*' terms, called **innominate** (or intermediate) terms. Whether termination is available for breach of such terms depends on 'waiting and seeing' whether the actual *consequences* of breach are sufficiently grave for the claimant. Its effect is still all-or-nothing; the difference is simply in the *timing* of the decision (ie at breach rather than at formation as for conditions and warranties). Diplock LJ explains in **Hong Kong Fir Shipping Co Ltd v Kawasaki Kisen Kaisha Ltd** (1962), that the legal consequences of the breach of innominate terms 'do not follow automatically from a prior classification of the undertaking, as a "condition" or a "warranty"'. It depends upon whether the breach has deprived or will deprive the claimant 'of substantially the whole benefit which it was intended he should obtain from the contract' (at 70). In that case, H chartered a ship (the *Hong Kong Fir*) to K for 24 months, but breached the term requiring her to be 'in every way fitted for ordinary cargo service' by failing to provide competent personnel to maintain the aged ship. The ship had many serious breakdowns and only spent two months at sea in the first seven months. The seaworthiness term was held to be an innominate term, the breach of which would only entitle the charterer to terminate if its consequence was so serious as to frustrate the commercial purpose of the venture. Upjohn LJ (at 62–3) explains:

> It is for the simple reason that the seaworthiness clause is breached by the slightest failure to be fitted 'in every way' for service . . . If a nail is missing from one of the timbers of a wooden vessel or if proper medical supplies or two anchors are not on board at the time of sailing, the owners are in breach of the seaworthiness stipulation.

It is contrary to common sense to suppose that in such circumstances the parties contemplated that the charterer should at once be entitled to treat the contract as at an end for such trifling breaches.

The essence of innominate terms is that they can be breached in different ways, resulting in consequences of varying seriousness. On the facts, it was held that in spite of the delays already occurring and likely to occur, the defendant's steps taken to remedy the failings and the length of the charter period remaining meant that the claimant was *not* substantially deprived of the whole benefit of the contract. Thus, the claimant's purported termination itself amounted to a repudiatory breach entitling the defendant to damages for loss of profit. These were substantial since the market had dropped significantly: indeed, the real motive for the claimant's attempted termination was to get a cheaper deal elsewhere.

In determining **whether breach of an innominate term entitles the claimant to terminate** the court must balance the position of the parties at the date of the purported termination. In *Telford Homes (Creekside) Ltd v Ampurius Nu Homes Holdings Ltd* (2013), Lewison LJ noted that the test for termination 'is the same test as that applicable to frustration. This sets the bar high.' Other expressions emphasise the **high threshold** for termination: it is said that the breach must go to 'the root of the contract',[7] be 'fundamental',[8] amount to 'a substantial failure to perform the contract at all',[9] or 'frustrate the commercial purpose of the venture'.[10] In *Telford Homes*, Lewison LJ sets out the nature of the multi-factorial assessment (at [51]–[52]):

[T]he starting point must be to consider what benefit the injured party was intended to obtain from performance of the contract. . . .

The next thing to consider is the effect of the breach on the injured party. What financial loss has it caused? How much of the intended benefit under the contract has the injured party already received? Can the injured party be adequately compensated by an award of damages? Is the breach likely to be repeated? Will the guilty party resume compliance with his obligations? Has the breach fundamentally changed the value of future performance of the guilty party's outstanding obligations?

On the facts of *Telford Homes*, the Court of Appeal held that a property company had not been entitled to terminate an agreement to take 999-year leases in four mixed-use blocks on the ground of the construction company's delay in building two of the blocks. Likewise, the buyer of a 125-year lease was held not entitled to terminate because the delay of one month on the completion of the building could not possibly be said to have deprived the vendors of substantially the whole benefit of the contract (*Urban I (Blonk Street) Ltd v Ayres* (2013)).

---

[7] *Cehave NV v Bremer Handelsgesellschaft (The Hansa Nord)* (1976) at 60, 73; *Federal Commerce & Navigation Co Ltd v Molena Alpha Inc (The Nanfri)* (1979) at 779.

[8] *Suisse Atlantique Société d'Armement SA v NV Rotterdamsche Kolen Centrale* (1967) at 397, 409–10, 421–2, 431.

[9] *Wallis, Son & Wells v Pratt & Haynes* (1910) at 1012.

[10] *Trade and Transport Inc v Iino Kaiun Kaisha Ltd (The Angelia)* (1973) at 223.

In practice, this high threshold of seriousness required, the wide range of factors considered, their uncertain relative weight, and the potentially disastrous consequences of an attempted termination which turns out to be wrongful will act as strong disincentives to elect termination in response to its breach.

12.2.3 **How are terms classified?**

Terms may be classified by: (i) statute; (ii) the parties' express agreement; or (iii) the court applying binding precedents or finding the parties' implied intentions. Awareness of the **relevant policies** is important in understanding what is at stake here. The ubiquitous tensions in contract law between certainty, fairness, and respect for the parties' intentions come into sharp focus here. Policies favouring *prior determination* (ie at formation) support the classifications of 'conditions' or 'warranties'; policies favouring *subsequent determination* (ie after breach) support the classification of 'innominate terms'.

(i) **Commercial certainty**: certainty supports prior determination because it enables commercial parties to know, immediately and unequivocally, how they are entitled to respond on the other party's breach. Certainty is particularly important (*Bunge Corp v Tradax Export SA* (1981) at 720):

(a) where the contract is one of a chain or 'string' of contracts because 'most members of the "string" will have many ongoing contracts simultaneously and they must be able to do business with confidence in the legal results of their actions', or

(b) where it would be difficult for the claimant and the court to quantify the loss suffered.

(ii) **Freedom of contract**: contract parties should be free to determine in advance which breaches will entitle the claimant to terminate, irrespective of its consequences.

(iii) **Avoiding bad faith terminations**: this would support subsequent classification; that is, as an innominate term. The potential unfairness of termination for 'technical' or unmeritorious reasons is instanced by *Arcos Ltd v E A Ronaasen & Son* (1933). The parties contracted for the sale and purchase of timber staves cut to 8/16-inch thickness. The buyers were allowed to reject the goods for being 9/16-inch thick (ie terminate the contract), although their real reason was to escape what had turned into a bad bargain. A fall in timber prices meant that the claimant could now buy wood cheaper than under the contract. The courts have made use of the innominate term classification to counter such economic opportunism. In *Cehave v Bremer (The Hansa Nord)* (1976), the parties contracted for the sale of citrus pulp pellets for £100,000 to arrive 'in good condition'. Meanwhile, the market price for pellets dropped to about £86,000. The buyers rejected the goods on the ground that some of the pellets were damaged. The seller then sold the pellets to a third party who resold them to the original buyer for about £30,000; the buyer used them to manufacture cattle feed, as originally intended. The buyer's termination was held to be unlawful since the term breached was innominate and the consequences were not sufficiently serious to allow the contract to be avoided 'according to the whims of market fluctuations and where there is a free choice between two possible constructions . . . the court should tend to prefer that construction which will ensure performance and not encourage avoidance of contractual obligations' (at 70–1).

(iv) **Upholding bargains**: dicta from *The Hansa Nord* suggest that courts should encourage the performance rather than the termination of contracts, unless the claimant has been substantially deprived of the benefit of the contract. This leans towards the innominate term classification. However, preservation of the bargain can also be achieved by classifying terms as a condition; this would discourage the *other party* from breach in the first place for fear of losing the contract.

The modern default position is to treat terms as innominate, unless a court is compelled to find otherwise by reference to statute, the parties' express provision, or binding precedent. The question is not '*why* innominate term?' but '*why not?*' As Lord Scarman said in *Bunge Corp v Tradax* (at 717), 'unless the contract makes it clear, either by express provision or by necessary implication arising from its nature, purpose, and circumstances . . . that a particular stipulation is a condition or only a warranty, it is an innominate term'. This tendency is certainly detectable in classifications by the courts, but it is even detectable where terms are classified by *statute* and by the *parties'* ostensible agreement (see 12.2.3.1 and 12.2.3.2). An overview is provided by **Diagram 12B**. The European Draft Common Frame of Reference treats all terms as innominate for the purposes of the remedy of termination (Art III.-3:502).

Diagram 12B Classification of terms

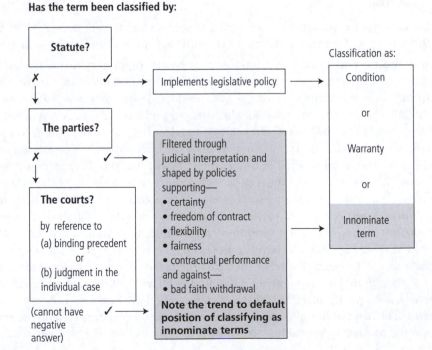

Has the term been classified by:

Statute? ✗ / ✓ → Implements legislative policy → Classification as:

The parties? ✗ / ✓

The courts? by reference to (a) binding precedent or (b) judgment in the individual case

(cannot have negative answer) ✓ →

Filtered through judicial interpretation and shaped by policies supporting—
• certainty
• freedom of contract
• flexibility
• fairness
• contractual performance
and against—
• bad faith withdrawal

Note the trend to default position of classifying as innominate terms

Classification as:
Condition
or
Warranty
or
Innominate term

12.2.3.1 Classification by statute

Statute may classify terms as either conditions or warranties. Recall that the Sale of Goods Act 1979 (see 10.4.2.1) *implies* into sale of goods contracts **conditions** guaranteeing that:

- the seller has *title* to sell the goods (s 12(1));
- goods sold by *description* correspond with their description (s 13(1));
- goods sold by *sample* correspond with the sample (s 15(2));
- goods sold in the course of business are of *satisfactory quality* unless the buyer's attention has been drawn to or the buyer's examination ought to have revealed any defect (s 14(2) and (2C)); and
- goods sold in the course of business are reasonably *fit for the purpose* that the buyer has made known to the seller (s 14(3)).

The Act also implies as **warranties** terms guaranteeing that:

- goods sold are *free from charges or incumbrances* in favour of third parties not disclosed or known to the buyer before the contract, and that the buyer will enjoy *quiet possession* of the goods subject to the disclosed or known rights of others (s 2(2), (4)–(5)).

There are no examples of statutes classifying a term as **innominate**, but this is the effect of **section 15A(1) of the Sale of Goods Act.** While breach of any implied *condition* entitles the buyer to *reject* the goods (ie terminate the contract), this section requires a *non-consumer buyer* to treat the breach as one of *warranty* (ie no rejection allowed) where the breach is 'so slight that it would be unreasonable for him to reject them', unless the parties otherwise agree. This would counter the unfairness of cases like *Arcos v Ronaasen*. However, section 15A(1) is *one-sided* in limiting the buyer's right to terminate, but not the seller's. Moreover, it is unclear when breaches will be regarded as '*slight*' (the difference between 8/16 and 9/16 of an inch may not be slight for certain uses).

12.2.3.2 Classification by the parties

In principle, it is always open to the parties to agree the status (and hence, consequences of breach) of particular terms (*Bunge Corp v Tradax* at 715) although, again, there are no examples of classification by the parties as innominate terms. Even apparently trivial terms can be classified as 'conditions', allowing termination for their breach. For example, in **Lombard North Central plc v Butterworth** (1987), B essentially agreed to buy on hire-purchase terms a computer from L, making quarterly payments for five years (totalling £11,680), time being 'of the essence' of the contract (ie timely payment is a condition). When the payments were almost complete, B was late with some payments and L terminated the contract. The computer was repossessed and resold for only £173. The Court of Appeal upheld L's termination and allowed L's claim to recover arrears as damages *up to* termination *and* claim *future instalments* as damages for loss of the bargain consequent on termination.

Thus, classification by the parties has the clear potential for unfairness. The stronger party can insist that even minor obligations of the other party are conditions, or can include a 'termination clause' giving itself a wide power to end the contract. This power can be exercised opportunistically (even for a trivial breach) to escape a bad bargain and so deprive the contract-breaker of its bargain. Courts have developed a number of **techniques for controlling the unreasonable creation of conditions and termination clauses**, although careful drafting may still evade the court's control.

(i) **Courts may find that the parties used the labels 'condition' or 'warranty' in their non-technical sense** (ie simply meaning 'terms') and not in their technical sense of determining whether there is a right to termination on breach; this leaves the court free to classify the term as innominate. In **Schuler v Wickman**, W had the sole right to sell S's goods in the UK for over four years. Clause 7 made it a 'condition' that W's two named representatives should visit particular manufacturers each week to promote S's goods; they failed to do so. The House of Lords denied that clause 7 was a condition in the technical sense, since this would turn even one missed visit (out of the 1,400 due over the period) into a repudiatory breach. Although Lord Reid (at 251) accepted that the parties' use of the word 'condition' was a 'strong indication', the fact that 'a particular construction leads to a very *unreasonable result* must be a relevant consideration. The more unreasonable the result the more unlikely it is that the parties can have intended it, and if they do intend it the more necessary it is that they shall make that intention abundantly clear' (see 10.5.2).

(ii) **Courts may treat termination under an agreed 'termination clause' as less remedially potent than breach of a condition proper**: thereby restricting the damages available. In *Financings Ltd v Baldock* (1963), B bought a van from F on hire purchase on payment of £100 immediately and monthly instalments of £28 for two years. Clause 8 gave F the express right to terminate the contract if any instalment was more than ten days late. F terminated the contract when B failed to make the first two payments and sold the van for £140. The court confined F to the recovery of the two late instalments but denied its claim for loss of *future* instalments (ie loss of the bargain); the latter was only available when terminating for a *repudiatory breach*, while F merely exercised a power conferred by the contract on an event that does not amount to a repudiatory breach.

On the other hand, if the claimant can terminate both under a termination clause and under the common law, the court will be slow to find that the claimant has abandoned his or her valuable rights under the common law. In *Stocznia Gdynia SA v Gearbulk Holdings Ltd* (2009), Moore-Bick LJ said (at [44]):

> If the contract and the general law provide the injured party with alternative rights which have different consequences, he will necessarily have to elect between them . . . but where the contract provides a right to terminate which corresponds to a right under the general law (because the breach goes to the root of the contract or because the parties have agreed) . . . no election is necessary . . . [i]t is sufficient for the injured party simply to make it clear that he is treating the contract as discharged.

(iii) **Courts may read down agreed 'termination clauses' to restrict their scope of operation**: in *Rice (t/a Garden Guardian) v Great Yarmouth BC* (2000), an agreement by R to maintain and manage G's sports facilities, parks, gardens, and playgrounds allowed G to terminate the contract 'if the contractor commits a breach of any of its obligations'. G purported to terminate the contract after serving a number of default notices on R. This was held to be unlawful since it could only terminate for a *repudiatory breach* and this had not occurred. Analogous to *Schuler v Wickman*, the court (at [18]) rejected a literal interpretation of the words of the termination clause as offending 'commercial sense'; R's performance involved 'a myriad of obligations of differing importance and varying frequency' which can be broken in many different ways with varying consequences typical of innominate terms. Likewise, Kitchin J noted that: 'the courts have shown some reluctance to interpret a termination clause in a complex contract containing many innominate terms as providing a party with the right to terminate for any breach, however minor' as this 'flouts business commonsense' (in *Dominion Corporate Trustees Ltd v Debenhams Properties Ltd* (2010) at [23]).

 Pause for reflection

1. The decision renders the termination clause meaningless since G could have terminated for a repudiatory breach anyway. A party seeking to rely on a wide termination clause would now be well advised to state expressly that he or she can terminate for 'any breach irrespective of whether it amounts to a repudiatory breach'.

2. The court's commendable aversion to interpretations that lead to very unreasonable results mirrors its *contra proferentem* construction of harsh exemption clauses (see 10.6) and *force majeure* clauses (see 7.4.1). It is motivated by the same concerns about inequality of bargaining power and the avoidance of harsh outcomes, which defeat parties' reasonable expectations.

3. In **'Termination Clauses'** in A Burrows and E Peel (eds), *Contract Terms* (OUP, 2007) 253, **Whittaker** examines the ways in which such clauses are controlled, including by invalidation under the Unfair Terms in Consumer Contracts Regulations 1999.

12.2.3.3 Classification by the courts

Where a term is not classified by the parties or by statute, the courts must do so. Where a *binding precedent* has classified the term, certainty generally requires it to be followed (eg time clauses are often treated as conditions).[11] However, Lord Wilberforce describes some previous decisions as 'excessively technical' and warned that they were open to re-examination by the House of Lords (*Smith Line Ltd v Yngvar Hansen-Tangen* (1976) at 998).

Where a term is previously *unclassified*, the default position is to treat it as an **innominate** term unless this is contra-indicated (*Bunge Corp v Tradax* at 717). Nevertheless, Lord Wilberforce (at 716) said that courts should not be reluctant to find a condition

---

[11] Eg stipulations in a time charterparty as to the date for payment: *Bowes v Shand* (1876–7); or in voyage charterparties, as to the time when the chartered vessel should be ready to load: *The Mihalis Angelos* (1971).

if the intentions of the parties so indicate, especially in the case of *time* clauses in *mercantile* (ie commercial) contracts.

In the last analysis, the court is making 'what is in effect a *value judgment* about the commercial significance of the term in question',[12] and different courts may reach different conclusions. Classification as a **condition** is more likely if the term:

- involves a single performance with a clearly specified time limit and sequence of performance (eg period within which events inhibiting performance are to be notified, an extension of time to be claimed, or the buyer is to have the option of cancelling the contract);

- can only be breached in one way;

- is vital to the contract; or

- is necessary for commercial certainty.

A term is more likely to be classified as **innominate** if:

- it can be breached in different ways with varying degrees of seriousness;

- performance is to take place over a long time and substantial performance has been given; or

- the obligation is loosely framed.

A **condition** was found in **Bunge Corp v Tradax**. The buyer of soya bean meal was required to nominate the *time* for shipment, giving the seller 'at least 15 consecutive days' notice of probable readiness of vessel(s) and of the approximate quantity required to be loaded'. The seller would then nominate a port to load the goods (shipment being required by 30 June). The seller treated the buyer's late notice on 17 June as a repudiatory breach. The House of Lords held the term breached to be a condition although it did not deprive the seller of substantially the whole benefit under the contract, because:

- of the need for certainty in commercial transactions, particularly those involving a chain of sales, when timely performance is vital and parties need to know where they stand when faced with breach;

- the seller's (claimant's) obligation to nominate a port and be ready to load was dependent on the buyer (contract-breaker) giving the requisite notice;

- damages for breach would be very difficult to assess; and

- precedents on similar time terms and predominant commercial practice.

In contrast, an **innominate term** was found in *Bremer Handelsgesellschaft mbH v Vanden Avenne-Izegem PVBA* (1978). Here, a time term in another soya bean meal contract required the seller to advise the buyer 'without delay' of impossibility of shipment because of prohibition of export. However, it did *not stipulate any time limit* by which the advice was to be given.

Even precise time clauses may be construed as innominate terms depending on their 'commercial significance'. In *Ioannis Valilas v Valdet Januzaj* (2014), the Court

---

[12] *State Trading Corp of India Ltd v M Golodetz* at 283.

of Appeal found that a dentist had not committed a repudiatory breach when he informed the practice owner that he would be making payments late because:

- time of payment was not generally of the essence in a commercial contract unless the parties had agreed that it should be. The requirement to pay on time was an innominate term;

- the effect of the dentist's past and threatened future breaches could not be said to deprive the practice owner of substantially the whole benefit of the contract. He had other sources of income and he knew that he would obtain that to which he was entitled in the end. His only likely loss was the loss of the use of the money in the meantime.

12.2.4 **Electing termination**

A repudiatory breach does *not* automatically bring a contract to an end. It gives the claimant a right to *elect* whether to terminate or to affirm the contract (even in respect of employment contracts: *Geys v Société Générale, London Branch* (2012)). Five points should be noted about electing to terminate (also known as 'acceptance of the repudiation').

(i) Termination must be **clear and unequivocal**: mere inactivity will not normally suffice. Election to terminate the contract must generally be **communicated** to the contract-breaker, but it 'requires no particular form . . . The aggrieved party need not personally, or by an agent, notify the repudiating party . . . It is sufficient that the fact of the election comes to the repudiating party's attention' (*Vitol SA v Norelf Ltd* (1996) at 810–11).

(ii) Termination can only come **after repudiatory breach**: in *North Eastern Properties Ltd v Coleman & Quinn Conveyancing* (2009), C's notice to N saying that C would deem the vendor in breach of contract and 'consider themselves discharged from the contract' if the properties were not ready for occupation within ten working days, was merely a statement of intention and not an effective termination since there was no right to make an election prior to the repudiatory breach.

(iii) The claimant is **not bound to elect at once**; he or she can wait for performance or negotiate in the hope of a settlement (*The Mihalios Xilas* (1978) at 1272). However, the innocent party who does not accept repudiation must remain ready and willing to perform. Further, as Rix LJ explains (at [87]) in *Stocznia Gdanska SA v Latvian Shipping Co (No 2)* (2002), the claimant runs a risk whilst making up their mind:

> If he does nothing for too long, there may come a time when the law will treat him as having affirmed . . . [Anyway, as] long as the contract remains alive, the innocent party runs the risk that a merely anticipatory repudiatory breach, a thing 'writ in water' until acceptance, can be overtaken by another event which prejudices the innocent party's rights under the contract—such as frustration or even his own breach. He also runs the risk . . . that the party in repudiation will resume performance of the contract and thus end any continuing right in the innocent party to elect to accept the former repudiation as terminating the contract.

In *Force India v Etihad Airways* (2010) Rix LJ adds that the length of time that a claimant may wait whilst making up its mind will depend upon the facts of each case: some cases 'may well be more or less complex and call for more or less urgency' (at [113]). On the facts, the claimant was entitled to wait and so had not affirmed the contract by virtue of their inaction.

(iv) The claimant's termination is valid if he or she is legally entitled to terminate even if his or her real motive is to escape a contract that is no longer advantageous because of market fluctuations and even if the **reason he or she puts forward** is:

- invalid (eg being mistaken);
- dishonest (eg *Arcos v Ronaasen*); or
- he or she gives no reason, because he or she was unaware of the good reason at the time of termination (eg ***The Mihalis Angelos*** (1971)).

In these senses, the phrases 'election' and 'acceptance of the repudiation' may be misleading since there is no need for any causal relationship between the repudiatory breach and the claimant's decision to terminate. Such 'bad faith' terminations are criticised for allowing parties to 'blow hot and cold'.[13] On the other hand: (a) it may be very difficult to determine a party's *real* motivation for terminating; (b) it is not clear that a claimant should lose his or her right to terminate simply because he or she was unaware of his or her right to do so when he or she offered a bad reason for terminating; and (c) *both* parties may have acted in bad faith (as in *The Mihalis Angelos* (1971)). The Article III.-1:103 of the European Draft Common Frame of Reference imposes a non-excludable 'duty to act in accordance with good faith and fair dealing'. This duty will bar termination for invalid or dishonest reasons.

(v) The choice, once made, is **irrevocable.**

12.2.5 **Loss of the right to terminate**

The claimant's right to terminate a contract may be lost by:

(i) **his or her own conduct**, eg in affirming the contract (see 12.3); by operation of 'waiver by estoppel' (see 3.3.2.1); or by his or her own subsequent breach making them liable for damages (*Fercometal SARL v Mediterranean Shipping Co SA (The Simona)* (1989));

(ii) **the defendant's performance** when it becomes due, in the case of renunciation or anticipatory breach;[14] however, once there has been *actual* repudiatory breach, the claimant's right to terminate is *not* lost by the defendant's cure of the breach. In *Buckland v Bournemouth University* (2010), the Court of Appeal held that the university's action in having the claimant professor's marking of examination scripts re-marked by someone else, behind the claimant's back, amounted to a breach of its implied duty of trust and confidence, entitling

---

[13] R Brownsword, 'Retrieving Reasons, Retrieving Rationality? A New Look at the Right to Withdraw Breach of Contract' (1992) 5 *JCL* 83, 92–3.

[14] *Howard v Pickford Tool Co Ltd* (1951) 421.

the claimant to terminate the contract. This right of termination was not lost although the university had effectively cured the breach by establishing a formal inquiry into the matter, which exonerated the claimant;

(iii) **the operation of a rule of law**, for example supervening frustration (*Avery v Bowden* (1856)), or section 11(4) of the Sale of Goods Act 1979 which deprives the buyer of his or her right to reject the goods if they have 'accepted' the goods even if they are ignorant of the breach. Section 35 states that the buyer is deemed to have accepted the goods when: (a) he or she so communicates to the seller; (b) the buyer's conduct in relation to the goods delivered are inconsistent with the seller's ownership; or (c) by lapse of time).

12.3 **Affirmation**

Rather than terminate the contract for the defendant's breach, the claimant may elect to affirm (continue with) the contract.

(i) **Electing affirmation**: the claimant must evince an unequivocal intention (expressly or impliedly) to continue with the contract, *with knowledge* of the facts giving rise to the breach; and his or her legal right to elect (*Peyman v Lanjani* (1985)). The claimant does not generally affirm the contract by mere inactivity (*Perry v Davis* (1858)) or by simply calling for performance: 'the law does not require an injured party to snatch at repudiation and he does not automatically lose his right to treat the contract as discharged merely by calling on the other to reconsider his position and recognise his obligation' (*Yukong Line Ltd of Korea v Rendsberg Investments Corp of Liberia* (1996) at 608). However, he or she *will* have affirmed the contract if he or she continues to press for, or accepts, performance.[15] Thus, in *Tele2 International Card Co SA v KUB 2 Technology Ltd* (2009), the Court of Appeal held that Post Office Ltd (POL) could not terminate for T's breach of a term because POL's delay of almost a year in giving notice of termination and continued performance during that time constituted affirmation of the agreement by election. POL was therefore in repudiatory breach. The existence of a waiver clause providing that delay or failure to enforce a provision should not prevent later enforcement, cannot negate an election to affirm (it is doubtful that any clause can). It only emphasises that an election to abandon a right to terminate requires a clear and unequivocal communication of an election.

(ii) **Irrevocability**: once the claimant has communicated his or her affirmation to the contract-breaker it is irrevocable, even without *reliance* by or detriment to the contract-breaker (*Peyman v Lanjani* at 493, 500). Lord Wilberforce said (at 398) in **Johnson v Agnew** (1980), on termination 'the contract has gone—what is dead is dead' (at least, its primary obligations). But if the contract-breaker *persists* with his or her non-performance or commits a fresh breach, the claimant can rely on this to terminate the contract.

---

[15] *Bremer Handelsgesellschaft mbH v Deutsche Conti Handelsgesellschaft mbH* (1983); *Davenport v R* (1877).

(iii) **The effect of affirmation**: both parties remain bound to perform their primary obligations ('an unaccepted repudiation is a thing writ in water'),[16] but the claimant is entitled to damages for any loss flowing from the delay (although logically not for loss of bargain). The claimant may also seek specific performance come the time for performance, unless the claim for *damages* indicates that the claimant is terminating the contract.

(iv) **Restrictions on the right to affirm**: faced with an anticipatory repudiatory breach, the claimant will prefer to affirm a contract, complete his or her own performance, and claim the contract price (ie the **'agreed price'**; see 14.1) where:

- he or she has incurred substantial expenses that would be difficult to recover as damages;

- his or her expectation of damages would be nominal (eg due to the mitigation requirement (see 13.2.5.1)), or too remote (see 13.2.5.6);

- termination would damage his or her *reputation*, for which damages are rarely available and difficult to assess (see 13.2.4.3);

- termination would put him or her in breach of contracts with third parties; or

- the contract-breaker has repudiated in bad faith (eg because of a personal dispute with the claimant) and not because the claimant's performance was unwanted.

However, the claimant cannot always affirm. In **White & Carter (Councils) Ltd v McGregor** (1962), M agreed to pay W&C to advertise his garage business on rubbish bins they supplied to the local council for three years. On the same day, M tried to cancel the contract but W&C refused. The latter continued with the advertisement and sued M for the agreed price. The House of Lords by a 3:2 majority upheld W&C's claim, but Lord Reid (at 431) set out two limits on the claimant's ability to affirm the contract (neither applied in this case).[17]

(i) Need **for the contract-breaker's cooperation**: in practice, the claimant faced with a repudiatory breach will often have no choice but to terminate the contract because he or she cannot complete his or her own performance without the contract-breaker's cooperation. On this basis, it has been hotly contested whether employment contracts are *automatically* terminated on a repudiatory breach. In *Geys v Société Générale, London Branch* (2012), the Supreme Court:

✗ rejected the automatic termination approach; and

✓ affirmed the general election approach.

(ii) **'No legitimate interest'**: the claimant cannot affirm if he or she has 'no legitimate interest, financial or otherwise, in performing the contract rather than claiming damages'. However, the threshold is a very high one (*The Oldenfield* (1978) at 374). Simon J said (*Ocean Marine Navigation Ltd v Koch Carbon Inc (The Dynamic)* (2003) at [23]) that:

(a) the burden is on the *contract-breaker* to show that the claimant has no legitimate interest in performing the contract;

---

[16] *Howard v Pickford Tool Co Ltd* (1951) at 421 (Asquith LJ).
[17] See *Hounslow LBC v Twickenham Garden Developments Ltd* (1971).

(b) it is not enough to show that the benefit of affirmation to the claimant is small in comparison with the loss to the contract-breaker;

(c) the exception to the general rule applies only in extreme cases where damages would be adequate and where an election to keep the contract alive would be wholly unreasonable—*White & Carter v McGregor* is problematic on this point since the court must impliedly have found that W&C had a legitimate interest in performing the unwanted services, although this could be seen as unreasonable and damages would seem an adequate remedy.

 Pause for reflection

White & Carter v McGregor is much criticised.[18]

1. The decision encourages *wasteful performance* contrary to the claimant's *duty to mitigate* his or her loss in damages claims (see 13.2.5.1). In contrast, no mitigation is required for affirmation.

2. The decision allows the claimant to increase the contract-breaker's liability by conferring unwanted goods or services.

3. The decision may amount to *indirect specific performance* of a contract when it would not be specifically enforceable (see 14.2.1).[19]

4. Article III.-3:301(2) of the European Draft Common Frame of Reference would reverse *White & Carter v McGregor*. It bars affirmation if:

   (a) the claimant could have made a reasonable substitute transaction without significant effort or expense; or

   (b) performance would be unreasonable in the circumstances.

On the other hand, *White & Carter v McGregor* can be *supported* on the following basis.

1. Contract law would fail to protect the aggrieved party's performance interest if it denies his or her right to affirm and perform the contract.

2. English law does not require the claimant to act reasonably in *selecting* his or her remedies (*White & Carter v McGregor* at 430, 445).

Subsequent cases illustrate the operation of the 'legitimate interest' factor. The question is whether, on the facts, the wastefulness of the claimant's continuing performance is completely *disproportionate* to its performance interest in earning the contract price. The scale is easily tipped in the claimant's favour.

✓ In *The Oldenfield* (at 373), the claimant owners under a time charter were permitted to affirm the contract because it would be difficult to find other employment

---

[18] See P Nienaber, 'The Effect of Anticipatory Repudiation: Principle and Policy' (1962) 20 *CLJ* 213; M Furmston, 'The Case of the Insistent Performer' (1962) 25 *MLR* 364; W Goodhart, 'Measure of Damages when a Contract is Repudiated' (1962) 78 *LQR* 263.

[19] In *Attica Sea Carriers Corp v Ferrostaal Poseidon Bulk Reederei GmbH (The Puerto Buitrago)* (1976) at 255.

for the ship, termination would put them in breach of other contracts, and damages would be hard to assess.

✓ Likewise, in *Reichmann v Gauntlett* (2006), a landlord was allowed to affirm and sue for unpaid rent where the tenants, a firm of solicitors shut down by the Law Society, vacated the premises. The landlord had a legitimate interest in affirming the contract since he foresaw difficulties in re-letting the property and could not be sure of obtaining damages for loss of future rent.

✓ In *The Isabella Shipowner Ltd v Shagang Shipping Co Ltd (The Aquafaith)* (2012), a vessel was chartered by IS to SS for a minimum period of 59 months. When SS attempted to return the ship three months early, IS was held to be entitled to refuse redelivery and to retain the prepaid hire. IS did not require SS's cooperation to continue with performance of the contract. Nor could SS's conduct in continuing with performance be described as 'perverse' or beyond all reason, or wholly unreasonable.

✗ In contrast, affirmation was denied in *The Puerto Buitrago* (1976). The charterer had returned the ship to the owner damaged and almost a year before the end of the hire period. Since repairs would have cost £2 million and the ship's value fully repaired was only £1 million, the owner could *not* insist on repairing the ship and charging hire for the charter period because the obligation to repair was not a condition precedent to the right to redeliver. The court added that the charter could not continue without the charterer's cooperation and that the owner had no legitimate interest in affirming the contract, although these statements do not clearly form part of the *ratio*.

✗ Likewise, in *The Alaskan Trader* (1984), the defendant chartered a ship to the claimant for 24 months but the claimant returned it after 12 months as it required extensive repairs which would take several months to complete. The defendant refused to accept the claimant's repudiation, repaired the ship, and kept it fully crewed and ready for the claimant's use for the remaining hire period. The arbitrator found this to be 'wholly unreasonable' and allowed the claimant to recover the hire for the period after the ship's return. While accepting the importance of commercial certainty and the difficulty of distinguishing between affirmation which is '*merely* unreasonable' (and permissible) and that which is '*wholly* unreasonable' (and impermissible), Lloyd J upheld the arbitrator's conclusion that the owner had effectively no legitimate interest in affirming the contract; the assessment of damages was not thought to present special difficulty even if the defendant's prospects of re-letting the ship were poor.

THIS CHAPTER IN ESSENCE

The key areas and core topics in this chapter are summarised in an easy-to-use list, ideal for revision purposes, on the Online Resource Centre at http://www.oxfordtextbooks.co.uk/orc/chenwishart5e/. Links to websites relevant to the topics covered and any updates to the chapter can also be found on the Online Resource Centre.

QUESTIONS

1 'Identifying when a party can terminate a contract for breach raises difficult technical and policy questions.' Discuss.

2 Should all terms be treated as innominate terms?

3 Ida, a gizmo manufacturer, hires Jack to deliver her gizmos to her customers in London for one year. The contract states that 'It is a condition that gizmos should be collected before 6 pm each day and delivered by 8.30 am the next morning.' Jack is late in two collections and three deliveries in the second week. Ida's customers have not complained. Meanwhile, Ida discovers a much cheaper way of making the deliveries. On Monday morning of the third week, Jack shouts sexist abuse at one of Ida's employees and Ida terminates the contract because of Jack's sexist views. Advise Jack.

4 Explain and distinguish each of the following, giving examples.

   (a) Termination, breach of an entire obligations clause, rescission, and discharge.

   (b) Breach, anticipatory breach, and repudiatory breach.

5 'The sanctity of contract requires, at the very least, that the innocent party be permitted to continue with the contract even if the other party commits a repudiatory breach.' Discuss.

 For hints on how to answer these questions, please see the Online Resource Centre at http://www.oxfordtextbooks.co.uk/orc/chenwishart5e/

KEY FURTHER READING

Liu, Q (2011), 'The *White & Carter* Principle: A Restatement', 74 *MLR* 171.

Smith, J (1997), 'Anticipatory Breach of Contract' in E Lomnicka and C Morse (eds), *Contemporary Issues in Commercial Law: Essays in Honour of A G Guest* (Sweet & Maxwell) 175.

Treitel, G (1990), '"Conditions" and "Conditions Precedent"', 106 *LQR* 185.

Whittaker, S (2007), 'Termination Clauses' in A Burrows and E Peel (eds), *Contract Terms* (OUP) 253.

13

Damages

'I want you to pay me money for my loss due to your breach'

13.1 **Introduction**

13.1.1 **Judicial remedies**

The vast majority of contractual disputes are *settled out of court*. Parties have every incentive to reach a compromise if at all possible, to avoid the significant time, money, general aggravation, and uncertainties inherent in litigation. Going to court is the 'nuclear option'. However, parties bargain in the shadow of the law. On breach, well-advised parties will negotiate settlements by reference to the remedy that the innocent party (the claimant) is likely to be awarded, with deductions for the risk of the claim not being proved and for avoiding the trouble and expense of going to court. If the contract-breaker (the defendant) is facing insolvency, the claimant will be forced to accept a much reduced settlement, rather than risk getting less or even nothing at all as an unsecured creditor.

Where the parties have not agreed on the consequences of breach or any agreed remedies are judged to be unenforceable (see 14.3), the law supplies *default rules* to determine the available remedies. The claimant's *self-help* remedy of termination, discussed in Chapter 12, is supplemented by various *judicial* remedies for breach.

(i) **Damages** compensate the claimant's loss of *expectation*. Exceptionally, in qualifying circumstances, he or she may be awarded:

- his or her *reliance* loss as a proxy for their expectation (13.1.3.3);
- *restitution* of the benefit conferred on the defendant instead of his or her expectation (13.3); or
- the defendant's *gains* from the breach (see 13.4).

(ii) In limited cases, the court may order **compulsory compliance** with the contract by an award of the **agreed sum**, or an order for **specific performance** or for an **injunction**. The court must also determine the enforceability of any agreed remedies contained in the contract (see Chapter 14).

Unlike *tort* actions (which prevent harm to the claimant) and *unjust enrichment* actions (which reverse the defendant's unjust enrichment at the expense of the claimant), the distinctive feature of the *contract* action, its unique claim, is that it purports to fulfil the expectations created by binding contracts. However, while there is a trend is towards greater protection of the claimant's interest in the defendant's performance, the overall picture still falls far short of perfect vindication. The questions for consideration in this chapter are:

(i) What *types* of loss are recognised and so compensable for breach of contract? To the extent that contract law does not recognise certain types of loss (eg *non-pecuniary losses* such as pain and suffering, disappointment, loss of reputation, and loss of enjoyment), the claimant's expectation is imperfectly protected.

(ii) How is loss *calculated*? Although expectation damages are available for every breach of contract, they often yield less than the value that the claimant would put on performance because of: (a) the way that loss is calculated (eg by the 'diminution of value' measure, which may yield less that the 'cost of the cure' measure); and (b) reductions due, for example, to the unforeseeability and avoidability of loss.

(iii) When and why might contract law allow departures from the expectation measure and allow awards based on *reliance, restitution, account of profits, or loss of opportunity to bargain*? The increasing willingness of courts to entertain such claims may strengthen a claimant's bargaining power in negotiating a settlement closer to his or her actual valuation of the performance.

13.1.2 Policy considerations

Contract law's commitment to the protection of an innocent party's interest in the performance of the contract is the starting point when considering the remedies for breach. However, it is not the only important value. Recognition of the competing concerns in this area helps us to understand the court's selection of the appropriate remedy. These group around three clusters:

(i) **The innocent claimant:**
  - protecting his or her expectation of performance and of what the performance was *for*;
  - acknowledging his or her real losses from breach (including non-pecuniary or intangible loss, eg pain and suffering);
  - protecting him or her from unfairness (eg by controlling exemption clauses); and
  - encouraging him or her to act and react sensibly in relation to the contract (eg by requiring mitigation and insurance of losses that may be too 'remote').

(ii) **The defendant contract-breaker:**
  - avoiding *unnecessary* interference with his or her freedom (eg by not compelling specific performance if the claimant can otherwise be adequately protected);
  - protecting him or her from the claimant's unforeseeable and preventable losses (eg mitigation and remoteness); and
  - signalling disapproval of the breach, especially where the claimant's loss is unclear (eg nominal damages, and stripping the defendant's profits from breach).

(iii) **Administration of law:**
  - responding to evidential and quantification difficulties, and the potential for fraudulent claims (eg reluctance to give damages for pain and suffering);
  - avoiding indeterminate liability and opening the floodgate to claims (eg again in respect of pain and suffering); and
  - preventing waste (eg the requirement of mitigation, refusal of specific performance).

13.1.3 Damages

13.1.3.1 Expectation, reliance, and restitution

In the celebrated article by **Fuller and Perdue, 'The Reliance Interest in Contract Damages'** (1937) 46 *Yale LJ* 52, the authors introduced the different possible measures of damages by reference to the terminology of 'expectation', 'reliance', and 'restitution'. The following illustrates their different effect, although it should be emphasised that not all are available for breach.

A buys a picture for £50,000 which *B*, a dealer, sells as the work of *C*, a famous painter.

(i) **A makes a *good bargain*** because, had the picture been genuine as *B* promised, it would have been worth at least £70,000. In fact, it is a forgery worth only £200.

- If *A keeps* the picture, *A's* **expectation interest**, aimed at putting *A* in the position he or she would have been in if the contract had been performed, is:

Expected value (£70,000) – the value received (£200) = £69,800

- *A's* **reliance interest**, aimed at putting *A* in the position he or she would have been in if *no* contract had been made,[1] is:

Amount paid (£50,000) – the value received (£200) = £49,800

- *A's* **restitution interest** if he or she *returns* the picture is aimed at preventing *B's* unjust enrichment at *A's* expense. *B* should return *A's* payment of £50,000.

If the contract was a *good bargain*, *A's* expectation interest will generally cover both his or her reliance and restitution interests; *A* would be reimbursed for the amount paid and other costs incurred, and would have made a profit.

(ii) **If *A* had made a bad bargain** because, say, the picture was in fact only worth £10,000 even if genuine, then:

- *A's* expectation interest is:

Expected value (£10,000) – the actual value received (£200) = £9,800

- *A's* reliance interest is:

Amount *A* paid (£50,000) – the value received (£200) = £49,800

- *A's* **restitution interest** if he or she *returns* the picture is:

The amount *A* paid = £50,000

A is clearly better off claiming reliance or restitution *if* either is available.

If *B* makes a profit by breaching the contract, say, by lending the picture to an exhibitor for £5,000, *A* may now be able to claim *B's* **profit from breach** or **damages for loss of hypothetical bargain** permitting *B's* breach, even if it caused no loss to *A*.

13.1.3.2 The contract interest: expectation

While Fuller and Perdue argue that damages should, and often are, aimed at the protection of reliance, this is powerfully criticised by **Friedmann**, in '**The Performance Interest in Contract Damages**' (1995) 111 *LQR* 628. Friedmann effectively defends the primacy of the expectation interest in contract damages, preferring the terminology of 'performance interest' to emphasise the claimant's right to receive that which was promised to him or her.

---

[1] But see 5.2.1.2(iii), compensation for the reliance of loss of opportunity to make an alternative bargain can mimic the expectation measure.

13.1.3.3 The role of the reliance measure

(i) Not an alternative measure of damages

It has been said that a claimant suing for breach of contract can choose between his or her expectation and his or her 'reliance' loss (*CCC Films (London) Ltd v Impact Quadrant Films Ltd* (1985)). However, this is misleading. The only circumstance in which a claimant would *want* to claim for his or her reliance loss is where he or she has made a bad bargain (ie where expenditure exceeded expected profits from the defendant's full performance). But this is the very circumstance in which English law prevents them from claiming the reliance measure (*C & P Haulage v Middleton* (1983)). The modern view, therefore, is that there is no alternative claim for reliance damages. The aim of compensatory damages for breach of contract is *always* to put the claimant in the same position *as if the contract had been performed* (*Robinson v Harman* (1848)). While the claimant's reliance may occasionally be awarded as *evidence* of his or her expectation loss where the latter is difficult to establish directly, the reliance loss is not an independent measure of damages. Thus, the claimant cannot invoke his or her reliance loss to get around the fact that they would have suffered loss even if the contract had been duly performed (ie circumvent a bad bargain); the expectation measure will require an award of nominal damages only.

In the High Court of Australia in *Commonwealth of Australia v Amman Aviation* (1991), Mason CJ and Dawson J (at 85) reject as inappropriate, 'the language of *election* or the notion that *alternative* ways are open to a plaintiff in which to frame a claim for relief'. In truth, 'damages for loss of profits and damages for expenditure reasonably incurred are simply two manifestations of the general principle enunciated in *Robinson v Harman*'. Likewise, in *Omak Maritime v Mamola Challenger Shipping (The Mamola Challenger)* (2010). Teare J held that 'reliance losses are a species of expectation losses and that they are neither . . . "fundamentally different" nor awarded on a different "juridical basis of claim"' (at [42]). How does this work?

(ii) The assumption that expectation would at least equal expenditure

Occasionally it will be very difficult for claimants to prove what position they would have been in had the contract been properly performed. One way around this evidential difficulty is to assume that *the claimant's profits under the contract (ie his or her expectation interest) would at least have equalled his or her expenditure in reliance on the contract (ie his or her reliance interest)*. This assumption even applies to expenditure incurred before contract formation, based on the unlikelihood of a claimant spending more on performing a contract than they were likely to gain from it. For example:

> ✓ in **Anglia Television Ltd v Reed** (1972), R contracted to star in A's film but repudiated the contract at the last moment. A, unable to find a replacement, abandoned the project. It was impossible to assess what profits A would have made if the contract had been performed. But A was awarded its expenses although these were incurred *before* the contract was made, since it was foreseeable that they could be wasted in the event of breach;

> ✓ in *McRae v Commonwealth Disposals Commission* (1951), CDC sold M a sunken oil tanker which turned out not to exist, although CDC had promised that it did. The value of the non-existent ship and its contents was held to be

too speculative for the purpose of measuring M's expectation interest. Nevertheless, the court awarded M's reliance loss, being: (i) the price paid to CDC and (ii) the wasted expenditure in attempting to find and salvage it.

It is fair to require the *defendant* to prove that the claimant is not entitled to the reliance measure because he or she has made a bad bargain, because it is the defendant's breach that has caused the claimant's evidential difficulty (*Parker v SJ Berwin & Co* (2008) at [77]).

13.2 Expectation damages for not receiving due performance

13.2.1 The compensatory aim

The normal measure of damages in a contract action is the *expectation* measure. The general rule stated by Parke B (at 855) in **Robinson v Harman** (1848) is: 'that where a party sustains loss by reason of a breach of contract, he is, so far as money can do it, to be placed in the same situation, with respect to damages, *as if the contract had been performed*' (emphasis added). The relevant 'loss' is the claimant's *expectation* from the contract, which is lost by the breach. Whilst damages in tort may protect *pre-existing* expectations (eg of earning capacity or of business profits) impaired or destroyed by the tort, the distinctive feature of a contractual action is that it protects expectations *created by the contract.* In this sense, it is 'forward-looking', while reliance and restitutionary damages, which aim to make the claimant no 'worse off', is 'backward-looking'.

Four points follow from the compensatory aim of contract damages, although each is subject to significant qualification:

(i) **Only nominal damages if no loss**: if the claimant has suffered no recognised loss from the breach, he or she will receive no substantial damages, but only nominal damages (usually £5). Common examples are where:

- goods are not delivered, but the claimant has not yet paid and can buy substitute goods for the same price or less;
- the defendant's defective performance is worth no less on the market than the performance due (ie there is no diminution of value, but see 13.2.3.2);
- the performance was intended for a third party so that the claimant suffers no loss (but see 13.2.4.4).

(ii) **No protection from bad bargains**: the primacy of the expectation measure means that the claimant cannot switch to a reliance claim in order to circumvent a *bad bargain* (see 13.1.3.3).

(iii) **No claim to the contract-breaker's gains from breach**: traditionally, damages are not measured by the defendant's gains from breach of contract (*Teacher v Calder* (1899)) or his or her savings (*Tito v Waddell (No 2)* (1977)). However, the House of Lords decision in *Attorney-General v Blake* (2000) now permits exceptional claims to some portion of the defendant's gains from breach (see 13.4).

(iv) **No punishment of the contract-breaker**: *Addis v Gramophone Co Ltd* (1909) bars punitive or exemplary damages (to punish the contract-breaker) in purely *contractual* action, even where the defendant's breach is deliberate and calculated to increase his or her profit by performing for someone else instead (*Cassell & Co Ltd v Broome* (1972)). However:

- as we will see, punitive considerations cannot be entirely excluded from the increasing recognition of *non-pecuniary loss* and the exceptional availability of gains-based damages;

- in *tort actions*, the House of Lords held (in *Kuddus v Chief Constable of Leicestershire Constabulary* (2001)) that punitive damages should be freed from the narrow circumstances in which they were available prior to *Rookes v Barnard* (1964). Rather, the question should be whether the case involves: (a) oppressive, arbitrary, and unconstitutional action by public officials, or (b) the defendant calculating that his or her wrongful conduct will make profits exceeding any compensation payable to the claimant.[2] There may be a similar development in contractual actions. As Lord Nicholls predicted: 'Never say never' (*A v Bottrill* (2003) at 456). The current position will push claimants towards non-contractual actions where a claimant can sue in both since punitive damages *are* available for claims in tort and equitable wrongs;

- the Supreme Court of Canada has affirmed the exceptional availability of restrained punitive damages to 'address the purposes of retribution, deterrence and denunciation' where appropriate. For example, $100,000 was awarded in *Royal Bank of Canada v W Got & Associates Electric Ltd* (2000), where a bank demanded repayment on the same day that it applied to put the debtor company into receivership. By failing to give the debtor reasonable notice of its application and misleading the court to induce it to grant the receivership order, the bank's conduct was a serious affront to the administration of justice and caused grave and irrevocable consequences to its client's business.

13.2.2 Basis of calculation: loss of expectation minus gains

The **basic measure** of the claimant's expectation damages is his or her loss of expectation minus any 'gains' made under the contract. The question is: 'How well off would he have *been* if the contract had been performed? How well off is he *now*? The difference is the measure of damages'.[3] An overview is given by **Diagram 13A**.

The **'plus' side** is the claimant's expectation loss from breach. A contract can give rise to two quite separate expectations: that of receiving the promised performance and that of being able to put it to some particular use. Loss of the latter, losses

---

[2] The Supreme Court of Canada has allowed punitive damages in these circumstances: *Royal Bank of Canada v W Got & Associates Electric Ltd* (2000); see J Edelman, 'Exemplary Damages for Breach of Contract' (2001) 117 *LQR* 539.

[3] J Smith, *The Law of Contract* (4th edn, Sweet & Maxwell, 2002) 217.

Diagram 13A Expectation losses: the pluses and minuses

✓ = Recoverable ? = Uncertainty over recoverability	IP = innocent party CB = contract-breaker

Compensatable loss: the 'plus' side	**Restrictions and deductions:** the 'minus' side

A. Loss of the performance
 	
✓ if conventionally measurable by diminution of value, or cost of cure
 	
? otherwise, recovery under *Panatown* 'broad' ground?
 	
B. Consequential loss (loss of what the performance was *for*, failure to achieve the *purpose* of performance)
This may take the forms of:
  not being better off:
    ✓ physically (eg health not improved),
    ✓ financially (eg loss of profits), or
    ? satisfaction-wise (eg enjoyment or amenity);
and/or
  being worse off:
    ✓ physically (eg building destroyed by breach),
    ✓ financially (eg wasted expenses, reasonable costs of mitigation, liability to third parties),
    ? satisfaction-wise (eg pain and suffering, physical inconvenience, damage to reputation).
	1. Costs saved by IP from terminating performance
	
	2. Benefits received from CB's part-performance
	
	3. Gains from breach or mitigation
	
	4. Failure to mitigate
	
	5. Generally loss measured at time of breach
	
	6. IP's contributory negligence
	
	7. Loss from intervening causes
	
	8. Loss too speculative
	
	9. Loss too remote

consequential on not getting the due performance, may comprise losses from *not being made better off* as expected under the contract, and losses from *being made worse off* than expected under the contract. For example, in ***Parsons (Livestock) Ltd v Uttley Ingham & Co Ltd*** (1978), P (a pig farmer) bought a food storage hopper from U (a manufacturer) to store pignuts. The hopper was installed defectively so that the pignuts became mouldy and many of the pigs died of a rare intestinal infection. On the 'plus' side, P's claim comprised of:

- not getting a hopper fit for the purpose (the promised performance);
- the dead pigs (consequential loss in being made worse off);
- the profits which would have been made on the sale of the pigs (consequential loss in not being made better off).

The *'minus'* **side** which can reduce the expectation measure includes the items in column 2 of **Diagram 13A** (discussed at 13.2.5).

13.2.3 The measure of expectation damages

Compensation for *financial* or *physical* loss is the predominant domain of contract law. *Parsons (Livestock) v Uttley Ingham* shows that the claimant can recover for loss of: the performance itself, not being able to put that performance to its intended use, and any additional costs wasted or incurred consequential on breach. Things get more difficult when at least part of the claimant's motivation for contracting is *non-financial*, so that his or her loss from breach is not readily measured in money (eg if some of the dead pigs had been much loved family pets). Contract law is much less prepared to recognise and compensate for such non-pecuniary loss. When this is combined with the other 'minus' side factors, which drive down the expectation measure (see 13.2.5), the result is a significant deviation from contract law's stated commitment to the protection of the claimant's expectation or performance interest.

> ### Pause for reflection
>
> We will see that some of the problems encountered by the courts arise from a certain ambiguity about the purpose of contract remedies—whether it is to secure the claimant's right to *performance*, or only to secure the claimant's *economic end result* of performance (his or her 'expectation'). In **'Performance and Compensation: An Analysis of Contract Damages and Contractual Obligation'** (2006) 26 *OJLS* 41, **Webb** argues that the word 'remedy' conceals which interest is being protected. There are two distinct contractual interests: in receiving performance (the 'performance interest'), and in being compensated for losses caused by non-performance (the 'compensation interest'). The compensation interest is not an alternative way of enforcing the performance interest. Webb suggests that the claimant should be able to claim both so long as there is no double recovery. Even if a claimant has suffered no loss *from* non-performance, he or she has still lost the performance due to them.

13.2.3.1 Minimum obligation undertaken

Two types of case can be identified. In the first, the contract requires the defendant to do *X* and the claimant has a reasonable expectation (but no contractual right) that the defendant will do *Y*. In this case, *the court should assess damages on the basis that the defendant would only have done what he or she was contractually obliged to do*. This is the minimum obligation approach. For example, in *Lavarack v Woods of Colchester Ltd* (1967). L was employed by W, 'at the rate of not less than £4000 per annum . . . and such bonus (if any) as the directors . . . shall from time to time determine'. When L was wrongfully dismissed, the Court of Appeal denied L's claim for damages in respect of the lost bonus because W had no contractual obligation to provide it.

In the second category of cases, the contract requires the defendant to do *X* but allows him or her discretion on how he or she performs it. In this case, *the court should assess damages according to how the defendant would in fact have exercised the discretion* (on the balance of probabilities approach). For example, in *Durham Tees Valley Airport v BMI Baby* (2010), BMI Baby contracted to operate flights from D's airport. In breach of contract, BMI withdrew from the airport but argued that, since the contract did not require them to operate a minimum number of flights, they were not liable for damages. The Court of Appeal rejected this, holding (at [79]) that the court must assume that the contract-breaker would have performed the contract 'in his own interests having regard to the relevant factors prevailing at the time'. The court 'is not required to make assumptions that the defaulting party would have acted uncommercially merely in order to spite the claimant'.

13.2.3.2 Diminution of value, cost of cure, or loss of amenity?

(i) The difference between these measures

The claimant's loss of the expected performance can be measured by:

- **'diminution of value'**: the *market value* of the performance the defendant promised minus that *actually* given;

- **'cost of cure'**: the cost of buying *substitute* performance from another party including undoing any defective performance; or

- **'loss of amenity'**: the non-pecuniary loss to the claimant in the absence of pecuniary loss (see (iii)).

Diminution of value and the cost of cure may produce the *same* amount. For example, according to section 51(3) of the Sale of Goods Act 1979, a buyer who has not received goods (worth £5,000) to which he or she is entitled, but who has yet to pay the contract price (£4,000), can claim the difference between the market price of the goods and the contract price (ie £1,000). This can be described *either* as the cost of cure (the buyer can add this sum to the unpaid price and buy from elsewhere) *or* as the diminution in the value between the buyer's entitlement (£5,000) and what he or she received (£0), taking account of what he or she would have paid under the contract for it (£4,000). However, in some cases, the two measures will produce very *different* results. In **Tito v Waddell (No 2)** (1977), a company obtained a licence to mine phosphate on Ocean Island, promising to restore the island afterwards by replanting 'coconuts and other food-bearing trees'. The company failed to do this and the islanders claimed the cost of cure ($A73,140 per acre). The court denied this because, by the time of the action, all the islanders had resettled some 1,500 miles away after their small Pacific island was devastated by the events of World War II. They were only entitled to the diminution of value ($A75 per acre), although there can hardly be a market for 'worked out plots of land in Ocean Island' (at 344).

(ii) How is the applicable measure decided?

Statute may prescribe which measure is applicable, for example a tenant's covenant to repair is assessed on a diminution of value basis (Landlord and Tenant Act 1927, s 18). Or, the law may adopt *conventions* or presumptions, which can be displaced in particular cases. For example, diminution of value is applied to *defective surveys* and the supply of *defective goods* (Sale of Goods Act 1979, s 53(3)). However, in the latter case, it is arguable that if an attempt is made to cure the defects at a *reasonable cost*, this should be recoverable, even if the cure ultimately fails (*Harling v Eddy* (1951)).[4]

The conventional starting point for assessing damages for breach of a **building contract** is the cost of curing the defect or completing the work (*Mertens v Home Freeholds* (1921)), even if this exceeds the enhancement of the claimant's financial position (ie the diminution of value). However, this is subject to the requirement of *reasonableness* as *Ruxley Electronics and Construction Ltd v Forsyth* (1996) shows.

(iii) *Ruxley Electronics and Construction Ltd v Forsyth*

R agreed to build a swimming pool for F for £17,797. The pool actually built was shallower than the specified depth but it was still safe for diving and F's property was no less valuable for the breach. Nevertheless, F claimed £21,560 as the cost of cure, to demolish and rebuild the pool to the specified depth. The Court of Appeal allowed this on the reasoning that F was contractually entitled to his *exact* preference on the pool's depth. However, the House of Lords supported the trial judge's conclusion that the cost of cure was *unreasonable* taking into account:

(i)   the claimant's *purpose(s)* in contracting;

(ii) whether the claimant has cured or *intends to cure* the breach; and

(iii) the *proportionality* between the cost of cure, the contract price, the benefit already received by the claimant, and the benefit he would receive from cure.

The extra depth stipulated constituted a loss of pleasure or amenity since F wanted the comfort of a deep pool (this is (i) above). The *cost of cure* is certainly the appropriate starting point where the claimant's purpose for a building contract is not purely financial. Examples are a contract for alterations to make a house 'more comfortable, more convenient' to the owner's individual preference (at 360), or a contract for expensive redecoration of a house in good decorative order to the owner's eccentric taste, even if it would *lower* the market value of the house (an ugly fountain, gaudy wallpaper, yellow and pink tiles and fittings throughout).

However, on the facts, the cost of cure exceeded the *extent* of F's loss because the court found that F had **no genuine intention to cure the defect** (this is (ii) above). While courts are normally unconcerned about what claimants actually do with their damages award, a claimant's intention to cure is *evidence* of the *extent* of his or her non-pecuniary loss flowing from the breach. If the claimant does not care enough to cure, awarding him or her the cost of cure while they keep the existing pool would over-compensate him. The court noted that R had agreed to F's request for a deeper pool at no extra charge after the contract was first made; that the builder had already rebuilt the pool once to rectify other defects and had reduced the price by £10,000 to compensate F for that disturbance; that F still refused to pay alleging various minor deficiencies; and that F's statements of defence and counterclaim made no mention of the pool's depth until five years later. The House of Lords refused to allow F's promise to cure 'to create a loss, which does not exist, in order to punish the defendants' (at 373).

---

[4] As where veterinary fees are spent yet the sick animal dies.

Given the benefit the claimant *had* received, the House of Lords thought the cost of cure **wholly disproportionate** to the disadvantage F suffered from having a pool 9–18 inches shallower than he wanted. This is (iii) above, F still had a useable and safe pool which enhanced the value of his property no less for its shallowness. As Lord Jauncey (at 357) said: '[a] failure to achieve the precise contractual objective does not necessarily result in the loss which is occasioned by a total failure' warranting the cost of total rebuilding. The court's stated concern not to over-compensate the claimant is consistent with a concern to **avoid unnecessary hardship to the defendant**, readily evident on the facts of *Ruxley*.

In contrast, the cost of cure was awarded in *Radford v de Froberville* (1977) where dF failed to build a boundary wall on adjoining land she purchased from R. Although the wall would not increase the value of R's property, it represented R's 'genuine loss' from dF's breach, in terms of R's (in fact, R's tenants) desire for privacy. However, if R had intended to sell his property, then his interest in the property would be purely financial and the diminution of value measure would have sufficed. Thus in *Birse Construction Ltd v Eastern Telegraph Co Ltd* (2004), Lloyd J held that it would be *unreasonable* to grant the cost of curing defects in the building constructed because: (i) it would greatly exceed the claimant's real loss; and (ii) the claimant was likely to sell the building without any discount for the defects.

In *Ruxley*, the House of Lords rejected the cost of cure measure as over-compensating the claimant, and the diminution of value measure as under-compensating him (it would render the personal preference 'part of the promise illusory, and unbalance the bargain' at 360). Their Lordships endorsed a third measure: damages for **loss of amenity** 'where the value of the promise to the promisee exceeds the financial enhancement of his position which full performance will secure'. Such an award 'is incapable of precise valuation in terms of money, exactly because it represents a personal, subjective and non-monetary gain' (at 360–1). The trial judges' assessment of F's loss at £2,500 was not challenged in the House of Lords.

It should be noted that the claimant who does not receive due performance may be judged to have suffered **no loss at all** whether pecuniary or non-pecuniary. In the famous US case, *Jacob & Young v Kent* (1921), contractors building a large house used a different brand of pipes from those specified in the contract. The owner of the house claimed the cost of demolishing and rebuilding the house with the correct pipes, but the New York Court of Appeals awarded only nominal damages since the pipes used were functionally identical with those stipulated and did not reduce the value of the house.

(iv) What does *Ruxley v Forsyth* establish?

(i) The narrower and preferable interpretation is that the case **simply extends the category of contracts for enjoyment** for which, exceptionally, the law already allows damages for non-pecuniary loss (see 13.2.4.1).[5]

---

[5] Lord Lloyd in *Ruxley v Forsyth* at 374; Lord Steyn at [21], Lord Clyde at [36], and Lord Hutton at [49] in *Farley v Skinner*.

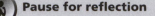

Pause for reflection

1. *Ruxley* shows that damages *can* protect the claimant's performance interest *without necessarily* enabling him or her to obtain the exact performance (the cost of cure).

2. Substantial damages are not given for the fact of breach *itself* (for which only nominal damages are available), but for *loss flowing from* the breach measured in money's worth. Hence, 'loss of amenity', 'cost of cure', and 'diminution of value' can be seen as merely different ways of achieving the same aim, namely, to compensate the claimant for the *extent* to which his or her purposes were left unfulfilled by the breach.

3. To modern eyes, the refusal to award the cost of cure in *Tito v Waddell (No 2)* gives insufficient recognition to the islanders' non-pecuniary interests in the restoration of their ancestral homeland. The court's conclusion that the islanders had no real intention to cure would not now be determinative: it merely shows that the claimant's loss may be *less* than the full cost of cure. Today, with better understanding of and sympathy for environmental issues and the spiritual value that indigenous peoples place on their land, a similar case may well be decided differently.

(ii) A broader and more radical interpretation of *Ruxley v Forsyth* is that it supports the **protection of the claimant's right to performance itself**, rather than just his or her consequential loss from not getting performance.

- In *Ruxley*, Lord Mustill (at 360) justified the loss of amenity award by reference to the concept of the 'consumer surplus' (not limited to the 'contracts for enjoyment' exception), which is triggered whenever 'the value of the promise to the promisee exceeds the financial enhancement of his position which full performance will secure'.

- In *Farley v Skinner* (2001), Lord Scott said (at [80]) that the claimant in *Ruxley* suffered *no* consequential loss consisting of vexation, anxiety, or other species of mental distress. He simply did not get the depth of pool he contracted for.

- In *Alfred McAlpine v Panatown* (2001), Lord Millett said (at 588) that 'viewed objectively, there was no loss of amenity' in *Ruxley*. 'The amenity in question was entirely subjective to the plaintiff; and its loss could equally well, and perhaps more accurately, be described as a defeated expectation.'

- In '**Contract Damages, *Ruxley* and the Performance Interest**' (1997) 56 *CLJ* 537, **Coote** argues that courts should be more prepared to protect the performance interest (by awarding the cost of cure) subject to reasonableness, rather than merely awarding compensation for the economic consequences of breach (the diminution of value). The question should be whether a reasonable person in the claimant's position, having his or her tastes and needs, would use the damages to effect cure.

> ⏪ **Counterpoint**
>
> These dicta are *not* taken to their logical conclusion. There is no support for protecting the claimant's performance interest by an *automatic cost of cure, or specific performance* (see 14.2). Three qualifications, explicitly or implicitly accepted, support the narrower interpretation (that *Ruxley* merely extends the 'contracts for enjoyment' exception).
>
> 1. The claimant must have a *provable* non-financial, subjective, or personal interest left unfulfilled by the breach.
>
> 2. Where that interest is valued at *less* than the cost of cure, the claimant's interest in literal performance of the contract cannot be protected since it does not allow him or her to buy substitute performance.
>
> 3. Loss of amenity only comes into play when 'there is no other way of compensating the injured party' (*Farley v Skinner* at [79]). Put this way, the award is less a principled protection of the performance interest and more a *long stop* to deal with deserving cases left without remedy by the dominant pecuniary conceptions of loss.

13.2.4 The problem of non-pecuniary loss

Breach of contract may cause non-pecuniary loss to the claimant whether *positive* (ie the failure to obtain satisfaction and enjoyment), or *negative* (ie the claimant's annoyance, anger, frustration, disappointment, distress, and loss of reputation from breach). In **'Contract Remedies and the Consumer Surplus'** (1979) 95 *LQR* 581, **Harris, Ogus, and Phillips** urge courts, in calculating damages, to take more account of the subjective value of the contract's subject matter to the recipient, over and above its market value; this is what economists call the 'consumer surplus' or 'personal preference'. To the extent that contract law traditionally does not recognise or undervalues claims for non-pecuniary loss caused by breach, the claimant's *performance interest* is unprotected.

(i) The general approach

In the leading case on damages for non-pecuniary loss of *Farley v Skinner*, Lord Steyn said (at [16]): '[t]he general principle is that compensation is only awarded for financial losses resulting from the breach . . . [Citing *Watts v Morrow* (1991)] as a matter of legal policy "a contract-breaker is not *in general* liable for any distress, frustration, anxiety, displeasure, vexation, tension or aggravation which his breach of contract may cause to the innocent party"' even if they are the foreseeable consequences of breach. Such loss can only be compensated if they fall within an *established exception*.

Canada and Australia take a more permissive approach. For example, in *Fidler v Sun Life Assurance* (2006), F was awarded $20,000 for mental distress caused by the insurer's refusal to pay disability benefit for five years, despite medical evidence of F's inability to work. The Supreme Court of Canada viewed the 'remedial ostracisation' of mental distress unwarranted. It contradicts the general principle of recovery for loss of reasonable expectations, rests on flimsy policy grounds, and is not followed by the High Court of Australia (*Baltic Shipping v Dillon* (1993) at [43]). Damages for mental distress were awarded in *Fidler* because: (i) an object of the contract was to secure a psychological benefit; since people buy disability insurance to avoid financial and emotional stress and insecurity, mental distress on breach is within the reasonable contemplation of the parties; and (ii) the extensive medical evidence of the degree of mental suffering warranted compensation. The European Draft Common Frame of Reference on contract law, expressly recognises that recoverable loss includes non-economic loss which 'includes pain and suffering and impairment of the quality of life' (Art III.-3:701(3)).

(ii) The policies in play

A number of concerns affect the law in this area.

(i) **Problems of proof and quantification**: claimants may fake or exaggerate their mental distress. Moreover, as the Law Commission points out, there is 'no standard measure of assessment by reference to which the harm can be converted into monetary form . . . This incommensurability gives rise to real danger of indeterminacy and of inconsistent awards'.[6] *However*, this should not bar recovery for losses which are proven, well recognised, and awarded in other areas of the law such as in personal injuries actions. Nevertheless, non-pecuniary loss for breach of contract will be more varied, and less likely to generate the sort of notional tariffs applicable in personal injuries cases.

(ii) **'Floodgates' and avoidance of hardship to the defendant**: since mental distress is all too foreseeable and common a consequence of breach, if damages were to be available for it, claims would multiply. Staughton LJ expressed his alarm at the prospect of every ship-owner in the Commercial Court, having successfully claimed for unpaid freight, adding a claim for his or her mental suffering whilst waiting for his or her money (*Hayes v James & Charles Dodd* (1990) at 823); Lord Steyn warned against the 'creation of a society bent on litigation' (*Farley v Skinner* at [28]). The legal response has been to confine recovery to exceptional categories ('pockets') and only extend recovery by analogy to them. *However*, contractual liability for non-pecuniary loss can only be owed to one's contract partner who must prove damage, causation, mitigation, and remoteness.

(iii) **Protection of the claimant's non-pecuniary motive for contracting**: Lord Mustill (*Ruxley* at 360) notes that the principle of *pacta sunt servanda* (agreements must be kept) would be eroded if the law did not recognise that consumers often make contracts that, although not of economic value, have value to them and for which they may have paid extra. The promisor should not be allowed to 'please himself whether or not to comply with the wishes of the promisee which, as embodied in the contract, formed part of the consideration for the price' (see also *Farley* at [21]). Most contracts made by most people (not acting in the course of business) are aimed wholly, or partly, at satisfying *individual preference* or improving quality of life (eg contracts made in

---

[6] Law Commission, *Aggravated, Exemplary and Restitutionary Damages* (Law Com Consultation Paper 132, 1993) at para 2.12.

respect of one's food, accommodation, clothing, employment, recreation, or provision for one's family and friends). The same considerations apply to contracts made from altruism to improve the *environment* or for other *good causes*. In all these cases, failure to protect the claimant's non-pecuniary interest in the performance of the contract *contravenes the compensatory principle* and allows the defendant to 'get away' with the breach.

13.2.4.1 Contracts for enjoyment or alleviation of distress

One recognised exception to the general rule against damages for non-pecuniary loss is where the *purpose* of the contract or of an important term is to provide enjoyment, peace of mind, or freedom from distress.

(i) Illustrations

✓ In ***Jarvis v Swan Tours*** (1973),[7] J (a solicitor) bought a package holiday with S. S's brochures promised a 'house party' with a variety of activities and entertainment (including a yodeller evening). In fact, there were only 13 people at the hotel in the first week, and only J in the second week. The Court of Appeal took account of the value of what he received (effectively nothing) and awarded J the sum he paid for the holiday; he was also compensated for 'disappointment, distress, upset and frustration'.

Damages for mental distress were also awarded where:

✓ a solicitor failed to take effective legal steps to protect the claimant from being harassed (*Heywood v Wellers* (1976));

✓ a solicitor's negligence resulted in the claimant's twins being kidnapped by their father and taken to Tunisia where he was awarded their custody (*Hamilton Jones v David & Snape (a firm)* (2003));

✓ a photographer failed to turn up for the claimant's wedding day (*Diesen v Sampson* (1971));

✓ a touring holiday was spoiled by a car purchased for the purpose from a seller who knew that it was not of merchantable quality (*Jackson v Chrysler Acceptances Ltd* (1978));

✓ an undertaker failed to inter a corpse properly (*Lamm v Shingleton* (1949));

✓ a cemetery owner failed to grant the claimants burial plots adjacent to their parents (*Reed v Madon* (1989)).

(ii) The non-pecuniary purpose

Ruxley v Forsyth can be seen as an application of this category because the stipulation as to the pool's depth was for the claimant's enjoyment or peace of mind (see 13.2.3.2(iv)). The House of Lords in *Farley v Skinner* relied on *Ruxley* to loosen the original requirement that the non-pecuniary purpose (enjoyment, peace of mind, or alleviation of distress) should be the 'sole' object of the contract (*Watts v Morrow*

---

[7] See also *Jackson v Horizon Holidays Ltd* (1975), at 13.2.4.4 on loss of performance to third parties.

(1991)). It is now enough if it represents **'a distinct and important obligation'** of the contract breached. This meets the injustice of *Knott v Bolton* (1995)[8] where a couple were denied compensation for an architect's breach in designing their 'dream home' because the contract *also* had an economic purpose. The House of Lords in *Farley v Skinner* accepted the criticism[9] that this made part of the claimant's expectations unenforceable. This injustice is reinforced when the claimant's non-pecuniary purpose would have been enforceable if it had been contained in a *separate* contract. In **Farley v Skinner**, F employed S to survey a property he intended to buy for quiet and peaceful weekends, expressly asking S to report on the likelihood of disturbance from aircraft noise. S reported that it was 'unlikely that the property will suffer greatly from such noise'. F bought the house and spent more than £100,000 improving it. In fact, the house did suffer from substantial disturbance during busy periods such as the weekends. The breach caused no diminution of value, since F did not pay more than the property was actually worth. However, the House of Lords upheld the trial judge's award of £10,000 for the loss of enjoyment caused by the noise.

Farley v Skinner was applied in **Hamilton Jones v David & Snape** (2003) where the defendant solicitors' negligence resulted in the claimant's twins being kidnapped by their father and taken to Tunisia where he obtained custody of them. Neuberger J (at [61], [63]) held that both parties 'would have had in mind that a significant reason for the claimant instructing the defendants was with a view to ensuring, so far as possible, that the claimant retained custody of her children for her own pleasure and peace of mind'. Neuberger J awarded £25,000 for her *financial* loss and £20,000 for mental distress. The latter figure was arrived at by taking into account her grief, anxiety, and hurt, the fact that the Fatal Accidents Act 1976 provides for statutory damages of £10,000 for negligence resulting in death of a child, and the fact that she still had some access to the twins.

When is the provision of enjoyment, peace of mind, or alleviation of distress a 'distinct and important obligation' under the contract? These are obvious in holidays, weddings, funerals, custody of children, and the like. In contrast, *Farley* (at [14], [38]) approved Bingham LJ's view in *Watts v Morrow*, that a house survey would normally not qualify. Less clear-cut are *Ruxley* (which rests on a distinction between a contract to build a swimming pool and to build one *which brings pleasurable amenity in its depth*) and *Farley* (which necessitates a distinction between an *ordinary* survey and one which ensures, inter alia, the prospective owner's quiet enjoyment). *Ruxley* and *Farley* give considerable scope for arguing that some aspect of the contract incorporates a significant non-pecuniary purpose. The problem is acute since all non-commercial contracts (indeed, in a sense, even commercial contracts) confer peace of mind which breach reduces or destroys. The courts will have considerable latitude in determining whether terms have an important non-pecuniary purpose. It is a question of degree and judgment. In *Farley*, Lord Hutton (at [54]) stressed the need for a clear test to

---

[8] Overruled in *Farley v Skinner* at [24], [41], [52], [93].

[9] D Capper, 'Damages for Distress and Disappointment—The Limits of *Watts v Morrow*' (2000) 116 *LQR* 553, approved in *Farley v Skinner* at [24], [51].

prevent damages being generally available for anxiety and aggravation caused by breach and 'to prevent the exception expanding to swallow up, or to diminish unjustifiably, the principle itself.'

Five factors **restrict the scope of recovery for non-pecuniary loss**.

(i) In general, *commercial claimants are excluded*. Lord Cooke notes that '[c]ontract breaking is treated as an incident of commercial life which players in the game are expected to meet with mental fortitude' (*Johnson v Gore Wood & Co (a firm)* (2001) at 108; see *Farley v Skinner* at [98] and *Hamilton Jones v David & Snape* at [64]).

(ii) Lord Hutton (*Farley v Skinner* at [54]) said that the non-pecuniary purpose must be: *important* to the claimant, made a *specific term* of the contract, and clearly *communicated* to the defendant.

(iii) The loss must have been *caused* by, and not be too *remote* a consequence of, the breach. In practice, this requires that the defendant knows the importance of the claimant's non-pecuniary purpose and so foresees the loss from breach. It was explained in *Farley* (at [104]) that damages were denied in *Johnson v Gore Wood* (2001), since 'it was not . . . remotely arguable' that J's alleged mental distress and anxiety was a consequence that 'was reasonably in the contemplation of the parties as liable to result from a breach' at contract formation. Likewise, damages were denied in *Wiseman v Virgin Atlantic Airways Ltd* (2006), because 'it would not have been in the contemplation of the parties that the mere fact of not permitting a passenger to board the aircraft for his return flight would lead to a breakdown in health' (at [19]).

(iv) The *awards should be kept low*; £10,000 was regarded as being at the top end in *Farley v Skinner* (at [28], [61], [110]), but note that £20,000 was awarded in *Hamilton Jones v David & Snape*. In *Milner v Carnival plc (trading as Cunard)* (2010), the Court of Appeal awarded the claimants £12,000 in respect of their unhappy time on the maiden world cruise of the Queen Victoria. They had paid some £60,000 and their legitimate expectations were 'sky high': they had been promised luxury, glamour, 'star treatment', and the 'experience of a life time'. Unfortunately they were unable to sleep due to vibrations and noise in their cabin and they disembarked 28 days into the 78-day cruise. In relation to the claim for damages for physical inconvenience, discomfort, and mental distress, the Court of Appeal sought to ensure a measure of consistency by having regard to damages awarded for bereavement and for an affront to feelings in cases of sex and race discrimination. The court noted the modest nature of these awards. Even allowing for the exceptional nature of the present case, the disappointment, distress, annoyance, and frustration in the present case is a less serious kind and does not equate with bereavement. In practice, the small awards will make non-pecuniary loss not worth pursuing in view of the potential costs and risks of litigation.

(v) *Other measures must be inappropriate or yield no substantial damages*. For example, in *Farley*, cure was impossible and there was no diminution of value and in *Ruxley*, there was no diminution of value and the cost of cure was inappropriate. Lord Scott (at [109]) said that to allow damages for both discomfort and diminution of value 'would allow double recovery for the same item'.

> ◀◀ **Counterpoint**
>
> Damages for both pecuniary and non-pecuniary loss were awarded in *Hamilton Jones*. If the facts in *Farley* remain the same except that F also suffers diminution of value, why should *both* types of loss not be recoverable? If your failure to lay the precise colour of tiles I order causes me *both* a diminution of value (because my house now lacks a matching colour scheme) *and* loss of satisfaction (in not living with my favourite colour), I should be able to claim both.

13.2.4.2 Mental distress consequent on physical injury or inconvenience

The second exception to the general rule against damages for non-pecuniary loss is where breach has caused personal injury (eg *Godly v Perry* (1960)), physical inconvenience, or discomfort.

(i) Illustrations
Modest damages were recovered where:

- ✓ a railway company took a family to the wrong station, leaving them to walk four or five miles home on a rainy night (*Hobbs v L & SW Railway Co* (1875));

- ✓ a man, his wife, and child were forced to live with his wife's parents for two years when a solicitor failed to obtain possession of a house (*Bailey v Bullock* (1950));

- ✓ the claimant bought a house in reliance on a negligent survey which failed to mention a leaking roof and an offensive-smelling septic tank. Damages were awarded for the distress and discomfort of living there and for the claimant's anxiety as to when repairs would be made since he could not afford them himself (*Perry v Sydney Phillips & Son* (1982)).

(ii) The scope of physical injury or inconvenience
Farley v Skinner extends this category insofar as disturbance by aircraft noise was classed as physical inconvenience: this was the secondary ground for the £10,000 awarded by four of their Lordships (at [30], [32], [57]–[60], [81]–[88]) and the primary ground for Lord Clyde (at [37]–[39]).

What amounts to *physical* inconvenience or discomfort?

- Lord Scott explains that the issue is not the types of inconvenience suffered, but rather how they were *caused*. Mere disappointment does not sound in damages even if it has led to a complete mental breakdown. 'But, if the cause of the inconvenience or discomfort is a sensory (sight, touch, hearing, etc) experience, damages can, subject to the remoteness rules, be recovered' (at [85]).

- Lord Steyn draws an analogy with causes which could constitute nuisance (at [30]).

- Lord Clyde thought it unnecessary to give a detailed analysis or definition beyond excluding 'purely sentimental' matters and mere 'disappointment'. The other Law Lords were also content to assess inconvenience on the facts of the particular case (at [35]).

Farley v Skinner seems a very borderline case; Lord Scott notes the 'evidence that many, perhaps most, of the residents in the area were not troubled by the noise' (at

[68]). Acceptance of physical inconvenience in the case must therefore be based on the claimant's *subjective experience* of 'real discomfort' and interference with his or her preference for 'a quiet reflective breakfast, a morning stroll in the garden' and pre-dinner drinks on the terrace. This increases the *potential scope* of this exception. Lord Cooke (at 108), dissenting in **Johnson v Gore Wood**, was prepared to extend this further by treating the claimant's *extreme financial* embarrassment as physical inconvenience and discomfort (the defendant's breach reduced him from a prosperous state to subsistence on social security benefit and led to the significant deterioration of his relationship with his wife and son). Lord Cooke said: 'the common law would be defective and stray too far from reality, humanity and justice if it remorselessly shut out even a restrained award under these heads'.

Pause for reflection

This analysis of the foreseeability (or remoteness) of loss shows the overlap between the categories of physical inconvenience and contracts for enjoyment, so that too much should not be made of Lord Scott's distinction between them (*Farley* at [86]). The measure of damages seems to be the same; Lord Scott's (at [107]) calculation of damages for *failure to receive intangible benefits* takes account of the distress, annoyance, or physical inconvenience from breach. Likewise, damages for *physical inconvenience* are assessed by reference to the baseline of freedom from aircraft disturbance (at [108]). In short, damages for *not being better off* includes being worse off, and damages for *being made worse off* depends on what you are worse off *than* (ie where you fix the baseline of entitlement).

13.2.4.3 Loss of reputation and breach of employment contracts

Some cases previously regarded as exceptional can now be seen as examples of a third exception to the non-recoverability of non-pecuniary loss; namely, where *loss of reputation* occasions *financial* loss to the claimant.

(i) Illustrations
Damages were awarded where:

- ✓ a bank wrongly dishonoured a cheque causing damage to the customer's reputation and credit rating (*Kpohraror v Woolwich Building Society* (1996));
- ✓ breach of contract to employ an actor caused loss of anticipated publicity (*Clayton & Waller v Oliver* (1930)).

(ii) No claim in employment contracts
Addis v Gramophone has long been regarded as authority for the rule that where an employee is wrongly dismissed, no damages are available for the employee's:

(i)   mental distress: *or*

(ii) loss of employment prospects due to the harsh and humiliating manner of his or her dismissal.

This is open to criticism. Why should employees be denied compensation for provable financial loss flowing from breach? Why is 'the contract of employment singled out for a special rule to the disadvantage of employees?' (*Johnson v Unisys Ltd* (2001) at [17]).

(iii) Qualifications on *Addis v Gramophone*

The scope of *Addis* is now confined as a result of *Malik v Bank of Credit & Commerce Intl SA* (1998) and *Johnson v Unisys*:

(i) **Causation**: in *Malik v BCCI*, Lords Steyn (at 38–9) and Nicholls (at 51) confine *Addis* to cases where the breach did not *cause* the loss of reputation. In *Addis*, the employer's breach comprised of failing to give the employee the requisite notice: this is remedied by damages based on payment for the notice period, whereas, the employee's loss flowed from the dismissal itself. As Lord Steyn explains (at 39): '[L]oss which an employee would have suffered even if the dismissal had been after due notice is irrecoverable, because such loss does not derive from the wrongful element in the dismissal. Further, it is difficult to see how the mere fact of wrongful dismissal, rather than dismissal after due notice, could of itself handicap an employee in the labour market.'

(ii) **Nature of the term breached**: *Addis* was further confined to cases of breach by failing to give *notice*. In principle, **Malik v BCCI** allows damages for loss of employment prospects where the loss flows from breach of the mutual *duty of trust and confidence*, a term now generally implied into employment contracts. In *Malik*, M and other senior employees made redundant following BCCI's insolvency, claimed *stigma damages* for being unable to obtain similar employment because of the stigma of being former employees of a bank widely known to have engaged in corrupt and dishonest practices, in breach of its implied obligation of trust and confidence to its employees.

Despite these restrictions on the *Addis* bar, the claim for loss of employment prospects is still very difficult to make out because:

(i) **Proof of causation is difficult**: in *BCCI v Ali and others (No 2)* (1999), Lightman J (at 115–16) held that since the decision to offer a job rests on the unrestricted choice of the employer (subject to anti-discrimination legislation), in the absence of clear evidence that the claimant had a real chance of getting the job which was lost because of the stigma associated with BCCI's breach, no damages could be awarded.

(ii) The implied duty of **trust and confidence is not breached by the unfair manner of dismissal**, independent of any failure to give notice (**Johnson v Unisys**). This is because the duty only exists where employment is *continuing* and not when it is being terminated since 'an employer who summarily dismisses an employee usually does so because, rightly or wrongly, he no longer has any trust or confidence in him' (at [78]). Their Lordships declined to imply a term requiring the power of dismissal to be exercised fairly and in good faith because, on the facts:

- the employer had a contractual right to dismiss without cause;
- it would raise extremely difficult questions on causation and remoteness (how is the psychiatric injury flowing from the unfair *manner* of dismissal distinguishable from the similar consequences of the dismissal itself, for which the employer is not liable?);

- its breach can give rise to huge claims (£400,000 in *Johnson v Unisys* itself), wholly disproportionate to the employer's fault and are likely to deter employers from hiring psychologically fragile persons;

- it would circumvent parliamentary intention manifest in the unfair dismissal legislation under which Johnson had already obtained the statutory maximum of £11,000 (*Eastwood v Magnox Electric plc* (2005), *Edwards v Chesterfield Royal Hospital NHS Foundations Trust* (2011)).

The net effect is that *Addis v Gramophone* continues to bar damages for unfair dismissal causing non-pecuniary loss and loss of employment prospects.

◼◼ Counterpoint

Lord Steyn *dissents* from this view in *Johnson v Unysis* (at [23]) and in *Eastwood v Magnox Electric* (2005). He observes the following.

1. A separate common law remedy would not amount to double recovery because the statutory regime:

   - does not allow recovery for non-pecuniary loss (*Dunnachie v Kingston upon Hull CC* (2004) at [38]);

   - does not cover financial loss from psychiatric injury (*Eastwood v Magnox Electric* at [41], [42], [45]) which is accepted as 'personal injury' in other contexts (*Page v Smith* (1966)); and

   - is capped so severely that it can only deal with 'cases at the lower end of seriousness'.

2. The implied duty of trust and confidence *should* apply when employment is being terminated since the obligation was originally developed in the context of constructive dismissal claims.

3. The current position can produce the *perverse result* that an employer is better off dismissing than suspending an employee because the statutory claim for unfair dismissal is capped, whilst the common law claim for unfair suspension (by breach of the implied duty of trust and confidence) is not (*Eastwood v Magnox Electric* at [32], [40]).

4. *Addis v Gramophone* rests on an outdated conception of employment; it does not reflect the modern recognition that 'a person's employment is usually one of the most important things in his or her life. It gives not only a livelihood but an occupation, an identity and a sense of self-esteem' (*Johnson v Unisys* at [35]).

5. *Johnson v Unisys* has attracted heavy criticism from distinguished and experienced labour lawyers including Freedland, Collins, Heppel, Deakin, and Morris (*Eastwood* at [43]–[44]).

13.2.4.4 Loss of performance to a third party

(i) The problem

A parent may make a contract to obtain music lessons for their child. Companies in a group may decide for reasons of convenience and profitability that one of them will contract for work to be done for another in the group. Where *A* contracts for *B*'s performance to be directed towards a third party *C* (hereafter 'third party contracts'), what damages can *A* claim on *B*'s breach? Since *A* will generally have suffered no direct *pecuniary* loss, the answer to this question informs the larger question of the extent to which contract law recognises a claimant's *performance interest beyond his or her expectation of financial gain*. The traditional rule is that a party can only claim compensation for his or her *own* losses, not for loss to third party beneficiaries (see 4.1.5.2).[10] In addition, a third party is traditionally barred from suing on contracts to which he or she is not a party (see Chapter 4 on privity) so that the rights generated by a third party contract cannot be vindicated by any effective remedy; they disappear down a 'legal black hole'.

(ii) Claims for the third party's loss

The most important exceptions to the general bar against substantial recovery in third party contracts (see 4.1.5 and 4.1.6) are:

- the *third party's own action* under the Contracts (Rights of Third Parties) Act 1999; and
- the *promisee's claim* under the *'Albazero* exception' (*Albacruz v Albazero* (1977) at 847) to recover damages for the third party's loss, *held in trust for* the third party.

(iii) The promisee's performance interest

The *Albazero* exception assumes that the loss belongs to the *third party*; the promisee sues on his or her behalf. However, it is arguable that the loss is more appropriately attributed to the *promisee*. For example, a mother who pays for treatment for her drug-addicted son would be astonished to be told, if no treatment is given, that the law regards her as suffering no loss. She made the contract to confer this benefit on her son; awarding *her* substantial damages would allow her to achieve this bargained-for result from someone else. Directing the damages to her son translates her gift into money, which is not what she wanted to give. Moreover, in the nature of addiction, this money is unlikely to be put to the original purpose.

In *Woodar Investment Development Ltd v Wimpey Construction (UK) Ltd* (1980), the House of Lords expressed dissatisfaction with the general failure to recognise any compensable loss to the promisee in third party contracts. However, when the opportunity arose to reconsider the matter, the House of Lords continued to apply the *Albazero* exception. The interest to us is in their Lordships' use of the concept of the **promisee's performance interest** to support the award of substantial damages to the promisee even absent any direct pecuniary loss. In *Linden Gardens v Lenesta Sludge* (1994), substantial damages were awarded under the *Albazero* exception. However, protection of the promisee's *performance interest* received guarded support from Lord Browne-Wilkinson (at 112), with whom Lords Bridge and Ackner agreed. Only Lord Griffiths decided the case on this ground (at 96). It is a moot point whether this line of reasoning has been strengthened by *McAlpine v Panatown*.

---

[10] See *McAlpine v Panatown* at 522, 563, 575, 580; but Lord Goff questions the force of the rule at 538–9, 544.

(iv) *Alfred McAlpine Construction Ltd v Panatown Ltd*: facts and the 'narrow' ground

Two contracts were made.

(i) The **main contract** under which Panatown (the promisee) engaged McAlpine (the promisor) to construct a new building on land owned by UIPL (the third party). Panatown and UIPL belonged to the same corporate group and the building contract was so structured to avoid payment of VAT.

(ii) The **duty of care deed** agreed between McAlpine (the promisor) and UIPL (the third party) which UIPL could assign to its successors in title.

Panatown claimed £40 million under the main contract for the cost of repairing McAlpine's defective work. A majority of the House of Lords (Lords Clyde, Jauncey, and Browne-Wilkinson) **denied the claim** as falling *outside* the *Albazero* exception, the so-called **'narrow ground'**, because:

- Panatown (the promisee) suffered *no* loss; and
- Panatown had no claim under the *Albazero* exception because, although UIPL *had* suffered loss, the duty of care deed gave UIPL a *direct contractual right* against McAlpine (the promisor): there was no 'legal black hole'.

▶◀ Counterpoint

The duty of care deed conferred significantly fewer rights on UIPL (only to McAlpine's exercise of reasonable care) than the main contract intended for it to get (eg strict liability in building, provisions on arbitration, and liquidated damages). Thus, the decision renders illusory the rights conferred by the main contract which exceeded those contained in the duty of care deed: *these* rights did indeed disappear down a 'legal black hole' (see further 4.1.5.2). On this point, *McAlpine v Panatown* is inconsistent with dicta in *Catlin Estates Ltd v Carter Jonas (a firm)* (2005), also decided on the *Albazero* exception. CEL sued CJ for substantial defects in the construction of a shooting lodge which emerged after the lodge was transferred to a third party, C. Judge Toulmin said that: even if CEL could claim under the Defective Premises Act 1972, this would not bar a substantial claim for contract damages since '[t]he principle that a party cannot bring a claim through a third party where it has a substantial claim on its own *must relate to a claim which can be brought on the same conditions as the original claim*' (at [301], [304], emphasis added).

(v) The 'broad' ground

In *McAlpine v Panatown*, Lords Goff (at 545–6) and Millett (at 585) held that substantial *damages should be awarded on 'the broad ground'* to compensate the *promisee* for the loss of his or her performance interest.

The status of the 'broad ground' depends on how Lord Browne-Wilkinson's judgment is interpreted (see 4.1.5.3). His Lordship agreed with Lords Clyde and Jauncey on the applicability and outcome of the 'narrow ground'. But he *also* held that Panatown's claim would fail even if he 'assume[s] that the broader ground is sound in law' because the duty of care deed exhausts the promisee's performance interest (at 577).

> ## Pause for reflection
>
> Lord Browne-Wilkinson's *application* of the broad ground is questionable for the same reason stated in the previous Counterpoint. Nevertheless, it is arguable that Lord Browne-Wilkinson's, albeit lukewarm, support for the broad ground combines with the judgment of Lords Goff and Millett to constitute *another 'majority'* on the applicable law, namely that the promisee's compensable performance interest may *in principle* go beyond his or her narrow pecuniary expectation. The judgments in *McAlpine v Panatown* can be represented as follows:
>
> **Applicable law**
>
> | 'Narrow' ground | 'Broad' ground |
> | --- | --- |
> | Lord Clyde | Lord Goff |
> | Lord Jauncey | Lord Millett |
> | Lord Browne-Wilkinson | Lord Browne-Wilkinson |
>
> **Application to the facts**
>
> | No substantial damages | Substantial damages |
> | --- | --- |
> | *On the narrow ground*: Lords Clyde, Jauncey, and Lord Browne-Wilkinson On the broad ground: Lord Browne-Wilkinson | On the broad ground: Lord Goff and Lord Millett |

(vi) The measure of damages on the 'broad' ground

A promisee's loss from breach, whether performance is directed towards themselves or a third party, can take the form of:

(i) loss of his or her pecuniary expectation from performance;

(ii) loss of his or her *non-pecuniary* expectation from performance; and

(iii) loss of the literal *performance* itself.

Which of these losses are recoverable and how are they measured? The short answer is that the apparent divergence of approach between their Lordships disappears on closer examination.

(i) **Pecuniary loss**: in third party contracts, the promisee will generally suffer no *direct* pecuniary loss from breach since he or she expected no improvement of his or her own financial position from the defendant's performance. Where he or she *does* suffer direct pecuniary loss, this is recoverable (eg where breach leaves the promisee's obligation to the third party undischarged (*Price v Easton* (1833)) or makes him or her liable to the third party).

Lords Clyde and Jauncey first appear to adopt a narrow 'balance sheet' approach recognising only pecuniary loss. However, they both (at 533, 574) accept that the claimant may claim the cost of cure *where he or she has or intends to cure*. Thus, the intention to cure *creates* a recoverable *financial* loss. This is reinforced by Lords Clyde and Jauncey's acceptance that damages *are* properly available for non-pecuniary losses (at 534) and that the intention to cure is subject to a reasonableness qualification (at 533, 574).

(ii) **Non-pecuniary loss**: *Ruxley v Forsyth* and *Farley v Skinner* make it clear that the law will protect a promisee's non-pecuniary interest, if it falls within the recognised exceptions. This may exist in third party contracts.

> ✓ Lord Griffiths instances a husband who contracts for repairs to the roof of the matrimonial home owned by the wife (*Linden Gardens v Lenesta Sludge* at 96–7).

> ✓ Lord Goff refers to the wealthy philanthropist who contracts for repairs, renovation, or reconstruction of the village hall belonging to the parish council or trustees (*McAlpine v Panatown* at 547–8).

> ✓ In *Jackson v Horizon Holidays Ltd* (1975), J obtained substantial damages for the grossly substandard holiday that he and his family endured: the case is interpreted in *Woodar Investment v Wimpey Construction* (at 283, 291, 293, 297) as recovery for J's *own* mental distress (including that caused by his failure to benefit the third parties), or as a case calling for 'special treatment' (eg contracts for family holidays, restaurant meals for a party, or a taxi for a group).

> ✓ In *Radford v de Froberville*, the landlord obtained the cost of the cure to provide his tenants with the benefit of having a boundary wall.

In all these cases, the promisee's loss comprises loss of satisfaction (enjoyment, peace of mind, or freedom from distress) consequential on the benefit not being conferred on the third party. Recovery for this is broadly analogous to that awarded in contracts of enjoyment (see 13.2.4.1).

(iii) **Loss of performance itself**: does and should the law protect the promisee's performance interest in the sense of protecting his or her entitlement to *literal* (*precise*) performance measured by the cost of obtaining substitute performance? Lords Goff and Millett's judgments in *McAlpine v Panatown* (at 595) first appear to say 'yes'. They emphasise that:

> ✓ the promisee's loss is principally of the performance *itself* (rather than of what the performance was *for*);
> ✓ the correct response to this is the cost of cure.

They cite in support:

> ✓ Lord Griffiths, who said that the husband contracting for repairs to his wife's house 'has suffered loss because he did not receive the bargain for which he had contracted with the first builder and the measure of damages is the cost of securing the performance of the bargain by completing the roof repairs properly by the second builder' (*Linden Gardens* at 97);

✓ Oliver J, who said *'Pacta sunt servanda . . .* if that which is contracted for is not supplied by the other contracting party I do not see why, in principle, he should not be compensated by being provided with the cost of supplying it through someone else or in a different way' (*Radford v de Froberville* at 1270);

✓ Wetmore J, who said that the promisee in a building contract is 'entitled to recover such damages as will put him in a position to have the building he contracted for' (*Allen v Pierce* (1895) at 323);

✓ *Ruxley v Forsyth,* interpreted as compensation for simply not getting the depth of pool contracted for (see 13.2.3.2). Lord Millett (at 588) comments that this 'loss could equally well, and perhaps more accurately, be described as defeated expectation'.

However, in *McAlpine v Panatown*, Lords Goff and Millett also accept:

• the reasonableness qualification in *Ruxley v Forsyth*, which assumes that damages may be *less* than the cost of cure (at 550–1);

• that the promisee's intention to cure is relevant to the reasonableness of a cost of cure claim (at 550–1, 592);

• dicta from *Radford v de Froberville* stressing that damages should only compensate for the promisee's 'genuine loss' and should not amount to an 'uncovenanted profit' (at 549);

• the famous article **'Contract Remedies and the Consumer Surplus'** (1979) 95 *LQR* 58, 58, in which **Harris, Ogus, and Phillips** state that the proper protection of the performance interest would make a significant difference only in a minority of cases; an automatic cost of cure award would make a radical difference (at 589);

• Lord Browne-Wilkinson (at 577) explains that:

> [t]he essential feature of the broader ground is that the contracting party A, although not himself suffering the physical or pecuniary damage . . . has suffered his own damage being the loss of his performance interest, ie the failure to provide C with the benefit that B had contracted for C to receive . . . it follows that the critical factor is to determine *what interest A had in the provision of the service for the third party C* (emphasis added).

Other considerations tell against a claimant's right to *literal* albeit substitute performance. First, it is inconsistent with the basic principle that a 'breach of contract may cause a loss, but is not in itself a loss in any meaningful sense' (*McAlpine v Panatown* at 534), so that damages are generally measured by the diminution of value (ie the difference between the money's worth of the promisee's *expected* welfare on full performance and his or her *actual* welfare on breach). Second, Lord Clyde (at 534) explains that while the promisee's *right* to literal performance is destroyed by frustration, it is not destroyed by breach: 'the bargained-for contractual rights . . . [remain] as the necessary legal basis for a remedy' (damages or specific enforcement). Termination of contract for breach extinguishes the contract-breaker's *primary* obligations, but replaces them by *secondary* obligations to compensate the promisee (see 12.2.1). Thus, the promisee's *right to performance* is *converted* at the remedial stage into a right to the *fruits of performance* and only very exceptionally to literal performance itself or its money's worth. Third, a right to literal performance is inconsistent with the *restrictions* on: (i) the measure of damages (eg by mitigation and remoteness, see 13.2.5); and (ii) the availability of specific performance (see 14.2).

Pause for reflection

There is *no* unqualified support in the authorities for the protection of literal performance. Rather, all the judgments in *McAlpine v Panatown* are broadly consistent with the recovery of pecuniary and non-pecuniary losses. The real differences are ones of *emphasis* rather than of kind.

- Judges who overtly support the narrow 'balance sheet' approach nevertheless concede that damages are properly available for non-pecuniary losses based on actual or intention to cure which is subject to a reasonableness qualification.

- From the other end, Lords Goff and Millett's starting point on the right to literal performance is not taken to its logical conclusion of an *automatic* cost of cure award. Again, the award is made to depend on the promisee's actual or intention to cure and the reasonableness of curing.

- The *convergence* makes non-pecuniary loss the appropriate locus for conceptualising the remedy for loss of performance to third parties.

13.2.4.5 The future scope of recoverable non-pecuniary loss

Ruxley v Forsyth and *Farley v Skinner* significantly extend the previous law. Even if we resist an automatic cost of cure award to a promisee (wholly appropriate in *McAlpine v Panatown*, where the commercial promisee neither paid for the original performance nor would pay for the repairs), we may be sympathetic to a more liberal approach to non-pecuniary loss than is hitherto recognised. Lord Millett said (*McAlpine v Panatown* at 592, citing Lord Scarman in *Woodar Investment v Wimpey Construction*): 'that a contracting party has required services to be supplied at his own cost to a third party is at least *prima facie* evidence of the value of those services to the party who placed the order'. To the extent that the law is more willing to award damages for non-pecuniary loss, it better protects the claimant's performance interest. However, the performance interest will only be fully protected if *all* the restrictive conditions are abandoned and not merely relaxed (eg the duty to mitigate; the limits on remoteness, specific performance, and the cost of cure).

Diagram 13B summarises the exceptional categories in which the claimant's non-pecuniary loss has been considered and has received some recognition. The shaded area denotes where loss is currently recognised and compensated for. The overlapping circles at the bottom right signify the uncertainty over the status, nature, and measure of the 'broad' ground in *McAlpine v Panatown*.

In '**Damages for Breach of Contract: Compensation, Restitution and Vindication**' (2008) 28 *OJLS* 73, **Pearce and Halson** argue that the purpose of contract damages

Diagram 13B Overview of recovery for non-pecuniary loss

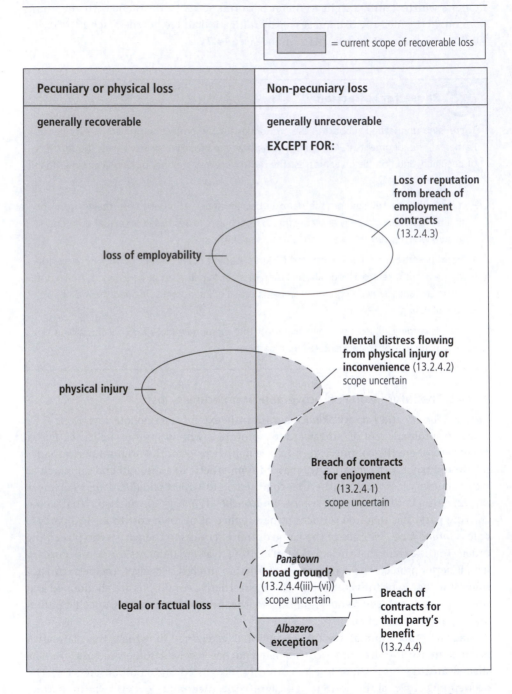

is not only to indemnify loss caused by the breach, but also to 'vindicate' the contractual right. The latter explains certain awards such as *Ruxley* damages, the broad ground in *Panatown*, and *Wrotham Park* damages (being loss of opportunity to negotiate for the release of the defendant from performance, see 13.4).

13.2.5 **Factors limiting the protection of the expectation interest**

Aside from restrictions on the *types* and *measure* of loss already mentioned, other rules further restrict contract law's commitment to the protection of the claimant's performance interest. The result is that the stated aim of putting an innocent party in the same money position 'as if the contract had been performed' (*Robinson v Harman* (1848) at 855) is merely the *starting point*. Ultimately, the claimant can only recover such of his or her losses as are *unavoidable*, are *provably caused*, and are readily *foreseeable* by the defendant.

The doctrines focused on the *avoidability* of the loss claimed are:

1. mitigation;
2. time for quantifying loss.

Other doctrines focus on loss caused by other factors:

3. intervening causes;
4. the claimant's contributory negligence.

Other doctrines exclude loss that is too:

5. speculative;
6. remote; or
7. long past (exceeding the time limit).

13.2.5.1 Mitigation

(i) The mitigation rule

The mitigation rule requires the claimant to act reasonably to limit or reduce his or her loss caused by the defendant's breach (**British Westinghouse Electric & Manufacturing Co v Underground Electric Rly Co** (1912)). Although this is often expressed in terms of a claimant's 'duty' to mitigate, it is not a duty that attracts liability on its breach; it merely reduces or negates the damages otherwise recoverable by the claimant. No duty to mitigate traditionally attaches to an innocent party's election to affirm the contract or to claim specific performance. Nevertheless, the desirability of mitigation explains why a claimant cannot affirm if he or she has no *legitimate interest* in doing so (because it would be very wasteful and grossly unreasonable, see 12.3).

(ii) The standard of reasonable mitigation

The burden is on the defendant contract-breaker to show that the claimant has failed to mitigate. The standard of mitigation required from the claimant is not high for it lies ill in the defendant's mouth to criticise the claimant's actions when this has been necessitated by the defendant's own breach. The claimant need not 'take any step which a reasonable and prudent man would not ordinarily take in the course of his business' (*British Westinghouse* at 689). For example, he or she need *not* take steps:

- which would entail substantial financial risks or involve complicated litigation (*Pilkington v Wood* (1953));

- which would require him or her to risk their commercial reputation (*James Finlay & Co Ltd v Kwik Hoo Tong Handelsmaatschappij* (1929));

- which he or she cannot afford; thus, impecuniosity, including inability to borrow, may excuse a failure to mitigate (*Clippens Oil Co Ltd v Edinburgh & District Water Trustees* (1907)); or

- while an action for specific performance is being determined (*Radford v de Froberville*).

(iii) The requirement of positive action

The first limb of mitigation requires the claimant to take *positive* action to minimise the loss flowing from the breach. What is required is fact-specific; however, in general:

- a claimant who does not receive the *goods or services* contracted for must make reasonable efforts to buy substitute performance (*Kaines (UK) v Osterreichische Warrenhandelsgesellschaft Austrowaren GmbH* (1993)); this will require prompt action in a volatile market (*Coastal (Bermuda) Petroleum Ltd v VTT Vulcan Petroleum (No 2)* (1994) at 635);

- a wrongly dismissed *employee* must make reasonable efforts to obtain suitable alternative employment (*Yetton v Eastwoods Froy Ltd* (1967));

- a claimant who sustains *property damage* from the breach should accept help to prevent further damage (*Anderson v Hoen, The Flying Fish* (1865)); and

- a claimant who sustains *physical injury* from the breach may be expected to undergo an operation to reduce or eliminate the injury unless the operation entails the risk of complications (*Selvanayagam v University of the West Indies* (1983)).

More controversially, mitigation may even require the claimant to *renegotiate the contract with the contract-breaker*:

- *Brace v Calder* (1895) held that a wrongly dismissed *employee* may be required to accept re-employment from his former employer unless their relationship has been damaged, the new job would involve a loss of status, or alternative employment is more permanent (*Yetton v Eastwoods Froy* (1967));

- in *Payzu Ltd v Saunders* (1919), S (suppliers of silk) wrongly insisted on cash payment on delivery, whereupon P sued for the difference between the contract price and the greater market price. This was denied because P's rejection of S's offer to supply the silk on cash terms amounted to a failure to mitigate its loss. The court held that, in *commercial* cases,[11] a party can be expected to consider and accept a reasonable offer made by the contract-breaker. The claimant may even be expected to initiate the renegotiation;

- in *The Soholt* (1983), the buyers of a ship who lawfully terminated the contract for late delivery were denied the difference between the contract price ($5 million) and the market price ($5.5 million) because they should have offered to buy the ship for the contract price adjusted to reflect the costs of delay to them.

---

[11] No such requirement attaches to contracts for personal services, *Clayton-Greene v de Courville* (1920).

> ### ⬦⬥ Counterpoint
>
> The law produces perverse results. Where the claimant fails to mitigate *in a rising market* by renegotiating with the contract-breaker, the latter gets to keep the benefit from the increase in the market price of the goods contracted for but not delivered. Thus, in *The Soholt* the sellers should have delivered a ship to the claimant, but sold it to another party for $300,000 more than the contract price *without* having to compensate the claimant, who then had to pay more to replace the ship in the same rising market.

(iv) Refraining from unreasonable action

The second limb of mitigation prevents any claim arising from *incurring unreasonable expenses* in mitigation. Again, what is reasonable is fact-specific, but examples of *reasonable* expenses include:

- ✓ advertising costs to mitigate the claimant's loss of business (*Holden Ltd v Bostock & Co Ltd* (1902));

- ✓ hire charges to replace an asset damaged or not delivered (*Bacon v Cooper (Metals) Ltd* (1982));

- ✓ the cost of printing new bank notes and of exchanging all old notes for new ones when printers wrongly delivered the old bank notes to criminals who put them into circulation (*Banco de Portugal v Waterlow & Sons Ltd* (1932));

- ✓ expenses in attempted mitigation even if it fails (*Esso Petroleum v Mardon* (1976));

- ✗ but, it was held to be *unreasonable* to take a loan at very high interest rates to release a ship, which had been wrongly detained (*Compania Financiera Soleada SA v Hamoor Tanker Corp Inc* (1981)).

(v) Gains from mitigation

Gains flowing *directly* from a claimant's mitigation is deducted from the claimant's damages. But no deductions will be made if the gains are indirect, merely collateral, or accrue from acts that are independent of, or too remote from, the act of mitigation. Thus:

- ✓ damages were reduced by the savings achieved when a defective turbine was replaced by a more efficient one that used less coal (*British Westinghouse*);

- ✗ proceeds of an insurance policy will not reduce the claimant's damages;

- ✗ *where supply exceeds demand*, the seller's damages for loss of profits are not reduced although he or she subsequently sells the car to another at the contract price because, but for the breach, the seller would have made two sales and two profits (*Thompson Ltd v Robinson (Gunmakers) Ltd* (1955)).

In *Lavarack v Woods of Colchester Ltd* (1967), the employer's breach released the employee from a clause prohibiting his involvement in other businesses:

- ✓ the court reduced the employee's damages by the remuneration he received from his new employer (a salary and half-share in a company);

✗ but no reduction was made for his profits from investing in another company, since this was too indirectly related to the employer's breach.

Where *A* delivers defective goods to *B*, which *B* sells on to *C* for more than their actual value, *Slater v Hoyle & Smith* (1920) permits *B* to claim the difference between the expected value and the actual value of the goods; it is 'immaterial that by some good fortune with which the [sellers] have nothing to do [the buyer] has been able to recoup himself what he paid for those goods'. However, the contrary was concluded in *Bence Graphics Intl Ltd v Fasson UK Ltd* (1998) where the buyer could only recover the price for the small quantity returned and for its liability to *C*.

 Pause for reflection

Atiyah (at 458) notes that the mitigation requirement 'makes a large dent' in the theory that the claimant is entitled to damages representing his or her lost expectations. If *A* refuses to perform her contract with *B*, but *B* can get substitute performance at the same price, *B*'s compensable expectation will be nil. Atiyah concludes: 'the reality is that the bindingness of executory contracts protects not the expectation of performance, but the expectation of profit; and even that is only protected so long as the promisee cannot secure it elsewhere'.[12]

What then is the justification for the mitigation rule?

1. *Fulfilment of expectations*: Burrows explains the requirement of mitigation as adding 'a supplementary policy to those policies justifying protection of the expectation interest . . . [Namely] that the promisee should not leave it simply to the courts to ensure fulfilment of his expectations, but should rather take it upon himself to adopt other reasonable means to ensure the fulfilment of his expectations'.[13] With respect, this seems to contradict (rather than supplement) the policies supporting the protection of the claimant's expectation interest. A party makes a contract *so that* the other party (backed up by the law), *not they themselves*, will fulfil their contractual expectation.

2. *Altruism*: Fried explains mitigation as a 'kind of altruistic duty, towards one's contractual partner'.[14] But why should an altruistic duty be raised in favour of the promise-*breaker* if, as Fried believes, promise-*keeping* is the essence of contractual liability?

3. *Efficiency*: mitigation is aimed at minimising wasteful conduct and encouraging efficient conduct. The concern to avoid waste is reflected in other restrictions on the measure of damages. Efficiency theories (see 1.4.3) reconcile this with the promisee's *right* to his or her expectation on the basis that mitigation leaves him or her no worse off: it is therefore said to be a 'cost-free' duty.[15] However, mitigation costs the promisee the effort of making a substitute contract and this will often not be trivial. Moreover, the rule bites precisely

➜

---

[12] P S Atiyah, *The Rise and Fall of Freedom of Contract* (Clarendon Press, 1979) 430.
[13] A Burrows, 'Contract, Tort and Restitution—A Satisfactory Division or Not?' (1983) 99 *LQR* 217, 266.
[14] C Fried, *Contract As Promise* (Harvard University Press, 1981) 131.
[15] C J Goetz and R E Scott, 'The Mitigation Principle: Toward a General Theory of Contractual Obligation' (1983) 69 *Virginia L Rev* 967.

> ➡ where the promisee is judged to have *failed* to mitigate and is denied some or all of his or her *provable* losses flowing from the breach: this clearly 'costs' the claimant.
>
> In 'Mitigation of Damages in Contract and the Meaning of Avoidable Loss' (1989) 105 *LQR* 398, **Bridge** observes that the duty to mitigate relaxes the strictness of contractual obligations. He considers arguments based upon factual causation, remoteness of damage, contributory negligence, and economic waste, and concludes that no single factor sufficiently explains the requirement to mitigate as a general rule. He suggests the relevance of judicial aversion to the claimant speculating at the defendant's expense, judicial promotion of self-help, and discouragement of passivity. Bridge also emphasises the importance of the expectation principle and of carefully defining the scope of contractual promises.

13.2.5.2 The time for measuring loss

Where the market for the subject matter of the contract fluctuates, the amount of compensation will depend on *when* damages are assessed. In a rising market (ie prices are increasing), the *earlier* the time fixed for assessment, the *less* will be awarded. Courts normally measure the loss at the earliest date that the claimant can be expected to mitigate (find substitute performance or take remedial action). He or she cannot sit back in the hope of claiming a greater loss at the date of the trial. Hence, loss is normally assessed at the *date of breach*, although a *later time* may be more appropriate (*Johnson v Agnew* (1980)) if the following apply.

(i) The contract provides for an event that occurs after breach but before the assessment of loss. In **The Golden Victory** (2007) (*Golden Strait Corp v Nippon Yusen Kubishiki Kaisha*), the charterer breached by returning the ship four years before the charterparty expired. Fourteen months later, the Gulf War broke out which would have entitled either party to terminate the charterparty. The House of Lords restricted damages to 14 months rather than four years of hire because contract damages should put the claimant in the position he or she would have been in had the contract been performed. The court should not shut its eyes to subsequent events which reduce the claimant's loss even if this may reduce certainty and give defendants an incentive to delay settling cases (see also *Ageas (UK) Ltd v Kwik-Fit (GB) Ltd* (2014)).

(ii) The claimant could not with reasonable diligence have discovered the breach at the time (*The Hansa Nord* (1976)).

(iii) The claimant reasonably waits to see whether the defendant will remedy the breach, or pending an action for specific performance (*Radford v de Froberville* and *Wroth v Tyler* (1974)).

(iv) The claimant cannot afford to take remedial action because of his or her own impecuniosity or inability to obtain credit (*Wroth v Tyler*).

Even if these factors are present, damages may still be reduced if the claimant unreasonably drags his or her heels through the courts (*Malhotra v Choudhury* (1980)).

13.2.5.3 Intervening causes

The claimant cannot recover more than nominal damages if no loss was caused by the defendant's breach. Neither can he or she claim for loss incurred but not as a result of the breach. In *Levicom International Holdings BV v Linklaters* (2009), solicitors were in breach of contract by not giving clear and proper advice but were liable only for nominal damages of £5 because the court found that, even given the proper advice, the claimant would not have conducted settlement discussions differently. Thus, L failed to prove that the solicitors' breach caused them any loss.

The causal link may also be broken by the occurrence of unforeseeable events.

(i) **Acts of independent third parties**: this will negate the claim unless the defendant was contracted to guard against that very occurrence (*London Joint Stock Bank Ltd v Macmillan & Arthur* (1918)). Thus, a house painter who leaves the house where he or she is working unlocked is liable to the owner for the value of goods stolen from it by a third party thief (*Stansbie v Troman* (1948)).

(ii) **Acts of God**: this describes natural or other unforeseeable external events. A party supplying an unseaworthy ship in breach of contract is liable for any losses caused by foreseeable difficulties at sea (*Smith, Hogg & Co Ltd v Black Sea and Baltic General Insurance Co Ltd* (1940)), but *not* if delay caused by his or her breach caused the ship to run into a typhoon; the delay is not of equal causal potency to the typhoon in causing the loss (*Monarch Steamship Co v Karlshamns Oljefabriker* (1949) at 215).

(iii) **Unreasonable acts of the claimant**: in *Lambert v Lewis* (1982), the claimant continued to use a trailer coupling after it broke. This severed the chain of causation between the defendant's breach (in supplying the defective coupling) and the loss claimed (for liability to persons injured when the coupling gave way). Damages were also denied in *Quinn v Burch Bros (Builders) Ltd* (1966) where the defendant employer's failure to supply a stepladder was held to be merely the 'occasion', and *not* the effective cause, of the employee's personal injury when the employee used and fell from an unstable unfooted trestle. Glidewell LJ (at 1374–5) said that the distinction between breach which (a) *caused* the loss and which (b) is merely the *occasion* for the loss depends on:

- the *likelihood* of the intervening cause;
- the *reasonableness* of the claimant's actions (*Galoo Ltd v Bright Grahame Murray* (1994)); and
- 'the application of the court's common sense'.

This uncertain formula blurs the issue of *intervening cause* with the issues of *contributory negligence* and *remoteness* of loss to which we turn.

13.2.5.4 Contributory negligence

At common law, a claimant whose negligence contributes to his or her own loss but does not break the chain of causation cannot have his or her damages reduced

(*Quinn v Burch Bros*). But can his or her damages be reduced under the Law Reform (Contributory Negligence) Act 1945? The answer, stated in **Vesta v Butcher** (1989), depends on the **nature of the contractual duty breached**.

✓ Where a *contractual duty of care* coexists with a *tortious duty of care* (so-called category 3 in the Law Commission's *Contributory Negligence as a Defence in Contract* (Law Com No 219, 1993), Parts III and IV) damages *are* reducible for contributory negligence where the claimant's action is: (i) for the tort of negligence (the Act explicitly permits this); or (ii) for breach of a concurrent contractual duty of care. For example, in *Trebor Bassett Holdings Ltd and the Cadbury UK Partnership v ADT Fire and Security plc* (2012) ADT supplied a tailor-made fire suppression system for TB's confectionery factory. ADT's breach caused a fire in the popcorn production area, which spread and destroyed the whole factory. The Court of Appeal upheld the finding that TB was contributorily liable for 75% of the loss because: it had negligently failed to segregate the production area from the rest of the building, failed to install sprinklers, and encouraged the spread of the fire upon its discovery by ejecting the entire load of burning popcorn and trying to stamp out the fire (this was held to be entirely predictable and did not break the chain of causation). ADT only undertook to exercise reasonable skill and care in the design of the system, not to guarantee the system's success.

✗ Where any *duty of care* is *purely contractual* (with no coexisting tortious duty of care; so-called category 2), damages cannot be reduced for the claimant's contributory negligence. A rare example is *Raflatac Ltd v Eade* (1999), where the acts of the defendant's subcontractor amounted to breach of the defendant's *contractual* duty of care but the defendant was not vicariously liable for the subcontractor's negligence. The Law Commission recommends that loss apportionment be extended to category 2 cases by analogy to category 3 cases, but this would make little practical difference given the rarity of category 2 cases.

✗ Where the *contractual obligation is strict* (so-called category 1), damages cannot be reduced for the claimant's contributory negligence. Most contractual obligations are strict: the defendant warrants the truth of something or guarantees a particular result irrespective of fault. In **Barclays Bank plc v Fairclough Building Ltd** (1994), a claim for £4 million damages for breach of a contract to remove asbestos from buildings was *not* reduced for the claimant's contributory negligence: the defendant had a strict duty to comply with the contract and not simply to take reasonable care. The Law Commission recommends *no change* here because:

- the parties' allocation of risk should be respected; and

- allowing loss apportionment in all three categories would transform currently straightforward cases into complex disputes about comparative blame, introducing intolerable uncertainty and hampering out-of-court settlements.

> ### ⏩ Counterpoint
>
> 1. Burrows supports a more radical extension of loss apportionment on the basis that the *proportionate approach* of contributory negligence is preferable to an *'all or nothing'* approach.[16] For example, in *Quinn v Burch Bros*, a fairer result would have been to reduce the employee's damages for its foolish use of unsafe equipment, rather than deny its claim altogether and shield the employer from all responsibility for its failure to provide safe equipment. The same may be concluded of a claimant who ruins expensive clothes by using a new iron on them, although the iron is clearly missing its heat dial and notice-ably defective in other respects.[17] The availability of contributory negligence has not prevented settlements in negligence cases. Moreover, uncertainty can be alleviated if the court makes clear that any reduction would be in 'steps', for example, in multiples of 25% rather than a complete spectrum between 0% and 100%.[18] Nevertheless, the concern not to undermine the parties' risk allocation in agreeing a strict contractual duty remains (although, arguably, it is already undermined by the rules on mitigation, time of assessment, and intervening causes).
>
> 2. The European Draft Common Frame of Reference stipulates that: '[t]he debtor is not liable for loss suffered by the creditor to the extent that the creditor contributed to the non-performance or its effects' (Art III.-3:704),

13.2.5.5 Speculative loss

The claimant must prove the extent of his or her loss. Problems arise when the law must quantify the claimant's loss of the *chance* of making a gain or avoiding a loss due to the breach.

(i) When is loss of a chance compensable?

✓ A claim will be excluded if it depends on very *remote* and hypothetical possibilities. For example, in *McRae v Commonwealth Disposals Commission* (1950), a salvor wasted money fruitlessly searching for the non-existent wreck of an oil tanker. His claim for the loss of profits expected from a successful salvage was dismissed as far too speculative, but damages were awarded for wasted expenses (see 13.1.3.3).

✓ Courts are not prevented from awarding damages just because there is an element of guesswork in the assessment. For example, in *Simpson v The London and North Western Railway Co* (1876), the defendant's breach prevented S from exhibiting his products at an agricultural show. S could claim loss of profits even though its quantification was difficult and speculative.

---

[16] A Burrows, 'Contributory Negligence in Contract: Ammunition for the Law Commission' (1993) 109 *LQR* 175.

[17] Law Commission, *Contributory Negligence as a Defence in Contract* (Working Paper No 114, 1990), para 2.9.

[18] A Burrows, 'Limitations on Compensation' in A Burrows and E Peel (eds), *Commercial Remedies* (OUP, 2003) 27, 43.

✓ In *Chaplin v Hicks* (1911), the defendant's breach of contract prevented the claimant from taking part in the final stage of a beauty contest where 12 of the 50 finalists (from 6,000 original entrants) would win places in a chorus line. The claimant was awarded damages for her loss of chance, assessed at 25% of winning the competition. However, *Chaplin v Hicks* 'does not offer a free pass to claims that the loss of practically any chance will be sufficient to found a claim to recoverable loss' (*BCCI v Ali (No 2)* at 113).

✓ *Allied Maples Group v Simmons & Simmons* (1995) confines damages for loss of a chance to cases where the causation of loss rests on the *hypothetical actions of a third party* (at 509–11). If there is a *substantial chance* (not merely a speculative one) that the third party would have acted to confer a benefit on or avoid a loss to the claimant, then the court can award a sum for the claimant's loss of a chance. In *Allied Maples v Simmons*, a solicitor's failure to warn his client about the potential liabilities of a company the client was acquiring meant that the latter did not try to negotiate a better deal with the seller. The court held that if the client could show, on the balance of probabilities, that: (i) they *would* have sought renegotiation with the third party; *and* (ii) they had a *substantial chance* of negotiating (it is unnecessary to prove that they *would* on balance of probabilities have negotiated) a better deal from the third party, then the court should quantify and award compensation for their loss of chance of doing so.

Confining damages for loss of chance to cases concerning the hypothetical actions of third parties *excludes* damages where the causation of loss:

✗ is a matter of *historical fact*; this category includes mostly tort cases where the defendant's negligence has reduced the claimant's chance of avoiding some physical disability (eg *Hotson v East Berkshire Area Health Authority* (1987) and *Wilsher v Essex Area Health Authority* (1988)); or

✗ rests on contingencies wholly within the *claimant's control* (eg *McWilliams v Sir William Arroll & Co Ltd* (1962), where the question is whether, had the employer provided the safety equipment, the claimant would have used it and avoided his loss). In these cases, loss must be determined on the *balance of probabilities*. However, such cases are better dealt with by proportional reduction for contributory negligence rather than wholesale denial.

(ii) How is loss of a chance quantified?

Quantification of the lost chance is necessarily speculative; it depends on the *value* of the expected benefit and the *likelihood* of the claimant actually getting it; 'the more the contingencies, the lower the value of the chance' (*Hall v Meyrick* (1957) at 471). The rigour with which the quantification issue is approached varies. In *Chaplin v Hicks*, the court seemed to proceed on the claimant's *statistical* chance of winning (as if she were a lottery player), perhaps to avoid assessing the claimant's 'merits' against any particular criteria of beauty. However, in *BCCI v Ali (No 2)*, where a former employee claimed that he could not get a new job because of the stigma of having worked for a failed bank known to have engaged in corrupt and dishonest practices, Lightman J refused to recognise any real or measurable loss of a chance of employment in the absence of *specific evidence* (eg the claimant's job application history and the claimant's suitability for specific jobs measured against the competition and the criteria of appointment) showing that the stigma attaching from the defendant employer's breach had *caused* the claimant *actual*, rather than hypothetical, loss (see 13.2.4.3). This shows the potential overlap between *causation* and the *measure* of loss.

13.2.5.6 Remoteness

The expectation measure would suggest that the claimant should be compensated for *all* provable losses flowing from the breach of contract, including physical injury, large-scale property damage, and anticipated profits from other transactions now disrupted by the breach (ie *all* the dominoes that fall, triggered by the initial breach). However, the law departs from this position (and so from the full protection of the innocent party's expectation interest) by relieving the defendant of liability of losses that are too 'remote' (only some of the falling dominoes 'count'). This means that losses genuinely sustained may be unrecoverable.

(i) The justifications for the remoteness limit

(i) It represents the liabilities that contract parties have undertaken responsibility for.

(ii) It alleviates the *potential harshness* of the expectation measure which may impose crushing liability on a defendant if it is imposed irrespective of the foreseeability of the loss, the disproportion between the contract price, and the size of the liability, and the contract-breaker's ability to bear or bargain around it. Wiles J illustrates such an unfair case: 'where a man going to be married to an heiress, his horse having cast a shoe on the journey, employed a blacksmith to replace it, who did the work so unskilfully that the horse was lamed, and, the rider not arriving in time, the lady married another; and the blacksmith was held liable for the loss of the marriage' (*The British Columbia & Vancouver Island Spar, Lumber and Saw Mill Co v Nettleship* (1868) at 508).

(iii) It encourages *efficient risk allocation*: if the claimant must disclose remote risks, the defendant has the opportunity to exclude or restrict liability for them or vary the contract price, and the claimant can insure appropriately.

(ii) The rule of remoteness

Baron Alderson (at 354) sets out the tests for remoteness in **Hadley v Baxendale** (1854). The defendant need not actively accept the risk of liability for particular losses; it is enough that he or she *knows* it is liable to result from their breach.[19] Recoverable loss is divided into two types:

(i) those 'arising naturally, that is, according to the *usual* course of things, from such breach of contract itself': knowledge of these losses is *imputed* to the defendant as a reasonable person even if he or she does not actually know it; and

(ii) 'such [loss] as may reasonably be supposed to have been *in the contemplation of both parties*, at the time they made the contract, as the probable result of the

---

[19] Confirmed in *GKN Centrax Gears Ltd v Matbro Ltd* (1976).

breach of it': the claimant must prove the defendant's *actual* knowledge of the special circumstances aggravating the claimant's loss.

These two rules are overlapping and not mutually exclusive, since what occurs naturally will almost always be in the contemplation of the parties. In **Victoria Laundry (Windsor) Ltd v Newman Industries Ltd** (1949), Asquith LJ said (at 539) that they express *the single principle* that the claimant can only recover such losses as were *reasonably contemplated* by the defendant, at the time of contracting, as liable to flow from the breach.

The Heron II (1969) clarified the following.

- *What must be foreseen?* The defendant is liable if, at the time of contracting, he or she 'contemplated as a serious possibility the type of consequence, not necessarily the specific consequence that ensued upon breach' (*Parsons (Livestock) v Uttley Ingham* at 813); that is, he or she is liable if he or she merely foresees the general *type*, even if he or she does not foresee the *extent*, of the loss.

- *How foreseeable must the loss be?* The required degree of foreseeability of the type of loss claimed is *higher in contract actions* (it must be a **'serious possibility'**, a 'real danger', or a 'very substantial' probability) than in *tort actions* (a *'slight possibility'* is enough) (*The Wagon Mound* (1961)). The same loss may be too remote in contract, but not in tort (see (iv)).

In sum, the remoteness test is that: loss is recoverable in contract if the defendant contemplated that *type* of loss as a *serious possibility* at the time of contracting, or *ought* reasonably to have done so.

(iii) The *Achilleas* modification

In **Transfield Shipping Inc v Mercator Shipping Inc (The Achilleas)** (2008), the charterers returned a vessel late in breach of contract, causing the owners to lose the profits on a lucrative follow-on charter. The owners were denied this loss of profits, although the arbitrators and the courts below found that the loss was clearly foreseeable under the first rule in *Hadley v Baxendale*. Lords Hoffmann and Hope (with the concurrence of Lord Walker) reasoned that it was too crude to rely solely on the foreseeability of the loss in question. The real question is what liability the defendant had assumed the risk for; that is, the contracting parties' *common intention* in respect of loss occasioned by relatively short delay in redelivery. Given the understanding in the shipping industry and the uniform dicta over many years in which judges said or assumed that the damages for late delivery were the difference between the charter rate and the market rate, this is the appropriate measure. The charterer could not reasonably be regarded as having assumed the risk of the owner's loss of greater profit on the following charter. Lord Rodger and Lady Hale also denied the owner's claim, but on the alternative basis that the loss was not foreseeable. This is unconvincing given the lower courts' finding that it *was* foreseeable.

In *Supershield Ltd v Siemens Building Technologies FE Ltd* (2010) Toulson LJ recognises that *The Achilleas* may not only result in narrower liability than the foreseeability test (as in *The Achilleas* itself), it may also yield wider liability (as in *Supershield* itself where the contract-breaker was held liable for a type of unforeseeable loss). Thus, 'the question of remoteness cannot be isolated from consideration of the purpose of the contract and the scope of the contractual obligation'.

> **Pause for reflection**
>
> 1. In *The Achilleas*, Lord Hoffmann sought to transplant the approach in *South Australia Asset Management Corp v York Montague Ltd* (1997). There the House of Lords decided that valuers were not liable for all the foreseeable consequences of their breach, but only for the consequences which they had assumed. Thus, recoverable loss was limited to the difference between the amount lent based on the negligent valuation and the amount that would have been lent if the correct value had been provided to the lender.
>
> 2. Lord Hoffmann criticises the foreseeability approach for being highly indeterminate and open to manipulation. However, his Lordship's own 'assumption of responsibility' approach can also be criticised for being: (i) too uncertain—there will usually be no direct evidence of the parties' intention as to liability and courts will inevitably have to rely on other criteria; (ii) unnecessary—this already happens under the rubric of foreseeability.

In *Sylvia Shipping Co Ltd v Progress Bulk Carriers Ltd* (2010), Hamben J did not see *The Achilleas* as heralding a new legal test of remoteness. The orthodox approach remains the standard rule. In most cases it will not be necessary for the court to consider the assumption of responsibility test because 'the fact that the type of loss arises in the ordinary course of things or out of special known circumstances will carry with it the necessary assumption of responsibility'. It is only in relatively rare and unusual cases that consideration of assumption of responsibility will be required. Namely, cases where the foreseeability test:

- leads or may lead to an unquantifiable, unpredictable, uncontrollable, or disproportionate liability; or
- would be contrary to market understanding and expectations.

In *John Grimes Partnership Ltd v Gubbins* (2013), Sir David Keene affirmed the emerging consensus that:

(i) Lord Hoffmann was not departing from the foreseeability test of remoteness, but merely rationalizing it on the basis of the parties' imputed intention in the ordinary case;

(ii) thus, the foreseeability test would not apply only if the circumstances showed that the parties could not have contracted on that basis.

In other words (at [24]):

Normally, there is an implied term accepting responsibility for the types of losses which can reasonably be foreseen at the time of contract to be not unlikely to result if the contract is broken. But if there is evidence in a particular case that the nature of the contract and the commercial background, or indeed other relevant special circumstances, render that implied assumption of responsibility inappropriate for a type of loss, then the contract-breaker escapes liability. Such was the case in *The Achilleas*.

(iv) Judicial discretion in applying the remoteness tests

Knowledge of the formal tests of remoteness (the verbal formulae) is only the starting point. Students must get a 'feel' for the way the test is *applied*. In particular, for the courts' considerable latitude in determining:

(i)   the type of loss that is *ordinarily* foreseeable to a *high degree*; and

(ii) the type of loss that is only foreseeable with *special knowledge* or disclosure to a high degree.

The remoteness limit can be reconciled with protection of the claimant's expectation interest by the reasoning that the claimant had no *real* expectation that the contract will protect him or her against such remote losses (Collins at 412–13). However, this simply begs the question 'why not?' Contract parties rarely contemplate breach, let alone the nature and extent of losses caused by breach. It is for the *court* to say what a *reasonable person* with the defendant's knowledge *should* have contemplated. In this way, the standard of the reasonable person may represent no more than the *court*'s conception of justice (*Davis Contractors Ltd v Fareham UDC* (1956) at 728). Thus, a finding that the loss was or was not reasonably foreseeable is really a statement of the *conclusion* reached and *not* the *reason* for the conclusion: the real reason must be sought elsewhere. The cases show that these include:

- whether the defendant was aware of the claimant's intended use for the subject matter of the contract;

- the defendant's opportunity and ability to negotiate around the risk (eg by increasing the price or restricting liability);

- the parties' relative abilities to estimate the extent of the risk and to provide for it;

- the defendant's expertise in the subject matter of the contract.

(v) Loss 'in the ordinary course of things': the first limb

✓ In **Victoria Laundry v Newman**, V purchased a boiler from N. N knew that V needed it for *immediate use* in V's laundry business. The boiler was delivered five months late. N was liable for V's loss of profits that it would *ordinarily* have made in this period, in view of the business relationship between the parties and N's expertise as qualified engineers.

✗ However, N was *not* liable for the loss of some *exceptionally profitable* government contracts due to N's delay because N knew nothing of them and could not be expected to foresee the loss.

✓ **Brown v KMR Services Ltd** (1995) approves the distinction made by *Victoria Laundry* between: (i) *ordinary* loss of profits and (ii) *exceptional* loss of profits (from particularly lucrative contracts) as different 'types' of loss, although it is arguable that (ii) is merely loss of the same type as (i) albeit to a greater extent. However, the case also illustrates the difficulty in making the distinction. B sought damages for K's negligence in failing to advise on the real risks of joining high-risk syndicates. K argued that the loss claimed was too remote because the run of major catastrophes was unprecedented and unforeseeable. This was rejected because the claim was only in respect of one *type* of loss, namely underwriting loss: this was entirely foreseeable and recoverable, although its *extent* was far greater than foreseen. Thus, courts can **increase the scope of recovery** under the first limb by emphasising that only the *broad type* of the loss suffered needs to be foreseen, and not the specific nature or extent of the loss or the exact way it arose.

✓ In *The Heron II* (1969), the claimant contracted for its sugar to be carried to Basrah for immediate sale on arrival. The sugar arrived nine days late, and the claimant was entitled to damages resulting from the fall in the market during the delay. Although the carrier did not know the claimant's intention, the court held that in view of its *past dealings* with the claimant, and its knowledge that there was a market for sugar at Basrah, 'if he had thought about the matter, he must have realised that at least it was not unlikely that the sugar would be sold in the market at market price on arrival' (at 382).

✓ In *Parsons (Livestock) v Uttley Ingham*, U supplied P with a defective hopper for storing pig food, the food became mouldy and 254 pigs died from a rare intestinal disease. The trial judge found that U could not have reasonably contemplated the serious possibility of mouldy pignuts causing such serious illness in pigs. Nevertheless, the Court of Appeal (at 813) allowed recovery because it was enough that U must have appreciated 'that food affected by bad storage conditions might well cause illness in the pigs fed upon it'. The claimant also recovered loss of profits on the dead pigs but not loss of future sales from rearing additional animals.

✓ In *Jackson v Royal Bank of Scotland* (2005), J imported dog biscuits from Thailand and sold them on to EB at a great profit. RBS disclosed to EB the extent of J's mark-up, in breach of its duty of confidence to J. EB thereafter bought directly from the Thai suppliers. J sought damages for the loss of repeat business from EB as loss arising from the normal course of things. The House of Lords held that 'loss of the chance or opportunity of repeat business should in principle be available, and that the issue in this case was for how long it was or should have been in the reasonable contemplation of the parties that the trading relationship would continue' at the time of formation (at [29]). Lord Walker quantified the loss at four further years at decreasing profit margins. Lord Hope stated (at [36]) that 'since the parties have the opportunity to limit their liability in damages . . . [i]f no cut-off point is provided by the contract, there is no arbitrary limit that can be set to the amount of damages once the test of remoteness according to one or other of the rules in *Hadley v Baxendale* has been satisfied'.

The courts can also **narrow the scope of recoverable loss** under the first limb by finding that the loss suffered was unforeseeable by the defendant, especially when his or her expertise and ability to meet potential liabilities is low.

✗ In *Hadley v Baxendale*, H's claim for loss of profits was denied where H sent a broken shaft from his mill with B, a carrier, to Greenwich to enable a new one to be copied. B's breach resulted in several days' stoppage in the mill. Although B knew what was being carried, that H were millers, and that the mill was stopped, the court (at 355) found the loss to be *outside* the first limb, since B was not specifically informed of the 'special circumstance' that he was carrying an article on which the operation of the entire mill depended (see also *Victoria Laundry v Newman* at 537), and B might reasonably think that H had a spare shaft or was able to get one or that other defects with the mill were stopping its current operation. Had he been so informed, B would have been able to limit his liability. It seems crucial to the denial of liability that, unlike the defendants in *The Heron II* and in *Victoria Laundry v Newman*, B was only a *general* carrier and so less able to foresee the effects of delay.

✗ The claim also failed in *Balfour Beatty Construction (Scotland) Ltd v Scottish Power plc* (1994) where disruptions in the S's supply of electricity to BB at a critical moment in BB's construction process meant that a significant part of the construction had to be demolished and rebuilt. Lord Jauncey (at 810) explains that remoteness depends on what the defendant can be taken to reasonably know of the other's activity:

> However, when the activity of A involves complicated construction or manufacturing techniques, I can see no reason why B who supplies a commodity that A intends to use in the course of those techniques should be assumed, and merely because of the order for the commodity, to be aware of the details of all the techniques undertaken by A and the effect thereupon of any failure of or deficiency in that commodity.

(vi) Exceptional loss: the second limb

The defendant who *knows* of *special circumstances*, which may increase the claimant's loss, is liable for it. The court can **increase the scope of recoverable loss under the second limb** by being more willing to *infer* the relevant knowledge from the circumstances.

✓ In *Simpson v London and North Western Railway* (1876), N transported S's sample of cattle food from the Bedford agricultural show to Newcastle for its agricultural show. The goods were marked 'must be at Newcastle by Monday certain', but did not arrive until the show was over. S was awarded the loss of profit which he would have made from the Newcastle show. Although S did not expressly refer to the show, the court was prepared to *infer* N's knowledge of this special circumstance because the contract was made with N's agent at the Bedford Showground, sent there specifically to attract such custom.

Conversely, the court may **narrow liability under the second limb** by increasing the specificity of the loss which must be foreseeable and finding such knowledge absent in the circumstances.

✗ In *Horne v Midland Railway Co* (1872), H had an urgent contract to deliver military shoes to London for the French army at an unusually high price. H sent them with M, giving notice that the shoes were 'under contract' and the date by which they had to arrive. The shoes arrived a day late and were rejected by the intending buyer; H resold them at a much lower price because demand had dropped due to the cessation of the war. H was denied the loss of profits from the lucrative contract ostensibly because H did not sufficiently disclose it. However, the dissenting view (at 144) that the loss claimed was *ordinary* and that, anyway, there *was* adequate notice under the second limb seems compelling: 'It is said that the defendants would not contemplate so large a loss from the notice that they received. If this notice be not sufficient it must be necessary in such a case to communicate the exact details of the contract. I cannot think this is so.'

Pause for reflection

The real reasons for denying the claim can be found in the court's reference (at 139) to: the defendant being a railway (ie a general carrier), the concern that it may be exposed to a flood of claims from customers, and the unfairness arising from the disproportion between the contract price and the potential contract liability. The US Second Restatement of Contracts, § 351(3), empowers courts to limit damages for foreseeable loss if justice so requires to avoid disproportionate compensation (ie an extreme disproportion between the price and the loss). The majority in *Horne v Midland Railway* achieved the same result by increasing the level of notice required of onerous or unusual potential liability. The same technique is used by courts to avoid binding a party to onerous and unusual terms contained in unsigned documents purporting to have contractual effect (ie by finding that the other party failed to satisfy the heightened requirement of notice, see 10.3.3.2).

The final example of the flexible application of the rules to achieve a just result is *Cory v Thames Ironworks & Shipbuilding Co Ltd* (1867) where TIS delivered the hull of a boat late. If it had been used as coal storage, as TIS believed, C would have sustained £420 of loss. However, it was intended for use in an innovative way, unknown to TIS, and C's actual loss was £4,000. This was held to be too remote, but the court awarded C £420, explaining that 'there can be no hardship or injustice in making the seller liable to compensate him in damages so far as the seller understood and believed that the article would be applied to the ordinary purposes to which it was capable of being applied' (at 190).

(vii) The test of remoteness where concurrent contract and tort actions exist
The Heron II requires a *higher* degree of foreseeability for recoverable loss *in contract actions* (the defendant must contemplate the type of loss as a *serious* possibility at the time of contracting) than in *tort actions* (only requiring contemplation of the type of loss as a *slight* possibility). Lord Reid justifies this on the basis that a claimant in the contractual context can protect him or herself by disclosure of unusual risks before contract formation (the defendant has the option of restricting liability for it and the claimant can insure), whilst the claimant in tort has no such opportunity. *However*, this distinction is inapt where the tortious duty

arises in the context of the parties' contractual relationship (see Scarman LJ in *Parsons (Livestock) v Uttley Ingham* (at 806–7)). The position is now stated by *Brown v KMR*: where the parties are in a contractual relationship, the *contract test applies* (requiring higher foreseeability or a stricter remoteness test) even where the claim is brought in tort.

Pause for reflection

1. In 'Remoteness of Damages in Contract and Tort Law: A Reconsideration' (1996) 55 *CLJ* 488, **Cartwright** explains that the foreseeability standard varies with the reason for imposing the duty or liability in the first place. Thus, where the duty is contractual or based on an 'assumption of responsibility' in tort, the question is the scope of the risks assumed by the defendant. In respect of tortious liability for physical injury, it is inappropriate to ask what liability the defendant has assumed, and compensating the claimant takes on more prominence.

2. The European Draft Common Frame of Reference shifts the inquiry to the *quality of the defendant's breach*. The foreseeability test limits recoverable loss 'unless the non-performance was intentional, reckless or grossly negligent' (Art III-3:703). An analogy can be drawn with misrepresentation where the remoteness limit is lifted in the case of fraud (see 5.2.1.2). This focus on *fault* can be justified. It is contract law's role to uphold the claimant's expectation; to the extent that the remoteness qualification aims to avoid harsh outcomes to the contract-breaker, it is much less compelling where the contract-breaker causes the loss deliberately or with gross negligence.

13.2.5.7 Time limit

The law discourages stale claims, because, as time passes, it becomes increasingly difficult for a defendant to produce the evidence to defend him or herself. The law draws a line beyond which a claimant cannot seek a remedy from the courts.

- Sections 5 and 8 of the Limitation Act 1980 provide that an action founded on a simple **contract** must be brought within **six years**, and one founded on a deed within 12 years from the date the cause of action accrued.

- The cause of action accrues in contract *when the breach occurs*, or when the claimant elects to terminate the contract for an anticipatory breach. In contrast, the cause of action accrues in tort when the damage is suffered, and in unjust enrichment when the defendant is unjustly enriched.

- Time runs even if the claimant was unaware or could not have been aware of the existence of his or her cause of action until after the time limit has expired. But where the claimant's action is based on *fraud* or *mistake*, or where the defendant has deliberately *concealed* facts relevant to the claimant's right of action, time only starts to run when the claimant *discovers* the fraud, concealment, or mistake, or could have done so with reasonable diligence (Limitation Act 1980, s 32).

However, this cannot prejudice the rights of third parties taking bona fide and for value.

- Claims in **equity** or for equitable remedies to which the Limitation Act does not apply are subject to the doctrine of laches (*Lindsay Petroleum Co v Hurd* (1874)). Thus, delay may bar equitable remedies such as rescission, rectification, specific performance, or injunction. The delay necessary to make it unjust to allow a claim to be brought must be judged against the particular circumstances of the case. This may be shorter or longer than the statutory limitation of six years (see 5.3.2.3).

13.3 **Restitution of benefits conferred**

The claimant will prefer to recover the benefit he or she conferred on the defendant under the contract where:

- his or her expectation and reliance losses are *too speculative* to quantify;
- the *benefit* conferred is substantially the claimant's whole *loss*; or
- the claimant has made a *bad bargain*.

However, restitution is only available for **total failure of consideration**. This occurs when the defendant has performed nothing of his or her contractual obligation (consideration). For example, if you pay me £200 for a bicycle worth only £100 but I fail to deliver, you are better off getting your money back than seeking expectation damages (£100).

13.3.1 **The contract must be terminated**

In general, restitution is only available if the contract has been terminated for breach (*Kwei Tek Chao v British Traders and Shippers Ltd* (1954)). The defendant's enrichment is justified by the contract until the contract ceases to govern the parties' rights and remedies; only then does the enrichment become 'unjust' and liable for return. However, if, exceptionally, the contract does not govern the benefit transferred, restitution can be awarded without termination of the contract since it would not undermine the contractual valuation and risk allocation (*Roxborough v Rothmans of Pall Mall Australia Ltd* (2001)).[20] Restitution cannot be claimed in addition to expectation damages if this would amount to double recovery (*Rogers v Parish (Scarborough) Ltd* (1987)): you cannot get back X (restitution) and claim what you gave X in order to get expectation.

---

[20] The part of the contract price understood by the parties to be payable as tax by the seller was held to be returnable when the tax turned out to be illegal because the contract did not provide for this eventuality: the basis for the payment had failed. See J Beatson and G Virgo, 'Contract, Unjust Enrichment and Unconscionability' (2002) 118 *LQR* 352.

> **Pause for reflection**
>
> Three related reasons can be put forward for allowing an innocent party to 'go backwards' by claiming restitution (and perhaps avoiding a bad bargain) once a contract is terminated when the contractual response characteristically projects the parties 'forwards'.
>
> 1. *The contract reason*: a contract is *two-sided*; the *purpose* of each party is to get the other party's reciprocal performance. Each party's undertaking is generally *conditional* on the other's *substantial* performance ('I will if you will'). Where one party does not substantially perform, the other party should be able to choose whether to go 'forwards' (claiming expectation damages) or 'backwards' (claiming restitution). In particular, the innocent party should not be forced to go forwards if it requires him or her to pay for performance that he or she does not get. The defendant should not be enriched by his or her own breach. The idea that 'you can't get something for nothing' is a contractual principle.
>
> 2. *The unjust enrichment reason*: failure of consideration is an *independent* cause of action in the law of unjust enrichment and should be available irrespective of the contract. The problem is that 'failure of consideration' and the bindingness of a contract address the same question (ie whether the *transfer of benefits* is justified) but point in opposite directions. A claimant's payment cannot simultaneously be justified by a valid contract *and* liable to be returned as an unjust enrichment. The contractual regime takes priority because the parties' autonomy should be respected. Thus, contracts must generally be set aside (terminated, rescinded, discharged, or rendered unenforceable) before restitution can be claimed.
>
> 3. *The pragmatic reason*: it is less objectionable to ignore the contractual allocation of risk and permit escape from bad bargains if the defendant has not even commenced performance. Moreover, restitution for *total* failure of consideration avoids quantification difficulties.

13.3.2 **Total failure of consideration in money claims**

Traditionally, a claimant can only recover *money* if there has been a *total* failure of consideration in the sense that he or she has received *nothing of* the performance they contracted for. Receipt of benefit does not bar recovery if it is not 'what was contracted for' on a proper construction of the contract (*Rowland v Divall* (1923)).

> **Pause for reflection**
>
> The requirement that the failure of consideration must be *total* is:
>
> 1. *Unfair*: a defendant may also be unjustly enriched where failure of consideration is only partial.
>
> 2. *Unnecessary*: if the real concern is that it is unfair to require the defendant to give back everything when he or she has conferred some benefit on the claimant, a set-off can be allowed. However, this does raise the difficulty of valuing *non-monetary partial* performances;
>
> ➡

➡

3. *subject to exceptions*:

- the Law Reform (Frustrated Contracts) Act 1943 (see 7.6) allows recovery (for money or non-money performance) even if the claimant has received some counter-performance before the frustrating event, although allowance must be made for this in calculating the restitution;

- recovery is allowed where mutual performances consist of money payments. In *Goss v Chilcott* (1996), G lent C $30,000 but the contract turned out to be unenforceable. G could recover the sum although C had paid two instalments of interest;

- non-money claims (see 13.3.3), if analysed in terms of failure of consideration, have never required the failure to be total, although valuation difficulties abound;

- in *Attorney-General v Blake* (2000), Lord Nicholls (at 639) suggests 'a part refund' for cases of partial failure of consideration. Where 'the defendant fails to provide the full extent of services he has contracted to provide, he should be liable to pay back the amount of expenditure he saved by the breach'.[21] Similarly, in *Birse Construction v Eastern Telegraph* (2004), Lloyd J (at [53]) said that 'in some cases it may be reasonable (or even proportionate) to award an amount so that the contractor does not get paid for what was not done';

- recent amendments to the Sale of Goods Act 1979 (s 48C) provide for *price reduction* or rescission in respect of non-conforming goods in consumer contracts (see 14.2.1.2).

4. On termination, the **European Draft Common Frame of Reference** requires mutual restitution of the benefits received, either in specie or in money's worth, *except* to the extent that 'conforming performance by one party has been met by conforming performance by the other' (Arts III.-3:510 and III.-3:511).

13.3.3 **The innocent party's claim for restitution of *non-monetary* benefits**

A party who has *completed* his or her non-monetary performance can sue for their expectation, the 'agreed price'. If he or she has *partially* performed before terminating the contract for breach, they can claim:

- a *quantum valebat* (the reasonable value of the goods supplied); or
- a *quantum meruit* (the reasonable charge for the services supplied).

For example, in *de Bernardy v Harding* (1853), H failed to pay dB for arranging the sale of tickets to see the Duke of Wellington's funeral procession. Alderson B recognised dB's right to sue for breach or to terminate, and sue on a *quantum meruit* for the work actually done. A difficult case is *Planché v Colburn* (1831) where P agreed to write a book for a series published by C, for £100. After P had done much work, C abandoned the project. P was awarded £50 *quantum meruit*, although he never handed over any of his work and could not be said to have conferred any meaningful benefit on the defendant.

---

[21] See the same idea in H Beale, 'Damages for Poor Service' (1996) 112 *LQR* 205 discussing *White Arrow Express Ltd v Lamey's Distribution Ltd* (1995).

13.3.4 The *contract-breaker*'s restitutionary claim

In principle, the contract-breaker should also be able to claim for failure of consideration to recover *money* paid under the contract once it is terminated (subject to the other party's expectation loss, if any). There are authorities supporting this position although English law has not adopted this reasoning. In *Dies v British and Intl Mining and Finance Co Ltd* (1939), D made an advance part-payment for ammunition but breached by refusing to accept delivery. D was allowed to recover his payment subject to B's damages claim (see also *Rover Intl Ltd v Cannon Film Sales Ltd (No 3)* (1989)).

It is arguable that the contract-breaker should also be able to recover *non-money* benefits for failure of consideration. However, courts have denied contract-breakers' *quantum meruit* or *quantum valebat* claims (see *Sumpter v Hedges* (1898)). Support for restitution of non-money benefits to contract-breakers has been given by the Law Commission (*Pecuniary Restitution on Breach of Contract* (Law Com No 121, 1983)) and by dicta in two House of Lords cases. In *Hain SS Co Ltd v Tate and Lyle Ltd* (1936), Lord Wright (at 612) said that a court should award a reasonable remuneration if a 'steamer carrying a cargo of frozen meat from Australia to England deviates by calling at a port outside the usual or permitted route' but the cargo is duly delivered with only a trifling delay, even if the contract can be and is terminated. In *Miles v Wakefield Metropolitan DC* (1987), Lords Templeman and Brightman took the view that employees who take industrial action by a 'go slow' are not entitled to wages, but should be allowed a *quantum meruit* for the reduced work done.

13.3.5 How much can be claimed?

Restitution is a type of reliance loss but since it excludes losses that do not end up as enrichment in the defendant's hands, restitution can be claimed alongside reliance if it does not amount to double recovery. However, restitution cannot be combined with a claim for expectation damages since this *would* amount to double recovery (*Rogers v Parish*).

Unlike claims for reliance damages on breach, claims for restitution on total failure of consideration *can* allow claimants to escape from bad bargains.

- In *Bush v Canfield* (1818), B paid a $5,000 deposit on an agreement to buy wheat at $7 a barrel. When C failed to deliver, B was allowed to recover his deposit although the market price had fallen to $5.50 a barrel.

- Claimants for the restitution of *non-money performance* can even claim more than would have been due under the contract. In *Boomer v Muir* (1933), M's breach entitled B to quit his work and recover $250,000 as the reasonable value of his work, although only $20,000 was due under the contract.

> **▶◀ Counterpoint**
>
> A distinction should be made between money and non-money claims for restitution. Allowing the claimant to circumvent a bad bargain by making the contract-breaker *return* the claimant's *payment* is arguably quite different from making the contract-breaker *pay* ➔

➔ *for* the claimant's non-money performance where the market value exceeds the contract rate originally agreed. Money *is* the measure of value conferred on the defendant, but the value of non-money performance *to the defendant* is the *contract* valuation agreed. Contract damages are determined by reference to the valuation contained in the contract even if the contract is terminated. Hence, the contract valuation should also act as a *ceiling* limiting any restitutionary claim. Consistently, Goff J supports *a pro rata contract rate* approach in the context of non-money claims on frustration (*BP v Hunt (No 2)* (1979), see 7.6.4.2).

13.4 **Account of profits and loss of bargain**

13.4.1 **The general rule and two exceptions**

The orthodox position is that damages for the wrong of breach of contract *cannot* be measured by:

- the defendant's *gains* (eg by making a larger profit from transferring his or her performance to a third party, see *Teacher v Calder* (1899)); or
- the defendant's *savings* (eg by incomplete or defective performance, see *Tito v Waddell (No 2)* (1977)).

This is subject to two exceptions.

(i) Where a breach of contract *also* involves a **breach of confidence or of fiduciary duty** the defendant must account for *all of their profits* to the claimant. For example, a defendant who accepts a bribe in breach of his or her contract of employment must hand over the bribe to his or her employer (*Reading v Attorney-General* (1951)) and a defendant who sells land he or she has already sold to the claimant must hand over its proceeds to the claimant (*Lake v Bayliss* (1974)).

(ii) Where breach of contract *also* involves the **use of or interference with the claimant's proprietary rights**, whether by trespass (*Penarth Dock Engineering Co Ltd v Pounds* (1963)), wrongful detention of goods (*Strand Electric and Engineering Co Ltd v Brisford Entertainments Ltd* (1952)), or breach of a restrictive covenant attaching to land (*Wrotham Park Estate Co Ltd v Parkside Homes Ltd* (1974)), the defendant is required to pay a *reasonable fee* for the use of, or interference with, the claimant's proprietary right, even if no loss is caused to the claimant's property. This award is now interpreted as *compensatory*, as the sum that the claimant might have demanded for the defendant's interference with his or her proprietary right.[22] In **Wrotham Park Estate**, W sold land to P, developers who made additional profits by building in excess of the restrictive covenant contained in the contract. W's application for an injunction to undo the breach was denied for social and economic reasons, but damages were awarded in lieu assessed at 5% of P's estimated profits.

[22] R Sharpe and S Waddams, 'Damages for Lost Opportunity to Bargain' (1982) 2 *OJLS* 290.

However, in *Attorney-General v Blake* (2000) the House of Lords awarded an account of profits for a simple breach of contract (not involving (i) or (ii) above).

13.4.2 *Attorney-General v Blake*: account of profits

In *Blake*, a double secret agent made profits from publishing his autobiography in breach of his contract of secrecy with the Crown and in breach of the criminal law. The House of Lords awarded the Crown an account of profits for breach of contract to meet the demands of 'practical justice' in the 'exceptional circumstances' of the case.

Their Lordships said that settled expectations in the commercial or consumer world would be undisturbed and that the majority of cases would remain unaffected. It is not enough for the claimant to show that the defendant's breach was cynical or deliberate, or that the breach enabled the defendant to enter into a more profitable contract. Their Lordships emphasised the *exceptional* nature of this award, adding (at 639) that it should only be available when:

(i) the ordinary remedies for breach of contract are 'inadequate';

(ii) the claimant has 'a legitimate interest in preventing the defendant's profit-making activity and, hence, in depriving him of his profit'; and

(iii) the award is consonant with the demands of 'practical justice'.

Courts must take a *'case by case' approach*, having 'regard to all the circumstances, including the subject matter of the contract, the purpose of the contractual provision which has been breached, the circumstances in which the breach occurred, the consequences of the breach and the circumstances in which relief is being sought'.

On the unusual facts of **Blake**, it was held that the Crown had a **legitimate interest** (in preventing its security and intelligence employees from profiting by disclosing information that they would not have obtained except by undertaking secrecy) to protect the operation of the secret services. An account of profits was awarded.

13.4.3 Relationship between *Blake* and *Wrotham Park* damages

Blake relied on the authority of *Wrotham Park* as a 'shining beacon'. The problem is that *Wrotham Park* only awarded 5% of the profit made and was clearly not a case of disgorgement of the whole profit as in *Blake*. Nevertheless, in *WWF*, Chadwick LJ said that while the two remedies 'may differ in degree', they have the same underlying feature; namely, as flexible responses to circumstances where the claimant cannot demonstrate identifiable financial loss (at [59]). However, the suggestion that the remedy of **account of profits** in *Blake* is compensatory is controversial. It could be said to deprives the expression 'compensatory damages' of any sensible meaning, since the remedy is assessed by reference to the defendant's gain, rather than the claimant's loss, from the breach.

In *Pell Frischmann Engineering Ltd v Bow Valley and PT Bakrie Interinvestindo* (2009), Lord Walker, giving the opinion of the Privy Council, implicitly regards the two remedies as distinct, noting (at [48]) that the authorities 'are not completely consistent among themselves (especially as to the circumstances in which the court will award an account of profits . . .)'. In *Vercoe v Rutland Fund Management Ltd* (2010), Sales J also appears to regard the two measures as distinct. He explains (at [340]) that where the claimant's rights are of a 'particularly powerful kind and his interest in full perfor-mance is recognised as being particularly strong', the claimant may well be 'entitled to a choice of remedy' as between damages, an account of profits, and a notional reasonable agreement to buy release from his rights. Further, '[t]he law will control the choice between these remedies, having regard to the need to strike a fair balance between the interests of the parties at the remedial stage, rather than leaving it to the discretion of the claimant' (at [341]).

- An **account of profits** may be more appropriate 'where the right in question is of a kind where it would never be reasonable to expect that it could be bought out for some reasonable fee, so that it is accordingly deserving of a particularly high level of protection' (at [340]).

- A **reasonable buy-out fee** will be more appropriate where 'one is not dealing with infringement of a right which is clearly proprietary in nature', such as intellectual property, and 'there is nothing exceptional to indicate that the defendant should never have been entitled to adopt a commercial approach in deciding how to behave in relation to that right'.

The outcome in *Pell Frischmann* further supports the distinctiveness of the two measures. There, P had 'pre-qualified' status to bid for a contract with N, an oil company, to develop an oil field. The defendants later entered into confidentiality agreements with P and agreed to work exclusively with P in a consortium to under-take the project. In breach of contract, the defendants entered a contract with N without P's consent. The Privy Council awarded P $US2.5 million as *Wrotham Park* damages although the defendants' actual profit was much *less* (between $1 million and $1.8 million) because the parties' negotiations prior to its breakdown showed that they had expected the contract with N to be much more profitable than it turned out to be. On this view, *Wrotham Park* damages is compensatory and not simply an award of partial disgorgement along a single spectrum ending with the total disgorgement in *Blake*.

Lord Walker explained (at [48]–[49]) that *Wrotham Park* damages (called 'negoti-ating damages' by Neuberger LJ in *Lunn Poly Ltd v Liverpool & Lancashire Properties Ltd* [2006] at [22]) represent such a sum of money as might reasonably have been demanded by the claimant from the defendant as a quid pro quo for permitting the continuation of the breach of covenant or other invasion of right. Both parties are to be assumed to act reasonably: 'It is a negotiation between a willing buyer (the contract-breaker) and a willing seller (the party claiming damages) . . . The fact that one or both parties would in practice have refused to make a deal is therefore to be ignored'. In *Vercoe v Rutland*, Sales J lists three relevant factors in determining the price of release (at [292]):

- the likely parameters of realistic commercial acceptability assessed on an objec-tive basis with reference to each party's position;

- any additional factors particularly affecting the just balance between the compet-ing interests of the parties, such as the claimant's delay;

- the court's overriding obligation to ensure that the award does not provide relief out of proportion to the real extent of the claimant's interest in proper performance judged on an objective basis.

In *Lane v O'Brien Homes Ltd* (2004), Clarke J said (at [30]), that the calculation 'is not a precise mathematical process'; 'at the end of the day the deal has to feel right . . . [the questions raised are] matters of judgment which are incapable of strict rational and logical exposition from beginning to end'. For example, in ***Experience Hendrix LLC v PPX Enterprises*** (2003), the defendant repeatedly and deliberately breached a settlement agreement on the royalties payable for the use of licensed material belonging to Jimi Hendrix's estate. It was impossible to quantify the claimant's financial loss from the breach. The court (at 843, 848) stressed the *commercial* nature of the contract: it did not involve anything as sensitive as the national security in *Blake*. The defendant would only be required to pay a ***reasonable sum*** assessed by reference to what the claimant could reasonably have demanded for use of the material. This was awarded in *addition* to an injunction against future infringements.

🧑 Pause for reflection

1. The compensatory analysis of the *Wrotham Park* remedy has been criticised as fictional where the claimant would not have contemplated selling the right to breach the contract, as in *Blake* itself. However, it is no different from many cases where compensation is awarded (eg for personal injury) where there is no question of the claimant permitting the defendant's breach.

2. Alternatively, Beatson explains this award as *restitutionary* in the *subtractive* (as opposed to the gain-stripping) sense of being *derived from* the claimant's dominium (although there is no diminution of the claimant's wealth).[23] Similarly, Edelman[24] interprets *Wrotham Park* awards as 'damages which reverse wrongful transfers of wealth from a claimant by subtracting the objective benefit received by the defendant' and believes they should be widely available. In contrast, he sees an account of profits as appropriate only when compensatory damages provide *inadequate deterrence* (consistent with *WWF*).

13.4.4 **How much should be awarded?**

There remains little consistency of approach to the issue of quantification. The best that can be said is that courts demonstrate considerable remedial flexibility. For example:

- in *Attorney-General v Blake*, Lord Nicholls (at 637) praised *Wrotham Park v Parkside Homes* without explaining why only **5%** of the profit was recoverable there,

---

[23] J Beatson, *The Use and Abuse of Unjust Enrichment: Essays on the Law of Restitution* (Clarendon Press, 1991) 206–43.

[24] J Edelman, *Gain-Based Damages: Contract, Tort, Equity and Intellectual Property* (Hart Publishing, 2002) 68, 83–5.

whilst recovery of the *whole* profit **100%** was deemed appropriate in *Blake* itself. The matter of quantum is left to the courts for determination according to the demands of 'practical justice';

- in *Esso v Niad* (2001), E sold discounted petrol to N, a petrol retailer, and N agreed to on-sell petrol at the price E stipulated. When N repeatedly charged more than the stipulated price, E was *awarded* N's excess profit; that is, **100%** of N's gain;

- in contrast, in *The Sine Nomine* (2002), charterers were *denied* any of the profits made by the owners who wrongfully diverted the vessel for more profitable use elsewhere. The arbitrators refused to strip the contract-breaker of its gains 'where both parties are dealing with a marketable commodity—the services of the ship in this case—for which a substitute can be found in the marketplace'. The arbitrator said (at 805) that 'the commercial law of this country should not make moral judgments, or seek to punish the contract-breakers';

- in *Lane v O'Brien Homes Ltd* (2004), L sold land to O for a housing development limited to the building three houses, but O built four houses in breach of contract. The award of £150,000 represents a sizeable share of the builder's profit (**30–50%**, depending on the cost of construction). Clarke J said that the calculation 'is not a precise mathematical process'; 'at the end of the day the deal has to feel right . . . [the questions raised are] matters of judgment which are incapable of strict rational and logical exposition from beginning to end' (at [30]);

- in **Experience Hendrix LLC v PPX Enterprises** (2003), the defendant repeatedly and deliberately breached a settlement agreement on the royalties payable for the use of licensed material belonging to Jimi Hendrix's estate. It was impossible to quantify the claimant's financial loss from the breach. The court (at 843, 848) stressed the *commercial* nature of the contract breached: it did not involve anything as sensitive as the national security in *Blake*. The defendant would only be required to pay a **reasonable sum** assessed by reference to what the claimant could reasonably have demanded for use of the material. This was awarded in *addition* to an injunction against future infringements;

- in *Pell Frischmann Engineering Ltd* (see the previous section), the Privy Council awarded P $US2.5 million in damages although the defendants' actual profit was between $1 million and $1.8 million.

13.4.5 **Why an account of profits?**

The uncertainty in quantification of damages measured by the defendant's gains from breach reflects the instability of its juristic basis. The main justification for awarding account of profits for breach of contract, stated in *Blake*, is the inadequacy of traditional remedies for breach. Contractual remedies may be inadequate because they do not adequately deter or punish the defendant's breach. This was identified by Lord Hobhouse (at 653) dissenting, as the primary motivation behind the majority's decision in *Blake*: 'the policy which is being enforced is that which requires Blake to be punished by depriving him of any benefit from anything connected with his past deplorable criminal conduct'. The public would be outraged if Blake were to receive his money.

▶◀ Counterpoint

A deterrence justification is problematic.

1. It contradicts the traditional *rejection of punishment* as a proper aim of contract law (hence no punitive damages are available).

2. It is unclear what *degree of moral blameworthiness* is required if the mere fact of the defendant's breach being cynical or deliberate is not enough.

3. A gains-based award bears no necessary *correlation* to the defendant's blameworthiness: it is only available *if* the defendant's breach generates a gain *and* when other remedies are inadequate.

The second justification for allowing an account of profits for breach of contract is the inadequacy of contract remedies to protect claimants. In *WWF (Nature) v WWF (Entertainment)* the Court of Appeal (at [58]) referred to Lord Nicholls' statement in *Blake* that 'the plaintiff's interest in performance may make it just and equitable that the defendant should retain no benefit from his breach of contract'.

▶◀ Counterpoint

In 'Restitutionary Damages for Breach of Contract' (1998) 114 *LQR* 363, I argue the following.

1. *Blake* is a questionable example of inadequate remedy. The Crown had a perfectly effective remedy: it knew about the breach and could have applied for an injunction to restrain publication; it merely failed to act until it realised the extent of Blake's potential profit. Moreover, it is hard to see what loss the Crown suffered from disclosures which were no longer secret.

2. The case creates an irrational picture of two quite *distinct* measures of money awards aimed at the *same* goal of protecting the claimant's expectation interest.

3. A gain-based measure bears *no correlation* to the claimant's interest and it is only available *if* gains are actually made from breach.

4. The availability of a gain-based remedy undermines the balance currently struck between conflicting policies. You cannot simultaneously (i) avoid waste, over-compensation, and harshness to the defendant (and so deny specific performance or the cost of cure) *and* (ii) protect the claimant's expectation interest (by stripping the defendant of his or her savings from not performing).

➡

13.4.6 **Protection of the performance interest**

Gain-based awards indirectly protect the claimant's performance interest by removing the defendant's profit-making incentive for breach. That being so, they inform the larger question of the extent to which contract law protects the claimant's right to performance over and above his or her right to the *fruits* of performance. In *Blake*, Lord Nicholls (at 637) sought to equate contract rights with property rights, which traditionally allow gains-based remedies. He adopts Smith's argument[25] that contractual rights should be protected as strongly against expropriation by the defendant, but he does not take this to its logical conclusion of allowing gain-based awards for every breach: they are only available for very *exceptional* breaches.

 Pause for reflection

1. If the concern in *Blake* is the inadequacies of contract remedies to vindicate the *claimant's loss*, the logical response is to address this *directly* (eg by increasing the recognition and measure of awards for non-pecuniary losses and, where appropriate, by increasing the availability of specific enforcement or cost of cure awards). It seems distinctly odd to allow a claimant to switch to a claim measured by the wholly unrelated *gains* of the *defendant*.

2. As a matter of policy, contract law has simply not valued contract rights as highly as proprietary rights. The choice is reflected in and reinforced by many features of contract law which are inconsistent with the protection of the claimant's performance interest. For example:

   (i)   no *punitive damages*;

   (ii) the severe limits on the availability of *specific performance* (see 14.2);

   (iii) *limits on the expectation measure* of damages (see 13.2.3–13.2.5);

   (iv) *restrictions on the right to affirm the* contract on anticipatory breach (see 12.3); and

   (v)   control of agreed damages clauses by the penalty rule (see 14.3.2).

3. These restrictions manifest the *balance* that contract law has struck between its commitment to the protection of the performance interest and the concerns:

   (i)   not to *deter contracting* by allowing remedies which are 'unnecessarily' oppressive to the contract-breaker;

   (ii) to *avoid waste*; and

   (iii) not to stifle wealth-creating economic activity.

The same policies should also inhibit the availability of gains-based awards.

---

[25] L Smith, 'Disgorgement of Profits of Contract: Property, Contract and "Efficient Breach"' (1995) 24 *Can BLJ* 121.

THIS CHAPTER IN ESSENCE

**online
resource
centre**

The key areas and core topics in this chapter are summarised in an easy-to-use list, ideal for revision purposes, on the Online Resource Centre at http://www.oxfordtextbooks.co.uk/orc/chenwishart5e/. Links to websites relevant to the topics covered and any updates to the chapter can also be found on the Online Resource Centre.

QUESTIONS

1 Where contract law awards reliance damages, restitution, or account of profits for breach of contract, to what extent, if any, is the protection of the performance interest undermined?

2 'Monetary awards for breach of contract should do no more, and no less, than compensate the innocent party for their loss.' To what extent is this true? To what extent should it be true? What other considerations, if any, affect the selection of remedies for breach?

3 'Contract law recognises non-pecuniary loss reluctantly and only within narrow confines.' Discuss.

4 Ken employed Lou to install a new kitchen and add an extension to the living room: he paid Lou £30,000 on completion. Advise Ken on the following facts:

(a) Ken is very annoyed to find that the plasterwork in the extension has been painted a slightly different shade from that stipulated. Ken has rejected Lou's offer to redo the plasterwork for an extra £3,000, and hired Milo to redo the plasterwork for £6,000.

(b) Completion is delayed, necessitating Ken and his family staying an extra month with Ken's in-laws in very cramped accommodation which caused great discomfort and distress all around. Moreover, the delay meant that Ken had to pay £500 for an alternative venue for his friend's wedding, which Ken had offered to hold at his house.

(c) After a few weeks, Lou's faulty wiring in the kitchen caused small sparks which ignited a gas leak that Ken had been meaning to fix for some time. The ensuing fire resulted in £15,000 worth of damage to the kitchen.

(d) What difference would it make if Ken has not yet paid?

5 Bugbusters won a major contract to clean 40 hospitals undertaking to meet ten specified targets. Bugbusters instructed its workers to meet only six of the targets, saving £30,000 over six months. The hospitals are outraged when they learn of the breach, but it is impossible to prove whether any additional infections have resulted. Advise the hospitals.

For hints on how to answer these questions, please see the Online Resource Centre at http://www.oxfordtextbooks.co.uk/orc/chenwishart5e/

KEY FURTHER READING

See generally, Burrows, A (2004), *Remedies for Torts and Breach of Contract* (3rd edn, OUP).

Bridge, M (1989), 'Mitigation of Damages in Contract and the Meaning of Avoidable Loss', 105 *LQR* 398.

Burrows, A (2003), 'Limitations on Compensation' in A Burrows and E Peel (eds), *Commercial Remedies* (OUP) 27–43.

Coote, B (1997), 'Contract Damages, *Ruxley* and the Performance Interest', 56 *CLJ* 537.

Coote, B (2001), 'The Performance Interest, *Panatown*, and the Problem of Loss', 117 *LQR* 81.

Friedmann, D (1995), 'The Performance Interest in Contract Damages', 111 *LQR* 628.

Fuller, L, and Perdue, W (1937), 'The Reliance Interest in Contract Damages', 46 *Yale LJ* 52.

Lord Hoffmann (2010), '*The Achilleas*: Custom and Practice or Foreseeability?', 14 *Edinburgh LR* 47.

Law Commission (1997), *Aggravated, Exemplary and Restitutionary Damages* (Law Com No 247, HC 346).

McKendrick, E (2003), 'Breach of Contract, Restitution for Wrongs and Punishment' in A Burrows and E Peel (eds), *Commercial Remedies* (OUP) 93.

Pearce, D, and Halson, R (2008), 'Damages for Breach of Contract: Compensation, Restitution and Vindication', 28 *OJLS* 73.

Rowan, S (2010), 'Reflections on the Introduction of Punitive Damages for Breach of Contract', 30 *OJLS* 495.

Webb, C (2006), 'Performance and Compensation: An Analysis of Contract Damages and Contractual Obligation', 26 *OJLS* 41.

Wee, P C K (2010), 'Contractual Interpretation and Remoteness', *LMCLQ* 150.

14

Specific and agreed remedies

'I want you to do what you undertook in the contract'

Protection of an *innocent party*'s ('the claimant') performance interest is evident in awards of damages to fulfil his or her expectation, or so it is often assumed. But the most obvious way of protecting a claimant's performance interest is to make the defendant perform his or her contractual obligations (although this will usually be later than originally specified). Specific performance is the most effective way of avoiding the risk of under-compensation via the operation of doctrines such as remoteness and mitigation that limit the award of damages. The parties may have agreed to pay money, or to do (or not do) something other than paying money; these are *primary* obligations (what the parties undertook to do) under the contract. In addition, the parties may also have expressly agreed on how any breach should be remedied (eg to pay a stipulated sum or to forfeit money already paid); these are *secondary* terms; they are the agreed *remedies* for breach of the primary obligations. The terminology of primary and secondary obligations is used in *Photo Production Ltd v Securicor Transport Ltd* (1980).

We will see that courts are very willing to award orders compelling the defendant to pay the agreed price. In contrast, orders compelling non-monetary performance (for specific performance or injunctions) are rarely given; many 'bars' obstruct such awards. In this sense, they are regarded as secondary or supplementary remedies granted at the court's *discretion*, with damages being the primary remedy. In addition, courts exercise significant although inconsistent control over the parties' agreed remedies. The questions to be considered are the following.

(i) To what extent does (and should) the law grant specific enforcement of contract?

(ii) How can parties control the consequences of breach and prevent under-compensation?

(iii) To what extent does (and should) the law permit the parties to agree on the remedies for breach?

(iv) What considerations influence the answers to questions (i)–(iii)?

14.1 **The agreed sum**

A contract may require the defendant to pay a specific sum: on the defendant's breach; on the occurrence of a specified event or condition that does not constitute breach; or as a deposit, pre-payment, or instalment. We will discuss these situations at 14.3 on agreed remedies. In this section, we will discuss the claim for the agreed sum (or price) on full performance by the claimant. As such, it is a form of specific performance. This is the most common claim for breach of contract. It is distinguishable from a claim for damages because the claimant need not prove any loss caused by the defendant's breach, merely that he or she has *earned* the sum by due performance. Moreover, his or her claim cannot be reduced for being too *remote* or for their failure to *mitigate* loss (*Jervis v Harris* (1996)). It is treated as a claim for the payment of a *debt* and this has many **advantages for the claimant**.

(i) *Availability of summary judgment*: the claimant can take advantage of a quick and truncated legal process with procedural advantages.

(ii) *Additional availability of damages*: the claimant can also sue for loss flowing from the defendant's failure to pay on time (*Overstone Ltd v Shipway* (1962)).

On the other hand, **the defendant's interests are protected by the following**.

(i) *Strict interpretation of the pre-condition for payment*: while courts have mitigated the 'entire obligations' rule by the doctrine of 'substantial performance' (see 12.2.2.1 III), the claimant must still give 'substantial' performance to trigger the defendant's obligation to pay. For example, full payment was *not* due in a contract to install central heating for £560 when defects amounted to 31% of the total price (*Bolton v Mahadeva* (1972)). But, full payment *was* due subject to deductions where the defects amounted to less than 10% of the value of the contract (*Hoenig v Isaacs* (1952)). The Unfair Terms in Consumer Contracts Regulations 1999 ('UTCCR') specifies as indicatively unfair (and invalid) any term 'obliging the consumer to fulfil his obligations [usually to pay money] where the seller or supplier does not perform his' (Sch 2 para 1(o)).

(ii) *Allowing the defendant's set-off*: the defendant can deduct what the claimant owes him or her from the sum to be paid, if it would be unjust not to allow it (*Federal Commerce & Navigation Co Ltd v Molena Alpha Inc* (1978)). A clause that bars this right of set-off was held to be unreasonable (and so unenforceable) under the Unfair Contract Terms Act 1977 ('UCTA') in *Stewart Gill Ltd v Horatio Myer & Co Ltd* (1992). Likewise, UTCCR identifies as 'indicatively unfair' terms that prevent the consumer from setting off his or her claim against the seller or supplier who claims against the consumer (Sch 2 para 1(q)).

(iii) *Restricting the claimant's right to affirm*: where the contract is repudiated, the claimant will be barred from rendering the performance no longer wanted by the defendant (and earning his or her right to the agreed sum) if he or she needs the defendant's cooperation to complete his or her performance or if he or she has no legitimate interest in wholly unreasonable and wasteful completion (see 12.3).

Pause for reflection

Courts are more reluctant to impose direct restrictions on the action for the agreed sum because to do so would overtly control the fairness of the contract, the balance exchanged. Whilst this allows the action for the agreed sum to be held up as the shining example of full protection of the claimant's performance interest, it is also at odds with contract law's restrictions on the protection of the claimant's performance interest manifest in: the calculation of damages awarded; the control of agreed remedies (secondary) terms; and restrictions on the specific enforcement of *primary* obligations which are *non-monetary*.

14.2 **Specific enforcement**

A claim to compel the defendant to do what he or she undertook to do may be for specific performance (ie for the defendant's performance of his or her *positive* undertaking to do something) or for an injunction (ie for the defendant's performance of his or her *negative* undertaking, to *refrain* from doing something). Monetary awards such as damages and the action for the agreed sum are *common law* remedies and available *as of right*. In contrast, non-monetary specific enforcement is historically available only in the courts of *equity* and is still regarded as an exceptional and *discretionary* remedy.

14.2.1 **Specific performance**

In *Beswick v Beswick* (1968), the House of Lords (at 90) held that specific performance should be ordered if it would 'do more perfect and complete justice' than an award of damages. In practice, the courts have developed settled principles, which are followed in all but exceptional circumstances. Nevertheless, the decision is ultimately a matter for the court's discretion.

14.2.1.1 Overview of limits on the availability of specific performance

A claim for specific performance is best understood by reference to the factors that weigh *against* the remedy. These 'bars' to specific performance are identified, instanced, and then further discussed:

- *14.2.1.2 Claimant-sided considerations*:
  - (i) adequacy of damages; (ii) lack of clean hands; and (iii) delay.

- *14.2.1.3 Defendant-sided considerations*:
  - (i) the contract is for personal services or to carry on an activity; (ii) impossibility and hardship; and (iii) want of mutuality.

- *14.2.1.4 Administrative considerations*:
  - (i) uncertainty; (ii) the need for constant supervision; and (iii) avoidance of waste.

The overlapping operation of these factors is illustrated by the leading modern case on specific performance, **Cooperative Insurance Society Ltd v Argyll Stores (Holdings) Ltd** (1998). In 1979, C leased out the largest ('anchor') unit in its shopping centre to A to operate a supermarket. A covenanted that it would, for 35 years, 'keep the demised premises open for retail trade during the usual hours of business in the locality and the display windows properly dressed in a suitable manner in keeping with a good class parade of shops'. The supermarket started to run at a loss with 19 years of the lease still to run; A stopped trading and stripped out the fittings. Since the supermarket was the main attraction in the shopping centre, its closure would undoubtedly impact adversely on surrounding shops and on C as the lessor of those premises. C's claim for specific performance was denied at first instance, granted by the Court of Appeal, and denied again by the House of Lords.

Supporting specific performance, the *Court of Appeal* emphasised:

- the *inadequacy of damages* in compensating C who faced enormous obstacles in proving what loss was caused by A's breach; and

- the *deliberate and cynical nature of A's breach*.

Against specific performance, the *House of Lords* played down these factors since both parties were large sophisticated *commercial* organisations who entered the contract for purely *financial* reasons, knowing that the remedy for breach of the covenant was likely to be limited to damages. Rather, emphasis was placed on:

- the settled practice against specific performance when this would require a defendant to *carry on an activity*, as opposed to achieving a result by performing a single well-defined act;

- the oppressiveness of requiring A *to run a business* under the heavy-handed threat of *proceedings for contempt of court* for which one may be imprisoned;

- the need for *constant supervision* (ie the likelihood of repeated and costly litigation over compliance) which is *wasteful* of the resources of the parties and of the court, oppressive for A, and *perpetuates a continuing hostile relationship*; this is exacerbated by:

- the *uncertainty* in the contract which makes it impossible to draw up the terms of any order with sufficient precision (eg as to the kind and level of trade) to enable A to know exactly what it must do; and

- the enormous *losses A would suffer* from compulsory performance (in refitting the shop at the cost of over £1 million and carrying on a loss-making business for the next 19 years).

The decision can be criticised for tilting the balance too far in favour of the contract-breaker. However, the risk of under-compensating the claimant must be weighed against the enormous scale of the loss that the contract-breaker is likely to suffer if forced to perform and the potential for continuing conflicts between the parties which require judicial and parties' resources to settle. As Lord Hoffmann said in the case (at 16, 18), the principles of equity have 'a strong ethical content', the application of which is influenced by moral values. The balance to be weighed will often be a fine one.

14.2.1.2 Claimant-sided considerations

(i) The 'adequacy' of damages

Historically, the basis of the equitable jurisdiction to order specific performance of a contract is that the claimant cannot obtain a sufficient remedy by the common law judgment for damages (*Harnett v Yielding* (1805) at 553). Hence specific performance is normally barred where damages provide an adequate remedy. The fact that the claimant can buy substitute performance in the market is the single most important bar to specific performance. Contrary to the *stated aim* of damages, this bar implies that contract damages may *not be* adequate to fully compensate the claimant. However, damages are not 'inadequate' just because the established limits on damages will reduce the amount awarded to the claimant. Damages have been regarded as *inadequate* in the following situations.

(i) **Unique goods**: the subject matter of the contract is **physically unique** if it has strong sentimental value or significance for the claimant and so is not replaceable in the market. It is not enough to point to difficulty in quantifying the claimant's loss since courts are very willing to overcome quantification difficulties (see 13.2.5.5).

- In relation to the sale of goods, damages will almost always be considered adequate. Heirlooms, great works of art, and rare antiques were commonly regarded as 'unique', although this category is sparingly used (*Falcke v Gray* (1859) at 658).

- Section 52 of the Sale of Goods Act 1979 gives courts the discretion to award specific performance for the delivery of 'specific or ascertained' goods (as opposed to generic goods).

Most notably, the adequacy of damages bar does *not* apply in contracts to transfer interests in **land** where specific performance is *routinely* ordered, even if the *buyer* attaches no particular significance to, or has no special need for, the land, as where it is only traded for investment. The *seller* can even obtain specific performance where the land is readily resaleable. The automatic availability of specific performance in land contracts has been explained in terms of: the court *deeming* interests in land to be unique; the rule that land contracts confer an immediate equitable *proprietary interest* on buyers; and the *mutuality* of granting the seller the same remedy as the buyer is entitled to.

⏩⏪ Counterpoint

The automatic availability of specific performance in land contracts should be *reconsidered*. While specific performance is appropriate where the buyer has some unique interest in the land or the seller cannot readily resell the land or wants to free him or herself from burdens attached to the land, commercial parties motivated by profit should normally be regarded as adequately compensated by damages.

Specific performance may also be available if the subject matter of the contract is '**commercially unique**'. The difficulty of obtaining a substitute may mean that the claimant's business will be gravely disrupted without specific performance.

- ✓ In *Sky Petroleum Ltd v VIP Petroleum Ltd* (1974), an interim injunction amounting to specific performance was granted to compel V to continue supplying petrol to S garage during the petrol shortage of 1973 when V was, in effect, S's 'sole means of keeping their business going' and S would otherwise be 'forced out of business' (see also *Howard E Perry & Co Ltd v British Railways Board* (1980) and *Thames Valley Power Ltd v Total Gas and Power Ltd* (2006)).

- ✓ Although damages are normally adequate in respect of *shares*, where substitution is *not* readily available (as where breach deprives the claimant of the controlling interest) damages may be regarded as inadequate and specific performance ordered (*Harvela Investments Ltd v Royal Trust Co of Canada Ltd* (1986)). This is consistent with the US Uniform Commercial Code, which requires uniqueness to be judged in the total situation (§ 2-716(1)).

(ii) **Non-conforming goods supplied to consumers**: sections 48A–48E in Part 5A of the Sale of Goods Act 1979 allow specific performance to be awarded to compel the commercial seller to *repair or replace* non-conforming goods sold to consumers, *unless*: (a) repair or replacement is impossible; (b) the remedy sought is disproportionate to the other; or (c) price reduction or rescission of the contract is more appropriate (s 48C). This statutory right is consistent with the scope of specific relief at equity since damages are likely to be inadequate for a consumer who buys a defective appliance. However, Harris notes that these sections make no reference to damages, and so must be regarded as a self-contained code; the court cannot deny *both* repair and replacement because damages would be adequate.[1]

(iii) **No other substantial remedy available**: in *Beswick v Beswick*, an elderly and ailing coal merchant sold his business to his nephew in return for various undertakings including a promise to pay his widow £5 a week after his death. When the nephew failed to pay, the widow, acting as the administratrix of his estate, claimed specific performance of the contract. The case raised the classic 'legal black hole' problem since the payments were to be made to the widow (a third party) who could not sue in her own right (the case predates the Contracts (Rights of Third Parties) Act 1999), and the husband's estate, which *could* sue as a party to the contract, had lost nothing by the breach. The House of Lords ordered specific performance to achieve a 'just result' (see 4.1.5.1).

Adequacy of damages is the main restriction on the availability of specific performance. But, even if damages are *inadequate*, other restrictions may 'bar' specific performance.

(iv) **The presence of a clause limiting or excluding liability for damages**: in *AB v CD* (2014), Underhill LJ explains (at [27]) that: 'The primary obligation of a party was to perform the contract. The requirement to pay damages in the event of breach was a secondary obligation, and an agreement to restrict the recoverability of damages in the event of breach could not be treated as an agreement to excuse performance of the primary obligation.' Where the only losses suffered were of a kind excluded by the contract, it would be unjust if no injunction to restrain breach pending arbitration (ie an order for continuing performance) were available, even for the most gross and cynical breach of contract. The bar of adequacy of damages should be applied in a way which reflected the substantial justice of the situation. There was no question of the parties' commercial expectations being undermined. The primary expectation was that the parties would perform their obligations. The expectations created by an exclusion or limitation clause were about what damages would be recoverable in the event of breach, but that was not the same thing.

(ii) The claimant's 'lack of clean hands'
The maxim that 'he who comes to Equity must come with clean hands' translates into a denial of specific performance where the claimant has induced the contract by unfair means even if the unfairness was not such as to render the contract void or voidable. Thus, specific performance has been denied where the claimant:

✗ unfairly hurried the defendant into granting a mining lease in ignorance of the value of the property (*Walters v Morgan* (1861));

✗ took advantage of the defendant's drunkenness (*Malins v Freeman* (1837)) or the defendant's mistake (*Webster v Cecil* (1861));

✗ during a petrol price war, subsidised all garages to which it supplied petrol in the area except the defendant who was forced to sell petrol at a loss; the defendant

---

[1] D Harris, 'Specific Performance—A Regular Remedy for Consumers?' (2003) 119 *LQR* 541.

switched to a cheaper supplier in breach of contract with the claimant (*Shell UK Ltd v Lostock Garages Ltd* (1976));

✗ artificially increased the sale price of his car and portable telephone business (calculated on the number of customers at completion date) by giving away free telephones to inflate the number of customers (*Quadrant Visual Communications Ltd v Hutchison Telephone (UK) Ltd* (1993)); and

✗ sought an injunction amounting to specific performance but were unwilling to assure the defendants of their own counter-performance. Not only must the claimant come with 'clean hands' but 'he who seeks equity must do equity' (*Chappell v Times Newspapers Ltd* (1975)).

While *inadequacy of consideration* is said to be no ground for setting aside a contract or refusing its specific performance (*Collier v Brown* (1788)), it will tell against specific performance if the court finds any trace of procedural unfairness (*Griffith v Spratley* (1787) at 389), bearing in mind that procedural unfairness itself is often inferable from serious substantive unfairness (see 9.4.3). Moreover, since 'equity will not assist a volunteer', specific performance is not available to enforce *gratuitous deeds* (*Cannon v Hartley* (1949)), or contracts for nominal consideration (*Jeffreys v Jeffreys* (1841)).

(iii) Delay, acquiescence, and termination

- The six-year limitation period which is generally applicable to contract actions does not apply to the equitable action for specific performance (see 13.2.5.7). However, like claims for rescission, it can be barred for delay. Traditionally, a claimant must show themselves 'ready, desirous, prompt and eager' to perform (*Milward v Earl of Thanet* (1801)). Thus, where the contract involves property of fluctuating value or where the defendant would be prejudiced, delay of more than a few months has been held to bar specific performance (*Glasbrook v Richardson* (1874)), but a delay of over two years did not bar the remedy in *Lazard Bros & Co v Fairfield Properties Co (Mayfair) Ltd* (1977) since 'it was just that the plaintiff should obtain the remedy'.

- *Acquiescence* occurs when the claimant leads the defendant to believe that he or she will not object to the defendant's breach. This will bar specific performance, particularly if the defendant has detrimentally relied on this belief.

- The claimant's *termination* of the contract will bar a claim for specific performance even in the absence of the defendant's detrimental reliance (*Johnson v Agnew* (1980)).

14.2.1.3 Defendant-sided considerations

The blameworthiness of the defendant's breach may *encourage* the courts to order specific performance (eg Lord Hoffmann's example of 'cases of gross breach of personal faith, or attempts to use the threat of non-performances as blackmail' (*Cooperative Insurance v Argyll Stores* at 18)). However, defendant-sided considerations generally operate *against* specific performance, revealing a concern in favour of the contract-breaker.

(i) Contracts for personal services or to carry on an activity

✗ *Cooperative Insurance v Argyll Stores* shows that courts will generally deny specific enforcement of contracts to *carry on an activity* because of the potential for continuing conflicts over compliance which will require court resources to resolve and, the oppressiveness of compelling the defendant to carry on the activity 'under a sword of Damocles which may descend if [he] . . . does not conform to the terms of the order'. The law is concerned to avoid undue interference with the contract-breaker's *personal* liberty if the claimant can be adequately compensated. This explains the long-established denial of specific performance in contracts of *personal services* lest they are turned into 'contracts of slavery' (*de Francesco v Barnum* (1890) at 438).

✗ Consistently, legislation prohibits orders compelling an *employee* to perform a contract of employment (Trade Union and Labour Relations (Consolidation) Act 1992, s 236). However, *employers* may be compelled to reinstate the employee (Employment Rights Act 1996, ss 113–17), although these provisions are relatively little used (perhaps as low as 3%, see *Johnson v Unisys* (2001) at [23]), since employees usually prefer compensation and a new start elsewhere once relations have soured, and employers may resist reinstatement by paying enhanced compensation. Nevertheless, courts will not prevent employers from dismissing employees where *trust and confidence has broken down* and conflict would be created or perpetuated. Specific performance is only appropriate where there has been no breakdown in the employer–employee relationship (*Hill v CA Parsons & Co Ltd* (1972) and *Powell v Brent London BC* (1998)). But, even if it has, specific performance may be granted to enable proper disputes or disciplinary procedures to be complied with, but *on terms* that the employee may not turn up for, and the employer need not provide, work (*Irani v Southampton and SW Hampshire Health Authority* (1985) and *Robb v Hammersmith & Fulham LBC* (1991)). As Megarry J explains (at 318) in *CH Giles & Co Ltd v Morris* (1972), the courts' reluctance to specifically enforce personal services contracts relates not only to the concern about constant supervision, but is:

> more complex and more firmly bottomed on human nature. If a singer contracts to sing, there could no doubt be proceedings for committal if, ordered to sing, the singer remained obstinately dumb. But if instead the singer sang flat, or sharp, or too fast, or too slowly, or too loudly, or too quietly, or resorted to a dozen of the manifestations of temperament traditionally associated with some singers, the threat of committal would reveal itself as a most unsatisfactory weapon: for who could say whether the imperfections of performance were natural or self induced? . . . However, not all contracts of personal service or for the continuous performance of services are as dependent as this on matters of opinion and judgment, nor do all such contracts involve the same degree of the daily impact of person upon person. In general, no doubt, the inconvenience and mischief of decreeing specific performance of most of such contracts will greatly outweigh the advantages and specific performance will be refused. But . . . it should [not] be assumed that as soon as any element of personal service or continuous service can be discerned in a contract the court will, without more, refuse specific performance.

✓ This bar is limited to services that are *personal* in nature. Thus, specific performance has been ordered in *building contracts* and *repairing covenants* where: (i) the work is capable of sufficiently precise definition; (ii) damages will be inadequate to compensate the claimant; and (iii) the defendant has possession of the land on which work is to be done so that the claimant cannot employ someone else to do it (*Wolverhampton Corp v Emmons* (1901); *Jeune v Queens Cross Properties Ltd* (1974)).

(ii) Impossibility and hardship

✗ Specific enforcement will be denied where performance is physically or legally *impossible*, as where: the defendant contracts to sells land which he or she does not own and cannot obtain (*Castle v Wilkinson* (1870)); the defendant assigns a lease without the necessary consent of the landlord (*Wilmot v Barber* (1880)); or the defendant agrees to sublet to the claimant, when his or her head lease prohibits subletting (*Warmington v Miller* (1973)).

✗ Specific enforcement may also be denied where it would cause the defendant *severe hardship*, far exceeding any uncompensable loss suffered by the claimant. In **Patel v Ali** (1984), the claimant sought specific performance four years after the defendant contracted to sell her home. By then, the defendant had suffered cancer necessitating the amputation of her right leg at the hip joint, had borne two more children (three in all), and her husband was adjudged a bankrupt and sent to prison. Moreover, her poor English made her highly dependent on the support of friends and relatives living close by, so that compelling her to move would cause a 'hardship amounting to injustice'. Goulding J (at 288) emphasised that 'mere pecuniary difficulties' are insufficient:

> [O]nly in extraordinary and persuasive circumstances can hardship supply an excuse for resisting performance of a contract for the sale of immovable property. A person of full capacity who sells or buys a house takes the risk of hardship to himself and his dependants, whether arising from existing facts or unexpectedly supervening in the interval before completion . . . [but] equitable relief may . . . be refused because of an unforeseen change of circumstances not amounting to legal frustration.

✗ On the facts, great emphasis was put on the claimant's *delay*, which reinforced the injustice of compelling the defendant to perform after all the unforeseeable changes over four years.

✗ However, hardship can operate *alone* as in *Denne v Light* (1857) where the court refused specific performance against the buyer who mistakenly bought landlocked farmland.

✗ In *Wroth v Tyler* (1974),[2] specific performance of a contract to sell land was denied because it would have required the defendant to take legal action to evict his wife and daughter from the matrimonial home.

---

[2] The wife had given notice of her rights of occupation under the Matrimonial Homes Act 1967, s 1(1), which protects her but not the daughter from eviction.

✗ In *Cooperative Insurance v Argyll Stores*, the House of Lords denied specific performance partly because it would cause loss to the defendant which would be 'enormous, unquantifiable and unlimited, as well as being out of all proportion to any
uncompensable loss' suffered by the claimant (at 909). Lord Hoffmann observed
that the availability of specific performance would, in practice, simply *strengthen
the claimant's bargaining power in settling the case*. That is, the claimant can charge
a sum for *releasing* the defendant from performance, which approaches the
defendant's *cost* of performance, far exceeding the *value* of actual performance
to the claimant.

(iii) Want of mutuality

It was once thought that specific performance would not be ordered *for* the claimant unless it could also have been ordered *against* them at the time the contract was
made.[3] *Price v Strange* (1978) now makes clear that the claimant is only barred if a
defendant, who is compelled to perform, would be inadequately protected should the
claimant subsequently breach.[4] Nevertheless, this bar seems too pro-defendant. As
Burrows notes,[5] it will already have been concluded that damages will not adequately
compensate the claimant, yet the court is prepared to deny him or her an admittedly
more appropriate and just remedy because of the mere *risk* that the *defendant* may not
be adequately compensated *if* the claimant subsequently breaches. The bar is more
understandable if the defendant's potential hardship (ie difficulty of proof and scale
of loss) greatly exceeds the claimant's.[6]

14.2.1.4 Impracticality and unsuitability

(i) Uncertainty

Specific performance will be an unsuitable remedy if the performance cannot be
defined with sufficient precision, although there was sufficient certainty for contract
formation. Contracts regarded as too uncertain to specifically enforce include: to
publish an 'article on jade' (*Joseph v National Magazine Co Ltd* (1959)); to build 'a railway station' (*Wilson v Northampton and Banbury Railway Co* (1874)); 'layout £1,000 in
building' (*Moseley v Virgin* (1796)); and to 'run a supermarket' (*Cooperative Insurance v
Argyll Stores*). As Lord Hoffmann said (*Cooperative Insurance v Argyll Stores* at 13), 'the
less precise the order, the fewer the signposts to the forensic minefield which he has
to traverse', the more the 'oppression caused by the defendant having to do things
under threat of proceedings for contempt'. Uncertainty also increases the likelihood
of further litigation.

(ii) Constant supervision

It was once thought that specific performance would be denied if it involves a continuous act. But this was read down in *Posner v Scott-Lewis* (1987), where a covenant
to employ a resident porter was specifically enforced since the contract stated the
required performance with *sufficient precision*. In *Cooperative Insurance v Argyll Stores*,

---

[3] E Fry, *A Treatise on the Specific Performance of Contracts* (6th edn, Stevens, 1921) 219.
[4] *Either* by ordering specific performance *or* by adequate damages against the claimant.
[5] A Burrows, *Remedies for Torts and Breach of Contract* (3rd edn, OUP, 2004) 493; A Schwartz, 'The Case
for Specific Performance' (1979) 89 *Yale LJ* 271, 301–3.
[6] E Durfee, 'Mutuality in Specific Performance' (1921) 20 *Mich L Rev* 289.

Lord Hoffmann (at 15) made clear that the 'constant supervision' bar refers to the *likelihood of repeated and costly litigation over compliance*, which is greatest where uncertainty surrounds what must be done. The general public interest in the *finality* of dispute resolution may require the claimant to settle for damages, although it does less perfect justice than specific performance.

(iii) Avoidance of waste

Specific enforcement may be denied where it would involve a significant waste of resources (ie when the cost of performance far exceeds the benefit to the claimant; the cost of cure is also denied for this reason, see 13.2.3.2). This rationale is sometimes obscured by talk of constant supervision or findings that the claimant has suffered no or little loss. Thus, in *Tito v Waddell (No 2)* (1977), the court declined to compel the defendant to incur enormous costs to restore and replant the island it had ravaged by mining because the islanders had resettled elsewhere. In *Cooperative Insurance v Argyll Stores*, the court would not compel a party to continue running a loss-making supermarket for 19 more years. The concern to prevent waste overlaps with the concern to avoid hardship to the defendant.

14.2.2 Injunctions

- A *mandatory injunction* compels the defendant to *undo* the effects of breaching a negative undertaking.

- A *prohibitory injunction* specifically enforces a contractual obligation *not to do something*.

Both are equitable remedies given at the court's discretion.

(i) Mandatory injunction

Courts are more reluctant to compel *positive* action by mandatory injunctions than to restrain some action by granting prohibitory injunctions. A court will generally deny a mandatory injunction and award damages in lieu unless the defendant has 'trodden roughshod over the plaintiff's rights' (*Luganda v Service Hotels Ltd* (1969) at 221) or the claimant would otherwise suffer extreme or serious prejudice (*Durrell v Pritchard* (1865)). In *Shepherd Homes Ltd v Sandham* (1971), Megarry J (at 351) said that the grounds for denying mandatory injunctions 'at least include the triviality of the damage to the plaintiff and the existence of a disproportion between the detriment that the injunction would inflict on the defendant and the benefit that it would confer on the plaintiff. The basic aim is to produce a "fair result"'. For example, in *Wrotham Park Estate Co v Parkside Homes Ltd* (1974), the court declined to order the destruction of 14 homes to enforce a restrictive covenant because it would be 'an unpardonable waste of much-needed houses'. In *Sharp v Harrison* (1922), the court refused to order the removal of a window built in breach of contract overlooking the claimant's property because no damage was occasioned; the defendant undertook to prevent any future damage by the continuing breach; and an order would inflict damage on the defendant out of all proportion to the relief derived by the claimant.

(ii) Prohibitory injunction

A prohibitory injunction is the main remedy to restrain threatened or future breaches of negative undertakings. As Lord Cairns LC said (at 720) in *Dolman v Allman* (1878) it will be granted *as a matter of course* and is not 'a question of the balance of convenience or inconvenience, or the amount of damage or of injury'. A prohibitory injunction may be granted to prevent the defendant from doing what he or she has *negatively* undertaken (eg not to sing for someone else, *Lumley v Wagner* (1852)), although the court would not order specific performance in respect of what he or she has *positively* undertaken to do in the same contract (to sing for the claimant). This is because granting a prohibitory injunction (rather than compelling positive action):

- seems less restrictive of the defendant's individual liberty;
- is less likely to run up against the claimant's duty to mitigate and the problem of constant supervision; and
- avoids the difficulty of assessing loss from breach of a negative undertaking.

For example, in *Araci v Fallon* (2011), F, a famous jockey, contracted with A to ride A's racehorse at the Epsom Derby and no one else's. The Court of Appeal granted a prohibitory injunction to prevent F from riding a rival horse because: even if the adequacy of damages were relevant, which it is not, damages were not adequate because it would be exceptionally difficult to calculate the loss that would result if the rival horse beat the claimant's horse, and nothing could compensate the claimant for losing the prestige that would flow from one of its horses winning the Derby.

However, the courts have refused prohibitory injunctions on similar grounds that would bar specific performance, such as the claimant's delay (*HP Bulmer Ltd v J Bollinger SA* (1977)), acquiescence (*Shaw v Applegate* (1977)), or lack of clean hands (*Grobbelaar v News Group Newspapers Ltd* (2002)), or the trivial nature of the claimant's loss (*Harrison v Good* (1871) at 352).

(iii) No indirect specific performance

The main reason against granting a prohibitory injunction is that it will amount to indirect specific performance of a contract for personal service (which would not have been specifically enforced). Thus, injunctions are denied which seek to enforce undertakings not to accept any other employment *at all*, as where X promises to work for Y for ten years and not to 'engage himself in any other business' during that time (*Ehrman v Bartholomew* (1898)). Granting the injunction will, in practice, compel X to choose between working for Y and starvation. However, injunctions to enforce undertakings to refrain from only *particular activities* will be granted if they will not *in practice* compel the defendant to perform his or her positive obligations. Thus:

- ✗ in *Mortimer v Beckett* (1920), an injunction to enforce a boxer's implied undertaking not to box for anyone else for **seven years** was denied because it would amount to indirect specific enforcement of a personal services contract;
- ✓ an injunction was *granted* in **Lumley v Wagner** (1852) to restrain W from singing for anyone else during the **three months** she had agreed to sing at L's theatre, although the court would not compel her to sing for L. The period was short and there was no risk of W's skills atrophying if she refused to perform;

✓ an injunction was *granted* in the questionable decision in ***Warner Brothers Pictures Inc v Nelson*** (1937). The court's view that to restrain Nelson ('Bette Davis') from working as an actress elsewhere for **three years** was not indirect specific performance because she could, at the height of her career, stop acting and do something else albeit less well paid, has since been described as 'extraordinarily unrealistic' (*Warren v Mendy* (1989) at 865). Recent cases take a more realistic approach;

✗ an injunction was denied in *Page One Records Ltd v Britton* (1968) where a pop group, The Troggs, breached a contract to be managed by and make records solely for the claimant for **five years**;

✗ an injunction was denied in ***Warren v Mendy*** where the boxer Nigel Benn breached a contract to be managed by the claimant for **three years**. Nourse LJ (at 865) said that 'an injunction lasting for two years or more . . . may practically compel performance of the contract';

✓ an injunction was granted by the Court of Appeal in ***Lauritzen Cool AB v Lady Navigation Inc*** (2005) to prevent ship-owners from using their vessels inconsistently with the contract, although its practical effect was to specifically enforce the contract. This is justified when, exceptionally, the subject matter of the contract is of particular value to the claimant and damages would be inadequate.

14.2.3 Damages in lieu of specific performance or injunction

Under section 50 of the Senior Courts Act 1981, the High Court has the *discretion* to award the claimant damages:

- in *addition* to an injunction or specific performance (eg for losses suffered from delayed performance: *Ford-Hunt v Raghbir Singh* (1973)); or

- in *lieu of* them where the discretion is exercised against granting them.

Damages in lieu of specific performance or injunction are said to 'constitute a true substitute for specific performance' (*Wroth v Tyler* at 58) and to be assessed on the *same* basis and subject to the same limits as common law damages for breach of contract (*Johnson v Agnew* (1980) at 400). Both have the stated aim of putting the claimant 'in the same position . . . as if the contract had been performed' (*Robinson v Harman* (1848) at 855), but neither is followed through to its logical conclusion. Damages in lieu of specific performance or injunction may be reduced by reference to remoteness and mitigation. Where breach causes no financial loss to the claimant, courts have awarded as damages in lieu of specific enforcement a 'reasonable payment' representing 'the sum which [the claimant] could have extracted from the defendant as the price of his consent [to the breach]' (see 13.4 and **Sharp and Waddams, 'Damages for Lost Opportunity to Bargain'** (1982) 2 *OJLS* 290). This seems sensible for, if specific enforcement is denied to avoid undue waste and harshness to the defendant, it hardly makes sense to compel the defendant to pay the monetary equivalent of specific performance. Analogous reasoning applies to the measure of damages in lieu of rescission in section 2(2) of the Misrepresentation Act 1967 (see 5.3.3.2).

14.2.4 Should specific enforcement be more widely available?

The case for a wider availability of specific enforcement centres around four factors.

(i) Inadequacy of damages

In '**The Case for Specific Performance**' (1979) 89 *Yale LJ* 271, **Schwartz** argues that if the law is committed to putting disappointed promisees in as good a position as they would have been in had the contract been performed, specific performance should be available as a matter of course. He reasons that:

- damages under-compensate in many cases where specific performance is currently unavailable;
- claimants would prefer to sue for damages if they are likely to be fully compensated since 'a breaching promisor is reluctant to perform and may be hostile'. Thus, if he or she chooses specific performance they should be able to have it;
- claimants have better information than courts as to the adequacy of damages and the difficulties of coercing performance.

> ### ◀▶ Counterpoint
>
> 1. On one view, specific enforcement may amount to 'over-compensation' because it allows the claimant to sell it for *more than* the *true* value of the performance to him or her (Lord Hoffmann in *Cooperative Insurance v Argyll Stores* at 15).
>
> 2. The current level of damages awarded represents a compromise between the interests of the claimant and those of the defendant. If we accept the validity of policies such as the avoidance of waste and undue harshness to defendants, and the desirability of mitigation of loss by the claimant, then under-compensation to that extent is inevitable. Specific performance should not evade such policies.

(ii) Protection of the claimant's performance interest

Friedmann argues that 'the essence of contract is performance. Contracts are made in order to be performed'.[7] Since factors such as prevention of hardship or economic waste do not prevent the formation of contracts, they should not bar specific performance either. Otherwise, it is questionable that the claimant has acquired a *right* to contractual performance. In '**Disgorgement of Profits of Contract: Property, Contract and "Efficient Breach"**' (1995) 24 *Can BLJ* 121, **Smith** argues that the right to performance should be elevated to that of a *proprietary right*; thus, if specific performance were too late or otherwise inappropriate, the claimant should be entitled to the defendant's profits from breach *as if* the defendant's performance (and hence its fruits) is already the claimant's property (see 1.4.5 and 13.4).

---

[7] D Friedmann, 'The Performance Interest in Contract Damages' (1995) 111 *LQR* 628–9 and C Webb, 'Performance and Compensation: An Analysis of Contract Damages and Contractual Obligation' (2006) 26 *OJLS* 41.

> **◀▶ Counterpoint**
>
> 1. As a matter of policy, English law simply has *not valued contractual rights so highly* as to coerce literal observance as a matter of course. Indeed the rule against penalties, forfeitures, and unreasonable deposits further undermines the claimant's performance interest by refusing to enforce secondary terms designed to deter breach of the contract's primary obligations (14.3.3).
>
> 2. Even those who support the primacy of the performance interest recognise the need to restrict the right performance in many circumstances (and to award damages as a 'substitute' for performance). For example, in **'Remedial Rights and Substantive Rights in Contract Law'** (2002) 8 *Legal Theory* 313, **Kimel** argues for a 'general presumption in favour of liberty'. So that where harm can be remedied in different ways, the law should opt for the one that interferes least with the defendant's liberty. It is more oppressive to compel specific behaviour than to require the payment of damages, particularly where the sanction for breach is contempt of court, potentially punishable by imprisonment. Indeed, courts may be more prepared to order specific performance if other sanctions (eg a fine or a monetary award to the claimant) are available, as in France or Germany.[8]
>
> 3. The claimant's performance interest must also be weighed against the social interest in the *finality* of dispute resolution, and the related interests in avoiding waste of judicial resources and ending hostile relationships, which may generate further litigation.

(iii) Efficient breach

In **'Specific Performance'** (1978) 45 *U Chi L Rev* 35, **Kronman** argues that the current pattern of protection by specific performance where the subject matter is 'unique', but otherwise by damages, is economically efficient and mimics what rational parties would have agreed beforehand. The theory of *'efficient breach'* supports a restrictive approach to specific enforcement. The basic idea is that contract law should aim at maximising overall wealth and this is facilitated if the law permits 'efficient' breaches of contract to enable commodities to move to those who value them the most (rather than keeping them with claimants just because they are entitled to them). This is only possible if damages rather than specific performance is the primary remedy for breach.[9] Thus, if I agree to supply a widget to you for £10,000, but Jack is prepared to offer me £20,000 for it, I will increase overall wealth by selling the widget to Jack and paying you damages for not supplying the widget, as long as that is less than £20,000. Jack and I are better off without you being any worse off. But I will have no incentive to breach if damages to you would equal or exceed £20,000.

---

[8] See H Beale, A Hartkamp, H Kötz, and D Talon, *Ius Commune Casebook on the Common Law of Europe: Contract Law* (Hart Publishing, 2002) 680–1.

[9] The efficient breach theory must also logically resist any gains-based remedy as an even stronger disincentive to efficient breach than specific performance.

> ## ◄► Counterpoint
>
> 1. Schwartz argues[10] that the routine availability of specific performance would achieve efficiency *gains* such as minimising the inefficiencies of under-compensation, reducing the need for liquidated damage clauses, minimising strategic behaviour, and saving the cost of litigating complex damage issues.
>
> 2. The efficient breach argument for current restrictions on the remedy of specific performance is difficult to assess (see 1.4.3). On the previous example, it is arguable that the widget would still move to Jack even with specific performance as the primary remedy. If Jack values the widget more highly than you, you would agree to release me from specific performance for *a share of my* gains and this is a fairer outcome. But the relative efficiency of this outcome must take into account the transaction costs of negotiating my release and making the new contract with Jack, which may reduce or negate any overall gain. This must also be compared with the efficiency of the damages remedy (ie the cost of negotiating a settlement or obtaining a judicial assessment with its attendant risk of inaccurate under-compensation). In the end, which remedy is more efficient 'depends entirely upon the relative transaction costs . . . [which can] only be determined inductively from empirical evidence'.[11] The matter remains inconclusive.

(iv) Comparative law

Other jurisdictions support greater use of specific enforcement. For example, in Scots law and in civilian systems, specific performance is the primary remedy. But, in spite of this apparent difference, there is significant overlap in the circumstances when specific performance will be denied. Article III.-3:302 of the European Draft Common Frame of Reference recognises a general entitlement to specific performance *unless*:

- performance would be unlawful or impossible, unreasonably burdensome or expensive, of such a personal character that it would be unreasonable to enforce it; or

- the claimant has unduly delayed in seeking the remedy; or

- the claimant 'could have made a reasonable substitute transaction without significant effort or expense'.

The open-textured nature of these considerations means that, no matter how the discretion is structured (whether as the primary or supplementary remedy), courts of all systems must engage in the same delicate balancing of competing policies on the facts of particular cases.

Different courts may reach different conclusions, as the progression of *Cooperative Insurance v Argyll Stores* up the levels of courts shows (specific performance denied at first instance, granted in the Court of Appeal, and denied in the House of Lords).

---

[10] 'The Case for Specific Performance' (1979) 89 *Yale LJ* 271, 277.
[11] I Macneil, 'Efficient Breach of Contract: Circles in the Sky' (1982) 68 *Virginia L Rev* 947, 957.

Nevertheless, it may make a practical difference whether the *presumption* is for or against specific performance since it determines which party has the effective burden of proving otherwise. In the Scottish equivalent of *Cooperative Insurance v Argyll Stores*, specific performance was ordered to enforce a covenant to keep retail trading premises open until 2009 (*Highland and Universal Properties Ltd v Safeway Properties Ltd* (2000)). The period of time was significantly shorter than in *Cooperative Insurance v Argyll Stores*, but the different starting point may also have been significant in a finely balanced case.

14.2.5 **Can parties agree to specific performance or an injunction?**

Subject to certain limits, parties can determine the remedies for breach by agreeing, for example, exemption clauses, payments on breach, termination clauses, or that a certain term is a 'condition' yielding the right to terminate on its breach.

However, courts have always jealously guarded their jurisdiction over the remedies for breach to prevent one party from exploiting the other's bargaining weakness or from abusing their rights.[12] Upholding an agreed specific enforcement clause would oust the court's jurisdiction to determine whether specific enforcement is appropriate *at the time it was claimed*. In *Quadrant Visual v Hutchison Telephone* (1993), the Court of Appeal (at 451) held that the discretion over whether to grant specific performance belongs to the *courts* and cannot be usurped by the parties. The court cannot be reduced to a 'rubber stamp'; 'its discretion cannot be fettered'. Injunctions are granted more liberally, and clauses stipulating prohibitory injunctions are persuasive although not determinative (*Warner Brothers v Nelson* at 221).

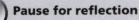 **Pause for reflection**

1. In *Quadrant Visual*, the refusal to enforce the specific performance clause was reinforced by the claimant's unfairness (lack of 'clean hands', see 14.2.1.2(ii)). Likewise, other policies against the award of specific enforcement should tell against the enforcement of an agreed specific enforcement clause.

2. However, if the only concerns are about adequacy of damages or 'want of mutuality', it is arguable that the courts should give greater weight to a specific performance clause. Just as courts accord a large *margin of tolerance* to agreed damages clauses (see 14.3.2) as genuine pre-estimates of the claimant's losses, a specific performance clause should be treated as a persuasive indicator of the claimant's loss, as long as the contract was not procedurally or substantively unfair at formation. At least, any doubts on these issues should be resolved in favour of the claimant when a specific performance clause is present.

---

[12] See generally D Friedmann, 'Good Faith and Remedies for Breach of Contract' in J Beatson and D Friedmann, *Good Faith and Fault in Contract Law* (Clarendon Press, 1995) 399.

Diagram 14A Approach to remedies problems

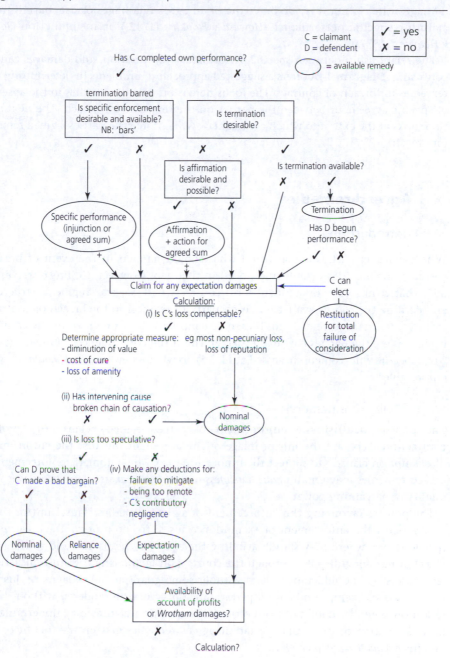

The presence of an *agreed damages clause* may be thought to impliedly oust the court's jurisdiction to grant specific enforcement, since the clause: (i) gives the defendant the *option* to perform or pay the agreed damages; or (ii) indicates that the agreed damages are adequate. However, courts are eager to preserve their jurisdiction over specific remedies and have interpreted agreed damages clauses as only indicating the *quantum* of damages recoverable *if* the claimant sues for damages; the claimant is *not*, by virtue of an agreed damages clause, barred from claiming specific performance (*Howard v Hopkins* (1742)) or an injunction (*Jones v Heavens* (1877)).

The relationship between specific performance, termination, and damages can be confusing. **Diagram 14A** offers a suggested approach to problems in determining the remedies for breach of contract. The focus here is on default remedies in the absence of specific agreement between the parties on the remedies for breach. The next section looks at the extent to which contract law will enforce the parties' agreed remedy for breach.

14.3 **Agreed remedies**

14.3.1 **Introduction**

Where contract parties are silent on what should happen in the event of breach, contract law provides default rules to fill in that gap. However, Collins observes (at 365) that a 'majority' of standard form contracts will 'seek to augment, structure, and confine the claims available to each party in relation to the breach of contract. In short, the normal remedy for breach of contract is that provided in the contract itself'. Where the parties *have* expressly agreed on the consequences of breach (aside from specific enforcement discussed at 14.2.5), to what extent *are*, and *should*, they be enforceable?

14.3.1.1 Policy considerations

The policies **against the enforcement** of agreed remedy clauses (to protect contract-breakers) are the mirror image of the arguments against the enforcement of exemption clauses (to protect the innocent party). The automatic enforcement of agreed remedies may entail *undue harshness to contract-breakers* where there was inequality of bargaining power.

The policies **favouring the enforcement** of agreed remedies clauses mirror those that support the enforcement of exemption clauses: freedom of contract; certainty (parties know where they stand); avoiding the costs (to the parties and to the judiciary) of resolving disputes through the courts; and facilitating certain transactions (eg lenders will be reluctant to lend without some guarantee of repayment, just as, in the case of exemption clauses, performance may not be rendered without limitation on potential liability). However, while exemption clauses may undermine an innocent party's contractual expectation, agreed remedies may ensure that he or she obtains *adequate remedies on breach*.

14.3.1.2 Types of agreed remedies

The main types of agreed remedial obligations are clauses relating to *money payments*; these may stipulate:

(i) an upper limit on the compensation payable on breach (ie exemption clauses);

(ii) a particular sum payable on breach (agreed damages);

(iii) a prepaid sum to be forfeited on breach (deposit); and

(iv) instalments to be forfeited on breach (forfeiture).

This section focuses on (ii)–(iv). Examples of other main types of agreed remedies are:

- *specific enforcement* clauses (see 14.2.5);

- *termination* clauses (specifying when a party can end the contract, see 12.2.3.2);

- clauses that alter *property rights* on breach (eg failure to pay timely instalments gives the seller title to the goods purchased or to the debtor's other property or both);

- subsidiary provisions for *third party guarantees* of the contract party's performance (see 9.3); and

- stipulations that any disputes arising should be resolved by arbitration in a particular *forum alternative to the courts*).

14.3.1.3 Primary terms with remedial consequences

We have already discussed some *primary* terms that have clear *remedial* consequences. For example:

- an *entire obligations* clause will relieve a party from paying until, at least substantial, performance by the other party (see 12.2.2.1 III);

- designating a term as a *condition* will enable the claimant to terminate the contract for its breach (see 12.2.4);

- a *force majeure clause* which discharges primary obligations on certain events prevents any secondary obligations from arising in respect of any failure to perform them (see 7.4.1).

A party may also retain or create *property rights* as security against the other's breach. For example, under *hire-purchase* contracts, the finance company retains ownership of the goods, leaving the debtor with only the possessory right which may be lost on breach; otherwise, he or she can purchase the goods at the end of the hire period for a nominal sum. Another common example is *home loans* that grant the creditor an equitable charge over the debtor's property. If the debtor defaults, the creditor can possess and sell the property to satisfy the debt.

Lastly, parties may agree particular *sums* to be payable either on the claimant's completion of performance (see 14.1) or on some event other than breach (see 14.3.2.3). In spite of the obvious remedial consequences of these primary obligations, there is a clear judicial and legislative *reluctance* to control them. This is in marked contrast to the greater *willingness* to control express remedial terms.[13] Consequently, the law in this area is tarnished by: the necessity of drawing artificial distinctions, avoidance devices, and inconsistent legal controls of functionally similar terms. **Diagram 14B** gives an overview of the different techniques used to determine the enforceability of different types of terms with remedial consequences.

---

[13] D Friedmann, 'Good Faith and Remedies for Breach of Contract' in J Beatson and D Friedmann, *Good Faith and Fault in Contract Law* (Clarendon Press, 1995) 399.

Diagram 14B Overview of primary terms with remedial consequences and secondary (remedial) terms

| | | | IP = innocent party
CB = contract-breaker
✓ = Enforceable
✗ = Unenforceable |

IP wants:	1. Monetary performance from CB	2. Non-monetary performance from CB	3. To withhold own performance
A. Enforceability of PRIMARY terms with remedial consequences	Action for the 'agreed sum': ✓ on IP's full performance (14.1), ✓ on other event not amounting to breach (14.3.2.3)	✓ *Specific performance* or *injunction* but restrictions on availability (14.2)	✓ *Termination* if CB breaches a term agreed to be (a) a 'condition' or (b) an 'innominate' term which substantially deprives IP of intended benefits (12.2.4.2) ✓ IP need not perform if CB breaches 'entire' obligation (12.2.2.3) ✓ Under *force majeure* clause
B. Enforceability of SECONDARY terms agreed to arise on CB's breach	✓ *Liquidated damages* clauses, ✗ *penalty* clauses (14.3.2) ✓ *forfeitures* clauses but subject to restrictions (14.3.3), ✓ *exemption* clauses but subject to restrictions (chs 10–11)	✗ Cannot fetter court's discretion by specific performance clause (14.2.5)	✓ 'Termination clause' but subject to strict construction and may not allow damages claim (12.2.4.2)

14.3.2 Payments on breach: liquidated damages and penalties

14.3.2.1 The penalty rule

The parties may agree the sum which should be payable by the contract-breaker. This secondary (remedial) *agreed damages* clause is distinguishable from: (i) an action for *damages*, which is the default money remedy; and (ii) an action for the *agreed sum*, which enforces the defendant's primary obligation.

The general rule is that an agreed damages clause is:

✓ *enforceable* if it amounts to '**liquidated damages**', that is, if the sum represents a *genuine pre-estimate* of the actual loss likely to be caused by the breach; and

✗ *unenforceable* if it amounts to a '**penalty**', that is, 'if the sum stipulated for is extravagant and unconscionable in amount in comparison with the greatest loss that could conceivably be proved to have followed from the breach' (*Dunlop Pneumatic Tyre Co Ltd v New Garage & Motor Co Ltd* (1915) at 87–8). The court will then award damages on the usual principles.

The distinction is said to depend on the parties' intention, but the parties' own **label** of 'liquidated damages', while relevant, is not conclusive (*Elphinstone v Monkland Iron and Coal Co* (1886)). The court may still decide that the term is really an unenforceable penalty. Traditionally, a term was enforceable if it was a *genuine* pre-estimate of the claimant's loss; the reasonableness of the pre-estimate is merely *evidence* of genuineness, so that a genuine, albeit unreasonable, pre-estimate would still be valid and enforceable (*Dunlop Pneumatic Tyre*). However in *Alfred McAlpine Capital Projects Ltd v Tilebox Ltd* (2005), Jackson J said (at [2]) that: 'the test does not turn on the genuineness or honesty of the party or parties who made the pre-estimate. The test is primarily an objective one [ie of reasonableness], even though the court has some regard to the thought processes of the parties at the time of contracting.'

It is for the party claiming that a clause is penal to establish that. Whether a clause is penal or not must be determined by reference to the contract as a whole in the circumstances and context in which it was made, especially the following overlapping factors (Lord Dunedin in *Dunlop Pneumatic Tyre* at 86–8).

(i) **Proportionality**: a clause is more likely to be penal if it lacks proportionality between the sum payable and the seriousness of the breach, as where 'a single lump sum is made payable . . . on the occurrence of one or more or all of several events, some of which may occasion serious and others but trifling damage'. Conversely, it will be regarded as a liquidated damages clause if the payment is proportional to the seriousness of the breach (eg £100 per acre of land not restored (*Elphinstone v Monkland Iron & Coal Co* (1886)), or £500 per week of delay (*Phillips Hong Kong v Attorney-General of Hong Kong* (1993)). However, in *Makdessi v Cavendish Square Holdings BV* (2013), the Court of Appeal held that a sum payable should *not* be presumed to be penal *just* because it is payable:

- for several breaches of varying severity;
- for different breaches of the same stipulation the effect of which may vary; or
- for breaches of different stipulations, if the damage likely to arise from those breaches is the same in kind.

But a presumption that the term is penal may arise if:

- the same sum is applicable to breaches of different stipulations which are different in kind;
- there is a range of losses and the sum provided for is totally out of proportion to some of them.

(ii) **Whether the amount stipulated is 'unconscionable'**: the further the stipulated sum deviates from the actual or compensable loss, the less likely it is that it will be regarded as genuine. In *Murray v Leisureplay* (2005), the Court of Appeal said (at [55], [111]) that 'the clause should be compensatory rather than deterrent'. Moreover, the court requires the parties to take account of the *duty to mitigate* when agreeing damages. Nevertheless, the importance of giving a **wide margin for error** is frequently stressed. *Dunlop Pneumatic Tyre* contains an example of an 'unconscionable' and so penal clause: requiring a builder to pay £1 million on breach of a contract for building work worth £50. The more difficult it is to estimate the consequences of breach, the more reluctant the courts are to second-guess the parties' estimation; thus, for example, greater leeway is given in services contracts where loss may be more difficult to assess.

(iii) The relative **bargaining power of the parties**: courts lean towards upholding stipulated damages clauses in commercial contracts, especially where the parties are of equal bargaining power and have had high-level legal advice. Lord Woolf stressed in *Phillips Hong Kong* that courts should adopt a 'hands off' approach unless the sums stipulated were *obviously extravagant* or there was *significant inequality of bargaining power*. His Lordship (at 55) said that 'courts should not . . . be too ready to find the requisite degree of disproportion lest they impinge on the parties' freedom to settle for themselves the rights and liabilities following a breach of contract'.

(iv) **Commercial justification**: in *Makdessi v Cavendish*, the Court of Appeal also considered the more modern approach (in cases such as *Lordsvale Finance plc v Zambia* (1996), *Cine Bes Filmcilik v United International Pictures* (2004), and *Murray v Leisureplay* (2005)) in which courts decline to strike down a clause as penal because there was a commercial justification for it.

> ✓ In *Phillips Hong Kong*, the court upheld the agreed damages clause in a road-building contract. The fact that the stipulated sum will exceed the actual loss on a number of possible scenarios (none actually occurring) is not enough to make the term penal, *unless* the sum was *extravagant* having regard to the *range* of losses that could reasonably be anticipated at the time the contract was made (at 58).

> ✓ Likewise, in *Murray v Leisureplay* (2005), Buxton and Clarke LJJ require any discrepancy between the liquidated and the common law damages to be 'extravagant or unconscionable' before it will be invalidated as a penalty (at [106], [114]). The Court of Appeal held that a provision in M's employment contract giving him one year's gross salary if his employer wrongly terminated was not penal. The terms 'were generous, but they were not unconscionable' (at [115]) because, in the context of employment contracts: it would be very difficult to pre-estimate M's loss on his dismissal, the clause saved time and expense, avoided uncertainty and damaging publicity, and an entrepreneurial company will provide a generous package to attract employees; although the agreed damages exceeded common law damages, it was not out of line with 'market expectations' (see also *Lordsvale Finance plc v Bank of Zambia* [1996] QB 752, 763–4).

> ✓ In *Dunlop Pneumatic Tyre*, the defendants bought tyres from the claimant and breached their undertaking, inter alia, not to sell them below the manufacturer's list price. The contract also provided for £5 to be payable for every tyre sold or offered in breach of the undertaking. The House of Lords upheld this sum as liquidated damages although the sum was payable on the occurrence of several events. The loss likely to result from any breach was difficult to assess and £5 represented a genuine attempt to value it.

✗ In *Makdessi v Cavendish* the Court of Appeal struck down a stipulated damages clause in a commercial contract negotiated by highly experienced lawyers on both sides because the amount was out of all proportion to the loss
attributable to the breach and acted to deter breach. The contract-breaker
stood to lose $40 million which went way beyond compensation.

14.3.2.2 The justification for the penalty rule

In *Makdessi v Cavendish* Christopher Clarke LJ said that 'the law of penalties is a bla-
tant interference with freedom of contract' (at [44]). What explains this anomaly?

(i) Preventing over-compensation

The idea here is that agreed damages should only compensate the claimant for failure
to receive due performance of the primary terms. Lord Diplock said in *Photo Production
v Securicor Transport* (1980) that an agreement must not impose upon the 'breaker of a
primary obligation a general secondary obligation to pay ... a sum ... that is manifestly intended to be in excess of the amount which would fully compensate the other
party for the loss sustained by him in consequence of the breach of the primary obligation' (at 827, 850). Thus, freedom of contract as applied to agreed damages amounts
only to a margin of error for *reasonable* estimations of common law damages when the
contract is made, although a wide margin of error is allowed.

(ii) Preventing punishment

The reasoning here is that the law should not punish breach of contract and the parties should not be permitted to punish each other. Compensation in excess of what a
court would award constitutes punishment.

(iii) Preventing indirect specific enforcement

The idea is that parties should not limit the court's discretion to grant specific performance by stipulating such a punitive payment that it practically coerces performance. However, there does seem something odd about invalidating a term designed
to encourage contractual performance.

(iv) Preventing unfairness

Unconscionability provides a broader rationale for the penalty jurisdiction.[14] It
is consistent with the origins of the penalty rule,[15] aimed at restraining creditors
from enforcing a term in loan agreements under which the defaulting debtor was to
pay a sum greatly in excess of the loan and interest. Collins[16] explains that 'courts
of equity prevented these actions on the ground that the loan agreement constituted an unconscionable bargain, and insisted that the only sum recoverable by the
creditor was the principal and the interest on the loan. These penalty clauses were

---

[14] Collins at 377; D Harris, D Campbell, and R Halson, *Remedies in Contract and Tort* (2nd edn,
Weidenfeld & Nicolson, 2002) 146; H Beale, *Remedies for Breach of Contract* (Sweet & Maxwell, 1980) 59;
M Chen-Wishart, 'Controlling the Power to Agree Damages' in P Birks (ed), *Wrongs and Remedies in the
Twenty-First Century* (Clarendon Press, 1996) 271.

[15] *Protector Endowment Loan & Annuity Co v Grice* (1880); *Re Dixon* (1900).

[16] Collins at 376; see also A Simpson, *A History of the Common Law of Contract* (OUP, 1975) 120; *Dunlop
Pneumatic Tyre v New Garage* at 85. Today, courts can reopen and revise such contracts under the Consumer
Credit Act 1974.

objectionable, therefore, as representing what today we would call an extortionate credit bargain.' In *Phillips Hong Kong*, Lord Woolf (at 57), adopting a passage from *AMEV UDC Finance Ltd v Austin* (1986), said that 'equity and the common law have long maintained a supervisory jurisdiction . . . to relieve against provisions which are so unconscionable or oppressive that their nature is penal rather than compensatory'. However, Shelton[17] argues that a test of unconscionability may be too vague for commercial comfort and may reduce English law's competitive edge. In **'Liquidated Damages, Penalties and the Just Compensation Principles'** (1977) 77 *Col L Rev* 554, **Goetz and Scott** take the view that economic efficiency is maximised by the enforcement of even penalty clauses, unless there is *procedural unfairness*. They are an efficient way for parties to insure against uncompensable losses and distinguishing them from liquidated damages necessitates an inefficient (costly) review of contracts.

14.3.2.3 The scope of the penalty rule: the jurisdictional question

The paradigm case for the application of the penalty rule is payments on *breach*, but the doctrine has also been applied to a clause which: (i) bars the contract-breaker from receiving a sum which would otherwise be due to them (*Makdessi v Cavendish*); or (ii) requires a transfer of property from the guilty to the innocent party either for nothing or at an undervalue (*Jobson v Johnson* (1989); see 14.3.3.2). Nevertheless, it does not apply to other common provisions that have the same effect as penalty clauses. Hence, the penalty rule can be easily evaded by redrafting the term in the following ways.

(i) Stipulating sums payable on events *other than breach*

In *Alder v Moore* (1961) a professional footballer received £500 from an insurance company on the basis that his injury had disabled him from professional football and that he would repay the amount if he resumed playing. The majority enforced the agreement to repay when the footballer resumed playing four months later. The penalty rule did not apply because the footballer never undertook not to play football again and committed no breach when he did. Likewise, in *UK Housing Alliance v Francis* (2010), F breached a 'sale and lease back' and UKH terminated the agreement, resulting in F forfeiting a large sum that he would later have become entitled to. The Court of Appeal denied that it had any jurisdiction to assess the forfeiture as a penalty, because it was triggered by the termination rather than the breach (although the breach triggered the termination).

(ii) Varying the payment due on events *other than breach*

Clauses that accelerate payment, give discounts for prompt payment, or provide for payment on an event not amounting to a breach can have the same effect as penalties. In **Interfoto Picture Library Ltd v Stiletto Visual Programmes Ltd** (1989), a contract for the loan of transparencies for up to 14 days included a clause stating that 'a holding fee of £5 plus VAT per day will be charged for each transparency' retained beyond that period. The clause was not held to be unenforceable for lack of incorporation

---

[17] 'Agreed Remedies: Comment' in A Burrows and E Peel (eds), *Commercial Remedies: Current Issues and Problems* (OUP, 2003) 222.

(see 10.3.3.2). Bingham LJ (at 445) said that the clause was also open to challenge as a **'disguised penalty clause'**. However, the Court of Appeal refused to widen the penalty rule in *Euro London Appointments Ltd v Claessens Intl Ltd* (2006). E supplied employees to C on terms that it would give some refund if the employment ended prematurely *and* C paid its fee within seven days of its invoice. C did not pay on time but argued that E's claim for the whole fee contradicted the penalty rule. Chadwick LJ disagreed, because the term 'imposes no obligation on the client' and could not be breached (at [19]).

The distinction between payments on *breach* and on *other events* also leads to perverse results in hire-purchase contracts. If a debtor ceases performance pursuant to a 'termination clause' the penalty rule does *not* apply to any agreed sum payable by him or her because he or she commits no breach (*Associated Distributors Ltd v Hall* (1938)). In *Bridge v Campbell Discount Co Ltd* (1962), Lords Denning (at 629) and Devlin expressed the view that the penalty rule should be applicable since, otherwise, 'equity commits itself to this absurd paradox: it will grant relief to a man who breaks his or her contract but will penalise the man who keeps it'.

Pause for reflection

The penalty rule is another instance of English law's piecemeal approach to problems of unfairness and throws up some familiar problems.

1. The restriction of the penalty jurisdiction to secondary terms is artificial since primary terms can perform an identical function and yet remain largely uncontrolled, as **Diagram 14C** shows. Penalties can be redrafted into primary terms (ie making the event that triggers payment *not* a breach) to evade the penalty rule. This mirrors the problem with the distinction between terms that exempt liability for breach and terms that are duty-defining (see 11.4.5.1).

2. The penalty rule can be reformed to cover clauses stipulating payment on *events closely allied to breach*, wherever 'the object of the disputed contractual obligation is to secure the act or result which is the true purpose of the contract' (Law Commission, *Penalty Clauses and Forfeiture of Money Paid* (Law Com Consultation Paper 61, 1975) at para 26). The High Court of Australia has taken this path in *Andrews v Australia and New Zealand Banking Group Ltd* (2012), stressing that it is the *substance* of the clause that matters, not the *form*. In contrast to *OFT v Abbey* (see 11.5.2), where the Supreme Court held that certain fees charged by the bank to its customers constituted penalties (eg over-limit fees) were *not* penalties because they were not charged upon breach, the High Court of Australia held that such charges *may* amount to penalties. The question is whether the stipulation is 'collateral' or 'secondary' to the primary obligation owed to the innocent party, and whether it imposes an 'additional detriment' on the contract-breaker. It remains to be seen whether this is a workable test.

3. An alternative is to abolish the penalty rule altogether in recognition that the parties' freedom of contract should extend from primary terms to remedial terms.

Diagram 14C Payment clauses and their tests of validity

	IP = innocent party CB = contract-breaker

Type of term:	Test of enforceability:
Agreed sum (CB's payment for IP's performance)	• No direct control
Limitation of damages (CB to pay less or nothing for IP's loss)	• Incorporation • Interpretation • UCTA or UTCCR
Payments on breach (CB to pay the agreed damages)	• The penalty rule • UTCCR (Sch 2 para 1(e))
Payments on other events (no breach so not a CB, but must pay if specified event occurs)	• No direct control at common law • UTCCR
Forfeiture (CB forfeits sums already paid to IP)	• Deposits: whether reasonable • Pre-payments: whether total failure of consideration • Instalments: whether retention is unconscionable • UTCCR (Sch 2 para 1(d) and (f))

14.3.3 **Forfeitures of payments**

14.3.3.1 Deposits and part-payments

An enforceable agreed damages clause requires the claimant to extract the sum *after* the defendant's breach. A better option is to obtain money *in advance* and refuse to return it (forfeit it) on a breach by the defendant. In general, an advance payment is:

✗ *not recoverable* if it is a **deposit**, that is, a sum paid as 'a guarantee that the contract shall be performed' (*Howe v Smith* (1884) at 95); but

✓ *recoverable* if it is a **part-payment** of the contract price, subject to the contract-breaker's liability to pay damages (*Dies v British and International Mining and Finance Co* (1939), see 13.3.4).[18]

The true nature of a payment is said to be a matter of construction of the contract.

---

[18] But, it is not recoverable if the part-payment is not just for the end product but also for work done or services provided (as with the design, building, and inspection of the ship) analogous to *instalments for services* rendered, *Hyundai Heavy Industries Co Ltd v Papadopoulos* (1980).

The law draws a distinction between a deposit payable *before* breach and agreed damages payable *after* breach, yet while both devices can unfairly penalise the defendant, only the latter is subject to systematic control. A jurisdiction to control **unreasonable deposits** was only recognised by the Privy Council in **Workers Trust & Merchant Bank Ltd v Dojap Investments Ltd** (1993).[19] There, a contract for the sale of land stipulated an unusually large deposit of 25% of the purchase price (almost $3 million). The balance was to be paid within 14 days, time being of the essence (ie a condition). The purchasers tendered the balance plus interest a week late, and the vendors terminated the contract, claiming to forfeit the deposit. The Privy Council advised that a payment is only a valid deposit if the 'sum is reasonable as earnest money'. A 25% deposit is unreasonable in view of the well-established custom for a 10% deposit in sale of land contracts and in the absence of any 'special circumstances' justifying its retention. The vendors were ordered to repay the amount after deducting its provable losses from the breach, which turned out to be less than 10% of the contract price. This decision rationalises the law by extending judicial control of unfair remedial terms from stipulated payments *after* breach to payments *before* breach.

In contrast, in *Union Eagle Ltd v Golden Achievement Ltd* (1997), forfeiture of a 10% deposit for the sale of a flat in Hong Kong was upheld when the buyer was *ten minutes* late in tendering the balance of the purchase price (amounting to $HK10 million). The Privy Council allowed the seller to terminate the contract because of the importance of certainty in commercial transactions (a seller needs to know immediately whether he or she is free to deal with someone else). The 10% deposit was forfeited as it was in line with well-established custom.

14.3.3.2 Instalments

A contract may allow the price to be paid in instalments and stipulate the forfeiture of all the payments if the defendant defaults on any one instalment.

- Where the contract is for **services** rendered over time in return for periodic payments, the sums paid are not recoverable on the payee's breach if they 'represent the agreed rate of hire for services already rendered, and not a penny more' (*The Scaptrade* (1983) at 703). The result may be different if the payments are clearly 'front-loaded'.

- Where a contract for the sale of **property** is terminated for the buyer's breach and the subject matter remains the property of, or is returned to, the seller, forfeiture of instalment payments presents a clear danger of unfairness to the buyer. Denning LJ compares the situation where the buyer defaults after paying 5% of the price, where forfeiture is not unfair, with the situation where the buyer's default comes after paying 90% of the purchase price, where forfeiture is patently unfair (*Stockloser v Johnson* (1954) at 492).

  (i) Where the buyer is *ready and willing* to resume performance, the court can relieve against forfeiture by granting extra time for payment (*Re Dagenham (Thames) Dock Co* (1873)).

---

[19] The decision mirrors the Law of Property Act 1925, s 49(2), and the Consumer Credit Act 1974, ss 90, 132, and 136.

(ii) Where the buyer is *not ready and willing* to perform, the majority of the Court of Appeal in *Stockloser v Johnson* held (at 483, 485, 489) that, in principle, the instalments are still recoverable if retention would be *unconscionable*, while Romer LJ (at 501) limited recoverability to cases of *procedural unfairness* in the form of fraud, sharp practice, or other unconscionable conduct (the forfeiture was enforceable on the facts absent unconscionability of any sort). This position was confined (by the Privy Council in *Workers Trust v Dojap*) to cases where the buyer had been *let into possession*, although it is unclear why this should make a difference. In *Jobson v Johnson*, the Court of Appeal cut through the categories. It set aside a term in a contract for the sale of shares by instalment payments which required the buyer, if he defaulted on any instalment, to sell the shares back for £40,000. The defendant defaulted after paying £140,000. Relief was granted for unfairness although there was no procedural unfairness in Romer LJ's sense, and although the clause involved a return of property and a forfeiture of payments rather than a payment of money.

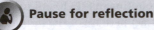 **Pause for reflection**

Like deposits, forfeiture provisions can have the same effect and purpose as penalties (*Jobson v Johnson* at 1041). Indeed, they operate even more coercively than penalties since one party already holds the proprietary interest in money or property, which is the equivalent of the agreed compensation. As Birks states, 'since the promised penalty cannot be claimed, the penalty which has already passed into the other's hands should be recoverable'.[20] There is no principled basis for different tests of validity for payments made *before* and those made *after* breach. The *same* test should apply to deposits, pre-payments, instalments, and sums payable on breach. It brings no credit to the law when artificial jurisdictional requirements can be evaded by shrewd drafting, and when functionally similar terms are subject to different controls.

THIS CHAPTER IN ESSENCE

online resource centre

The key areas and core topics in this chapter are summarised in an easy-to-use list, ideal for revision purposes, on the Online Resource Centre at http://www.oxfordtextbooks.co.uk/orc/chen-wishart5e/. Links to websites relevant to the topics covered and any updates to the chapter can also be found on the Online Resource Centre.

---

[20] P Birks, *An Introduction to the Law of Restitution* (Clarendon Press, 1989) 215.

QUESTIONS

1 '*Cooperative Insurance Society Ltd v Argyll Stores (Holdings) Ltd* (1998) has tipped the balance too far in favour of the contract-breaker.' When are specific performance and injunctions available, and when should they be?

2 'Contract parties enter contracts to get performance and not damages for non-performance. Therefore, specific performance, and not damages, should be the main remedy for breach.' Discuss.

3 Explain and distinguish each of the following, giving examples.

(a) An exemption clause and a penalty clause.
(b) A penalty clause and a liquidated damages clause.
(c) A deposit and a part-payment.

4 Should parties have greater freedom to agree on the consequences of breach?

5 Are the following terms in a contract between Nick and Olga enforceable? What further facts do you need to know?

(a) A term stipulating that 'if Olga breaches clause 8 then Nick can specifically enforce the term *or* is entitled to the sum of £50,000 as Nick chooses'.
(b) A term stipulating that 'On the occurrence of circumstances specified in clause 8 Olga must pay Nick £50,000.'

 For hints on how to answer these questions, please see the Online Resource Centre at http://www.oxfordtextbooks.co.uk/orc/chenwishart5e/

KEY FURTHER READING

See generally, Burrows, A (2004), *Remedies for Torts and Breach of Contract* (3rd edn, OUP).

Friedmann, D (1995), 'Good Faith and Remedies for Breach of Contract' in J Beatson and D Friedmann (eds), *Good Faith and Fault in Contract Law* (Clarendon Press) 399.

Goetz, C, and Scott, R (1977), 'Liquidated Damages, Penalties and Just Compensation', 77 *Col L Rev* 554.

Kronman, A (1978), 'Specific Performance', 45 *U Chi L Rev* 35.

Rowan, S (2010), 'For the Recognition of Remedial Terms Agreed Inter Partes' 126 *LQR* 448.

Schwartz, A (1979), 'The Case for Specific Performance', 89 *Yale LJ* 271.

Smith, S A (1997), 'Performance, Punishment and the Nature of Contractual Obligation', 60 *MLR* 360.

APPENDIX

ADDITIONAL CHAPTERS

Additional chapters accompanying this text can be found at
www.oxfordtextbooks.co.uk/orc/chenwishart5e/.

@ Incapacity

This chapter examines a basis for invalidating an otherwise valid contract based on
the claimant's lack of capacity to make the contract in question. On the one hand,
the law should protect those whose self-protective abilities are impaired to an unacceptable degree. On the other hand, the law must also have regard to the interests
of those who have dealt fairly and in good faith with the incapacitated party. Thus,
although an incapacitated person is logically *incapable* of giving valid consent (rendering the contract void and of no effect), the legal consequences of incapacity often
vary. Recognised categories of personal incapacity are infancy, mental incapacity, and
significant impairment by drink or drugs.

(i) **Children**: the law adopts a strongly protective attitude to minors. In general,
minors can enforce their contracts, but are not bound by them unless they ratify
the contract after reaching 18 years of age. Exceptions have been created to protect those who deal fairly and in good faith with the child and to allow children
to enter 'beneficial' contracts. Thus:

(a) *contracts for 'necessaries'* (widely interpreted) are, binding if they are beneficial to the child, but not if the terms are harsh or onerous;

(b) *contracts beneficial to the child* overall are binding, for example contracts to
obtain education, training, employment, medical care, and legal advice;

(c) *contracts involving land, company shares, and partnerships* bind the minor
unless he or she repudiates the contract before or within a reasonable time
of attaining majority.

A contract not binding on the child may still generate *non-contractual obligations* such
as to make restitution of benefits received under section 3(1) of the Minors' Contracts
Act 1987.

(ii) **Mental incapacity, drink, and drugs:**

(a) a person lacking capacity under the *Mental Incapacity Act 2005* cannot make
a valid contract although he or she remains liable to pay a reasonable price
for 'necessaries';

(b) incapacity due to mental infirmity, drink, and drugs renders a contract voidable if the claimant's condition is known to the other party;

(c) *lesser impairments* (short of incapacity) by those who appear sane are subject to the doctrine of unconscionability as discussed in Chapter 9.

(iii) **Companies and public authorities**: limiting the capacity of such *non-natural persons* is necessary to protect those on whose behalf they act (eg shareholders, lenders, taxpayers). For example, *public authorities* cannot make a valid contract if they act beyond their powers. Possible hardship is mitigated by allowing recovery of money paid and property transferred under void contracts unless this would amount to indirect enforcement of the contract.

Illegality and public policy

The so-called 'illegality' doctrine represents the most open and direct interference with contract parties' freedom to determine the *substance* of their contracts. The law's refusal to facilitate immoral or reprehensible contracts means that courts will neither *enforce* an illegal contract nor order the restitution of any money or property transferred under it.

Statutes may prohibit the *formation, purpose, or performance* of certain contracts. Examples include prohibitions on the trade of certain weapons and body parts. The categories of common law illegality reflect changing social and moral values. They include contracts which:

- commit or further a criminal or civil wrong;
- interfere with the administration of justice;
- prejudice the state, such as trading with the enemy in wartime;
- prejudice family life;
- unduly restrict personal liberty, such as contracts of slavery;
- further sexually immoral purposes, such as prostitution;
- are in restraint of trade whereby one party agrees to restrict its freedom to trade or conduct its profession or business in a particular locality for a specified time. Such restraints are invalid to the extent that they are unreasonable.

The effect of illegality varies. The relevant statute may stipulate the consequence of the illegality (eg impose a penalty or bar enforcement). Otherwise, the court must decide on the same general principles as apply to common law illegality. The rule of thumb, that courts will not enforce contracts expressly or impliedly prohibited by statute or contrary to public policy, is subject to exceptions. Thus, for example, a claimant can enforce an 'illegal' contract:

- where the purpose of the illegality is to protect a class of persons to which the claimant belongs;
- if its illegal part can be severed; and

- if the claimant is ignorant of the illegal manner in which the other party is performing an otherwise legal contract.

In all these cases, enforcement must *not subvert the policies underlying the illegality.*

Exceptionally, a party may be able to claim restitution of the benefits he or she conferred on the other party under an illegal contract where he or she:

- is less blameworthy than the defendant;
- has *withdrawn* from the transaction in time; or
- can establish a legal or equitable *proprietary right* to the property independent of the illegal contract.

INDEX

In this index the following abbreviations are used:

C(RTP)A   Contracts (Rights of Third Parties) Act 1999
LR(FC)A   Law Reform (Frustrated Contracts) Act 1943
UCTA   Unfair Contract Terms Act 1977
UTCCR   Unfair Terms in Consumer Contracts Regulations 1999

Note: Page numbers in this index which are preceded by a 'W' (eg W1, W2) indicate where topics are covered in the chapters that appear on the Online Resource Centre. These chapters cover Incapacity and Illegality.